As Far A

Can Tell

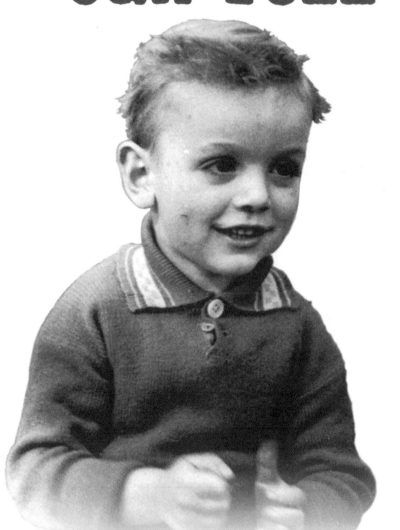

RALPH McTELL

First published in two volumes by Amber Waves,
an imprint of Heartland Publishing Ltd,
in 2000 and 2002.

This edition published by Leola Music Ltd 2008.

ISBN 978-0-9549540-2-4

Extract from Lunar Lullaby ©1974 Misty River Music Ltd used
with kind permission of the publisher.

Designed by Peter Thaine.

Printed and bound in Great Britain by Biddles Ltd
King's Lynn, Norfolk, England.

www.ralphmctell.co.uk

For Mum and Bruce

contents

Egg   1
Soft   9
Frank   25
Accident   33

Night duty   42

Magic   45
Jock   49
God   57
Woods   69

As if in sleep   87

Helmet   92
Yoyo   102
Shave   107
Fairies   117
Warts   134
Picnic   147
Stone the crows   164
Hedge   169
Straws   175
D-day   179
Wolf   191
Puggy   197

Old Puggy Mearns   203

Facts   206
Ice   218
Cadets   232
Haircut   236
Town   245
Hard   252
Needlework   263
Out   269
Wolfie   275

PLATES   *BETWEEN*   276-277

Tech   277
Girls   284
Guitars   290
Brighton   298
Singer   308
Whitgift   316
Olive Tree   322
Max   326
Pad   337
George   343
Gill   351
Shiver   361
Robbery   374

Olé	386
Riviera	392
Returns	400
Podger	407
Engaged	414
'Oggin	423
Grapefruit	432
Dumper	438
Reg	449
Amaranthus caudatus	459
Harmony	462
Olaf	471
Disharmony	477
Crossroads	488
Bosporus	502
Spies	508
Tenner	518
Tubs	528
Waterloo	535
Timber	544
Matuzzi	550
Musketeers	556
Joints	564
Nanna	572
Fin	579

As far as I can tell
Is all that I can say
A million miles on down the road
Twelve thousand days away

Mirror held to mirror
As far as I can tell
At this glimpse of eternity
I fumbled and they fell

Between these shards restored
Lies truth in splintered cracks
As far as I can tell
Remembered light refracts

And shadows cast by doubt
Move by the soundless bell
The sun tolled ringing earth reveals
As far as I can tell

preface

Most of my songwriting is autobiographical. The incidents described in my songs became songs because it was possible to contain the poetry or symmetry of a story within the confines of the song format. The stories in this book also have a kind of poetry, insomuch as there had to be a reason for writing them down other than pure chronology.

The first story I wrote for this memoir was called 'Picnic on the Playnies'. It is about a day out with the kids in the street when we attempted to cook over an open fire by the farm (the sewage farm!). The 'poetry' in this story was centred on the young boy (me) observing Maureen, who had decided to be mother to us all and do the cooking. When she cuts herself preparing the food and her blood drips into the chip pan, her small sacrifice becomes a mystical communion as one by one we receive the chips. It is the nearest we will get to sharing her body (except for Bobby Best, if he is to believed). The blood and body of Maureen in a starling-whitewashed arbour of elderberry bushes: adolescent stirrings around the fire: laughter and smoky tears – it is far too much to cram into a song.

Once I started writing, I found I loved recounting these moments and I experienced a total suspension in time as I worked. I could clearly hear the voices of the characters mentioned: in some cases, I could even smell them. So lost was I in the writing that I was transported back and confused by time and memory. Sometimes this was a wonderfully intoxicating experience but sometimes there was a hangover and a melancholy for lost moments. Some names had to be changed to protect the guilty and a few incidents omitted to protect the innocent. No matter how difficult recounting some stories was, writing them down was pure pleasure. More episodes began to arrive as I wandered back and forth from my first memories at eighteen months to my time in Paris in the mid-1960s. All these stories were sent to my dear friend Nick Evans.

Nick, who died in 2005, worked with Jeff Horne at Heartland Publishing Ltd and they were keen to publish the stories. The problem was in the editing: there was so much material that we all wanted to keep, and often chronology was needed to make sense of the incidents and to connect the narrative. In the end we decided to divide my writings into two books.

The first volume, Angel Laughter, was published by Amber Waves, an imprint of Heartland, in October 2000. It covered childhood from my earliest recollections until, after serving six months in purgatory, I left the Infantry Junior Leaders Battalion of the army in 1960.

The second volume, Summer Lightning (also published by Amber Waves) came out in 2002 and dealt with the next five years. In that book, I recounted my adventures until I met my wife Nanna in Paris in 1966. Music had always been an interest but from my teens the guitar increasingly took over my life and turned me in a direction I am still following.

Now the two volumes have been combined and, with some additional passages and a selection of photographs, published by Leola Music Ltd. As Far As I Can Tell takes the reader from my early childhood to meeting Nanna and the brink of my career as a professional musician and songwriter. From that point on my musical career ran in tandem with my life with Nanna and my family.

That is our story: this autobiography, however, is mine.

There are many people I have to thank. Firstly, of course, my mum, who as well as providing me with the best she could throughout my childhood got me out of the army thereby allowing my subsequent life to take the course described in this book. I thank Jack Elliott for his marvellous guitar playing and singing which inspired my striving in music. Woody Guthrie's inspirational songs planted dreams of the road and showed me the dignity of the working man; Woody also demonstrated one did not need to be a great musician to be a great songwriter. I thank all my blind, black, dead heroes – men like Blind Boy Fuller, Blind Blake and the Rev Gary Davis – for their joyous, complex, fascinating, sexy exploitation of the acoustic guitar. Bob Dylan not only brought me his majesty and street attitude but introduced me to the harmonica harness thus freeing me from the bent wire coathanger. Thanks, too, to Wizz Jones, Davy Graham and Bert Jansch, who proved that British lads could write songs and play a peculiarly British guitar music.

Above all, though, I thank the 'cast of thousands', those many friends who moved in and out of my life through music. They know who they are. But if I had to single out one from them all, it be Mick ('Henry') Bartlett, who died in 2001. Henry accompanied me on my early recordings and many of my live performances as well. We drove all over the place with just a few bob in our pockets, accompanied by music, laughter and friendship. It is to these essentials, and to Henry in particular, that this autobiography is dedicated.

egg

✪

Sunshine pours in
through the top half of
the basement windows. The
light is slightly diffused through
floral curtains. Their background colour
is a creamy yellow and swirls of flowers
grow from unnaturally green stems. Below
me is a table, dark brown in colour, and at one
end stands my mother in a long-sleeved smock-
type apron that buttons up to her neck. She leans
over a small enamel dish with a blue line around
the edge. There is no tablecloth but there are place
mats made of thick cork for things to stand on.
Making his way to the chair on the other side is my
father. He is wearing a light short-sleeved shirt, open
at the neck, and his face and arms look very brown
contrasted against it. His hair is very dark and he
is smiling slightly. He sits down, and my mother,
with surgical precision, slices open the golden
brown pastry crust and removes its
supporting structure. To my utter
amazement she fishes out...
an egg cup.

A car door opens on to a huge expanse of grass. In the distance is a thin line of trees, leaves trembling. In front of them stands a fairground in full swing; it's loud even though it is far away. I turn to reach for my mother's hand but she is getting out of the car with a bundle in her arms and does not have a hand free. I drop my arm and stare at the shawl that is wrapped around my little brother, Bruce. I look at him as if for the first time. A bigger hand takes mine, and looking over my shoulder, my mother is smiling at my father and me as we walk off toward the tents and rides.

❀

A noisy puffing steam train is standing at the station platform. As we draw near, the volume is almost deafening. I grip the hand that holds mine harder. The noise is frightening but it unaccountably makes me smile. A man leans out of the tender and pushes his leg into a huge boot that is fixed to the wall and swings out of the compartment toward the wall. He connects a large hose to the tender and there is acknowledgement between him and my father.

❀

I'm sitting watching my parents get dressed. Even though there is no fire in the grate, they still stand in front of it to put on their clothes. They both dress with their backs to me but eventually I see the bits they modestly try to keep from me. My mother's body is very white, my father's only white in parts; the rest of him is sort of yellowish-brown and his hair is very black and curly.

We have a carpet in the living room. It is old but it is between us and the floorboards under which the mice hurtle about. Sometimes we hear them scurrying along between the stud walls and overhead between our ceiling and the floor of the family upstairs. Their scampering feet drives Meemo the cat crazy because he can't get at them. Meemo is very soft and sort of a sandy colour.

❂

I'm sitting on the floor when my father comes into the room with something in his hands. He sets it down. It's a tiny puppy with black and white markings. Some words are exchanged between my parents and the puppy pees on the carpet. He's very young and just sits there. I'm intrigued but not excited as he waddles about the room.

❂

Bruce has a cot in the corner of the small room adjacent to the living room and I have a noisy bed that creaks and pings with each move I make. Bruce has bronchitis and the Valor stove has a threatening witch's kettle on it which hisses venomous breath into the room. The air is slowly being starved of oxygen by the naked paraffin heater flame. Soon I develop bronchitis too, and our mother is nearly beside herself with worry. Sometimes above our combined wheezing I can hear her crying in the next room.

I love Saturday night bedtimes the best because we have clean sheets, and they are cold and make me want to breathe on my hands to stop my teeth going on edge, but after a while they are not so cold and I draw the old army blanket, which is under the patchwork bedspread, up to my chin and rub it on the skin just below my bottom lip and feel quite safe.

❂

We are always in bed at the same time and Mum always tucks us in and kisses us goodnight. She keeps the blackout curtain at the window to "help us get to sleep." In the spring and summer months there is always a chink of tantalising light which creeps in somewhere and the sound of the other flat dwellers passing through the yard. Occasionally there is even the odd visitor who descends the steps to our front door and in so doing has to pass our window. These footsteps are exciting and scary because it might be my father come home. Usually it is Mrs. Leisk from over the road.

❂

There are no pictures on the walls of our flat. The walls in Mum's bedroom are grey; so is the hall, and the front room is yellow distemper. We do not have a kitchen but we do have a scullery which was obviously used to keep skulls in. I expect they were lined up in rows in the cupboard that we are not allowed to use. There is a single cold tap with a brass handle that hovers over a huge yellow sink at one end of the room under the window. Next to this is a gas stove and next to that is a copper boiler that does not work, then a table that Mum prepares food on. The room has a stone floor and it is always too cold to eat in there.

4

Once every couple of weeks my mother does a wash. It is a huge job and makes me feel sad to watch her boiling up kettle after kettle of water, then using the soap whisk to try to get a lather and the little bag of blue to make the grey colour look white. There is a mangle in the yard next to the kennel in front of the Anderson shelter. Red chapped winter hands hang out the washing and the clothes prop hoists everything above the dustbins that have a strange smell all year round that strangely I do not find offensive.

❂

Every so often Mum paints the stones in the hallway with red ochre. It is so dark that you would never know that they are red but she insists that we will keep our standards up by such disciplines. White hairy fungus grows on the walls of the hall and in the toilet that we are told is poisonous and must not eat. Naturally because it grows so plentifully I decide to try it and I can state that it tastes salty and that it is not poisonous. Once we even had toadstools growing in the lavatory above the cistern.

❂

Next door is a home for wayward girls. They walk around in grey uniforms and are rigorously kept in line. At the back of their institution are some tennis courts and often in the summer evenings we can hear the plop of tennis balls being hit across the net and occasional little cries of elation and disappointment. These only serve to remind me that there is more left to the day, and resentfully I wonder how long it will be before we can stay out until it is impossible for anyone to see to play tennis.

Mr. Fox from upstairs comes down one day to apologise for something. His voice is slurred and he is swaying about and Mum shouts at him for causing a leak and water pouring through the scullery ceiling. I think she is very brave to shout at Mr. Fox and admire her for standing up to him. I afterwards realise that Mr. Fox had been drinking and my mother does not approve of drinking. In moments of desperation she tells me that she could be playing the piano in pubs instead of looking after us. On the face of it I cannot see anything wrong with this as pubs seem to be such jolly places where people are singing and laughing. I always was attracted to them and when I was out and about on my own I would always pause outside to listen to the atmosphere within.

✪

It is so cold in our room that we can pretend to smoke cigarettes and blow smoke from our mouths except that it is steam really. Our noses are always cold in the morning but the rest of us is warm in our squeaky, pingy beds. The secret is to get up and get dressed quickly; although it does not warm up the room much, we can stand near the paraffin stove that Mum lights before we have to get out of bed. I always stand too near it and burn myself, especially on the underside of my forearms when I am pulling on my vest. This makes me jump and angry when it happens and I feel stupid and I hate the stove, but it is our only morning warmth. When it does not seem to be working, I touch the top, but it always is and it burns my fingertips and makes a nasty smell and my finger prints are all smooth for a while. Sometimes I pull a hair from my head and hold it above the stove and see how near I must bring it to the top before it begins to writhe and shrivel in a strange death dance.

Mum buttons us up against the cold and she puts little Bruce on the seat on the back of her bicycle. We trudge through the snow to the nursery about half a mile away. Each time we say goodbye to her I wonder if she will come in the evening to collect us. She always does, so each day begins with sadness and closes with joy. Sometimes Anita from across the road collects us from the nursery and stays with us till Mum comes home. She's ten years older than me and goes to the Old Palace girls' school.

✯

At the nursery in the mornings we all march round and round in the room and pretend we are a band. One of the children pretends to play a shiny flute; I long to play it too because it is so shiny but I never get a go. In the morning when we arrive we all have to have our hair combed. I don't like this because ours is already done at home and they use a very fine metal comb that is dipped in some cloudy liquid and it smells of toilets and makes your hair go hard. They try to make us eat porridge but it makes me vomit so I am excused as Mummy give us Weetabix before we leave home. I don't like Weetabix much either. Bruce can eat his with warm milk but warm milk makes me sick. I think Mum would like me to eat mine with warm milk. It seems to warm her up to see us eat warm things in the morning but I drink warm tea with sugar and milk and Bruce drinks warm milk with sugar.

We are usually the last two to be brought home from the nursery, and in the evening before the other mums collect their children we eat a quarter of a slice of bread and margarine with either a single date or a piece of cubed cheese, or sometimes a single slice of cold boiled beetroot, which makes our lips red like lipstick. It has a strange sweet taste, but not sweet like jam which Bruce loves and not savoury like cheese that I love, and I don't think that I like it very much. But at least I don't throw up.

✸

Fixed to the wall of the living room is an old dark brown wooden cabinet with shelves. In the centre of the middle shelf there is a small pot in which sits a blown goose egg. It has female features painted on it and its huge eyes have long lashes. When we eventually leave this place my mother discovers some jars of pickled onions in the back of the cupboard. The onions are as dark brown as the woodwork. She had made these for Frank, my father, because they were his favourites. We eat them and they are delicious even though they are at least ten years old.

∾

soft

The protected enclave that was The Waldrons was a strange mixture of social conditions and classes. During the reign of Henry VIII it was occupied by Sir Henry Carew, who used it as a game reserve, and it remained a private road until the beginning of this century.

It was enclosed by a wall and accessed by two gates, one at the Duppas Hill Lane entrance and the other at the hill that ran down to Southbridge Road. For many years it was a very upmarket street and it even had its own policemen who occupied a peculiar octagonal cottage at the Duppas Hill entrance. One could imagine these private police officers in top hats chasing boys who climbed the walls or gates in search of apples from the gardens or the chestnuts that fell in profusion each autumn in the Spinney, the miniature woodland in the middle of The Waldrons.

By the time Bruce and I were growing up there the cottage was derelict, although this was not unusual in post-war Croydon, where the remains of bomb-damaged and deserted properties littered the area. In Victorian times it was still a rather grand residential street, but as wars and recessions produced housing shortages, more ordinary folk started to populate the imposing old houses, and buildings that once housed one family and their servants now provided homes for dozens of people.

As I grew up I became aware of the different types of people living around us, from comparatively wealthy ones, who kept their houses and gardens beautifully, to the poorest underclass—what would now be called problem families. But everybody rubbed along with each other somehow. There were spats and a few drink-induced quarrels up at the top of the road, but things got patched up pretty quickly, and in spite of genuine poverty in many of the homes, everyone considered themselves better off than those who lived in the estates around the 'Old Town'.

Many of the streets on the Salem Place estate had such a reputation that I was scared to enter them. There was also an area at the side of Holloway's yard where a few really rough families lived, and I avoided this as much as possible, sometimes taking the long way round to get to the shops that served the district. Once as I hurried past on my way to the shops, one of the front doors was open. There was rubbish in the hallway and no carpet, and the walls were cracked and crumbling. It was not that different to our place except that it was above ground, but it was obvious that those living there couldn't have cared less about the state of their home.

As I glanced furtively in I could see a small kid sitting on a toilet at the end of the short corridor. His name was Raymond, and he was a horrible piece of work. Once, though, even I felt compassion for him when, to impress a couple of girls, his older brother picked him up by pressing his hands over his ears and exerting the kind of pressure you would use to pick up a line of books. The kid let out the most piercing, blood-curdling shriek I had ever heard. Tears spurted from his eyes like water jets as soon as his feet left the ground.

Just past this boy's house was Warren's, the greengrocer and general store, and next to their shop was a small newsagent. Both shops had chewing gum machines and with patience and the right degree of intuition you could sometimes arrive when the arrow on the handle faced forwards. This entitled the lucky penny spender to an extra packet of gum. Once I got there and found both machines in this position—but I only had one penny, and by the time I'd raced back to get a friend to invest, the arrows had been moved on!

Down on Southbridge Road was Bowman's the bakers, and past St. Andrew's Secondary Modern school was a post office, an antique shop, newsagent and Martin's the greengrocer, who also had stalls down at Surrey Street market. The Martin boys were a tough little bunch, and Terry, who was in my class, had the nickname Pongo. I longed to have a nickname (but not 'Pongo').

Mr. Harris ran the newsagents; he was quite a jovial man but I didn't like the way he said things to my mother. Once he tickled her over the counter, and although she said nothing at the time I knew she didn't like it and said he was "too familiar." He twisted everything around into a double entendre and Mum found him distasteful. Mrs. Harris wore lime-green frocks and had a great goitre below her chin that wobbled like a turkey's wattle when she spoke, which frightened me a little.

But we still had to go there. I liked it best when people were paying their newspaper bills and I had to wait in the shop smelling the mixed scents of chocolate, toffee and boiled sweets stored in glass jars on shelves behind the wooden counter. These essences were blended further with tobaccos and loose cigarettes, and the smell was intoxicating. I couldn't wait to start smoking.

Our house, number 30 The Waldrons, was a huge property owned by Mrs. Cox who lived at number seven across the road. It was divided into rooms and flatlets and we were in the basement: a damp, forlorn place. Above us were the Connaughtons, and across the hall was Mrs. Williams, a retired fortune teller whose uncle wrote a book on the search for the Indian rope trick called *A Magician in Many Lands*. She loaned it to me once and one of the pictures in it showed 'before and after' poses of a man sentenced to be hacked to death, which unsettled me for a very long time. Above her lived the Miss Dickinsons, across from them was Miss Elwell, and on the floor above lived Mr. and Mrs. Clarke (she was the married sister of the Miss Dickinsons).

Meemo the cat died one Christmas Eve when he got a fish bone caught in his throat.

Tyler, the puppy, was a cross between a Labrador and a bulldog; my father got him cheap because all the other pups looked like bulldogs or Labradors but this one had a bulldog's body and a Labrador's head. The lady who sold him to us named him Tyler after the peasant revolutionary and his black and white flag.

He was a great house dog; though he was never really a friend to Bruce and me, I know he was a comfort to my mother in her dark and lonely days after my father left us. He was my mother's dog and fiercely protective of her. Once when she had left Bruce and me in the old pram outside the library at Croydon Town Hall with Tyler tied to the railings, she came out to find that a whole line of people had been kept out of the building by our ferocious guardian, who had decided that Mum should be allowed to choose her books alone.

Tyler spent most of his days in his 'kennel' which was a crate in front of the old air raid shelter. He was firmly chained to his kennel and was quite snug inside. He let me go in once but it was a bit smelly and once was enough. His chain was long enough for him to scare the dustmen who had to walk past him to collect the bins.

If Bruce and I were in the basement when my mother came home, we would hear Tyler's tail banging out a rhythm on the side of his box like a drummer to announce her return. I don't recall Mum taking him on long walks but perhaps these took place when we were in bed.

Sometimes Mr. Douglas would call round, and Mum, pulling on her old leather jacket, would tell us that they were going for a little walk, adding, "As you can see, we're not going anywhere special." Bruce and I would have loved her to go somewhere special with Mr. Douglas, as he was someone we both liked. He smiled a lot, Mum seemed to like him and he liked her, even in her old jacket.

We wondered if they would get married, hoping that they would because we liked him better than our own dad and were glad that he made Mum happy. But she found out that he was already married, and he never came round again. All three of us were sad about it.

At first Bruce and I had a potty each but I was literally elevated to the lavatory proper once I was big enough not to fall through the seat. There we had to sit until both of us had performed, which sometimes took a long time. Mum put us together for this activity as we were both scared of this end of the flat. Whilst we waited, grunted and strained, we sang little songs to ourselves or made up quizzes. Bruce discovered that if he banged his fists on his knees it sometimes helped him go, and thereafter if we got impatient we would both sit there drumming away until we had a result.

Often to while away the time I made up stories modelled on the ones our mum told us from Beatrix Potter or Allison Uttley. Mine concerned two characters called Piggy and Goat, and these yarns meandered on and on until I had managed to perform, whereupon my story would be abruptly drawn to a close with "and they all lived happily ever after." Poor little Bruce, however, sometimes had to sit there for so long that his little bum was stuck to the rim of the pot. Whatever he had done, my mother always said, when she looked in, "Oh my Godfather Dick!"

I was spared this declaration of approval because I could pull the chain. For a long time I wondered who our godfather Dick was, but although his name was mentioned a lot (along with Jack Robinson), we never got to meet him.

In those hard grey days after the Second World War it did not seem appropriate to show signs of affection. There was work to be done, a country to rebuild, deprivation to be dealt with stoically, and if you couldn't afford things you made do.

Everyone was more or less in the same boat, and because clothes and many other things were 'on the ration' you seldom saw anyone wearing anything new, which particularly suited our fairly dire situation. Shoes were made to last longer by cutting out the toes to make summer sandals, and clothes were adapted, lengthened, shortened or completely transformed. Old skirts became trousers for small boys, and no-one was too proud to accept hand-me-downs. Our general shabbiness was probably worse than many and our circumstances poorer, but my mother still insisted we held our heads high as a family.

When couples went out, mother and father walked arm-in-arm but seldom held hands. Courting couples lay and canoodled on the grass of Duppas Hill long after they should have caught pneumonia from the damp. Children clutched their mothers' hands on the way to school, but the goodbye kiss was administered perfunctorily at home where no-one could see it. As children, we were reassured of our parents' love by much more subtle signs: coats being buttoned up and shirts and vests being tucked into trousers; shoelaces being tied properly in double bows, in mysteries of routing that was far beyond the logic of small boys; hair being brushed or combed; sandals being buckled; and occasionally spit being administered to handkerchiefs by fastidious mothers in the street to clean our faces.

We knew these signs were love tokens and had to be content with them. At nursery school Bruce and I were separated from our mum all day and we both took comfort wherever it came from. Sometimes it was worth taking a tumble just to have someone fuss over you when you scraped your knees.

Around the nursery was a large garden, and whenever the weather was warm enough we were taken outside to play. It was always slightly hazardous playing under the trees in late autumn, as the remains of fruit attracted wasps and sometimes a child was stung. The initial shrieking usually subsided as quickly and abruptly as it had begun. I managed to get stung by a bee right under my left ear lobe and, although it hurt unbelievably, I did not cry.

The nurses painted it with something purple and I felt brave like a wounded soldier. In fact one of them told me I was a brave soldier and that kept the tears away. I loved being comforted, and although cuddling the children was rare, there were small signs of affection from those in charge of us: a hand rubbed over our lysoled hair; a hand guiding us up the step or leading us in games or little dances.

Although we often sat close to our mum or even shared the same chair, I do not remember her cuddling us or stroking us. Our intimate moments with her were mostly as she read to us in the evening; and often while she was reading I would just look at her and think how wonderful she was not to send us away so that she could go down to the pub and play the piano for all those happy people who sat in the smoke and left their kids outside with a glass of lemonade and a bag of crisps or an arrowroot biscuit.

I did envy them the crisps and lemonade though.

The head of the nursery was called Matron and she wore a white coat. She was nice to us, but she had hair as short as a man, which confused me a little. Later I heard that she was a replacement for the old matron who was addicted to pethidine. She had asked Mum to get a prescription for her and Mum's boss had realised it was forged. When she'd been rumbled, she just moved on and there was very little scandal and no detrimental effect on the children.

One day by the heavy gate at the entrance to the nursery, I failed to notice that the gate was swinging toward me. It had an iron latch which fell shut on a clip to lock it. If only my head had been almost up to the latch instead of one inch above it, the latch would not have hit me in the forehead, making a hole right through to the bone. I do not know why it was not stitched. Perhaps there was not enough skin, or perhaps Matron would have got into trouble.

Strangely it was not the pain of the wound that upset me but the anxious faces of those who tried to stop the bleeding. The hole healed up reluctantly, only to be reopened several years later. I was tracking the path of a stair rod that had been thrown up at a conker tree to knock down some immature horse chestnuts. Round and around it twirled as it ascended through the leafy branches. Round and around it went as it descended, finally landing in exactly the same place on my forehead as the gate latch had done. That *really* made me feel sick.

The young girls who looked after us were called nurses and they wore grey uniforms, white hats and black stockings. They were all pretty and smiled and laughed a lot. Once when Bruce was crying a little as we sat on the ledge into the back garden I told him he was a "miseryguts."

"What did you call your little brother?" asked the nurse.

"Miseryguts," I replied, and it made her laugh so much I said it again, and that made Bruce upset, but we soon comforted him and it was all right. I loved it when the pretty nurses laughed.

One day a man came to the nursery and did a Punch and Judy show. It was a bit frightening but we loved it when we could finally understand Mr. Punch's words, and we all said, "That's the way to do it!" in his nasal whiny voice. But if I said it at bedtime Bruce didn't like it so much, so even though I should not have done so and I knew it worried him, I would still say, "That's the way to do it!"

Because of the dark and other things it was always hard to close the door on the day, even after Mum had read us a little story and allowed us to talk for a while. Bruce's voice would start to get drowsy and I would dread the approaching silence. Finally, when I could keep him awake no longer for company, we would say goodnight. Even this was extended by me to make it last longer.

"Goodnight Bruce."

"Goodnight Ralph."

"See you in the morning."

"See you in the morning."

"Hope you have a good night."

"Hope you do too."

Then after a short pause, and in a nasally voice, "That's the way to do it!"

After a calming down period the whole thing would begin again. Later on this rigmarole would be even more extended by the addition of our prayers.

"Have you said your prayers yet?" I would ask Bruce, and at first we would repeat together the going home prayer from school:

"Lord keep us safe this night,
Secure from all our fears,
May angels guard us whilst we sleep,
Till morning light appears."

One night I suddenly decided to announce that I would say my own prayers and in silence in my mind. I asked God to bless everyone that I knew and liked and then everyone I didn't mind too much. This soon gave rise to anxiety, as I would wonder if I had forgotten anyone and if God would think less of me for forgetting.

My litany soon got shortened to "Bless everyone in the world except the woman who went off with Daddy." I never asked God to bless him, but I didn't ask him not to. I would finish this off with an audible "Amen" and invite Bruce to say his own prayers. For a long time we did them separately so that God would not have to de-scramble them, but this I realised was probably unnecessary as there were bound to be other children saying prayers at the same time, and he could cope.

Of course I saw angels but they afforded me scant comfort. They were yellow and dark brown in colour, the colours of twilight when the creeping night sucks the life colour from the day. They never spoke, but hung motionless in our grey bedroom near the wardrobe and communicated amongst themselves like dutiful Nannies, more out of obligation than real love. They did not trouble me and I did not trouble them, but I was glad they were there.

I saw God only once and that was in a dream. I was still at nursery school and it was a sunny afternoon near the wooden climbing frame. There were several knotty apple trees in a cluster at one end of the garden, and a couple up by where a few children sat playing on the grass. There was a clear sky with just a few traces of cloud very high up. As I gazed absently at the space between earth and sky, I became aware of a trouser leg stepping out of nothing as if on an invisible ladder. At the end of the trouser, which was very dark green in colour, was a dark sock inside a black lace-up shoe. The trouser was soon matched by another, and to this was added a body and finally a head with a pleasant but unremarkable face.

"Hello children," smiled the man, "I'm God."

"Hello God," we chorused, unfazed for the most part.

"Are you having a nice time?" asked God.

"Yes!" we shouted in the manner we all use for communicating with children's entertainers.

"I just thought I would come down and see if you were all right," said God, smiling broadly from under a small moustache. Something on his lapel was drawing my eye, and though I couldn't read, I recognised it as the identity number of a Green Line bus driver. This was corroborating evidence to the dark green uniform that he was wearing. He's not God, I thought, he's a bus driver, and although Green Line bus drivers were a superior class of driver to the regular red bus driver it still did not explain his ability to descend from the sky from an invisible ladder. I was puzzled.

"Well, I must be going," said God. "Goodbye, children."

"Goodbye God!" we all shouted back, and I watched as he reached out for an invisible rung and slowly ascended into oblivion, his body disappearing into the same emptiness between the sky and the ground. All this took place at a disappointingly low level from the grass we were sitting on. In spite of his uniform I realised that it must have been God, for how else would he have been able to appear and disappear like that. As I grew up and saw other, more traditional depictions of the supreme being, I often felt like telling people what he really looked like. Until now I have kept it to myself.

One afternoon after we had all been woken from our nap after lunchtime at the nursery, one of the pretty young nurses led several of the children in a game of chase. As we wove in and out of the apple trees chasing and laughing, we all tumbled and fell and the game became one of rough and tumble. This was unusual because normally everything was a little formal. It was fun falling down and sometimes landing on her, and up we got and round the trees we went, and falling on her and feeling her softness was all I wanted to do. After a particular fall I was the first to get up, and as she rolled with some of the other children shrieking and laughing, her dress had ridden right up her thighs and I stood and gazed at all the wondrous clips and paraphernalia that held her nurse's black stockings up. She wriggled her legs to free herself from the remaining children who were still clambering over her and I became even hotter, and a strange new feeling spread all over me and I liked the feeling but somehow knew that I was not supposed to have it. I thought I would like to marry her and find out more about all these wonderments that ladies had under their clothes.

Once a man came with a donkey and he gave the children rides on its back, but he ran out of time and neither Bruce or I got to ride him. It was nice to look at it though, and in spite of his scruffy coat it had friendly eyes and very long ears. When it had finished giving its rides the man let him wander through the grass, and while it was nibbling, the donkey allowed its penis to emerge. I was absolutely astounded by the length of it and tried to stand in front of the animal in case one of the pretty nurses saw it and was shocked. A long time after that the same thing happened with the coalman's horse, and one of the kids tried to flick a stone at it as it dangled half way to the ground. Creeping nearer to get a better shot at it, the marksman was lucky not to get soaked by an enormous torrent of urine that suddenly splattered all over the road and seemed would never end.

Kids seemed to have all manner of diseases and skin complaints then. There would always be someone with Gentian Violet painted on their faces or their heads close-cropped to discourage nits or fleas. Some kids had perpetual snot hanging from crusty nostrils. Instead of expensive cotton handkerchiefs, I carried a ripped-up square of old bed sheet and at times of winter colds I would pull this out to wipe my nose, only when no-one else was in sight. Otherwise the dried-up piece of what felt like cardboard would remain in my pocket.

Our road was a loop with an exit at one end for pedestrians and a private road into the back of a residential hotel. Between the alley known as the Waldrons Path and the hotel entrance were a few houses divided into flats, and on the other side of the hotel rear entrance was a white house which Mum called the 'Halfway House'.

This was as poor a place as I had ever seen. It was divided up into single rooms for problem families, single mothers, deserted wives, and sometimes families with nowhere else to go. The women were expected to share a gas cooker on the landing, and two toilets supplied the whole house. I don't know if there were any bathing facilities, but few of us had bathrooms in those days anyway. Some of the families who lived there were noisy, often rowing, occasionally drunk and different to the rest of the road. They were also intriguing to me and I found several friends there.

There were three pretty Anglo-Indian girls and their mother; a family from Devon with an Italian name; and a woman who, it was rumoured, had an affair with a man of eighty. She had subsequently given birth to a severely handicapped boy whose name was Roger. At the time he was called a spastic, and the assumption was that he was an idiot. In fact he was a highly intelligent, strong and muscular boy, who in spite of his ungainly walk, dribbling and contorted features managed to roam all over Croydon, where he was admired for his determination and great sense of humour. Roger turned his disabilities to his advantage and wore short pants long after the accepted period for change had passed. He practically had a beard before his mum got him his first long pants.

There were also lots of Irish. In those early years after the war, families moved from the republic to find work and in the chronic housing shortages afterwards accepted the worst kind of accommodation. I think there was always compassion for families, but single men were resented, and I can clearly remember the adverts which persisted for years in shop windows offering rooms for rent with the by-line 'No Irish Need Apply'.

One such family lived in the halfway house with a lot of kids, the oldest being Michael, who must have been about seven or eight. He was a slight boy but tall for his age, with deep brown eyes and dark freckles. He wore a pair of plimsolls until his toes poked out of the ends, with no socks. The people in the road got him a pair of second-hand shoes, and until he had been at school a week, he wore the same pair of swimming trunks for the whole summer although we were nowhere near any water.

I never got close to him, but we all sort of played together and somehow I got to play regularly in the rambling back garden. This originally had a beautifully terraced, landscaped Victorian elegance, but was now overgrown with rhododendrons and the paths were slippery even in summer. Next door was condemned as a property and was known as the Haunted House. Our games often spilled over into this place, and when I was very brave I forced myself down into the cellar that was full of fever water and felt the presence of a ghost.

One summery evening I sat with Michael on the periphery of a group of older children. They were playing a new game about dares, truth and promises, and us younger ones were not allowed to join in. This in itself was exciting because there was something else happening, and there was an edge of danger in the softening, midge-filled shadows. The boys' laughter was deeper than usual and the girls' was more shrieking. At one point one of the girls chased after one of the boys and kissed him on the mouth. Michael and I looked at each other and grinned.

Suddenly Wendy, one of the girls, called Michael over to where they were all sitting and I followed on curiously to see what might happen. Without any warning Wendy and another girl grabbed Michael, and while one of them tickled him the other pulled down his trunks and wiggled his willie between her thumb and forefinger for a few seconds. All of them hooted with laughter and for a second Michael giggled too. Suddenly he burst into tears and they let him go. I was terrified and ran home in a state of shock and excitement. Michael and I never spoke about this humiliation, though I wanted desperately to know what thoughts had gone through his mind while it was happening. Soon afterward Michael got trousers, and later the whole family moved away.

Old Mr. Cox, the landlady's husband, used to work at the bottom of the back garden and had made a sort of shed out of some pieces of air raid shelter. In the summer he was usually stripped down to his woollen vest and flannel trousers, and although he tried to tiptoe past Bruce in his pram, the dog would bark and wake Bruce. He would bawl and my mother would tut-tut and come out and rock him until he went back to sleep. Once Mr. Cox invited me to his shed, and poured me a cup of sweet tea from his thermos into a beautiful little china cup with a poppy printed on the side of it. I thought it was one of the best things to do, sitting in his shelter sipping tea. He spoke to me, but it was one-way conversation as he was quite deaf and could never make out what I was saying. I hoped Mr. Cox would invite me again but he never did, being too busy growing things on the patch of ground that my father had once worked. Eventually this piece of land was sold for a building plot, and I was convinced that the builder had used my swing frame for a door lintel as we watched the house rise out of the vegetable plot.

One day from the bedroom window we saw a plump red-headed boy in the back garden.

"Mummy, there's a boy with red hair in the garden," I alerted her.

"It's Mrs. Cox's grandson," she said, and turned to look at him from the window. "Look at him, the fat pig."

I was surprised at this remark and have often sought to justify it. Was it because his slight stoutness was proof that he was getting enough to eat, when in our own lives it was a double struggle for us, first to afford the right food and secondly getting us—or me at any rate—to eat?

My mother told me that at one point after my father left us that the doctor simply said, "If you don't get this child to eat soon he will die."

I was first force fed at nursery school and the feeling of that spoon being rammed down my throat only made me vomit up what little they had managed to get down me in the first place. Sometimes I would manage to keep food down all day only to throw it up at night.

Mrs. Cox's grandson wandered aimlessly about the back garden for the next couple of days with no-one to talk to. He was a lot older than me, but mustering the courage from familiarity of surroundings, I finally went out to him where he was walking in the bushes by the reformatory next door and said hello to him.

"Hello!" he said back to me, as nice as pie.

"My mum says you're a fat pig," I told him, and immediately realised it was not the right opening thing to say.

"Does she now?" said the stout redheaded lad with a grace and aplomb that astounded me. We spent the morning getting on quite well, but the age gap between us, not to mention my opening remarks, precluded a deep friendship from burgeoning. I told my mum what I had said and her conclusion was that we would probably be thrown out on to the street.

I lost my appetite completely and hardly slept for the dread of being kicked out. In my convoluted prayers I wrestled with the concept of honesty over diplomacy. For the life of me I cannot think what possessed me to tell him her remarks. Visions of the three of us plodding round the streets, with Tyler the dog barking at everyone we spoke to, and our pathetic possessions heaped on the old twin pram, woke me sweating to find that I had peed the bed. This was a habit that took a long time to fix.

All kinds of things are written about this problem now but the truth is that I was scared to leave the safety of the bed. I believed that even if I did not have to brave the freezing unlit hallway to the bathroom and used the bedside chamber pot, I could still be pounced on by the witch (one night a witch had leaped out of the wardrobe and pinned me to my bed and breathed noxious vapours into my mouth and made my eyes run. She had cackled and laughed at my terror as I lay just a few feet from my sleeping mother and brother).

Around this time another thing began to happen. Often during the day I would seem to hear people talking in low babbling whispers, like conversations coming from down the hall of some building. It was impossible to pick out the words, and that made it even more maddening.

I suppose I became used to hearing the voices. Indeed I may have almost encouraged myself to hear them. From my favourite hymn at school, about God calling to Samuel (*Hushed Was The Evening Hymn*), I hoped that he might call me in a voice that others could hear.

I convinced myself on more than one occasion that God had spoken to me through my mind and advised me to become a missionary to far-off lands. Whether this form of ministry had greater attraction than the regular church because of the element of travel, I cannot now say. All I do remember is that I truly believed God had spoken to me, and when I later realised that he probably hadn't and that it was wishful thinking, I was filled with horror that most of the misguided despots of the world, the causers of such misery to the human race, based the legitimacy of their actions on the conviction that God had told them it was what he wanted them to do.

I needed to believe there was a God and that he heard my prayers, and I liked praying. Sleep always came to me with difficulty, but praying helped. My worst fears were that Mum would leave us, or send us to a 'home', but I also feared for people in general and children in institutions especially; people with no-one to care for them.

I balanced all this caring with resentment at rich kids and privilege, and was quite sure that I would have the last laugh in heaven if I was good. It is a hard lesson to learn that goodness is rewarded by death in the same way as wickedness.

Our landlady, Mrs. Cox, also became a figure of hatred for taking rent off my poor mum, in order that we could live in that dismal freezing damp basement that I missed so much when I was later in hospital. Once, when I took the rent across to number seven, she opened a drawer in her kitchen that seemed to me to be full of half crowns. I nearly passed out at the sight, and certainly had never seen so much money in my life before. If she had so much, why did she need our pound per week? I later realised this old lady was quite philanthropic in her way and, amongst other small acts of comparative generosity, organised a Coronation party for all the kids in the street.

I was also angry that young soldiers died for old generals, although this did not stop me wanting to be one—I suspect it was to prove that I could be tough and manly. Some hopes, when on most occasions the plaintive call of the *Last Post* could, and still can, reduce me to tears.

The angels around the bottom of the stairs who whispered to each other did not bother me, because I could dismiss them, but the voices I began hearing seemed much more sinister. They took the form of muttering and murmuring in tones of discontent. They sounded like the noise you might hear at the beginning of a concert on the radio before the instruments tune up.

Every now and again one voice would rise to the surface, and I would be just about to catch the words he or she was saying when it would disappear in the general hubbub of sound. This voice was the one that particularly disturbed me. I was never sure whether I was being warned, threatened, advised, or admonished. Sometimes the voices would begin at full tilt and other times they would slowly increase in volume. This mostly happened when I was on my own.

Sometimes they were talking directly to me and their message would be frustrated by my inability to catch what they were saying. Most often they were talking conspiratorially, as if they were discontented. Was it with me or the world? Were they coming to get me, or planning my rescue? I could not tell, and asked my mum what they meant. She advised me that they probably would soon disappear, and that she would ask Mr. Strong at work (the assistant dispenser). She had earlier explained my curiosity about erections as having excess acid in my body. I knew that rhubarb had acid but I liked rhubarb, so I resolved not to ask about that again, and live with my erections. This was very different. I don't remember what Mr. Strong's advice was, but the voices continued and only stopped when they were ready.

Somewhere along the road Mum had bought us an old piano from the junk shop at Reeves Corner, and I loved it. It cost about eight pounds and it was definitely for me, as Bruce had absolutely no interest in it. I would spend hours playing tunes with one hand, and sometimes the voices would stop abruptly whilst playing, and sometimes they would start whilst playing. Sometimes I tried to shout them down, or sing loudly to drown them. Later, when I began to get used to them, I tried to listen in case I could learn what they were trying to tell me.

On the whole, they frightened me and I wondered to myself if I was going crazy. We had a crazy woman who used to walk through The

Waldrons from time to time and I didn't want to end up like her. She wore a mauve hat and her stockings were all loose and she had red lipstick smudged on her mouth and she was mad and I had nightmares about her. I liked happy shows on the radio because they chased these voices away. I loved people who laughed a lot because they chased them away too. But sometimes the voices would appear in the middle of these moments as well.

The voices ended finally as I entered my teens, but at this early stage I found I could sometimes drown out the noise if I hummed to myself. My preferred method of making them go away, however, was to whistle.

Men, and to some extent women, used to whistle then and they don't now. Perhaps it is because of the constant noise pollution, or more likely because people look at you if you whistle. I was coming home one day from Duppas Hill park when I first got a sound from my pursed lips. In the beginning I could only get one note out, but by the time I got home I could manage a bit of a tune. Naturally I wanted to share my new skill with everyone and wanted all my friends to be able to do it too.

I tried to explain the trick but it is impossible to explain how to whistle. You just have to walk around pursing your lips and looking stupid blowing away, until that first reedy note emanates from inside your head, and then intuitively you can eventually call up any note or any pitch you want without even sliding up to it. Soon you develop your own tone, and the popular melodies of the day were very accessible.

The impression this gave was that I was a sublimely happy child as I wandered about the place whistling away, but the truth was sometimes a little darker. Indeed, when a song came out with the words, "I whistle a happy tune so no-one will suspect I'm afraid," I was comforted that others might be hearing these scary voices too. I whistled all the time and was particularly impressed by a performer on the radio called Ronnie Ronalde who could almost warble like a real bird. Could you, I wondered, make a living from whistling? I thought that would be marvellous, so I practised all the more.

❧

frank

"Y̶ou sound just like your father," my mother would say, as I whistled my way round the house or along the road from school. I liked to think that I had got something that was good from him.

The hurt that he had caused us all was immeasurable. It affected us on an almost daily basis; from the moment we were awoken to go to nursery school to being the last ones collected from it, we were reminded of his lack of commitment to our well-being. In his actions he had denied us the comfort of having a mum at home. The intimacies between us all were always strained by both my mother's exhaustion and her duty to take care of us, and we were always aware of it.

The night my father first left us I was in their room. Whether I had come in to see what the noise was about or whether I was in there when the noise started I do not know and my mother does not remember. She was sitting on the bed, crying and shouting, and my father was angry. Though I have never been able to recall the actual sound of his voice I know that it was moderate and warm, but this night it had an added intensity. As the row went on, no-one seemed to notice I was there. I stood motionless, watching these two people shout and plead and deny and assert in a tableau that I had never witnessed before.

"You dropped the letter behind my back," wept my mother. My father just stood there, pale and with thunder in his eyes, and his brown skin looked yellow in the light from the forty watt filament in the clear glass bulb that lasted for years afterwards, its curly red image of points hanging like a crown between the two terminals inside the vacuum. Suddenly he seemed to notice me for the first time, as my mother's body shook with sobbing. He turned and grabbed the door handle.

"I'm leaving!" he shouted.

"Frank!" cried my mother.

There was a mighty slam of the heavy front door before a deafening silence as we waited for a change of heart and direction. It did not come, and with a huge desperate sob my mother collapsed on to the bed and cried and cried.

Hardly able to take it all in, I crawled up on to the bed, the strange feel of the knitted spread in blue with brown and white stripes feeling comfortless to my skin as my mother seemed to be burying herself deeper and deeper into it.

I reached over her back, her feet still dangling over the side of the bed and said, "Don't worry Mummy, I'll look after you."

As I uttered the words I was surprised by the way it sounded, for as they were being said I really meant it. After they had been spoken I realised the magnitude of the statement, and it had made my mother cry even more and that in turn made me cry. Bruce slept through it all.

By the few accounts that it is possible to draw on, my father did love me. He often took me to work, and I used to sing for his work mates in the cafe. He was close to a Jewish family who were tailors in the high street, and the lady of the house made a big fuss of me too. I remember being in their place, which was very dark and shadowy but not a bit scary. Their shop was near to a chiropodist. In the window of this shop was an anatomical diagram of a foot and part of a lower leg that is imprinted on my memory.

The chiropodist was called Miss Roberts. My father was conducting an affair with her even when my mother was in hospital having Bruce, and I had been sent into the care of a Mrs. Hayes. I can only surmise by what went on that all did not run smoothly between him and his mistress even after he left us.

Often my dad would be back at our place when I got in from school.

I cannot explain how, but I always seemed to know that he would be there, and my whistling would drain away before I got to the steps to our flat. The effect of his visits was to suck the energy from our little family. It would be smiles when we got in and a little chat, they would talk, and then he would go and she would cry. Sometimes they would shout and she would cry. It was terrible, and in the end I was frightened of him, not from any threat of violence but for all the pain that would ensue when he had gone. He had begun to put on a lot of weight, and although he was under six foot tall my mum says he got up to fifteen stone.

One morning he was in the flat wearing a dark suit and in need of a shave. I guess he had fallen out with his new partner and was living rough in the woods and made his way to our place still confident in some sort of welcome. By this time he had acquired an old motor car and a shotgun; later he arrived with a black dog that had been bitten by a snake and asked my mother to fix it up for him.

I have several clear memories of him that I know are accurate, and I still have tangible proof of one of them. My mother never gave us extra pennies for sweets; we had our sixpence pocket money, and because we ran errands for the whole street we picked up a few more coins this way. What we did have was a sweet tin. My mother kept everything in jars or tins to protect them from mice or dirt or fingers, and at the end of the day she would reach for the tin and dole out a sweet each. It never occurred to me to steal one, and we looked upon the treats as confirmation that she still loved us or that we had been good. My father was home, and in a genuine effort to get to know me had taken me down to the local shop, and after picking up a packet of cigarettes had asked me if I wanted a sweet. In those days a penny could buy you a gobstopper, a packet of YZ chewing gum, two flying saucers or four blackjacks.

I was so taken aback that I did not know what to ask for, so I said, "A flying saucer please?"

"Is that all you want?" he asked me, smiling at the same time.

"Yes thank you," I replied, and he duly parted with the ha'penny required, half smiling and shaking his head disbelievingly. I crunched up the rice paper outside and frothed the sherbet inside and spoke no more words to him. He asked me if I liked school, or some other inane enquiry, and I nodded.

The next memory is of being told how to hold a cricket ball. This was probably, on a scale of one to ten, about minus five on my list of ways to improve my knowledge. Of all the men I know who have been brought up by single mothers, I am the only one that has any interest in sport at all, and that only really began when I had children of my own. I threw like a girl, and have never had good hand to eye co-ordination. These skills, such as they are, had to be acquired by imitation, bluff and sheer bravado in my early teenage years, and I was not really found out until I played football for the pub team—and then my weaknesses were put down to my veteran status.

"You have to keep the ball behind your back until the last minute, so the batsman won't know what kind of ball you're going to bowl him," explained my dad conspiratorially in my ear as he pushed my hand firmly behind me.

"Now take your run up and swing your arm over and spin the ball," he instructed. I had only a passing interest in hitting anything with a bat and when we five-year-olds played we only threw underarm. I duly tried to please him, but the ball, instead of going toward the piece of planking that he had set up as a wicket, flew straight up in the air. My father laughed and I went red with embarrassment.

"One more," he encouraged. This time the ball shot out sideways at right angles to the intended direction, and as I got more and more flustered the situation just left me until I was close to tears. To my relief he abandoned the exercise.

It was coming up to Christmas one year, and the stores were full of the usual toys and games ready for the festive season. I had spotted a child's tool set comprising a small hammer, a saw, set square and so on, neatly arranged in a presentation packet. I decided that if I was armed with this item I could make every other toy I ever needed and proposed to ask Father Christmas for it when I sent my list up the chimney.

Halfway home from school I sensed my father would be at home, and sure enough when I got there his brightly painted old Wolseley was parked outside. After saying a resentful hello, I retreated as normal, but at some point he found me and in his effort to make conversation asked me what I wanted for Christmas. I told him I was hoping for a tool set, and he asked what I wanted that for, but I couldn't tell him as it suddenly sounded stupid. Instead I just said I wanted to be a carpenter. This seemed to meet with his approval and he told me to come with him to his car. After rummaging about in the back, he presented me with a small picture fram-er's hammer with the nail lifter broken off, a hacksaw, a screwdriver and a mortise or saw gauge made from two pieces of wood.

"There you are," he said, "now you've got your tool set." I looked down at my collection of scrap instruments, and wondered how far I would get with my plan to make everything we ever needed with such items. I think I knew even then that what I really wanted was the pleasure of unwrap-ping the tools rather than using them. I still have the broken hammer!

I do not feel able to press my mother on their relationship during these years. They were estranged and he was living with someone else. Although there are strong indications that she would have willingly taken him back, it was not to be and hopefully he enjoyed seeing Bruce and I from time to time.

Once he came to see us and took my mother to school where they both watched me leave the school gate and go dancing a 'happy to be going home' sort of dance, which resembled the Morecambe and Wise jig. I had become convinced that I had almost discovered the secret of flight at this time and may have actually been in experimental mode. My mother told me that my dad wondered if I was the 'full shilling' at the time.

On another occasion he joined us for tea, and as Bruce and I sat eat-ing our bread and jam he flew into a rage because Bruce had his elbows on the table, and he tied his arms to the chair with the straps from our recently acquired bus conductor's outfit. This was a terrifying experience for us both, as we had seldom seen a man in real anger before. My father's temper was dreadful and years later my mother tried to rationalise it by telling us of his war experiences, but at the time it must have been hard to cope with even when they were happy together.

She told me once how he had mistaken one of his friends sitting next to her in a car for someone else and punched the guy out through the car windscreen. He had lost his sergeant's stripes twice, for fighting and for attacking an officer. There was also violence against my mother and ac-cording to his mistress he tried on more than one occasion to strangle her. I am in no doubt that had he really wanted to, he would have done so. I can only take it that reason and compassion were also part of his character. In spite of his imprisonment and subsequent hospitalisation after the war, he was utterly fearless and with good reason. He was a good athlete and regimental heavyweight boxing champion.

He was also an above average cricketer, and was invited to play for the MCC, which he derided by saying, "I'll hit them if they get someone else to run for me."

As a result of a boxing injury when he collided with the corner post he could only blow smoke from one nostril. He told my mother that he only wanted one kid, although once Bruce had arrived it was he who named him, as he did with me. When he was on the move we were always getting letters asking for bills to paid, as he chose to give our address to avoid ever being caught up with. I believe he did the odd bit of time for minor street trading offences and I also have a memory of a suitcase full of lions made from pipe cleaners. Our neighbours across the road remember him getting their two girls to sew up some material in the shape of animals, that were then stuffed elsewhere and sold from suitcases on street corners. At one point he even acquired an electric motor and fixed it to their old treadle machine to speed up the operation.

After he left us Bruce and I never had a single birthday card or present from him, and I know that he never gave my mother a penny towards our keep. She would never lie about such a thing. The penultimate time that I saw my father was in 1951, when he arrived one day out of the blue to take me in his car to see the Festival of Britain, the great exhibition on the south bank of the Thames. The only trouble was that it was not yet built, and as we wandered round what was a giant building site I wondered if he was planning to take us on all the magical rides and amusements that would one day be in place. On the way back home he took me to a café where he bought me fish and chips. I could barely manage the knife and fork, and when he dropped me off he had a go at Mum about my table manners, which forged another quarrel and my voices came back again and I wished he would just leave us alone.

The last time I saw my father he was sitting opposite my mother by the wall. The old table had been moved across the room and now occupied the wall area next to the condemned room which was the bedroom I shared with Bruce. Now under the window was an older styled 'put-u-up' or sofa-bed with wooden arms and covered in a pink material with a thirties type pattern on it. I sat there listening to the conversation as if I was not there and once again it turned to Frank coming back to us and got more heated. The voices in my head got louder and louder and still I could not hear what they were saying. Suddenly I burst out with a string of invective that stopped both my parents in their tracks, and they just turned and stared at me.

"Why don't you just go and leave us alone?" I shouted, my voice trembling. "You only make Mummy cry and that makes us all cry. You're no good! None of the Mays are any good! Why don't you go away and leave us alone?"

My speech went on for much longer than this but these are words that I clearly recall. Perhaps this is hardly surprising. All the time that my unbroken string of tormented sadness was being transformed into words that had been unrehearsed, other voices were encouraging me, all of them talking at once. It wasn't just my own voice I could hear as I spoke but lots of voices, and though I could not hear the actual words they seemed to be saying *Go on, tell him all those thoughts and feelings.*

The words flew out from my lips and my temperature was rising and a dark redness becoming black was enveloping me. I was frightening myself.

Where were these words coming from?

Why had I chosen this moment to let it all go?

Why weren't either of them saying anything to me?

Why are these tears falling out of my eyes and splashing on my bare knees?

Where is all this snot coming from?

For a few seconds the two of them sat there staring at me as the tears of rage and anger burnt down my hot cheeks.

My father turned to my mother and said quietly, "Did you tell him to say that?"

"No of course not!" she answered.

"No-one told me to say it!" I sobbed. "You just make us cry and we don't want you and we don't need you!"

I shook the words out of myself and sat with uncontrollable anger and sadness pouring out of me.

"I think you'd better go outside now, Ralph," said my mother. I left the room and found the piece of old bed sheet in the pocket of my jacket and blew my nose and wiped away some of the tears. Soon afterwards I heard the front door slam and my mother starting to cry, and I knew that

I would never see my father again.

In our darkest days when Mum was too ill to work, she finally went to an interview with the National Assistance Board. I found her back at home. She had been crying and was still in her best frock from the interview.

"They said, 'Go and find your husband, Mrs. May'," was all she managed to tell me.

What could I do except try to be good? I was still unable to eat much with any relish; although Bruce was becoming well built I was always a bit on the skinny side. Mum eventually found work as a charlady and scrubbed doorsteps and skivvied for some people, so once again we were self-supporting, although the struggle was hard and joyless.

Thank goodness for the radio, where you could hear people laughing at comedians who told jokes that I could not really understand, and music that made you feel good. *Take It From Here*, *Ray's a Laugh*, *Variety Playhouse*, *The Al Read Show*—I listened to them all.

I loved *Children's Hour,* and the recollection of the dramatisation of *Winnie the Pooh* still gives me a warm feeling. I can remember the sound of the actors' voices though the memory of my father's has gone forever. David Davis sang the Pooh songs, Norman Shelley played Pooh, and Wilfred Babbage played Piglet. Babbage also played the schoolmaster in *Jennings at School*, and his exasperation at Jennings' mistakes and his catchphrase, "You silly little boy!" made me laugh out loud.

At that time I thought I would have loved to have gone to boarding school and find a stupid friend like Jennings' friend Darbyshire, but I was soon to find just what being away from those I loved was really like.

∾

accident

St. Peter's Primary School was no more than a rather large house, so
the transition from the nursery school I'd attended up to then, which was
just up the road, was not too traumatic. To get there I only had to cross
one road with very light traffic on it. Nevertheless I still managed to walk
in front of an ambulance one day.

Fortunately the driver had seen me from a long way off, ambling across
the road looking in the opposite direction, and timed our meeting just
before I reached the other kerb before giving me the slightest toot on the
horn to let me know how foolish I had been. My face was still red when
I got through my front door.

My first teachers were kind and I soon learned my numbers and letters. In fact I still think of my letters and numbers in terms of the colours
in which they were printed on the walls of our first year's class with Miss
Gun.

The whole of the basement area doubled as the school dining room
and it was here that I had to wrestle with the problem of school dinners.
I found it impossible to keep the food down even if I managed to get it
past my lips, and became quite adept at shoving food on to my neighbour's plate when they weren't looking.

Once this ruse had been tumbled, I began trying to hide various foods under mashed potato or even hollowed-out boiled potatoes, but this too was discovered. My next plot came to grief when the paper bag in my pocket containing the mash and carrots burst during playtime, making me smell like a pig bucket for the afternoon. Next I tried to swap places to where the tables joined and for almost a week I was successful at dropping my food through the crack between the tables and on to the floor. Eventually by elimination the phantom food flicker was traced back to me and I was summoned to see the headmistress, Miss Clifford.

"Hello Ralph, have you been throwing your food on to the floor?" she asked me very gently. She was a sweet lady with dark hair and a slightly hooked nose.

As the realisation hit me that I had been caught almost red-handed my face responded in sympathy. My body began to ignite somewhere above my navel and rose upward like ink across blotting paper. As it reached my neck and drove quickly over my chin and up my face, the sudden evacuation of blood from my lower body began to cause a trembling in my legs, and my hands assumed the temperature of school milk bottles in January covered with a light dew.

I looked straight into her kind eyes, holding on to her desk with my wet cold hand and hardly able to stand or control my legs. My eyes, their lids throbbing, had now involuntarily filled with water and were about to overflow. My voice had all but dried up, and when it did come I hardly recognised the hoarse croak that emerged from my glowing head.

"No Miss," I managed. It was my first lie.

"All right Ralph," she said, "it must have been someone else."

I couldn't believe it. Of course she knew it was me, but I think she also knew that I had suffered enough and that I would never do it again. I don't know how I got my legs to walk out of that room, and I didn't eat school dinners again until I went to John Ruskin Grammar School. In fact it was walking home to cook myself my sausage with peas and potato that I nearly got hit by the ambulance.

In February 1950 Mrs. Leisk, Mum's cherished neighbour and confidante, was looking after me during the early half-term holiday. Mum was at work and Bruce was in nursery school. I had turned five in the previous December and had been at St. Peter's for the first few weeks of the new year.

Mrs. Leisk was a tiny woman. She had been deserted by her husband

and was as joyless as the grey basement flat she occupied with her two daughters, Valerie and Anita. Both girls were older than me and very pretty, and went to different schools. Anita, the elder, sometimes used to collect Bruce and me from the nursery, and occasionally acted as baby-sitter.

Mrs. Leisk prepared her food with a great deal of care and originality for the times, and tried to persuade me to eat dishes like stuffed toma-toes. It was hopeless though, and after managing her potatoes there was little more I could force down.

There was nothing for me to do all day except look at books, which were mostly for girls. I was not allowed to play in the garden. There was a box of old birthday cards; one in particular had a drawing of a man having a drink, and when you tilted the card his glass appeared to empty (it was a small plastic holder full of orange sand), which amused me for a little while.

This particular Saturday Mrs. Leisk took Valerie and me into Croy-don to look at the shops. It was raining, and as we walked down Crown Hill we paused to peer into a sweetshop window. It was an old-fashioned confectioner's, and I was still holding on to the belief that if you looked pleadingly enough through the glass, a kind person would stop and buy you some sweets.

We were there for some minutes when I was aware of a loud revving of an engine followed by a crash and a blow to the small of my back. Someone—Valerie, I think—screamed, and as I looked round for her I was aware that the whole pane of glass in front of the shop had come loose and was about to fall out of its frame. I couldn't move, as something huge was pressed up behind me, and the pane of glass crashed down on my legs.

Because of the angle at which I was standing, the glass acted like a guillotine and sliced down the inside of my thigh, slashing straight through my overcoat and short trousers and into my leg. I don't remember the pain at this point, I just remember seeing a great flap of skin hanging down from my leg, and the flesh beneath it that was so shocked it had not yet begun to bleed.

I was very frightened and took a step backward before falling on to the shards of glass behind me. I could see that Valerie had become wedged at the knee between the two shops and was crying loudly. People were running about, and two or three of them came to help me. One man laid the torn piece of flesh back over my leg, then they lifted me into the sweet shop and laid me on the floor.

A lorry owned by a firm called Crippen had pulled out from the store across the road and turned left to go up Crown Hill, but had misjudged the turn. It had then mounted the pavement, hitting Valerie first and then the shop front and me almost at the same time. As the glass had fallen out on to me the lorry had moved back, enabling me to stagger a few steps backward before I fell over. The driver had been drinking.

At about four fifteen that day, Anita was leaving her school at the Old Palace. She decided to go home via Surrey Street and saw the huge crowd that had gathered to gawp at the incident. She realised there must have been an accident, but cycled on home, unaware that it involved her mother, sister and me.

While I was being comforted by those in the shop and the ambulance was making its way to the scene, blood continued to pour from another unseen wound in the back of my other leg. I lay there quite still, and the familiar smell of chocolate and tobacco mixed with lemon drops and toffee were as loud to me as the voices that attempted to stop my tears and assuage my fear. Shortly after the ambulance arrived from the nearby Croydon General Hospital I passed out.

I'd lost a lot of blood, and as I came to in a lift going to my recovery ward the two orderlies were talking to each other, assuming that I was unconscious. One of them asked the other if he thought I would make it. The other orderly just shook his head.

The injuries needed over fifty stitches, and a draining tube was fitted. I woke up in a children's ward with a protective crate over my legs and some kid screaming up at the end of the ward. The next few days are lost to me, but I do remember that on awakening all I wanted was to see my mother. My legs were both swathed in bandages and I don't recall any pain. The nurses told me not to move my legs, and I tried to stay as still as I could for as long as I could. I suppose that being used to nursery made me adapt quickly to the nurses on the ward.

There were two sisters on the ward, who were very strict. The night sister was the gentler of the two, but all the nurses were wonderfully kind and compassionate toward their charges, who ranged from about four years old to thirteen. My bed was against the wall facing the window which looked out on to the car park a couple of storeys below.

None of us were allowed visitors in those days and for the life of me the only reason that I can think of is that it may have upset us to see our loved ones. For me and my already insecure nature it was a very unkind rule and I was desperate. Each evening I asked for my mum, and although they explained that all the children were in the same situation, I was not the only one who cried himself to sleep for several weeks.

My right leg, which had received the worst injury, had become infected and when I first saw the wound I nearly passed out with shock. Somehow the stitches had not held, reopening the cut, and a huge scab measuring about an inch wide had formed. It was decided not to restitch the wound and nature was left to take its course. A drain had been inserted and each day when they changed the dressings the nurse would pull a little more of the tube from my leg and cut it off.

At first I was sure that this tube was part of me and hoped to impress the nurse by my bravery. I think what really impressed them was my putting up without complaint the amount of penicillin I had to be injected with to disperse the infection. My behind must have looked like the top of a pepper pot.

Slowly I grew accustomed to the routine of hospital. There was no TV or radio and time hung heavy. I longed to get up and walk, but the nurses all said I must wait. Being so young friendships were not struck up and conversation was very limited. Children came in and out for tonsils or adenoids or appendectomies and occasionally for road accidents.

I only remember three patients clearly: the little boy in the bed on my right and the two older boys at the end of the ward. These two were both accomplished artists in my mind. They whiled away the hours drawing, one of them specialising in drawing various parts of ladies' anatomy, which he held up to us little kids to see our reactions. He also drew hands, usually with a cigarette burning between the fingers.

I admired his talent greatly, and would loved to have become his friend if I had been able to walk down to his bed. But he decided that he could have more fun tormenting the smaller kids by telling us that the men in white coats were going to take us away to the lunatic asylum. I had no idea what this meant, but it terrified me, and because I showed it he did it all the more.

Eventually I hardly slept for fear of capture, and on top of this there was the warm milk incident. As if the food was not horrible enough (sago, rice, semolina and tapioca pudding being a speciality of Croydon

37

General), the evening's close was announced by the delivery of a glass of warm milk.

I could not even manage my mother's milk puddings, so the hospital had no chance. For a while the nurses tried to force feed me but they finally abandoned this and I was allowed to pick at whatever I could manage to swallow. But warm milk at the end of the day was too much—and they only collected the cups when they were empty.

The little boy in the bed next to me was called Stephen; I may have felt badly off, but this lad didn't even have a teddy bear, or any interest in one. On his locker he had some *Picture Post* magazines, but no toys or anything else to occupy him. It didn't seem to bother him; perhaps he was very ill, but he hardly spoke and just lay there looking at the walls all day.

After throwing up my milk a couple of times and still not being excused taking it, I hit on a plan. When Stephen turned to drink his milk I slipped mine into the top shelf of his locker, and in the business of cup collection afterwards, its disappearance was not noticed. This simple deception went on for almost two weeks, by which time his top shelf was full and I had begun to use the bottom shelf as well. The only trouble was that each time I opened the door a terrible smell emanated from within.

With several kids incontinent on the ward there was always a strong smell of some description and this one went by largely unnoticed. Of course it was bound to be discovered eventually, and one morning when the nurses were tidying all our beds for matron's inspection the contents of Stephen's locker were revealed.

"Stephen, what on earth have you been doing?" asked the horrified nurse as the discovery was followed by the stench of rancid milk.

"Nothing, miss," said the poor little chap, his eyes widening in astonishment as beakers of different colours containing stinking milk in various states of decay continued to appear from within like tricks from a clown's pocket. I lay on my side pretending to be asleep, though somehow my pounding heart seemed to be connected to my eyelids and I was unable to stop them fluttering; at the same time my temperature was rising and my colour changing.

"It wasn't me, honest miss," came the plaintive cry from the next bed. Finally I could stand it no longer.

"It was me," I suddenly blurted, with tears and sweat pouring from my crimson face. The two nurses looked at me, but it was no use rebuking me as I was clearly suffering enough.

"Never mind Ralph," they said kindly. "It's a good job we found it before matron did." With that they hurried off to get a bucket and clean up the odd spilt one. Stephen looked at me with a puzzled look on his face and one of the two older boys who had gleefully been watching the whole incident said in a loud voice, "Now they're definitely coming to take you away."

I was utterly miserable but managed one small heroic act when Matron asked Stephen what the terrible smell was.

"It was me," I whimpered guiltily.

"Well, next time you ask for a bedpan a bit quicker." Then turning to the nurse, she added quietly, "You can see to him after I've finished..."

My terror of the two older boys had become so marked that even the nurses noticed it, and I was moved to a smaller ward with only two other children. The days passed slowly, and once the older boys had been discharged I was moved back in to the main ward.

Mum had got me some books I could read, and I already had my shawl, a bedraggled piece of pink blanket that would have needed plastic surgery to separate me from, but for some reason all I really wanted was a fountain pen, which I used to ask for all the time.

Miraculously one arrived, but without any ink. The nurse who looked after me said that my mum was going to send it down the phone to me, and as she took it from me it fell on the floor and the top broke. She returned it to me with a piece of plaster round the cracked part with 'Ralph' written on it, and the whole thing had ink in it and I was happy for a while, although I knew that you could not send ink down the phone.

One day they wheeled my bed to the window, and there in the car park below stood my mum with Bruce, and they waved to me and I waved back. It was the first time I had seen them for six weeks, and it was too much for me and I started to cry and had to be consoled. I cried myself to sleep again for the next few days.

The infection eventually cleared and a nurse was instructed to remove the huge scab from my wounded right leg. I had to be quite brave, I was told, as it would hurt for a little while. It actually hurt quite a lot and underneath looked pretty horrible too. As it was prised off it stuck to the soft tissue underneath and pulled apart like someone pulling apart a Mars bar. I was nearly sick, but as a reward the nurse pulled out the last of the drain tube and told me that I could soon try to walk.

Later on that day two nurses lifted me from my bed. I had only a light covering over my right leg, and apart from the constant itching as the scar healed there was no more pain. I tried a few steps but was unable to support myself; it was a scary feeling. I could move my legs but there was no strength in them. The nurses sensed my anxiety and laughed gently. They told me I'd soon be going home when I could walk a little better, and over the next few days I did improve. When I'd completed a few steps I was trembling and exhausted, but excited too as I knew that I'd soon be home with Mummy and Bruce and Tyler and Timmy the new cat.

You never say goodbye properly to those who care for you in hospital. For you it is a unique moment. They have helped you get well and now you must go. For the staff however it is just another day. Your sense of occasion is seldom theirs.

I was discharged from hospital on 13th April 1950. Seeing my mother again with Bruce's old green pushchair was wonderful. I couldn't walk and had to be pushed. It was all so unreal as we wheeled out into the spring sunshine. As we moved out of the car park, however, the noise of the buses and trams became almost unbearable. Everything was bigger and louder than I remembered it. For fifteen weeks I had been isolated from the world and to re-enter was terrifying. By the time I got home I was shaking, and for many weeks afterwards I was scared of the traffic. At one point when I was being pushed to the shops I even got scared of old 'Maida' the milkman's horse, and I was told not to be silly by Mum. I remember thinking that perhaps I was milking the situation a little, and from that moment I began to get better. I had a fairly bad limp and turned my foot inward a bit, but I had some boots that were not unlike the support boots I'd worn when I was younger and slowly my confidence returned.

I had not been home more than a few days when Mum mentioned that I was going to be sent to the seaside to something called a 'convalescent home'. The word 'home' filled me with dread and I began to shake with fear.

"Why have I got to go?" I wondered.

"So that you will get well quicker in the sea air," said my mother.

"Will you be coming?" I asked with more hope than expectation.

"No, of course not, Ralph—who would go to work and look after Bruce?"

An old brown suitcase was slowly being filled up with clothes and shoes wrapped in newspaper and all my garments were marked in Indian ink with my name in block capitals: R. MAY. I was terrified that if I went I may never be allowed to come home, and although I would have loved to go to the seaside the prospect of going alone with another bunch of strangers just filled me with morbid dread.

Luckily my tonsils became poisoned! I also developed a chest infection, and because of the amount of penicillin that I had ingested it was considered wise to let me beat it off by natural means. This meant that regretfully I would not be allowed to go. For a limping, frightened, infected boy, I think I was never so happy in my life.

Recently the correspondence that took place between my mother and her solicitor Mr. Barnes, concerning the accident and its consequences, came to light. With no telephone, their letters were exchanged at one a week, and I now have them all. At the end of it I was awarded three hundred pounds, whilst the driver was fined forty pounds and had his licence endorsed. My mother received ten shillings and sixpence to cover the cost of her fare to the court and loss of earnings. At that time she earned two pounds nine shillings a week and our rent on the basement was one pound!

night duty

Her desk lamp throws a pool of light
That travels halfway up the door
Her face above its shade in shadow
Lights her hands, spills on the floor

And as she moves the faintest breeze
Not strong enough to move a leaf
Yet rustles through her dress and leaves
The lightest touch upon my cheek

In the half light from her desk lamp
I see the clock upon the wall
Its hands are moving, time is passing
Like an injured snail's crawl

Children's sleeping cries and whimpers
Not enough to make her look
The maintenance of steady breathing
Keeps head and pen poised over book

In the half light she stands up
Glides over to the infant's cot
Reaches in and feels his forehead
To find that it is slightly hot

Thumb and finger on his wrist
Shoes more silent than her dress
Reads thermometer and twists
The watch that's pinned upon her breast

Holds the top from off her pen
Between her teeth and slowly writes
"Temperature is slightly up
Seems to be more quiet tonight"

Hangs the clipboard on the hook
On silent shoes and whispering dress
Around the ward takes one more look
Before returning to her desk

I knew it wrong but could not help
But wish that I was ill as he
And that it was my brow that felt
Her finger's touch so tenderly.

That heard the whisper of that dress
As she leaned across the bed
A measure more like a caress
That touched that tiny sleeping head.

❧

magic

$\mathbf{M}$y full recovery was very slow and my voices persisted, but soon I had another helper to drive them away. At the age of seven, just before the inevitable dawned upon me that Father Christmas might not exist, I paid a visit to his grotto in Kennard's department store in Croydon.

Admission was sixpence each, and I was given a plastic four note harmonica. I was always aware of extra expenses that my mother incurred on Bruce and I after we had our pocket money, but that wasn't why I set about getting a tune out of it. I just played the squawky thing all the time for the love of it, and eventually a tune arrived. I can still recall the thrill of getting *Hot Cross Buns* out of the thing, and it was not long before all I could think about was getting a real shiny metal harmonica. The one I craved was made by Hohner in Germany, and several of the boys at school had mouth organs made by them.

I had seen one in Surrey Street market on a toy stall which was an Aladdin's cave out on the street for small boys. The chap who ran it was called Charlie and he spoke in a high pitched nasal monotone and wore a very thin moustache. His toys ranged in price from sixpence to about two pounds. These more expensive items were on sale in his shop and not on the stall. He had some saucy novelties like the Mannequin Pis statue that embarrassed the hell out of me because you could see the little boy's willie. You filled the little doll with water and pressed his rubber hat and he peed for you.

The stall also sold some erotic dolls that if you pressed them their swimming tops came down and their breasts inflated, which I thought was quite exciting. Inside the shop amongst the comics and toys nestled glamour magazines such as *Spick* and *Span* and the naturist periodical *Health and Efficiency*. Once Bruce and I found one of these mags out in the park and pored over the carefully airbrushed photos of naked ladies playing tennis and volleyball. Of course Mum found some of these pictures in the back pocket of Bruce's trousers and we were asked why we wanted to look at pictures of naked ladies, a question to which it is impossible to find the right response.

After Saturday morning pictures I often hung around the stall daydreaming and watching nasal Charlie occasionally demonstrating his wares. Along with cap guns and spud guns, water pistols and masks, lay a shiny harmonica. It was slightly curved in shape like a smile, and it cost two shillings and elevenpence. On the box it had a picture of a boy with a feather in his hat playing in a woodland, and fluttering all around him were tiny birds drawn to his playing. I loved this object. I dreamt about it. I could hear the sweet music from inside its reeds. I would be that boy, wandering the pathways of Croham Hurst with wild birds all around me singing gratefully to me for sharing my music with them.

Two and eleven. It might as well have been a two pounds eleven. On my sixpence a week it would mean me forgoing Saturday morning pictures for nearly six weeks, and we were in the middle of a wonderful Flash Gordon serial at the moment. Mum had always encouraged us to save our pennies and on checking my errand money I found that I had nine pennies. I was encouraged and let it be known amongst the friends that I was open to offers for work.

Running errands for people on the street usually earned one penny tip, but this source had dried up. Then fortune smiled on me in the form of Mrs. Williams who asked me to be her regular errand boy. From then on until she died I went upstairs to the back of the ground floor where she lay, not quite bedridden.

Each Saturday morning early I collected her shopping list written in her shaky Victorian copperplate. For this job I received the princely sum of one shilling—I was rich beyond compare. Even my mother could not hide the surprise at this huge wage, but the old girl's weekly shopping was more than two huge bags full and I had to rest on the way back with the handles of the shopping bags cutting into my hands. She might have been frail but there was nothing wrong with her appetite.

What was also unusual was that the coins she paid me with were all old shillings, with the lion on the back and George V on the front. Now I guess she might have been raiding an old money box of her own from some long ago period. Perhaps that was why I got a shilling; maybe she had only saved shillings. I would have been very happy with sixpence and in a way that is what I got.

"Well you better save half of that for the future," Mum advised, and I did. In fact I saved all of it and in less than three weeks I was the proud and tuneful owner of a 'Song Bird' harmonica.

I parted with the money and collected the instrument in a plain brown paper bag, ran up to the top of Scarbrook Road and took out the box, fumbling with the lid and staring with absolute joy at the precisely wrought tiny piece of German engineering. I put it to my lips and blew the first notes. It sounded so sweet to me that I was lost for the next quarter of a mile, only hiding it as I got near to Pump Pail and the rough kids on the Salem Place estate. Then it was up the hill to The Waldrons, tootling and playing all the way. On arrival at the door of the basement I was only slightly disappointed that I was not surrounded by flocks of appreciative birds.

I went to school playing it, and played it at school, and came home from school playing it, and in the evening I played the harmonica. I played all the time, pop tunes, nursery rhymes, movie themes, anything. When Granddad came he taught me *Sally Go Round the Jam Pot* and was quite impressed with my efforts. Just like thousands of other small boys I loved the feeling of being able to play almost without thinking any tune (without sharps and flats) and I even wrote a melody of my own that I can still play. Everyone thought me such a happy child—if I wasn't playing the mouth organ I was whistling and if you pointed a camera at me I would grin for you. I still do.

The truth is that these activities did drive my voices away and filled me with great happiness. The comments that I got from people lifted me, and music gave me a discipline and sense of worth that has never really gone away. I kept the Song Bird in its box until the box fell apart, and from then onwards it was always in my pocket.

One night by the fire I was pressing the shiny top of the harmonica

I whistled first in nineteen fifty
A windy day on Duppas Hill
And from then on I whistled daily
And happily for me do still

This whistler's mother often said
Your father he was just like you
His hair was curly yours is not
But he was always whistling too

Laddered painters worked and whistled
Milkmen trilled their daily round
Postmen tunefully delivered
Grocers whistled by the pound

Whistling trains and kettles chorused
Rag and bone men clanged and yelled
Factory work started with whistles
Busses stopped by dings and bells

Harmonicas played on the wireless
Chromatically correct the tunes
Of Tommy Reilly Larry Adler
Or Max Geldray with the Goons

In whistling commune with the birds
In the woods at Croham Hurst
It seemed no breath entered or left me
Without making music first

The wind that stirred my silver Songbird*
Transformed to notes that fell like beads
Into the pool of sounds and voices
Contained among its trembling reeds

* The Songbird was a harmonica made in Germany

near my eye and I imagined that I could see forests and rivers in the close reflection. Soon I could see herds of deer and buffaloes and by just twisting the instrument one way or another all sorts of different scenes moved before me. I told Bruce about it and offered him a look but he couldn't see the images that I was able to. When I took it back I was able to see some of what had passed before, but on subsequent days I was unable to call up the picture. I have never forgotten the effect, though.

If music was magical, then magic was just as important. I probably first saw a conjuror at school or nursery and I was hooked immediately. In the wonderment that was Kennard's department store, near the rear entrance on the street level, there was a small counter with a red-faced gent who wore a yellow bow tie and spoke with a northern accent. It was his job to demonstrate the jokes and tricks beloved by small boys everywhere. After Saturday morning pictures I would stand in front of his stall for hours watching him perform with the three egg cups or walnut shells, disappearing sponge balls or card tricks. For the most part I was to remain mystified, delighted and frustrated as I tried unsuccessfully to duplicate his skills. Whenever I asked anyone how they were done I was fobbed off with the phrase 'sleight of hand'.

I wondered what it meant and where you could get a sleight from? The tricks on sale were always about the half crown mark but by saving and running errands I was able to purchase one or two of them. As you might expect, once the secret had been revealed to me I always performed the trick too quickly, but eventually I learned to practise a bit more before performance, and was quite adept in my little deceptions. The thrill of successful completion was always worth the pounding heart and sweaty fingers.

My mum belonged to the public library, and once I had exhausted all the children's books on magic I prevailed upon her to get me some from the main adult section. I would pore over these books for hours and some of them would have pictures of long-dead Edwardian exponents demonstrating the effects.

The explanations would appear under headings such as Effect, Apparatus, and Method. Usually my heart would sink after 'apparatus', where the list of requirements for a particular trick would appear:

1) nitrate of potash;
2) a silver candelabra;

3) a sheet of vellum (calf skin is preferable); and so on...

However, I would still read on to find out how it was done, even if I never had a chance to perform it. This interest led to puppetry—glove puppets in particular—and I acquired a Coco the Clown from Surrey Street, and later even an Archie Andrews ventriloquist doll. Soon I was putting on shows for the other kids in the street, and gradually I collected more puppets and the plays became more elaborate. I was always trying to make things, but my dreams of carpentry have continued to elude me and it would not be right to blame my father's tool kit entirely. Most of my work would have been made from old cardboard boxes, as I would construct machines based on Flash Gordon and old Batman or Rocketman serials from Saturday morning pictures. These designs were made more interesting with morsels of the junk that inevitably fell off lorries delivering scrap to Holloway's yard at the end of the road.

Our financial situation was constantly held up to us and to my certain knowledge Bruce and I never asked for so much as a one penny chew from our mother. We were aware of the heartache such a request would bring. Besides, we did all right—Mum made home-made cake, sometimes with an egg; we had a sweet tin from which were doled out sweets when we'd been even better than usual; and our friends in the street were always getting the odd penny or tuppence to buy sweets with. Both Bruce and I became very good at pleading from our more affluent chums:

"Can I have one?"

"Oh go on, just one..."

"Ahh go on, I'll be your best friend."

"All right then, how about a lick?"

And, more desperately, "Can I have that when you've finished it?"

❧

jock

My mother had managed to get a job at Wilkes the chemist on Parchmore Road on the first of December 1947, my brother Bruce's first birthday. The shop was on the corner of Beulah Road, and faced the police station where the motorcycle section of the division was based. We used to watch the police motorcyclists going about their business, zooming in and out of the place on their maroon-coloured Triumphs.

The chemist's was now owned by a Mr. Waters and on the labels to his medicines he was referred to as the proprietor. He resembled a character out of an Ealing comedy, with prematurely white hair, large-gapped teeth and glasses without rims which slipped down his nose so that he always had an enquiring look whenever you spoke to him. His air was that of an old Church of England parson, complete with a drip on the end of his nose. He was a kindly but frugal man, thinking nothing of transporting cylinders of oxygen on the crossbar of his bike to needy recipients, but at the same time only providing old telephone directories for toilet paper in the outside loo. He had a reputation for believing sob stories, much to the annoyance of Mum who felt that we had genuine need, and he was always loaning people cash on the promise that they turn to Jesus and promise to repay when able. They seldom did either.

There was little or no heating in the shop, and the women were

49

always complaining of the cold. They might have actually got somewhere if old 'Strongy' had ever backed them up. Mr. Strong was the unofficial dispenser. He made up the medicines, officially under supervision from Mr. Waters, or later on Mr. Jones, who were both qualified dispensers, but usually it was he who did the lion's share.

The chemist's shop in the late forties was a substitute for the doctor's surgery, and in many cases preferred to it. People would come in to discuss very intimate subjects with some of the staff. My mother became an unofficial diagnostician; in particularly difficult cases she would refer to Mr. Strong, who in turn on particularly tough questions might speak to Mr. Waters, but only to confirm his own diagnosis. The shop had its own range of patent medicines and often if they did not have what was needed they might "make you something up."

Strongy was a Liverpudlian, and Bruce and I both thought he spoke funny. He was a short, wiry, stooped man, losing his dark hair. He had one of those unattractive moustaches that looked like the end of a paintbrush; it grew straight out as if daring anyone to kiss him under penalty of being poked by his wiry bristles. Poised like some caged bird, his plumage a distressed white coat with sleeves too long and his scraggy neck thrust forward out of a collar that was always too big for him, he worked away out of sight but not out of earshot of the customers who queued on the other side of the partition. Weighing minute portions of this and that, a jar here, a bottle there, he moved like some strange alchemist, weaving spells next to the sink with the small brass cold water tap.

"Hello terrors!" he would greet us through clenched teeth as we walked round the back of the shop to where he was working.

"Hello Mr. Strong!" we'd chorus back smiling.

We could tell that he was smiling too under that moustache. Two kids less like terrors would be hard to imagine, as both of us were very shy and strongly disciplined by our mum. There is no doubt we were very well behaved, we dare not be otherwise, but we both understood the nature of our circumstances, and really did try to help as much as we could to make life no harder than it was already. This did not stop us loving to be called 'terrors'—it made us feel rebellious and dangerous. Strongy had that typical Liverpool sense of irony and dry humour that passes as everyday banter up there, but was not always understood by Bruce and myself. Perhaps he thought we ought to be more daring, or maybe he was trying to indicate that he knew how tough Mum was and was trying to show solidarity with us. We were both very fond of him, and very occasionally he would pay a visit to our dismal flat. His pet names for the two female staff were Blodwyn (Mrs. Owens) and Fan (my mum).

My mother's demeanour was so different whilst at work and it was easy to see why she was so popular with everyone. Confident and breezy and always attractively made-up, she exuded confidence and vitality. I thought she looked so pretty and glamorous and such a pity that it was always zapped out of her by the time she had pedalled the five miles home in all weathers.

As she hung up her white coat and put on the old leather jacket and scarf for the bike ride, she left that other persona behind. By the time she arrived home she had cycled away from her other identity and ridden into that of dutiful Mum with all the cares and responsibilities of raising her two boys.

One evening as she cycled off precariously carrying a rare bag of coal on her back, Mr. Waters called her back, and the rest of the staff thought he might give her a lift home in his motor car. Instead he reorganised the strings and supports she had constructed to carry the coal bag, and gave her some pieces of cardboard to place under the strings so they wouldn't cut into her quite so much. Old Strongy just shook his head incredulously as Mum cycled off into the evening gloom. By the time she got home her hands were nearly dead from where the string had cut into her shoulders, impeding her circulation.

Such pains were soon forgotten in the glow of the supplemented fire. It was always a bit more cheery with a knob or two of coal to supplement the hissing of the damp wood from our Saturday outings at Croham Hurst.

The reps that came to the shop would often treat the staff to free samples of cosmetics, although I heard Mum's reservations over at least one of them who was getting too familiar. The shop gave her a purpose and allowed her to enjoy the banter and gossip that is the oil to ease you through the day. The wages were pitiful but she enjoyed huge respect from the people who used the place and often they would ask to speak to her when they wanted advice or needed an intermediary to the dispenser.

The other lady at the shop was called Jessie Owens. She was a widow and had only just about been forgiven for being Welsh (my father had left us for a Welsh woman). Mum continually found fault with her, but they are still friends at the time of writing and correspond regularly.

Mrs. Owens was an austere-looking woman who had been a nurse. She reminded me a lot of my ward sister at hospital. She was always nicely made up and quite proper. She wore horn-rimmed glasses and had her hair swept back in a bun; her voice was resonant and slightly haughty to my ear, but really it was just the accent and the fact that she sounded different.

Bruce and I had been in nursery care from the first day Mum worked at the chemist. At first she was not able to get us in, as these places were reserved for unmarried mothers. Thanks to our landlady Mrs. Cox, however, she managed to get us both placed. In the early days we were taken in the old twin pram; later when Bruce was bigger Mum would get us dressed and load Bruce on to the little seat on the back of her bike, then with me in tow she would plod up to the nursery before cycling off to work.

Once inside the chemist's she would don her starched white coat, put on make-up and go out to meet the public. This was her stage and she relished the part, reserving complaint for when she got home exhausted. I guess most people knew her circumstances, but this must have added even more to her charisma as she was always so positive whenever we went to the shop, so much so that it was hard for me to recognise her as the same person.

People were supportive in practical ways, passing down old clothes and comics for us boys. Sometimes we would get some old Dinky toys that a kid had got fed up with, and once a builder named Phillips, who was doing up he house where we lived, dropped a load of old toys off for Bruce and me and it was like Christmas coming early.

The reason we went to the shop was to get our hair cut for free, at 'Jock's Gentlemen's Hairdressers'.

"Two halves to the clock, please," was our request and destination on the bus from Croydon. The clock was the Thornton Heath clock tower at the end of Parchmore Road. From there we walked down to the junction of Beulah Road and carefully crossed the busy junction to the chemists.

Once Bruce and I had greeted everyone at the chemist's shop, Mum would usher us out into the barber's next door. Jock would look up expectantly as we came in, and I'm sure his face always dropped a little when he saw us. He would gesture with a sideways nod of his head to a place where we would sit until the last customer had been attended to.

"All right dear, I'll send them through when they're done," was all that he'd say, the scissors snapping without any break.

Jock was one of the old-fashioned, old school, no-nonsense barbers. His shop was plain, not to say spartan. The interior was painted in green and cream gloss paint, with a row of chairs along one wall and two elaborate barber's chairs facing three huge mirrors.

Adverts for Brylcreem, Seven o'clock and Gillette razor blades hung on the walls, with the sombre face of King Gillette himself looking disdainfully down on us, whilst bottles of green liquids and other unguents stood on the glass shelves in front of the mirrors. In silver vases, waxed spills stood waiting for the odd customer who required a singe, and hanging next to each chair was a huge leather strop. In the centre of the wall hung a price list:

GENTS 2/6
BOYS 1/6
SHAVE 1/6
SINGEING from 9d
SCALP MASSAGE 1/-

I never saw anyone get a scalp massage, and as my only previous awareness of the scalp was through cowboy and Indian films, I wasn't particularly sure that I wanted to. The only thing that appeared to be missing from a previous age was the jar of leeches. Outside twirled the slowly revolving barber's pole of red, white and blue which signified a long forgotten commitment to perform this grisly operation.

Jock's partner in the business was Pat, a northern Irishman who would look up and acknowledge Mum as she provided a little feminine presence in this male enclave. All the men's heads would look up at the same time, and then seeing that the lady had two little lads would return to the *Star*, *News*, *Standard*, *Sporting Life*, or one of the tattered copies of *John Bull* or *Picture Post* that used to absorb me for the hours we would sometimes have to wait before Jock would be ready to see us.

Often by the time we got our hair cut the two barbers would have been on their feet for nine hours or more. At this end of the day our treatment was perfunctory but still kindly, Jock with his smiley mouth and somewhat gruff exterior, sandy-haired and smelly of breath, whilst Pat with his curly blonde hair parted almost in the middle would ask trivial little questions in his slow baritone whilst he snipped away.

Jock had to succumb to elastic stockings in the end. Pat's leg situation was even worse and he was on the point of having to stop work altogether, when a local engineer came up with a stool that revolved around the barber's chair. It had a wheel which ran on a track, and its uniqueness made the local papers. Pat had his photo taken on it, and for years a fading newspaper picture of it was stuck in the corner of his mirror, but in all the time we went there I never saw him use his mobile stool. This of course meant that he actually walked further than before, because he had to negotiate the stool whenever he moved round to the client's other side.

Whilst waiting to be called, I listened, enthralled by the rhythm of the place as snips and clips interchanged with mechanical shears. The stropping of razors, the scrape of steel on necks, the smell of hair being singed or lather being applied on stubbly chins and the elaborate preparation of hot towels that preceded it. The jovial banter and whispered asides that often resulted in huge guffaws and an imaginary tear being wiped from the corner of Jock's eye at the telling of some risqué story.

"I'll tell you that one later Pat!" he would call to his partner with a big stage wink.

"Oh aye," Pat would respond in his deep sonorous tone. Sometimes the two men would hit synchronicity and two customers take the chairs at the same time and then I would watch to see which would finish first. Usually it would be Jock. Quite often the men waiting would motion to each other, letting someone go in front of them if their preferred cutter was still busy. I usually got Jock whilst Bruce usually got Pat.

The sense that we were in a show was never very far away, because it was only rarely that anyone sitting in the shop joined in with the banter up front: this was Jock and Pat's show, and those allowed to join in had to be in the chair.

To a small boy it was amazing how knowledgeable they both were, able to switch from horse racing to football, politics to humour at the flash of a scissor blade, and all the time Jock's keen sharp brown eyes were on the door as he clocked the entry of each customer. There was the slap of the pomade bottle and the slurp as he rubbed his hands together before massaging it vigorously into the scalp of his customer, then the flick of the sheet as he dusted the hair from the collar of the man before leaning conspiratorially toward his ear with the enquiry that has become a cliché:

"Something for the weekend sir?"

I wondered what it could mean, as the electric clock with the Silvikrin advert and a pretty girl's picture on its face soundlessly ticked away our waiting.

A local caricature artist was sometimes employed to enhance any special announcement to be made in the shop, and one notice is still very clear to me: it was a picture of a railway carriage disappearing down the track in a landscape, and perched on the buffers were Jock and Pat, Jock on the left one and Pat on the right. Both had on their white coats, with combs and scissors flying from overall pockets as they clutched their suitcases to themselves.

Above the picture the legend read: 'Jock and Pat are taking their holidays from…' and then the dates that the shop would be closed.

This of course seemed perfectly natural to me as I had been brought up on Saturday morning pictures and Jock and Pat were obviously no different to Laurel and Hardy, Martin and Lewis or Abbott and Costello, and like them they probably slept in a double bed (I knew that Jock was unmarried) and why wouldn't they go on holidays together? I did have a problem about their safety travelling by this method, and wondered if we had been able to afford to pay for our haircuts, they may have had enough money to buy tickets for seats on the train.

Finally our time would come and sadly the show would end the moment we climbed into the chairs. Jock would work away quickly and efficiently, with only a cursory question or two as to how things were. Usually the conversation would be between him and Pat as they summed up the day or spoke about things that were beyond the ken of two small boys.

After the electric shears they would progress to the scissors and then the dreaded hand clippers that seemed to pull as many hairs out of your neck as they managed to cut. So as not to trouble Jock too much, Bruce and I often ended up with the longest hair in the school and so as Jock didn't have to see us too often, we regularly left the barbers with the shortest cut he could charitably get away with! Then with the slapping on of some sweet-smelling brilliantine that set hard as soon as it was put on, and the brush and comb treatment that parted and persuaded boyish locks into thirties footballers' styles (which always made me feel that I looked a bit simple), we were done.

Usually after thanking Jock profusely, as we had been taught by our mum to show gratitude for all kindness, I would try to push the swept-back majority of my parted hair into a quiff before it set like concrete. We would then troop back into the chemist's to be admired and called 'terrors' again by Mr. Strong before walking down to Thornton Heath clock tower to catch the bus back to Croydon High Street. With the walk home through the old town, sometimes Mum would have beaten the bus and arrived before us. The fire would be alight and although the room would not yet be warm there would always be a cosier glow to tea time. Then perhaps a bedtime story, with the tiny particles of hair now lodged in the collars of our pyjamas scratching and rubbing our shaved necks.

Jock continued to cut our hair until a couple of years before I joined the army. Around the time I was thirteen, some of the boys were coming into school with hair that had been 'blow-dried'; I had been looking for an excuse to change hairdressers and this was it. Bruce continued for a while, but soon he too stopped going all the way over to Thornton Heath and the chain was broken. It sounds strange, but such is the vanity of youth, I often wondered if Jock was disappointed that we stopped going to him.

There were many such small considerations shown to Mum, Bruce and me, but this was a practical piece of help and a kind gesture by an honest, hardworking and decent man. Pat was eventually forced into retirement because of his legs, and bachelor Jock finished up a married man after all when he married Mrs. Owens from the chemist's shop next door. They retired to Scotland, where he spent a few happy years before succumbing to a heart attack. The twice widowed Jessie now lives in Wales with her niece.

god

They must have told me about God at nursery school. How else would I have recognised him when he came to visit us in the garden? I learned more at school, and began to enjoy the stories we heard there.

The first story that really impressed me was the parable of the feeding of the five thousand. Obviously Jesus, like me, was very interested in magic and miracles. Turning water into wine was actually a trick that you could buy from a company called Ellisdon's in High Holborn, who advertised their products on the back of comics. Then there was raising the dead and making the blind see, and although his ultimate suffering was deeply disturbing to me, he even managed a miraculous resurrection. It always puzzled me how his disciples had to be convinced that it was him, and as for Mary Magdalen not knowing him in the garden and thinking he might be the gardener, *well!*

In spite of my uncertainty about his finale there was no doubt in my mind that he was a wonderful man, and my outrage at the injustice of his sentence, and subsequent awe at his compassion for the perpetrators stayed with me for many years. These thoughts were further reinforced by Chad Varah's illustrated bible stories on the back of my hand-me-down *Eagle* comics.

Crosses filled me with horror, and images of a broken man hanging on them gave me nightmares, while stories about his exploits filled me with admiration and pictures of his deeds were an inspiration. We always knew when we were going to have a religious lesson, because the teacher would place an old-fashioned scroll of linen pictures over the blackboard. He would turn it to a particular illustration representing a miracle or parable and tell us all about the woman who searched diligently for a sixpence, or how Jesus walked on water. It was not until later, in Miss Smee's class at Howard School, that some of these miracles were explained.

"There might well have been only five loaves and two fishes to start with," said Miss Smee, "but people might have been made to feel ashamed when they saw the generosity of that small boy and so added their sandwiches and tea over to make up the twelve baskets that were left over.

"Another thing you will find in the bible is that they are very fond of certain numbers like twelve, seven, and forty. It doesn't mean that they were exact figures, it's just like we have twelve months in the year and also twelve pennies in a shilling."

I am sure these pearls were supposed to be wisdom but they were all part of the mystery to me. Jesus had such a kind face and was usually portrayed in a slightly feminine way, apart from his wispy beard, which looked as though he had never shaved. Pictures of him always slightly disturbed me, yet I derived a great deal of comfort in believing he existed—the corollary of which was the enormous void that occurred when I realised that he probably did not. Or if he did, he was probably not the son of God, because God probably did not exist.

My first Sunday School was at the end of our road and was part of the Congregational church in Croydon. Miss Daisy Bales was in charge, with a young man called Mr. Cawthorn and a tiny lady with very bow legs called Miss Argent helping to run things. There was a lot of happy songs including *Jesus Wants Me For a Sunbeam* and my favourite, *You in Your Small Corner and I in Mine*. For some reason my mum decided to be a Sunday School teacher for a short while. She enjoyed good hymn singing and there was plenty of that down at the main church. Her strict discipline and very assertive manner with her girl charges at the Sunday school won admiration from the other teachers and respect from the sometimes naughty girls.

I was often a bit embarrassed by her assertiveness with them, but they seemed to love her and run to her when she came into the yard in which we held our meetings. Miss Argent was scared of my mum at first and then jealous of her control, especially over the unruly Linnaker family. Mr. Cawthorn, who was prematurely bald and wan, was gentle and not very good at keeping us interested. Miss Bales was tanned and prim with white hair and piercing blue eyes, looking like a seaside landlady, with the addition of that Christian shine that sits smugly on the faces of some true believers.

Those who attended were a mixed bunch, and I suspect now that the children were mostly there so that their mums and dads could have a Sunday afternoon cuddle in private. Given the state of housing at that time, privacy would have been at a premium. One family called Dowser had seven boys and at last Mrs. Dowser had given birth to a little girl. Mr. Dowser seemed to be relieved and everyone thought perhaps they would stop having kids; after all, they weren't Catholics. The seven boys said little about their sister, but eventually it emerged that she was really another brother and their mother was advised to stop dressing the poor little chap in girls' clothes. She refused to do this, however, and for the sake of the family she was indulged until the youngest Dowser began to attend school.

After a slight altercation with Michael Dowser (who was second eldest) in the play area which resulted in him having six stitches in his head, I began not going to Sunday School. Shortly after that, Mum stopped teaching there, although I think she still occasionally went to services in the main church.

I occupied my new-found leisure with roller skating trips and explorations further afield, but one afternoon as I was coming out of school, a man with a small moustache and a microphone, whose name we found out later was Mr. McKay, was standing outside the school gates speaking about a new club that was being set up in a Children's Church.

He promised discussion groups, gym equipment, outings and entertainment. As I stopped to listen and watch, it was apparent that his audience was not the slightest bit interested. I was filled with compassion for the poor bloke. I made a mental note of the address and on the appointed day turned up at the Mint Walk Mission with Bruce and another kid, to find that, apart from an older boy called Philip who came from the Old Town area, we were the only responses he'd had.

He started off by asking us to pray and thanked God for directing our little lost souls to the Mission, while we stared around at our surroundings.

The front edifice was made of corrugated tin sheets in the approximate shape of a church. The centre part was indeed a full size, if small, place of worship, and on each side were smaller wings. One was used as the children's Sunday School on one side, and the remains of what must have been an Edwardian boys' club on the other. We all met in the boys' club part. On the walls were various slogans urging us to be good, not drink and repent. From the rafters hung two or three climbing ropes. There was an old pommel horse, and in one corner stood an intriguing machine that turned out to be a bar billiards table.

Mr. McKay was a working-class Christian man driven by an upper working-class wife who was an enthusiastic evangelical lady. She also supported another fervent evangelist, the Reverend Frank Bustin, and a lovely old lady organist and shining Christian in the form of Mrs. Lily Adlam, who they were all slightly in awe of. A Miss Paul conducted the Sunday morning school. Strangely none of them had children of their own, although Mr. and Mrs. McKay had a temperamental adopted daughter called Brenda.

We were gradually introduced to all these people as they were part of the condition for entry to the boys' club. Mr. McKay promised talks on any subject we wanted "from sport to atomic piles."

"Okay then," said Philip aggressively, thinking that Mr. McKay knew nothing about them, "atomic piles!" Undaunted, however, our leader promised that if we returned next week he would have a talk ready for us. After our first meeting neither of my two conscripts wanted to return, which placed an even bigger burden on me. I could not let the poor bloke down and managed to get someone else to come along to the club the next week, where Mr. McKay warmly greeted the three boys who had shown up. After wandering around the dusty apparatus for a while we were given a glass of orange juice cordial.

"Nice orange juice cordial," I enthused to my unenthusiastic mate. Mr. McKay called us together for his discussion group.

"Now last week, as you may recall," he began, "young Philip here said he wanted to learn about atomic piles."

He pulled out a little red notebook in which he had prepared his talk on the subject, and folded it over to the right page.

He went on, "Now atomic piles are very special piles. We're not talking about the piles what you get up your bottom..."

At this point I lost it completely. Although I tried to follow his rambling discourse I could not get over the opening line. He had done little pencil sketches to elucidate certain points, and I was touched by his efforts although I retained none of the information.

The following week's group was only attended by two of us, and his talk on racial discrimination opened with the line, "Now a lot of people don't like coloured people who are all God's children although some of them do stink a bit and I should know because I was with some of them in the war..."

I lost it again, and after one more week the boys' club was abandoned.

By this time, partly out of curiosity but mostly out of obligation, I had started to go to Children's Church. The room was a miniature of the main building and the whole thing was run by Miss Paul. She was a small lady, quite young, who wore no make-up and had a rather large chin and tiny gaps between her teeth that gave her a rustic appearance. She always wore a hat in church and lived not far from us, in a small house near St. Andrew's school, with her epileptic brother.

The Sunday morning shows were jolly events, and the characters were from a different culture to anything I had known. Miss Paul bought little prizes out of her own money for children who memorised texts, and for years I had a New Testament that I got from her for learning the names of all of the books of the Old Testament off by heart (for fear that no-one else would bother to have a go).

Miss Paul's simple faith and purity was deeply touching to me, and her distress, when her brother was in the middle of a fit, all the more bewildering a reward from God for her kindness towards us.

Once I pushed through a crowd of people who had gathered down near Reeves Corner to stare at her poor brother lying in a pool of blood, thrashing around on the pavement while she stood there with tears pouring down her face waiting for the ambulance to come. God, I increasingly thought, was moving in very strange ways.

By now I was in the grip of evangelical fever and all I wanted to do was to get people to the Sunday school, not just because of a heightened religious conviction but because these people were so nice I wanted them to feel better. None of my mates had any real desire to attend, but at one point I cajoled at least ten new faces with promises of God knows what to induce them to come down to the Mission.

Somehow I got my best friend Charlie Ranger to go one week, and it was the week Mr. Hugget was to speak to us. Mr. Hugget's talks were always animated, with illustrations that he pulled out of a battered suitcase and stuck on a felt board. He was also a passable piano accordion player and he belted out his choruses with gusto. We had to join in with just as much gusto, or we would have to do it all again. He was a large man and wore a brown suit with brown glasses to match. He spoke with all his teeth showing and spat a little at the same time; often when he had come to the end of his sermon he would have little flecks of froth at the corners of his mouth. His hair was always cut too short so that it stood up at the crown, giving him a slightly boyish appearance, but I always enjoyed his little moral tales.

Mr. Hugget had set up his felt board and was rummaging around in his battered briefcase for his props. He kept looking up toward Miss Paul and was looking increasingly perplexed. To fill in some time Miss Paul thanked a girl called Moira, who had brought in some Michaelmas daisies to brighten the room, and informed us, "I think it was Shakespeare who said, 'One is nearer to God in a garden than anywhere else on earth.'"

Then Mr. Hugget blurted out, "I've brought the wrong lesson!"

He sat there with his briefcase on his knee and his top teeth resting on his bottom lip in a foolish grin, blinking myopically through his brown glasses at Miss Paul. She was unable to offer any advice, and he suddenly said, "Oh, I'll give them the one I've brought anyway."

There then began a discourse on the Evils of Drink.

This was a talk that he had obviously given many times before and he warmed enormously to his task. He slapped diagrams on the felt board and told us the proportions of water to alcohol in the average pint of beer and that alcohol was basically a poison and what brewers should really say in their adverts was that they sold Best Poison.

At this last statement Charlie, who had been silently chuckling for most of the talk, almost exploded, and an unbelievable amount of snot spurted from his nostrils causing us all to crack up at the back. Although Miss Paul regarded the matter in hand as serious it was not half as serious as the matter that Charlie had in his hand.

By now tears were running down my face, which made Charlie laugh all the more as I frantically searched for my bit of dried bed sheet to offer him. Charlie had no handkerchief, and the more he tried to clean himself the worse it got and the more it produced. Mr. Hugget responded to the merriment that he believed he had caused by becoming even more animated and began using bigger and more emphatic gestures on his felt board, so much so that his trousers began to work downward and he had to hitch them up before carrying on. This exposed his socks, one of which was shorter than the other, sending Charlie into more paroxysms of laughter until he had to leave the room in order to clean himself up.

"And that's why you should always avoid alcohol!" shrilled Mr. Hugget triumphantly.

He was now bathed in a light sweat, with his trousers hitched a little too high, his glasses awry and steamed up in the cold room, and his hair at the crown standing straight up. At this point Charlie re-entered the room and the sight of Mr. Hugget almost started it all off again, but by now the accordion was being strapped on again and we were getting ready to sing our closing choruses.

In spite of having so many laughs that day I could not persuade Charlie to come again.

By the time I was at grammar school, Sunday had become the busiest day of the week. In the morning I was up and off to the Mission to keep the numbers up, and after half an hour I dashed off on foot to St. Andrew's in Southbridge Road where I climbed into my cassock and surplice to sing in the choir. In the afternoon there was Sunday School back at the Mission, and in the evening there was Evensong back at St. Andrew's. What with all my homework as well, something had to give, and in the end I chose to leave the choir.

There were several reasons for this. Much as I enjoyed all the ceremony of a fairly high church, there was some conflict with my budding socialist beliefs, and even though I was at a grammar school now there was still a bit of snobbery involved, especially about my luminous green teddy boy socks. I was politely asked to stop wearing them, but how else was I to get the lovely Marion to notice me?

Marion was the choirmaster's daughter and she was so pretty it hurt. At practice she would come in wearing her school uniform, and then put on a little make-up before fluffing up her hair in the changing room mirror. I used to watch her with deep appreciation, but she only had eyes for an older boy called Clifford. She was supposed to sing with the boy sopranos but somehow she never stood close to me. I would probably have fainted if she had. I thought she had the sweetest voice.

None of us could read music, although we held the books in front of us and pretended that we could. The choirmaster was a kindly man, but his support was more visual than anything else. One of the two big songs we worked on was *Oh For the Wings of a Dove*. Our music master at school had played us the version by Ernest Luff and I thought it was marvellous. The trouble was that none of us were good enough to do it, so Marion sang it. I admired her even more. We boys approximated behind her as "the godless came fast" and the congregation seemed to approve at the Christmas concert. There was a sprinkling of other girls but none as pretty as Marion.

One day one of the bigger boys contrived to lock her and Clifford in one of the cupboards, and they stayed in there a long time. When they came out they were a little bit flushed, and I knew by looking at her that she had liked being in there with him. Then her dad found out and went crazy at everybody. I was fed up and knew that she would never be mine even when I got my long trousers, so I left and concentrated on falling in love with girls on the bus to school. I never managed to speak to them either.

It was getting difficult for me to equate my religious beliefs to my growing political sense. Constantly I asked myself, "What if?"

I tried to ponder on eternity and got scared. I thought about death and the sacrifice of soldiers and then the sacrifice of soldiers who did not believe in an afterlife. And then the voices would come back.

Ronald Patterson was a skinny kid who lived up the top of the road. He had a little sister called Susie who sometimes played in our garden, and we thought it possible that under the right circumstances she might show us what she had under her knickers. Ronald, on the other hand, was pretty much despised for being a sneak and a coward who threw stones at other kids and ran away.

He was like a magpie; you felt that if you got near enough to him to put salt on his tail he wouldn't be able to run away, but no-one ever got near to him. Even when he ran the odd errand, if one of us gave chase to get even with him over some ancient feud, he would wait tantalisingly until we were nearly level with him before he'd dart off like the wind.

Ronald Patterson was a tormentor, who would hide behind bushes and fire staples with elastic bands at you so that you could not figure out where they came from, or sneaky water pistol jets, hitting you from directions that you could not work out and even if you did and spotted him you couldn't catch him. From these distances I couldn't even be sure what he really looked like except he was very skinny with long running legs and a pasty complexion. I always knew it was him, however, because he wore his school raincoat and cap all year round. And we still couldn't catch him.

One afternoon in our back garden Susie obligingly revealed some of the mysteries of her hidden places. I considered it fair trade on the 'I'll show you mine if you'll show me yours' basis but it still wasn't enough, especially as Susie had already some knowledge of boys through her horrible sneaky little brother Ronald. Nevertheless it was exciting and I looked forward eagerly to whatever might happen next.

Unfortunately our activities had been spotted by old Mrs. Williams upstairs, who told my mum, who was furious but only accused me of trying to make Susie go to the lavatory. I felt really chastened and it was quite a long time before I tried to learn more about the mysteries of the female form. Maybe as long as a month. After a lot of nagging and pleading, Lilian who lived across the road obliged me with a quick peep. I was glad about this particular revelation as her dad hated me and Charlie and called us louts, which we weren't. He was always chasing us out of the garden. Once in a blind rage at both of us he called Charlie a slob and Mrs. Ranger (Charlie's mum) went mad and called him all the words she could manage without actually swearing.

"When I think of my husband slobbing *(sic)* his guts out in the desert for the likes of you it makes me feel sick," she told Lilian's dad. She was brilliant, and although her face was red and she had tears coming down her face and he was pale and shaking, we knew she had won and I was very impressed.

I told Charlie that Lilian had shown me her things and we both thought it was great to get one over on her dad. Later on Denise showed me as well. Denise was a bit of a surprise, because when I was made to sit next to her after some minor misdemeanour in class, she offered to show me before I had asked. This was all very exciting and the more so because you knew that the feeling you were having was one that you were not supposed to have.

In history lessons girls sitting together would often titter at Greek statues and this smacked of humiliation to me, as if they were mocking all masculinity. I searched in vain for pictures of female equipment and in the end was forced to add a pencil line here and there to pictures of naked ladies to get my own back and pass the books across the back of the room to even more titters. Was it all the more exciting because they understood that I had knowledge of such things?

Of course this very natural curiosity and delightful reciprocation was somehow at odds with my religion and produced a great deal of tension as I wrestled with the spiritual over the flesh. In the end Mrs. Patterson heard about the garden adventures and wanted me given a good hiding, but Mum would not hear of it so long after it happened and I resolved to try and curb my curiosity. Ronald had found it a good excuse to fire more stones at me and he was a pretty good shot. I probably thought I deserved to get hit and did little in the way of getting even.

It was early on in my Mint Walk Mission days when the Rev. Bustin came out after Sunday School and asked the children present if anyone wanted to "take Jesus into your heart."

I wondered what it could mean and how many of the kids would stay behind to do it. At the end of the session all the kids got up and went and I realised that no-one was going to take Jesus into their heart.

I felt so sorry for the Rev. Bustin that I went up to him and said that I would do it. I'm sure he was a kindly man and he believed in the word literally. Most recently he had been put in a spot by Philip, the oldest boy at the Sunday school, who like me was beginning to have serious doubts about everything we were being taught. One afternoon Mr. Bustin had come into our lesson and asked if there was anything we wanted to ask him about the bible.

Straightaway Philip said, "I have a question!"

"Go ahead then, Philip," said the reverend.

"Okay. If Adam and Eve had two boys, Cain and Abel, where did their wives come from?"

I was staggered that I had never thought of that one and neither had any of the other kids. How was Mr. Bustin going to get out of this one? I thought he would say that the theory of evolution was the truth, and that Adam and Eve's story had been constructed for the children of Israel to understand, but he took on the question and gave the implausible answer that they would have had many daughters as well, and that times was different then, and that...

"That's incest!" interrupted Philip knowledgeably, and then not waiting for an answer he demanded, "What about amoebas and life beginning in the water and that we are all descended from that?"

We all looked up expectantly.

"That is also in the bible," he said. "Read Genesis chapter 1, verse 20."

We did and it said, *And God said, let the waters bring forth abundantly the moving thing that hath life.*

It also went on about fowl of the air as well, but obviously this ambiguous reference could refer to an amoeba. I was amazed and Philip slightly disgruntled by Rev. Bustin's biblical knowledge, but in the end I favoured Darwin over Moses. The banter between them continued for a bit, and I suppose as far as points scored it was a draw. However I still felt sorry for the Reverend; not only was he beaten by the first question, but Philip did not return to church the following week.

My willingness to 'take Jesus into my heart' would, I hoped, lift his bruised spirits. He did seem pleased as we marched purposefully into his little room at the back of the hall. I do not know what I expected to happen next, but having made the decision I suddenly felt strange as if I wasn't really in control of events. Would there be the sound of rushing wind and fire or would a white dove sail through the window? I hoped not as the window was firmly locked shut. Would he want to see my privates? Again I hoped not, although it was probably all right to show them to a priest.

Once inside the meagrely furnished room we both knelt down and he began praying. I don't remember what he said, but the attention I was getting was wonderful and his strong voice intoned a rambling prayer, the kind that evangelical priests seem to be able to knock out without thinking too much.

After a little while he placed his hands on my head and called out, "If you want joy, real joy, let Jesus come into your heart!"

It was a genuine feeling of elation that I had at that moment, with the Rev. Bustin praying just for me. This was the second time, after my speech to my father, that I had actually made events in my life change by an intentional act. I was pleased with my decision as all my sins were forgiven, and I was sure that included getting girls to take their knickers down and that I would not be drawn away by the delights of the hidden female bits.

I resolved to tell Mum as soon as I got home and felt sure she would be proud of me. I ran home as usual but there was a difference in my step, a lightness and a feeling of relief that I had seldom experienced before. It was a lovely summer evening and the warm air of the day was hinting at a cool twilight. I crossed Southbridge Road and started up the hill to The Waldrons when halfway up I spotted the unmistakable form, still wearing his cap and raincoat, of the sneak Ronald Patterson.

I couldn't believe my luck. He was ambling up the hill alone, and I was behind him and the last person he expected to see was a deadly enemy like me. Stealthily and lightly I increased my pace, my smelly plimsolls making no sound. I nearly blew it at the last when I crunched a pebble but as he turned around to see what had caused this solitary note, I was on him. I had him by the collar of his mac and before he could pull away from me I had his arm. Now what was I going to do?

"Don't hit me don't hit me!" he begged.

I looked at him. He was older than I assumed, or at least he looked older. I had never been this close to him before.

"You little rat," I said, "you're always throwing stones at me. I'm going to smash your face."

"Don't hit me!" he pleaded again. "I won't do it again I promise."

I still had him by the belt on his raincoat and was floundering about as to what punishment I was going to inflict on him when I remembered that I'd just taken Jesus into my heart. What should I do? I really wanted to give him a slap or at least show the other kids that I had caught the little runt (actually he was nearly as tall as me).

My senses were on overload. I had just had a religious experience and now the thrill of capture. I could, if I had wanted to have the satisfaction, have given him a belt, but what about my heart with Jesus in it? Feeling him begin to tremble and seeing the fear in his eyes, I felt my anger being replaced by pity. In the end I just gave him a push that sent him one step off the pavement and let him go. Like a flash he was off, and as he skidded round the corner into The Waldrons, I wondered if I would get an extra credit from Jesus for my mercy.

What I did get was a rock on the side of the head from Ronald the next time I ran an errand for Mrs. Williams. Still, his sister had shared some mysteries with me. Altogether I supposed that it served me right.

woods

Miss Elwell was a seamstress at the Sleepeezee factory. People said that she was a hard and conscientious worker. She lived upstairs, on the floor above the ground floor, which was a half storey above us in the basement flat. From her tiny single room over the grand, columned front door, she had good views of the road and front garden. In the room was a small cooker, and her bathroom was shared with the Miss Dickinsons who lived across the hall.

She was petite with a sallow complexion and deep brown eyes; she seldom smiled, her gleaming false teeth hiding behind very thin lips. Her hair was dark and parted on the right side, its style unchanged since the thirties; although she never attended a hairdresser it still retained an echo of those days. Her movements were quick and nervous and her voice surprisingly deep for one so slight.

Miss Elwell affected to talk 'posh', often adding aitches where there were none and dropping them where they were supposed to be. She called a certificate 'sustificate', a chimney 'chimley' and Westminster 'Westminister'. She did all the overtime that was offered and her simple dream was a cottage in the country with a rose round the door; for this she scrimped and saved every penny. It was a task that would have daunted most people but Miss Elwell was deeply motivated; she needed to be as her boss Mr. Price only paid her five pounds a week. She had no friends and never left her room except for the bathroom and work. In September 1947 my father left us for good and Miss Elwell became my mother's friend.

In my memory she was always in our place, but the first time she padded down from upstairs was shortly after my dad left. For reasons that I can only imagine, she admired my mother greatly and was moved to try to comfort her. Perhaps it was Mum's strength not to give in, or her determination to raise these two little ones by herself. Or maybe she was drawn to Mum because of her own inherent distrust of all men (except Mr. Price). There was a rumour that Miss Elwell had been jilted, and her judgment that all men were swine had now been confirmed by my father's desertion.

Both women were working class, but Mum had the broadening experience of 'service' and had learned etiquette and style that raised her practicality above many of the families around us. Perhaps Miss Elwell picked up on this as she showed the younger woman a deference and undeclared admiration that I was always aware of.

1947 was one of the coldest winters on record, and indeed it was a terrible time to be left alone in a cold basement with two kids to keep warm and fed. Like millions of others we had no hot water, and everything we needed, from tea to washing, had to be boiled on the gas stove. There was a fireplace in one room, and we had a paraffin stove that sucked all the oxygen out of the air, burnt curious little fingers, and smelled. It didn't warm the room, but it stopped frost forming on the bedclothes and gave a comforting pattern on the ceiling as the flickering wick threw shadows through the vents at the top.

In those tear-drenched early days of being alone, Miss Elwell's deep tones sought to comfort Mum as she tried to come to terms with what had happened to the three of us. How had she not realised what was going on? Surely Frank would be back, if not for her then for the two little boys that he seemed so proud of.

All the trappings of a young couple were in evidence in our flat: the slow acquisition of a few bits of furniture; photos on the mantelpiece alongside the round mirror on which he had painted butterflies while in hospital. On the hearth stood two boxes that he had covered with plate copper and decorated with a hammered-out picture of two galleons. This had been done with a punch and a small panel-beating hammer from materials found at work. Mum used to joke that he often found things before they were lost! In front of the fire lay the rug that he had also made as he got well again.

There were pickled onions in the cupboard and meat on Sundays. Though there was nothing that could be said to be new in their possessions, there was the promise of things to come, and because of the garage connections at work, he said it would not be long before they had an old car to get about in.

One day, before the winter had really set in, Miss Elwell suggested a walk in a place she knew beyond South Croydon station. It was called Croham Hurst and was an area of unspoiled hills and woodlands in the middle of the suburbs, with Croydon on one side and Selsdon on the other.

Mum had grown up in the country and walking seemed to help pass the dark hours away, and sometimes she would forget the cold basement that was even colder without him, and so the two friends began the walk to the woods that was to become a Saturday afternoon ritual for the next ten years. Mum loaded Bruce and me into the big twin pram, and with the dog in tow, let 'old Elwell' lead the way.

The route took us up the Waldrons Path and past the nursery school that Bruce and I attended. From there it was down Nottingham Road, across by the Swan and Sugar Loaf, up the slow incline to Croham Road and finally to the woods.

As you entered them on this side there was a drinking fountain, with behind it some toilets, and facing you a steep hill of round pebbles with a footpath leading off to the left. Once climbed, the top revealed a high small plateau of stones and grass, with the ground sloping away to the right. In front was a magnificent view of the surrounding countryside with buildings and homes, and in the distance more trees disappearing into blue grey horizons.

The melancholy of autumn cannot have been the best time to have undertaken that first visit, but perhaps Mum found a reassurance in the almost rural atmosphere, the wet leaves clinging to the wheels of the old pram and her cheeks flushed with the exertion as she pushed us both through the dank sweet beech woods to where the thin sunlight beckoned us to the top.

Here and there she would recognise a late wild flower; she even stopped and picked up a few chestnuts under a tree and with a stick opened them and popped them in her pocket. Almost without thinking she placed the piece of wood on the pram 'for the fire', and with Miss Elwell pointing the way they should go, memories from happier times replaced the ever-present sadness she was feeling.

She paused to change Bruce's nappy at the entrance as they were leaving. A soft-spoken uniformed park keeper stopped to pass the time of evening, and Mum was relieved that he did not question the small bundle of old wood that she had absentmindedly collected for the fire and placed on the top of the pram.

By the time the little party left, it was almost dusk and with a lightened heart the four set off on the two and a half mile journey home. Mum was hooked.

From then on the trip to the woods was a regular event. It began as a sort of meditational stroll to take her mind off her situation, in the way that people in shock occupy themselves with a trivial task just to keep busy, but it ended up almost the highlight of our week. The discreet collecting of old bits of wood gave way to quite brazen displays, as gradually both Bruce and I were able to walk home and the old pram became loaded up with wood. Sodden as it often was, this would supplement the few bits of coal, and hiss and fizz flickering comfort right through the week until the next outing.

The journey through the houses suddenly gave way to allotments by the railway and lanes that led up past where the new St. Peter's school would be built, and then the last little lane would give way to the entrance and we would scamper off on the familiar paths that became the extensions of our imaginations. Gradually we learned every climbing tree in the wood and where you could run the fastest downhill amongst the pebbles, slipping and sliding with glee and shrieking with delight as the feeling of almost flying possessed us. By the time the trees hove into view Tyler would be practically hauling the lot of us in his anxiety to get into the trees and smells and re-anoint his favourite places.

Mum had begun to take a thermos of tea for herself and a bottle of National Health diluted orange juice for us two. Then there were a few sandwiches added, Marmite for me and jam for Bruce, and we would pause usually by the same tree for our picnic. This in itself was exciting because Mum had always wrapped up the sandwiches in little parcels and the two of us would sit to undo them, a little like Christmas once a week. When Mum had her tea she would make a bit for Tyler and he would finish off the remains, slurping it noisily out of the lid of the old red flask.

As soon as we had eaten we would be off again on our adventures until it was time to load up the pram with twigs and fallen logs and troop off home tired and happy.

We soon became known to the keepers. They had a small hut which was of immense interest to a little lad like me. Inside was a small table and a couple of chairs, and facilities for making tea. Their uniforms were navy blue and buttoned right up to the top, and they wore caps with shiny peaks. The one who had spoken to Mum on our first visit was called Mr. Bachelor, and his boss was Mr. Sweetman; both were old soldiers from the First World War. Mr. Sweetman had lost an arm in the trenches and wore a false one with a brown leather glove stretched over a wooden hand that, once we realised what it was, Bruce and I found rather scary.

Both men were extremely kind; Mr. Sweetman bore himself more militarily and was less warm to us kids, but Mr. Bachelor was the sort of old boy that was born to be a grandfather. Both men quickly worked out our circumstances. Without fussing over us they always managed to bump into us somewhere on the Saturday and we loved to see them.

As we grew, Bruce and I made new friends and they joined us on our outings to the 'Hurst'. The first to do so was Richard Ranger. The Rangers lived in the next house, which was almost a mirror image of ours, and their rooms corresponded to Miss Elwell's plus a partition which gave them an extra room. Mrs. Ranger was a kind and intelligent woman who soon replaced the ageing Miss Elwell on our walks. She and Mum would talk all the way there and back about everything and nothing, while us boys would get on with the serious business of tree climbing, hide and seek, cowboys and indians or whatever else had fired our imaginations that particular week.

Richard was persuaded to come unwillingly at times, and I distinctly remember my mother telling her friend to "leave the little grizzler" who had decided that he wanted to be carried the last half mile to the woods. Later we were joined by Mickey Sparrow and his brother Paul and various other children from the street, until a veritable little army of waifs made the journey after Saturday morning pictures and Saturday lunchtime.

By now we were all well acquainted with the two park keepers, especially Mr. Bachelor who had metamorphosed into 'Uncle Charlie'. He would often talk with us all and occasionally sit down while we were having our sandwiches. One day he asked Mum if she'd like any apples, and when she said that she would, he told us to go to his home which was close by and ask Nellie his wife to let us collect some windfalls.

On our way home we diverted to the address and knocked on the door, which was opened by a pretty young woman with a lovely smile. This was Ella, Uncle Charlie's younger daughter. She invited us in and introduced us to her mother Nellie and her sister Doff (Dorothy), who was sitting on the back lawn of the lovely big house. Her two children, Robert and Mandy, were running about with their cousins Brian and Maureen (Ella's children).

Beyond the lawn were some vegetable patches and two intriguing sheds, and beyond these were several trees with vivid red apples growing on them and littering the ground. We ran over and eagerly scooped up apples with scant regard as to their worth or quality. Mum patiently told us not to be greedy, and soon we had more than we could eat before they would have rotted. Everyone was so kind and friendly and they asked us to call again. It was the beginning of a family friendship that, in spite of many changes of circumstances, survives to this time of writing.

The apples were taken home and sorted; many of them were wormy and had maggots but there were still enough to provide us with a little treat. The flesh was yellow and sweet and they were awesomely red and autumnal in colour. Before they were all eaten we visited again, and soon we were calling round for Sunday teas.

Nellie was Charlie's second wife but the mother of the two girls. Ella was married to Alf and the young couple shared the house with Nellie and Charlie. Brian and Maureen were striking children; in the summer their skins were dark brown and their hair almost white. Nellie was from Tewkesbury and was slightly deaf, which may have been a good thing in this noisy, happy household.

I had never before been where everyone laughed so much. Even our childish puns were roared at by the grown-ups and it was a marvellous feeling to be able to contribute in this way to the general merriment in the place. Alf was such a happy chap with his sparkling eyes and deep voice, while Charlie had an almost soundless chuckle and his eyes wrinkled and sparkled with mischief. Nellie's laugh began slowly and seemingly later than the rest but it went on longer than everyone else's to make up for it. Brian laughed as readily as all of them and Maureen, even at the age of three or four had a warm, smoky laugh.

But the laugh beyond all laughs came from Ella. Just to watch her was a pleasure; she was quite stout, though she had slim legs, and when she began, this joy bubbled up from somewhere under her apron to such a huge gurgling, open-mouthed, head-back, thigh-slapping expression of well-being that I waited with eager anticipation for each new beginning, and they were never far apart.

I loved those visits. We thought of the Thorpes—Uncle Alf and Auntie Ella—as real relations, and Brian and Maureen as cousins. Told of the arrival of a new baby for Ella, we waited as part of the family for its safe delivery, and they arrived fairly regularly: first Susan, then Pamela and finally Sandra.

Although they all lived together, the house was divided so that Auntie Nellie and Uncle Charlie had their own front room and Ella and Alf had theirs. This meant that we might be invited by either part of the family and take tea in their respective front rooms. I preferred having tea with the older side of the family simply because Ella used sterilised milk that made the tea taste odd, but the sandwiches were made with real butter and tasted wonderful.

This kind and generous family were not wealthy in any material sense. Alf cycled to work at the water board and Charlie (in semi-retirement) worked 'up the woods'. Their combined wages would have been about enough for one modest small family, and of course compared to us they would have been rich, but Alf hardly had a drink; they spent everything on the children and the family, and saved not a penny. If they didn't have the money, they didn't buy the goods.

Each year Ella and Alf managed a caravan holiday with the kids so Nellie and Charlie could have a peaceful break at home. But they missed them terribly after a couple of days and looked forward to their return. We got cards on our birthdays and little presents at Christmas and were as welcome as any family member to their happy home.

We had always had some fireworks for bonfire night, but no bangers as they frightened the cat and dog. But the first year we went to Ella's and Alf's made up for all the silent ones before. Alf had made a huge pile of timber and sticks in the back garden and laid out rocket launching positions and boards to fix Catherine wheels to, and there was a Guy Fawkes effigy seated in an armchair waiting to be burnt.

Bruce and I happily donated our five shillingsworth of Roman candles and Vesuviuses, threepenny Catherine wheels and Flowerpots to the fireworks kitty, and joined our 'cousins' for the display. Alf started off the proceedings with some small fireworks (probably ours) and then lit the monster bonfire. As the flames illuminated the garden you could see the whole family bright-eyed in the autumn air and the outline of the runner bean poles in the vegetable garden.

Then the display proper began whizzing and fizzing. The sickly smell of cordite and powder filled the air with a delicious sense of danger. Then a huge explosion as the first of the bangers went off to shrieks of delight and amazement, and wheels whirled and volcanoes erupted and sparklers spat and candles sprayed—and then more bangs and whizzes and spinning wheels and flames and faces warmed by the bonfire as rockets stitched the sky with stars and shared the airspace with rockets launched from all over the country.

Around late September sweet shops began to stock fireworks, and even if you had forgotten the time of year you would soon realise it, as random bangs and explosions occurred around the time schools closed for the day. Little groups of boys spent loose change on penny bangers instead of four-a-penny blackjacks or chewing gum.

Stories abounded of boys who had tied ten and even twenty bangers together to see what would happen, and tales that filled me with horror of pigeons with legs blown off and cats minus tails. It was years before I found out that legless pigeons are usually suffering from a parasitic illness akin to leprosy and that there is a breed of cat called a Manx. There was one up the road that belonged to someone and I always reserved a special pat for the poor thing, believing it to be maimed by fireworks. Bruce and I were not allowed bangers as Mum did not like them. It was just a small detail but I felt and still do that it was one of those little things that make boys raised by mothers alone different to those raised by both parents.

Mum only liked the pretty ones and I suppose I did as well; half the fun of a banger is not knowing that it is about to go off, and once it has there is no more to look forward to. With the non-exploding type you got real value for money, and we would all pass comment on the ones that carried on long after they should have finished, or the ones that seemed to start again when you thought they had fizzled out. Bruce and I pored over the biscuit tin of fireworks for days before the event reading the instructions and trying to imagine what the effect would be. The price of each device was marked on the side, and I was certainly aware of the cost and that it was all going up in smoke. We also had to light them only one at a time.

Uncle Alf, on the other hand, was into showmanship, and two, three, or even four were the norm. It was extravagant and wonderful, and even at that young age I think we both understood that it was generosity of spirit and pure fun rather than wealth and display that were at the heart of the matter.

Homemade cakes were doled out and the grown-ups had tea with sterilised milk and there was more merriment as Guy Fawkes himself was hoisted up on to the flames and cheers from everyone as he caught fire. I watched in a trance of happiness only allowing the horror of what was happening to intrude on my dreaming as his mask caught alight and his body collapsed into the flames.

Another fizzing rocket left the garden and exploded in a cascade of stars which in turn exploded again into greens and reds falling toward where we stood but vanishing before they touched the ground. All around me was joy and laughter; oohs and aahs emanated from mouths permanently half open, and even Mum was caught up in the display.

Then this hum began again in my head, but this time it did not frighten me. I suppose I was getting used to it by now, and anyway I had company, and it was much more frightening when I was on my own. I looked around to make sure no-one else could hear it, as the fireworks flashed and banged and faces hypnotised by the display and flames beamed from every part of the garden. Coats were handed round as the nip of evening produced the odd shiver amongst the happy group, and then Uncle Alf brought out Mrs. Fawkes and she too was put on to the fire, still sitting in the other armchair that had to be got rid of, to more merriment and sleepy cheers.

When it was over we still had to get the bus home, and Mum said that she thought it was an awful waste of money to spend all that only to watch it go up in smoke, and that made me consider the wastefulness of the event. But the hum in my head had stopped, and both Bruce and I agreed that this was the best fireworks we had ever been to in our lives and once home I fell asleep with stars bursting before my eyes as I involuntarily replayed the evening. Dreams of people being consumed in flames gave way to children's laughter, apples, and cake. And Nellie, Charlie, Ella and Alf: names to draw up to your chin like blankets and wrap around your worried head until you fell into a blissful sleep.

Our trips to the woods were not stopped even in the middle of winter. On many occasions we ate our sandwiches in the snow! This was when our need for fuel was at its highest, and Uncle Alf had kindly and cleverly made us a proper wood collecting barrow out of the old twin pram. It measured about four feet long by three feet wide and about three to four feet deep. He was a real handyman and this barrow was perfectly put together in one of the two sheds that stood in their back garden. It was painted green and Mum had got an old light green bedspread that she used to cover the top, to hide our spoils from prying eyes on the way home.

At the end of our picnic Mum would call all the kids together to help fill the barrow. We all learned pretty quickly the type of wood that she wanted, and filling the barrow took no time at all. She would break off huge limbs of dead trees by wedging them in between a cleft in a couple of trees and leaning on them till they snapped. I was very proud of her strength and practised doing the same, but I wasn't nearly big or heavy enough.

Mrs. Ranger was now our permanent companion, and although she did not collect wood for herself, she helped with the loading. On the way home, the smallest ones in the party would be hoisted on to the barrow and off we would go. Once a kindly policeman held up the traffic so that we could cross the road. There were eight of us on this trip: Chick Edgerton, Richard Ranger, Mickey and Paul Sparrow, Bridget Brosch and her little brother Lenny, and Bruce and me. As we passed the policeman in the middle of the road, he leant forward to Mum and in a conspiratorial whisper said, "Blimey love, I hope they ain't all yours!"

I distinctly heard him and Mum burst out laughing; it was wonderful to see her happy like this. From then on, when we went on our outings with several kids in tow she would preempt curious glances by stating, "Don't worry, they aren't all mine!" and people would smile or make a little joke.

Chick's real name was Douglas Edgerton, but no-one referred to him as that. I really envied his nickname; it seemed to imply that everybody liked him, and that he was little, lovable and cute. Actually he was all these things and cheeky too, with dark curly hair. He came to the woods with us on several weekends and endeared himself to my mum on the first occasion by referring to the anemones, one of the first signs of spring, as 'enemies' and telling her that they were his mother's favourite flower.

On the way back from the Hurst we would stop and Mum would buy us a penny lolly. For some reason I always chose the blue one, which was supposed to taste of peppermint but didn't. And very occasionally we might get a Walls ice cream. At this time there was a character called Tommy Walls who was a kind of superboy hero. He was featured in a strip cartoon in the *Eagle* comic and he was used to promote the product. By making the sign of a 'W' with your fingers and thumbs you were supposed to be able to fly. Without telling anybody that I was trying it out I would run around the corner frantically making 'W's and trying to launch myself into the air. Often I thought that I had achieved a hint of levitation, and though I plainly had not quite mastered the technique, I knew that I was close.

I always had a vivid imagination, which was further fuelled by the radio programmes where of course we had to imagine what everyone looked like. Mum read to us no matter how tired she might be, and we loved this moment more than any other. We believed in fairies, pixies, Jesus, elves, Father Christmas, goblins, ghosts, magic and some things called the woodcraft tinys. It was hard to form a distinct picture of these creatures, but I knew for certain of their existence as I often made shelters for them and placed food inside, which was always taken by the morning after they had visited.

I never quite sorted out the relationships in this world of fantasy, and knew that somehow Jesus might be the odd one out—yet there was something that brought them together. For instance, was a goblin bigger than an elf? Did elves marry fairies? Were fairies and angels related? Why were there no pictures of Jesus with pixies and goblins? Was God a bit like Father Christmas? And so on. In my imagination they all had a place, and that place was the woods.

The seasons were more marked in Croham Hurst, and the physical changes in nature were pointed out to us by our mother. She delighted in naming all the flowers as they appeared and she knew all their country names. The first leaves on the hawthorn were called 'bread and cheese' and were to be nibbled and enjoyed as the first fruits of spring. It was with a mixture of bemusement and pity that our Croydon pals viewed some of this knowledge and behaviour. We ate blackberries in the early autumn, picked the odd mushroom from Duppas Hill, collected conkers from everywhere and saved them till they were as wrinkled as Aunt Naomi. Sweet chestnuts could be found in the Spinney and in the woods, and I even ate beech nuts, though they were fiddly and unrewarding, so most of our friends didn't bother with them.

Coltsfoot, anemones, speedwell, campion, dead nettle, lords and ladies, cuckoo pint, violet and bluebell and dozens of others were all eagerly greeted as they came forth. We learned the names of the poison ones like deadly nightshade and briony (I nearly ate one of these berries once but Mum stopped me and I was quite convinced that she had saved my life). We made tunnels stretching for what seemed miles in the bracken and played games, oblivious of the little scratches to legs and hands that are the inevitable badges of such fun. Once Bruce picked up a piece of wood for the fire that was full of red ants, and Mum had to strip him naked to beat the little biters off him, and he cried as much with embarrassment as pain.

We fell in stinging nettles and found dock leaves to stop the stinging. The occasional wasp sting was borne manfully, eventually. We got clawed by brambles and after the brown scabs had peeled, wore with pride the little white scars that were left for the summer until they faded with our tans in the autumn. We looked for badgers, rabbits and foxes but saw none; made friends, quarrelled and made up again. Sharing this place with new acquaintances was like showing them your favourite toys. It was done with such pride. Along the bridle paths where the branches met overhead, secret tunnels were found. Short cuts were discovered and we would jump out on Mum and Mrs. Ranger after waiting for them to round a bend in the track. They usually obliged with the right expression of surprise and we would scurry off to the next hiding place. We developed muscles like knotted rope, as we dried out the dampness in our bones from the dismal flat, on the hills and amongst the trees and gullies of the Hurst.

Our friendships with the Thorpes and Bachelors flourished and Bruce and I loved going there for tea. Auntie Ella was a wonderful cake maker, and we loved to hear her and her mother Nellie laugh. In fact we both conspired to make them laugh if we could, because that made us laugh as well. Once, after going to the outside toilet together I said that Bruce did a wee like a watering can; Auntie Nellie nearly had a seizure, and her infectious cackle soon had the whole house rocking with merriment. Mum was fairly strict, so it was a tremendous release to get away with some very slightly risqué things.

Brown as berries we ran through the early summers, Red Indians streaked with blackberry juice, and as the summer moved to autumn running knee-deep in dry leaves as the anticipation to our shared December birthdays prepared us for the excitement of Christmas.

The first Christmas after my father left, there was no money and my mother's family made no attempt to offer any help at all. Her weight dropped dramatically, and the few photos of her taken at the time make her look as if she is suffering from some terrible wasting disease. She has often told me that the Christmas dinner comprised of one lamb chop that she was too sad and distraught to eat. Thankfully this is one memory I do not share. Things improved, and though out of necessity our Christmases were frugal to say the least, we always had a chicken after that, and the holiday was hugely enjoyed just the same.

The Christmas thrill is still there after all this time, and I love the atmosphere of street markets at that time of year. Strings of lights over the stalls as the costers try and offload their wares at knockdown prices so that they can get home and enjoy the fun; people rushing about doing their last minute stuff, kids all shiny-faced and eager.

One year Mum bought a bargain bird, only to find when she got it home that it had not been drawn, but thankfully Mr. Connaughton obliged and the bird had an onion stuck inside its body cavity. In the absence of a fridge it was hung in the 'coal hole' next to the scullery, and by pushing open the coal hole door you could glimpse the chicken's ghostly, white form hanging by a string in the gloom like a lynched corpse, contrasted against the blackness of the interior. It actually frightened me to look at it, so I stopped peering round the door. Nevertheless sometimes just before sleep the image would return long after it had been eaten and enjoyed.

We knew that Christmas was nearly here when, on getting up one day, we would find the front room decorated with paper chains and garlands. Mum always told us that the fairies had done it and we had no reason to disbelieve it as she was certainly too tired to do it after she got in from work. The decorations were always the same year after year; she had collected them once after a dance. They were carefully put up with drawing pins and after the twelve days had passed carefully packed away again for the next year. By the time they were finally thrown away, they were positively peppered with pinholes at each end of the streamers, and the centrepiece, an old bell in purple and yellow concertina-ed paper, was falling apart.

We always had a tree—or some branches held together to look like a tree—which was decorated with tinsel and coloured balls, two red plastic horses, and a fairy on the top that for many years I was convinced was a real one. We had nuts and raisins, non-alcoholic ginger wine, and raisin wine which we drank out of tiny glasses feeling rather sophisticated as we did.

Mum would listen to the Queen's Christmas message and talk with relief about how much better she was than the old king, who had a stammer and used to make her all hot with embarrassment with the long pauses between words as he fought to utter the next one. We hung pillowcases up and always got presents to open in the freezing morning of Christmas Day. We had to unwrap them carefully so that the paper could be used again; it is a habit I still haven't properly broken.

We had no TV but I think we must have seen so many shows and programmes at neighbours that I certainly don't have any recollections of missing it. We played cards and board games and Mum played too. The fire would be on all day and the flat would feel warm; we could toast bread on a toasting fork made from twisted copper wire whilst Tyler slept and Timmy, the cat who had been brought in to replace Meemo, purred. We all loved Christmas and we were all happy together; it would be difficult to think of a closer time for Bruce, Mum and me because for those couple of days we would all be together with no work to separate us.

Miss Elwell would come down in the evening and sit and talk around our meagre fire as she did on many occasions. One year she helped us blow up balloons to complete the decorations the fairies had put up, and I would play my treasured harmonica for everybody whether they wanted me to or not.

Then one year we were invited to Auntie Ella's for Christmas.

There were no buses on Christmas Day, so we walked there, and with each step our anticipation grew. From the moment they opened the door to greet us, there was jollity until it was time to go home. The house was festooned with tinsel, paper chains, streamers, cards, and a huge decorated tree with lights of all different colours; there were snowflakes and toys and presents everywhere. The children's faces were flushed with excitement and they seemed to have been looking forward to seeing us as much as we them. There was a roaring fire that was so hot Bruce and I dare not stand too close to it.

Although the children had opened their presents long before, there were a couple of parcels under the tree for Bruce and me, and even a little extra something for Brian and Maureen so that they did not feel left out. Alf and Ella were typical of many working-class families in that they spared no expense at Christmas for their children; and as each new baby arrived, they bought a brand new pram and complete new layette. Bruce and I had never seen anything to compare with the lavishness of their generosity and we were treated so kindly it moves me to think of it still.

When it came to the meal, I was totally unprepared for the sight of the table groaning with all the vegetables, and when they brought in the turkey, I could not believe my eyes. The image of this huge bird had an effect on me akin to watching an expert magician pulling off some amazing trick. I just sat there with my mouth hanging open. There were so many things that I could not eat through fussiness that my plate comprised peas, roast potatoes and gravy, with slices of white and dark meat. It was heavenly, and I resolved if ever we got some money we would have turkey every day.

After we had eaten everything, I had to go to the loo and this meant going through the dining room of Nellie and Charlie, and to my astonishment their table was almost as laden as ours had been, and they had a turkey as well. It was like a scene from a Norman Rockwell painting, and became more so as the afternoon became evening and Auntie Ella started laying the table for tea. There were sandwiches and jellies, mince pies and trifles, and a home-made Christmas cake the size of a car wheel, beautifully decorated by her with twirls and furls of sweet sugar icing over marzipan.

I have never liked marzipan, but Bruce loved it and we traded his icing for my marzipan and all were happy. Then came the Christmas log which was another of Ella's creations. It was a kind of sponge cake covered in chocolate, and perched on a twig on top sat a little robin. After tea, when our fears of being sick had been averted by trying to be still and play some games, we watched the TV which sat in the corner. Then, just when we thought it could not get better, in came Alf, squeezing past the door wearing the most spectacular piece of equipment I had ever been close to in my life.

Bruce and I watched in amazement as room was made for him to stand where all could see through the haze of cigarette smoke that filled the happy room. Three out of the five adults smoked: Mum smoked her Weights, and Alf and Charlie, who both smoked Ringers tobacco, offered each other their tobacco tins in turn. Then Alf let out the longest sigh on his piano accordion as he charged the bellows, ready to perform.

Alf was not a big man, about five foot six I would guess. He was wiry with swept back straight fair hair, a small nose and twinkling blue eyes already quite lined by smiling. He was a wonderful dad; kind, generous, warm, and one of those blokes who seemed to be able to do anything with wood, from making our barrow to the most complex building of sheds, without the aid of plans or designs—and once erected, everything fitted and was sound.

Charlie and he had cultivated the piece of ground at the back of the garden and it was neatly laid out with winter vegetables in lines. In the summer there would be runner beans and carrots replacing the last of the sprouts that we had eaten a few hours ago. Alf was a real man and here in the ample bosom of his family, admired in every corner, his small but strong frame supporting the instrument that, with the bellows stretched out, must have been the size of a radiogram, he stood poised to play.

As the first notes of *Run Rabbit Run* emanated from the front of the machine, all the children looked at each other and grinned. The reeds rang and we were witness to the loudest music any of us had ever heard. You just had to smile with the magnitude of it all, and soon all of us were singing along. It was wonderful to see Mum joining in and all the adults and children so happy.

Behind the great wheezing monster, Alf's neck strained as if to avoid the constant stream of cigarette smoke that drifted into his screwed up eyes from the roll up that was hanging from the corner of his mouth. Someone brought him an ash tray and he rested the cigarette for a minute whereupon it went out and in between each number he relit it and placed it back in the ash tray. Song followed song and the noise level increased as the kids' voices were raised above the music.

After about an hour, the combined weight of the instrument and the previously consumed Christmas fare took its toll and Alf had to rest. I wanted to know all about it, and as I sat at his knee he patiently explained what all the buttons did and where the air inlet valve was, and even let me finger the notes and hear the noise it could make. Then there was more tea and biscuits before the mighty accordion was returned to its case for another year and we all had to say goodnight and begin the long winter walk home to the cold of our flat in the basement. We spent several Christmases with these wonderful people and though I remember so much I do not remember a single journey back to our place. The memory too full of wonder, I should think.

One January Miss Elwell died of a massive stroke, upstairs and alone as usual. After the post mortem (she was fifty-five years old) a search was conducted to find if she had any relatives. The spelling of her name was unusual and there were few pretenders to her pitiful estate. By dint of her self-sacrifice and frugality she had managed to save nearly three hundred pounds toward her cottage in the country, and for that money in those days, she probably had enough to have bought one. Instead, after much searching, her savings went to the Crown. Mum remarked on that final ignominy with irony as 'old Elwell' was a republican and would have rather given it away than let "that bunch of parasites" get hold of it.

Miss Elwell was the first person that I would really miss. True, my father's mother had passed on but I did not know her. Miss Elwell's slippered tread down our dark stair was something I would miss, or not understand properly, for a very long time. Why had God allowed this to happen? Had she been guilty of some terrible hidden crime?

The sudden death of anyone who is not at the 'fullness of time' is impossible to explain to children whose logic has not prepared them for the random nature of premature departure. Just when the notion of crime and punishment may have been taken on board, along comes this wild card. The result is anger mixed with a feeling of betrayal and bewilderment. I was deeply troubled by Miss Elwell's death and surprised by my mother's tears. It was not the loss of a companion that saddened her, although I know she missed her; but in our own circumstances of slender hope for an uncertain future, Miss Elwell's failure to see her simple dream come true almost knocked the hope out of everybody.

After the twelfth night, we took down the decorations for another year, some of the balloons by now hanging like wrinkled breasts that we occasionally saw on old African women in nature films. I remembered that Miss Elwell and I had blown them up together. It fascinated me to think that these receptacles contained her breath and I asked Mum if we should keep one so that she was always with us. Quite rightly Mum told me not to be so macabre, whatever that meant (though I understood what it implied) and we threw them away. But instead of popping the last one, I made a small hole in the top with my teeth and as Miss Elwell's last breath whistled out, I took a deep breath and held it for as long as I could. It awed me to think that she sort of had one last gasp, and that somehow I had communicated with her.

It was the last year that the fairies put up the decorations.

~

as if in sleep

Trundling through the bridle paths,
Too low for horse and rider now
Even in the warmest summer,
Ruts that never quite dried out

As sunlight trickled through the branches
That grew on both sides of the track
And overhead met in the middle,
Curled, entwined and doubled back,

The children skittered off the pathway
Joined the grown-ups further on
Where the light streamed through the beech leaves
Robin Hood and Little John

The curls of bracken barely showing
Whipped off by swishing hazel shoots
Sharp as blades with patterns carved
By the tribe of Croydon Sioux

On bows and arrows fired and found
Amongst the brambles, sticks for guns
And the dried yolk from the eggshell
That fitted on a small child's thumb

Amongst the willow herb and bracken
Evening insects buzzed and humming
Grip upon the day had slackened
Knowing night was surely coming

A breeze blows up and through the birches
Stirs cathedrals of pines
Wafts through copses still as churches
Above the ferns a child's head high.

Leaf mould underneath the beeches
Sweet decay perfumes the eve
The last sun's ray stretches and reaches
Stragglers who are last to leave

Residents of sandy banks
Badgers, voles and all their kin
Poke out their noses left and right
Venture forth and sniff the wind

Birds are jostling for branches
In oaks and elms and silver birch
Rabbits wash, sat on their haunches,
A fox begins his nightly search

Sunlight fell upon the sandstone
Shadows spread on breakneck hill
(Where someone jumped once for a wager,
The man survived, the horse was killed)

Now the woodcraft tinys come
That live among the roots of trees
Goblins, fairies, elves and pixies
Moved by curiosity

To go out in that other world
Where only children understand
The mysteries of the absurd
Explained away by mortal man

They clamber over garden walls,
Or float like dandelion seed,
Plant toadstool rings upon the lawns
And hide important things you need

And if they're caught when sun has risen
They must stand like statues still
With foolish grins in flowerbed prisons
Waiting patiently until

Shadows blue at evening free them
To the woods from whence they came
Children know this for they see them
In gardens all along the lane.

Back in the woods, lain on the heather
As if in sleep a child lay
No frantic calling would awake him
Creatures sniffed and ran away

And the moon above the pine trees
Let gentle light upon his form
Mr. Latimer would find him
On his rounds tomorrow morn

At once the woods were changed forever
Playtime shrieks not sound the same
Each and every cry examined
Was it for joy or was it pain

For if a child stays as a child
It's often said that he is touched
By fairies who would keep him so.
The love they feel for children's such

That they can't bear to let them grow
And keep one for themselves sometimes
Playing tricks to let us know
That they remember carefree times

They did not tell us where it happened
But soon we knew his age and name
And the man–child that had done it
All the pity and the blame

Was laid at doors in roots of trees
And dandelions cursed again
And garden gnomes were trapped forever
In flowerbed prisons down the lane

∾

helmet

The period after my father left home was made all the more difficult for my mother, as there was no apparent family support from her relatives up in the Cotswolds. Mum could always find excuses why Grandma and Granddad never offered any tangible help, but it didn't wash with me. These early years were spent without a real sense of belonging to a larger unit of blood relatives, as neither our father's or our mother's families did very much to reassure us that we were not alone in the world.

Mum always said that the Mays were too ashamed of what had happened, and the Mosses could do nothing as Grandma wouldn't allow it. There was probably some truth in the former, but as for the latter, I can't see myself letting my daughter get on with things on her own the way my grandfather did, whether he was under his wife's thumb or not. I did not resent him, partly because Mum was always singing his praises, and truth to tell he was a dear if dour old man and a true Victorian county man, who had learned etiquette and manners whilst in service as a butler/valet to a gentleman from Holland called van Roulte. Grandma was a working-class Tory; although she too had been in service, her mother had run a small shop in Hammersmith, and she had done the same in Brackley from the front room of their house in Banbury Road.

We had visited my other grandmother, Grandma May, in hospital where she was confined with debilitating arthritis. It was a sunny day, and she sat upright in bed in an uncluttered ward, with a blue shawl around her shoulders and a white bob cap on her head. I remember sitting on her bed and having to be removed because of the pain my weight caused her arthritic legs.

We brought her a pot of jam with a golliwog on the label. At home I had a golliwog, whose name was George. Later, Mum and I were walking in Park Hill in Croydon when I saw some black men for the first time. They were among the first of the Commonwealth students to arrive in England, and as they drew near I turned to my mother and caused her embarrassment when I told her to "look at the real live Georges."

Grandma May cried when it was time for us to go, and died soon after our visit. Mum says she died of a broken heart because Frank left us.

Granddad May had been an engine driver all his working life, and thought it was just grand when he finally left the steam engines for the comparatively genteel work on the electric trains that ran from West Croydon to Wimbledon. Eventually we were to move to the Miller Road estate that was bordered on one side by that very line, but by that time Granddad was long dead. Mum said he could not live with his sadness, and though he survived his first wife for a long time we did not hear from him much after she passed away. We visited him a few times and I was fascinated by the white ducks he kept in his back yard with only a basin of water to paddle about in.

Once in happier times my father had smuggled me on to the platform of East Croydon station and hoisted me on to the footplate of the *Brighton Belle*, a famous steam engine that Granddad drove to Brighton. Sadly I was too young to remember this, but I do recall my dad taking me to watch the trains there on later occasions, and once seeing an old stuffed German Shepherd dog in a glass case; it looked alive, but I knew it was dead.

My dad had a sister called Ivy, who died giving birth to her daughter Shirley. Grandma May said that God took Ivy because Granddad loved her too much and did not love Frank enough. This story always frightened me. Ivy was certainly very beautiful; we had a picture of her in an old frame on the mantelpiece, but it always faced the wall.

Bruce and I slept in the condemned room next to the living room until it was just too wet to be used for anything but keeping our toys in (we called it our Playroom after that, though an unhealthier room for play it would be hard to imagine. In it I used to listen to an old radio plugged into the electric light socket. From then on, until we finally left The Waldrons, we slept in Mum's bedroom).

Both of us suffered from bronchitis, and the Valor stove that was to keep the chill off the room also burnt up oxygen as it caused the steam to emanate from the long spouted kettle that was our sleeping companion for several winters.

Comforts were small but much appreciated, and among the biggest of these were the stories that Mum always found time to read to us, no matter what time she got in from work, before we were sent to bed. It was usually Enid Blyton's *Famous Five* or *Secret Seven*. She read so well that we would always plead for just one more chapter, and nearly always got one.

Mum really enjoyed these moments when she too could escape from the drudgery of our existence and be a kid again where there was still hope and optimism. Sometimes she would read Grimm's fairy tales, but their morbidity was sometimes more depressing than our own reality, and several times these were abandoned for lighter stories. I know that this was as much for her sake as it was ours. I was a sad case really, often troubled by nightmares and no doubt traumatised by my parents' split; very insecure and full of self-doubt and frightened by Mum's occasional threats to run away and leave us. This really did scare me. I would sometimes pump away at Bruce until he was aware of the enormity of this proposition, and soon we would both be howling and needing reassurance that her departure was not imminent.

I cannot for the life of me now think that Bruce and I ever did anything so bad as to warrant such a desperate promise, but her life must have seemed like a never ending descending tunnel of darkness at times. Mum was a one-man woman, and when Dad went, he turned the light out. What glimmer of hope Bruce and I produced was not strong enough to light her way forward.

In the winter Bruce and I would inevitably be the last ones indoors, unless Mrs. Sparrow allowed us to stay in and watch television. She put up with loads of kids from the street and we sat politely on the floor with Mickey and Paul and assorted others, loving the Lone Ranger and the Cisco Kid.

It was warmer in the Sparrows' house but I cannot remember where the warmth came from—perhaps it was from all the kids in the one room. Eventually it would be time to leave and we would reluctantly cross the road back to number thirty. Sometimes we would sit under blankets in the big armchairs by the still unlit fireplace listening to the radio. When we were older, I was allowed to lay the fire after first cleaning out the ashes.

The sound of the old split coal shovel on the grate used to make my teeth go on edge, but I could wrap up the cinders as professionally as a worker in a fish and chip shop. When we were very small, well before we could tell the time properly, Mum would stick two pieces of paper on the old American wall clock to tell us when to light the fire that she had laid in the morning before she went off to work. We had the same system for lunch during the school holidays: on the table would be two packets of sandwiches wrapped up in waxed paper, and next to them a bottle of diluted National Health orange juice (we would have had the cod liver oil and malt in the morning).

We would sit there, tummies rumbling, watching the slow movement of the hands before starting our meal: Marmite or cheese for me, and jam or jam for Bruce, although we never ever started before the hands said we could.

Sometimes we would go for picnics and persuade some of the other kids to come with us—after all, our lunches were already packed. Off we'd go, perhaps on our noisy old roller skates, sometimes not very far at all and other times to the far ends of the earth like Beddington Park.

Our imaginations were fuelled by the bedtime stories and fired by what we saw at the Saturday morning pictures. Even the trailer of a forthcoming film would have a profound effect, *The Hunchback of Notre Dame* being one that kept both Bruce and me awake and scared. Sometimes a radio play such as *The Nine Tailors* would haunt me for months. I remember the first episode ending with a body being exhumed and the coroner saying, "My God! Who would want to smash in his face and cut off his hands?"!

Mrs. Connaughton took me to the pictures some Saturday nights. We grew up in the golden age of westerns and great cowboy epics; bows and arrows, cap guns and catapults (hidden) were our stock in trade. Bruce became an expert on the tribes of the American Indians and built Fort

Apache on top of the old Anderson shelter in the yard above Tyler's kennel. Bare-legged and scabby-kneed we roamed the Croydon ranges, ran errands for pennies, and every now and then went totting for paper and rags to sell to Holloway's or Gurney Whites on Southbridge Road. We would have loved a 'telly' and were offered one by a neighbour who was updating, but Mum declined and it was years before we acquired a flickering ghostly black and white set of our own.

Once or twice my maternal grandparents came to visit, and once after my accident I stayed with them at their place in Brackley.

In the black, smelly coal shed of my grandfather's house, reeking of decay, dried onions and impotence, I was reverent. After all this was his storehouse of fuel and he had shovelled it to keep his family warm. He and Grandma also had a cellar, and one day I went down there in the dark with a box of matches and found a sit-up bath and an old bird cage amid the dust. I didn't stay long, perhaps two matches' worth of light, but I saw enough to know that I did not want to know whose bath or whose cage they might have been.

Convalescing at their place, all I knew was that I should be respectful, which I was. I was respectful of my bed that I could not wait to get into even though it was hard with the sheets smelling of Grandma and Granddad's house. The dreams that normally tormented me changed shape in the countryside and I missed the sound of my brother as I awoke in the little room that my mother and her sister Olive shared some thirty years ago. This was the room in which they planned their escape to run off with the gypsies, away from the drudgery of their existence. Stories of how hard they both had to work in order to satisfy their mother filled me with dread, and were often repeated to remind Bruce and I as to how lucky we were. We knew how lucky we were.

Grandma and Granddad did not know how to be with children. The deep tick of the mantelpiece clock measured the silences between them. Grandma expressed surprise at almost everything with her "Well I never" and Granddad expressed virtually nothing. He was the strong, silent type. Well, silent mostly.

One day he carefully built a cement step by the box hedge and I watched in admiration as he scooped shovelfuls of mortar into a carefully shuttered mould. Sadly before it set I managed to accidentally step on it and ruin it. He was very kind and did not shout at me. I'd like to think that I was forgiven for an careless child's mistake, but even at the time I suspected (in my own childish way) that he was so used to being nagged and dumped on that he would have said "that's all right" if someone had pretended to have accidentally sliced off his penis. That night I lay awake for hours thinking about Granddad.

The whole house smelt of paraffin, which they used to fire their old cooker, and old age. Grandma had even restricted the meagre warmth from the tiny fire in the living room by the application of tea leaves and old wet potato peelings wrapped up in newspaper and placed at the back of the grate ("To keep the fire in," she explained when I asked why, helpfully pointing out that the wet bundle consistently failed to ignite).

There was no TV and the two-valve radio was only used to check the horse racing results. Grandma liked a flutter, rarely more than a bob or two, but often regaled us with the story of how she had gone to the post office to place a bet and spotted a paper aeroplane on the floor. Believing this to be an omen she hastily changed her bet and placed ten bob on a horse called Airborne which came in at fifty to one.

On Sundays Granddad took the *News of the World* for its unbiased political opinion. There were few books, and neither he or Grandma went to the pub which was only next door. I was packed off to bed with my premature nightmares long before I was tired; I missed my home a lot and cried a good deal. Granddad and Grandma didn't know, and I was aware that I couldn't return home as there was no-one to look after me there.

In the evenings Granddad would reread the newspaper and puff on his Woodbines or his 'makings'. Grandma would prod the dishes in an old enamel bowl of tepid water; the very same one that she used for washing her feet. There was no bath and the toilet was outside with no light in it. I tried to go during the hours of daylight, sitting there humming loudly and peering through the cracks in the door for the reassurance that there was still light outside.

There were a few objects in the house to stimulate my imagination. On the mantelpiece in the front room, on either side of the clock, were two shells brought home from the First World War. I hoped they weren't live. One night I thought of them exploding and making Granddad's Woodbine fly out of his mouth with shock and it gave me the giggles for a bit. Then I began to worry that they might explode, then I reasoned that the fire in the grate below was never going to get hot enough to make them go off, and then I fell into a fitful sleep.

But there was precious little to occupy my time with except my fantasy of being a cub scout. Granddad made me an old push cart and helped me pretend; dressed in my St. Peter's School cap and a blue knitted sweater, I marched up and down the Banbury Road pushing my cart. I had an old gas mask bag over my shoulder, with a piece of newspaper rolled up as a loaf and another rolled up in the shape of an egg inside. Granddad cut out some bits of green paper, and these I stuck in the tops of my socks to resemble the chevrons that the cubs used to wear at that time. I was left completely on my own, and the deserted pigsty at the top of the garden became my hut and the street outside my parade ground.

It was pretty miserable but at least Mum had a bit of a break whilst I was supposed to convalesce. She had brought me to her folks on the train, and although I was still terrified of traffic, the ride on the steam train from Marylebone to Brackley had been wonderful. I was still walking badly and it was decided that I should have a new pair of shoes, which were duly purchased from Mr. Knibbs. I had doubts about these shoes from the off as they had chisel toes (instead of a conventional round toe, these were cut square across the front), but they were new and they were the only pair in my size. I remember wondering at the time how long they'd been waiting to get rid of them on some poor out-of-towner like me. Anyway they were bought for me and everyone remarked on how unusual they were and for such a 'bargain' price. Lying in what had been her room when she was a little girl, all I could think of was a desperate longing to be back with Mum and Bruce in my condemned room where the smell of wet walls was preferable to the smell of Grandma's paraffin cooker and cabbagy kitchen and outside loo with the shiny paper and no lights.

One morning I was outside on parade in full get up when I was approached by two local lads.

"What's on here then?" murmured one of them as he eyed me up and down. I smiled nervously and wondered if they were going to hit me.

"Who are you?" asked his mate, who was looking at my shoes curiously. I thought at the time, because of what everyone else said, that he was probably admiring them and so felt a little bold as I answered.

"I'm a wolf cub."

"Are you now?" said the first one. "Then what's that on your cap? You ain't got no wolf badge." Of course I knew that I hadn't, because I was wearing my green school cap, and in the place where the badge would have been there was my school emblem of the crossed keys of St. Peter. Before I could explain the discrepancy, the second boy offered the explanation that I was a schoolboy at the Cross Keys. It was easier to agree, so I did.

"What's in yer bag then?" continued the first one.

"Just some bread and an egg," I said brightly, not expecting the matter to be pursued.

"Let's 'ave a look then," said the second one, and with that plunged his hand into the bag and pulled out the news paper that had been my egg but that now closely resembled a newspaper. Throwing it down on the pavement he plunged his hand once more into my bag and this time pulled out my loaf of bread that now even closer resembled a newspaper.

"Where's your egg?" demanded the second one.

Seeing the difficulty of explaining the situation I blurted out, "I've eaten it."

The two of them looked at each other suspiciously, then at me.

"You're not from rahnd here are you?" said one.

"No, I'm from Croydon," I replied. I could have said Dar-es-Salaam for all the clarification it made.

"Where's that then?" said the bigger one of the two. He was beginning to get on my nerves, especially as I didn't know how to explain where I had come from.

"You have to go on the train to Marleybone." I pronounced it the way Grandma always did, hoping that they would understand.

"Which way is that?" they wanted to know. I pointed in the direction of the station and then attempted to indicate the direction in which supposed we had come but I became confused and my pointing arm was gesticulating all over the place and I was becoming more helpless and confused. The two boys had plainly never heard of Croydon or Marylebone and cared even less once it was established that I was not a near local. In my experience, near locals are in more danger from their close neighbours than foreigners—unless there are a lot of them.

"Where are you going with that cart then?" they asked me.

"I'm going camping," I answered thinking this would impress them, but even as the words left my lips I knew I'd made a mistake.

"Camping?" they chorused. "Where's your bloomin' tent then?" I must have gestured in desperation to my empty cart because they both started to laugh and ridicule its lack of any content. Then they noticed my shoes.

"What the bloody 'ell are those?" laughed the bigger one.

"I bet he's a dancer!" suggested the other one, giggling.

"Yeah, are you a dancer mate?" echoed his friend. By now I was crimson with embarrassment and close to tears, as I instinctively put my hand up to hide my 'woggle'. Yes, dear old Granddad, in an effort to keep me authentic, had cut off the end of a toilet roll and stained it brown with some boot polish before slipping through the ends of the rolled up scarf that was my pretend neckerchief to complete my ensemble. I needn't have worried because luckily they had discovered the bits of green paper stuck in my socks and were now almost helpless with mirth.

Plainly I was perceived as posing no threat, and after pulling my cap down over my eyes they left me alone. As I dragged my cart and hurt pride back into the garden and furiously wrestled with the toilet roll woggle, I found myself muttering all the things I should have said.

After one or two days in the back garden I ventured back on to the street again but I was not troubled by the local boys, I guess the word was out that there was a simpleton staying at the Mosses' house and they left me in peace.

Grandma and Granddad tried to be nice, but their own kids had been encouraged to leave home by the age of fifteen so the house had been empty of children for a very long time. It was a quiet and comfortless place. I suppose there isn't a lot to say to each other after so long. The clock on the mantelpiece loudly ticked away the minutes that seemed like hours, and the two polished shells guarded its sacred duty to remind me of how long I'd been away from home and how long it would be before I returned.

Above the old sink were a pair of gas masks from the Second World War, still hanging up just in case. The real treasure however hung in the coal hole. There on its own shelf sitting amongst the dust of years was a wondrous item. It was a German officer's helmet from the first world war. Sometimes when I was feeling brave I would take it from the shelf and hold it in my hands and concoct heroic adventures around it. Granddad had a picture of himself taken during the war. He was in full battle dress; my aunt Olive stood by his side and Grandma held my mum as a tiny baby on her knee. Granddad was in the Middlesex Regiment; his battalion were supplied with bicycles and were nicknamed the Dunlop Brigade.

Putting all these various elements together I attempted to explain Granddad's silences. He had probably wrestled the German general from his horse and thrown him on to the ground. His last bullet spent, he disposed of him with his bare hands and hid the helmet in his 'old kit bag' for a souvenir.

More likely he had exchanged the item with another soldier, perhaps by cleaning his kit for him. I will never know what really happened.

Years later, when they emptied the sparse contents of the house after Grandma died, I slipped into the coal shed and took Granddad's helmet. The house was stripped bare of my grandparents' few remaining belongings, and even the old lino off the floor was ripped up. Upstairs in an old bedside table I found a souvenir of Grandma. It was a nipple protector. I mused as to which of her children had been denied the tender comfort of a soft breast whilst feeding. I think it must have been my own mum. I threw the thing away as we left number 63 for ever. I kept the helmet for years, as it slowly dried out and all but disintegrated, until it was finally lost during a move to our present home.

yoyo

Saturday morning pictures was eagerly anticipated all week. Talk about 'the flicks' occupied playground and evening games in the spinney (the name given to the collection of quite wonderful chestnut trees that formed a central sort of island in the Waldrons).

Charlie Ranger, an older boy next door, had taken me to Saturday morning pictures for the first time when I was about six years old. The name on the outside said Gaumont but it was always called the Odeon. We had neglected to tell anyone where I had gone and in absolute desperation the police had been called and a search begun for me. This had made me feel quite important. I don't remember feeling remorse for this neglect of responsibility.

Once mum had realised that I would come to no harm, I became a regular at the Odeon. It was at the foot of Crown Hill at the junction with Surrey Street market just opposite where I had been knocked down by the lorry a couple of years previously. Indeed, the queue to get in ran alongside the wall opposite the Times Furniture shop from which the lorry had emerged.

Hundreds of us formed an orderly line buzzing with excitement as to whether the goody or the baddie in the serial had got out of the speeding car before it plunged over the cliff. Inside, the chatter became deafening and the heat from our anticipation warmed up the seats that smelt of grown ups, cigarettes and sweat. After an eternity of waiting the lights would go down in the auditorium and come up on the stage to illuminate a portly man wearing a suit and bow tie. He was called The Chief and I think he had a microphone with which to address us. He would introduce the films we were to see and tell us what was on the weekly program in case we could persuade our parents to bring us to a show during the week.

In those days the picture houses were nearly always full and a different kind of excitement was obtained by attending the evening programs. It was almost obligatory to smoke and if a film failed to keep my attention I could be entertained for short periods by watching the beams of light assume various colours as they projected through the clouds of smoke that filled the whole auditorium. I had been to a film one Sunday night with Mrs Conaughton who lived upstairs. I remember the smell and atmosphere but not the film. I am almost sure it was at the Davis Theatre, once the biggest cinema in Europe.

If we had joined up to the Saturday Morning Picture Club and it happened to be our birthday, we would receive a birthday card entitling us to free entry that week. All the birthday kids would be summoned to the stage and the other kids in the audience would have to sing Happy Birthday. If we fooled with the words we had to sing it again. It was especially marvellous because you could spend your normal sixpence entrance money on sweets from the British Home Stores next door.

There was a lady on the sweet counter who somehow had taken a shine to our little crew. My pocket money was nine pence. It was sixpence to get into the cinema, which meant we had threepence to spend. Even in those days there was not much for threepence in British Home Stores. When we told the lady that was all we had she miraculously filled up paper bags with huge lumps of jaw-breaking toffee and odds and ends of broken sweets. We became regulars at her counter on Saturday morning and as news of her generosity flowed through our little gang, the line at her counter grew embarrassingly long. Somehow she managed to keep us happy. One day, however, she wasn't there. We asked where she was and were told she had left. I was convinced that she must have been sacked and blamed myself. I wondered if they thought she was stealing from the shop. It worried me quite a lot.

When our little supply dried up we had to be even more careful with our remaining pennies. Bubble gum was good value but gobstoppers were even better. We would usually have one each for a penny and they would sit against our cheeks like giant cysts. If someone didn't have their own gobstopper, someone would share theirs. The idea was that the original owner could enjoy it until it changed colour and it was then passed to the next one until it changed again and he got it back. Frequently the round and slippery gobstopper would slip from fingers and land on the carpet where it collect fag ash and fibres none of which daunted the sharers of sugary delights in the dark. The same applied to chewing gum; the original purchaser would enjoy it until the flavour was chewed out of it then it would passed to the next one. Sometimes the owner would give you one tablet of Beechnut and have the other three for himself. I would chew these with my front teeth. My mum was against gum as she was convinced it gave you stomach ulcers and I was convinced that they would kill you. But I still chewed gum and blew bubbles with it too. She found out that I was buying bubble gum because when the bubbles burst they left a coloured residue of rubber around the lips that only mums could see.

After his greeting and announcements The Chief would instruct us to sing songs, the words to which were projected on the screen. If we didn't sing with enough gusto we had to sing them again – this brought loud groans from the kids. We sang 'Margarita Picking Plums With Me' and the hymn 'Jerusalem' which I liked even then. "Bring me my arrows of desire…" I loved bows and arrows. Red Indians all had bows but Robin Hood could split a willow wand with his. I could hit a tree at about twenty feet. Once I accidentally shot a boy in the forehead. Just for bravado, he walked around for a minute or two with it sticking out of his head. Later a boy at school lost an eye in a similar incident; thankfully I was not the archer that time.

On Empire Day, someone wearing traditional costume would sometimes visit us from an empire country. People with darker skin were still rare before the waves of 1950s immigration although we sometimes saw African students or Sikh salesmen selling stuff out of suitcases around the streets. These exotic people were a splash of colour on Saturday mornings and we clapped and cheered them too.

Finally, the cinema would go dark and the show would begin to a deafening roar from the kids. Usually there'd be a cartoon to kick off the show – Bugs Bunny, Mickey Mouse or a similar favourite. Then there would be a comedy short like the Three Stooges or Laurel and Hardy (my favourites). This would be followed by a serial – and yes the guy always jumped out of the car before it went over the cliff. The kids all hooted and shouted out things like "that wasn't in the last episode." I still remember the titles of many of those serials: Rocketman, Purpleman, Superman, Flash Gordon, Batman, and Charlie Chan.

The main feature was usually a cowboy adventure or a comedy. However, occasionally there would be a drama; these were least liked by kids who only craved action or laughter. The films often provided the themes for our games through the week and they also formed the basis of our knowledge about native American culture, warfare, punchlines and lots of other stuff you do not learn at school. Love scenes, particularly scenes with kissing, were greeted with howls of derision. I wondered why film kisses did not end with the usual pop or lip smack. Grown ups only seemed to press their lips together then stop. How strange!

It was about this time that a yoyo craze began. I am pretty sure there had been one before but this time it was promoted at Saturday morning pictures. At the heart of this craze was a brand-named yoyo – the Lumar 99. It cost half-a-crown (two shillings and sixpence in old money or twelve-and-a-half pence now).

A yoyo promotional film was shown every Saturday featuring an expert called Pickles. He was a rather tubby chap who looked like he still lived with his mum with a slight stoop and a white sweater. He could perform amazing tricks with the yoyo including looping the loop and the 'flying saucer'. We were all smitten.

As usual I could not afford a real Lumar 99 but I bought one in similar colours from BHS and practiced and practiced until the string had several knots in it. It wasn't until I borrowed a proper 99 that I discovered the secret for making it spin at the end of its string enabling those seemingly impossible feats. I finally obtained the right kind of thread and could occasionally get mine to spin. The BHS yoyo cost half the price of the 99 and was very light in construction but in spite of its limitations I was able loop the loop although both 'walking the dog' and the 'flying saucer' eluded me.

One Saturday morning The Chief announced there was to be a yoyo competition and there would be prizes. I practiced and practiced and the next Saturday I got through to the next round with fairly rudimentary tricks. The next week turned out to be the final because only three of us had made it past the first stage. The prizes were exhibited on the stage. There was a cricket bat and a painting-by-numbers set. I had my eye on that. The Chief and a representative from Lumar supervised the competition. The third boy was soon eliminated; now it was just one more trick and the winner would be decided.

The yoyo man asked us to loop the loop and the other boy went first. He was just as nervous as me and he dropped his catch. It was my turn. With my heart beating in my ears accompanied by the noise from the kids who just wanted the show to start. I walked forward to the light. "Go on in your own time," whispered the Lumar man. I flicked my yoyo up and down to make sure the string was not tangled and then did a loop the loop. It wobbled a bit but I caught it! The kids all yelled, mostly I suspect because it meant the show could start. I was the winner and I looked around at the painting by numbers set. Then I heard a voice.

"Just a minute son, can I look at your yoyo?" I showed him my sweaty red and white tin yoyo with its knotted string. "Where did you get this?" he asked, "This isn't a Lumar 99."

"No it's from British home stores" I replied. He turned to my defeated opponent . " Is yours a Lumar 99?" The boy confirmed that it was. I was disqualified! I trooped off the stage with nothing and the other boy chose the cricket bat. I didn't want the cricket bat anyway.

These experiences are supposed to make a man of you, but I was glad of the dark of the cinema for a while.

shave

Mum's sister Olive had left home to work in service at fifteen, and somewhere along the road had met and married Reg who came from Standlake in Oxfordshire. They had two daughters, Christine and Susan, who were one and three years older than me. They were very striking girls, both blonde, but Susan had black eyebrows and beautiful blue eyes and a nervous chuckle, while Christine was very pretty and had a delightful sense of humour. I was especially fond of her.

The first time we stayed with them was when they lived in a council house at Ruscote Avenue in Banbury. I can only remember a little of that visit but my impression must have been good because I know I was very excited when Mum told us we were going to spend a little while with them during our summer holidays. They had moved to a new house in West Street backing on to a recreation ground, beyond which were the goods yards and shunting tracks for the railway.

Bruce and I were given the back bedroom. I think this was the first time we were together without Mum, and everything was different. First of all there was a bathroom, which meant we could have a bath. There were girls' things about the house and Susan had pin-up pictures of Audie Murphy and James Dean on her wall, and there was a piano in the front room where nobody used to go. I spent hours tinkling away there and

Auntie never told me to stop. That room smelt of furniture polish and coal and everything was in its place with polished brass and shiny wood-work. Both girls were having piano lessons from a man who may have been a little effeminate; I heard him described once as looking like 'a water lily floating down West Street'.

The house smelt of bacon and frying pans on some days, and at tea time we had bread and real butter with little Dairylea cheese wedges and vegetables from the garden and allotment; and here was the biggest dif-ference from our own family: this one included a man, and he was our Uncle Reg.

Reg was tall and slim with slightly receding hair and thin lips. His parents had paid for him to have all his teeth out for his twenty-first birthday 'so as to avoid any trouble later on,' and he spoke with what to us at first was an impenetrable Cotswold accent. He also worked nights. Uncle Reg had a shed in his garden where he performed shed rituals—that is to say, no-one knew what he did in there. Most men in those days had sheds where they made things, and to me it was the epitome of male-ness with its strange implements on the wall and the smell of oil and wood and sawdust and metal, and lots of old tobacco tins with names like 'Ringers A1' printed on them which were full of screws and nails.

Some men had mild pin-ups on their walls, and Mr. Humphries next door to No. 55 had that famous picture of Marilyn Monroe on his shed wall. For a while sheds were quite exciting, not least for their sometimes erotic content.

Perhaps because he had daughters, Reg wasn't totally at ease with Bruce and me, but he did try. He used to take us to his allotment, and some years ago before he died I jotted down this little memory in rhyme, meaning to send it to him:

My Uncle Reg grew a little fruit and veg
Out on his allotment,
And a carrot wiped clean
On the side of my jeans
Was part of my summer contentment.

…but I never did.

Uncle Reg worked nights at the aluminium factory, and didn't rise until early afternoon, when he would descend to the kitchen and prepare for the day. Bruce and I used to love this time, and would often arrange to be back indoors to observe the ritual.

First there would be the quick patter of carpet slippers coming down the stairs to where I sat waiting expectantly. The door would fly open and there, in trousers and string vest with hair all over the place, he would appear. I did wonder if he arranged his wispy locks to amuse us, but realising that we were not so important to him that he felt it necessary to entertain us from the moment he got up, I guessed that he must sleep with the window open. But there wasn't a gale every night, so it remained a mystery how his hair could be quite so violently disarranged.

His teeth would still be in a cup on the windowsill and his eyes, still slightly swollen with sleep, would blink rapidly as if annoyed with their betrayal of his slumbers. With genuine affection he would notice me in the corner, and as he reached for the kettle would say something which sounded to me like, "Gom mon dew nib Brutus," (he always called my brother Bruce 'Brutus').

"Oh, he's over in the rec on the swings," I would hazard.

"Im gom pooh gert bon frit farl I shouldn't wunner."

"Umm," I might offer.

"In up tom bing bong dayn lotment," said Uncle Reg looking at me directly.

"Oh yes, I'll go and tell Bruce, I'm sure he'd like to go," I answered, recognising the word allotment. It was only slightly better when he put his teeth in, and I'm not sure if he ever had both sets in at the same time anyway. Uncle fascinated me when he ate, because his usually immobile mouth would assume miraculous contortions as he chewed.

As he poured a little water from the kettle into the bowl he would usually say something else as part of the prevarication process before the delicate operation of shaving began.

"Ooh tal Brutus oy god bam blot dig nob nelly ban bog oryte."

"Yes uncle," I would say hoping that this was the correct response.

Once this next operation was finished the teeth would be in and I would be in with a chance. He nearly always repeated anything important anyway. If his lips had moved it would have helped, but I'm sure he could have said "bottle of beer" with no movement. At the time I was trying to master ventriloquism with a miniature version of Archie

109

Andrews purchased from Surrey Street market toy stall for twenty-three and six—fourteen and sixpence less than the store price. I was very proud of finding this particular bargain as Mum bought it for me for Christmas one year.

After a thorough wash and much slooshing, Uncle Reg would dab his face dry and throw the towel over his shoulders. Then picking up the kettle again, he would pour some water into a special large mug containing his shaving soap. Easing back his shoulders, he would exhale with a sort of a cough and take one or two steps up and down the kitchen.

Reaching for the shaving brush, he dipped it into his washing water, shook off the surplus, and whisked it rhythmically in the mug. To this day I have never seen anyone get a better lather on a brush before a drop was put on his face; the foam would be overflowing like a frothing firkin of best Belgian beer.

Another few steps up and down as he whisked, then whap! as the first brushful hit his face and the massaging into his stubble began. Uncle's stubble was awesome and every night it grew with a determination that gave him a complexion like Bluto in the Popeye cartoons. Today a beard might have been an option but not then; every morning, or in his case afternoon, one's masculinity was reaffirmed by this ritual of mortifying the flesh—quite literally in Uncle Reg's case. When all that was visible were his two eyes and the tip of his nose, framed by the mad hair, he would pick up the razor and stare at it a moment with the hatred of a weightlifter about to try and beat his personal best. With a few more steps up and down the kitchen, a deep breath and a little froth blown from his lips, his eyes would narrow to slits as he looked once more at the libelously named 'safety' razor and then in a quick rehearsed movement lift it up and stroke down from the top of his ear to his chin.

Three things happened simultaneously: there was a sound like ripping calico, or finger nails on a cheese grater, his toothless open mouth acting as a resonator for this dreadful sound; the first drops of blood appeared; and a short gasp of pain emanated from his foaming lips.

He took a few steps, then back at the mirror performed the same stroke on the other side of his face, and the same thing happened again. The teeth-on-edge noise, blood and a muted gasp. A few steps back and forth before he went for the moustache area on his top lip. This was accompanied by little intakes of breath with each short stroke and more droplets of blood.

Next came both cheeks. He was working quicker now before the blood dripped onto the string vest and it was up with the chin to tauten the skin and the bloody instrument of torture was dug into the whorls and eddies of whiskers that flourished in dense thickets in the lines that connected his chin to his neck.

With each noisy jarring stroke the gasps became louder until they were real cries of pain, the razor now flying along as the task neared completion. Then with a bang he threw down the implement on to the draining board and lifted up both hands full of water and threw it over his face. As he repeated this, the sudsy water turned pink. I could feel my colour draining away as uncle took a few more steps and then picked up the brush and re-lathered his face.

For him the worst was over. The foam on his face became dotted with leaks from all the little nicks in round one, but now he was on the home stretch and sometimes would hum a little something or talk to me through gritted gums and woolly froth.

"Ger schtiff lat Rutus ginks lar gog ler gargoyle," he offered.

"Umm…" I replied noncommittally.

"Well?" he grinned enquiringly at me.

"I didn't quite catch what you said uncle," I explained apologetically.

"Oy said," he began only this time speaking very slowly, "Ger schtiff lat Rutus ginks lar gog ler gargoyle."

Recognising the shorthand for Brutus I offered to go and get him and this seemed to satisfy him, though he did mutter mysteriously under his breath and foam, "I bet 'e will."

Once more the shave began, only this time it was much quieter, the length of the bristles now shortened and like piano strings the longer they are against the sound board the deeper the note. The sound now resonating from uncle's mouth was like someone sandpapering a tobacco tin.

Finally the shave was complete, and if the blade had been new it would now be useless, but I never saw uncle change a blade so I can barely imagine his pain. As he stood there, blood dripping and foam everywhere on his visage, he looked as if he'd done six rounds with Rocky Marciano.

Uncle was resigned to his daily torture and undaunted he threw the weapon down on the draining board like a weightlifter throws down the bar when he fails to make a lift, and rinsed his face once more in the water that by now resembled what you'd find in a beaten boxer's bucket. Then, taking a piece of Bronco from the toilet, he would tear off little bits and dab them on his tongue before sticking them on all his little wounds to stem the flow.

What a man! How I admired him! I wondered how long it would be before I would be shaving; not too long, I hoped, or else I might have to get a tattoo.

These days with Olive, Reg and my cousins were probably some of the happiest of our young lives. There was an order to each day and Bruce and I, long able to organise ourselves, were about our business and only came in at teatime. Auntie was kindness itself and though she sometimes got cross, there were none of the rages we had got used to with our mother.

Once I heard Olive tell Mum not to be so hard on Bruce and me, telling her we were "really good kids", and once I heard her threaten Christine and Susan with the words, "If you don't behave I'll send you off to your Auntie Win [our mum]".

That soon shut them up. I actually found this reassuring as I know we both tried to be good, but with all she had to cope with, Mum was sometimes hard to please.

We attended their local Saturday morning pictures and wandered through their market that had gypsies selling herbal cures, and we ate fried potato scallops on the way home, past the smelly brewery and the big rec where the magnificent steam locomotives thundered through on their way to London.

There was a brook there and we went fishing for tiddlers and sticklebacks and redthroats, and once we put a dragonfly baby in with our catch and it slaughtered several of the fish before we could remove it. It dug these horn-like things into their throats and it upset us all greatly. We wandered the fields and played games, fished in the rivers, climbed hills, ate watery homemade ice lollies that a lady made in her fridge and charged one penny for, had tea with the family and finally fell asleep to the sound of trains shunting trucks and carriages way across the rec, their puffing shuddering steam and smoke occasionally blowing smoke rings into the red green blue gold summer night sky and guiltily I wished we could stay here forever.

Uncle and Auntie were very kind and used to help an old couple called

Woodward on an unpaid basis, Reg doing the garden and Olive doing the housework. Quite why they felt obligated to do this I don't know, but people generally seemed to help each other more then, and favours done were usually returned.

Reg was also a voluntary bell ringer, and one day took Bruce and me to see them practise. Just past Banbury Cross, a little way back from the road, stands the beautiful St. Mary's church. Its circular shape and mellow sandstone made it something of a landmark.

When we went in to climb to the belfry the church was surrounded by very ancient tombstones but later, to my horror, they were mostly dug up and turned into paving around the periphery of the church where the soft stone soon relinquished their memorials to passing feet. As a child I found myself doubly worried by what became of the remains beneath the stones and the final anonymity for them once their names had vanished. This rekindled memories of *The Nine Tailors* for me. As we entered the tiny bell space the noise was unbelievable, and partly because of that and partly from the sight that greeted us, both Bruce and I looked at each other and grinned.

There must have been eight bell ringers there; most were men but there was at least one lady, and they shouted their greetings to Reg and acknowledged us with smiles. Reg took his place among them and added his bell to their cacophony. I could perceive an order to the peal but the rhythm was very irregular. All the pullers were red-faced and sweating with the exertion, and many of the men were in some state of disarray: stretching up to pull the ropes resulted in trousers and shirts parting company, and what seemed like acres of underpants had become exposed.

Bell ringing is a two-handed job, so there was no possibility of adjusting one's dress until the session ended. The bell ropes had sheepskin grips of red and white and it was confusing to note that the 'clang' did not synchronise with the pull but at a little time after; this is because the bell is attached to a beam which is rocked by the rope, and as the bell tilts so the clapper hits the side.

Watching them all working together, it was as if there was a time delay and the soundtrack was a couple of frames behind the action. All this only added to the confusion of the senses, and a comic ingredient was added to the scene when Uncle Reg's trousers slipped from his skinny waist, staying precariously balanced on his hips as he puffed and sweated with the rest of them.

Bruce and I gazed in wonder as the weight of the bells practically lifted the men off the ground. We were allowed to hold on to a rope and were actually elevated a few feet, a marvellous experience. It was probably the loudest thing we had ever heard up until then, but more was to come as one of the blokes left his post and, taking Bruce by the hand, led us up a narrow wooden staircase to the place where the bells were fixed.

As we climbed through the little trapdoor the noise was literally deafening. The swaying of the huge bells and the terrifying din awoke the memory of the *Hunchback of Nôtre Dame* trailer. We were almost hypnotised by the rocking motion of the bells themselves; I began to feel dizzy and very frightened, and Bruce even more so, as I used to tease him about the Hunchback. At home I'd made a haunted house out of our damp old 'playroom', where I'd fixed up some cocoa tins which I'd told him were the bells of Nôtre Dame, and he'd been so scared that he wouldn't go in until I'd removed them, but now I was as glad as he was to get down from there.

Banbury's other claim to fame, after the famous nursery rhyme, is that it boasts the biggest cattle market in the country. We went several times, but that used to make me sad as I soon released that, in spite of Auntie telling us otherwise, some of the animals were not going to new homes but were destined for mint sauce and mustard. Nevertheless it was exciting watching these huge beasts slipping and slithering down the ramps of lorries and to hear the squealing of pigs, the crying of calves and the mournful moaning of cows recently separated from their offspring.

The air was full of Woodbine and pipe smoke, and it stank of shit as terrified animals evacuated their bowels in the strange environment. Gumboots squelched through the unspeakable mire and red-faced men spoke and joked in loud hearty Cotswold accents whilst auctioneers gabbled in high speed code that both mystified and amazed us. I was staggered by the size of the balls on a bull, and when I heard the price of a calf, I seriously wondered if we could accommodate it in the back garden at home.

I had been unlucky with pets at that time, as a rescued kitten that I'd attempted to rear had all but died on me. I'd only fed it on Puffed Wheat (I had presumed that because our own master mouser Timmy liked this breakfast cereal that a kitten would love it). His cries had revealed his whereabouts in the old bedroom, his life was saved and a new home found for him.

Not so my pet jay, a full-plumaged fledgling who had miraculously avoided the attentions of our cat and survived for three days perched on a waste pipe in the area around our basement. On the third morning I had gone out to feed him with some bread (which they don't eat) and as I got right up to him he just made a strange cry, lifted his lovely wings and placing them over his head in a final display, dropped dead in front of me. I was inconsolable and cried on and off for several days. It would have been bad enough finding him dead but for him to wait for me before dying was cruel. I blamed myself, though I could not have provided the meat that he required for his survival as we only had meat once a week ourselves and we gratefully ate all of it between us. All things considered, perhaps a calf was not a good idea.

Beyond the cattle market was Uncle's allotment, and in neat rows his crops were displayed: runner beans, lettuce, carrots, parsley, onions and even flowers all shared the bit of ground. Reg would take his single-bladed old knife and cleanly cut a lettuce to take home or scrape a carrot for us both. Never before or since did a carrot taste so good. As the summer wore on we began to understand his speech more, and he was never less than enthusiastic when he spoke to us boys. He also grew some vegetables in his back garden, from which a gate led out to the rec, a huge piece of open ground. It was largely unsuitable for football (which didn't interest us anyway) as the ground had been pushed up in undulating waves to assist drainage, but it was always well used by local kids.

One evening Uncle asked if I could ride a bike. I told him that Mum wouldn't let us have one because we lived in town, and he said that I was old enough to learn anyway. So after tea one warm evening he wheeled his old 'sit-up-and-beg' out of the shed through the back gate and into the park, where I clambered aboard. Supporting me upright by holding the saddle, he ran along till I had enough speed to balance and then let go in the time-honoured way.

I was amazed at uncle's stamina, as I was now pedalling at a fair lick. What a man he was! I shouted that he should let me try on my own. Not getting any response, I glanced back to see him back at his garden gate and realised I had been on my own and self-propelled for a while. I immediately fell off. Unhurt, I got back on and Uncle pushed me and away I went. Then he taught me how to get on and off, and soon I was riding all by myself all over the rec. What a feeling of freedom and speed! The whole thing was exhilarating. I had to be called in to go to bed or I would have cycled till dawn. Sweaty and tired I fell asleep with a grin as wide as a cycle chain.

Bruce learned at the same time, and though we didn't get our own bikes for a number of years, we now had the skills to begin our rehearsals for leaving home.

I never saw any open display of affection for each other from either Olive or Reg. I suppose they just rubbed along like some old-fashioned couples did before separation and divorce became so commonplace, and Auntie never seemed to bother about trying to make herself glamorous. Her hair was sort of parted and rolled up at the back, and she wore a crossover apron all day. She looked a lot like Mum, but she laughed more readily and was always kindly without being over-fussy. She wore the same sort of underwear that old ladies did, sensible stuff made out of cloth, whilst Mum wore embarrassingly scanty (for the time) nylon bits of frippery. The lascivious Mr. Humphries next door always had a comment to make, and I think Mum sort of enjoyed the mildly risqué remarks.

"I can always tell when yer sister's 'ere because of the washing on the line," he would chuckle.

I quite enjoyed the thought that he found Mum sort of sexy. She did try to impress in certain ways as if to test her attractiveness, and she always wore make-up and dressed up smart for work, as far as her wardrobe of hand-me-downs would let her.

fairies

The most famous resident of The Waldrons was a pre-Raphaelite style painter called Cicely Mary Barker. This sweet lady was tall, but almost bent double with a terrible stoop. She was rather splay-footed with large feet, and always seemed to be smiling, her large teeth protruding slightly. She wore a huge-brimmed straw hat and strode on her errands with purpose and gentility. Perhaps because of her stoop she did not seem to recognise individual children, though she knew many of us; she never spoke to us, but you sensed that she liked the fact that we were there playing in the street. Maybe it was that permanent smile.

Miss Barker is known all over the world for her illustrated books for both children and adults; her 'Flower Fairy' stories and poems are the best known. Our neighbour Mrs. Leisk's two attractive daughters, Anita and Valerie, posed for two fairies each, and Anita remembers having to stand holding a broom pole to represent a flower stalk. She was the Tottergrass fairy and her sister the Pansy fairy.

Contrary to rumour, Miss Barker did not make the costumes that the children wore. Her models wore their own clothes, and the gossamer threads and petals were added from her imagination afterwards.

She had also illustrated a children's bible that had been written by her sister Dorothy. The two sisters looked after their very elderly mother who wore frightening surgical boots, one of which had an extended built-up sole made of cork. The three of them lived in genteel order right at the top of the street and directly opposite the Halfway House with all its concomitant pandemonium.

She had a studio in her back garden, and one day she approached Mum and asked if I would be allowed to pose for her. The Flower Fairy books had by then been completed; instead, the character I was modelling was a little boy in a country smock and hobnailed boots, in a story about a swan. Bruce also modelled for her, and we became a composite figure. She usually stood to draw and she had half glasses that her stooped frame peered over. I preferred it when I was facing away from her, as when I had to look straight at her I sometimes wanted to laugh. Her gaze was very different to the way one would look at someone if they were having a normal conversation, and with her protruding teeth she did look a bit odd. For a long time I didn't see the paintings, only the drawings. One was a profile, and for the first time I saw the shape of myself sideways on—or was it Bruce?

On the wall of her studio she had fading newspaper cuttings with pictures of Brumas, the polar bear cub at London Zoo, and although they were beginning to go yellow she kept them there to keep her young models' attention.

Perhaps because she guessed that I would be interested, she let me look at her sketch books, and I marvelled at her ability to reproduce faithfully likenesses of everyday objects.

Once when needing to draw a pair of boy's leather boots, she had journeyed all the way to Cumberland, believing that boys there still wore them for everyday use, only to find when she returned that a lad across the road whose name was Roger Conio wore them all the time. She was able to chuckle at this, which I thought quite remarkable. I realised she must be rich to be able to travel so far just to draw boots, and my suspicions were proved correct when, after the posing was finished, she gave me four shillings and sixpence and allowed me to keep the jeans that I had worn for the drawings.

Eventually I did see a painting from these sessions when she exhibited a portrait of me in an show that was held at Allders department store, and I was very excited about seeing it. I was wearing the hat and smock that I wore for the sitting, and with great pride and a loud voice I announced to all nearby that it was me in the picture. A lady leaned toward me to verify my assertion and smiled.

I believe it was Miss Barker who was instrumental in getting me into the choir at St. Andrew's, because she was upset when I left. I love her pictures of the flower fairies because of their originality but mostly because she draws out the beauty of the street urchins who posed for her, some of whom I can still recognise from kids in our road.

For many years I thought that Valerie Leisk was the model for the Snowdrop fairy, and even though she didn't pose for this particular one, it is one of the sweetest paintings. Even at the time it reminded me of Hans Christian Anderson's *Little Match Girl* and I used to wonder if her bare feet might be cold in the snow.

I've mentioned before that my mother read to us every night; I remember that halfway through reading one of Anderson's stories she suddenly put down the book and said that she could no longer continue reading them because they were so unremittingly miserable and were enough to give anyone the willies. I was surprised but glad and we moved on to Enid Blyton or something a bit more cheery. She always said that it was to protect us from having nightmares, but I had them anyway. I suspect it was to stop her having them herself.

Mum needed escape from the drudgery of her life, and in a way I think reading these and other 'Sunny Stories' reminded her of protected but happy times in her youth when she worked as an assistant to the old Nanny that raised the young Marquis of Hertford. There must have been books available suitable for the young aristocrat, and Bruce and I in our poverty-stricken surroundings inherited the love of those safe and sensible, and often very funny, reading lists.

Perhaps this influence made us a little bit softer but the fact that our country-raised mother taught us by repetition all the names of the wild flowers we came across as we played up in Croham Hurst, Bruce and I picked little bunches of flowers for her and did not in the least consider it unmanly. This was a definite perk of being brought up by just a mother, although I think that shedding this softness made the pain of entering the real world with its macho values that bit more difficult.

Eventually both Miss Barker's old mother and her sister Dorothy died. The old house must have been too big for her, and the last time I saw her—though she didn't see me—she was wearing a huge pink straw hat and striding splay-footed down Violet Lane. I think she bought a little house there and retired. It really could not have been more appropriate.

Earning money as a model for Miss Barker was not going to provide a regular income—we always needed a few pennies more. Mum gave us pocket money that started off at sixpence a week, but as that was consumed by Saturday morning pictures it was soon raised to ninepence, giving us a surplus of threepence. These were the pennies that should have been used to buy luxuries, but from the beginning we were encouraged to save them. This meant that we always had enough to buy her a Mother's Day box of chocolates or a hyacinth for her birthday, and we were very happy to do it. She was always very appreciative of her little presents and handmade cards, even when Bruce made one with a bomber plane delivering her birthday wishes.

Mum also paid for the sweets in the sweet tin, plus the occasional Mars bar that was carefully cut into as many as eight sections and shared out through the week. She also paid for our weekly comic, *The Topper*, and later *The Beezer* as well. On trips to the woods we would get the odd ice cream, and with neighbours always asking us to run errands for a penny or tuppence reward, we were more or less on parity with the rest of the kids on the street. But we could always have done with more.

One day I suggested that we have a go at raising some extra money by totting. Mum was not at all keen on the idea, but relented when she realised we would only be collecting paper salvage. With Bruce in tow to give me confidence we began knocking on the doors of the friends in the street. We progressed to those we did not know, and soon we had enough paper to go to Holloway's yard.

Holloway's was a scrap metal business. They also dealt with rags, newspaper and woollens. It meant that there was a constant throb of noisy activity at the end of the street. A non-stop parade of horses and carts, open lorries and even blokes with hand carts made their way to deliver the scrap that afforded many of them a living.

As we nervously made our way inside, the rough-looking blokes who worked there gave us odd looks, but seeing us with our bags of paper, one of them told us to go up to the paper scale and wait. Across the yard was a man working at a machine that chopped up pieces of metal as if it was plasticine. We both stared transfixed at its awesome power until the operator gave us a big wink and we grinned back.

Next to his machine was an open arched doorway, and through it a tunnel that led to a room in a cellar under the road. There was movement down there and as I focused through the bright sunlight of the afternoon I could see a woman with a curious hooked knife tearing rags in the gloom with a single light bulb above her head. She pulled the shapes of old garments, sleeves flapping, from a huge pile on the floor then hooked them up and slashed at them with this wicked looking knife. As they flailed about they looked like people hanging there, and I looked away. A cigarette dangled between her lips and I thought it must be the saddest loneliest job in the world.

As we stared, a man came up and tipped our pathetic bundle on to the scales and weighed it without a word. He wrote something on a piece of paper, handed it to me and told me to go up to the office and get it cashed.

With one last glance at the woman in the rag cellar I scuttled off up the wooden steps and gave the lady in the office the slip of paper, in return for which I received one shilling and eightpence. I hurried back to Bruce and we scurried out of the yard. It was so much money we decided to save it and put it in our money boxes that Uncle Reg had made out of cocoa tins.

That evening Bruce and I sat putting our ten pennies each into the slot in the top and listened to the satisfying clank as the hit the bottom, then we took the lid off and did it all again. The next day I changed my pennies into halfpennies so that I could count twenty coins in and out of the money box.

After a few days we tried again but not nearly so much luck, and some of the people said that we were a nuisance. We left the paper at home and resolved to try further afield. We were only moderately successful, lacking the bravado of some lads. We did, however, collect some rags and separated the woollens because you got more for them, and were even offered an Anderson shelter which we weren't able to dismantle. A pity, because we would have made a fortune out of that.

Eventually the blokes down at the yard got fed up with us too and started to take the mickey.

"What have you got in there, son," one of them asked, "loose cigarettes?" All his mates laughed, and although I'm sure she wouldn't have been able to hear, the woman in the rag cellar looked like she was laughing as well. We both went red, and after I got our money we did not go back totting for several years until after we had moved.

Some time later I had a dream about a mad woman in a cellar who hooked bodies of children up on a hook and slashed at them with her wicked crooked knife and I knew that we'd had a narrow escape.

In November 1952 something unthinkable happened. A policeman, Sydney Miles, was shot and killed, allegedly by two youths attempting to rob a sweet wholesalers not far from where we lived. We did not take a daily newspaper but we knew everything about what was going on because people talked about it endlessly.

We all knew that Christopher Craig had shot the policeman and some knew that Derek Bentley was epileptic and mentally about eight years old; at some point he had visited the chemist where my mother worked and had to hand over a note for the things that the family needed. Craig's elder brother Nivan had also been in the shop and been pointed out to my mother by the dispenser Mr. Strong as being "a bad lot."

Everyone was appalled at the death of a policeman, but the trial was over so quickly that I think everyone was in a state of shock.

No-one really thought Derek Bentley would be executed. Mrs. Connaughton brought down the paper with the terrible news of the 28th of January. There was that same smudged and grainy photo of the young Bentley, cigarette dangling from his mouth in an arrogant laddish pose which suggested toughness and mischief at the same time.

Now the paper told me that Bentley was dead. In response to all my bewilderment and the awful silence that followed the news all my voices were murmuring at the same time, and I begged for an answer with every look that I could give my family and the few grown-ups that we came into contact with.

My mother could only wearily manage, "Well at least now it's over." How wrong she was.

Mr. Diamond moved next door in the basement flat. He was a nice man, who unfortunately had lost his wife recently with polio and had three little ones to raise: Nicholas and Geoffrey, who were respectively two and four years younger than me, and a brand new baby called Linda. He also had his mother and father-in-law to help look after the children, who seemed incredibly sad.

I took it upon myself to welcome the boys to the street. I had just learned a new swear word, which I was sure was not as meaningfully bad as bleedin' or bloody, and decided to use it at every opportunity. Because the boys took a little while to settle in to their new home and life without mother, it was a few days before I actually had a chance to speak with the two of them. One morning on the way to school I spotted them hand in hand on their way to my school, and ran to catch them up. They both had on their new school caps and looked very apprehensive as I shouted hello.

"Are you going to fucking Howard's school?" I asked cheerfully, enjoying my new word. Recoiling slightly with the shock of being so familiarly addressed they nodded.

"That's the same fucking school that I fucking go to!" I confessed. "Is this your little brother?"

"Yes," said Nicholas, looking even more nervous and probably wondering if this foul-mouthed maniac might eat his small sibling. Geoffrey smiled a toothy smile.

"I've got a little fucking brother as well!" I announced as we drew near to the school gate. Further attempts to converse were put aside as we went into our respective classes, but I felt I had gone some way to assure them that there was a friend nearby.

On the way home from school that evening as I was balancing on top of a fucking garden wall, Christopher Bond questioned me on my new all-purpose adjective and to the wisdom of using it at every opportunity.

"Oh, it doesn't mean any fucking thing," I said, adding, "it's only like saying flipping which is probably a worse swear word."

"I don't think so," said Chris, "anyway I wouldn't say it to my mum."

"Oh, my mum wouldn't mind," I said, secretly wondering if I should dare and deciding not to.

Unfortunately the word slipped out later that evening in a moment of exasperation when some cardboard contraption I was making failed to work.

"I can't find the fucking scissors!" I exploded.

There was a sudden hush like the world coming to its end.

I realised at that exact moment that Chrissie Bond had been right, as my mother looked up from the fireplace and asked slowly, "What did you say, Ralph?"

"I can't find the scissors," I replied, as the colour drained from my face.

"You said something else as well," she said. "Another word."

"Oh that, it's a new word we say at school when we can't find things like where's the *flucking* scissors," I said, heavily emphasising the L which is usually left unpronounced in normal speech.

Of course it was no good and Mum saw right through my pathetic excuse.

"If I ever hear you use that word again, Ralph, I'll wash your mouth out with carbolic soap. No-one ever uses that word in front of me. Your father did once and I told him the same. Don't you ever use it again, do you hear me?"

"Yes Mum," I agreed, and I thought to myself, that was flucking close.

As Christmas grew near it occurred to me that with my new found skills on the mouth organ there might be a chance of earning a few pennies by carol singing. I spoke to Bruce and said that if we got Mickey Sparrow along and a couple of other kids, I could play the mouth organ and they could sing and we were sure to make some money because most carol singers didn't have anyone to play for them. Bruce could see that we might be in with a chance, so we had a rehearsal. It was only then that a slight doubt entered my mind.

If you have music in you then you are blessed, and if you can make music as well you are doubly blessed. If you like music but cannot make it, at least you have partial blessing, but if music means nothing to you at all then pity is all that should be accorded you. Unfortunately my two accomplices fell into these last two categories. Bruce liked music but could not really find the notes, and seldom got off in the right key even with me trying to indicate higher or lower with my eyebrows as I blew as hard as I could to try and give him an anchor to the tune. Mickey hated to sing anyway, and when we finally got him to oblige he sang everything on one note not daring to move from the safety of the one he had found. This was especially difficult for me, as I started to think that they were doing it on purpose.

"NO!" I would shout, breaking off to join them in a bit of singing.

Bruce would wrestle his way up to the right key, but as soon as I left to return to the harmonica he would flounder and Mickey would drone on with his one note dirge. Neither of them wanted to go out and try it, but after investing all this time I was not going to give in.

I realised even before we embarked on our mission that my eyebrow signals would be redundant in the dark, and I had to come up with an alternative. Bruce suggested using hand signals, but I was not so good at these for some reason and occasionally moved my hand up for a down note which, when corrected in mid-note, tended to reduce Bruce's effort to a yodel. Mickey didn't even try to follow and continued to drone away, but at least he had most of the words.

Then I had a minor brainwave. For our birthdays both Bruce and I had received a small torch. This had been a great choice as it was supposed to give us the confidence to negotiate the dark passage to the bathroom past the stairs. It did not manage this entirely but it did help in using the bedside chamber pot. I had missed it several times and fairly recently had managed to pee in my shoe that I had pulled out by mistake. Bruce and I entertained each other with light shows and I found another way of fear transference when I discovered that if I slowly moved my open hand over the beam reflected on the ceiling I could say that the monster was going to get him as my hand assumed gigantic proportions before smothering the torch lens and reducing the room to death and blackness. Eventually this game palled and I stuck various shapes on the front of the lens to scare him or entertain us both but nothing worked quite as well as the 'haunted hand'.

By now Mickey was adamant that he did not want to go carol singing even with the untold riches we had told him would soon be his. I pondered on those whose parents gave them the odd penny and thought that he was a bit spoiled. Certainly his younger brother was. If Paul was to so much as whimper, his mum or Midge (his unmarried aunt who lived with them) would give him some money and we would all troop after him down to Warren's sweet shop for a lick of his sherbet fountain or whatever he bought.

Mickey was finally persuaded to come when I made Bruce give him his torch. I explained I would need mine so as they would be able to see my eyebrow conducting and clues as to time. We had rehearsed several carols including *Once in Royal David's City* and *While Shepherds Watched their Flocks by Night*. We considered who might be the most sympathetic to our music of the people in the street, and eventually decided that our landlady Mrs. Cox was probably going to be our best bet.

After one more rehearsal of our dismal chorale, and with a somewhat heavy heart, we trudged across the road to number seven and climbed the steps to her front door. We started off with *Once in Royal David's City* and I thought it sounded dreadful, so I stopped it after the first verse and we went into *While Shepherds Watched* which sounded even worse.

There was nothing for it but to knock on the door after several what seemed like minutes of banging, ringing and waiting the door was finally opened by old Mr. Cox who was, you may remember, virtually stone deaf.

"Yes!" he bellowed, looking down at the hapless three.

Bruce stuck out his hat as he'd been instructed to do, and the old man looked at it for a second or two before he said, "It's not mine."

"No, we know that," I shouted, "we're carol singing and we want some money." Then I remembered. "Please."

"I can't hear what you're saying," said the old man, "I'll get Mrs. Cox to see you." Off he went down the hall to where the old couple sat in their kitchen, which was as far from the front door as you could get in their apartment. No wonder the old man couldn't hear us.

"Hello Ralph and Bruce," said the old lady, "and isn't that Mickey with you?" She peered at the three of us in a curious but kindly manner. "What can I do for you?"

"We're carol singers, Mrs. Cox, and we've just sung a load of carols and we were hoping for some pennies."

"Are you?" she beamed, "well I didn't hear anything as we were in the back end so you better sing me some now that I am nearer to you."

The ensemble looked crestfallen but we had gone this far and so I boldly struck up again with *Shepherds*. After some frantic eyebrow movement my choristers reluctantly joined in halfway through the second line. With an audience, my wayward harmonisers went a bit quiet on me, and I thought we sounded somehow vaguely Scottish as my reedy mouth organ squawked out the tune whilst these two droned on below.

We had not even begun verse two when she walked off to get her handbag, and coming back, took out her purse and gave us two pennies. That seemed to be the going rate as the night progressed. One lady complimented me on my playing but said nothing to the drones, who by now were fairly philosophical about the enterprise. One man came out and started laughing right in our faces and gave us two more pennies to sing one verse again while he dragged his wife out to hear us. She laughed at us as well. Several times Bruce got the giggles, which made Mickey laugh, and our shape was clearly beginning to suffer, as well as a kind of exhaustion setting in.

Looking back I think our presentation would have been more suited to Hallowe'en than Christmas, my torch shining from below my chin giving my already contorted face an eerie strangeness. My eyebrow signalling had given me a headache, and my body was aching from willing on my unenthusiastic and mournful sounding vocalists with every spasm and shoulder flick I could muster. Halfway down Violet Lane we had all had enough, and Mickey wanted his split there and then so that he could go to the shop. I think we finished up with a shilling or so each.

Summer games took place in the Spinney. As you looked at it from our gate there was a postbox that I fell off from time to time, and just beyond it a huge ibrox or evergreen oak. I also fell off this once and tore a lot of skin from my backside, which would have been more bearable if Mum had not insisted, to my utter embarrassment, on showing Mrs. Connaughton.

This was our adventure playground; there were trees and bushes and a store for the road sweepers to keep their dust cart in, and in the autumn there were chestnuts and conkers. Around the perimeter the road became our running track and the bushes provided cover for games of a more enquiring kind. Once in the middle of my becoming a boy detective I discovered a whole pile of what I took to be blood-soaked bandages. I was totally convinced there had been a murder or at least a stabbing (Mrs. Connaughton had told us about a knife fight down at the pub in Salem Place the previous Saturday). For the life of me I could not understand the reluctance of any of the adults to take my find seriously, but eventually someone must have done. I was told not to go near them and that they would be dealt with, which they were. It was years later before I realised they were used sanitary towels.

As the nights drew in I was forced to keep the games going longer and longer; if our friends got bored they would just peel off and go and watch telly so I had to be good. The alternative was to sit indoors waiting for the hands on the old American clock to reach the two bits of paper that had been stuck on the seven and twelve to indicate seven o' clock. This was the time that Mum left work, and usually it meant that the fire had to be alight and going well by the time she came in exhausted through the door.

Sometimes Bruce and I would sit under a blanket together until the time was right, then I would do the honours and light the old newspaper and damp wood in the grate and hope for the best. Mum was good at laying fires and to this day so am I. It was rare that we needed more than one match to get it going. Our cat Timmy was a better frogger and toader than he was mouser, and ceaselessly dragged in the bodies of dead amphibians for my mother's approval. But we loved him anyway and I was convinced that he was the prettiest cat in the world. He would sit one side of the fire and Tyler the other.

One night as Mum prepared some tea for us all I was dreamily gazing into the flames while Tyler was sitting with his back to the fireplace. Suddenly, without any warning or provocation, he lunged forward and bit my face.

It was an extraordinary thing to have done. His teeth closed around the inside of my left lip and his top teeth under my left eye. As soon as the bite was made he let go and I recoiled backwards in a state of shock with blood spurting everywhere. I must have screamed, and my poor old tired mother came rushing in and in utter disbelief surveyed the scene in front of her. Bruce explained what had happened and Mum tried her best to stop the bleeding before we all trudged up to Croydon General Hospital. Luckily the evening casualty room was quite slow that night, but the smell of ether and disinfectant got to me, and I began to tremble as the dreadful memories of my stay there came back.

The wound to my upper lip took three large stitches—but should have had more—and the top injury just one. The thing I remember most was the feeling of having manly bristles on my upper lip in the form of the thin wire stitches that were inserted and the fact that the young nurse who administered the tetanus injection broke off the needle in my leg and they had to use pliers to pull it out. My biggest fear however was for Tyler. Mum, naturally, was furious but I knew how she loved her dog and I had to think of an excuse for his behaviour.

In the end the story I made up went along the lines of, "I was stroking Timmy as he sat by the fire and the buckle of my sandal accidentally pressed on Tyler's foot which caused him to jump at me in pain and jealousy."

It was a bit thin, and I suspect that she knew it all along, but it gave her the excuse not to have him put down.

On my return it was as if nothing had happened between us two. Tyler greeted everyone with his normal wood-splitting tail wagging and must have been surprised at the coolness of the welcome he got in return. I enjoyed my hero status a little as well, especially as it could have been viewed as if I had been in a manly scrap of some sort. I think I even put on a little swagger as I walked.

On the weekend as usual we went up to the woods and as usual ran about playing games and climbing our favourite trees. It was a normal sort of outing except towards the end of the afternoon I began to feel very strange. By the time we were ready to leave and begin our homeward journey I had begun to look ill enough for my mother and Mrs. Ranger to be concerned. I was very dizzy and hot and my colour was deserting me.

Soon I was unable to walk and they lifted me up on to the wood barrow and hurried to the nearest phone box. By now I had gone a sort of grey colour and had all but fainted. How Mrs. Ranger got the wood barrow home with her push chair I don't know; I had passed out by the time we got back. The ambulance arrived and took me off; as it neared the hospital I had begun to come up in a rash, which then started to turn into small blisters. My mother was almost beside herself by the time the doctor had seen me and declared that I must have had an overdose of the tetanus injection.

This diagnosis was confirmed by our own wonderful Dr. Martin, whose sonorous Welsh tones gave us all such confidence to get well: "You see, my dear, it appears that they gave him rather too much of the serum for anti-tetanus and now the poor boy has the illness proper."

I can't say that he ever soothed me with that clear penetrating enunciation of his, but he did inspire confidence. He always wore a suit and half-rimmed reading glasses in gold frames. He had grey hair and very dark eyes with eyebrows that seemed permanently furrowed with care. I imagine he used the same voice to tell you that you were dying as he would to tell you that you were going to survive. His delivery lacked any trace of sentimentality and he would deal out admonishment in the same tone as praise. Everyone loved and feared him in equal measure.

The only time there might have been a hint of embarrassment shown on his part was when Mrs. Sparrow was safely delivered of her third child. Dr. Martin helped bring him into the world and Mrs. Sparrow insisted that the little boy be named after him. On hearing that the good doctor's first name was Lambert, she compromised and named the child Paul Lambert Sparrow.

I eventually regained consciousness in the small ward that I had been placed in three years previously to avoid the tormentors of the children's ward. For the next few days I was woken every few hours to receive doses of antibiotics. It was touch and go for a while, but I was soon home again, although much weakened by the experience. I began to feel quite guilty about these mishaps and paradoxically realised how lucky I had been.

Not very long afterwards I arrived late home from school to find quite a little crowd gathered at the top of the basement steps. Poor old Tyler had gone crazy and had attacked everyone who had gone close to him. My mother and the vet were there already and she was the only one that could get anywhere near him.

The diagnosis was an inoperable brain tumour and Tyler was put to sleep. It was tough on all of us, and a replacement dog that the vet provided us with was too boisterous for Bruce and I to handle and we had to give him up too. Still we had Timmy the cat, and soon I had pet mice and even a guinea pig.

Several of my school friends had joined the cub scouts. I had longed to be a cub since before my accident. I suppose it should have been a warning to me of all disciplined activity, but I continued to confuse obligation and duty with being good or correct. The mysteries of 'sixers' and indecipherable songs like *Ging Gang Goolie* left me bewildered and embarrassed, and the sausage-cooking outing was a washout, during which I lost my penknife and my pocket money.

The games, devised I guess to foster a team spirit, were lost on me, as I had no desire to win apart from running races, which are not team sports. The only thing I really remember was the cub play, where I was given a walk-on part on the small stage at the scout hall. It was a play about a man who hears the football results on the radio, realises that he has won the pools, and then one of the kids finds the coupon in his pocket and they are not instantly wealthy after all.

The audience found this very funny but I thought it sad, especially if my mum had done it and we'd had a chance to escape from poverty and then I'd found the coupon in my pocket. It did not bear thinking about and I wondered which might be the best form of suicide and how I could explain or ever come to terms with my slackness.

At one point Brian Atkins, who was at my school, got up and sang a song in a beautiful boy soprano voice, and all the mums cooed and aahed at him. He was a slim blond boy with an angelic face, and I was jealous of both his voice and the effect it had on his audience. That night I practised singing like Brian Atkins and learned *Golden Slumbers* which I sang to Bruce on many goodnights.

After a while I thought I was probably good enough to join a choir. The best church choir was thought to be at the Croydon Parish Church and Miss Barker was kind enough to ask if I could join. She told us with some small embarrassment that they only took Grammar School boys and I was still at primary school. I thought this unbelievable. Did Jesus really worry what school you went to I order that you might sing his praises? I doubted it. Other forces were at work here, so I applied at Miss Barker's favourite church where she had designed one of the stained glass windows and was accepted.

By now I was involved with three churches: the Mint Walk Mission, the Congregational Church and the Anglican church at St. Andrew's, as well as the cubs. Of course one of them had to go, and just before Mum had scraped up the few coins for my second-hand cub uniform, I got into a small scrap with a boy outside the cub hut. I took a swing at him with the wolf's head on the pole that we had to march with, he ducked, and with my usual co-ordination I managed to hit the gate pillar, causing the wolf's head to burst just above its right eye. A pile of stuffing fell out on to the road and I thought it best to go home and construct an excuse as to why the cubs and I were not really suited.

For some time I had been having doubts about my future with this organisation, because I had been taken at my word when refusing payment for my errand running, saying that it was "my good deed for the day"; and now I was being run ragged with the neighbours always asking for me to go to the shops so that they could avail themselves of my free service.

Needless to say Mum was disappointed, but we sold the cap for two shillings and I wore the jersey without the badges for a long while.

Eventually, some months after my tetanus scare, I was well enough to have my tonsils out. For a hospital veteran like me it was a doddle. Nine days inside and ice cream to eat with jelly—no problem! This operation was done at Mayday Hospital, where my brother was born. It made a nice change to be in a new hospital, and I was also one of the oldest on the ward at nine years old.

When the Sparrow family acquired a TV, a dozen or more kids would troop or sneak into their tiny front room to watch the Lone Ranger and Tonto or the Cisco Kid. It was great to sit amongst them and stare at the black and white screen, but part of me missed the outdoor games that we seemed to play more before the TV arrived.

We never ran out of things to do in our street. Bows and arrows, soapbox carts, roller skating and for a short time roller skate soap boxes, where we took the wheels off a pair of skates and fixed them crudely on to wooden axles so that the trolley was only about an inch off the ground. Not only did this add greatly to the sense of speed but it made a fearsome noise as well. You could get two trolleys out of one pair of skates.

Probably one of the best presents Bruce and I ever got was a pair of rubber-wheeled roller skates. I travelled miles on my skates and led a troop of kids with me into uncharted territory, often miles from where we lived, and somehow got us all back home again. Of course skates were not as good as they are today, but that feeling of speed and silence, where we felt we were able to speed the world up to the tempo we wanted it to go, was marvellous. Often at the end one of these epic trips, long after I had taken the skates off, I could still feel the motion of moving. Just like when you come off a ship and you can still feel the motion of the vessel. The one small hitch with rubber wheels was when a tiny piece of grit or small stone got under your wheel it stopped it dead. This did not necessarily tip you up, but worse, it spoilt your rhythm.

Wheels gave us freedom and I longed for a bike, but Mum made it quite plain that after my accident I would not get a bike until I was at least twelve years old. The waiting was torture.

Much later there was a push scooter craze and again I was off for miles and miles of pavement travel. My fear of traffic all but a memory, my legs grew hard and strong, and if I wasn't on wheels then I was running.

And if I wasn't running I was blowing. My enthusiasm for the harmonica had stayed with me, and eventually led me to persuade my mother to fork out the sum of twenty-nine and eleven for a hefty looking instrument, the Super Chromatic.

Around the age of eleven my friend Charlie Ranger got a ukulele, which cost thirty-seven and six.

By this time (it was now the middle fifties), Elvis had arrived on the scene, and the guitar, like Elvis himself, became king. It is hard to overstate the impact Elvis had as far as the guitar goes. Prior to this, the instrument of the working class would have been either the piano accordion (for portability) or the piano, for the pub sing song. The guitar was a rare bird, and its place in the orchestra or bands of the day not properly understood beyond a few jazz aficionados. The main reason being I suppose that you could hardly ever see or hear it. You couldn't hear Elvis's either, but you could certainly see it, and it was sexy.

I was intrigued, and after some persuasion managed to get Charlie to swap his uke for my harmonica. This did lead to a slight altercation between our mums over the discrepancy between the two prices, but it was resolved and I kept the mysterious stringed implement.

After we moved, I learned to play it with the help of the George Formby Ukulele Method. Although it was all but a guitar in miniature, I can't say it was in any way sexy.

According to the George Formby book, all you had to do was to tune the strings to the tune of *The Campbells Are Coming,* then put one finger on the third fret of the first string and by strumming in a downward movement you obtained the chord of 'G'. It worked! Next came a two-finger chord of 'C' and then a hard three-finger chord of something strangely labelled 'D7'.

Put them together with the words under the picture of the chords, and out came *Way Down Upon The Swanee River*. It was fantastic. I was away almost immediately. Thankfully I could hear when the chord was right or wrong, and within a few days could just about accompany all the new skiffle hits on it.

Skiffle had arrived about this time with the marvellous Lonnie Donegan version of *Rock Island Line*. It is hard to think of a better beginning to this movement. I loved this track and played it over and over again with that slow build-up of speed until my green felt ukulele pick was a blur in my hand. I was soon playing Buddy Holly tunes as well on this plinky little instrument.

∾

warts

Howard Junior School was an ordinary Victorian building in Dering Place, Croydon. I was transferred there, with other children from the immediate area, when St. Peter's School closed.

It had separate entrances for boys and girls and one for 'mixed infants'. I started there at the age of about six and a half, in Miss James's class, and from there went to Miss Burt, who had eyes of different colours and who wore her hair in a bun. She walked with great strides and her face went a little red whenever she spoke to one of the two male teachers in the school.

Miss Burt introduced us to the stories of Brer Rabbit, which I loved. I was by now reading very fluently, and my writing was good if not particularly neat. My spelling was reasonable and I looked forward to the next year when we would be given pens and inkwells to use.

Around this time, in the early 1950s, appeared the great London smogs. We were all used to fog, and as kids we loved to run and disappear from each other in the playground, only to reunite with our friends from a different direction. Fog enhanced some of our games and enabled you to be part of magic. I loved the eeriness of the shapes of trees in the Spinney or the muffled outlines of the few cars in the street and the way colour was almost reduced to black and white. Usually the sun burned the fog away by morning playtime.

Smog, however, was different.

Smog settled on Croydon like a wet blanket of smoky smothering cloud. At first it was funny because two or three paces away from you, your friends disappeared entirely, but at its worst you really couldn't 'see your hand in front of your face' if your arm was outstretched.

Traffic all but stopped and only valiant bus drivers crawled along familiar roads using their sixth sense and memory to guide them to the next paraffin flare. Inching your way to school, holding on to garden walls and straining your ears for oncoming vehicles, tested your hearing and faith to the utmost. Over everything hung an eerie muffled silence.

Then people started to die. The old were particularly at risk. Bruce, Mum and I, all of whom had suffered with bronchitis, began coughing. Mum tied scarves around our faces, and by the time we got to school there were black sooty stains where our mouths and noses had drawn in the filthy air.

When the newsreels of the time were shown in cinemas, they produced a few laughs as you could not really see what had been filmed, and people once again seemed to draw reserves of fortitude from their remaining vestiges of wartime spirit.

My best friend at this time was Chick Edgerton, who was distantly related to the Leisks, our neighbours across the road. Chick was considerably shorter than me, but he was a very fast runner. He also did well at simple hand-to-eye co-ordination, which I was hopeless at, but we became pals anyway.

One day during the lunch break we were running around the junior boys' playground, fairly bored, when Chick thought it would be a good idea to do something naughty. We decided to write down all the rude words that we could think of on a piece of paper and show it to one of the little girls in the playground next door. We got quite excited by the prospect, and using a stub of pencil and a scrap of paper we scrawled down words like: winkle, bum, titty, pee, fart.

With each new word we had a giggle, and when we ran out of naughty body parts to list we went on to swear words like: dam *(sic)*, sod, bugger, fuck.

We knew these were bad but had not the faintest idea what they meant.

Our laughter now attracted the attention of a red-haired boy called Terry, who was a real handful and a little slower at reading than Chick and I.

He wandered over to us by the playground wall and wanted to see what we were doing. Because we were both slightly nervous of him we handed him the paper. This was a big mistake. Terry looked at the wobbly writing and made no sense of it whatsoever. The fact that we were laughing at our rudeness was lost on him, but he rightly presumed that we were up to something. Unfortunately, because he couldn't read, he mistakenly thought we were laughing at him and his eyes narrowed as he considered what to do. Suddenly he took off across the playground.

Chick took off after him like a rocket. Terry knew he could not outrun Chick, and now thinking this was a great joke he ran straight up to the dinner lady, Mrs. Holder. After tormenting little Chick by holding the piece of paper above his head, he was just about to run off when Mrs. Holder snatched it out of his hand, unfolded it and silently read my childish hand.

She looked at Terry and asked, "Did you write this?"

"No miss," he said, "it belongs to Chick and Ralph."

She looked up and motioned to me to leave the refuge of the wall I was trying to climb into. Once I was by her side she read the list again as if to reassure herself that such awfulness warranted the decision she was about to make.

"Go and stand in the hall by the cloakroom," she ordered.

Hardly believing the sound my heart was making, we both went and stood where she said, minutely examining the green gloss paint. We stood fairly close together, but such was the discipline in the school we hardly dared try to talk to each other. Outside, the distant but still exuberant sounds of the playground seemed a long way away.

I don't know if Mrs. Holder planned for us to see the headmaster, but on his way back from lunch he had to walk past us on his way up to his study.

George Wilson was a smallish, slightly pompous man with slicked-back brown hair and a pencil moustache. He always wore a suit, and liked to think that he possessed a sense of humour. We had a boys' football team, but neither of our male teachers were very sporty and Mr. Wilson's most oft repeated euphemism for losing hopelessly at our matches was, "We didn't quite manage to win but it was a very good game!"

As he walked past us I noticed to my horror that he held our pathetic scrap of paper in his hand.

"Come with me, you two!" was all he said.

We dutifully followed him up the three flights of stairs to his room. He told to us to wait outside his study, where we stared at a picture of boats by Van Gogh.

After several more minutes we were summoned in to the small room. Mr. Wilson turned to face us and asked which of us had written these words on the paper. My heart was making so much noise that I hardly could hear myself answer.

"I did."

"What did you do?" he asked Chick.

"I helped him," said my friend. Chick looked so relaxed, I felt I would be all right once the shame of being caught had gone. Without another word our headmaster went to a cupboard by the wall and took out a long thin cane. It had a small piece of string tied round the top and I noticed that it was split quite a long way down its length.

"Hold out your right hand," he ordered Chick, who did so without hesitation. Then, spinning quickly on his toes and giving a little jump, Mr. Wilson brought down the cane on Chick's hand with a swish and a slap that I can still hear. I instinctively looked at Chick's face: not a sign of pain, thank goodness. Then, as I kept looking, I saw all the colour drain from his face, as with no change of expression huge tears welled up and overflowed his eyelids, splattering on to the floor. His hand had clamped up but I saw no more as I was ordered to hold out my own hand.

Mr. Wilson seemed pleased with his effect and with a flourish of a man who takes a pride in such things repeated the little twirl leap and contact with my hand. I had never experienced such a shock before. The cane not only stung my hand like an army of wasps but it gripped it momentarily between the split and must have pulled at the centre of the stripe it left on my palm. My hand clenched and I wanted to put it under my arm but was forbidden to do so.

Our headmaster then put the cane back into the cupboard and told us, "Let that be a lesson to you both. Now go back to your classes."

Tears were silently pouring down our cheeks but I could make no sound except a kind of muted sob. The pain was unbelievable and was getting worse. I could barely open my hand to look at the damage. I felt sick and violated. Somehow I got through the afternoon, and from across the classroom I could see Chick trying to prise open his own hand to look at what had happened. On the way home I stared at my hand. Across the palm was a thin pinched red line and each side of it was a white one. By now the weal had swollen up, and opening and closing the hand was painful.

By the time Mum came home from work the redness around my eyes had disappeared and I managed to keep the whole event secret from her. The pain lasted until well into the evening and I was sure that my mother would see the mark. Even at bedtime my hand still throbbed, and in the morning there was a slight blue tinge as the bruise began to appear.

The next day, apart from comparing the marks to our hands, Chick and I did not speak to each other. It was as if we might inadvertently pass more trouble to one another. Most of our friends knew what had happened and sort of sniffed around us the way animals do, keeping a distance from one of their number who might be mortally wounded. Terry was really upset by the incident, but could not articulate his contrition for our punishment. It was nearly a week before we were both free from pain and could use our hand for writing properly again.

Teachers usually dealt summarily with classroom offences but this was one of the few times I remember the head caning such a young pair of children.

It was not until much later that I found out that many of the teachers were members of some brethren sect. I have no idea if that was what gave them the right to be quite so brutal with some of us. There didn't seem to be an undue emphasis on religious education at the school, but there was a very strict regime and a high degree of expectation backed up with very firm handling. I was certainly anxious never to be caned again, especially on my hands. The preferred way of quick summary punishment was to have your sock rolled down and be hit on the calf muscle two or three times with a ruler.

Miss Smee had no need to threaten any of us with violence, as her reputation was awe-inspiring. I dreaded going into her class, but as an A-stream child I was expected to pass the 'eleven-plus' exam for grammar school selection, and Miss Smee had certain methods that had proven very effective.

She was one of the old school, who believed that children should not speak unless they were spoken to. It took her ages to learn our names and she never discussed anything with us. She played the piano with great ferocity, seated on several thick books to raise her up to the required height.

She was very keen on singing, and to help us open our throats, she forced a ruler between clenched teeth and rattled it up and down until our mouths were open wide enough to let out our praises. Those of us who were unable to hold a tune or who refused to try were called 'growlers' and no more was asked of them. The selection process was to walk down the line whilst we were singing and to send any out-of-tune offenders to one side.

Our classroom was an old laundry, and there was an inscription to that effect over the door. The desks were on two levels and Miss Smee conducted her lessons from street level. She had two mobile blackboards, one on each side of her desk, and behind the one on her left was a sink with hot and cold taps. Miss Smee used to smoke Churchman's cigarettes, which were quite strong; she would have frequent coughing fits which were quite productive and by nipping behind the blackboard she could expectorate into the sink. Some of the more sensitive pupils were nearly sick when she did this, but I was inured to it by my mum's ferocious cough from her roll-ups.

Miss Smee made us collect waste paper and milk bottle tops. I got over the paper obsession, but milk bottle tops stayed as part of our family duties for years, and it was only when I found out that it took three railway trucks filled to the brim to pay for one guide dog that I stopped collecting and made donations instead. It was wonderfully liberating to stop hoarding silver paper.

Miss Smee constantly preached the virtues of National Savings, and excelled at teaching us mental arithmetic by saving the lesson until last in the day or last before lunchtime. No-one was allowed to leave until so many correct answers had been achieved. The calculations had to be done at speed, as she rattled off the numbers like someone reading the weather forecast: 6 plus 9 minus 3 times 2 plus 6 divided by 3... and so on.

Her voice was gruff and masculine, with a broad local accent that mellowed on school open day to that of a sweet old lady. I was hardly able to believe my ears as the old tartar sweetened the parents and even managed a smile, revealing teeth the colour of mahogany.

No-one was allowed to interrupt her lessons, and hands raised for requests when no question had been asked were largely ignored. This had dreadful consequences for me.

One morning after break I suddenly needed to pee. I tried not to think about it but the more I tried, the more I was sure that I could feel my bladder filling up. There was ages to go before lunch break and finally I was forced to raise my hand to be excused. Miss Smee was in full flow on some subject, and though she must have seen my hand, now waving with anxiety, she steadfastly took no notice. Now my knees were unhelpfully knocking together rhythmically as I tried not to concentrate on my growing discomfort. Soon my other hand was forced under the armpit of the raised one in order to give it more height and I was leaning slightly to one side. Next I was bouncing to the rhythm of my knocking knees, and my face was getting red, but still there was no acknowledgement.

Finally I could stand it no longer and got up and ran down to her desk.

"Please Miss," I began, "may I be ex..."

I got no further because she rounded on me.

"How dare you interrupt my lesson. Get behind the blackboard!" she ordered, and miserably I crept behind it, wondering what would happen next. For a moment. standing was a little easier, but within a few seconds I was back hopping from one foot to another. I had on a pair of brown corduroy short trousers that my mum had made for me from an old skirt from the lady upstairs. It had a pocket in it and I thought that if I were able to reach in maybe I could hold my willie and stop myself peeing.

Unfortunately the pocket was rather too short to reach the vital part and as I struggled in my desperate dance to find myself, my concentration was unable to focus on both needs and I peed myself. At first it was such a relief and the sound of the pee so alien to classroom noises that no-one noticed it. I stood there watching it happen and wondered if it would ever stop. Within a few seconds I realised that it never would, and after several gallons had splattered over the stone floor, and with a cry of woe and humiliation, I ran for the swing door and pushed it the wrong way before bursting out into the playground and running to the boys lavatory. Whereupon I stopped peeing. I stood in front of the urinal and pulled up the side of my trousers and of course there was nothing left to do. I felt so miserable I wanted to cry. Suddenly the thought of going back to class was too much, and with my damp brown corduroys flapping round my skinny legs I hoofed it off home.

Mum was very sympathetic and the next day went in to see Miss

Smee, who professed to understand, and when at last I could be persuaded to swallow my humiliation and return to school I was amazed that no-one ever made any comment about my accident.

I was not the only one to pee in Miss Smee's class. Shortly afterwards Susan Hayward did a silent pee whilst sitting at her desk and then my friend Vernon Burford obliged, and by so doing cemented a friendship which survives to this day!

Meanwhile, in Mr. Ogle's class Trevor Gunther pooped his pants. Once I had heard about poor Trevor, a mere piddle on the floor was nothing and I started to get my confidence back.

My humiliation had been exacerbated by a growing awareness of girls, and not just wanting to look at the hidden parts; I genuinely wanted them to like me because I was certainly attracted to several of them in my class.

We had to do country dancing on Friday afternoons and this was both a joy and a curse. A joy because it meant I might have the opportunity to dance with Sandra Williams. When I returned to school after peeing on the floor I was placed next to Sandra and instead of being embarrassed at having a piddler sitting with her she told me she was glad that I had been put there because she liked me. This was a tremendous boost to my ego, and I immediately decided I liked her as much as Irene Wood, a very pretty blonde-haired girl who lived not far from us, near the wooden houses on Southbridge Road.

Things should have been looking up. Girls liked me and although it would have been sissy to have admitted it, I liked girls. Of course all the boys hated country dancing, and I agreed with them that it was stupid, and we had to dance with girls that we did not like, and sometimes these girls smiled at us in a way that made us suspicious. Sometimes their hands were sweaty and sometimes they held too tight, but every now and then, one of the pretty ones would have soft sweet hands and I would get a warm feeling when I touched them. Which is where the curse came in. It should have been wonderful, but for one small problem, which eventually became several small problems.

Warts.

Just as I was able to enjoy the tactile sensation of fleeting touches with the prettiest girls in the class, a series of warts arrived on my hands, causing me deep embarrassment. Naturally I thought that everyone could see them, but what was worse, the girls might be able to feel them.

The first wart appeared near the first joint of my right thumb, and then one came on the back of the same hand. Another appeared on my left hand, and then one in the palm of my right. As if this wasn't bad enough, people insisted on telling me the folk law of warts.

"Have you been playing with eggshells?" was a frequent question, first asked by my mother but repeated by several others. There were also the country variations to deal with.

Uncle Alf suggested, "Rub them with a bit of raw meat and bury the piece as far away from the house in steps as you have warts on your hands. Do this during a full moon and when the meat has rotted the warts will have rotted too."

This sounded promising as it hinted of magic and spells. The trouble was that in our family we hardly ever had any cooked meat, and rubbing it with a sausage or a piece of spam did not promise the same mystical effect. Somehow Mum got me a piece, but even as I was rubbing it on I started to have doubts. In the end I expect a fox dug it up and ate it, as the warts stubbornly remained.

Uncle Charlie told me to rub them with elderberry leaves. This left green stains on my fingers and hands.

Someone else told me to cut notches in an elderflower stalk (one for each wart) and bury it, then when it had rotted like the meat, my warts would be gone.

Granddad suggested that I had probably been playing with toads.

Grandma agreed and said there was only one thing to do and that was to rub them with elderberry juice. This I did as it was plentiful and cheap: there were bushes in berry all around us. It stained my fingers and hands purple, but apart from showing everyone where the warts were sited, failed to have any effect.

Back in Croydon, Miss Elwell from upstairs helpfully suggested strangling them. By this time I felt this would be a suitable punishment for all the misery they had caused me. The problem with this method was getting the cotton round the thing in the first place. After considerable patience on the part of my mother, we succeeded and eventually the wart on my thumb dropped off only to be almost instantly replaced by another.

I think people started to make up cures for me to try. When someone suggested putting the same number of cherry pits in my shoes as corresponded with the number of warts I had, making me barely able to hobble to the front door, I finally gave up and we went for the more conventional method of burning them off with acid. This was painful but it almost succeeded.

Unfortunately, before they were ready I would pick them and they would bleed, and apparently (another bit of wart folklore) wherever a trail of blood from a wart stops, another wart will appear. So I finished up with twelve of the horrid little bastards over my fingers and hands.

My warts had got the better of me and Mum had to arrange surgical treatment to have them removed.

Weeks of treatment at King's College Hospital in Dulwich came next where my warts were electrocuted, burnt, needled and painted. Blisters were lanced and infections treated. Old warts died; new ones arrived. It was misery because nothing worked and even the surgery only seemed to make them pop up somewhere else on my hands.

Even thus afflicted I still sort of looked forward to Friday afternoons and dancing about with the pretty girls in the class. I felt I had come up with a suitable way of disguising my afflictions by offering my preferred dancing partners, instead of an open hand, a rather unfriendly fist for them to hold. This can't have impressed the objects of my desire, but I guess girls are used to boys being scared to show their deeper feelings, and no-one ever asked me about my style as we hopped about the floor to the music from an electric gramophone. I would jealously watch where my favourite girls were in the room, and in the meantime give my open hand to Nancy Wayklin or Maureen Prendergast.

In the end, in a fit of anger and panic, I scrubbed the warts away with a piece of pumice stone, which made the bathroom look like an axe murder had taken place, and they never came back.

Our last class at Howard School was run by Mr. Harvey. He was very tall with a large head and dark hair. The school had a very high pass rate for the eleven-plus and he must have been under a lot of pressure to get results. This is no mitigation, however, for his appalling behaviour toward some of the children in his care.

Although there was another male teacher, Mr. Ogle, at the school, Mr. Harvey was the first male adult since my father that I had ever been in regular daily contact with. His reputation preceded him, but for our first few days he was so gentle and softly spoken that many of us began to think that maybe all the reports had been exaggerated. Miss Smee's approach had probably toughened us up, and although I never saw any real affection given to the children by any of the staff, up until we were nine or ten there had been an attempt to haul all the kids along together. Now we were blitzed with work, and those that fell behind were almost written off by Harvey as he strove to get eleven-plus results.

Before our actual exams there was some light relief in the form of a school pantomime. Mr. Harvey scripted a version of *Babes In The Wood*. It was very funny and parodied many of the school characters, especially Miss Smee, who Mr. Harvey was in awe of. In the panto she was clearly recognisable as Miss P. Nut. She even had a servant carrying books about on a cushion mimicking her piano playing position.

Mr. Harvey cast the play and all his favourites got major parts. When it came to the two robbers, he chose Ronald Strudwick for one of them...

"...and the second robber will be Ralph May."

I couldn't believe that I had been picked to play a part. What was more, the role was a comic one, so it meant that Mr. Harvey thought I was funny. I liked that perception even if I felt sad a lot of the time and heard strange voices. I began to think I was a devil-may-care character and for a while I started skipping to show that I was light of heart.

The play began with Ronald and I walking backwards toward each other and bumping into each other, which gave us our first laugh and made me feel wonderful.

I also got to play the mouth organ. In those pre-rock'n'roll days the hit parade comprised some dreadful material and at the top of the charts that year had been a song called *Where Will The Baby's Dimple Be?* I was supposed to play it on stage and one of the teachers had written out all the words on the blackboard. It was great when we played for the school children as everybody joined in, but in the second performance when the parents came to watch, most of them just sat there. They applauded me when it was over but didn't join in at all.

This was my first public performance and I can still see one mother's face staring at me while I played. She had a puzzled look and I was not sure how to interpret it. Perhaps I was well received in part because my right hand was swathed in a huge crepe bandage to protect it from my recent wart surgery. Perhaps they felt sorry for me.

The panto was a big success, but our moment was soon over and the oppression really began. I don't remember any more stories being read to us, and all our lessons were about sharpening up our IQ. We had endless tests of the type we would face for our examinations and all levity seemed to leave the class.

I cannot imagine what horrendous things the class could have done to send our teacher into almost uncontrollable rages, but somehow we managed it. I can still see the look of terror on Victor Sageman's face when he was being shouted at from close quarters; in a temper Mr. Harvey's complexion went purple and his insane bellowing must have been heard all over the school through the partitions that separated the classrooms. His reputation was well known by all the kids who slowly worked their way toward their final year at junior school.

He often used a slipper on the boys. One of his favourite tricks was to line up more than one offender and punish the first one but not the other; but because the boys were bent over they had no means of knowing whether they were to receive the punishment or not. His greatest venom was reserved for two kids in the class, Stephen Gardener and Dawn Bates. In the end Stephen developed a stammer because he could not pronounce his "th" sounds, and after a particular session of torment, ran away from class and never returned.

Stephen was a war baby and never had a dad. He had been to my house on several occasions and although I saw him quite a few times over the years, he appeared not to recognise me. This was strange as we had only sat two rows apart in school. He was a gentle lad but a bit over-weight; he got a job working down Surrey Street market and eventually had his own stall. I always recall him telling me about some sour-faced individual: "He's so horrible even his friends don't like him!"

At least Stephen survived with his dignity. Poor Dawn suffered the whole year she was in the class.

Dawn was a skinny girl with mousy hair tied into two pigtails. She lacked grace and charm and was a rather plain kid. She always seemed to work hard and had travelled through the school with me, although I didn't even notice her until our last year. For some reason Mr. Harvey hated her, and because she was a girl he could only hit her around the head, which he did frequently. Why cases of child abuse are seldom reported by children may be partly explained by the whole class's reaction to these mental rages which Harvey seemed to go through. After throwing Dawn about the room, and on one occasion banging her head on the radiators, we just sat in stunned silence. For a long time afterwards the atmosphere was one of terror with hardly a flicker of movement among us.

Whatever Harvey threw at the poor girl she weathered and tried to get back to the safety of her desk as if it would protect her. Once she repeatedly scrambled back on to her seat only to be thrown out of it on to the floor again, and back she crawled while Harvey grabbed at her hair and hurled abuse at her at the same time.

I cannot think what caused these rages and why she was treated this way, but it was horrible to watch. It was made even worse by the way he returned to normal after such episodes. He would begin talking in a voice of oily calm and even joke with one of the brighter children, usually one of the boys. This would produce a forced laugh from the recipient of his attention, and as Mr. Harvey's complexion returned to normal so did the atmosphere in the class. I could not take my eyes off the man during these bouts, and it was not until another form master in class 3D at secondary school struck Chris Masters full in the face with his fist and made his nose bleed that I have been so scared of an adult.

Harvey went on to become a headmaster at another local school.

❧

picnic

After years on the housing list our number finally came up, and Mum, my brother Bruce and I were moved from our semi-condemned basement flat in The Waldrons to Miller Road, a council estate off the Mitcham Road in Croydon. It heralded a major change in our lives.

Number 17a was known as the show flat; it was the first one to have hot water and an indoor bathroom separate from the lavatory. At last I was able to have my first bath in my own home. It was luxury. My mum had often had baths at Mrs. Leisk's across the road, but Bruce and I had always had to make do with the tin bath and a couple of kettles of water.

The estate teemed with life and vigour of a very different sort to that which we had become used to. My mum had accepted the flat after biking over to see it, and as the three of us stood in the little sitting room overlooking the chimneys of the Croydon 'A' power station and in the shadow of the gasholder (we called it the 'gasometer') that dominated the estate, she burst into tears.

"Never mind Mum, it'll be all right," I said.

"You don't understand, boys," she sniffed, "I'm not sad, I'm so happy."

From that moment on I knew we were all going to be OK, but I also knew it would still be tough; even as we had come in to check the place over I had heard the language the boys were using on the street, and it wasn't the same as the way they spoke where we came from.

On the day we moved in I heard a boy playing the mouth organ, and behind the enormous overgrown hedge that ran down the lane between the houses I sat on my doorstep and played a song I knew. Within a few seconds a voice enquired through the hedge who it was playing, and that's how I met Tony Potter, his brother Jamie and their friend Benny. The Potters lived over the road and Benny lived at 11a which was the mirror image of our flat at the other end of the block.

Benny had a moderately bad stammer, which meant he had to kick start most of his sentences with "and", but this had still proved difficult so he had found it better to add a "g" to the vowel, hence nearly everything he said started with "gan-gan". Benny was an ideas man, and without ever assuming the mantle of leadership, his influence on our activities was immense. He also had an uncanny knack of coming up with nicknames that stuck.

At The Waldrons I was one of the older boys, but here we were all about the same age; Tony was a year older than me and Jamie and Benny were a year or two younger. We were all 'bulge' babies, fathered by servicemen back from the war, and there were loads of us. We had street cricket and elaborate games of Release-O and Tin Tan Tommy Knob; we played Knock Down Ginger and had raids on the council dump that was just down the road in Factory Lane, where we nicked bits to make bicycles.

The older boys were all 'Teds' and a couple of the really ancient ones, like Paul Potter and Harry Barnet, were in the Merchant Navy. Some of them went to boys' clubs where they did weights or boxing, and it was all very laddish. So different from the insularity of The Waldrons, a world of its own where the very poor still rubbed shoulders with some of the comparatively well off; here everyone was poor and working class, and I felt it prudent to knock about with some of the younger boys whilst I found my way.

Beyond the Purley Way and the power station lay the factories that employed many of the people from the estate, and just beyond the factories stood the sewage farm. In another direction there was the skinning factory at the edge of the estate, and not far from that the corporation dump and the knacker's yard, and we often joked about always knowing which way the wind was blowing.

Before hanging out any washing Mum had to wipe the soot off the plastic clothes line, and if that did not mark the sheets there was always the chance of an aerial bombardment from Mr. Kelly's pigeons, which exercised around the smutty air of the estate. Sometimes fumes would waft across the estate and make us feel dizzy and nauseous, but most of the time we took no notice.

In front of the sewage farm was a patch of waste ground, completely overgrown with scrubby trees and elderberry bushes, and in front of this was a huge crater from a wartime bomb aimed at one of the factories, which some of the older boys used to trial their illegal motorbikes.

Over to the left of the main plant there was a small detached three-bedroomed house and a little garden with a few apple trees in an otherwise overgrown wasteland. This was always referred to as 'Farmer Brown's orchard'. I never queried it at the time, but looking back it was almost certainly a name that Benny thought up: we were at the sewage farm, therefore the man who lived there all the time must be a farmer, and all farmers are called Brown. It's obvious really.

This whole area Benny had christened the 'playing fields' because they were fields where we played, but they were always referred to as the Playnies. The boys used to go there on a regular basis for a number of different activities: mucking about, meaning just going across to see what would happen; racing our home-made bikes around the crater; or occasionally making raids on Farmer Brown's orchard.

Early on in our friendship Benny asked us if we'd ever seen any 'johnnies'. I said that I probably had but I couldn't remember exactly, so Benny offered to take us. Once across the Purley Way we walked down the railway tracks that served the factories, across the 'white road' and straight on, with the playnies on the left and the processed waste fields on the right, where tomato plants grew in abundance in the summer (even after all the treatment of the sewage the tomato seeds stay potent and ready to germinate).

Just before the sewage farm proper was a railing across the road and an inspection platform. From here it was possible to watch the raw sewage flow into the plant. After staring in wonder at the size of some of the stools that flowed past I was ready to leave, but Benny insisted we must wait as we hadn't seen any johnnies yet. I wondered what he meant. We didn't have long to wait, for very soon a used condom floated past, closely followed by another and another.

"Cor look at that one!" yelled Benny, "and that one, fuckin' 'ell 'e must 'ave 'ad one like a rollin' pin!" Then he burst into his whistling laugh.

"There goes another one, coo look at that. What would you do if you 'ad one like that?" At last I realised what we were looking at. It was a truly humbling experience for a twelve-year-old. These things were enormous, and it forced me to ponder all sorts of things that I was only just ready to grasp. The younger Benny had even more to perplex him—or rather, less.

The Potters who lived opposite were a very unusual crowd. Mrs. Potter was of Anglo-Indian descent and liberally used Indian words in her speech. Mr. Potter was largely out of work with his chest, which he made sure would stay that way by smoking Capstan full strength cigarettes. I remember sitting in their spartan front room one afternoon with the sun streaming in through the windows, watching him exhale as much smoke as the steam coming out of the cooling tower chimneys, and wondering how he managed it. His hair was a grizzled grey colour. I never saw him with his teeth in and I never saw him smile.

It was rumoured that they were a rum lot and that Mrs. Potter had been involved in some street trade during the war, but it only added more spice to my imagination. Paul, the eldest boy, as I mentioned before, was away in the 'merchant'; Albert was semi-delinquent, dangerous and frightening; Tony was handsome and honourable; and Jamie was a moaner and hadn't been circumcised properly. Benny said that when he had a piss, the end of his willie blew up like a balloon. There was one girl in the family, Donna, who was very pretty and sexy and didn't live at home; Benny said she was 'on the game.'

The Potters also had a dog, imaginatively named Spot. He was a cross between a wolf and a collie, so Jamie said.

"He must be a wallie then!" said Benny, which almost caused a fight. Spot was largely concerned with homosexual activities with other dogs, but if none were available he would spend most of his day rubbing the mange patch on his back under the bars at the end of the alley. The bars were placed at each junction throughout the estate to stop the kids running out into the roads.

Sometimes the boys would go 'shtrewing' and this was where Spot came into his own; he was reckoned to be the best shtrewer in the neighbourhood. The first time we went across to the playnies to go shtrewing I was puzzled, but later horrified at the sport which awaited me. Once on the playnies we combed the waste ground for old bits of corrugated metal and formed a circle around its perimeter. Spot would be alert and waiting for his moment.

One of the boys would call "Ready!", the sheet would be flipped over and if there was any 'shtrews' underneath, Spot would have them.

I had enormous problems with this. Although my brother and I had been brought up in poverty in most accepted definitions of the word, our mother had always made sure that our imaginations were richly stimulated by reading. She had read to us from a very early age and no matter how tired she was she always found time for a couple of chapters of something before bed.

I'm sure Mum was motivated to read to us not only for educative reasons, but to escape the drudgery of our grey existence and to perpetuate a feeling of childhood optimism; and through the stories I had always vaguely thought of small creatures as living in little warrens and houses in tree trunks, with a set of values and morals not unlike those instilled in us at Sunday School. For me to see tiny shrews and field mice ripped apart by mangy old Spot was more than I was ready for.

We were also keenly aware that we were under scrutiny from the lads, especially Benny. I had quickly decided not to copy their accents, but this was easier said than done. The boys on the estate used wonderful language. They littered their speech liberally with swear words, especially "bleedin'" which my mother hated the most; but more interesting to me was their use of Romany words among the slang terms. Thus a dog was a juk (rhymes with hook), rain became parni in the sky, and a stranger was always a mush (like bush).

They also used a good deal of cockney slang which was all new to me, and I began to feel that we were quite genteel by comparison. I can remember listening in awe as the boys recounted the episode where Freddy Barnet and Robby Elmwood attempted to climb the gasometer at the end of Miller Road. The boys had to climb very narrow, almost vertical ladders up about four stages.

"'alf way up Freddy's bottle went," said Benny, "an' 'e 'ad to come dahn."

Why he had to take a bottle with him I couldn't understand, or what difference it would have made if he lost it, but so impressed was I with the bravado that I pressed him to explain.

"What, he took a water bottle with him or something?"

"No, 'e shit 'isself," Benny explained.

151

Gradually the mysteries of rhyming slang were revealed to me. Bottle and glass equals arse, so saying your bottle went meant your arse went. Having plenty of bottle meant not shittin' oneself—in other words, courage.

I don't know whether Freddy actually defecated with fright or was just too scared to continue. I made up my mind anyway that one day I would climb it—and I did, and ran across the wobbly dome on the top. It was a great buzz, and my bottle held.

Our gang was made up like this: Benny, Jimmy and Ronnie Barnet, my brother Bruce, Tony and Jamie Potter, Jimmy Wren (cousin to Benny) and sometimes little Bobby Best, who was the youngest. Of course there were girls in the street but the boys had long grown out of their company. Well, the youngest ones had, and the older boys would have liked to play different sorts of games but were not quite sure of the rules. It was a strange feeling, noticing that you were suddenly growing interested in a girl who, only a term or two before, made you so irritated that you could hardly bring yourself to speak to her.

The girls down our street were the Longhurst girls, whose parents did not allow them to play with any of us, Amy Blair, Maureen Forester, Pat Elsie, Jeannie Wren, Charlotte Price who was very strange, and little Lucy Best who was as pretty as her brother was plain.

Maureen was fifteen and just about to start work in one of the factories beyond the Purley Way. She arrived at the bars one day to mind one of her little brothers, when the idea of the picnic on the playnies came up.

"Everyone's got to bring an egg," said Benny. Bruce and I were crestfallen. "Or a potato," he added, quickly perceiving that we might have a problem with the egg. Benny was like that; seemingly of average intelligence, he was capable of great and quick understanding, and his sharp observation gave him a pragmatism that would make sure that he would get his way.

Benny was chubby with cherubic features, blond curly hair, a little hooked nose and lips that were never closed. This sometimes gave him a vacant look, but he never missed a trick and his eyes were always darting about, taking it all in. His mother was a large-hipped woman, slightly reserved and prone to gossip, while his dad walked like a sailor and kept pigeons. He had a centre parting and was kindly, and Benny had a brother called Robert who was deaf and dumb.

"We could 'ave a fire over there, no-one would mind," said Benny, "an' we could cook things, it'd be a right laugh."

We all thought that it would be a laugh but nothing was finalised until Maureen suddenly said, "I'll be your cook."

That was it, suddenly we were motivated and the news spread rapidly. Soon a little gang had arrived and everyone was talking about what they were going to bring and what a great laugh it would be and that we ought to leave Spot at home because he didn't like fires, and so on.

The next day saw us all arriving in dribs and drabs until we were assembled loosely under the 'white trees'. The whole area was like another planet; the trees actually had white leaves and it was only much later that I realised this was because of the thousands of starlings that gathered there to feed on God knows what at the sewage works, along with the seagulls so far inland.

There was just a light breeze which occasionally rustled the trees, and a hot sun sat high in a blue sky as we scurried about collecting bits of wood. Benny and I had found an old dustbin with the bottom rotted out of it, and we judged that it would make a great burner. We stood it on four bricks, and paper and twigs were placed in the bottom. Maureen laid out her kitchenware: a large saucepan, some butter or marge which was already beginning to melt in its paper, and an old black frying pan.

"Right, let's have all the food," she ordered.

All the food? What food, I wondered, as I laid my potato on the ground next to the melting butter that had now got some twiggy bits of grass mixed into it. Bruce laid his potato next to mine.

"That's a big one," I found myself saying, "I hope Mum won't remember it and notice it's gone." Bruce looked worried for a moment.

Next came Ronnie who had both an egg and a potato, which he laid next to Bruce's. A little too close; Bruce was forced to move his a little further away so they didn't get mixed up. Bobby Best had an egg and a potato, and so did Jimmy Barnet; Jamie Potter had only managed a potato and half a loaf of stale white bread. All of this was laid out on the ground and we all stood back to admire our banquet in waiting. By now a little more twigs and grass had made their way into the butter as Maureen gently lay down her own egg and potato.

All this time Benny had been watching everyone's contribution without uttering a word. When he was sure that there was nothing left to be laid alongside the rest, he slowly put his hand in his pocket, and with a little flourish pulled out a potato that was about half a pound on its own. Then from his windcheater top pocket he carefully removed an egg and placed it next to the others, and finally, with a dramatic "dah dah", he spun around to face us all, reached into his other pocket and pulled out a sausage!

"You flash sod," muttered Ronnie as Benny waved his prize in front of us all held between his finger and thumb.

"I bet you nicked that," said Jamie.

"No I never," said Benny.

"Yes you bleedin' did!" said Jamie this time even louder.

"You ain't 'alf a lie," spluttered Benny again (he never called anyone a liar, always a 'lie').

I was dreadfully jealous as we only had a sausage if there was an 'r' in the month, and then only one each, but I said nothing. Maybe he might give me a bite of it later, I thought, and immediately realised how stupid this idea was.

Benny was taking huge delight in our envy and was now holding the sausage in front of his flies and waggling it rudely at Maureen. I looked anxiously at her to see what her reaction might be; she told him not to be a dirty little devil but she was laughing at the same time. I began to think how pretty she was.

"It looks like yours, Jamie," said Benny.

"Piss off!" said Jamie, more angry than embarrassed.

"At least this one don't blow up at the end when I 'ave a piss," taunted Benny.

I noticed Maureen looking puzzled by this remark, and felt very uneasy, but only for a moment as Jamie suddenly leapt at Benny, hitting him in the belly with his head. Although Benny was a solid sort of boy, the sheer surprise of the attack set him off balance and he was forced to take one step backwards to remain upright.

In doing so, he trod on Bobby Best's egg. Benny looked dismayed as nearly everyone else started to laugh at his predicament, which only increased as little Bobby flew at Benny and tried to grab him round the throat. Based on their size there should have been no contest, but we all knew about Bobby's legendary temper. He was capable of fearsome rages and was totally fearless with regard to his own safety, and amazingly hardly ever came to grief in spite of having a go at boys a lot bigger and older than himself.

After a little struggle we managed to prise them apart, and Maureen said that Bobby could have her egg. I began to think how *kind* and pretty she was.

After the dust had settled and Benny had satisfied himself that the egg could not be salvaged in any way, it was decided to light the fire. Everyone wanted to do this, so in the end Maureen said that as Bobby had lost his egg, he should be the one to strike the match. There was no argument with this, and with one match the old dustbin's contents were ablaze.

Unfortunately so were the lower branches of the tree under which we had built our kitchen. None of us had thought about the siting of our fire, and with the summer sunshine and hot weather, everything was as dry as tinder.

"Sssssssssssssssssssssssshit!" stammered Benny and backed away from the inferno that was now crackling and roaring inside the old bin, treading as he did so on Jamie's bag of stale bread.

Before another fight could blow up, Jimmy Barnet came from nowhere and kicked the dustbin on to its side so that the remaining contents spilled on to the ground, then grabbing hold of an elderberry bush yanked off a branch and began beating the flames out on the tree above our heads. We all followed suit and eventually managed to put out the blaze.

When everything was once again under some sort of control we all looked at each other and began laughing.

"Di'n it bleedin' go!" marvelled Benny.

After the excitement we resited our stove in a little clearing, gathered up the trampled bread and potatoes, poured the now quite melted butter into the black frying pan and began again to collect wood and scraps for the fire.

Ronnie and Jamie meanwhile had started a game of knife throwing. The idea was that you aimed the weapon as near to your opponent's foot as you could, and where the knife landed you took up that position, your legs gradually getting further apart until one of you fell over or received a stab wound to the leg or foot. It seldom came to this though, and the game was usually abandoned after a few rounds.

"You'll 'ave to lend me the knife," announced Maureen. "I forgot to bring one for the potatoes."

The boys handed it over and sidled off into the bushes. I watched Maureen set about peeling the potatoes, which proved difficult because, although the knife had a sharp point, the cutting edge was very blunt. Maureen was reduced to laying the spud on the ground and sawing at it, which made for a lot of waste. The resulting square peeled items were further sliced into chips, and each one was then wiped on her dress and stored in the frying pan with the melted butter and twigs.

Suddenly there was a sharp cry as Maureen's grip slipped and she sliced into her finger. It bled profusely and I felt quite sick and thought I was going to pass out. Luckily Benny, who had been arranging his sausage and two of the eggs somewhat genitally, had a handkerchief. I say 'luckily' reservedly, because Benny was one of those kids who always seemed to have a runny nose. His mum insisted that Benny carry a handkerchief with him at all times, and it was a well-used item that was reluctantly accepted by Maureen.

I couldn't bear to watch as she wrapped the rag around her finger, so I busied myself with lighting and tending to the fire. Once again the flames crackled and roared and soon they were leaping above the top of the bin. The heat was ferocious and Maureen was beaten back from her stove until the flames died down. I watched fascinated as Maureen valiantly moved toward the heat, holding the saucepan in one hand and shielding her face with the other. Someone had turned up an old aluminium milk crate and slung it on top of the bin as a kind of grill, and Maureen carefully placed her frying pan on top, moving back with her eyes streaming.

Amongst the sticks and general rubbish collected for the fire was an old tyre, which was now burning merrily with thick black smoke and giving off a terrible smell. Undaunted but beginning to perspire with the heat and pain in her finger, Maureen changed position with the wind, and I could see her face now lined with tracks of her smoke-driven tears.

Intermittently she darted toward the swirling pan to prod a chip with the knife that had wounded her. The hankie bandage was by now drenched in butterfat, and trailed into the pan as blood from the cut dripped in amongst the cooking potatoes. Maureen began to look as if she had been in a fight; her hair was drenched, her face was smeared with soot and blood, the bandage flapped loosely on her damaged finger and a steady stream of tears ran down her cheeks. I thought she looked beautiful and was almost overcome with compassion, but I also felt sick.

The boys were slowly drifting back from what they'd been doing in the bushes, and Benny and little Bobby returned from throwing stones at the johnnies. Ronnie and brother Bruce had returned from Farmer Brown's orchard with some tiny little scrubby green apples, which everyone started throwing at each other.

The sight of poor battered Maureen only stopped them for a while as everyone engaged in a funny little ritual dance around the fire in order to avoid the black burning rubber smoke that seemed to follow us wherever we went.

"When we eatin'?" someone demanded.

"When we 'avin' our eggs?" asked the egg owners.

"When they're bleedin' well cooked," came Maureen's harassed reply.

"I'm starvin'," muttered Benny. "Can I 'ave mine now?"

"Look," said Maureen, "they ain't even cooked yet."

"I don't mind, I'll 'ave em raw," said Benny hungrily.

"Yeah, let's 'ave em now!" we all chorused.

At this point Maureen was happy to concede defeat, and one by one we queued up to take a chip or two each. Pierced with the wounding knife, basted in gravy made from her own blood and butter, we attempted to eat our scalding rock-hard potatoes. There was many a burnt lip and scalded tongue, to say nothing of terrible swearing from young mouths of tender skin who had dropped the food on to the jungle floor and tried to wipe off the grit only to find that the spud was inedible.

By now all our eyes were streaming as we sat Indian-style with black lines down our cheeks, spitting out bits of twig and grit round the fire.

Benny handed Maureen his egg, which she broke expertly on the side of the pan and tossed into the now burning fat. Benny grinned round expectantly at the rest of us when Jamie sullenly pointed out that he hadn't got a plate to eat it off. A moment of anxiety crossed Benny's face, then he jumped up and quickly disappeared into the bushes, arriving back a few seconds later with a bit of an old cardboard box about the size of a saucer. He offered it up to Maureen, who somehow managed to slide the egg on to it, leaving most of the gravy in the pan. For a moment Benny looked triumphant, but while he was gloating he took his eye off the 'plate' and his slippery feast slithered off and on to the dirt floor. Everyone guffawed and hooted, and for a moment I thought Benny was about to burst into tears.

Then defiantly he muttered, "I'm still goin' to eat it!" To our assembled amazement he picked up the egg by its white and, after dropping it once more and then picking off the worst of the dirt, popped the whole lot into his open mouth like a mother bird feeding her young.

Suddenly the other egg owners were not interested in having their eggs after all. Although nothing was said, we were all pretty impressed by Benny's defiance. Maureen had certainly had enough of her role as little mother and was sitting down inspecting the soiled nature of her light sweater, picking little bits of twig from it and lightly flicking at the butter-splattered stains that had landed on her breasts. I wished she would have let me help her.

Ronnie and Jamie had wandered off again to light up a fag and little Bobby Best had disappeared somewhere with his egg. Benny and brother Bruce were lobbing bits of wood into the fire. I was chatting with Jimmy while secretly admiring Maureen and wondering what we would do next, when an egg came hurtling through the trees and hit Jimmy smack in the forehead.

There was a moment of stunned disbelief as we all realised the enormity of the situation. Jimmy Barnet was easily the best fighter pound for pound on the estate; he boxed for the boys' club and fought at just about any other opportunity as well. If the egg had hit anyone else there would have been enormous hilarity but now there was silence.

It was a silence that stilled the birds in the bushes; a silence that quelled the chattering flames; a silence that stopped the sewage flowing in the farm. The sun momentarily hesitated in its passage across the summer sky. We thought about the great Kenny Manley fight on the Canterbury Road rec, and the time he almost killed Rory McLean in the snooker room at the Rectory Manor Boys Club by locking his arms round the legs of the table so that he could exert more pressure round the boy's neck he held between his thighs. Two grown-ups had had to hit Jimmy with billiard cues to make him release the kid, and that was all because Jimmy thought Jamie had called him a guttersnipe. It's very doubtful that anyone in our neighbourhood would have used such an old-fashioned word, but it was well known that if you wanted to put Jimmy into an uncontrollable rage all you had to do was to address him thus.

I have often wondered what Jimmy imagined a 'snipe' was. Could it have been an evil rat character that lived in the gutter and survived off the spittle and waste that found its way there before being flushed down the drains, or was it some huge indefinable monster of his imagination? Certainly I would never know as I was far too scared to even mention the word within several miles of his hearing.

Perhaps he saw it the way I saw the 'ape of the lights'. My old Grandma was a Victorian of high moral principles and iron discipline, whom her daughter (my mum) hated, it seemed to me and Bruce. She was a Hammersmith native born and bred, and her speech was littered with superstitions and colourful sayings like, "He's as soft as an a'porth o' lights!"

'Lights' were the lung offal that was often boiled up and fed to the domestic pets of the house, and whoever it was she was referring to was obviously as soft as one halfpenny worth, but to me for years it was King Kong draped in fairy lights. It didn't seem silly to me at the time. I will always wonder what Jimmy saw.

Suddenly an anguished cry burst from the bushes.

"Sorry Jimmy, it was me, I was aiming at Ralph, I never meant to hit you, honest Jimmy, you got to believe me!"

Recognising the voice as that of little Bobby, Jimmy slowly stood up and without wiping away the egg walked over to where Maureen was sitting and picked up one of the remaining eggs.

"Come here, Bobby," he said, his voice showing a menacing calmness which struck terror into all our hearts.

"Don't 'urt 'im Jimmy, please," said Maureen quietly.

I tried to speak but only a croak came out, so I shut up and watched as if in a trance as the only moving thing on earth advanced slowly toward where the cowering Bobby was quietly snivelling. Jimmy bent down and, placing his hand in the bush that held the offender, slowly lifted him into view by his ear.

A new episode of Edgar Lustgarten's *Tales of Scotland Yard* was already taking shape in my mind: I could hear his sombre tones and clear diction announcing the horrible Murder On The Playnies and how after a gruelling cross-examination in the witness box I had finally admitted that it was my fault, and that if the egg had hit its intended target little Bobby would still be with us. I began to shake but was unable to move; like everything around us we were frozen in time.

Jimmy, still with the evidence of the direct hit on his forehead, brought the distressed figure of Bobby to the remains of the fire. Looking up to confirm that we all had his attention, he pulled Bobby's trousers out at the back and placed the egg in his underpants and under his bottom, then tweaking the ear slightly in an upward direction he leaned forward and said in a voice of utter calm, "Sit on it."

Immediately the earth started moving again as little Bobby looked up at Jimmy and realised he was going to live after all. One by one all of us began to laugh as little Bobby, only too glad to play his part in the situation, slowly and theatrically sat down on the ground. None of us heard it break, but we all saw the expression on his face as the goo spread between his legs.

As the sense of relief spread through our little group, a bit of knockabout bravado ensued, and just as Jimmy had refused to wipe off the egg from his forehead until he'd had his retribution, so Bobby bore his punishment manfully and left the shells inside his trousers. Benny suddenly remembered his sausage and after cutting off a stick and sharpening it to a point, picked up the twiggy pink member and after a lewd waggle at Maureen, pierced it with his stick and started to cook it over the dustbin. Most of the tyre had been consumed, but there was still a smell of burning rubber permeating the air along with that of the pork sausage. The others drifted away out of nose-shot of the cooking and I watched Benny twirling his treat over the flames that were still occasionally firing up as drops of fat hit the embers below.

"You fancy 'er don't ya?" he asked me. "I seen ya lookin' at 'er tits. I bet she's got nice tits, but you're wastin' yer time boy, she fancies that kid Pepper, the one that goes out with Gillian Pallister, she's got the best tits on the estate."

"How do you know?" I demanded, embarrassed and blushing so deeply my face nearly bled.

"'ow do I know what?" asked Benny innocently. "That you fancy Maureen or that Gillian Pallister's got the best tits on the estate?"

"About Gillian," I mumbled.

"My mate's 'ad 'em out, one in each 'and, they're like that!" Benny described the size and weight with his free hand.

This was too much for me. I was getting aroused by all this talk and the heat, and I was just about to turn and join the others when I noticed that Benny's stick was burning and his sausage was on fire. I don't know whether he was following my gaze but he looked back at his stick just as the flaming morsel fell off the prong and into the fire. I quickly turned away so that he wouldn't be sure if I saw the tragedy and went to join the others. They were playing a game that was getting a little bit too rowdy for Maureen's liking, and I could see that I was not the only one to find her nearness stimulating. In those days most boys wore Y-fronts and some lads nothing at all underneath and a few of us were already teenagers and arousal was easy to spot. Suddenly we were joined by Benny.

"How was your sausage, you greedy fat bastard?" shouted Jamie.

Only I knew that the hurt look in Benny's eyes had nothing to do with the insult, but was entirely due to the loss of the item in the flames of the dustbin.

"Don't you worry about my sausage, mush, what about your balloon dick sausage," spluttered Benny.

"Yeah, show 'er your knob," suggested little Bobby to Jamie, and everyone sniggered. Maureen had a mixture of feigned shock and curiosity, and we all looked at her expectantly to see how she would react.

"I've seen a dick before," said Maureen.

"Yeah, but not like Jamie's," Ronnie and Bobby chorused together, and everyone sniggered again.

"Look you lot, I've 'ad enough of all this talk," said Maureen, "I'm goin' 'ome," and with that she turned back toward the dustbin and her few utensils.

The afternoon was coming to an end and a balmy breeze was rustling the leaves of the elderberry bushes. The acrid smell of burnt rubber had been replaced by a real wood smoke scent in the air, shadows were lengthening and all of us were in various states of dishevelledness, Maureen amongst the worst of us. A handful of swallows were swooping above the sewage works and the tired and smoky band of kids from Miller Road were reluctant to call it a day.

"I got an idea," said Benny, and he whispered his plan to us all.

Maureen was inspecting the cut on her hand as we approached, the old dustbin lay on its side and our pitiful little kitchen was dismantled and ready to be carted off home. I had my instructions and when all the boys were in position I nonchalantly asked Maureen if we should put the fire out.

"Oh yeah," she said, "I almost forgot about that." Then I banged the frying pan with a stick really loud which was the signal to begin and with a jump Maureen swung around to find a circle of boys all peeing on the fire, then on my next bang on the pan, they divided the circle and folded back to reveal Jamie in full flow and ballooning willie in hand.

It was pretty impressive. In the company of the rest of the boys the last remnants of Jamie's inhibitions were shed and he peed with great force and brio, and the fire hissed in response. Maureen on the other hand turned tail and ran out of the trees and bushes into the open, hair flying and shoes slipping, soon to be followed by our gang.

I paused to pick up the bits and pieces and her jacket before chasing after them all. Just before the bomb crater she was brought down by Ronnie, and the others all fell on top of her. Amongst a great flailing of arms and legs could be heard a lot of laughing and giggling, but by the time I'd got there most of the lads were back on their feet. Maureen was crying with what looked like tears of laughter and relief that nothing had really got out of hand, and we all set off again toward the railway line and the bridge over the Purley Way.

We must have been quite a sight as we traipsed up the lane to our street, covered as we were with bits of straw and grass, streaked with dust and soot, smelling of smoke and rubber, with bloodshot eyes and bramble scratches, fingers stained with berry juice and stomachs rumbling.

As we got nearer home I found myself walking with Benny and little Bobby.

"I nearly got an 'andful di'n I," said Benny, "but that Jimmy Barnet could see what I was after an 'e pulled me off of 'er."

Little Bobby was quiet for a while, then he said in a voice that trembled a little, "I felt 'er tits."

We both looked at him for a second or two, then he giggled and shook with mischief. Bobby was the youngest of the lot of us and it was he who had the prize we all wanted. It was years before I was ever to feel such jealousy again.

Never did such a lot of us ever go to the playnies again, and Maureen soon started going out with a boy from the next street. We were never really friends in the same way, but she always spoke to me when we met. I loved the sound of her morning chatter with friends at the bars at the end of the lane, and their laughter coming home from the factories near the old playnies. But she never knew how I'd once felt.

Jimmy went on to become a fine amateur boxer, little Bobby vanished from my ken and we heard that Ronnie had died prematurely with the same heart complaint that killed his sister Pam. Tony Potter joined the

Royal Navy at the same time that I joined the boys' army. Jamie surfaced again at his sister's place, coincidentally above my mother's new flat in Thornton Heath, where the noise and 'entertaining' nearly drove Mum crazy and we had to get her moved to save her sanity.

Benny lost his deaf brother after a fit when the boy turned twenty-one. Benny himself married a girl at the top of the road, and as far as I know still lives there.

❧

stone the crows

Just before we moved to Miller Road we became aware of a way of earning some pocket money by an easier method than totting or running errands. Somewhere down the end of the road near Holloway's yard a rather strange little family lived in a basement like ours. The husband (and father of the three girls who lived there) was an agent for a toy company that was responsible for hand painting tiny toy soldiers, cowboys and Indians. The models were made of the then-new plastic and were very detailed and sharply moulded.

The man would give Bruce and me a gross of these figures, supply the paints and instruct us not to use another colour until the first one was dry. We would collect them from his crowded dimly-lit basement room and he would remind us that paint was expensive and that the gold paint for military buttons was particularly dear. He would also remind us of the strict quality control that he exercised. If things were not up to the exacting standards required by the company, we had to do them again. This rarely happened because our young eyes could see all the detail and we wanted the money. I wish I could remember how much we were paid but I cannot. I do know that it was labour intensive and that it was a pittance if you judged it by the hourly rate for completing the job.

I tried to figure out quick ways of doing them but there wasn't a quick way. I tried tackling only the difficult ones because they paid more money (guardsmen with groups of gold buttons) but that took even longer. Sometimes, I admit, I was a little slapdash but I got away with it. Crouching red Indians with full headdress, soldiers, cavalrymen, cowboys, some on horseback. I got to know their faces and all the details of their features. I came to hate them all but it was pocket money. There was always just a little tension as the agent man scrutinised the returned figures but we got our few shillings and returned home with another load.

After we had moved to our new home on the council estate, my homework from grammar school forbade street association and there was no spare time for me to be painting soldiers. Bruce continued for a while in our cramped bedroom whilst I struggled to lock out the sounds of the kids playing in the streets outside.

Because I had been selected for early GCE examination by the second year, we had hours of homework to contend with each night. I was totally wrapped up in our estate culture and it was agony hearing the boys hooting and laughing to say nothing of pretty Anne Webster sitting on the bars outside watching them with her friend Linda from the next road. Nearly the whole street attended Lanfranc school down the road and they never had any homework to do. Bruce would soon be attending another grammar school but at this time he could run with the pack and I was so jealous and aware that I envied the carefree ways of the secondary modern school system.

I missed the street cricket and strange games like Releaso and Tin Tan Tommy Nob which had rules that we were supposed to absorb by osmosis. Then there were the bikes we made up from parts we got from the rubbish tip. We'd creep past the watchman at the council yard gatehouse and nick bits for our own customising.

We would play extended games over by the sewage farm and venture further afield. Sometimes we would cycle to Earlswood lakes to swim in the tickly waterweed infested ponds. We were never bored. These daydreams forever got in the way of wrestling with the totally incomprehensible electro-chemical equivalents or kinetic friction or algebra and trigonometry. What possible use could there ever be for logarithms? Then there was Anne Webster and her friend Linda to complicate the equation still further.

One early afternoon on a Saturday both Bruce and I were indoors for some reason. There was a loud ring on our wind-up doorbell followed by a knock on the letterbox. I knew immediately it was not someone that we knew because you come to recognise people by their knock or ring. I went downstairs and opened the door.

There were two women standing there. One was quite a bit younger than the other and was wearing slacks. The older one was about mum's age but more dressy and wearing more make up. After saying hello they asked if mum was in. I called up to her and she came down to the front door. Before they had exchanged any words with each other I knew who they were. "Please go to your room Ralph I will call you in a minute," said mum.

I went into our crowded bedroom and sat down on my bed. Bruce looked up at me from his bed where he was painting soldiers. I said something like: "I think that's the woman that our dad ran off with." Then there was a tap on the door and mum told us that the younger lady was going to sit with us and that she would tell us what was going on after a while. There was no need; I already knew but I did not know why they were here.

The younger woman attempted to make conversation with us. "What lovely soldiers you have. Are they yours?" I explained we painted them for pocket money. I wanted her to know that we were poor, that our dad had left us penniless, that we were robbed of a dad. I wanted her to know Bruce and I worked so that we did not have to ask mum for anything, especially money. There was barely enough room for two beds and two boys in the tiny room and we were not used to anyone visiting us in there. We were locked in with a stranger while we heard the mumble of voices in the next room.

Finally, Mum came into the room. She was crying and the other woman looked tearful too. Mum told us the visitors had come to tell us our dad had been killed.

I did not cry but listened in a state of utter incredulity. I had always planned to sort things out with my dad. These feelings ranged from beating him up to begging for a reason as to why he had left us. I could not believe mum's tears, after all this time she was weeping. So was this other woman and mum was being sympathetic to her. I can hardly remember her face although I can remember the younger woman. Here was mum consoling the woman who had 'stolen' her husband and offering sympathy and kindness.

I had been told that the woman was Welsh but I heard no trace of a Welsh accent. She showed me a photo of my dad taken at a village fete. He looked much like the other photos I had seen. She explained that I could have this one as all the other photos had her in the picture too.

Time seemed suspended and I cannot truly remember the order of events or who said what. My heart was beating fast: it is now as I write. I felt deeply angry, cheated, frustrated, puzzled and empty at the same time. This was not how it was supposed to be.

After mum had signed some papers the woman and her friend left the flat and mum related the sorry tale she had been told by my father's partner whose name was Roberts. Until that day, none of us had seen or heard anything from my father since my outburst and the black cloud of anger that had enveloped me and gave me words to say when I was six. Mum sat there with her red eyes and told us both what had happened.

It seemed after my dad had left us he had settled in Brighton for a while before moving to a little village called Loughton in Sussex. There he became a butcher and apparently settled down to life of the community. He had no more children but had sort of adopted two boys approximately corresponding to Bruce and me in terms of age. These boys were the children of neighbours of theirs, and now I was angry with them for holding his affection.

No birthday or Christmas cards ever came. No letters of explanation or excuse and we did not even know where he was living. Occasionally mum received notice of a fine not paid or a bill for something or other; he still gave our address as his own but we never knew where he was. It appeared he'd been on the run and in and out of court for various petty offences but mercifully not for physical harm. The woman had told mum that he had tried to strangle her, and mum told her that he had been violent to her too. I wished he had strangled the woman, it was all too strange and I had never had these feelings before. I thought about him and once again tried to remember the sound of his voice. Once, when my mother had asked him to look at my fingernails to see how close they resembled his own, he had looked up and smiled saying "Stone the crows!"

My dad had spent many years as a soldier and always wore army boots for work. He was still prone to black moods. He also had affairs and had recently had one with the girl in the butcher's shop.

He had made his own meat defroster at his butchers shop. He had been trying to repair a fault in the defroster unit when he slipped off the ladder and grabbed a live wire. The force of the electric shock had thrown him from the ladder to the other side of the shop and when the girl assistant ran to him she too was thrown across the room from the electricity he had absorbed. The death certificate put the cause of death as asphyxiation. He died on 31 August 1958. His death had been reported in the *News of the World* and it even used the name Frank May. My mum had discounted it because my dad was a master mechanic not a butcher.

This was not the way it was supposed to be. None of the questions I had stored up would ever be answered. My shaky belief in God wondered if this was divine retribution for leaving us. Perhaps the biggest shock was to see how mum had reacted. She had always hoped he would return one day. As for the other woman, she was bereft and mum had shown her an understanding, which amazed me. She had referred to her in the most dreadful terms at times and here she was signing legal papers and sympathising. I was sort of affected by her loss too, but my overriding emotion was one of being cheated out of a reckoning. Now I would never know if I was like him, how his voice sounded, if I could ever have forgiven him for leaving, whether we might have become friends. The photo revealed little and I lost it soon afterward although I carried in my wallet another photo taken when he was in the army. In the picture he was aged about sixteen, full of life and looking dangerous and handsome.

I now realise that from this point onward my education began to collapse. There were extended periods of dopey dreaming and a deep confusion settled on me about the equation of what my family obligations were against my academic ability and willingness to apply myself to school work.

I also felt very alienated from many of the boys at school and out of kilter with my perceived social class. I recognised I belonged more to the Mitcham Road estate than to the lower-middle-class background of most of the grammar school boys. Naturally enough I gravitated toward others like me at school and we formed a little clique of cycle-shed smokers and after-school cigarette sharers that eventually spilled over to evening get togethers, cinema and occasional homework sharing.

❧

hedge

It was accepted that after the war a lot of kids were brought up by grandmothers, aunts, and in some cases even by neighbours. The idea of extended families is not really new and you don't have to go very far back in most families to find a child that came into the world before its parents were married.

On the Miller Road estate there were several children who were brought up by their grannies. One of these was Charlotte Price. She was an odd child and spent most of her time on her own. Her old grandfather was a complete eccentric, but he had died just before we moved to the estate. Stories abounded about him and his wife. In spite of our common financial state, they seemed a different class from the rest of us, and were reportedly old-style revolutionary socialists. Some of the older residents in the road confirmed that the old man used to wait till the sun went down in the summer and stand naked at their bedroom window playing the violin. I couldn't decide what was the funniest aspect of this activity: the nakedness, the timing, the violin or just the display. The old ladies talked about it and laughed behind their hands at the memory. He was known as Pop Price.

His wife, Charlotte's grandmother, was odd as well. She wore an assortment of brightly coloured clothes and hats and was the most bowlegged person I had seen since Miss Argent at my first Sunday school.

All the elderly women on the estate were given the honorary status of Granny, and within three houses lived Granny Wren, Granny Cockell and Granny Price.

The former two ladies had total respect from all the kids, and the pair of them used to take turns keeping an eye on all the games that took place on the road. A couple of words from either in the way of remonstration would be obeyed with little dissent. Both of them used to lean on their garden gates, and Benny said that their arms had gone bad from all the leaning they had done.

Granny Cockell was very elderly with only two teeth on the bottom left of her mouth. Her voice was stern but not loud, and she sometimes had to issue her rebukes more than once.

Granny Wren had more teeth, was somewhat younger and walked with a brisk shuffle to the shops and back. She was very Romany-looking and had a voice as gruff as an old soldier, but her eyes always had a twinkle and she laughed off comments on her deep tan as having picked up its Mediterranean colour from "walking up and down the Mitcham Road."

Granny Price, on the other hand, was a genteel old girl; she had very little authority over us kids and none at all with Charlotte. Her amazing rolling gait made her unmistakable from hundreds of yards away. Although quite elderly she carried her bags of shopping in both hands and swayed like an Indian bullock up Factory Lane with her load. Charlotte never went shopping and threw massive tantrums against her granny whenever she was asked to do the smallest thing. The only time she was respectful was when her mother paid the odd visit to the estate by taxi.

"She's on the game," said Benny. He said that about so many people that the statement was beginning to lose credibility, but there was no doubt that Charlotte's mother was like nothing we ever saw on the estate. The taxi would pull up and in a swirl of fur coat she would alight and pay the driver through the window using currency of such high denomination that none of us recognised it. Her hair and make-up were always immaculate, and she swept into the end of terrace flat like an actress. She had a fabulous figure and invariably wore sweaters that showed it off as her elegant fur coat opened and flapped in the breeze. Like Charlotte she had intense eyes under the make-up and the glasses she sometimes wore. Charlotte's eyes just looked small, and she wore her glasses all the time to help correct a slight squint.

These visits never seemed to last very long, and soon the cab would return and she would be whisked off ("back on the game," said Benny), leaving a slightly pink-eyed squinty girl standing forlornly at the gate watching her mother drive out of sight.

At twelve, Charlotte was much taller than the other girls, and while many of them were now adding little fashion accessories to their dress, she was still being dressed as a child with her bright red hair tied in a ponytail, or sometimes in plaits which suited her less. Other girls were starting to get noticed by the boys on the street, but not Charlotte, who still wore ankle socks, little cotton dresses tied with a bow at the back, and a ribbon in her hair.

All the houses and flats on the estate had privet hedges in front of them, and because our house bordered the alley, we had the longest hedge to cut. We also had the bluntest shears with which to do it.

When we first moved in, it took Bruce, Mum and I three days to work our way down the outside and a week to trim the inside, after which we just about kept it in check. Most of the hedges of the houses on our side of the road were nicely trimmed. One or two on the other side were positively ornamental.

The Prices' hedge, however, was dreadful. It had grown up and out and drooped over the pavement and into the garden in a tangle of dense branches, and as spring gave way to early summer it was plain that something had to be done. It was difficult to drop hints, and even when old Granny Price was forced to walk in the road to get past the hedge, she seemed not to notice. Finally one warm evening Granny Wren stopped her in the street as she was returning from the shops.

"Your bleedin' 'edge needs cuttin'," she suggested. Granny Price put down her bags for a moment and squinted up at her hedge.

"My goodness, yes it does!" she said, as if noticing it for the first time ever. "I'll have to see if I can find the shears and sort it out."

Granny Wren gave a gruff chuckle at the acknowledgement and resumed leaning on the gatepost. Granny Price picked up her bags and slowly waddled through her gate.

The cutting of hedges seems to work like the domino effect. Someone does theirs, and another follows suit, and in most cases a lazy neighbour is eventually shamed into cutting his hedge by the neatness of those either side of him. In the case of the Prices this was slow to happen, and it was not until we had broken up for the Whitsun holiday and all our hedges were trimmed that old Granny Price was seen by us kids valiantly hacking a hole through her gateway.

It was a warm afternoon and the old lady had adopted a short-sleeved sweater and floral apron to embark on this task. As I watched I realised her shears were even worse than ours. The scissors seemed to merely grip the fronds of privet and I watched transfixed as huge flaps of fat beneath her upper arms wobbled and shuddered when she tried to rip the branches from the main body of the hedge. Our game of street cricket came to a pause as one by one we stopped to watch her efforts.

"We ought to offer to help," I said.

The rest of my mates looked at me incredulously and then Benny shouted, "You should let Charlotte do that, Granny Price!"

When the old lady finally realised that she was being addressed, she conceded that Benny was right and slowly turned and spoke to Charlotte who was playing quietly in another part of the garden. There then followed a one-sided shouting session as Charlotte loudly protested that she should not do the work. This petulant voice was something we had got used to, and it was a fact that Charlotte's protests were always louder when she knew that some of us kids were listening.

Suddenly there was a noise none of us had ever heard before from over the jungle of privet as the old lady finally snapped and a clear voice rang out, "You take these shears young lady and begin cutting that hedge NOW!" This was followed by a slapping noise and a shriek.

Us lads all looked at each other and grinned. *She had it coming* was the silent agreement among us all, and soon through the hedge came muffled stuttering sobs, of hurt pride more than pain, accompanied by rhythmic clipping noises.

Our game of cricket wandered aimlessly on, and gradually through the hedge Charlotte's sobs turned to little tuneless humming noises as the cutting settled into a neat regular pattern. The sun grew warmer and us lads slipped off our shirts, to expose singlets and skinny chests with arms in various shades of brown.

As our game dwindled toward its close, Charlotte's red hair began to show above her hedge, and as she worked her way backwards and forwards along the front facing the road, more and more of her face appeared, now slightly flushed, and then the tops of her bare shoulders. Then from behind the foliage she began cutting from the bottom of the inside to the top in great strong chops of the shears, all the while singing her tuneless little song.

From time to time I glanced at her progress, and as she cleared away the leafy outgrowth from the inside border it was possible to make out her movements through the lace curtain of the depleted front foliage. She bent to pull some leaves from the ground and I suddenly noticed that she had taken her top and skirt off and was cutting away stripped to the waist, wearing only her school knickers.

Several other lads had noticed at the same time because the bowler had paused to look, effectively stopping the game. There was nothing unusual in children running about in their knickers and nothing else during the warm weather, but what had made this different was that Charlotte was suddenly no longer a little kid. The sight that we could so tantalisingly glimpse was of a beautiful coltish young girl, her flaming red hair tossing from side to side with her movements and her young breasts bouncing in time with each swish of the blades. To the sound of a cricket bat hitting the pavement the entire team crossed the road as one to the Prices' hedge.

"'ow's it goin' Charlotte?" asked Benny as nonchalantly as he could. Charlotte looked up surprised by the proximity of the voice.

"Who's that?" she squinted over the newly-cut top. Ordinarily Charlotte looked better with her glasses on, but now the fact that she wasn't wearing any added to her 'natural' look. The streaks of dust in the beads of perspiration and her quizzical peering, to say nothing of the lines down her cheeks from the smack that had so chastened her, made me feel a little protective toward her.

"'ow's it going?" asked Benny again.

Now Charlotte recognised the voice, and could make out the forms of the half dozen or so boys that were pressed up against the hedge trying to look over the top. Charlotte delighted in the attention; I was simply overwhelmed and feeling a little light-headed. Suddenly one of our number appeared with a pair of shears and began cutting the front of the hedge enthusiastically, and from where I and one or two others were standing more of Charlotte's gorgeous form began to emerge. In the next few minutes hedging shears were appearing from sheds all up and down the road as eager lads jostled to work next to the redheaded girl.

Some of the boys engaged in brief competitions with her to get her breasts to move more by snapping the shears shut more fiercely. One of them suggested she use his shears as they had just been sharpened, and she eagerly accepted. Soon there was a boy on each side and another three in front of her, all snapping and cutting away as Charlotte giggled and thrilled to all the attention she was getting. I hung back but could not take my eyes off her.

It was only a car horn that alerted any grown-up to this fun. As usual the boys had set up a wicket in the middle of the road and put various markers to denote lines and boundaries, and the car refused to drive through them. No-one was prepared to give up his position near to Charlotte to move them either.

It was Granny Wren who shouted to us, "Move that bleedin' wicket out of the way!" and noticed the crowd of boys all working in the hedge.

"What's going on here?" she wanted to know, her suspicions aroused by this unusual enthusiasm for work. By this time Granny Price had come down but saw nothing unusual in the boys' interest. In fact she went so far as to thank us all.

"I think it's very nice that Charlotte has so many nice friends willing to help her," she said.

Granny Wren left the authority of her gate and in slippered feet came to inspect the scene. She was quick to realise the attraction, and shaking her head slightly in disbelief at the naiveté of the old lady, pushed past us lads and told us to clear off whilst she spoke to the older Price. In rebellious, sulky little groups, the boys stood in the road and watched as Granny Price told Charlotte to go upstairs and change. Without a murmur the young girl turned and went to the front step, but just before she went inside, she paused and gave us all a wave. Perspiration had rivered lines down her face in the dust from the privet hedge and traced patterns across her breasts, and as she waved they gave one last jiggle and she was gone.

When she came back outside, she was washed and wearing her little girl's dress with the bow at the back. Although we all knew what lay underneath, she was once again on her own when it came to friends. But for a brief moment she was the undisputed star of the road. None of us ever forgot that preview of what to expect when we had girlfriends of our own, and Granny Price got respect and her hedge cut.

straws

Like kids everywhere, I longed to work at the fair, and we only lived a mile or two away from Mitcham Common where the Easter and Whitsun Fairs were held. At the age of about twelve I acquired my first black shirt with a button-down collar; I had a shilling tin of lavender brilliantine, home tapered trousers, and my tie knotted the wrong way round so that the thin end faced the world, and in my mind I was a Teddy boy.

I thought Teds were the best thing. Of course, I had no money to dress like they did and I had no beard to grow sideburns either, but I could make up a pastiche of what they wore and practise the way they walked. Teds always worked the fair; they had tattoos and took incredible risks standing on the whirling machines, leaning against gravity and nicking a bit of small change from the excited punters. They looked so cool as they made the girls scream with excitement, pushing the Waltzers round so that the rib-crushing centrifugal forces made them shriek as the air was forced out of their lungs. Dresses went awry and we caught tantalising glimpses of what we were not really supposed to see as the music roared out of the fairground speakers: *I Found My Thrill On Blueberry Hill...*

The posters announcing the fair would appear a few days before the advance party arrived with some of the heavy machinery and one or two trailers. It didn't matter that you knew they were coming, you still got the same rush of excitement at the thought of all that colour and noise. The caravans ringed their position like wagons in a western film as they built up the site from within the protection of their walls. At night lights were seen in these trailers and eventually television aerials were in evidence alongside the elderly but immaculate Scammells and Albions that hauled the fairground rides to each new destination. The Common was our domain all year but when the show people arrived it was definitely theirs.

None of my mates dared break through the cordon of trailers and trucks, and in any case each one seemed to contain a dog with a bark loud enough to knock down the walls of Jericho. One night, however, I did creep inside the cordon on my own whilst my mates stood at a discreet distance. It was a strange sight that opened up in front of me: all the stalls were covered up and only the lights from inside the caravans illuminated the scene. Then some monster dog began a frenzied barking, and I was only just back to my friends before a couple of men appeared with the beast at the rim of the vehicles and let us know if they ever caught us again they would set the dogs on us.

Stories of the fabulous amounts of money to made at the fair abounded, and I decided that it was time I swallowed my shyness and tried to get a job on one of the glamorous rides. I would be able to buy a pair of black jeans which I would have tapered like Rory McLean, only not so tight, and stand leaning backward on the Waltzer making the girls scream. They would admire my skills of balance and manliness and also my honesty. I would not fiddle the change that the boys handle with distracted indifference (I was always convinced they would forget mine, but I always got it). If there were no jobs on the Waltzer, there was always the Whip or the dodgems.

The job I got was on the Pick-a-Straw stall. By the time I applied, everything exciting had been taken by much older lads. I'd gone up to the Duck Shoot stall and asked the bloke in charge and a young lad if there were any vacancies on the rides. I must have sounded posh to them and the lad nearly had a fit of laughing, but he told me to go and see his auntie on her stall. She asked me if I could give change and was I honest, and said she wouldn't tolerate any nickin' or fiddlin' and took me on to start that same afternoon at one o'clock.

There followed one of the most miserable weeks of work I have had before or since. Although disappointed by my failure to secure a glamorous job, I was still quite pleased to have got something. I began to wonder how much money she would give me, as this had not been discussed. I was sure I would have enough to get a Teddy boy suit, but more than that I had no idea.

The job was simple enough. All I had to do was to walk round and round the stall carrying a large mug stuffed full of drinking straws and shouting, "Pick a straw!" for which the punters paid sixpence. Hanging on the uprights that supported the roof were prodders made from bits of coat hangers; the participants would insert these into their chosen straw and poke out a piece of paper with a name of an old movie star printed on it.

If their name corresponded to a name on the stall, then that would secure the item represented by that film star. So if you pulled out Dale Evans you would get a pencil sharpener, and for Bing Crosby you got a 48-piece tea service. It took me two or three days to realise that there were probably no Bing Crosby names in the straws. At first I was more excited than the punters as they poked out their tickets, craning my neck to see if they had won it. It soon became obvious that the whole thing was a con and that there were far more Tab Hunters (no prize) than there were Dale Evanses.

I felt so bad in the end that I began telling little kids not to spend their last sixpence there, as I couldn't bear to see them go away with nothing. Once I gave away a chipped and battered plaster elf to a little girl who had lost to Tab Hunter, and the old girl even questioned me about how I had got rid of it. I blustered some excuse which she grudgingly accepted. In spite of this apparent disloyalty, the old girl was pleased with me and after the fourth day could even remember my name, though she still called me 'boy'. I can only think that in spite of me actively discouraging speculation at the stall, her profits were up, simply because I didn't steal from her.

Her oafish nephew got me to part with my collection of second-hand comics, which he promised to return. I soon realised that he couldn't read and that he liked to look at the pictures, but it kept him off my back and once or twice he let me have a free go on the .22 rifle range, which I was surprisingly good at (I was useless at most hand-to-eye sports).

I only stayed the week, and by the Saturday I couldn't wait to get away, but I couldn't leave until I'd been paid. The music had been irresistible, but the weather had been miserable and rainy, the girls and boys that nightly thronged the rides had not even noticed me, and as we wrapped up the stall for the last night and I prepared to receive my wages, the old girl addressed me.

"Well boy, you've been a good kid and I've talked to me old man and we'll take you on with us if you like. I know your old mum is 'avin' a struggle with two boys at 'ome and I should know 'cos I've raised four meself. Now you tell 'er that we'll look after you and you'll get your proper schoolin' and proper food an' you'll travel everywhere we go. We're off to Southampton after this and you can leave with us tomorrer if you want it, now what do you think?"

As she made her little speech she counted out in half crowns the sum of twelve shillings and sixpence and pressed the large coins into my hand. The mixture of emotions at this time was extreme. This woman was more or less offering to adopt me and take care of me, and I could become a traveller and be free as the other lads who worked the rides and drove the wagons and trucks. I could wear my hair long and greasy and live on hot dogs and candy floss, I could meet hundreds of girls and become experienced and get tattooed and have an earring put in. I could leave the council flat and be free.

Not on twelve and sixpence a week I couldn't. I counted the coins in my pocket again. I couldn't believe it—twelve and six! A whole week standing under a soggy canvas poking out a mug of 'lucky' straws at people and not cheating the old girl and this was my reward. I stood outside her trailer and mumbled about not being able to leave as I had to attend school and look after my little brother. She once again told me that I would get all the schoolin' I needed with them. I thought of her strange offer of motherhood, then of the callous exploitation of my honesty and stupidity, and a tear trickled down my cheek. She didn't notice.

I managed a goodbye and thank you, and without looking back at me she said, "We leave tomorrow at eight, if you want to come and yer mum says okay, be 'ere an' we'll take you with us." Behind her at the caravan table the old man was looking at the paper, and he slowly shook his head from side to side and blew out a cloud of Old Holborn smoke.

"Bye boy," he said. I walked away from the fairground angry and confused, and when I got home I lied to all my mates about the money I got paid and then realised that her oafish nephew hadn't even returned my precious comics.

d-day

"Have you ever 'opped the wag?" asked Benny nonchalantly one evening. We were all leaning on the bars that were situated outside our tiny flat. They were there to stop kids running straight out into the road from the alley that ran down the side of the houses and the kids sort of met there and hung around while they waited for inspiration to hit them as to how to spend their time.

"'ave you ever 'opped the wag?" I turned the expression over in my mind. This was a new one on me and Benny was always doing this. He seemed to have a vocabulary that was all his own. All the other kids knew his words but seldom used them. It took me weeks to work out what a 'juk' (the Romany word for a dog) was. 'oppin' the wag? Could it be rhyming slang, I wondered, all the kids used this cockney derivative. Wag, bag, fag, shag? All these thoughts raced quickly through my mind. I drew a blank but already Benny was starting again.

"'ave you ever 'opped the wag?"

It was probably some sexual thing, I decided, so it was probably best to deny it. I answered as lazily as I could, "No," then added, "not really."

There was a pause and Benny said, "Either you 'ave or you ain't."

So I said, "No, definitely not."

He kicked a small stone into the gutter and said, "Well you ought to,

179

it ain't 'alf a laugh."

There was a short hesitation as I pondered what it could mean when he offered, "We could both do it, it's more a laugh if we both do it."

Oh Christ, I thought, it *is* a sex thing and Benny wants us to do it together. I was constantly amazed at Benny's precociousness, as he was only eleven but seemed to know so much. After a while I asked when he was thinking of doing it. This seemed to be the safest way of continuing the enquiry without committing to the act.

"I was finkin' Wednesday," said Benny, and for the first time he looked round at me and I saw not a hint of embarrassment at his proposal. It was still term time, and as we went to different schools I asked what time he wanted to do this thing.

"All day of course!" was all he said. All day? What on earth could it be about? I kicked a small stone into the gutter and turned round and looked down the lane.

"Well, I couldn't do it Benny, you know I have to go to school."

"Exactly," said Benny, "I know, that's why I said it. It's Derby day." He pronounced Derby like the Americans do. I was more perplexed than ever, this wag 'opping was somehow connected with horses and I was becoming even more wary.

Then Benny asked, "'ave you ever been to the Derby?"

I turned round to face the road. "No, I haven't been interested in it."

"It's only up Epsom. We could go and 'ave a laugh," he said without stammering.

"Look Ben, I have to go to school, I already told you."

"Yeah, you could 'op the wag, an' we could go." Oh Christ, we were back to 'oppin! Then it dawned on me that he meant me to play truant.

"You mean to bunk off school, don't you?" I said with relief.

"Yeah," said Benny, turning round to face down the lane, "Let's both 'op the wag."

And 'op the wag we did. In the end it was Benny, Ronnie, Bruce and me that 'opped the wag that June morning and met down at the tiny station at Waddon Marsh. This was the first stop on the loop line to Wimbledon, and the regular train service added character to our estate. Years before, my paternal grandfather had considered his train driving career hit the heights when he was promoted to the electric service and he could wear a collar and tie to work, returning home almost as clean as when he started. The train was only ever two coaches long, and after rush hour it was often completely empty. We climbed in and immediately Benny started to behave badly. He threw his legs up on the seat opposite and pulled out a packet of Weights.

"'oo wants a fag?"

"Stop showin' off," ordered Ronnie.

"I ain't showin' off," said Benny, "if you want a fag you can 'ave one that's all I'm sayin'."

He only had a pack of five, so we all took one, leaving him with one for later. I was the only one who could inhale the smoke, and soon our little coach was full of cloudy fumes.

"You can't even take it down," teased Ronnie, as Bruce and he puffed away with much flicking of ash.

"Yes I fuckin' can," said Benny.

"Let's see you then you lyin' git," said Ronnie. Benny attempted a tiny inhalation but predictably ended up in a coughing fit, which caused Ronnie and the rest of us much amusement.

As the train pulled away from the next stop, Beddington Lane, Benny said, "We got to change at the next station, Mitcham Junction." Just before the train drew in Benny threatened to pull the communication cord, but we stopped him and I breathed that he better behave or we'd leave him on his own. For the next part of the trip he sulked a bit, but he was no trouble.

It was a beautiful morning as we left the station and asked a man the way to the racecourse. At first he must have thought we were taking the mickey, and then seeing that we were genuine he stated deliberately that to follow the crowd might be a good idea. I was embarrassed that I hadn't thought of that, it was so logical.

We dropped in behind a group. I was surprised at the numbers of folk that were moving toward the downs. We all looked at each other and grinned the way kids do when there is excitement in the air. I rattled the loose change in my pocket and wondered how far I would get on three shillings and sixpence; I bet myself that Benny would have at least ten bob and I was right.

Benny had his first toffee apple at eleven o'clock and his first candy floss shortly afterwards. Now he's down to nine shillings, I calculated, as I resolved not to start spending until we had achieved parity. That meant he had to spend another five and six. It was going to be a long afternoon.

We entered the downs at the top, where hundreds of cars were parked, and the level of conversation rose around us as people glimpsed the course and the sweep of the scenery that warm sunny morning. Over in the distance could be seen the tops of tents and a few fairground rides; in fact it looked bigger than our own Mitcham Fair, one of the high points of our social calendar.

"Come on," shouted Benny, "look at all the bleedin' tents over there." We quickened our pace slightly, but there was so much to look at I wanted to take it all in. Soon our pace had slowed again. All around the top, people were gathered in groups as tipsters shouted that they had the sure winner of this or that race. I wondered why, if they knew they would be willing to pass on such valuable information for a paltry half crown. Not that a half crown was all that paltry, especially if you only had a few bob to your name like me.

As we edged along, gawping at everything we came across, a huge crowd was listening to Prince Honolulu. Not that they had much option but to listen, his voice was so loud.

Every time he hollered, "I gotta horse, I gotta horse!" the crowd smiled and acknowledged his famous cry. I remember him as being very big, with a huge voice and a head dress of exotic feathers. In his hand he held a brown paper envelope in which he swore that he had the name of the Derby winner. There was a steady stream of takers for this prize, and as I watched it dawned on me that he only had to list all the horses, and as long as that number of people bought his tips, one of them would be a very satisfied customer. In fact he was part and parcel of the entertainment as we moved along through the happy crowd.

Soon Benny had his first hot dog, and Bruce and I pretended not to notice as the first little jabs of hunger reminded us that it was mid-day. Couples and groups sat all around us on the grass, with everything from a sandwich to small hampers of food and bottles of warm beer; and way over by the track, the crowds were being drawn to the rails like iron filings to a magnet.

Benny ate another toffee apple and washed it down with a bottle of R. White's cream soda, which he offered round and we all gulped down a few sickly mouthfuls. As the horses pulled in the punters, so the music of the fair drew us to the rides above the course. It was a proper fair, with side shows as well as rides, and us kids were in our element.

Benny and Bruce invested in a ride on the 'chairoplanes', and while that ride was going on, I planned to visit a tent that promised the longest rat in the world. I was just about to pay my tanner when I heard some kid say to his mate that he could see where they had sewn two rats together, and what was the point of seeing a rat floating in a lot of yellow liquid? The picture on the outside showed a terrier cowering in terror before a snarling rat of gigantic proportions, not some mouldering specimen in a bell jar.

I was relieved at saving my sixpence, as I had once before succumbed to curiosity at Bognor and parted with hard earned pennies to see the two-headed calf. The pictures on the display outside showed rosy-cheeked children stroking the heads of a beautiful young creature, but on entry to the booth, all that was on display was a jar about the size of a pickle jar at the fish and chip shop, in which floated the tiny embryo of an aborted two-headed something or other. It was about the size of a puppy and had been disembowelled and sewn up with some white thread. It was as much as I could do to force any food down me for several days.

Benny and Bruce had been on their ride and were both eating candy floss.

"That was terrific weren't it, you feel like yer flyin'," enthused Benny, looking over at Bruce for confirmation. It might have felt good, but I thought Benny was looking a little dodgy myself.

Then there was a hammer and bell machine, and skinny blokes with brown arms and ghostly white bodies in string vests made the bell ring, whilst bigger blokes failed for some reason. I watched the abstracted way the barker broke the fall of the striker with a stick, just before it returned to rest. He took the sixpenny toll with the same hand as he used to hand the punter the hammer, and didn't even look at the geezer as he continued his urging to "Try your strength!" or "Ring the bell, impress the gels!"

I looked around, but there were no unattended girls for me to impress, and the hammer looked too heavy for me to lift, let alone hurl over my shoulder and on to the spigot of the machine.

I almost blushed at the thought of the humiliation if I failed to get the clapper to move, and my fears were vindicated when Ronnie, after some prompting from Ben, decided to have a go. He had to hold the hammer so near the head in order to lift the thing that it had no travel to gain momentum, and the hammer merely fell on to the spigot sending the clapper all of twelve inches up the fifteen feet of the graduated board.

"Weaklin'!" crowed Benny, gleefully reading the classification of effort from the board.

"Fuck off," countered Ronnie, his face more red with effort than embarrassment. Benny was giggling and sweating at the same time; Ronnie made a lunge at him and Bruce and I pulled them apart before anything happened. It went a bit quiet for a moment as we sauntered round the various stalls. A little way off from the rest was a bloke dressed for some reason as a cowboy and speaking in a cod American accent.

"Guess your age! Guess your age! Only one shilling!" All he had by way of props was a box that his punters stood on, and then he walked round them assessing their age. As a backdrop to his box, the rules of his gig were set out: *If I cannot guess your age within two years you can have your money back.*

"D'you fancy a go, Benny?" I asked.

"Not if he takes two years to guess it, we're only 'oppin' the wag for a day," observed Benny cleverly, though it took me a minute to work out what he meant. I wished I was as fast as Benny.

"I don't do kids," muttered the cowboy from the corner of his mouth, his accent suddenly more English. The others began to drift away, and I watched as a few punters duly parted with their shillings to be told what they already knew. He appeared to get all the ages right, and it crossed my mind that if he guessed a woman to be younger than she was, she might be so grateful that she would pretend he got it right. The longer I watched, the more impressive it became; he was getting all the ages right, and in the short time that I watched he must have earned about ten or eleven shillings. I was very impressed.

He must have seen how intrigued I was. During a lull in his labours, he turned to where I was standing and from the corner of his mouth whispered cryptically, "You have to look around the eyes. It's the eyes that tell the story," and then he was back to work.

I grinned and went red. He walked round the back of the customer and gave me a large wink, as I was now privy to the secret. Again he was on the money, and another shilling went into his pocket. I wandered away, wondering if he had a son to pass on these skills to. Perhaps he had been waiting for the right kid to come along to pass on these age-old secrets, and he had chosen me. I was flattered and couldn't wait to try it out on someone.

Suddenly I realised I had lost the others. I gazed at the throngs of people milling about and a panic hit me. Onions and cigarette smoke and sticky smells were on the breeze, and Little Richard records crackled above the general noise. Other voices closer to my head were all talking at the same time and I felt a little dizzy.

"Come over 'ere Ralph," spluttered Benny, snapping me out of my distancing feelings, "there's some tarts in a tent over 'ere wiv no cloves on." He raised his eyebrows and pursed his lips and blew a gasp of air through the small gap between them.

"They're stark fuckin' naked!" He burst out in a huge guffaw.

"What are you talking about?" I said, still coming to from my away moment. I was really pleased to see him and as usual his enthusiasm was very contagious. Bruce looked a bit embarrassed but I still looked to him for confirmation of Benny's assertion.

"What Ben's saying is that there's a striptease tent over there," and he gestured with his hand. Without saying anything, we all wandered off in that direction.

Outside the small marquee was a little man with a huge voice drumming up an already interested group of punters, while we lurked at the back. His spiel indicated that these three lovely girls would reveal all their charms in discreet artistic poses for the price of two shillings.

I felt my own hand check the few coins in my pocket and looked at the others.

Benny said, "Two bob to look at them old birds, you must be jokin'. One of 'em looks as old as my mother." This was probably true, but another one was so pretty, with dark hair and a sweet smile, that I had nearly fallen in love with her before the barker finished his pitch. Soon the men in the crowd started to pay their two bobs and I stood watching them file into the tent.

Ronnie turned to Bruce and Benny and said, "They won't let us in anyway, we're too young. Let's go on the dodgems." I told them to go and I would wait for them here. The three of them took off in the direction of the cars while I stood outside the tent, listening to the lascivious murmurings and chuckles emanating from within.

Other noises mingled with the crowd, and voices again muttered just out of earshot inside my head. The thought of the men leering at the pretty girl disturbed me, but the thought that I could see her naked exerted a greater pressure on my adolescent body. After what seemed like an age, the flap opened on the tent and the men emerged, blinking slightly in the sunshine and grinning to each other.

The barker came out and once more began drumming up the crowd with his well worn patter. He was assisted once more by the one who was as old as Benny's mum, who also took the money on the door, and she was joined at the entrance by another slightly younger girl with a fairly large nose. Finally my pretty one came out, to a few wolf whistles, and that was it. I plunged my hand into my pocket and grabbed the two bob bit, and as soon as some of the men had paid their entrance I joined in the queue, and the lady who was as old as Benny's mum took my money without looking at me.

Inside the tent the heat was overpowering. All the men lit up at the same time and began jostling for position. I worked my way to a corner, and by standing on tip toe and craning my neck I could see the stage quite well. The barker climbed on to the tiny stage and stood in front of the curtain, which looked like a stained bed sheet with a small triangular tear, revealing a small amount of movement behind it. The lady who looked as old as Benny's mum scurried back out of the tent, allowing a flash of sunlight on to the tawdry scene within. Another flash of sunlight indicated that she had arrived at the backstage area and the barker began a short spiel.

"What you are about to witness is an artistic display of some of the world's finest paintings depicted in living tableaux form by the lovely ladies you saw outside. Because the great artists of the past found naked-ness to be quite acceptable, some of the poses you will witness will contain nudity. We 'ope that this will not cause offence and must point out that to conform to the guidelines of the 'ome Seckertary there will be no movement allowed during the performance. I thangyew."

From somewhere behind the scenes an elderly gramophone struck up and the man announced, "Salome with the 'ead of Samson!"

He reached up and drew back the sheet to reveal the lady who was as old as Benny's mum, sitting on a red cushion dressed in her briefs and holding a dinner plate with the head of an old shop window mannequin wearing a black wig. Apart from her briefs and a silly smile she was na-ked. The act of holding up the plate had raised one breast slightly whilst the other one drooped forlornly. Her skin was as white as my mum's, in contrast to the ruddy complexions of the men around me and my own spring-browned arms. There were several nasty bruises on her arms, and a large one on her thigh that she had tried unsuccessfully to disguise with make-up.

A sort of groan came from some voices in the audience, the curtain was hastily drawn over the proceedings and the barker announced, "Thangyew laydeez an' gennermen! And now we present the 'and maidens of Aphrodite!"

Once more he drew back the curtain and there sat the lady who looked as old as Benny's mum on an old gold-painted chair, the girl with the big nose holding a long handled fan, and the one I was in love with now sitting on the red cushion with her back to me. She held what looked suspiciously like a coal scuttle imploringly toward Aphrodite. I wondered if they were related; could that have been her mother she was facing? All three were topless, but I could not see the pretty one's charms from the position she held.

The barker closed the curtain once more and announced, "Thangyew laydeez an gennermen. And now we present 'The Birth of Venus'." He drew back the curtain and there was the same woman, this time wearing a huge wig which she held coyly in front of her privates whilst balancing on a dustbin lid, representing a shell.

The curtain was drawn back again and the barker bellowed, "Thangyew laydeez an' gennermen, and now we present 'The Toilet of Venus'."

"Oh fuck that," said a voice in front of me, "I suppose the old bird'll be sitting on the bog now!" and some of his friends laughed. The curtain was drawn back and there sat the lady who looked like Benny's mum with a different wig on. The pretty one was holding a mirror in hands that trembled slightly (I loved her more than ever for this) and the one with the big nose held a sort of comb to the older one's hair.

"They all look bloody silly if you ask me," an old geezer in front of me remarked, but I was transfixed by the young girl's figure. For the first time I could see her breasts. They were small and round and firm and I was dizzy with all sorts of emotions. The voices grew louder in my ears and the heat of the tent and the cigarette smoke swirled and the record player scratched on and the barker went, "Thangyew laydeez an' gennermen..."

Sweat poured from my forehead as the curtain swished closed again.

"An' finally the Three Graces thangyew!" With that, the torn curtain was pulled back to reveal the three of them, naked, in the pose of the famous statue. The one who was as old as Benny's mum faced the audience, a judicious crossing of her legs concealing the part that most had paid to see, and the one with the big nose and stubble armpits had her head turned heavenward with a look of what I supposed was to represent divine inspiration but looked more like a mad woman to me.

I had eyes only for my love, who looked wistfully over one shoulder with a cardboard lute under one arm. I could just see one breast and her bottom and her pretty smile, and just before I passed out the curtain swung back and the barker shouted that the show had ended but we were welcome to call again.

I was almost carried outside in the rush to escape, and sat down on the grass in a state of shock and excitement. Men around me were grumbling and laughing but no-one seemed really to mind. I was slowly returning to reality; all I could see were the cadaverous white bodies with their thumb marks and bruises and the tatty surroundings and cheap props and torn drapes, then breasts and bottoms and pretty smiles. I was smitten.

"Look what fuckin' Benny's done !" Ronnie's voice was very loud in my ear. I turned round to see Bruce laughing silently as Ronnie pointed to his shirt which was covered with the contents of Benny's stomach.

"I couldn't 'elp it could I, it was all that banging about in the bumper cars weren' it?" said Benny with not much hint of contrition.

"Yeah but you could have turned the other way couldn't you? You twat," Ronnie added for good measure. I was glad to get up from my position and to laugh along with the others. Ronnie took off his t-shirt and his body was as skinny and white as the older men in shirt sleeves or vests, although the rest of us had the beginnings of tans as all the bits that poked out were getting brown. We strolled happily amongst the crowds until we found a standpipe amongst the trailers and caravans. Ronnie rinsed off most of the puke and we all had a swig of water, until a fearsome-looking old woman saw us and threatened to turn her dog on us.

"All right missus, keep your fuckin' 'air on," shouted Benny, and then he took off leaving the rest of us standing like idiots before following him, laughing our heads off.

Some way below us the racing had begun, but we took little notice. The crowd noise came to a crescendo as the horses reached the winning post. The sun continued to pour down on us all as I tried to digest what had happened to me and then suddenly I saw her. Not the object of my desire, but the old girl who had given me the job at the Mitcham Fair the previous year.

And there she was, a year on, in front of me and even in the hot afternoon sun she still wore the same fawn-coloured overcoat she wore every day. Ominously there was no sign of the old man with his duck stall and I wondered if the cough had carried him off. Her skin was even greyer than I remembered it, and even from a distance I could see that her deep brown eyes had no life in them. As she wandered around the stall like a goldfish, her gaze stopped for a second in my direction. I thought that she had recognised me, but her eyes moved on to others in the crowd, each person viewed as a sixpence.

I drew a little closer, and there at the back of the stall was the same tea service with Bing Crosby written underneath. Now you could get a tiny plastic Barbie doll for Dale Evans, and on the floor scattered around the stall was the name Tab Hunter. I looked around for the others. Benny and Ronnie had made it up, Benny was eating another hot dog, and they were both laughing with Bruce, who had also recognised the old girl.

"Did she know you?" he asked.

"I didn't speak to her," I replied, and the four of us began the long walk back to the station. We all had a drag on Benny's last crumpled cigarette, and the journey back to Waddon Marsh Halt was altogether quieter than the outward one had been.

In my dreams the young stripper came to visit me and begged me to rescue her from her wicked mother, who owned a pick-a-straw factory where she was made to work long hours. She told me that she had seen me in the tent and had followed me home. She was prepared to live in our shed and to live off stolen breakfast cereals until we could find somewhere of our own, and to prove it she was about to let me do something with her, but we were already lost on an open common where we found a plate containing the head of Benny with a fixed leer on his face. I felt compelled to take it home with me and give it to his mum. I placed Benny's grinning head in a carrier bag and hurried across the open ground.

Suddenly I'm on my own, with Benny's head banging against my thigh uttering his prelude to speaking from inside the bag. "Gan gan gan…" it goes, in time to my step. Where has she gone? The sound of horses' hooves make me turn round to see her naked on the back of the leading horse. She is pursued by the barker and the one who looks as old as Benny's mum. As she draws level with me she leaps from the horse into my open arms and I am consumed by her softness and we fall to the ground.

We roll in each other's arms down the grassy bank and something is happening to me. Breasts the size of toffee apples float in my head, then hot dogs, and before the dream is consummated I awake with proof of my coming adolescence. I can see her still, though I couldn't tell you which horse won the Derby.

~

wolf

One morning, it must have been in the winter holidays, the kids gathered on the street bars outside our flat. As usual, we talked and joked and woke up to the new day and thought about what we might do that morning. As we leaned on the bars, we noticed the shuffling walk of Teddy Wolf coming towards us.

He sidled up to the bars, stood there and pulled out a flattened cigarette from a packet of Player's that looked as though he had sat on them. As he struck the match we could see his hands shaking so much that he could barely line up the match with the end of the cigarette. He took down a huge drag and blew the combination of steamy breath and smoke out in an enormous cloud. Benny mimicked the action with an imaginary cigarette and a couple of the younger ones copied Benny. I was fascinated, though, as I had never seen anyone shake like this man was shaking.

Teddy was about twenty-two years old and therefore not really a contemporary of any of the kids who knocked about with the older brothers of our friends on the estate. The boys that Teddy would have known were either in one of the services, in prison, or else had married and moved away. Teddy had not grown up on the estate and his past was not known or much discussed. His hair stood up in a grown out crewcut and was pushed back off his forehead, his skin was deathly pale, and he wore a thin 'Raindrop' fabric semi-Ted suit. His shirt was white and open at the neck and it was clear that he had no vest underneath. He finished his Player's and stubbed it out on the pavement, grinding it into the asphalt. Benny did the same with his imaginary dog-end.

"Anyone got a smoke?" asked Teddy without really looking at any of us. We felt flattered and grown-up to think that he might assume we could supply him with a fag. After a few seconds silence he pointedly looked at each of us, until Jimmy Wren offered to get one from his sister Jeannie.

"Go on then mate," said Teddy urgently, and lifting his empty hands to his lips blew steam through them. Benny copied him.

"You look like you're freezin'," observed Benny, "Ain't you got no coat?"

Teddy said nothing, and at that moment Jimmy returned with a cigarette with a filter tip that Teddy broke off before lighting it up with his trembling hands.

"I slept out last night," said Teddy Wolf, "in her shed."

"In 'er shed?" guffawed Benny, looking around at us with his eyebrows raised to share his incredulity.

I frowned at him to shut him up, and Teddy drew another deep drag on the cigarette before flicking it almost to the other side of the road.

"Where was I supposed to go?" he asked distractedly. "Where could I go? I ain't got nowhere I could go," and he swung round and looked pointedly at Benny. "Can I come round your house?" Benny looked embarrassed.

Teddy had not stopped shaking all the time he had stood with us. His collar was turned up on his jacket and his hands were pushed deep into his pockets. The suit would have provided a little style but no warmth at all. Shoulders hunched, eyes frightened and so alone you could feel it, Teddy Wolf *was* James Dean.

I looked as deep as I dared into Teddy's eyes and all I could see was desolation. There was this man with no-one to turn to except a bunch of little kids. We all stood silent watching him shake. Any moment now he has to stop, I thought, but the trembling persisted.

"Has anyone got another fag?" he asked.

Little Jimmy produced another Bristol that he had planned to smoke himself, but even at nine years old he realised that Teddy's need was greater than his own.

"Why did you sleep in 'er shed?" said Benny at last.

Another cloud of steam and smoke was exhaled across the road and Teddy replied, "I 'ad to leave and there weren't nowhere else to go."

"Where were you staying?" persisted Benny.

"With Poppy," said Teddy.

And then something happened. From the corners of both eyes, huge tears formed and splattered down his cheeks and splashed unchecked on to the freezing pavement. The strange little gathering looked at each other and wondered what could it be that would make a man cry? Benny at first grinned sheepishly and then even his expression gave way to one of concern.

There was no sound coming from Teddy as he stood there, just a slow rhythm of silent sobs shaking his torso against the faster shivering of the rest of his body. Without a word little Jimmy Wren climbed up on to the lower of the two bars to reach the shoulders of the crying man, and laid his hand on them. The effect of this was that a cry of such pain erupted from the throat of Teddy Wolf that it frightened us. A cry that tore the child's voice from within his grown-up body, his broken heart robbing him of the dignity of privacy. All the sadness spilled out on to the open street.

"Ain't anyone got an 'andkerchief?" asked someone, and we all instinctively looked at Benny, whose mum always made him carry one. Benny reluctantly half pulled it out of his trouser pocket and inspected it to see if it was still flexible, but his cousin Jimmy pulled it out the rest of the way and crammed it into Teddy's hand. Teddy absently started to use it.

"What can you do if you love someone and they kick you out? What are you going to do?" he sobbed. "I love 'er and that's it."

He blew his nose so violently that we all winced.

"Who is it you're talking about?" Benny wanted to know.

"Poppy, Poppy Spinner," said Teddy.

"Poppy Spinner, what, her who lives in Euston Crescent? Olly, Olly Voil?"

"Yeah, Poppy Spinner," he said, and then turning round again to focus on Benny, "what did you call her?"

"Nuffin'," said Benny, casting his eyes down.

Suddenly we all knew the cause of this broken heart, Olly, Olly Voil. Benny it was who invented nicknames for everybody, and with patience you could work out the logic to their origination. For example, the old girl who lived diagonally opposite me on the other side of the road and the corresponding bars, was known to all the kids on the street as Shanny, or from Benny, "old Shannybags." She was a tough old bird who terrified us kids and used language that I for one had never heard coming from any woman before. She lived with her elderly and very infirm brother, who seldom ventured out beyond the front door.

We were convinced that she was a witch, and if a ball landed in Shannybags' garden that was where it stayed. It was Benny who detected her different accent and decided she was Irish and that her name was Annie. So she became 'Irish Annie' and later 'Shanny'. It took me years to work that one out.

Poppy Spinner was very tall and slim; she was about thirty-three and had two daughters. She was tidy and neat, and her little girls were plain but always spotlessly clean, as they had to be because they had two different fathers and Poppy had never been married. There was no particular stigma attached to unmarried motherhood on the estate; there were several that we all knew about, and just as many more who were being raised by Grandma and Granddad or even married aunts and uncles. It was just that Poppy kept herself to herself, managing all the while to keep her little ones looking as if they had a dad's wages coming in as well.

There were a number of rumours about the children, one of which suggested that it was a friend of her father who had made her pregnant first, and she dare not say for fear her old man would have killed them both. For me, this story elevated her to saintly proportions, heroically bearing her secret to protect her father from greater hurt.

For three years she never looked at another man, and then met a lad from a few streets away who swore he loved her. At length she gave in to his incessant pleading, only to find he had enlisted in the army and was killed out in Cyprus during the troubles with EOKA. Everyone knew this story, but it was never confirmed or denied by the relatives, who still lived on the estate.

Poppy was thin and wore glasses, and she had a retroussé nose; to Benny her name sounded like Popeye, so obviously she became Olly Voil!

Her downstairs flat was like a doll's house; you could almost smell the furniture polish as you walked past. Her windows were always sparkling clean and decorated with spotless nylon nets. The two little girls shared a bedroom with their mother, and this enabled Poppy to make her second bedroom available to a single gentleman, for whom she would provide an evening meal.

This of course was all against the council regulations, but Poppy was otherwise a model tenant in every way, and no-one would have dreamed of grassing her up. Most of her gentlemen were older and just passing through, but somehow this time her system had broken down and she had taken pity on poor Teddy and allowed him to lodge with her.

Naturally people talked. Teddy was not from our area and he didn't know anyone; he didn't drink and all he wanted to do was stay in after his tea and watch a bit of TV with Poppy and the two children. Eventually Poppy told him to go down to the pub, just to get out for a bit. Reluctantly he did so, only to scurry back to his little nest on the crescent.

He started to do little jobs for her, like trimming her hedge, or putting the milk bottles out, occasionally washing up and sometimes buying a little box of sweets for the girls. People still talked, but it was warmer talk along the lines of, "So what if he is a bit younger than her, look at so and so, she was fifteen years older than him," or, "Ain't it wonderful how he looks after them girls. They think the world of him you know."

Whatever went wrong happened quickly. One day it was right; the next it had all changed.

We looked at the young man in the grey morning. It was still early and the watery winter sun was just piercing the clouds over the gasholder. The sunlight made him appear even more pathetic, as the redness of his eyelids and nostrils contrasted with his sallow complexion and the new day's stubble on his chin.

"What are you going to do?" I ventured at last.

"Dunno," came the eventual reply.

"Are you going to sleep out tonight?" I asked.

"I'll have to, ain't got nowhere else." He seemed to shiver harder at the thought of it.

Benny was looking bored and several of the younger ones were fidgety. They had been reverent to his distress but now there were things to be done, games to play, shtrews to catch, and the morning was getting to be warm enough to start all those juices flowing.

"We've got an old blanket in our shed if you want it," I offered.

Teddy said nothing and the kids began to peel away. I still felt I should stay and soon I was the only one at the bars.

"Have you got a fag mate?" he asked me.

"No, I'm sorry," I replied. He reached down to one he'd finished earlier and rolled the end in between his finger tips and got enough to light and pulled a few more drags down to the filter and beyond before flicking it away.

Then pulling the collar of his raindrop suit up, and without acknowledging any of us he uttered two words as one, "See-ya." He turned in towards the sunlight, thrust his hands deeper into empty trouser pockets, and walked off in the direction of Factory Lane.

Benny came up to me. "You won't see him again," he said, watching the figure move off away from us, and we never did. People talked like they do. Some said he topped himself by jumping in the water at the foot of the gasometer where a body would never have been discovered. Some said he moved to Brighton. Certainly Poppy and her little girls moved away and no word of explanation was ever uttered.

∽

puggy

Our home in Miller Road had a fireplace in which we were obliged to burn smokeless fuel. There was an irony to this, as all around us chimneys belched out a cocktail of obnoxious gases. From our front room window we could clearly see the main Croydon power station, a masterpiece of thirties brick architecture and a tribute to the skill of the old bricklayers. From our bedroom windows we could make out the chimneys of the B power station in Factory Lane.

Some Saturday mornings we would see a few kids coming back round the end of the road with prams full of coke. I asked the lads on the estate where they had bought it from, and they told me you could get it as a by-product of the power generation down on the Purley Way. We still had the wood barrow that Uncle Alf had made for us from our old pram, so the next week Bruce, Benny and I went down to get some fuel.

Whenever I see old Soviet Russian films glorifying industry, I think of this area of Croydon. All around us there was bustle and noise. At the bottom of our lane there were steam trains as well as electric services, and across Purley Way there were service steam engines delivering coal to the power station. As we walked down Factory Lane you could clearly see, through the shutters of the workshops, the gleaming turbines with polished copper pipes making energy. The hiss of the cooling towers and the constant flow of trucks delivering garbage to the corporation dump was punctuated by factory horns and hooters, whilst down the street boys revved and tuned old motorbikes and screamed up and down showing off their machines. It was all such a contrast to the sedate Waldrons.

As we entered the gates of the power station and headed to the coke dispensary, huge machinery clanked and thundered on either side of us, cranes dealt out huge quantities of coal and diggers pushed it into place. Steam hissed and everyone had to shout to be heard as they delivered their order. They had a minimum of what they would sell, so we had to ration our visits.

Once we had the hang of lighting the fire, we had warmth none of us had ever experienced before. Our new living rooms were half the size of the ones we had come from and we were all as snug as bugs in rugs. Our bedrooms were still cold and damp, however.

One day in conversation Benny told us about Puggy Mearns. Benny was like that, he would let you make a mistake before telling you that he had seen it coming, or let you go one way and then tell you the way that you should have gone. After you had paid so much a pound for apples, he would tell you where they were cheaper.

"Ol' Puggy Mearns sells coal an' that," he said one day out of the blue.

"Puggy?"

"Ol' Puggy Mearns sells coal an' 'e ain't got no eyes an' 'e's deaf as a post."

Benny chuckled mysteriously.

"What was his name again?" I asked and Benny repeated it several times before I could understand what he was saying. For all I knew he was making it up; Benny was the creator of many of the nicknames on the estate, like 'Shannybags'. But this part of Croydon used many words that I have not come across since, and I knew by now that to 'pug something up' or 'pug it away' meant to hide something. Could Puggy have something to do with hidden things, I wondered? Benny either failed to catch my drift or was deliberately unforthcoming.

"Is he cheaper than down at the power station?" I asked.

"About the same but it's worth it just to look at 'im. 'E's only got white eyes, no middle bits like we 'ave, an' 'e's got an ol' woman what 'e shouts at all the time an' 'e shouts at everybody an' it ain't 'alf scary an' 'e's black like the bleedin' coal an' all."

Benny had done it again. He took a huge interest in everything around him, and once again had whetted our appetites to see this character. Blind Puggy Mearns. He sounded like some character out of Robert Louis Stevenson.

In fact, Puggy Mearns turned out to be real. He had a coal yard down on the Mitcham Road. You entered by two wooden gates into a cobbled yard. In front of you was a giant heap of coal that spilled out from under a slate roof into a covered area, from where old Puggy Mearns served his reverential customers. I say reverential, because usually when we queued up for anything there was a lot of banter and small talk among the clientele, but not in Puggy's yard.

I took my place at the back of the small line of people, and soon someone joined on the back of me, and to the background sounds of a shovel being scraped across cobbles and its contents being dropped into a metal pan, we slowly moved forward. As we neared the front of the queue I noticed that Benny was getting quite excited as he guessed what my reaction might be, and I could hear him trying to suppress nervous laughter. Every now and then I could hear an old, but not frail, voice bellow out, "That's a pahnd ain't it?" or "That's a ten bob right?"

We turned the corner and I could see the form of the old man as he bent to shovel up another load. By now I was bursting with curiosity to see what he looked like. From the back he seemed to be about five foot six. He had on the remains of an old suit jacket, and his ancient trousers were tucked into an enormous pair of wellington boots. On his head he wore a coalman's peaked cap, with a flap down the back to prevent the dust from going down his neck. He swung the shovel away from my direction on to an old scale, and to check if he had the right weight he touched the scoop with a black grimy hand to see if it was level.

As his customer handed him a note, Puggy Mearns leaned forward in the direction of the donor and bellowed, "It's a pahnd ain't it?"

"Yes," answered the customer.

"EH!?"

"Yes it's a pound," repeated the customer, a little louder.

"Go on then," said Puggy Mearns, "she'll give you yer change," and he motioned with his head in the direction of an old woman who sat at a small table with a cash box on it.

The sight of her made me jump and do a double take. She was as dirty as the old man and covered with a film of coal dust. Her fingers and nails were black and her skin was pale and grey. As she doled out the change her husband pocketed the pound note and this seemed to be their way of handling the money: if you paid in coins you gave it to the old girl and if you paid with paper you gave it to the old man.

I shuffled forward a few feet, unable to wrest my gaze from the old lady. She reminded me of someone from my past and I couldn't think who it was. I turned back to express my incredulity at her appearance to Benny and as I did so I looked up to where Puggy Mearns had come into my eye line. In spite of all that Benny had said, I was not prepared for the sight that stood in front of me.

Puggy had swung around to confront his next customer.

"Yus?" he barked and I stood frozen to the spot.

There almost in front of me was the most terrifying individual I had ever clapped eyes on. He must have been all of eighty years old and weighed about ten stone. In spite of the coal dust, there was enough hair showing to indicate that whatever he had under the hat ought to have been white. His skin was pallid, with all the larger pores completely filled in with black. Around his mouth was coal dust set like mascara round an eyelid closed on an empty socket, for he had not a tooth in his head.

But his eyes, oh Christ, his eyes were awful. They were both completely covered by cataract. Each eye was as if someone had placed a sixpence in a saucer and poured a little milk over it. Just below the surface two pale irises, now as grey as the rest of his skin, stared unblinking and unseeing into the gloom of his shed from the sockets in his head. The dust had long since ceased to irritate the skin and there was no trace of redness to show any inflammation, whilst settled into the corner of each orb was a lump of coal grit big enough to throw on a fire.

Suddenly it was my turn to address him as I wheeled the old barrow up to the scales.

"Yus?" barked Puggy Mearns.

I don't know if it was terror that made me respond the way I did, or fear of being shouted at again. I was almost as tall as the old man and my wide eyes had not left his sightless ones. I leaned toward where his ear should have been and to my horror I saw that under his cap there was just a hole that led down some sooty passage into his head. As I recoiled from the orifice I hardly recognised the sound that came from my lips in a sort of strangulated yell.

"Half hundredweight of coal!" I screamed, and as a polite afterthought, "please!"

The old man bent to his task without a flinch. Amongst the acrid smell of accumulated coal dust there was also the faint smell of urine. I stood back to allow him to expertly balance the scale and handed him the ten shilling note.

"Ten bob ain't it?" he bellowed.

"Yus!" I yelled back.

"She'll give you your change." He motioned to the old girl as he pocketed the note. As I wheeled the old barrow over to her I recognised her as the witch that jumped out of the wardrobe at me when we lived at The Waldrons, and a shiver went down my back as her cold grey hand plonked out the silver change.

"What'cha say?" hollered old Puggy Mearns at his next terrified customer. "Speak up why can't yer speak up like that last bloke what's the matter wiv everyone these days. You have to shout or I can't 'ear a bleedin' word. What'cha want?"

Once again the two sightless orbs instinctively rolled upwards as if to seek divine explanation.

As Benny and I wheeled the barrow out of the yard and into the thin sunshine outside, we grinned at each other. I couldn't think of anything to say for a while; it was like some miraculous escape from hell for me.

I kept thinking of old Puggy Mearns and his wife climbing out of their dusty bed from under their black sheets, eating crushed coal nuts instead of corn flakes off dusty plates, sprinkling coal dust on everything before they ate. I wondered if they ever bathed, or perhaps like summer birds they had dust baths and then sprinkled coal dust in places usually reserved for talcum powder. Had they ever made love? Perhaps they 'smoked' in bed! When he blew off perhaps he blew smoke rings from his bottom. How did he lose his teeth? Where did his ear go?

We had crossed the Mitcham Road before I could say anything at all, and then all I could manage was, "They were both filthy," and then, "those horrible eyes and no teeth."

"I bet 'e sucks raw eggs," said Benny inexplicably.

"I wonder what his sheets look like?"

"I wonder what 'is underpants look like?" said Benny, and we both guffawed.

"An' I wonder what 'er pants bleedin' look like?" said Benny, and suddenly we both wanted to change the subject.

"I suppose it doesn't matter to him if it's day or night," I thought out loud, "he can shovel away by moonlight and he wouldn't know. I wonder if he was always blind. Do you think he knows what she looks like?"

"I bet 'e don't know about washin' 'isself. An' she ain't goin' to tell 'im is she, 'cos that way the old girl don't need to go down the bag wash an' she saves money."

"Maybe he has a bath in the summer when the people don't need coal."

"Yeah," said Benny.

We rounded the corner into Miller Road.

"I told you 'e was bleedin' scary didn' I?" said Benny.

"Yeah, he certainly was horrible," I answered. "He wasn't stupid though. I mean he kept all the money didn't he?"

"Yeah," pondered Benny.

"Next time we'll take Bruce to see him."

"Yeah," said Benny as he peeled off to his house.

"See you."

"S-s-s-see ya," said Benny.

❧

old puggy mearns

Old Puggy Mearns was born in a coal mine
Damp dark noise level
Holler and shout
North south east
Without a pick or shovel
His teeth went west when he gnawed his way out

Old Puggy Mearns works in the coal hole
Cobble clatter shovel splatter
All night long
Sunshine moonlight
It really doesn't matter
If you can't see the present and the past's all gone

Old Puggy Mearns had a dad who was a sewer rat
Slimy slithery
His mother was a mole
Great big hands
With skin all leathery
Handy sort of grabs when you're shovelling coal

Old Puggy Mearns never has his klobbah washed
Squeak squelch rustle bustle
Smelly old clothes
When he sits down
Little clouds of dust'll
Rise from his collar and vanish up his nose

Old Puggy Mearns if you ever tried to bath him
Slop slurp fizz bubble
He's bound to have a fit
Wright's coal tar
Wouldn't get you out of trouble
Blocking up the plughole with his sludge and grit

Old Puggy Mearns has never ate an apple yet
Sucks on a lump of coal
Before he starts
Coal dust breakfast
Coke in the sugar bowl
Breath like an ashtray and smoky old farts

Old Puggy Mearns has got a dirty old woman
Sits in the corner
Smells like the drains
She has to look at him
He's never seen her
He keeps the pound notes she gives the change

Old Puggy Mearns ain't got a proper ear
Waxed up sooty little
Hole in his head
Deaf as a slag heap
Oil black dribble spittle
Burn him in the fireplace when he's dead

facts

The effects of such episodes as Mr. Harvey's abuse in our last year at Howard Junior School are somewhat ameliorated by the realisation that there are girls in the world, and by the age of eleven I had been in sort of love with a dozen or so. It was usually centred on one particular feature that the girl possessed: her lips, her eyes or maybe her hair; the way she laughed or appeared not to notice me; her brashness or shyness. Or her changing shape.

Allison Rees had breasts at the age of ten, and by the time I left Howard School many of the girls were, as it were, sprouting. I asked the worldly-wise Chick Edgerton about girls changing shape as he had a sister, and somehow we got on to the subject of Miss Collet, who was very glamorous by our school's standards. She was young and very pretty, often wearing red which contrasted beautifully with her shortish blonde hair and dark brown eyes. She had the most pointed breasts we had ever seen, the points pricking provocatively at her red sweater.

Chick explained, "That's because she's got braziers *(sic)*." He wasn't sure exactly what they were but explained that they were principally invented for skiing. I have pondered this statement many times over the years and have come to the conclusion that her shape must have confused him and perhaps he was thinking of the Dolomites.

Originally I'd been offered a place at Archbishop Tennyson School, a secondary selective, and after my initial disappointment at not making it through to grammar school, I was content within myself that I would be able to handle what I supposed might be an easier level of work. This easing of the pressure meant that I passed the eleven-plus exam and Mum duly gave me the watch she had been given for passing the equivalent exam twenty-eight years earlier. I was extremely proud of the watch, although I did think after a while that it might have been more masculine in appearance.

When the letter came telling me that I had been awarded a place at John Ruskin Grammar School I was both thrilled and apprehensive.

One of the worst aspects for me in going there was the thought that there would be no girls at the school. I had to be content with dopey daydreams about pretty girls on the bus on their way to schools further up the road from our own.

It was in the first year at John Ruskin that I first heard the expression 'facts of life'. I became intrigued because amongst some kids these words always produced nudges and sly smiles. What did they know that I didn't?

One of the other schools in Croydon had decided to tell its pupils about the Facts, and I searched out one of the kids and asked him what they were. I don't think he properly understood or was really interested, and he just answered that it was "where babies are made." I suddenly realised that I had no idea how where or why babies were made—I just assumed that when you are married they arrived in due course. Some people were unable to have them because the lady had something wrong with her, and sometimes a lady had babies without being married because she had loved someone very much and it had happened without them getting married. I guess that was the closest I came to understanding.

I talked about it to my friends that had come up with me from Howard School: Vernon Burford, Michael Schwartz and Andrew Smith, but they could throw no light on the matter.

Help was at hand from an older boy called Cook. This lad was in the third year and was part of a pack of kids who were always grabbing other boys by the genitals. He befriended some of the first year boys; perhaps he was attracted to them in some way. He never interfered with them and seemed quite a kind and caring boy to me. He made it his business to tell Michael Schwartz the whole story, and although we got all the technical information second-hand from Michael, it was pretty close to correct. On the way home on the bus that evening Michael told us the Facts.

I sat there open-mouthed. I was shocked, fascinated, sickened, excited, and had to say that I could not believe it. As the story unfolded, I found myself thinking about all the people I knew and tried to imagine them making love. It didn't add up. Try as I might, the thought of my grandparents doing it or my uncles and aunts was impossible to picture. I started to run through images of people in my street and the same incredulity hit me. Then I thought of some of the girls at school and got a funny feeling. I thought of Brigitte Bardot and hoped that it might be true, and then I had to change the subject or at least try to make us all laugh.

"It can't be true," I said. "Can you imagine my mum doing that?"

"Can you imagine *my* mum doing that?" asked Vernon, whose mum was a lot older than ours and almost crippled. None of us could possibly imagine Vernon's mum allowing anyone to do that to her.

"Well can you imagine my mum or dad doing it either?" asked Michael Schwartz and suddenly we all fell silent, because that's exactly what we could imagine Michael Schwartz's parents doing.

After a couple of seconds of non-confirmation from any of us Michael asked us, "What are you all thinking?"

Suddenly I burst out laughing and said, "What if it's true?"

We looked around the bus at the passengers. and began asking each other, "Do you think she does it? Do you think he does it? I bet he's never done it."

A fat man got on and we all said, "He couldn't do it even if he wanted to!"

Next morning as usual I saw Michael Schwartz on the bus with Andrew, and the look on Michael's face confirmed it.

"It's true," he said.

I looked at Andrew and Andrew nodded.

"My dad says that you do it on your honeymoon, and at first you don't but then you start to think that you would like to, and then you do it and it is a gift from God."

I started to think of Andrew's mother and father and I just could not picture them doing it. Then I thought of my own parents and I could sort of see my dad doing it but not my mum, and then I thought of Mr. and

Mrs. Schwartz doing it.

And then a pretty girl got on the bus and I *knew* that was how it was done.

Suddenly I understood why people tut-tutted when a girl had a baby when she was not married, and wondered where I might find one who might do it. What did it feel like to do it? All the films and jokes that were half understood before, I understood more fully and then another girl got on the bus and I wondered if she did it.

Derek Lester's sister was having a baby and she was only fifteen. So she'd done it!

I suppose most of my childhood ended right there on the 130 bus to New Addington.

In 1957 I had reached class 3U, which was the cramming stream for university entrance. It hadn't taken long to work out that I wasn't going to make the grade, and I'd decided to discharge myself. The only really surprising thing was that I had the courage to do it without consulting anyone. I just walked into the headmaster's office after break one morning and told him I had to leave, as I couldn't stand the pace of work or the commitment to the extra load that we were expected to cope with each evening.

The headmaster's name was Lowe and he reminded me a little of my Granddad in appearance; he was a dapper man with an air of calm authority. I suppose he could see the anxiety in my eyes, because he treated me very kindly as I told him my story; he even went so far as to tell me that I shouldn't have been put in the university stream as my second exam results were not quite up to it—I had come eleventh in my first exam and seventeenth in my second. I was a bit put out at this news, but soon realised it would soften the blow when I had to tell Mum.

Mr. Lowe asked me what I wanted to do when I left school, and without a hint of embarrassment I replied that I would like to be a missionary. He was taken aback slightly by this, as even in 1957 there was not much call for these people—at least not in the way that I saw the job. I had always been keen on religion, but at this time I was in the midst of a religious fervour: I'd joined the Scripture Union where I had to read the bible every day, and on Sundays, as described earlier, I was rushing around Croydon between Mint Walk Mission, Sunday School and St. Andrews Church Choir.

On top of this, my voices hadn't yet stopped, and above my bed at home I had assembled a number of religious artefacts including texts, pictures of Jesus, a crucifix and some beads—not altogether with my mother's approval, as she thought it smacked of Catholicism. I used to lie in bed and pray great long rambling prayers, which gave me comfort in my insecurity and darker moments.

Mr. Lowe handled my surprising answer with aplomb.

"Are you good at Latin?" he asked.

"Yes sir," I answered. I was indeed top of the form in that subject.

"Well, that should come in handy," he responded as he groped (and failed) for something further to say.

The result of the interview was that I was transferred down to form 2W.

Standing there nervously in front of the head, I was painfully aware of my distressed—as in, poor but honest—appearance. The first brand new clothes I'd ever had in my life should have been my school uniform, and I recall Mum sitting there in our damp basement looking at the list of items that we were supposed to buy from Horne's on Lower Crown Hill, and almost crying because there was no way we had money for any of that stuff. I wished I'd never passed the exam and was feeling thoroughly miserable and a little angry that the school would send this to someone like us.

Thankfully help was at hand, for at the bottom of the page was a list of part-worn items that were offered to help poor families like ours. When I entered the headmaster's office I was still wearing the same (secondhand) jacket I'd had in the first year; the badge which Mum had sewn on was now grey in the white bits between the shield, under which was written "Age Quod Agis"; and I was still squeezed into one of the two drip-dry shirts that we had bought to start my grammar school career. My shoes were a slightly more elaborate Teddy boy style than was properly sanctioned, and my trousers, well, they had a story all of their own…

When we lived at The Waldrons, the top floor flat was occupied by Mr. and Mrs. Clarke. Mrs. Clarke was the married sister of the Miss Dickinsons, who lived below her. She had congratulated me warmly when she'd heard that I passed the eleven-plus exam, and it was she that gave me the trousers, my first pair of long trousers. They had belonged to her only son, who had been killed in the war as a navigator in a bomber plane. As she handed them over to my mother with this tale she burst into tears, and my mum said how much we appreciated the gift and that I would treasure them.

I was very moved by this experience. A boy's first long trousers are an important moment in his life; they are an affirmation of approaching manhood and a celebration of his departure from childhood. Mine, however, were an artefact of a dead eighteen-year-old hero and when I wore them I was conscious of bearing the mantle of his sacrifice. Although they were styled in the Oxford bag style of the thirties, made from the itchiest flannel known to man and were two inches too short for me, I had a duty to wear them. After all, what was my discomfort and embarrassment compared to his sacrifice? Mum had got round the problem of length by sewing false turnups into the bottoms, which she assured me no-one would ever notice. This assertion however proved false as they were noted by some bully the first day I wore them.

"What are you wearing brat?" he shouted. All first years were called "brats" and this was encouraged to some extent by a few teachers.

"They're my false turnups," I replied helpfully.

"False Turnups!" the bully exploded. "Oi come and look at this fellas! The brat's wearing False Turnups in his trousers, let's de-bag him!"

Fortunately for me the bell went for the end of break and I was spared the humiliation of having my pants pulled down by these older boys. I made a note of this particular one anyway, and some time later I sorted him out, which took a good deal of bravery on my part. I lived in fear of retribution for a whole term, but like most bullies he didn't bother me after I had faced up to him.

After I'd successfully negotiated myself down from form 3U to 2W, our school year decided to have a party, and our kindly form master Percy Wright asked us all if we could contribute a 'turn' or two for the entertainment. Enquiries amongst my contemporaries revealed that several boys in my class could or would play if we could get it together, so we formed a skiffle group, with Chris Ricketts and Derek Roach on uke and ukulele banjo and someone I've forgotten on tea chest bass. We submitted our idea to Mr. Wright, and he demanded an audition in his physics lab after school.

We were all as nervous as could be as he perched himself on the lab desk and told us to commence. I am sure he was astonished at the volume we managed, but we certainly swung and he coloured up and was unable to stave off a grin although he tried turning toward the blackboard so that we should not see it. After racing through our first number he stopped us halfway through *Oh Boy* with a wave of his hand, and we waited until he said, "OK you can play," and then quietly, "Well done, boys. Go along then May, and take your band of tub thumpers with you."

We might as well have been handed a record contract, we felt so good. We met after school for smokes and rehearsal at Derek's place, where his father was warden of what was then known as a spastic centre. We had a great time practising and wheelchair racing; there were extensive grounds and even a tennis court (though I didn't play); and all the time Mr. Roach was keeping a weather eye on us and telling us about his cycle racing days, when racing bikes were fitted with wooden rims. He was a very kind man and he shared his Capstan Full Strength cigarettes with us. It was a matter of young male pride to smoke these fearsome tar-laden monsters without hiccuping or coughing, which we did. These days on Oakhill Road were some of the happiest at school for me.

The concert arrived, and although the other kids had to wear school uniform, we were allowed to dress more informally. With our plinky plonky sound, we were the undoubted hit of the evening. It was a wonderful feeling seeing our pals gyrating to our music, especially as we were standing on the same stage in the school hall from which our headmaster delivered his warnings, speeches, sermons and exhortations. We only played five tunes, but the evening belonged to us.

The next day it was back to normal and this would-be heartthrob was falling in love with another girl on top of the 130 bus to New Addington...

Tom Shaw joined form 2W shortly after I did. From the moment he walked into the class he stood out, with his almost film star good looks and his school badge sewn on to a double-breasted jacket. His hair did what he wanted it to do and he was already shaving at least part of his face. Tom was a year older than the rest of us. He had recently returned from America and spoke to no-one, which just added to his air of cool. He was seated in the desk in front of me and I was determined to make him my friend.

With his fingers deeply ingrained with nicotine from his American Chesterfield cigarettes, he was drawn into the smokers' group comprising Les, Vernon and myself, and was the first boy I'd seen who could gently expel the smoke from his lips and inhale it gracefully up both nostrils. Tom didn't just inhale the smoke, he almost ate it. Each time he lit up he seemed to find a new trick to convey his deep satisfaction with the habit. Tom was an elegant smoker; each time he took out a cigarette he tapped it on the flat side of the box, so that a tiny rim of paper could be turned in to prevent strands of tobacco getting stuck on his lip.

He had a Ronson Variflame gas lighter which had a perfectly measured flame and always lit first time. On a still evening behind the bike sheds he could produce beautiful large smoke rings, and indoors he would make tiny rings by tapping his cheek gently with his finger. He would flick the ash off his cigarette any number of different ways, from gently removing it with his little finger or thumbnail to tapping lightly on the top of its length. Just before throwing it away he would sometimes grip the end between his bottom teeth and his lower lip and turn it into his mouth whilst the thing was still alight.

Tom's mother allowed him to smoke at home, and as if all this was not exotic enough, she was a divorcee. Divorce still carried a racy image in those days, and a bit of a stigma. Most unhappy couples just rubbed along in misery or, as in our family, one of the partners left home. The implication of divorce was adultery and this was quite exciting. The only other divorced person I had known was Mrs. Leisk but she could not be described as exotic, and anyway she had divorced her husband for his affair. I always wondered if it was Mrs. Shaw's own affair which caused them to part.

Tom's accent had no trace of Stateside twang, but there was a sophistication about him that went beyond his one year seniority, and maybe because of our similar parental circumstances we were soon good friends and joined the school army cadet force together. Neither of us had any interest at school outside of the army cadets but we did share a sense of humour. It was not long before Tom stayed over at my house and my mother, who found him very handsome, used to give him tea and put him up on the sofa. In those days all mums were addressed as "Mrs. —" and Tom was very polite and charming, which impressed my mother. It was a long time before I met Mrs. Shaw.

One day Tom's elder brother Roy, who was a young officer in the merchant navy, returned from sea and gave Tom a present that totally confirmed Tom's superiority. Somewhere in his travels Roy had acquired the first transistor radio that we had ever seen. By today's standards it was quite large, but in 1957 it seemed minute—battery-powered radios at that time were the size of small suitcases. As the kids gathered round to marvel at this gadget in the playground an idea was forming in my head.

It has to be said that form 2W was beginning to get a reputation (confirmed the following year in form 3D) of being one of the worst behaved classes in the school. I would prefer it to be described as mischievous, and the challenge we set ourselves—and I was one of the prime movers—was to make our misdemeanours as subtle as possible.

We were genuinely fond of many of the teachers we were able to fool. Mr. Neal was a very dark-haired man who dressed in a comfortable tweed jacket and corduroy trousers. He took the class for English and he had a warm mellifluous voice that often nearly lulled me to sleep. We decided it was to be him who would be amazed by this little wonder.

Our classrooms were quite modern and the blackboard occupied most of the wall we faced. To the right of the board was a switch which controlled the three radio stations on the BBC, with the loudspeaker high up on the wall. It was a bright morning as Mr. Neal breezed into the room, his gown flowing behind him.

"Good morning boys!" he said with that mixture of authority and confidence that today he was going to get through the lesson without it descending into noise and anarchy.

"Good morning sir," we chirped with unusual enthusiasm. He looked up suspiciously, alerted to the change from our usual desultory response, and I thought I could see just a hint of optimism that perhaps we had decided enough was enough and that we were all going to start to work like grammar school boys were supposed to. He turned and began to write something on the blackboard about clause analysis.

Tom switched on his radio at a very low volume so that you could just hear the sibilant sounds of voices through the tiny speaker. The class was eerily quiet as we waited to see the teacher's reaction. As his handwriting moved over to the right hand side of the board he put down the chalk, reached over to the radio switch and turned it one click. Tom responded immediately by synchronising his off switch at the same time and the tinny noise stopped. No sooner was Mr. Neal back writing when on came the radio again.

"Somebody turn that thing off," said our teacher, and one of the boys got up and walked to the switch and pretended to turn it off. The pattern was set, and no sooner was the teacher's back turned than on came the radio. I still don't know if he had sussed exactly what was going on, but he must have been a little suspicious at the absence of talking, as we all strained in the quiet to enjoy his bafflement at the sounds which he presumed were coming from the speaker on the wall. Once the class work was set he sat down and looked at us all and especially those he knew to be ringleaders, but we buried our heads in our work—as much to disguise our sniggering as to avoid his search. Now the radio began its journey around the room being switched on and off by fingers under desks. The effect was perfect, and Mr. Neal duly obliged with all the range of expressions we would have asked for.

Annoyance gave way to curiosity, and when he asked plaintively, "Does it appear to anyone else that the sound is coming from all four corners of the room?", it was all too much for Les at the back who just exploded into one of his deep guffaws, and that started us all off.

"Just what is going on?" asked Mr. Neal as he stood up and wandered round the room with the radio following behind him, being passed from hand to hand and switched on and off in an aural game of hide and seek. Finally he swung round in the right direction just in time to catch Tom receiving the radio. He pounced and took it from him.

"What on earth is this?" he said in genuine astonishment, and instead of being angry he was totally amazed at the technology behind the prank. He could have confiscated it, but instead he asked to borrow it to take to the staffroom during the break.

Shortly after this incident Tom took me to his place, where I met his mother. She and Tom lived in an upstairs privately rented flat on the London Road in Norbury. Inside it was quite chaotic and I seldom stayed overnight there.

Mrs. Shaw had more than one man friend, and although Tom never talked about it I knew that he was a little embarrassed by her. I was intrigued because Mrs. Shaw was completely different to my mother. She was small, though putting on a little weight, and she wore glasses with thick black rims. She never cooked anything, but she liked a drink, and she also liked men. My mum, on the other hand, cooked, hated drink and hardly ever went out with blokes—my brother and I only wished she would.

Tom's mum was a bit coy the first few times we called round, but she soon accepted my visits and didn't try to put on any airs, with her eyes swollen with sleep, a cigarette in her mouth and that sexy early morning rasp in the voice. She had a strong Liverpool accent and spoke in a whiny, sing-song sort of way. She wore a smart suit to work, but at home I never saw her wearing anything other than her nightie, and her thick black hair was always mussed up by sleep, or lack of it. She had an unmerciful cough and smoked all the time, and was often very seriously hung over when we made our late morning calls round at the flat.

Her latest beau was called Arthur. Working-class and worldly wise, he was smartly turned out in a way that suggested that, though he might not be actually involved in crime, he would definitely know a few strokes. He always wore a bow tie and his sideboards were longer than they ought to have been for a man in his late forties.

Mrs. Shaw was always saying that she was going to throw him out or chuck him in, but the truth is that Arthur kept her laughing, and although they were too old to be sexually exciting to a teenage boy, it was titillating to know that they were in a relationship for the pure fun of company, drink and sex, as opposed to the worthy obligation of keeping a home together solely for the purpose of raising children. Or living my mum's seemingly joyless, husbandless existence as she worked to feed us and dutifully see us through into the world.

Arthur belonged to a breed that I am not aware of any more. There was no doubt that he had been a bit of a lad in his time but he was sort of settled in his ways now although he'd never married. He might have admired younger women but one suspected he was perfectly happy with older ones, who were grateful for his attentions and made very few demands on his time.

They were an odd couple. Tom's mother would have been described as a handsome woman in Victorian times. From her appearance—the black hair and eyes, a slightly aquiline nose and full lips—I guessed that her origins were Mediterranean. Arthur looked so English as to be a caricature of one of the betting fraternity, with a centre parting, blazer and slacks. He smoked Senior Service and always obliged us two thirteen-year-olds with smokes, and if he was waiting for Mrs. Shaw to go out he would talk to us about some of his escapades. I found these stories hilarious and daring, although I guess that Tom felt he might be trying to win him over by being nice. I didn't hear it as being patronising, as even at that young age I had seen enough to know that Arthur had absolutely no intention of ever getting permanently hitched to Tom's mum.

～

ice

Mrs. Shaw was the catering manageress at Streatham Ice Rink. Her office was upstairs in the far right corner of the ballroom that most people attending the rink did not know existed. Behind this door was the catering area, and in the corner of this room was her inner sanctum, where she had access to a safe and a strongly locked cupboard where the spirits and cigarettes were stored. I often found myself staring longingly at the cupboard.

"It's a good job you haven't got X-ray eyes, Ralph. You'd burn your way right through that padlock," she would say to me. It was to this office that Tom and I were summoned one day, and Mrs. Shaw offered us both a job.

"We need some help clearing up the cups down on the rink," she said, "and there's some washing up and general cleaning in the kitchen there too, and there might be some weekend work doing weddings up here if all goes well. It'll pay ten shillings for Wednesday evenings and a pound for all day Saturday. And you can start this Saturday."

It must have taken me a hundredth of a second to say yes, but Tom strangely declined. I suppose it was the idea of being under his mum again, but that didn't bother me and I jumped at the opportunity.

"You are a lazy bugger, Tom," she moaned as she led us downstairs to the rear of the rink to meet Alice the tea lady.

I liked Alice immediately. She deferred madly to Mrs. Shaw, screwing up her eyes and smiling ingratiatingly, but she had her pride all right. Slight and wiry, though stooped, with her hair parted neatly on the side and a kind of Esme Cannon twitter, she took tiny quick steps wherever she went, like someone who not only knows where they are going, but wants to get there quickly and get on with the next thing even quicker.

Alice worked in a continuum, each action leading to another. Even when it was time for a fag she would pick up a rag and start wiping the metal surfaces down, whilst running a bucket of water for me to wash down the floors—which we had to do at least once every skating session.

On weekdays outside of school holiday times she managed the tea bar on her own, but she was glad of my help and I was very happy working with her. She was one of the sweetest ladies I've ever worked with. Alice's patience was extraordinary as she taught me how to mop and wash floors properly, how to make the tea in the big pots and stack the shelves with bottles.

I learned how to carry crates of Pepsi-Cola by squeezing four bottles in two hands so that the bottles themselves gripped the wooden partitions that prevented them breaking against each other, and was soon able to stack them ten high using this method just like the delivery men. I loaded the fag machines and took out the empties and collected tea cups from all round the rink, and if it was quiet (which it seldom was) she would tell me to go for a skate. I even got quite proficient, given the horrendous condition of the wobbly-sided hacked-out things that passed for figure skates there.

I have loved skating rinks ever since those days, I think because they are romantic places for kids. There is a sense of fun, danger and sex in the freezing air, and flushed faces as kids learn the art of display and flirting, intrigues and spills. I quickly became aware of the culture of the rink and the wonderful diversity of characters there. Since moving from the comparative gentility of The Waldrons I had met some rough and ready people and was fast becoming a young man. Those closest around you hardly notice the changes going on, but as I entered the rink, I was fair game to the old girls at the tea bar. I was still taken aback, however, by old Mary and 'young' Margaret.

Mary was five foot tall and weighed about seventeen stone. She must have been in her early to mid sixties. Her grey hair was probably quite long, but as soon as she had married she'd rolled it up in a loose bun to be practical, and there it remained. To denote rank she wore a blue and white striped overall with a whitish apron. Alice only ever wore white as did I, a usually ragged but clean starched jacket. Old Beatrice, the washer-up, wore menial green.

Beattie, as she was always known, could have passed for Alice's mother. She was about the same stature as Alice but even more stooped, and had one of those London accents that have all but disappeared. Sometimes you can hear it on old music hall artists' recordings of comic songs. The 'r' is rolled and the accent is far more animated than now. It was the only thing that was animated about Beattie; she moved incredibly slowly, but the other women liked her and probably kept her with them out of kindness. I think Beattie must have had the prototype National Health false teeth: they were as white as snow with bright red gums, and as she spoke there was a constant battle to keep them in place.

Because of the general jollity of the place there were a lot of smiles, and this too was a hazard for Beattie: several times I saw the top set fly out of her mouth into the washing up water, as something Mary or Alice had said made her chuckle. There would then follow a fairly frantic search among the cups and saucers before that which was lost was found, rinsed and returned, rejoicing, to join the other ill-fitting bottom row. It was a good job the punters didn't know.

Beattie was occasionally short with me, and when angry it sounded as if she had a marble clattering around in her mouth, as she battled to keep both sets in place whilst still sounding stern enough in her rebuke. Lip-reading would have been out of the question as her lips had become prehensile and were able to grasp under and over the two sets of teeth to stop them leaving her mouth altogether. Beattie would not have looked out of place in a hospital bed. She wore slippers and hardly ever came out of her still room area, except when I would bring her a cup of tea. She would pick it up and sip it then without a word walk over to the urn and tip it away and proceed to make a fresh pot.

"Never give a worker a stewed cuppa char," she would intone wisely.

Later Mary showed me how to make an individual cup of tea without a pot, for when one of the big bosses came down: take a big tea strainer and fill it up with tea, slowly dribble boiling water through the leaves so that the tea brews as it goes into the cup, then add just enough milk to get it to the right colour.

From then on that's how I did Beattie's tea, and I think by the end she liked me, though she never got my name right, either deliberately or because she thought Ralph was too posh. I was sometimes Alf, and when it suited her the odd compromise Rilf was used.

Mary also always wore carpet slippers for work, with thick brown stockings. She had a huge bosom that she used to wave her hand in front of to show if she was working too hard, and she called everyone "darlin'". Mary was unwilling or unable to walk at anything faster than a slow sauntering shuffle, like Indian ladies in saris in summer, although she still made a slight breeze when she moved past you because of her density.

Mary's favourite adjective was "bleedin'" and away from the customers' ears she used it a lot. Mary had a great sense of humour and a sense of irony to go with it. She also learned very early on that it was easy to make me blush especially where sexual matters were concerned, and she never let an opportunity go by without trying it on.

"What's that in your pocket, darlin'?" she might say.

I would look down in all innocence and reply, "Nothing, why?"

"I thought you was trying to steal a bottle of Pepsi."

"Now come on Mary," I would say, "you know I wouldn't take anything without asking."

"Well what's that long thing I can see in your trousers? Perhaps it's a tube of Smarties. Let me have a feel to see if you're tellin' the truth."

By now of course I had sussed what was going on, and so had the others. Old Beattie would just grin and tut-tut, shaking her head without looking round, but Alice would giggle and put her hand to her mouth and give Mary a playful slap and tell her she was awful. If Mary saw me so much as put my hand in my pocket she would enquire after my 'thing'. I was a source of amusement to the old girls, but Margaret was a different matter.

Margaret was the sub-manageress in the tea bar and upstairs bar; she was unhappily married and always dressed to kill, with loads of make-up on. She was a tough south London girl in her early forties, and her only blemish was that she had lost a leg in a motorcycle accident when still a young girl.

The leg had been amputated just above the knee, but by wearing a skirt that was a little longer than fashionable, she was able to disguise it until she had to walk any distance. The knee joint was operated by throwing her leg forward which, even when she was trying to be sexy, gave her a rather too military gait for most of her intended prey. However, Albie the dustman found her the most attractive woman in the world, and though I never actually saw him skate, he never missed showing up at any session that she was on.

I could see that Margaret had no intention of ever running away from her marriage, and though she often feigned irritability with Albie always hanging about, in reality she loved it. Albie was about twenty-eight and not terribly bright; his face had the appearance of being crushed in the tube train doors, as his features were sort of pushed together, but bone and muscle had got in the way and this had forced his eyes to jockey for position on his face. It resulted in a slightly crooked smile and eyes at different heights. The overall effect was that he looked both dangerous and puzzled at the same time.

Albie was still a Teddy boy; he wore a drape jacket and chukka boots, and his hair was his crowning glory in an elaborate Tony Curtis style. Once I had shown the proper respect and awe for him, he trusted me and I found him to be a simple but honourable friend. Albie was totally besotted by Margaret and he saw no imperfection even in her purposeful walk. Sometimes they would go for a drink together, but Albie wasn't really a drinker—he would have gone anywhere just to be near her. Drink helped Margaret to sin a little.

Mary was always telling Margaret she should oblige him, but somehow Margaret kept him at bay with hints and teases that he must have loved, for he stayed true to her all the time that I knew them both.

Mary also told Margaret that I was fair game and at fourteen quite a big boy for my age. To them I must have had 'innocent' written in huge letters across my forehead. Margaret joined in the fun, especially on Friday or Saturday nights when she often went up to the licensed bar and had just a little too much. She would come down to the tea bar looking a little flushed and send for me in the kitchen, then ask me to reach some item on the shelf behind her. As I raised my arm she would deliberately press herself up against me or let the back of her hand brush against my trousers, which always made me jump. This was a cause of much merriment as I fumbled or dropped whatever I was supposed to get down for her.

Another favourite stunt was to wait until I was on my hands and knees loading up shelves with bottles of Pepsi or lemonade and step over me so that my head was practically inside her skirt. For some reason this amused them the most, and whilst I was there, not daring to move in case I should see where Margaret's stump fitted into her false leg, they all believed I was scared to look up any further for other reasons. I suppose they were partly right, but my biggest fear was that Albie might see her doing this and kill me in a jealous rage. Margaret was delighted with the results of these little scenes and it didn't really trouble me, but I did wish I could control my blushes (which were the principal reason she played these games).

She and Mary were always thinking up new games for me to fall for. When Mary wanted me to mop the floors she would say, "Now darlin', go and get your big long thing and bring it out here!"

The mop lived in a special type of bucket which had a grille welded to the side that you could press the head on to squeeze the water out of the fibres. When I had filled it with water and bleach and brought it out to begin washing, she would instruct me thus:

"Now take your long thing and dip it into that hole [the open side of the bucket]. Now push it in and out slowly—not too quick or you'll spill all your stuff over the floor. That's right, in and out, ooh ain't he got a lovely twirl on that long thing of his."

Another time Mary asked me to go to the fridge and get the ham out to be cut. With no reason to expect anything unusual I opened the big wooden door and moved to pull out the ham. The sight that greeted me took me by surprise for at first I had no idea what I was supposed to be looking at. There in front of me sat two hams turned on their sides and stuck between the two was a Pepsi bottle. I turned round to look behind me where Margaret, Mary, reluctant Alice and old Beattie stood for a second as they burst out laughing, and then it dawned on me that this was an erotic catering sculpture of Pepsi penetration of female genitalia. As the back of my neck went a deep red so their merriment increased. I was rooted to the spot until Alice walked over to the fridge and, reaching over my shoulder, pulled out the bottle. Beattie's teeth had remained in place but Mary was crying with laughter and so was Margaret. For me it was embarrassing but in a strange way liberating. I wondered with trepidation if it really looked like that.

Some time afterward the first wedding reception took place at the upstairs ballroom overlooking the front of the rink. It was a big do, with a sit down dinner before all the speeches. I was waiting at table, wearing a really good white coat and black cavalry twill trousers with black suede shoes. I was absolutely fascinated by the whole event; everyone was happy and jolly and all the catering staff came out to look at the couple as they sat eating their wedding supper. After the usual remarks about how pretty the bride looked and how handsome the groom, one of the waitresses remarked how well they were all tucking in to the food and drink, and Mary remarked, "Well I hope she saves some room because she'll be chewing on something else later!"

This remark brought peals of laughter from several of the women around but only bewilderment from me. What could it mean? Then I recalled a primitive drawing on the ceiling of the gent's toilet in the Duppas Hill recreation ground. I had to go and get a cold drink to calm myself down but the image stayed with me a long time. A photo of the happy couple was blown up and displayed in the foyer to promote the facility upstairs, and whenever I glanced at it I wondered if she did save some room.

I worked at the rink during school holidays as well as the weekends, and soon I was immersed into ice skating culture. On holiday morning sessions young middle-class kids had private instruction in figure skating circles and figures of eight, monotonously spinning slowly round and round, feet changing direction in the same place each time. Sometimes ice dancers would get the rink for themselves; I remember Diane Peach and an effeminate man called Peter, and although it was not something I would brag about to the boys I enjoyed watching them. All the girls who figure skated wore these little skirts that made their legs look lovely and long, especially when you added the height of the skate. It was often a different story when on the odd occasion you caught them in their normal dress, and the long-limbed glamorous dancer turned out to be a tiny little doll with a big bottom. Some of the girls' thighs were awesome.

The two different types of skates defined how hip you were. The ones available for hire were worn-out cheap figure skates with no support left in the sides, and all the beginners wore these. The hip boys only used hockey skates, which were altogether more macho and American-looking, and some boys had even acquired American high school jackets for wearing on the ice. Every afternoon they cleared the rink for the speed skaters (mostly lads), and this was really exciting as they whizzed round the ice at breakneck speeds and impossible angles.

For these sessions the music stopped, which was a blessed relief. The sounds were provided by two blokes on organ and traps; no doubt they were competent musicians, but for kids in the fifties there could be little in the world more embarrassing than Buddy Holly tunes played on a Wurlitzer theatre organ. However, when I occasionally see a baseball game and hear the sound of organ and traps, I am transported through time back to the rink, and instead of nauseating me, the sound gives me a warm nostalgic glow.

After a while during these music-free speed sessions I found I could keep up with most of the hockey-booted lads on a pair of borrowed figure skates from the hire shop. There I had become acquainted with a strange bloke who first told me that it was possible to kill a man with a single blow from an oriental sport called 'karachi', and one day he would show me the dark secret if I was sworn to secrecy. He was one of those who like to work in dark holes in the ground, and in this case he must have also loved the smell of feet.

In those days the ice rink was painted in strange thirties abstracts in orange, dark greens and browns and there were couples in fumbling embraces and contorted positions in every corner. Rumours abounded of girls who would let you, and although it certainly looked as if they were, I doubt seriously if a couple could have actually got away with it. But there was certainly a sexiness to the place. My own favourite fantasies were two lovely south London girls, both pretty as a picture but tough too. They dressed the same with shoulder-length brown hair, matching high school jackets, tight blue jeans and white hockey boots. I think it was the white boots that did it. They were the sexiest things on the ice but they never saw me, even on the odd occasion they came up to the tea bar to order a couple of Pepsis.

"That'll be one and six please," I would say provocatively, only they didn't notice. They moved languidly about the ice, completely at home on it, and only quickened their pace to get out of the way of some of the blokes, whose main reason for being there was to speed up to a couple of girls and screech to a stop, spraying ice all over everyone.

Apart from the general kids' recreational skating, Streatham also had a professional ice-hockey team, cleverly named Streatham. They were mostly Canadians, but included a crowd favourite called Danny Wong, whose feats were apparently the stuff of legend. Their arch rivals were the Paisley Pirates from Scotland. I only saw one match at the rink; most of the hockey games were on Wednesday nights, and from the tea bar they were not really visible. Anyway, team games failed to interest me until many years later, when I was too old to compete.

Boxing, however, was another matter.

In the middle of my time working at the rink, one of Britain's best boxers fought at Streatham. His name was Dave Charnley, and the atmosphere generated on those nights has lived with me ever since. I have never boxed myself, but my brother Bruce did a bit at school and my father was regimental champion at his weight. I did some sparring at the boys' club, but I was too unco-ordinated for the instructor to take me further, and truth to tell I was not unhappy. The sport, though, has fascinated me from about about the age of eight, when I got my *Freddie Mills Boxing Annual*, and I still love the old pictures of fighters on the walls of pubs and theatres.

The two fights I saw were towards the end of the 1950s. Rock'n'roll was established, teenagers had been invented, and the drab dark greens and browns of home decor were slowly being replaced by bright primary colours. Italian wallpaper had arrived, but the hangover of wartime austerity remained and a lot of working-class men were slow to adopt change. Dry-cleaning had been around for years, but few men ever had a suit dry-cleaned and many were the trousers that shone in the daylight from the accumulated dirt in the material. In the winter men wore big old overcoats, stored all summer in mothballed wardrobes, with scarves and caps or trilby hats, and all men smoked.

I cannot tell separate incidents from the two bouts I saw, but I do remember the totally different atmosphere in the rink as the crowds poured in for the event. The normal teenage babble, and kids' playground noises echoing off the ice and banging round the high ceiling and walls, was replaced by the animated but deeper rumble of men's voices. The ice was boarded over and the whole place was warmer than usual. The crowds grew, and as everyone lit up their cigarettes, the lights pierced the darkness like beacons searching for lost souls in the fog. Damp clothing warmed up and the smell of wet wool was added to tobacco and sweat. When at last Charnley entered the ring, the biggest shout I had ever heard in my life up to that point roared in my ears, and as I watched from the vantage point of the tea bar, I soaked up every bit of the action like a dishcloth and revelled in the maleness of it all.

After the first fight, Margaret took the victorious Charnley some tea and a couple of Pepsis, but the boxing fraternity has just as many superstitions as showbiz people, and women are considered unlucky in a boxer's dressing room. Margaret was not allowed in and had to march back to the tea bar without sharing in the glory—no mean feat for a woman with one leg and all those stairs to climb. Charnley, it appeared, liked ice cream after a fight and she almost had to carry the whole lot back again, but of course I was sent for to take it. At the next fight I remembered his preference and I asked if I might be allowed to go up and deliver it. Margaret confirmed that she wasn't bleedin' well going up there again, so Mary gave me six tubs of assorted flavours (strawberry and vanilla!) and I trooped off upstairs to the changing room behind the bandstand.

Inside the tiny room, surrounded by some of the biggest men I had ever seen, sat the tiny champion. At fourteen I was already as big as him. As I was ushered into the room his back was toward me, and I saw that he was still suffering from teenage acne. He seemed so pale and vulnerable still in his shorts and boots, with these cigar-smoking camelhair-coated admirers around him. Through the thick tobacco haze you could still smell the rubbing liniment and wintergreen that the champ had been anointed with before his ritual.

At first they tried to take the ice cream off me, but I suddenly heard a voice asking if I might be allowed in. I was surprised to find it was my own.

Charnley must have heard my plea, and said, "Let the kid inside," so I got in and handed him the tubs of ice cream and told him how much I appreciated the fight. Not that I saw much, but that's how I got to meet him and it was a great moment for me.

At the first Streatham fight a boxer called Mancini was on the bill. I watched him get beaten on points, much to the disappointment of the crowd, as in spite of his name he seemed to be a local. As the next bout was to begin, the small group who had come to get teas dispersed, and I started clearing the cups away. An unshaven bloke appeared at the counter.

"Cup of tea, son," he said quietly.

I poured him a cup from the big teapot, and as I asked for his sixpence I looked closely at his face.

Blimey, he looks as if he's been in a punch up, I thought. There were contusions under both eyes and a couple of nicks above the left, but it was the look in his eyes that struck me most. It was a forlorn, lost look, and the pain expressed in it was not a physical one but more like a wound to the soul.

"Weren't you just in the ring?" I enquired hesitantly.

"That's right, son."

"You're Mr. Mancini, aren't you?"

"Yeah," he answered and moved to take the handle on the tea cup and lift it to his lips as his eyes looked down and away from me. Before he could raise it up to drink I grabbed it from him and poured it away, then using Mary's method I made him a fresh cup and handed it to him.

"That's on the house," I said magnanimously, and put a sixpence of my own into the till.

"Thanks son," was all he said as he raised his head in acknowledgement. But his eyes still looked into his cup and he slipped off into the shadows to drink it on his own. I never forgot that moment and the lesson it offered: if you lose your fight you have to buy your own tea!

Afterwards I told Mary about it and she said I'd done the right thing and made me take my sixpence back.

Towards the end of my time at the rink I was getting bored and a little lazy. This probably irritated Alice and Mary, who became a little more removed and stopped their constant teasing. It upset me a bit, but time was moving on and there were other things to do. I just did not have a clue what or where they were.

One day Tom's mum sent for me and asked if I'd like to work at Wembley in the car parks for the Cup Final. The job paid thirty shillings for the day, which was a ransom in those days and a third more than I made at the rink. She told me I'd got the job on her recommendation for my honesty. Tom too had a job there, and the two of us set off on the Saturday morning very early around 6 o'clock. Luckily, because it took us two hours to get there, arriving on time at eight. I let Tom do the map reading as I was not prepared to be the one to get us lost, so I didn't complain. It was good to have something on the person whose hair did what he wanted it to do.

At the stadium we were split up and I was assigned to the bicycle and car park, where I was met by Don, a miserable bloke with the skin on his face and arms already brown from the early spring sunshine, like a deck-chair attendant. He was cockney and his bald head was as brown as his face, which surprised me as most of the time he wore a cap and a white coat.

I was surprised how many people came to the Cup Final on bikes, especially as it was the Rugby League Final and both teams were from up north.

"It's a fuckin' long bike ride from Sheffield!" observed my colleague, as he demonstrated the ticketing method I had to learn. Bikes cost six-pence for the day and motorbikes were a shilling. My mate was pissed off most of the day because he normally worked in the car park, where cars cost more to leave.

He had a little fiddle going, which he felt he had to let me in on. Each bike had two tickets issued when they paid their money over. One of them had glue on the back which enabled it to be stuck on to the bike. The other ticket was to be kept as proof that it was your bike.

"'ere's what you do," said Don. "When they pay you just give 'em one of the tickets and then you can keep the other ticket and sell it to the next geezer. That way you keep half the money you take for yourself. Easy ain't it?" He had a self-satisfied grin.

"Oh yeah?" I said, smiling nervously. Inside I was mortified; this was definitely stealing and I, who had never stolen so much as a glance up until now, was supposed to go along with such villainy.

"What if someone wants both tickets?" I queried.

"Nah, nobody's ever caught on, they're all too wound up for the game. They just take whatever you give 'em and piss off up to the entrance door. If someone starts to read what it says on the ticket you just ask sort of casual like, 'Whereabouts are you sitting mate?' Then they pull out their ticket and show you and then you tell them where to go to get in, they put their tickets both together for fear of losing them at the last minute and then they fuck off to the game," he explained.

I told him I didn't think I would be able to do it. This of course imme-diately made him suspicious, thinking that I might grass him up.

Desperate to reassure him that I had no intention of grassing, I groped around for an excuse and came out with, "I'm a deeply religious person," and when that didn't seem convincing, I added, "a catholic." I don't know where my conversion to Rome came from, but at that moment it seemed a convincing word to use.

"So am I a catholic, what's that got to fuckin' do with it? You'll learn son, you'll learn. Everyone's bent, you 'ave to nick a little bit 'ere an' there if you're goin' to get on. You'll learn. Fuckin' catholic—so fuckin' what!" he muttered as he walked over to a newly-arrived cyclist.

Eventually he was mollified and we were back on fairly friendly terms, although I knew he thought I was a bit odd. I offered to give him the other halves of my tickets, so that although I was an accessory to the crime I was innocent of profiting from it.

The incident was soon pushed into the background, for it was a beautiful sunny morning and soon there was a steady stream of customers for spaces. Then as the day wore on spectators began to arrive on foot or from buses. I was fascinated by these strange northern aliens with their broad accents and funny suits. Our Latin master, Mr. May, was from Sheffield so I knew the accent already, and everyone had heard Wilfred Pickles, but here were *thousands* of them. The disarming directness and openness of these strangers contrasted so much with the caution of the London men that I knew that I wondered if they were all a bit simple. Certainly none of them would have been a match for the sly bastard I was working with.

Not only that but they had such tiny feet compared to southern men— or at least that's how it looked to me. Most of these blokes were wearing what looked like a version of the demob suit, which was still fairly common in those days, except that for some reason the ends of their trousers were wider than the way we wore them in London. This may have accentuated my perception of the size of their feet, because for a long time afterwards I would confidently inform people that northern men had smaller feet than their southern brothers (strangely enough, years later I read an article which stated exactly that, though by this time I had stopped repeating my assertion).

At this time I had absolutely no idea about, or interest in, team sports and so the magnitude of the occasion was lost on me. I do however remember the roar of the crowd whenever the play picked up, and it was even bigger than that for Dave Charnley.

A couple of weeks later it was the FA Cup Final between Luton Town and Nottingham Forest, and back came all the suits and small shoes. Don trusted me enough to leave me to do the bikes on my own and went off drinking with some mates, but in the evening he reappeared and I was allowed into the central cashing up place, a small nondescript building on the outside of the stadium. There queues of attendants stood in line waiting to hand over the cash for the day.

Because Don had not made any cash himself on the day, having been out having a drink, he let me take our pittance in to be weighed with the rest, and the sight that greeted me on the inside of the low building I will never forget. Several cashiers were behind a long table counting out the money as it was emptied from satchels and tipped on to the surface. The place was full of blokes smoking as if the sight of so much money made them all nervous; in a curious way it reminded me of the boxer's dressing room. Paperwork was filled in and forms signed and people whistled in and out at amazing speed. All I can remember is the piles of notes, mainly ten shilling ones but pounds as well, and mountains of florins and half crowns spilling almost on to the floor. My mouth must have been wide open as I gawped at all this treasure on show.

"Come on son," said an official, "if you're finished get your docket signed and get out, there's a good boy."

I got my docket signed and was duly paid my thirty bob. I said my goodbye to Don, who wondered if I'd be working there any more.

"By the way, who won the match?" he asked. I had no idea, but someone shouted, "Forest," and he perked up.

As we left the treasure house he leaned over and beerily informed me, "Well I'm a tenner up on the day, 'ow about you?"

"I done all right," I said, jangling my thirty bob inside my pocket and patronising his grammar at the same time.

"You're learnin' then," he chuckled. "Everyone's bent, they all learn in the end, fuckin' catholic or not."

∽

cadets

I joined the army cadet corps at school as soon as I was old enough, at the age of thirteen. By this time I'd discharged myself from class 3U, but my trousers were still making me an object of ridicule, as I had not yet grown out of even their extended life and length. It was hard enough as it was coming from Miller Road with all the mickey-taking; at that time I was the only boy in my road going to grammar school, and the conflict of cultures between the street and school was being won hands down by the street.

I loved my new surroundings, and I knew the idea of joining the army cadets would get around the estate and would temper the swot image I must have had already. We met every Friday after school and paraded in the school playground. Some boys brought their uniform to school in bags so that it would still be smart for inspection, but I wore mine all day as even the itchy flannel khaki was more comfortable than the false turnup trousers. I supposed it was partly my already gangly shape but I never really looked right, and try as I might I could never win the Best Turned Out Cadet prize. This was always won by my mate and smoking companion, Tom Shaw.

Tom seemed to get everything right: his beret fitted better and it suited him, his trousers were the right length, his gaiters always sat properly on his beautifully polished boots, and his belt didn't sag like mine. We both spent hours pressing our uniforms with wet cloths and brown paper, but mine always looked a bit sad when it came to parade, whilst Tom's was immaculate. I did admire him but I was always jealous of his handsome appearance.

Our leaders were two teachers named Mr. Catchpole and Mr. Maggs. Mr. Maggs only had his left arm, having lost his right at the battle of Arnhem. This earned him a great deal of respect from the boys, and I for one was in awe of his small silver hook and scarred face. For one term he took us for Latin, but as the whole class were so bad at it we were forced to drop the subject en masse.

I was entertained and diverted by most of the activities of the cadets: marching, shooting in the .22 rifle range in the bike sheds, rifle drill and armoury training. I even enjoyed cleaning my kit, especially the leather boots. This was an amazing process: first you took an old spoon that you heated up in a flame, then you pressed this on to the toecaps and heels of the uppers, then you took lots of black boot polish (Kiwi, not Cherry Blossom) and smothered the tops and heels with this. You repeated the procedure until virtually all traces of the dimples in the leather had disappeared; then began the meditative process of polishing little fingerfuls of polish mixed with spit and water until a shine began to appear like glass on the toe caps of the boot. It was a slow laborious job, but it gave enormous satisfaction as the results started to appear.

I achieved marksman status with the .22 rifle and first class status with the .303. We all went away on camp and had a great time; I got to fire a Bren gun and I passed an armories course, and sometime later we went to Lulworth Cove where we got to fire two pound shells and a whole belt of machine gun bullets with tracers. I also learned to play the bugle and was made bugler for the school company. We went on school parades, church parades, and once marched through Guildford, the home of the Queen's Surrey Regiment. It was grand, and there was only one problem: Lieutenant Bisham.

Something I was to notice at many other times in my life, although I was not to work out its significance until much later, was that a disproportionate number of boys who were drawn to the cadets came from one parent families. Tom, like me, was raised by his mother, and there were other boys like me and Tom in the company; we were the ones Lt. Bisham came after. He was an unsightly man with huge pebble lenses in his glasses, a very ruddy complexion and a hooked nose. He was dark-haired and a little stout and he couldn't pronounce the 'th' sound. He lived in Selsdon with his "muvver".

Lt. Bisham got to know all the boys in the company who didn't have fathers, and over the course of a few weeks he would call round to their houses and introduce himself to the harassed mums, who were only too glad to receive the interest of an avuncular older man who obviously had the welfare of their boys at heart. His chat line would be something like:

"Hello Mrs. May, my name is Lieutenant Bisham and I'm with the Queen's Surrey Army Cadet force. Since young Ralph has joined it has come to our notice that you are bringing up the boy on your own. We like to keep a bit of an eye on them as they enter teenage, to both their school work and their moral development."

His first visit was invariably in uniform, which gave him an air of authority and easy access to any home of this type. I know many of the mothers found him distasteful, but harassed as they were it never occurred to them that his motives were anything other than what he had stated.

Once indoors and after some small talk about school, he would ask the mother if he could have a word with the boy "on his own." She would readily comply, then when they were alone he would begin his interrogation.

"Well Ralph, how are you enjoying the cadets?"

"Very much sir, thank you."

"Are you getting on with your lessons as well?"

"Oh yes sir."

"Are you a good boy Ralph?"

"Yes sir I think so, I try to be sir."

"I mean, are you ever a naughty boy Ralph?" he smiled knowingly.

"What do you mean naughty sir?"

"You know Ralph, do you ever—"

He paused here for a moment.

"—touch yourself?"

Oh my God what did he mean? Had someone told him? Did anyone know?

"I don't know what you mean sir," I blushed.

"I think you do Ralph," he said, leaning forward in his chair. "Do you interfere with yourself, Ralph?"

"Oh no sir, I never do sir," I lied. "I know it's wrong sir, I would never do such a thing."

I had no need to feign shock as I was absolutely devastated by his questions. There was no way that I could tell my mother about it, and that's how it was for all of us miserable little sinners. Always the same questions asked several times a session, then he would say that he was glad that you were a good boy and try to tickle you on the ribs before taking his leave, making sure that he could call again.

We all knew this activity must be wrong, but none of us lads could see what he got out of it, and our Company Sergeant Major told us that one day we would understand. Camp was particularly harrowing, as he would pick on one boy after another, and these tickling games became little power battles; as long as we didn't fight back too vigorously he seemed satisfied and he never touched any of us in an intimate way. Even so, we all hated him but didn't know what to do about it.

Many years later I heard that he had overstepped the mark and was made to leave the cadet force. He was one of the slimiest bastards I have ever met, and although none of us were harmed in either an intimate or physical way, he got his kicks out of an exploitation of our weakened family status and he was part of our loss of innocence.

❧

haircut

As much as I loved the cadets, I hated school. I slipped from near the top of my form to near the bottom in three years, and it slowly dawned on me that I would have to make some changes.

For some time I had been noticing adverts in the papers for boys' service in the army, and one day as I was slipping further down the ladder of failure I filled in a form and sent it off. My learning curve had all but vanished at school, and all I wanted to do was play practical jokes and have a laugh all the time. At one time Tom and my other best pal Les were also thinking of leaving with me, but in the end they both stayed.

After receiving a lot of paperwork from the army, it was not long before a recruiting sergeant called round to see me and my mother. I guess it was pretty routine for him calling on boys from council estates, but it all suddenly changed when he heard that I was at grammar school. At first he tried to convince me to attend the Welbeck College military school, but that just sounded like more of the same to me. Against his advice, I opted to join the Infantry Junior Leaders Battalion as a boy soldier in the Queen's Royal Surrey Regiment.

This decision was not made lightly, and in fairness to Mum she pressed me many times to make sure that I really wanted to go through with it. My mind was made up though, and anyhow hadn't my estranged dad done the same thing, and hadn't Uncle Ray signed up at thirteen, and wasn't my younger brother Bruce trying to get into the Navy on the *Arethusa*? No, there was no turning back, although I did still have a few niggling doubts.

I enjoyed the next few weeks because suddenly I was someone different. I had made a decision to leave home and family and become a soldier. Some of my mates were still half talking about doing it, but I had actually gone through the whole bit except for the medical and swearing in.

The most memorable part of the medical was the eye test. After what was the most extensive examination I'd ever had, the doctor casually asked me what service I'd applied to join. When I told him that I planned to make the infantry my career he was surprised, as in all his twenty-odd years as a military doctor, he said, he had never come across any lad with better vision than mine. He wondered if the Air Force would have been a wiser choice. To me the RAF was still the 'Brylcreem brigade' and an upper-class service: this misapprehension was due to all the bloody war films I'd been subjected to as a kid, and I was quite surprised when I later met up with some airmen to find that they were as working-class as I was.

Anyway a compliment was a compliment, and I felt as if I'd somehow had something to do with it.

The swearing in was a different matter entirely. I was summoned to West Croydon recruiting office and there, in the company of two recruiting sergeants, I swore to be loyal to my Queen and Country and signed on for six years with the colours and two with the reserve.

Except that I hadn't. After I'd signed my name I noticed that instead of six years the sergeant had written *nine* and two with the reserve.

I immediately pointed out the error, expecting him to say that he was sorry and to amend the document, but instead he just smiled, pulled the paper away and said, "Don't worry about that son, you'll get paid more!"

And that was that. He gave me an old hat badge of the Queen's Surrey Regiment, which he said had belonged to him when he was doing his service, and wished me good luck.

I was now a soldier, and I slunk home with a very heavy heart indeed, the enormity of my decision slowly starting to sink in. Although deeply touched by the sergeant's gesture regarding the hat badge, I felt cheated. I would now be twenty-four by the time my service was up, and the two years on the reserve would make me twenty-six, but at least I would be home then. Christ, I was already counting the days till I got out and I hadn't even arrived at the camp yet.

The next few days sped past and off I went to say my goodbyes to all my old school friends, most of whom I would never see again. Some of my teachers wished me good luck (and under their breath good riddance no doubt) but one of them, Mr. Field, just looked at me incredulously and said, "What! Why are you joining the army? You're certainly capable of eight O-levels."

"I don't think so, sir," I said.

"Nonsense May, of course you are! But if that's what you want to do, good luck to you." He shook his head in bewilderment.

My God, another compliment, why hadn't anyone said these things to me before? I felt even more wretched, and went through the school gates for the last time without a backward glance.

Friends in the street were used to boys leaving, and my friend Tony Potter from across the road had already gone off to join the Navy. I left to join the battalion on May 8th 1960 with a small bag of belongings including my boot polish, brushes, and a towel still clearly labelled in my mum's handwriting R. MAY, which had been prepared for my convalescence that never was after my road accident when I was five. After a manly but grinny handshake from my brother Bruce I turned to say goodbye to my mum. She gave me the first big hug I could ever remember and kissed me on the mouth.

"Take care of yourself, son, and don't forget to write," she said, looking quite tearful. I was so surprised by her reaction and this highly demonstrative show of affection that I nearly decided to stay.

As I left for Paddington up the garden path of 17a Miller Road I could almost hear the *Dam Busters March* being played on harmonicas. I looked to see if Amy Blair was watching me, but she must have been at school. I was fairly sure she liked me just from her glances, although we had not yet spoken as she lived so far away across the road. And now she would be even further away. My heart weighed twice as heavy as my bag.

The train journey from London to the west country is lovely and I am now very familiar with it. This was my first time, however, and although the countryside looked beautiful I was full of trepidation about what was in store for me once we arrived in Plymouth. For a long time I paced up and down the corridor and had cups of tea in the buffet till I couldn't drink any more.

Standing in the buffet car in a grey suit was a tall skinny lad with dark greased hair and brown eyes that sloped slightly upwards. He had a small mouth and a London accent.

"You joined up as well mate 'ave ya?"

"Yeah, that's right," I said, and told him who I was. "Are you going to Plymouth as well?"

"Yeah, I bin watchin' you moochin' up an' down so I thought I'd ask."

"What lot are you going in?" I asked him.

"I'm in the Middlesex Regiment," he announced.

"I'm in the Queen's Surreys," I said. "What's your name?"

"Brummel's the name," he replied, "but all my mates call me Beau."

"Oh. Why's that then?" I asked stupidly.

He gave me a quizzical look and said suspiciously, "Because of Beau Brummel, I suppose."

I wished the ground would swallow me. This was not the first impression I wanted to make; in the army I could be anyone I wanted to be, I could bring all my new-found street cred to my new situation and here I was making my first encounter with a fellow soldier and I'd failed to see the obvious connection with his famous namesake.

I could imagine him introducing me to other blokes, saying something like, "This is Ralph, he's from Croydon," then adding under his breath, "he's a bit slow on the uptake, but what can you expect from someone called Ralph who comes from Croydon."

I imagined everyone nodding sympathetically, and made up my mind that I would change my name to something more exotic and lie about my origins. Of course this was after I'd already told him my name was Ralph and that I hailed from Croydon. I also realised that I would probably have to stop saying my prayers at night and start swearing a lot.

The rest of the journey passed quite quickly and soon we were getting off the train at Plymouth. We had all been told we would be met, and so as the other passengers left the station a small unimpressive knot of skinny, nervous-looking young men grew on the platform. An old sergeant in the uniform of the London Irish Rifles arrived and called the roll. We had to answer "Here sir!" in a very loud voice.

"He looks old, I think he must be fuckin' deaf," said Beau, leaning into me.

"Not so deaf I missed that," uttered the sergeant. "What's your name lad?" he asked, looking directly at me.

239

"Me?" I asked incredulously.

"Yes you lad!" bellowed the sergeant to the red-faced lad on the platform of Plymouth railway station with the new recruits all looking at me, and now all the disembarking and embarking passengers staring as well.

"My name's May," I croaked.

"OK, Murray," sneered the sergeant, "I'll deal with you later," and he looked down his list. "Wait a minute," he said, "there's no-one down here called Murray."

"No sir, my name's May," I trembled. "M-A-Y." I spelt it out.

"That's not how you spell Murray boy," he seethed, "that's May."

"I know sir, that's my name."

"I hope you're not going to be a troublemaker May or Murray whatever your bloody name is boy, because you're in the army now lad and we have a way of dealing with smart arses like you!" As he uttered this chilling threat he wrote something down on his clipboard.

"Right you lot, form twos and follow me."

We half marched and half ambled out of the station and into a military coach that took us to Plummer Barracks at Crownhill. As we got off the lorry to view our new home the old sergeant leaned toward me and said, "All right Murray, I'll be watching you."

I looked over at my new friend Beau desperately, but he just grimaced and shrugged his shoulders in apology. We filed into the ground floor of Z Company barrack room and met the other lads who'd arrived at different times during the day.

"What a fucking great start!" I said to Beau. It felt great to say Fucking as well. It would be used a great deal over the coming months—and as it turned out it wasn't such a bad start after all.

I looked around at my new surroundings and noted the different types of boys there. We were all shapes and sizes, though there was no-one very overweight, and some looked far too small to have left home. Some wore glasses, one or two looked quite a bit older than the rest, a few had tattoos and several like me had Teddy boy haircuts.

We were all soon called outside and ordered to line up in loose military fashion. There was another roll call and we were introduced to our platoon sergeants. Mine was called Boon and the other one was called Roberts. They were the army's version of 'good cop bad cop'. Boon was short and wore a beret with a hackle in it. He spoke with a measured west country accent and was turned out immaculately. He had very light blue eyes like my uncle Alf and seemed aware of the trepidation of his new charges.

Roberts's eyes on the other hand were completely hidden by his slashed peak cap. He was in the Welsh Guards and was even more immaculate than his partner. When he issued words of command his voice, devoid of any compassion, divided into two parts, one with the tone of a shovel being scraped along the ground and the other a screaming falsetto. He scared the life out of all of us, and was probably the sort of NCO who in time of war we would have followed anywhere.

As we made two ramshackle lines, the two sergeants moved down the line looking at us and occasionally shaking their heads in mock disbelief that they were expected to turn us into soldiers. In well-rehearsed moves the two of them looked at each other and clicked their tongues in despair. I half smiled to myself in congratulation that I had recognised this performance as a deception when suddenly Roberts rounded on me, and singling out two other lads as well, bellowed, "You you and you! Haircut! Now!"

I noticed all three of us had longish hair, but more importantly we had elaborate styles. Mine at the time was what was known as a drainpipe, which consisted of two rolls of hair turned into the middle and a DA at the back with a Boston. I was first up in the chair, and the barber leant toward my ear chattily, asking, "How would you like it sir?"

I naively replied, "Well, I suppose trim up the sides and take a little off the top."

I can still remember the horror I felt as my vanity shorn off me. His electric shears zoomed straight up the back of my head and I instinctively grabbed at my head as if it had been cut.

"Oh dear," he said, "it seems my hand slipped!" to nervous laughter from the other two lads who by now had been joined by one or two more. I told him to take it all down short, and although I hated the way it looked, I felt a certain bravado and in the next day or so we all looked the same. The rule, as explained to us, was that whatever was below the beret line, the army wanted, and we could keep whatever was left. One boy called Weller was so shocked by the sight of the first returnees from the barber that he decided to have it all off, and they duly obliged. He thought this very funny, and so did I as he had a big round face like a football, and shorn of his blond hair he looked like Charlie Brown. I got to know him straight away and we were soon friends; he was in the Royal West Kent

Regiment and his name was Robert, "but everyone calls me Sam."

"Why's that?" I asked.

"Because of Sam Weller," he explained. Beau was in earshot and I was sure he would later tell Sam that he had the same trouble with me and his nickname. When Sam asked me my name I was determined to have a nickname too, so I replied, "Ray." It was all I could think of.

"I thought you said your name was Ralph," said Beau.

"Yeah, Ray is sort of short for Ralph," I explained.

"Is it? I thought it was short for Raymond," said Sam.

"Yes, and Ralph as well," I said, and gambled, "I mean, how many Ralphs do you know?"

"None," they both responded.

"There you are then!" I said triumphantly, and from that moment on I was always Ray. The only trouble was that I didn't respond to it very well, so as well as being known as someone who was a bit slow on the uptake I was also thought to be a bit deaf as well.

That evening we were issued with underclothes and fatigues, two pairs of boots, socks, brown army plimsolls, knife, fork and spoon, and bed-clothes. We were ordered to bed and allowed to talk for a while before lights out. I lay there in the gloom and didn't sleep too well, as a feeling of foreboding crept over me.

The next day our training began in earnest. We were obviously undrilled, so to give us some sort of order we were bidden to run every-where at the double. We did PT rigorously and attended a rudimentary educational class, and it was here that I realised I was one of the few boys that was literate. I might have been bad at school but here there was no-one to touch me.

To be truthful I was horrified. There was nobody that I could talk to on more than a superficial level, and it was only really tolerable when I was joking with Sam. Some of the other boys had begun to realise that this was going to be tough and we found that most of us had signed on for nine years and two in the reserve. Then somebody pointed out that the two years we would serve as boy soldiers didn't count, and that in reality we were going to do eleven in uniform. In fact on the third day I went and spoke to Company Sergeant Boon, and all but broke down as the helplessness of my situation dawned on me.

He was, I think, a kind man in private, but here there was a strict

NCO relationship that was never allowed to develop into anything other than formal, and he was unable to comfort me in any way.

On the parade ground we were bullied and sworn at just like recruits always have been, but some of the oaths were appalling when used against these young boys, the idea being to break you down in order to build you up. Humiliating and physically demanding punishments were handed out, like running round the parade ground with your rifle held above your head, or standing to attention perfectly still for inordinate lengths of time.

We were not supposed to be hit, but on occasion we were. I was ridiculed for being unable to straighten my arms properly when marching, and whacked with a pace stick several times by the RSM before he realised I was unable to make them any different. I was also smashed across the knuckles for not having my thumbs pointing down the seams of my trousers. The physical torment was just about bearable, but the verbal abuse was awful. Sergeant Roberts's voice of command was awesome. He would walk up to the offending soldier, stand nose to nose and bellow at the top of his voice his favourite insult: "The best part of you, boy, ran down your mother's leg!" Or occasionally, "When you were born they must have thrown away the baby and kept the afterbirth!"

You invariably had to repeat it to the whole battalion. Once I was ordered to march out to the RSM and tell him that I had grass growing out of my hat badge. Most of the accusations were made up to keep us terrified, and though we all worked at our kit for at least an hour every night, it was never enough to satisfy our sergeants.

We were told that from now on the army would be our mother and father, and even then I realised the humiliation, the uniform, and the regimen were all designed to strip away our individuality and to mould us into a cohesive unit. Every opportunity was taken to humiliate us. There was a lot of excitement in the barracks when we were told that we were going for a run across Dartmoor, but that changed to embarrassment when we heard that we were to run in army boots. The sight of fifty to sixty lads dressed in baggy army shorts and red shirts with army woollen socks and hobnailed boots, clattering over pavements and rocks and moorland, lives with me still. The whole purpose of the exercise was to break in our 'best boots'. Henceforth these would only be worn for parades; our second pair would be worn every day and would be broken in gradually.

After that run many boys had to wear plimsolls until their blisters and ripped toes had healed up, and only the very serious cases ever got as far as the doctor. In any case, you had to convince your Company Sergeant that you were ill before he would let you report sick anyway.

Our uniforms were First World War type and very itchy; how I longed for the Clarke boy's Oxford bags. We had two service dresses, both identical, but we did not have to wear the puttees, thank God. The Army generously paid us, whether we were awake or asleep, threepence an hour, earning us about two pounds a week. Out of this, one pound was saved and the other spent mostly on cleaning equipment: boot polish, Brasso, Blanco, whitener for our SDs and yellow dusters for polishing. We all became good, eventually, at ironing and we all had to shave every day whether we had any whiskers or not.

Our barrack rooms were kept spotless (but not spotless enough for our sergeants), and the washrooms were scrubbed daily with bass brooms. We were expected to attend to our own cleanliness, but because we did PT most days we showered automatically. Some lads, however, were simply not used to bathing and had to be reminded by the others.

After three weeks of unbelievably hard training, we were to be allowed to visit the town for the first time. We were given strict instructions not to visit Union Street, and to keep up the process of humiliation we had to go out in military uniform, so that everyone in Plymouth would know that we were raw recruits. But not even this could dampen our eager anticipation for the weekend ahead.

◦〜◦

town

For the last few days before being allowed into town, the talk was only about one thing: what we were going to do on our Saturday out. Boys' talk inevitably gets around to one thing and the lot in Z Company were no exception. I think most of us were virgins, but only one or two admitted to the fact, and it was obvious to anyone that we were inexperienced boys.

As fifteen-year-olds, we comprised all stages in male teenage development, from lads who looked as if they were wearing their first long trousers, with no facial hair and unbroken voices, to boys who shaved every day, spoke in deep manly tones and had muscular physiques. Not to mention those who had appalling complexions, terminal acne, halitosis, and who were suspected of perpetual masturbation. One Geordie lad was threatened with being put on a charge for the offence of having 'filthy flesh' and ordered to have instruction on how to remove blackheads with a key!

Inevitably all conversation turned toward sex, and the bedtime banter before lights out grew more and more lurid as boys would take it in turns to tell of their conquests, real or imagined. I suspect many tales were based on fact, but some were pure fantasy. One lad's story, however, had the ring of truth about it: his name was Malcolm Pringle and he was from Norfolk.

Malcolm had a picture of his girlfriend in his locker and he talked about her with genuine affection. I wanted to know all about her and he was willing to share details with me, albeit a little reluctantly—after all he was talking about the girl he loved. I was deeply envious of Malcolm as it became clear that he really did have a proper sexual relationship with this girl, for Malcolm himself was no oil painting. He had the biggest head in the platoon and had to have his beret specially ordered for him— and then it had to be stretched—and his SD hat had to be specially ordered too.

The other noticeable feature about him was his enormous feet; he took size fourteen, and the only thing the army had that would fit him were army issue brown plimsolls or 'pumps'. Poor Malcolm had to do all his early drill training in these soft shoes, which was faintly ridiculous as we had to bang our feet down with tremendous force when coming to attention. I am sure he must have damaged his spine before his two pairs of boots finally arrived.

Malcolm was odd in other ways too. For example, he thought that the army food was really good, and he always ate it all up and anyone else's leftovers as well. He was also one of three boys in my platoon who could neither read nor write. I was stunned by this fact, and it only served to make me more angry at the way I'd been conned into thinking that you had to pass an entrance exam to get into this mob. How the hell had these boys managed to get in?

Letters from home arrived for me on a regular basis and always moved me to tears as they were signed off "with fondest love, Mum." I also persuaded a friend from home to get me a pen friend so that I could pretend she was my girlfriend, and I loved getting her letters. As my friendship with Malcolm grew, he confided that he would like me to read him the couple of letters he had received from his girlfriend, and that's when I discovered that he was illiterate.

Malcolm's girl was called Pam. Her letters were written in big round shapes; they told of things back home but were quite short, although she always signed off that she missed him and sent her love. Malcolm then asked me to write his letters back. I was already writing for another lad called Rex to his mum, but Malcolm wanted me to write love letters!

This proved to be much harder than it sounds, because he could not dictate very well, so in the end I got him to tell me of his feelings and composed the letters myself, reading them back to him when they were finished. This method had two effects: firstly Pam's letters got much longer and more passionate, and secondly Malcolm always broke down and sobbed after I had expressed his feelings for him. After no more than a couple of these intense missives I no longer felt able to continue this correspondence, as I'd started to look forward to her replies.

Another reason was that one day whilst Malcolm was talking to me, he confided that Pam was not the best shag he'd ever had—that distinction belonged to his sister. Malcolm obviously saw nothing wrong in this, or in the fact that his father was also having sex with her, and looked genuinely puzzled by my reaction. Even after he explained that she was quite happy with the situation it still didn't seem right to me. For a fleeting moment I considered asking Malcolm if she might accommodate me, but as I looked into his tiny eyes set into his huge head it occurred that she might look just like him, and I thought better of it.

At last our Saturday arrived. Rex, Beau, Sam, Malcolm and I filed into the guard room for final inspection and insults before being allowed out into the city of Plymouth for a few hours release. Naturally we headed for Union Street, where we found a tattoo parlour, and all of us resolved to get a tattoo next time out. Drink did not really interest us at this time, so we just wandered about soaking up the late spring sunshine in our itchy SDs admiring every female between thirteen and twenty. We puffed away on our fags and tried to look manly, worldly and cool all at the same time, as we slowly guffawed our way up to the Hoe overlooking the harbour.

Someone had a camera and we posed for photos. There were young couples walking hand in hand, a sprinkling of matelots and marines, and servicemen in civvies, easy to spot by their savage military haircuts, all milling about on the clipped grass on the promenade.

Late in the afternoon we noticed a group of three girls and the dare was on to go and chat them up. I think at this point it is important to say that, although I had lusted after Amy Blair and various other girls on the bus going to school, I had never actually spoken to a female of my own age since reaching puberty. The reasons were complex and common to thousands of young men, but of course you don't know that at the time, believing only that the pain is unique to yourself and the exquisite agony of sexual awakening is the punishment you have to bear for having such wicked thoughts. I had been led by my friend Tom Shaw to believe that the size of my nose would seriously undermine any attempt to pull a girl;

I also had a few spots on occasion and had resorted to crossing to the opposite side of the road whenever I saw a pretty girl coming toward me.

Suddenly all the bawdy barrack room talk vanished into the air as my mates found excuses not to intervene, and it was left for me to make a move on the three girls. Leaving my friends I sauntered over to them; strangely, they neither recoiled in terror, burst out laughing or pointed at my nose. On the contrary, they seemed quite coy and tickled that we were interested in them. It has to be said that they were not great lookers, but they were our age and they were female.

Sam had crept up to join me, and although I have no recollection of how the chat-up line went, Sam was most helpful when he removed his cap to reveal his largely bald head. His hair was growing but it was so fine and light in colour that it still appeared to be shaved. At first this made the girls scream, but then they laughed and that settled Sam's role in the proceedings: he was to be the comedian and I was to be the intense, cool and debonair one. It is of course not possible for an overexcited fifteen-year-old to be any of those things, let alone all at once, so I tried to gather all the information I had learned from the other lads' talk in the barracks (first of all you've got to split them up, next keep them laughing, feel their tits outside of their bra before you go inside it, blow smoke into their faces to make them want to shag you, and so on).

I decided to save the smoke-blowing for later, as it was windy up on the Hoe and rather public, but I did get mine away from the other two, and we went for a stroll. I learned that her name was Bev Winterburn and that she lived over the water in Turnchapel and that her last ferry was about to go. As I walked her down to the jetty she took my arm and I asked if she would come to the pictures with me on Wednesday. She said that she would and we arranged to meet outside of the Drake cinema at about two o'clock.

I kissed her on the mouth (almost), said goodbye and as soon as I was out of sight from where I'd left her I raced up to the Hoe to find my pals and tell them what had happened, that she was a dead cert and I was meeting her in the week. My mates looked pissed off, except Sam, who had decided to pretend he was a nutter and was making himself dribble and speaking loudly as if he had a hare lip and was desperately trying to be understood. This diverted attention from my good luck and we all finished up laughing our way back to barracks. The only other one of us to get a date was Malcolm.

248

For the next few days I was in a state of total sexual anticipation. In my mind this girl was metamorphosing into the most glorious creature who ever lived, with the darkest eyes, the brownest hair, and the most perfect breasts and lips, with a sexy Plymouth accent thrown in. By now, of course, my missed kiss had turned into a full scale grope, and I was able to compete on terms with the other lads as we discussed our erotic adventures.

Wednesday finally came; a big day because it was the first time we were to be allowed out in our own civilian clothes. I had black suede shoes and black cavalry twill tapered trousers, a white shirt with cutaway collars and a Slim Jim tie, and a black and grey striped Italian three button jacket. My hair had grown sufficiently to do something with it, I was shaved and aftershaved and with a bounce in my step and wings on my heels I made my way to the cinema to meet my girl.

When I got there I realised I hadn't bothered to find out what the film was, and as the couples met each other outside I tried to contain my anxiety that perhaps she wouldn't show up. My eyes scanned the people swarming around the cinema but there was no sign of my Bev, just a couple of sailor boys, a dumpy little thing in a yellow frock, two other girls who were soon met by two boys and another boy about my age.

Gradually everyone drifted into the cinema, and still no sign of my Bev. The two sailors flipped a coin and then went inside, the boy my own age was finally met by his girl and after giving out at her for being late, they too disappeared into the cinema. I was alone except for the dumpy little thing in the yellow dress, who was standing at the opposite side of the picture house entrance looking at me.

I was wondering if she had been stood up as well, when she suddenly smiled and said, "Hello Ray. I wasn't sure if it was you without your uniform."

I was stunned. Here was my Bev, totally transformed. When we had met a couple of days before, she had been wearing a dark green cardigan and skirt with very little make-up, her lovely brown hair loose over her shoulders. What stood before me now, tottering slightly in white high heels and a yellow frock, was a different person, a little dumpy thing whose newly-permed hair was set in tight curls. She was covered in make-up and I had completely failed to recognise her. She must have spent hours on this effect, but I was depressed. Where was the siren I had given my heart to, the country girl with flowing hair, laughing brown eyes and huge tits? Gone, and in its place this travesty. She took hold of my arm and we went inside, where the film had already started.

As we sat down, her stiff petticoat bounced up on her lap and a little puff of talcum powder seemed to shoot out of her collar. Sitting there in the dark, I tried to remember the procedure for seduction as described by the various blokes in the barracks. The horror of her transformation was easier to bear in the cinema, and at last I managed to get my arm round the back of her seat in a nonchalant but unnatural move. Once there I was terrified about what to do next. Was I supposed to touch her hair or her arm? I knew there was a routine but it had escaped me in the heat of these moments.

Then I remembered: start at the top, hair first. Gingerly I raised my fingers to caress her curls, and as I did so I got another shock—the curls seemed to be made of wire. I had never heard of hair lacquer, and she had used about a tinful, which had made her hair feel as if she was wearing a crash helmet. I recoiled in fright and was left with my arm hanging over the back of her seat, too scared to move it and not quite knowing what to do next. Gradually my arm started to go to sleep and I lost all sensation of feeling in it as it was pressed against the back of her seat. Pins and needles began to set in and I was experiencing considerable discomfort, so I decided to withdraw the arm until it regained its blood supply and try again later.

Unfortunately my arm now felt like someone else's, and in attempting to haul it back over her seat to my side, it seemed to acquire a life of its own and thrashed about alarmingly, giving her a hard dig in her right ear. Mortified by this assault I apologised profusely, touching her shoulder and turning her face to mine, whereupon she lunged forward thinking I was about to embrace her. Our mouths met in a sickening crunch and we sprang back from each other to check our teeth.

Soon we were at it like every other couple in the dark and I prepared to make my next move toward the upper body, but this too resulted in confusion as she seemed to be entirely encased in sheet metal (I realise now that it must have been one of those bras that encircle the midriff to suppress undesirable bulges). She had metamorphosed into an armadillo.

At the end of the film we emerged mole-like and blinking into the warm spring evening, and my heart once again sank at the image before me. There was no doubt that our first encounter had been fairly passionate and promised more, but the truth was that I didn't fancy her any more.

The next day I wrote to her and made some excuse about not being able to meet her. When I next went into town I met another girl called Glenda, and we arranged to meet and go to the fair on the Hoe the next weekend. I wrote and told Bev that I was being sent to Oswestry as part of the advance party for our move to Parkhall Camp, but she saw me on one of the fairground rides with Glenda and wrote me a broken-hearted letter. I eventually realised what a sweet girl Bev really was, and that Glenda, who was so sexy, was actually going out with different blokes every day. She even got my name wrong on our last date before we moved camp. So now I'd had two girlfriends but no carnal knowledge—though none of my fellow boy soldiers knew that—and unbeknown to me there was some resentment growing.

✺

hard

Once we had passed out of Z Company and joined our training companies, we were bossed about by older boy soldiers, who were addressed as Junior Corporal or Junior Sergeant, and they tried with some success to be even worse than our senior NCOs. Fairness never came into it, and you were expected to put up with whatever prejudice the junior NCOs had. Complaint was a sign of weakness; it was your ability to take it that counted.

Junior Corporal Mostyn hated me on sight, and did his best to make my life even more miserable than it already was. I suspect it was because I was at least six inches taller than him. I suppose I should have read the other signs of resentment toward me and one or two of the other lads as we took our places with our training companies, but I didn't.

I was billeted next to an older, very capable lad called Derek, who was in the Dorset Regiment. We got on very well, and I just tried to carry on with a life that was making me more and more depressed. He realised that I was desperate to get out of service, but he also knew that my situation was hopeless. He managed to keep up my morale most of the time, and besides there were boys who were in a much worse position than I was.

Junior Private Bonney was from the intake before mine, but had been in my company before being placed under arrest for self-mutilation. The poor kid was entirely unsuited to military service, and any psychiatrist would not have allowed him to join up. The trouble was that the army simply did not have the mechanism for dealing with this type of case. The story went that shortly after Bonney had passed out of his training company he'd started to behave oddly, at first by not getting out of bed in the morning in fear of the terrors that awaited him through the verbal abuse from the senior sergeants. It was only his neighbour who had saved him on numerous occasions by literally hauling him out of bed before the sergeant came into the room with the usual order, "Hands off cocks and on with socks."

Gradually Bonney failed even to respond to his fellow soldiers' pleas to get himself together. The next sign was that he started to drink Brasso, the cleaning fluid we used for our brass buttons and belt clips. Maybe he thought he would get drunk by doing this, but he just got sick and vomited. He then started to disobey orders and began slashing the soles of his feet with razor blades so that he wouldn't have to drill.

Finally someone found him trying to hang himself in the washrooms, and he was deemed a risk to himself. He was thrown in the guardhouse, charged with self-inflicted injury, and put on RPs (restricted privileges). His boot laces were removed and he was marched down to the canteen where he had to eat his meals with a provost sergeant and a corporal watching every move, in case he tried to smuggle a knife or other dangerous implement back to the cell.

Bonney was a sad character, a tussle of dark curly hair, sallow complexion, skinny as a rake and huge dark sad eyes, and the way he was treated was a crime of unbelievable cruelty. The sight of this sixteen-year-old boy shuffling down to eat in the mess with his army boots gaping laceless and his old fatigues, his eyes dead and hardly noticing his surroundings, was unspeakable. Everyone agreed that Bonney was a nutter and most of us felt pity for him, but I doubt many realised he was paraded nightly for our benefit.

One night I came into my bed space and was getting something out of my locker when Derek whispered to me, "Watch out Ray, they're coming for you. Don't look round, just listen to me, can you hear me?"

"Yes," I said, wondering what on earth he could mean.

"You're going to be charged and put in a kangaroo court. You'll get a whacking and if you plead guilty that's probably all that will happen. They're going to do Alan as well."

"What are they charging me with?" I whispered as I began to shake.

"You're going to be charged with being a rookie and there's nothing you can say or do about it. So no more questions, just be ready."

I turned round to look at him but he would not look me in the eye; he was tight-lipped and grim faced and I noticed that he was putting on an odd combination of uniform. Our bed spaces were down at the far end of the barrack room and there was a lot of activity going on at the other end. I wanted to see what was happening but Derek, sensing this, shook his head to warn me against it.

Suddenly there was the order, "Attention. About turn. Quick march!" and the sound of two soldiers marching down the centre aisle grew louder and louder in my ears until they came to a stop at my bed.

"Junior Private May. Attention. Put your beret on and fall in with us." There was nothing to be done and, with one of the boys trying not to laugh, we marched like prisoner and escort back to the top of the room. Here two large tables had been set up, and seated behind them were three older boys dressed in a variety of strange bits of uniform and made up hat badges. In the middle sat the biggest bully in the company, a bastard in the East Anglia Regiment, and he was flanked by an Irish boy called Brady and another lad called Curry from one of the Lancashire regiments.

The East Anglian Bastard slapped a spoon on the table.

"This court is now in session!" he bellowed. "Junior Private May, what is your number?"

"23783801!" I shouted back.

"Two three seven eight three eight zero one Junior Private May you are charged with being a recruit. How do you plead?"

"You know that I'm a recruit," I said nervously. "What is all this about?"

The bastard leaped to his feet and pressed his face to mine.

"Shut your fuckin mouth you fuckin bastard May and just answer the fuckin question will you! I bin waiting for this you fuckin bastard, are you guilty or not guilty?"

"Guilty I suppose," I said.

"Guilty or not fuckin guilty you fuckin bastard!" he screamed and at the same time landed a tremendous blow to the side of my head with his fist.

"Guilty," I said.

At this admission my arms were taken and tied behind my back. They pushed me down between two beds, and my head was placed in the middle, held between the two steel frames that supported the springs. Then someone ripped open my shirt pulling most of the buttons off, and a box of Swan Vestas was produced. Without any instruction from anyone about a dozen matches were struck and whilst burning were stuck into my chest. I managed not to cry out because I was terrified about what other humiliations they had planned for me.

My chest now resembled a pin cushion, although I couldn't see this at the time and struggle was both futile and painful. As my head was held back at an acute angle I could not see who exactly my tormentors were, but it seemed that most of the platoon had been roped in. Suddenly I could feel my trousers being pulled down and I kicked out violently, only to be given a punch in the face by the East Anglian Bastard, and then I was aware of some liquid being poured over my genitals. This turned out to be the whitener that was commonly used to whiten our belts for our best SDs.

I was released from the bed's grip and turned over, and my shirt ripped from my back. They pretended to put a hot iron on my back as a brand mark; although they didn't actually plug it in, the coldness of it made me think I was being burnt. I was then turned over again. This time the East Anglian Bastard grabbed my hair and proceeded to hack off a four inch square right in the front above my forehead. That *really* hurt. He then gave me one more dig before I was dismissed and led back to the washrooms to try to clean myself up.

I felt completely desolate, and as I scrubbed away the whitener that had been used on me and saw in the mirror the extent of my tonsorial mutilation, the tears welled up and poured down my face. No-one came in to see me, and I had a few minutes to get myself together before I heard the same orders being bellowed from the barrack room, only this time they were coming for Alan, whose bed was across from mine.

In spite of what I'd just gone through, I went in to see what new tortures they had planned for him. Apart from blacking his balls with Kiwi boot polish, they cut his hair off just like mine, but instead of sticking lighted matches on his chest they gave him six lashes with a rifle strap before letting him go. All of this happened within half an hour and it all had a dreamlike quality to it. The whole room was involved in some way and when it was over the place was eerily quiet and blokes didn't speak to each other. I started to go over to talk to Alan but was cautioned not to by Derek. I saw Alan's pain, and long after lights out and the others were asleep I could hear him crying quietly to himself.

For some time there had been rumours that the whole camp was to be moved to a new location. These were now confirmed and the destination was Oswestry, a small market town in Shropshire. I was still besotted with Glenda and needed an excuse not to go on an outward bound course on Dartmoor when Curry, who it transpired had done the intimate punishments on Alan and me, suggested a method by which I could report sick.

"Its called spooning," he explained. "All you have to do is wrap your hand up in a wet towel and then I hit you with a spoon and slowly your whole hand swells up and it looks like a fuckin' balloon and the doc doesn't know what it is and you get put on light duties."

I realised this was a ruse to get back on terms with me, but I was desperate to see Glenda again so I agreed to try the treatment. After applying the towel the spooning began. By Christ how it hurt. When Curry had exhausted himself another lad took over and after fifteen minutes I could bear it no longer and gave it up as a bad job. The pain was excruciating but the desired swelling had not occurred. I was resigned to going on the course after all and was standing at my locker with my door open when I felt a blinding pain across my arm. I fell down under the force of the blow delivered by the East Anglian Bastard who had crept up along side my bed space and swung the bass broom over his head and brought it down with all his weight on my skinny forearm.

"There you are May you fuckin' bastard that ought to get you out of goin'," he cackled.

Before my eyes my arm started to swell. Miraculously it wasn't broken, but the pain was unbelievable. I reported sick the next day and the doctor asked me how it happened.

"I fell down the stairs sir," was the response I'd been told to use.

"And who cut your hair?" he demanded.

"I did sir," I lied.

"I see," said the MO—and I'm sure he did—but he put my arm in a sling and I was put on light duties for a week. The rest of my platoon went off to Dartmoor and I got Wednesday in town to meet Glenda.

Needless to say, she wasn't where we arranged to meet, and my misery was complete when I saw her arm in arm with two regular sailors walking into a pub. On the bus back to the barracks I thought of Bev and felt bloody awful about what I'd done, but I managed to content myself with thoughts of the battalion's move to Shropshire. With some relief I noticed my arm was already feeling better and it would not be long before my first home leave was coming up. I decided I would ask Amy out and see if there was any way I could arrange to get some money together to buy my discharge.

There are two things I remember about the move: a senior officer had to sign for the train; and I saw my uncle George working laying track as we passed through my childhood holiday home of Banbury.

Parkhall Camp was not as austere looking as Crownhill, but it had been empty for some time and lacked the comforts of a more lived-in barracks. I was billeted next to an older boy called Spike. He was taller than me and had large teeth, but he was a good-natured bloke with a ready laugh and had been a keen cyclist before joining up. We got on fairly well, and with the aid of brushes and brooms and heavy use of the 'bumper', a weighted device that was swung vigorously back and forward across the floor to produce an unbelievable shine without polish, we soon had the place depressingly like our old home. By now we had been joined by a new intake of lads. I couldn't help thinking what a motley lot they looked and by comparison how soldierly we had become, but I still hated it and all my waking hours were becoming obsessed with how to get out.

In our company there were a few boys from the Irish Republic, where they were allowed to volunteer at fourteen. One of these boys, called Digby, was a very good hammer thrower and was being trained up to represent the army in his specialised sport. The other boy was from County Ofaly, and one night I heard him discussing his plans once he passed out from the IJLB. After a day or so I approached him and asked him about what he'd been saying.

"Are you really not coming back after leave?" I asked innocently.

"Who feckin told you that boy?" he wanted to know, his eyes narrowing and his fists clenching.

"Don't worry, I won't say anything," I said.

"You're feckin right there," he said, "if you do you'll have no feckin teeth left to say anythin at all wid."

257

"It's just that you said that once you're in the Republic they can't get you back here to England," I explained.

When he realised I was genuine, he became quite talkative and told me how, after getting his lance corporal stripes in England, he would automatically get one stripe in the free state army, and that I probably could do the same if that was what I wanted.

This was an impossibly long shot, but I was so desperate to get out that I thought I would try anything. I lacked the courage to pretend to be mad, unlike one of the new intake who had already begun talking to himself and had begun to cut his arms with his dinner knife. Another boy had cut his hair by himself to give him a crazed appearance, and was carefully mimicking all the symptoms of a brain tumour so convincingly that he was eventually discharged.

My day to day routine was getting harder and harder to cope with, and it was only the thought of summer leave which kept my spirits from disappearing altogether.

At last leave came and we were doled out our holiday pay and issued with travel warrants. In spite of my hatred of military life, it was still important to impress my friends at home, and in common with quite a few other boys I had made some slight modifications to my uniform. The peak of my cap had been slashed—the corners had their stitches removed and the peak tucked up so that it resembled a guard's hat, forcing one to look out at the world from underneath the peak—and I'd fixed collar dogs on my shirt collar points.

I took my best SD trousers and best boots carefully in a bag all the way home and changed into this dog uniform in the toilets at West Croydon. From there I marched all the way home and up Factory Lane hoping to catch a few admiring glances, but there was no-one about as I rang on the door of 17a Miller Road.

At least Bruce seemed to be impressed. I went outside and smoked a Park Drive on the bars and looked in the direction of Amy Blair's house. Soon I heard the babble and chatter of the girls coming home from the factories, but was overcome with shyness and went indoors. I sweated in my heavy army uniform until my mum came home and said it was nice to see me. Everything was as I left it, and family life attempted to carry on as it had up until that point, but actually nothing would ever be the same again.

The first thing I noticed was how slow everything had become. I was full of energy and could barely saunter anymore; on the way to the Black Boy pub down Factory Lane I found myself striding ahead of the Marsden twins and then walking back again to rejoin the group.

It was the same when we went up to Mitcham Common on Sundays to watch football. I was never really that fascinated anyway, but it was something to do in the bleak afternoons after *Ray's a Laugh* on the radio; we'd sit in the café on the edge of the common and while away an hour or two over a cup of tea before going out to the pictures in the evening. I'd be pacing up and down the touchline as if I was really agitated by the state of play, rather than confused about my real plans to leave the army forever while at the same time pretending that I really liked it.

Pretty soon I plucked up the courage to ask Amy out, and she readily agreed. I guess I'd always known that she would say yes, and anyway I was considerably more experienced now than when I'd left. Amy was a very pretty girl with lovely brown eyes and a nice figure, but we found little to talk about, and although we had a few snogs in the dark I was shattered to find how quickly my long-held passion began to wane.

The most awful thing was that, terrible though army life was, the thought of knocking about with my old mates on the estate was almost as daunting; things were changing fast and I was having a job keeping up with them.

Back at the battalion I wrote to Amy a couple of times, and though I ached for letters back I can't say that they really fuelled my fantasies about girls, and my need for a girlfriend was starting to dominate my every waking moment.

On my first weekend leave in Oswestry I went out with a bunch of lads and cruised the town. It was a Sunday and there were drink laws that sent the Welsh pouring over the border in order to get a drink in England. Pubs didn't really interest me and anyway we were all under age; besides, I had other agenda to pursue.

As we ambled around the little market town I got separated from the others and found myself back at the railway station (maybe subconsciously I was still planning my escape), but there was no-one there—except the prettiest girl I'd seen all day. She was dark and slim with shortish brown hair, and was wearing a yellow frock with a blue jacket. Whether out of desperation, or confidence now that my mutilated hair had grown back, I can't say, but I found myself talking to her.

To my delight she talked back, and she was bright and she laughed at my attempts at being funny, and she wasn't fazed at my being in the army. I must have used this as the final test of our attraction, but she didn't even bat an eyelid when I told her.

She was waiting for the train to Llangollen, and I stood and waited with her. I knew we were hitting it off together, and rather than wait until her train arrived and I had run out of conversation, I suddenly blurted out, "Can I meet you next Saturday?"

"Yes, if you like," she answered.

"Where?" I enquired, my pulse beginning to race.

"What about here at the station, there's a train that gets in at ten past three on Saturday afternoon," she smiled.

I wanted to kiss her goodbye right there, but thought it might be a bit premature.

"I'll see you here then," I said. "Don't be late!"

"I won't," she said.

With that, I turned on my heels and with a forced air of casualness strolled out of the station. When I was sure that I was out of her eyeline I jumped in the air and ran all the way back to Parkhall Camp, feeling the happiest I had felt in the whole time I'd spent in the service. No-one had to tell me, I was definitely In Love.

The week seemed to drag by and I was constantly losing attention over petty things. On Friday morning I committed a minor infringement to do with my locker and was charged with some form of idleness, resulting in restricted privileges.

Saturday duly arrived and I got into my best grey Italian suit, spent ages disguising the cropped piece of hair in the front of my head, cleaned my teeth twice, shaved and aftershaved, and reported to the guardroom to check out for my longed-for Saturday tryst.

"Name?" shouted the sergeant.

"23783801 Junior Private May sir!" I yelled back. He looked down his clip board.

"There's no Murray here!" he shouted back at me.

"No, May, M-A-Y," I spelt out for him. There was a lengthy silence as he lip read the contents of his list. Finally he looked up.

"Who's been a naughty boy then?" he leered. "You're down for RPs. Report to the cookhouse at the double!"

"But sergeant—" I protested.

"At the double Murray, in fatigues Murray and any more talk laddie and I'll put you on a charge!"

There was nothing I could do. Perhaps if I got to the barrack room there would be someone to ask if they would convey a message, but when I got there only Sam was sat on his bed doing his boots, his moist lips even moister from spitting and polishing.

"Are you not going out?" he asked.

"No," I responded, "I've got kitchen RPs."

I trudged down to the cookhouse and wept great big soppy lad tears as I stood loading potatoes into the peeler and the first girl I loved slipped from my grip forever.

For years afterward I wondered if she ever turned up, and whichever way I viewed it, it broke my heart. If she had just been humouring me and had no intention of keeping our date it would have been bad enough, but what if she had turned up, all pretty and made up, and stood and waited and waited before catching the train back to Llangollen? I could not bear to think about it. Whenever I see that lovely Welsh name I think of her, but I'll never know what she was called and she will never know my nickname was Ray short for Ralph.

The cooks were regular soldiers from the Catering Corps. Some may have been conscripts, as it was the last year of national service, and they looked down on the boys with as much scorn as pity and had very little to do with our lot at all. I can only recall one of them, a corporal. He had a very white face with two tiny eyes that stared at certain boys with a look that made me feel a little unsure. Now here he was in front of me telling me what to do and fixing me with his beady little eyes; he always stared at me whenever he was aware that I was in his sight.

I think at that moment if he had made an advance toward me I would have stabbed him with my potato peeler, but I needn't have worried as the sight of my snotty nose and woebegone look seemed to put him off. Homosexuality was not evident in the barracks, although there were certainly some lads who were uncertain of their orientation. Sex was a solo affair for most boys, and obsessive masturbators were soon identified and the piss taken out of them by the rest, who were masturbating just as much but hadn't been caught in the act.

Its funny how you can sense something unusual is about to happen when the pressure builds up and a sort of unease spreads through the rooms of the barracks. So it was this particular time, when in the afternoon on a hot spring day a diverting rumble ensued from the room across the hall. Someone shouted "Fight!" in our room and we all rushed into the next one to see what was happening. Right by the door a young lad called Barker was being held down by four lads, and my first reaction was that he was about to be branded or tortured in some way, but then through the crowd of boys appeared Curry.

Someone ripped open Barker's trousers and Curry grabbed hold of the poor lad's dick and began to masturbate him. Barker's face was a strange mixture of fear, embarrassment and an odd sort of pleasure as Curry manipulated the lad to an joyless climax. Suddenly all the boys got up and left the kid on his own to clean himself up, and Brady the Irish boy slipped Curry five Park Drive cigarettes.

I could not see the point of this action; I never worked out why it took place or what was to be proved or disproved. At my school there was a little homo activity that mostly consisted of grabbing of genitals and the general argy-bargy that goes on in playgrounds everywhere, but this was different and humiliating and scary and sad and dirty. For a long time afterwards Barker was on his own and for a while so was Curry; the difference was that Curry couldn't have cared less what anyone thought, but Barker's eyes were often red from crying.

$\backsim$

needlework

Curry would do almost any thing for a smoke. His nickname was Twos Up, which translates as 'seconds'. For example, if you were using a broom to sweep your bed space and someone shouted "twos up" it meant that they had next call on the broom. Curry called twos up on everybody's cigarettes, and if someone already had a twos up on your fag, he would have twos up on your twos up. He was the first bloke I ever saw smoke a cigarette end fixed on a pin or between the prongs of a fork, so desperate was he for his nicotine.

Because of the lack of money and our age, drink did not play a large part in our activities. Cigarettes, on the other hand, were at a premium. I don't recall a boy who didn't smoke, and I was no exception. I had now settled on about ten a day; having delayed my first until after breakfast I could get through the day on four more, and smoke the other five during the evening.

Payday was on Wednesday, so everyone was desperate for fags on Tuesday when the money had run out. From very early in my life I had been taught the value of money and how to save, and this frugality enabled me to adapt very quickly to overcoming this problem. Just saving cigarettes till payday would not have helped, as anyone knowing you had them would simply take them off you. Even smoking one would be an embarrassment, as you would be constantly asked for "twos ups". My way around this was to buy a packet of five Park Drive on Wednesday and hide them in the toilets above the cistern; then when I needed my last cigarette, I would creep in to the bog and smoke it. Nearly always someone would wander in and shout, "Twos up on your fag!" and I don't think I ever stubbed out a cigarette myself on a Tuesday. In retrospect it would have been easy to have become a 'baron' as the going rate for a whole snout on Tuesday was at least two on Wednesday, but I was only interested in feeding my own habit.

However, I did find another way of earning a few extra shillings. One evening I decided to taper a pair of jeans. No-one showed me, I just worked it out. First I turned them inside out, then when I had decided on the width I wanted to have at the bottom, I drew a line with a ball-point pen up to the knee and sewed up to it in tiny under and over stitches. The only problem area was where the inseam had to be oversewn, but I got around it and by skilful pressing (by now we were all experts) the effect was all right.

One lad had been watching intently while I was sewing. When I'd finished he admired the look and asked me to do a pair for him, offering me five bob. I was happy to oblige, and after a while I acquired a longer needle and the price had risen to seven and six. Even Brady wanted a pair done. I was getting behind with my cleaning and polishing, and to be honest I was getting pissed off with doing it, especially as Brady had not yet paid me for his.

I tried being a bit more forceful about asking him.

"I'll knock yer feckin teeth down yer troat," he said. I decided that being company tailor was not the life for me.

I had to wait a while to get my revenge, but the opportunity came when he promised me a quid if I would do another pair for him. Up to then I had always left the old material in place inside the jeans or trousers, but this time, knowing he would never pay me, I asked if he would like me to cut off the waste. He thought it would be a good idea, especially if I were to taper them right up to the crotch.

Taper them I did, only this time I made them almost skin tight. It was particularly difficult sewing round the crotch, as three seams meet there, and I was glad that he had agreed to let me cut out the spare material as it made it easier to stitch.

I finally completed the job and handed them over. I can see him now, forcing the black jeans on with an anxious look in my direction as he pushed his large feet through the bottoms. They looked very uncomfortable round the privates, but to my relief he seemed to like his exaggerated profile. Norman Case from the Buffs Regiment was with me when Brady tried them on, and like me he had little time for this bully.

"They look really great," he enthused.

Brady looked at us both, but seeing no trace of a smirk, his own impression that he looked pretty snazzy was confirmed. He changed gingerly out of the garment, promising to pay me next week. Once we were sure he was well and truly out of earshot we burst out laughing at the thought of his appearance.

Between Norman, Sam, Rex, Beau and myself, we persuaded the other lads not to laugh at him when they saw him wearing them on the weekend. Somehow everyone managed to look the other way as Brady got dressed and left the barracks for town. Luckily, being an older boy he no longer needed to check out with the guardroom, or someone might have laughed and spoilt our enjoyment of this moment. From a distance he looked as if his bare legs had been painted black, and the tightness of the crotch was forcing him to walk in a very strange way. I was almost helpless with laughter and so were Sam and Norman.

"You want to watch it, Ray," said Rex, and my laughter suddenly stopped as the possible consequences dawned on me.

I didn't see Brady return to barracks but I heard from a couple of different sources the same story—unfortunately too late to prepare myself for my reward for his humiliation. I was queuing for breakfast when I heard my name called. I looked round and an awesome blow caught me full square in my face, making my nose bleed and eyes run. It was of course Brady, and as I washed myself down in the washroom afterward I was comforted to hear the tale of his undoing.

Brady had got into town all right, but his own discomfiture had been amplified by the stares of others; finally some girl had laughed at him and his embarrassment, which forced him riskily into a pub. Seating himself on a stool his bulging crotch had released itself from my sewing and so had half the stitching down one leg. An attempt to pin up the damage had resulted in a minor piercing injury, the inevitable unravelling began, and a drunk and dishevelled Brady crept back after dark with the remains of his trousers flapping in the night breeze.

No further punishment was enacted on me, and no-one ever asked me to tighten their jeans again. Sam once or twice told me to ask for my money, but I preferred to let that one go.

Once when I was at school I found a little drawing of a girl in a sarong with a palm tree in the background. I was so impressed with it that I kept it for a while, not just for its erotic content but because it was so well drawn. Whenever I found myself doodling I would attempt to reproduce it from memory. Not with any great success, but a stylised version of it began to emerge and could on occasion lead someone to believe that I could 'do drawing'.

At some point my little south sea island girl had been seen and I was approached by Nick, a lad from the Ox and Bucks Light Infantry, who asked me if it was true I could draw. With some modesty I replied that I could do a little bit. He asked to see some and when I showed him some doodles he was impressed enough to ask if I could do him a drawing of an anchor. He seemed happy with my effort and asked in a matter-of-fact way if I would tattoo it on him. At first I thought he must be joking, but he was deadly serious.

"But I can't do a tattoo," I said.

"Course you can, all you need is a darning needle and some Indian ink."

Now I have to confess that I'd always been fascinated by tattoos and on my first day out of barracks down in Plymouth had tried to get an appointment at Rex Zeta's establishment on Union Street. Unfortunately on the Wednesday I was to have been marked, a sailor lad had passed out in front of me and Mr. Zeta had cancelled the rest of the day's appointments as a precaution in case the lad had needed medical treatment. In those days an infected tattoo could be classified as self-inflicted injury, and the forces were actually against lads marking themselves, not realising that apart from giving themselves some individuality when the army tried to make everyone look the same, it was also a rite of passage.

As it transpired I was lucky to miss out, as in the world of tattoo artists Rex Zeta's work is not much admired. There were some lads in the company who had great work on their arms: a boy from Huddersfield in particular, who wore some beautifully drawn birds; and another cockney lad who had some work done by an artist on the Waterloo Road.

When I realised that this chap was serious, I picked the brains of all the tattooed boys in the company as to how it was done. They were mostly unable to say except that it didn't hurt. This was hard to figure out as it became obvious that from all they said that it was necessary to draw blood, and it was the blood mixing with ink under the skin that made the mark. I began by practising on myself and the first thing I realised was that I could not decide what design to have but I did learn to minimise the pain and got to be able to prick the skin quite fast and soon I was ready to have a go. Wisely Nick had decided to forgo the large anchor on the forearm in favour of a smaller version on the second joint of his thumb.

On the appointed evening in front of a small crowd I laid out the tools of my new trade on the table that doubled as both writing and ironing table in the middle of the room: Indian ink, darning needle (jeans tapering, for the use of) which was a little blunt but a good size, a ball-point pen and a towel. After drawing the little anchor in biro I commenced tapping away with my blunt needle and ink. Luckily Nick bled easily and the job was soon done, the whole thing being the size of a thumbnail. As the scab peeled off it was clear that my dots weren't close enough to-gether and another session was called for.

The end result was quite effective, and probably my best work. I was pressed to do more and thankfully most of my efforts were very small and were reasonably good as far as prison type tattoos go. There were how-ever one or two minor exceptions, where what looked good on paper did not translate well to the flesh.

One bloke wanted my Hawaiian girl on his forearm, and in spite of my trying to talk him out of it, his mind was made up and reluctantly I had a go. I remember this for two reasons: (a) because it was so hard to draw blood from his arm—the needle was getting blunter and blunter—and (b) because the way he placed his arm on the table meant that when it was finished and his arm assumed its normal position, the island girl had a twisted appearance with more voluptuous hips than were intended.

Thankfully he never noticed it himself, for when he lifted his arm up to see it, the tattoo distorted itself back into its original state. He never had the face drawn in, though; I think he'd had enough after the hour or so it took to get the ink into his arm.

The tattoo I remember the best though was for poor redheaded Dennis, a lad in one of the Lancashire regiments. Dennis was incredibly thin and pale, a slow and serious boy with a continuous slight tremor that shook his body as if he was cold. I asked him about his shaking and he said that he always had been like it. I wondered again at this army that was happy to take all of us misfits.

Dennis had decided to have a skull and crossbones with the words 'Death or Glory' written in a scroll underneath. The needle by this time had become almost too blunt to push through a piece of paper, but for some reason I had not thought to change it. To make it still more difficult, Dennis's arm was so thin that the crossbones had to be very small to fit on it, and the scroll had to start on the underside of his arm to get the words on so that they were legible.

As I banged away at his sad little stick-like arm with my head down, an extraordinary thing happened: when I started filling in the hollow eye sockets in the skull Dennis's voice began to trail off and he stopped shaking. I finally noticed this and looked up at him to ask if he was all right, but he could only nod through clenched teeth, and when I had finished the word 'Death' he suddenly shouted, "STOP!" unable to stand the pain any more.

Unfortunately I had also pricked a large vein on the underside of his arm, which decided not to stop bleeding for quite a while. It was all pretty gruesome and effectively stopped my career as a skin artist. It may have been the sight of Dennis bloody and tear-stained, or perhaps just my bad draughtsmanship, or even this half tattoo of a skull with the word 'Death' written underneath it. I didn't get around to drawing the crossbones, and as far as I know Dennis never added the 'or Glory' to the design.

out

In spite of what you might call these lighter moments, I found my situation increasingly desperate. The realisation grew that I would have to do something radical if I was to get out of the army.

In terms of female comfort, things were pretty grim too. Oswestry as a town was provincial but at the same time inured to squaddies, and some of a town's naiveté disappears as it becomes used to the exuberance and energy of young over-trained soldiers on the lookout for adventure and/or sex.

Nevertheless, one rainy night I met Linda, a plain, slightly dumpy local girl. She was already going out with a lad from Wakefield who I knew vaguely by sight from B Company, though I didn't know this at the time. She had a lovely laugh and a pretty Welsh accent, and that first evening I walked her back to her place, which smelt of washing and ironing and clothes drying and made me think of home.

"This is Ray, Mam," she said.

"Hello," said her Mam, hardly looking at me.

It was late and I had to get back to barracks so I made my excuses and moved toward the door.

"Can I see you again?" I asked.

"If you like," she replied. "There's a dance on Saturday at the town

269

hall, we could go there."

We had a little kiss on the doorstep and off I went back to the camp.

The next weekend I met her and we went to the pictures. I don't remember the film but I was allowed to pay for her; in fact she never paid for anything during the time we went out together. On the way back to her house she suddenly asked, "How old are you, Ray?"

"Eighteen," I lied.

"Oh that's all right then, only I don't go out with boys who are younger than me see," she explained. Then—I don't know where the idea came from—I suddenly said, "I've already got a kid. Would you like to see a picture of him?"

She looked a little taken aback at this but managed a curious, "Yes, if you like."

In my jacket pocket I had a wallet that my father had made either when he was in the desert or when he was in prison, and in this wallet I had a picture of myself as a baby that I'd brought with me from home. I showed her the photo under a street lamp and she even said that he looked a bit like me. Then, taking hold of my arm, she said that she was going to break it off with the lad from Wakefield and go steady with me.

Linda was eighteen and had expensive tastes, as I found out when she ordered a milkshake that cost half a crown. However, I was flattered and on the way back to her house I joked about her soon to be ex-boyfriend, saying that he was a bit thick and that his eyes were too close together. I was full of confidence now that she had plumped for me, and by my little deception she would know that I had carnal knowledge and would eventually expect some consummation of our relationship. I was really on a promise, and there was only a little resistance when I felt her breasts as we kissed goodnight.

When I had joined up the track most played on the NAAFI jukebox was *Three Steps to Heaven* by Eddie Cochrane. Then it was *Cathy's Clown* by the Everly Brothers, and now it was *Only the Lonely* by Roy Orbison. I wonder if all teenage songs are as appropriate to each generation as they seem to have been for mine.

The Saturday hop was great and they played *Only the Lonely* at least half a dozen times which meant that I could hold her close and shuffle around the brightly lit room. I was definitely getting somewhere, I could feel it and even in my thick grey Italian suit pressed up against her so could she.

When I called for her on the Sunday her mother said, "She's gone out with Mick and she won't be seeing you no more."

I was stunned and just stood there with my mouth open.

"But why?" I asked, almost unable to believe my ears.

"She found out you were only fifteen and she don't go out with boys younger than her. I'm sorry Ray, but you shouldn't have told her lies. Don't worry, you'll soon find a girl of your own age," she added comfortingly.

After a miserable night back at the barracks I was standing in the breakfast queue when a sharp dig in the ribs made me swing around to confront Mick.

"Tha's bin sayin' I'm thick," he declared in a loud voice.

"No I haven't," I countered cleverly.

"Tha's bin sayin my eyes is too close together tha 'as," he added.

"No I haven't," I repeated. I just couldn't think of anything else to say and anyway I expected my life to end at any moment as I was sure I was about to be stabbed by him with his dinner knife and fork. Instead he just looked at me and appeared to be searching for something to say.

He finally managed, "Well tha doesn't fookin want to either or than eyes'll be too fookin close an all!"

And that was it. I turned away expecting to feel the eating irons to be thrust between my shoulder blades but they never came, and for all I know Mick and Linda went off to be a couple while I slipped gradually into a deep depression.

In my desperation I began to write home to my mother, telling her just how unhappy I was and more or less promising anything if she could get me out. At first her letters were homely assurances that things would probably pick up, and that it was normal to see the worst of things from time to time and so on. These letters only added to my frustration. I was becoming more panicky by the day with my inability to convey my desperation. Now the army was a prison from which I had to escape or go mad.

My letters became longer and more emphatic. A couple of them spanned more than eight pages, and the tone became increasingly hopeless as I tried to press my case more urgently. Whatever the cost I must get out.

In the end Mum turned to her brother (Uncle Ray) for advice. He helpfully suggested she should leave me in to make a man of me. The poor bastard had joined the navy as a child of thirteen, and my brother Bruce had almost joined the navy training ship *Arethusa* but thankfully stayed at home.

My mate Sam had also been growing disaffected with military life, and when he realised that I was determined to leave, he embarked on a similar course—that of obtaining the then huge sum of fifty pounds to buy his discharge. I had as much chance of raising that sort of money as raising the Titanic, and again had to resort to begging Mum to try to get it for me, but only after I finally convinced her how essential it was for me to get out.

My life was falling apart; boys that I had previously got along with began to drift away from me, I stopped bathing regularly and lost interest in everything. All I could think of was escape. I smoked whenever I could and begged twos ups from the other blokes. Somehow I avoided getting put on a charge for generally being depressed and dirty, but one day Beau came into the washroom and said that some of the boys were about to organise a regimental scrubbing.

I don't know how this sort of information is passed down, but this particular punishment is also about humiliation. The victim is usually jumped by four or five others, stripped naked and thrown on to a table; buckets of cold water are thrown over him and then Vim or some other detergent, and then he is scrubbed with a bass broom. I had to discover who was behind this move and was upset to find that Rex was the proposer. I went to him and confronted him, telling him that I'd thought of him as a friend and threatening to get each and every one of them back if they were to carry out their plan. By the end of this speech I was in tears, but I knew that Rex could see that I was truly at the end of my tether. Although the proposed scrubbing never took place, my friendship with Rex and most of the others was at an end and would never be repaired.

Finally a letter arrived from my mother telling me that she had borrowed the money from her boss on the condition that I would return to school and attempt to get some O-levels, and that I would get a weekend job and pay off all the money in less than a year. I know that I have experienced happiness since that letter, but until that moment it was the biggest high I had ever felt. I rushed to tell Sam, who had also been promised money from home, and we danced about with glee.

I immediately wrote back to thank Mum and promised to comply with all the terms. Sam and I were placed on discharge fatigues as the army tried to humiliate us further, and we weren't allowed out until our papers were in order. One day when we were on garden fatigues, Sam gave lip to a sadistic Scottish sergeant, who struck Sam a fierce punch on the side of the head. Though we were sometimes pushed around or given the odd dig with a pace stick, I'd never before seen a boy physically abused by an adult sergeant.

As the pain took hold of Sam's emotions and tears streamed down his face he yelled, "Right you fuckin' bastard I'm reporting you for that I've got four witnesses and they'll back me won't you lads?" and he turned around to us for support.

"Yeah Sam, don't worry, we saw what happened," we agreed. Somewhere in barrack room mythology the idea had emerged that you needed four boy soldiers to charge one grown-up NCO. The sergeant looked at us all and very slowly turned round and went inside the sergeants' mess, returning a few seconds later with another sergeant.

"Did you see me strike this soldier, sergeant?" he enquired, not looking at his colleague but just eyeing us back and forth through narrowed eyelids.

"No sergeant, I certainly did not," was the deliberately delivered reply. The situation was hopeless and we knew it.

"Now get on with your work or you'll all be on a fuckin' charge!" he bellowed. The two of them grinned at each other, and we were left in no doubt that for a few more days the army still had the upper hand.

At last the day arrived and Sam and I were ordered to get into best civvies and report to the battalion commander's office. We were marched in one at a time, and the commander asked me my reason for leaving. I told him I had secured a place at Croydon Technical College, then he handed me a reference, my pittance of saved pay and a travel warrant, and I was dismissed and officially out.

I waited excitedly for Sam to emerge from his farewell interview and asked him what he had said when the CO had asked him what his future plans were.

"I told him I was going to get a good job working on the barges down at Gravesend!" laughed Sam. We said goodbye to a couple of lads that weren't otherwise engaged, and Norman Case asked for our addresses. I gave him mine and he wrote once or twice, but I didn't bother to keep up with the correspondence as I had other agenda by then. Sam, who had little time for Norman, gave him a made-up address in Gravesend.

Now Sam and I were off out of the barrack gates and standing on the side of the road heading toward the railway station. It was overcast and there was a stiff breeze, but to me the sky had never been bluer or the air warmer. I looked back at the poor hapless bastards on guard duty, and already their brown uniforms were assuming the anonymity we give soldiers so as not to grieve for them as individuals. Birds were singing in the fields around Parkhall Camp, soon two beautiful blonde girls would pull up in a pink Cadillac and ask us where we wanted to go and did we want to have sex with them and we would say yes and they would have loads of money and I breathed great lungfuls of free Shropshire air and the taste of freedom is real I can swear to it.

What actually happened is that we hitched a lift on an open back lorry, and standing up behind the cab with the wind in our faces, we hollered and sang all the way to the station. I have felt freedom and exhilaration many times since, but never so strong and in equal measure as on that ride. We had cups of tea and biscuits on the train and talked excitedly all the way to Victoria station, where we were to go our separate ways.

We entered the busy station in the late afternoon. An announcement called the Gravesend train, and as Sam ran to catch it I suddenly realised I only had this imaginary address he had given Norman. I didn't know it then, but I wouldn't see him again for twenty years, by which time I would have a son named Sam and a new name.

$\backsim$

wolfie

Five years later I was travelling on a huge crane fitted with caterpillar tracks which was moving at about four miles per hour along the road from Thessalonika to Athens. I had been hitchhiking for hours and this piece of plant had passed me several times, offering me a lift that I had already declined. I had got a few lifts but my progress was slow.

As I saw its lumbering form coming my way once again I decided to clamber aboard. There, hidden amongst the machinery and curled up in a foetal position, was a young and totally spaced-out German called Wolfgang. He had been travelling for a few years and was as skinny as a rake with, shorter hair than was normal for that time. He wore a t-shirt and waistcoat, black trousers, sandals and a tiny hat like the ones the black guys wore at home.

Wolfie spoke English with a slight American accent and a trace of a lisp. Some of his adventures were incredible, but he told them with no attempt to impress; it was just his reality he was keen to share, and he seemed to be amazed and delighted by each new experience and acquaintance that came his way.

Today he was riding a crane, tomorrow it could be a Ferrari, and some weeks previously in Afghanistan it had been in an oven-like compartment on a steam train. He was unable to get out of this until the locomotive stopped, which it mercifully did before he succumbed and was cooked alive. He was clearly not over this trauma yet, and every now and then he would leave his womb-like spot on the crane and we would both walk alongside the vehicle.

Wolfie earned his living on the road as a pavement artist, and apart from a tin whistle and a few items of clothing all he carried were his chalks. He also had one book with him that bore the stamp of a secondhand dealer in Rangoon: Brendan Behan's *Borstal Boy*. Wolfie insisted that I take it as a parting gift when I left his company to hitch to Istanbul. I tried not to accept, but sometimes on the road where friendships are struck that you know are not to become lifelong companionships, the taking or receiving of small gifts symbolises the transitory nature of the friendship between two people and eases both consciences as they part, probably never to meet again.

"Good luck, my friend, and may the road be good to you; and when you read this book you may think of me."

I still have the book, I loved reading it, and all I can say is that I would have swapped my time in the Army for a spell in Brendan's borstal any day.

✹

Upper left: Ralph aged about 20 months
Upper right: Bruce (left) and Ralph (right) with mum
Lower: Bruce, Christine, Ralph, and Susan with Patch the dog at West Street Rec, Banbury, in 1951

Upper: Ralph is wearing a tie and is seated in the second row at Bramley H nursery in 1948. *Lower left:* 'Stinging nettles' - Bruce, Susan, Ralph ar Christine at Brackley in 1949. *Lower right :* ' Bow and arrow' - Ralph and Bru at Croham Hurst, Croydon, in 1951

Upper left: Junior Private May 23783801 at Plymouth Hoe in 1960. *Upper right:* Ralph aged 18 at Miller Road, Croydon with the 12-string Harmony guitar. *Lower left:* Ralph with his treasured 6-string Harmony Soverign at Whitgift Arms, Croydon. *Lower right:* Olaf and Ralph at the Ponte Vecchio, Florence, in 1964

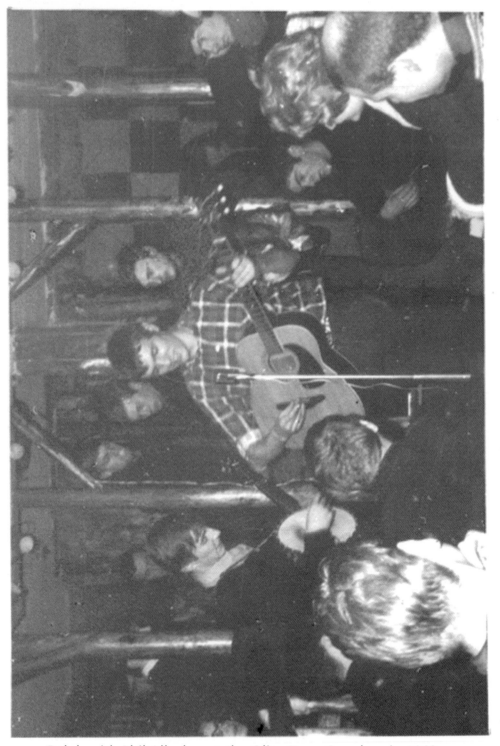

Ralph with Phil Allacker at the Olive Tree, Croydon, in 1962

tech

I walked from West Croydon station with my small bag of possessions, and with every step relished my familiar surroundings. It was the late autumn of 1960; my summer leave seemed an age ago and I took delight in the rattle and noise of the town. The contrast with the weekly visits to Oswestry was marked, the noise of the terminal gradually diminishing as I walked the route of the 64 trolley-bus. With each step homeward I left the life of the last few months further behind me.

Even as I write of these moments some forty years later, I can think of no subjectively longer six month period. My army days seemed more like two years; it had been a quantum leap towards manhood, as had been the jump from the relative gentility of the Waldrons, where my first memories began, to the Mitcham Road estate, where the warm feelings I held for it almost overwhelmed me. I could already see the giant gasholder under whose shadow we lived in Miller Road. It looked fat and friendly as I headed expectantly in its direction.

Familiar streets, familiar smells, everything was different and yet nothing had changed. As I walked over Pitlake Bridge I bumped into someone who did not even know I'd been away.

The traffic noise subsided as I approached the walk up Factory Lane past the working men's hostel. No cars passed me. The throb of the B power station grew louder then diminished, drowned in the hissing of the old wooden cooling towers and the clatter of the trucks into the council dump. Familiar sounds singing me home.

As the end of Miller Road came into sight my pulse rate quickened at the thought of number 17a and seeing Mum and Bruce again. The last few steps towards the gate produced a great grin of expectation at the welcome I would get as I crossed over the threshold of our upstairs two-bedroom flat and on to the green, green linoleum of home.

Against everyone's advice, my mother had borrowed the money from her boss Mr. Waters to buy me out of the army. She had made it clear to me that I would have to pay it back, and that I would also have to return to school in order to complete my O-level studies. I had readily agreed to this. I had served my time (six months), successfully pleaded my case to my dear mum, and not attempted suicide or self-mutilation (several lads had done this and about twenty were AWOL when I left Parkhall Camp).

The doorbell was answered by Bruce, grinning a toothy hello. I hopped up the stairs in three steps to give my mum a homecoming kiss.

"You'd better put your things in your room," she said rather coldly after a perfunctory peck. I realised that, far from being any kind of hero, my return was regarded as failure, and she had decided not to make my transition to civilian life a smooth affair. I have to say this pained me, and not for the first time I was shocked at my inability to convey the hell wrought by my own demons to others.

I contented myself for the first few days renewing old acquaintances. Just about everything was different to the way I had left it. For a start my little brother was now quite big and had already established himself at his grammar school. He had new friends and was playing rugby for his year (I had absolutely no interest in any team games at this time); he had recently discovered that he had hair and was combing it; he was wearing long trousers and his voice had broken. We never went about together after this, at least until my musical adventure became professional.

Re-establishing friendships was difficult. So little had happened to my mates and so much had happened to me. Just walking down the road together, I wanted to break into a run. I was teeming with energy, and the feeling of freedom was so prolonged and heady that I managed to put my cool welcome behind me. I took delight in everything around me and was sure I could make up lost ground at the college. Most of my mates were already at work and settling into the 'light and bitter, brown and mild' routine, We soon drifted apart, also forever.

The deal I had struck was that I would attend college—Croydon College of Technology, with a one day release for an A-level in art at the adjoining art school—and attempt to salvage something out of what was, after all, a grammar school education. The plan was doomed to failure.

Croydon Tech was a state of the art establishment. It catered to a tremendously varied bunch of students, and their range of studies went from engineering to the arts and secretarial courses to English and girls (studied by exotic Iranians). The art college was bridged by means of the canteen and there was an air of exuberance and ease about the whole place. It is hard to think of a more different environment to that of the camp. A few weeks previously I had been a number and a name, I'd responded to a self-administered nickname ('Ray'), and was screamed at from morning to night by mad men and boys who wore stripes on their arms. Here my hair began to grow back to the Tony Curtis-style late teddy boy look. I was addressed as Mr. May by my tutors, and everywhere and on every stair, corridor and room were girls. Girls, girls, girls.

Pretty as pictures, all sticky out petticoats, heavy eye liner, back-combed hair, girls, girls, girls.

Giggling, smiling, whispering behind their hands, collecting in groups, sashaying into the canteen, dancing in the common rooms at their lunch breaks to *Hit The Road Jack* and *Rubber Ball* and *Midnight in Moscow*, girls girls girls.

Just swishing past girls in the corridors, traces of perfume or the scent of shampoo, the rustle of clothing, all these things had a devastating effect on the newly released prisoner from Shropshire. By the end of the first week I was in love with four girls and had not spoken to any of them. After a few days some of them smiled in recognition. I blushed until I burned. Concentrating on anything in lesson time I found nearly impossible as my eyes and thoughts would settle on some sweet thing in a soft sweater or pencil skirt.

There was also the matter of my £50 debt and the need to repay my mother's boss, Mr. Waters. Luckily work came in the form of a gardening job for a certain Mr. Tickle who had a small electrical winding factory near to mum's chemist shop.

The Tickles lived in a beautiful house in Riddlesdown Road, in an outlying area beyond south Croydon. It had a huge, well ordered back garden with a large lawn, greenhouses and carnation beds. The soil was chalky and hard to dig, but I was still fit from the army; I liked being out in the open and I enjoyed the bike ride to and from the place.

There were two Mr. Tickles, father and son, and both were bird fanciers. Around the garden were aviaries containing all manner of parrots, cockatiels, amazons, and mynah birds. There was also a family pet named Joe, a very old African Grey parrot who was allowed to wander up and down the apple tree branches, and spent most of the time saying, "Come on down you naughty boy."

He found it difficult to climb down the tree and would, when distressed, order himself back into his cage with, "In your cage, Joe."

On my first morning, anxious to impress, I threw myself into my work and had not noticed the passing of time until Mrs. Tickle called me for a break with some tea.

"Ralph!" she called in a clear high voice, and from that moment on the mynah birds called my name at random so that I never knew whether it was her calling me or not. Even when they went out I would beaver away as hard as I could in case I got fooled into assuming it was the birds calling me. These same birds could perfectly imitate the sound of the car pulling up and the application of slightly squeaky brakes, so for me there was no chance of pausing to relax even to smoke the odd Park Drive.

Once unbeknown to me a young couple were staying at the house when the family had gone out. I kept up my normal work rate all afternoon, and just before the Tickles returned, the young bloke came out and asked me if I ever slowed down or took a break. He said they had been watching me from a bedroom window. I was pleased to be so commended for my efforts, and it was only on my way home at the end of my eight hours' work, when I could hardly push the pedals on my bike, that I found myself wondering what he'd been doing in a bedroom all afternoon while I sweated away behind the old lawn mower and rake.

Oh well, the first part of the journey home was all downhill and there was Saturday night to look forward to. There is always Saturday night to look forward to.

Saturday night seldom lives up to expectation; I suppose that's why we look forward to it, the next forever holding the potential to be better than the last. Ours would be spent at the Gun or other local pubs where I renewed old school friendships with Derek 'Les' Lester and Vernon

Burford. We would catch a jazz band somewhere, or shoot up west to Goodge Street and Fitzrovia.

Traditional jazz was enjoying its revival. I had liked this music since I was introduced to it by Vernon when I was eleven years old. His older brothers had quite a few records by Chris Barber and Lonnie Donegan; I knew these tunes and could identify the difference between a trombone and a trumpet, and to my new friends must have seemed quite knowledgeable.

There were all sorts of different dance steps available to the uninhibited, from the intricacies of the Cy Laurie steps, done against the beat at a furious speed, to the more ungainly 'skip jive' favoured by ravers. There do not seem to be any filmed records of these dance fads, but I thought them very stylish and sharp, especially performed by some of the couples. The added attraction was that girls were swirled around very fast and revealed all sorts of hidden paraphernalia of stockings and suspenders to the delight of leering students.

There were a couple of real creepy blokes who could not dance but asked girls to join them in the breaks in the common room, and these girls accepted. I couldn't believe how uncool these geezers were. I was too laid back to show any enthusiasm for this venture and although I had made the beginnings of fumbled exploration whilst 'away', I was still hopelessly shy. I decided to make notes and practise some steps in the privacy of my own bedroom.

The problem here was that I did not have my own bedroom. There was only a foot or so gap between my bed and Bruce's, and this hardly allowed room enough for the rather galumphing prancing about required for Trad. Nevertheless, I practised my reverse turns, often cracking my shins on the old iron bed runners. Once I rehearsed a few steps out in the yard one evening until spotted by Mrs. Bradley, who surprised me whilst silently taking in her washing and observing me from behind the privet hedge. It is very difficult to convert a full flying Trad jive with an invisible partner to the earnest search for something you have mislaid around the dustbin area of the yard, and my sheepish grin did not do much to convince her that I was all right. She bolted the back door once inside.

There was a parallel interest in Thirties jazz around this time, and a band called the Temperance Seven played a dance at the Denning Hall. The evening was called, somewhat inexplicably, 'Votes for Women 1913'.

The admission charge was two bob and the evening was subscribed mainly by the art school students. I thought the event was fantastic; I enjoyed the high camp of the band, but mostly I loved the music. The musicians were fabulous. They even had fabulous names like Alan Swainston-Cooper and Cephas Howard, and Whispering Paul McDowell, the vocalist, was so cool. The band performed in what looked like Edwardian costume and their playing was peerless. Soon the Temps had a number one hit with *You're Driving Me Crazy*.

Amongst the audience were some beatnik types from outside the college, including one quite famous raver called 'Little Ray'. The kids at the art college were different; they wore strange clothes—and what were those fabulous jeans they were wearing and where could you get them? Levis were forty two and sixpence a pair, which was double the cost of their rivals. Some boys had been to Paris to buy them. I had wanted a pair since I saw my first James Dean film.

Somehow I secured a small grant to assist Mum with my education and this was in part used to pay back some of the money I owed her. This meant that with incredible frugality I could spend some of my money on the odd item of clothing, usually from Millets, and buy my smokes and an occasional 45 record out of my gardening wages. I was one of the poorer kids at the college—but not as poor as Squeeb.

Squeeb came from New Addington and was a very bright lad full of confidence and fun, with jet black hair and slightly puffy eyes which gave him a frog-like appearance. He had small teeth and his hands trembled, but if he was nervous he certainly did not show it. I fell in with him, and being from the same social class we hit it off quite well. Squeeb chatted in a matey way to everyone and they responded to him in a usually friendly way. There did seem to be an enormous gap in social standing with the majority of kids coming from posh outlying areas of Croydon, but this did not daunt Squeeb, who bantered his way with them all. With boys and girls it is not all one way traffic and I guess some of the girls were interested in finding out about the new kid (me). They did this through Squeeb.

I was still at the stage of colouring up whenever I was spoken to, and although these girls were so pretty, they were out of my class and I looked elsewhere. As far as appearances went, I resembled more the boys on day release from the engineering school, who were proper lads, but I was with the kids who were studying the arts. Somehow the class structure seemed to prevail and like sought out like, except for Squeeb who pitched at everything and went out with no-one. Somewhere in those first few months I went out with Judy, Jenny, Angela—and eventually Roberta. But the first one I remember was Cleo.

∾

girls

Cleo threw herself at me at the end of a dance. Actually, she nearly threw up on me, and because she seemed a little worse for wear I walked her home. My affectionate little goodnight kiss did not end there as she suddenly sobered up and pressed me in a scary clinch that I managed to self deny, playing the double bluff that if she was that pissed she would not remember it and I could deny that it ever happened.

Judy was addicted to dance. At lunchtime in the common room, to the sound of a cheap record player, she would perfect her laconic, languid routine. Boys did not dance in the bright midday sunlit room that was reserved for us to spend our lunch hour in, so Judy danced with Susan, who was quite possibly the sexiest fifteen year old I have ever seen, before or since. They had the knowledge, of men, that is, in the biblical sense. Or so I thought. I was wrong about both of them, but more wrong about one than the other.

Susan was stunning in every regard; her naturally very blonde hair was parted down one side so that the majority of her fringe fell across her pretty face. She was forever pushing it back and unselfconsciously putting it behind her ear, which had the effect of making her look gauche and vulnerable. Her small blue eyes were nearly always smiling and she had teeth that were white and prominent; not quite Brigitte Bardot but also not quite Joyce Grenfell.

She had a husky laugh and a wonderful figure with huge breasts. Every boy in the place fancied her gutless. Both girls were working class but Susan fancied the most drippy boys in the college, hooray Henrys and chinless wonders from the suburbs. I stood no chance. I went for Judy.

Judy was something else; slim to a ridiculous degree, and her bust was almost non-existent. Her grey eyes were sleepy and heavy-lidded, and her hair was thick and styled in what was beginning to be known as the Mod girl look. She had a slight stoop to her shoulders and showed just the right amount of disinterest to make her interesting.

We went out quite a few times but it was all a bit fraught; at sixteen I was still encumbered with virginity, and although I once wormed my way into Judy's sleeping bag, I only ever got inside her bra—and there wasn't much there except two rolled-up handkerchiefs.

She did accompany me once down to Brighton on a rave and we shivered underneath the pier on the cold pebbles in March. A sleeping bag is like a giant condom, for unless you plan well ahead there is nothing much you can do once you are both in it except try to keep warm. So much for another Millets bargain! We slept, I suppose, but the next day, tired and unfulfilled, was the beginning of the end. Judy ended up going out with (and eventually marrying) one of the boys in engineering.

Jenny was sweet: she reminded me of a Sunday school teacher I once had. She loved me because I comforted her when Ricky Tyrell packed her in.

Ricky was a boy from the other side of the tracks, confident beyond his years and extremely funny. He had straight, wispy hair, tiny slits for eyes and a square English face. He wore a sports jacket and straight trousers and looked quite conventional, but his sense of humour was wicked. Once whilst watching a particularly ungainly girl jiving around the common room, he turned to me and said above the noise of the Dansette, "My God, Ralph, she looks like a ruptured camel with his hump on fire!"

One day a rumour started circulating around the college about some film extra work. We found there were auditions taking place somewhere near Dulwich. I was only too ready to try our luck, as the amounts being talked about were up to five pounds a day.

We embarked on a bus and train journey that took about two hours, and finally arrived at a tiny one-roomed office above a tobacconist shop, where a middle-aged lady with dyed black hair and a deep masculine raspy voice sat behind an overflowing ash tray and told us she hadn't the slightest idea what we were talking about.

"You are an agent aren't you?" asked Ricky. She replied that she was, but had no extra work, although she thought that we were two nice boys and she would put us on her books.

"What are your names?" she asked.

"Ricky Tyrell," answered my friend.

"Don't I know that name?"

"Yes," said Ricky. "My great- great- great- great grandfather Louis Armstrong shot the two little princes in the eye in Epping Forest and is known in history as one of the most heinous and vile aristocrats of all time. He was imprisoned in Thornton Heath clock tower before being transported to Virginia where he made some amends and a small fortune by discovering the pork pie."

We never heard from her.

I don't know if it was the disappointment at not launching his movie career, but things quickly fell apart with him and Jenny after this. Jenny had saucer eyes as big as my mother's, and to see her cry brought back painful memories. Gradually she replaced Rick with me in her affections and the responsibility was too much for me. One day she pointedly told me that she had fallen for someone else, and although I guessed it was me, I pretended to be happy for her and wriggled away from the situation.

When I told Ricky of these events he said, "Christ, how must she feel being rejected by two of the best looking blokes in the college?" I could not believe this remark for he was no oil painting either. The two of us began to drift apart after that, and apparently Jenny cried for a fortnight.

Angela had enormous breasts, but I was put off by her very thin legs. She was pretty and outgoing, with masses of curly dark hair, and had a lovely laugh that cracked when she chuckled. She was adored from afar by Spike, who had a Plan. He had found out that Angela was interested in me, and as he was besotted with her, persuaded the three of us to go to the cinema together. When I turned up he had quite a pretty girl in tow, and somehow engineered it so that I sat next to her whilst he sat with Angela.

Immediately the movie started, he fell on Angela, who resisted for a while but, assuming we boys had cooked this up between us, eventually responded to Spike's advances. Meanwhile I sat glumly with Gina. The poor girl was upset at my lack of interest as she had rather liked me, and Spike persuaded me to write to her explaining things. I helpfully sent a brief note along the lines of 'one man's meat is another man's poison', which I am sure helped to restore her self confidence in no time.

Roberta was quite simply the most stunning looking girl in the Tech. She was taller than any of the other girls at about five foot nine, with huge eyes and flaming red hair. She was on a secretarial course. She had a beautiful figure and always dressed as if she was going dancing instead of going to school. Her friend Tina was smaller with massive back-combed hair and wore more eyeliner than Dusty Springfield. The two girls were inseparable, and in a way Tina successfully minded her statuesque friend as she moved about the college attracting wolf whistles and remarks from just about all the boys. Like everyone else I fantasised about Roberta; you simply could not help it. Those huge blue eyes and that figure, and in spite of everything a gentle shyness about her. Tina strutted along basking in Roberta's reflected presence, and some of the more astute lads reckoned that Tina was a teaser and probably would never come across. The two of them danced together and sat together in the canteen and walked together, Roberta in pastel blues and Tina in dark greens. They were impressive.

One day I was sitting with some friends in the canteen when Tina strode over to us and rolled up her sleeve to reveal several finger-sized bruises.

"Can you see these?" she asked.

"Yes," we chorused.

"Do you know how I got them?" she demanded.

"No," we all chimed.

"From her," she gesticulated with a nod of her head in Roberta's direction. We all looked at Roberta who blushed prettily and turned away towards the door.

"Every time she sees you," she said, looking at me, "she grabs my arm and says, 'I want him!'"

There was a loud "Phwoarr" from all my mates.

"Please ask her out, Ralph—she's hurting me and she really likes you," implored Tina.

The lads on my table were guffawing and slapping me on the back. I was grinning stupidly and you could have lit a match from my burning cheeks.

"Go on!" roared my mates. "Go and ask her, go on, get stuck in!"

I was embarrassed, frightened, flattered and excited. I smiled foolishly at the wonderful Roberta and lip-read the word from her across the crowded canteen.

"WOOF."

I thought perhaps she couldn't pronounce her Rs properly and was trying to say Ralph. A small speech impediment was not going to stand in the way of a possible revealing of unthinkable delights to come. She smiled at me and for the rest of the afternoon I thought about her and her impediment, wondering if I should address her as 'Woberta' to put her at her ease. I met her later that day after lessons and asked her if she would like to come out with me for a walk before she took the bus home.

"Woof."

"My name is Ralph," I said.

"I know," she said. "Woof woof."

As we walked away from the college, some of the boys were calling after us. Roberta took no notice; she was used to producing this kind of attention. I looked at her again.

"Woof woof," she said.

By the time we had crossed the road she had hold of my hand. Cars were switching on their lights and the winter evening was drawing in. I had no money and nowhere to go, so we headed for the Town Hall gardens and sat on a park bench.

"Whereabouts do you live, Roberta?" I asked.

"Woof woof," she replied.

Then she said, "Norbury."

"Oh, what bus do you have to catch?" No answer. I tried another tack.

"Why do you keep saying woof?"

"Woof woof," said Roberta.

"Roberta—" I began.

"Woof woof woof," she said and then as I made a slight move she kissed me. This was a big kiss. It went on for a long time. Christ she was powerful. And probably the same weight as me, although I did have a slight height and reach advantage. But the first round was definitely hers.

Eventually I staggered from the Town Hall gardens and saw Roberta on to the bus and said goodnight.

"Woooof," breathed Roberta.

I commenced my walk home. I was aware of an aching below the belt which had started somewhere during the tenth round, and by the time I crawled through the front door I was in agony.

In the morning at college I resisted the opportunity to satisfy my leering mates with details of my encounter and simply told them that I had walked her home. We went to the pictures later in the week, but the story was much the same and with nowhere to go I felt I had lost that bout and Roberta's stamina and strength had finally won the day. I decided to throw in the towel, much to the incredulity of all the blokes I sat with. I told Roberta I had met someone else.

Years later I met her in the post office in Croydon when my first son Sam was in his pram. We chatted and she was just as sweet and lovely as I remembered her. I said how nice it was to see her, and we just said goodbye.

Woof woof Roberta.

guitars

I was gradually learning not to burn up every time a girl smiled at me (I haven't quite got it cracked yet, but I'm getting better). I had plenty of new friends and was moving easily about the college and in the main attending my lessons, which had nothing like the strict discipline of school. The freedom was intoxicating. Instead of the smell of Lysol and carbolic and the rub of serge trousers and clatter of army boots, this place flounced with pretty girls and perfumes and the ease of jeans and desert boots.

I became involved with the culture of common room and refectory. What interested me was the jazz club, which took place on a Wednesday evening after last period. There were a few who were only following the current musical trend through the trad jazz revival, but there was a small minority intent on taking the club towards the very modern—and even that floundered when Dave Brubeck got into the charts with *Take Five*. We just stood around chatting whilst listening to the likes of Thelonius Monk and Eric Dolphy and secretly hoping for some King Oliver or Freddy Keppard to relieve the intensity. Anyway we felt fairly hip.

Mostly the blokes wore the usual jeans and stuff, and even collars and ties like the Modern Jazz Quartet, but some also wore corduroy jackets and woollen sweaters or ex-military gear and combat jackets. Some of the lads cut their own hair with razors and a comb, or got their mates to do it for them. Footwear was mainly brogues, plimsolls, or winklepickers. Levis with a combat jacket and Clark's desert boots became my gear; I blended in almost anywhere.

One evening at the end of a jazz club session the DJ, Robin Langer, played an EP called 'Muleskinners' by Ramblin' Jack Elliott. It practically cleared the room, but I was captivated. I wanted to hear it again and again, and finally I prevailed upon Robin to let me take it home with me. A journey that would last the next forty years had now begun.

A few months before joining up in the army, I had acquired a guitar from Kennards, the big department store in Croydon. It was the cheapest of the cheap and was made of plywood by 'Egmond Frères' of Belgium, and it cost £5. It really was a piece of crap and could barely be held in tune, but there was that twang to it and I loved the ritual of stringing it, and the packets the strings came in, which held the promise of Superior Tonal Quality from the manufacturer. I had bought strings from the old boy at the store before, one at a time for my one string fiddle that Grandad had given me, but at fifteen now felt ready to start playing on six strings. Unfortunately the guitar was almost impossible to play and eventually it was put to one side.

That night, when I returned home from the jazz club, I played *San Francisco Bay Blues* from the EP on my pathetic little turntable about twenty times. Finally I picked up the plywood guitar that had been lying dormant for so long while I'd been away and painstakingly tuned the strings to something like concert pitch. I realised that Jack Elliott was playing in the key of C—but what were these other chords?

Slowly—oh so slowly—I worked out all the changes, and found chords that I had never found before. Looking back, I was lucky to have been able to do this, because I discovered how to make the notes without chord diagrams. For years I did not know the names of the chords I was playing. After a couple of days, I could play the tune recognisably enough to know I would have to get a better guitar. The strings had started to cut my already sore fingers, and if you cut your finger tip you can bet that the wound will perfectly accommodate a guitar string—very nasty.

My mission in life now was to find a guitar that sounded like Jack Elliott's. This proved impossible, but I settled on a £15 Voss guitar from Potters Music in South Croydon. It stayed in tune and I could not put it down. My college work suffered terribly, but I was lost in this wonderful music. I took the instrument to college and played it every break and lunchtime in the stairwells between floors, my coterie of pals sitting around smoking cigarettes and encouraging my efforts. I worked my way through all the songs on Elliott's 'Jack Takes The Floor' LP; my favourite was *Cocaine Blues*, which I found I could copy from the record quite easily, even though it was the first fingerstyle guitar piece I had ever heard. My pals were even more impressed.

Suddenly we were into mock O-levels. I took French, English, Maths, History, English Literature and Art.

I only passed English Lit and that because I loved poetry (not something you bragged about in Croydon). My worst failure was with maths: eight per cent for the entire exam. I was not altogether surprised that I was summoned to see Dr. Waring, our head of department.

"Well Mr. May," he began, "I expect you know why I have asked to see you."

"Yes sir."

"I am afraid that I won't be entering you for the actual exam."

The thought of failure and disappointment for my mother's sacrifices welled up in me.

"Why can't I take the exam sir?"

"Because you only got eight per cent."

"But surely that shows I got something right sir?"

"Mr. May, I am aware of your circumstances and I took the trouble to try and work out your thought processes in all stages of the paper. I am afraid, however, that they eluded me and although you showed your thought processes they defy logic in the mathematical sense. You simply cannot be creative with maths; there is only one answer and that is the right one."

"Yes, I accept that sir, but surely there is a glimmer of hope," I said as a weak smile spread hopefully across my anxious face. "After all, I did get something correct. I mean eight per cent is better than nothing."

"True," said Dr. Waring. "But the only thing you got right was the date and your own name, and as I've never awarded zero before I gave you eight per cent out of pity."

My crest had fallen to the floor. "I see," I murmured.

"Good luck with the rest of the exams," smiled the benevolent doctor as I scooped up my crest and pushed it into the back pocket of my newly acquired Levis. At least Mum would understand, as she was no good at algebra. I then resolved not to say anything about the mock exams but to wait for the real thing.

Two of my more important haunts over the next few years were the Whitgift Arms, a pub at the foot of Scarborough Road in Croydon old town area (of which more later), and a small but influential coffee bar called 'Under the Olive Tree'. The Olive was somewhere we used to go to after a few drinks at the Whitgift, and was run by an upper class couple called Parker.

In the ground floor sitting area was a splendid juke box which contained records by Muddy Waters, Woody Guthrie, Big Bill Broonzy and Howlin' Wolf. There was a coffee machine and one-armed bandit, rumoured to contain a £40 jackpot of sixpences visible behind a two-inch thick glass plate. Bruce, my younger brother, was working behind the bar with another school friend called Rick, and apart from having fun and meeting girls, they were also making a little pocket money.

Downstairs was a tiny parquet dance floor with a small raised platform round the outside, and on several nights a week a remarkable DJ called Dave King played even more remarkable records that must have been flown in from the States exclusively for him. I heard many future hits at the Olive Tree long before they ever got heard on the radio.

I have to say that I was less than interested in the music of the day, having by this time heard Ramblin' Jack, Jesse Fuller, the Carter Family and even old-timey banjo playing. Almost every waking hour my guitar was glued to my hand as I struggled to unravel the mysteries of the acoustic instrument that had taken over my life. I had developed a type of fast bluegrass flat picking, which may not have been of much musical value but impressed the shit out of my friends. I was never as moved by this stuff as much as the real mountain music, but everything I heard led me on to more wonderful discoveries, and as I was drawn deeper into the music I met more and more people who miraculously liked the same things.

My rambles with Les 'up west' to Soho and the area round it had brought us into company with lots of new acquaintances. For the most part we wandered around the pubs and bars of Fitzrovia. Sometimes we would hear a bit of music emanating from a bar or pub and go in to check it out.

That's how I first saw Buck Polly and Pete Brown. Both these two had busked around Europe, and Buck had achieved mythical status through an outgoing cockney personality allied to a western-styled wardrobe and the ability to play some tunes on the twelve-string guitar. It is impossible to explain the effect all this music had on me—sometimes it was just the sound of the instrument that knocked me sideways. Buck was the first person I ever saw play a twelve-string.

On the air in and around Finches on Goodge Street was the sweet essence of marijuana, and without ever having tried it, I knew that was what it was. Through discreet enquiries we found the name of a bloke who sold ten-bob deals. When we tracked him down, far from looking the depraved monster of movie depictions, he turned out to be a bit moddy, with slightly back-combed hair and aged at least seventeen or eighteen. He wore a light blue raincoat and was somewhat smarter than the beatnik crowd that frequented Finches at that time. I realised, not for the first time, how out of place Les and I looked in our Croydon modes. He asked us for our money, which we handed over in a sweat, and from inside the mac he produced two deals beautifully folded in newspaper to an intricate envelope; he had a special poacher's pocket sewn into the lining for this purpose. Les and I nervously went outside to smoke our first spliff. We wandered around Great Newport Street, and there in an alley near the Lamb & Flag I joined the three papers together as I had seen others do. Les carefully emptied the whole of his deal into the Rizlas and I began to roll. Just as I was about to glue the parcel together, a couple of cops walked past and glanced up the alley.

"Oh shit," said Les as he noticed them. "Quick, we better go!" Suddenly the rollup split and the weed went everywhere and we started to run as the two cops returned to look up the alley. We had a good start on them and, charged with the extra adrenaline from our attempted criminal act, we made our escape into the Saturday night throngs of people in Soho. Relieved at our escape we both started laughing, especially as I had my deal safe in my pocket.

We retraced our footsteps to Goodge Street and there in some quieter back road we rolled up again. The joint was pure grass—we had not put any tobacco in it—and greedily we both started pulling away. The effect was pretty immediate and I felt a change in my perceptions quickly—although Les did not. This is often the case with first-time smokers, and his puzzled expression made me laugh—which made *him* laugh. Soon the pair of us were wracked with hysterical giggles, exactly as we had been in chemistry class when we made laughing gas and gulped in huge lungfuls of air. *Every*thing was hilarious. In the end we had to sit down on shop window ledges to get our breath, only to go off again at the slightest thing.

"Look at him!" Les would say, and suddenly an ordinary bloke would become an object of total hilarity and we would be fighting to gain control of our breath once again. The problem was exacerbated by Les's laugh, a deep rumbling chuckle. If someone has a laugh that makes you laugh what chance have you got?

I began to get scared. Would I ever return to normal? We began walking, trying not to look at each other for fear of starting to break up again. For a while we sat on the kerb on Tottenham Court Road just watching the traffic, the rainy streets reflecting neon and car lights.

I got back to Croydon still quite early and had a slight problem trying to give the ticket collector my bus ticket instead of a train ticket. There was a copper standing next to him which increased my temporary confusion, but soon I found the right item and began walking back to Factory Lane and home. Saturday nights would never be the way they were again.

By now I was taking the guitar down to the local pubs and playing quietly in the corner, the same tunes over and over. Gradually one or two other guitar players drifted in to the scene. I was getting a bit of a reputation as a flat picker; love for this music and that of the Carter Family and Woody Guthrie became almost an obsession. I tried playing with different materials like collar stiffeners from shirts so that I could pick up speed. I cut up my set square from geometry and made plectrums out of it. I used thin card and almost any flexible material would be worth investigating as to whether it had the potential to make me sound better. Then I got a thumb pick and some metal finger picks.

About the same time and unbeknown to me, other boys of my age had also signed up to this style of music. We would meet eventually at the Olive Tree, where I would make friends that would take me further into music and travel, and around this time I wrote my first fan letter to Woody Guthrie. I was already getting fed up with the sound of the Voss guitar and I knew I must get a better one. I now knew that the sound I was after came from what were called 'jumbo' or 'dreadnought' guitars, and the first one I heard was played by Max Faulkner, a brilliant flat-picking guitarist whose hero and sometime teacher was Steve Benbow. His guitar was a Levin. It was made in Sweden, not America, but it sounded like Jack's, Woody's and all my new heroes'. It cost £45 new, which may as well have been £45,000 for all that I could afford it, but I knew I'd have to have one.

Somewhere into the picture came Mick 'Henry' Bartlett. Almost everyone called him Henry because one night in the Duke of York, Horse-Head Clive happened to remark that he looked like Henry VIII, and the nickname stuck.

Henry's enthusiasm took us both all over south London in various battered old cars to listen to blues, R&B, folk or jazz in clubs and festivals, and just about anywhere music was played that fitted his exacting standards. He never learned to play a conventional instrument, but he formed numerous bands in his career and recorded on at least four albums, including two of mine. I don't remember him ever complimenting me directly, but by his willingness to share his musical passions with me I presumed he must approve of my efforts. Henry played the jug; a stoneware one was his favourite, although I do remember one time at a session down at the Folk Cottage in Cornwall he was forced to play the plastic container that contained the chemical fluid for the Elsan Rural karzi.

One day Henry took me up to the King and Queen, a pub in the Edgware Road near Marble Arch, to see two young guys play: Tony Wilson (last heard of as a music writer living in Dublin) on guitar and Phil Allacker on banjo. Tony was playing a Harmony Sovereign guitar, and to me it sounded even better than the Levin; it was also cheaper at £35 and it was made in America. I resolved to save for one of these.

Henry introduced me to Phil, a gentle, serious soul who, like me, believed that music could somehow save us all from whatever it was we all needed saving from. Phil's taste was purer than mine; the very mention of bluegrass music would cause his face to change shape and reveal his disdain for the corruption of frailing and drop-thumb banjo. We hit it off well, and soon worked out some numbers together. I don't know whether or not it was this that prompted Henry to take the plunge into promotion, but he later negotiated the use of the Olive for a Sunday afternoon folk and blues session. This was the first of many ventures into running music clubs in pubs, barns and village halls with no real intent to make money; the music always came first.

After nine months' work and frugal balancing I had saved up £29. The guitar seemed as far away as ever when a friend told me of a second hand bargain in Ivor Mairants Musicentre in Rathbone Place. He had a Sovereign in the window for exactly £29! I went up the next Saturday morning with more money in my pocket than I had ever had before. I walked in at opening time and Ivor himself served me, letting me into the little store room at the side of the counter. I sat down and started to play. It was like heaven, the bass strings booming, the top strings ringing.

After what seemed like a quarter of an hour Ivor tapped on the door and said, "Well son, what do you think?" and before I could reply he added, "Only we are about to shut the shop—it's a half day on Saturday."

It was not the first time that time itself had been suspended by music. I bought the guitar, and Ivor threw in a Hamilton capo and a soft case. As I journeyed home it would have taken a plastic surgeon to remove the smile from my face.

A week or two after my happy Saturday a friend came up to me in college and asked.

"Didn't you used to be in the IJLB, Ralph?

"Yes," I replied (already it seemed like another life ago).

The friend said nothing and handed me the Evening News. On the back page in the stop press was written:

"There is to be an inquiry into the Infantry Junior Leaders Battalion at Parkhall Camp in Oswestry following the suicide of a second boy soldier in the last two months. The Junior leader who has not been named belonged to 'A' Company and was enlisted in a Scottish regiment."

∾

brighton

Some people are born hitchhikers. I was definitely not one of them. The first lift I ever got was on a truck outside Plummer Barracks when I left the army. It was exhilarating for so many reasons, not the least being that Sam Weller and I were on the back of the lorry leaning over the cab as the wind in our faces blew away the dreadful memories of the past few months; it seemed to whistle freedom's song as we rattled and laughed to the train station and our homes.

At college back in Croydon I had fallen in with a nice bunch of kids who were a little bit more daring than most of the middle class teenagers and late developers that attended the place. We all liked jazz and frequented pubs and clubs that played Trad, and two friends called John and Wendy (already a couple at sixteen) often danced the manic skip jive. It never looked cool, and it was certainly too elaborate for me. In spite of home practice sessions with half glances in the 'utility' wardrobe mirror, I used to mix up the bits that the boy was supposed to do, and anyway it was years before I would have had the nerve to ask someone up to dance.

I did think of taking lessons, but schoolboy memories of enrolling with my mate Tom Shaw at Fred & Cynthia's School of Ballroom Dancing (over the top of Burton's the tailors in Crown Hill, Croydon) came flooding back. A desperate attempt to meet girls, it had proved to be an absolute joke, although it gave us the chance to dress up smart and to smoke in a debonair way and look sophisticated.

The natural selection process decrees that any girl who is halfway attractive will not have to seek out a mate, because sooner or later she will be approached by someone, and even if the attentions are unwelcome, she will begin to acquire communication skills in dealing with it. This is not so with boys. Of course it is easier to make an approach to a girl if you are presentable and are able to do so without frightening them, but what if your affliction is shyness? This of course meant that the girls at the dancing school were either there because they really wanted to learn how to dance or, as seemed more credible looking at them, had never received the attentions by normal means from the opposite sex for reasons of size, halitosis or contemporary standards of beauty.

However, most of the handful of lads that were at the dance lessons were, like Tom and me, reasonably nice looking but incredibly shy. Except for Gerald. Gerald wore thick glasses which still hadn't enabled him to see that his teeth needed cleaning, his sweater that had been sweated in was often tucked in his trousers and sometimes, even more off-putting, only tucked in at the back.

We all wore hair cream in those days, but Gerald used Vaseline—and even that couldn't damp down the dandruff that powdered his shoulders. Gerald had been to classes for years and was completely lacking in tact or inhibition when it came to girls. After the instruction period, there would be three dances to close the session: a foxtrot (which was always going to be beyond me), a quickstep and a waltz. My only hope was the waltz, which I could make a reasonable stab at so long as it was in a straight line. Tom and I would stand in the shadows at the back of the room watching the hideous Gerald dancing with the girl of his choice, invariably the one we had hoped to have the last waltz with.

After four weeks we both quit. Apart from the small selection of 'talent', Fred our perfumed instructor was having far too much fun dancing the girl's part and teaching the boys, whilst his colleague, a large lady who was always in her ballroom gown, danced solely with the girls. A peculiar case of role reversal.

Barney Matthews not only liked jazz but had interests along the lines of the Beat scene that was beginning to attract me. Of course my main interest was getting laid, but although partially liberated by my army experiences, I now had to learn new approaches to girls with names like Thalia and Glennis who lived in the posh suburbs of Woodmansterne and Tadworth. This was much harder than I thought it would be, as I know they viewed me as a bit of an oik. These were mostly the girls doing O-levels but the college was full of girls. As soon as I saw someone I wanted to get to know, I looked around and found someone I wanted more.

The influence of Barney, John and Wendy had a calming effect on me (unlike that of Les). Our trips around local clubs drew me into a wider circle of acquaintances, and soon we were travelling further and further afield for our entertainment. One weekend Barney and John suggested that we hitch to Brighton for a change of scene, as they had heard through the grapevine that something was happening down there. We agreed to meet every hour on the hour at the Palace pier.

I was partnered by Barney on that trip and I remember the buzz when we got our first car. It was only going twenty miles down the road, so we had to try again somewhere near Gatwick airport. What do you know—we stopped a Bentley. Beginner's luck maybe, but it's not the sort of thing you ever forget. However, it was not long before I found that I'd used all my luck on that first trip.

Our driver was a pleasant chap and very proud of his car. He took the machine up to ninety miles an hour, which was the fastest I had ever been moved in my life. As I leaned back in the big leather seats I began to feel that the world was opening its arms to me and that my new adventure was just beginning. Once at Brighton, we met all our friends and just hung about on the seafront shivering or crowded into steamy cafés to drink a cup of tea. The weather was cold and damp, but we felt free and full of life.

This jaunt became a regular event as winter gave way to spring in 1961, and for some reason more and more kids seemed to be making their way down to Brighton. Most excitingly for me, a good number of them were 'beatniks'. I had decided that these were the people I wanted to be with, and as my confidence grew, so did my hair. One day I was cutting the hedge around our flat and Mrs. Potter walked past up the lane and muttered as she passed, "You're looking more like yer mother every day Ralph!" I was *so* pleased.

Some of the kids had blanket rolls and were sleeping out overnight, so the next requirement was a sleeping bag which I bought from Millets for 37/6.

The first night I slept under the Palace Pier was in the March. I almost froze to death and my back has never been right since. It took me years to realise that there are two things you should never economise on: your shoes and your sleeping bag.

Almost every weekend we would travel down to the seaside and stay overnight. Soon I was travelling on my own, and gradually I got used to always being the last to arrive at the pier. By now I knew where to find everyone, and sometimes after hanging around all day in a windswept and interesting mode, we would find our way to the Three Pigeons coffee bar. There was an open fire somewhere in the place, and soon our young faces were glowing and our hands throbbing as life returned to frozen extremities. At length the dreaded journey back would have to be undertaken and we would slip away singly or in pairs to face the headlights of cars on the London road. Frequently I would walk well beyond the Brighton gates and wait for hours for a lift, but the weekend I decided to partner Les must have been the record.

Les was only marginally worse than me when it came to lifts but he was blessed with more patience. This particular day, there was not much happening and we had decided to meet some other friends at the Whitgift back in Croydon, so we left early.

Of all my friends at school I loved Les the most. He was a true individual and always went his own way. At the age of twelve Les was utterly fearless. He had a racing bike, stripped of all but the essentials, that consisted of two wheels and a front brake with a fixed gear rear wheel. The saddle was set right up in the air and the handlebars were set as low as they could be. I used to watch in awe as he mounted the machine and his legs slowly propelled him up to a fantastic speed. The road outside our school was on a very steep hill and as the one cog on Les's bike only had about ten teeth, by the time his legs were flying up and down at a sprinter's pace, he must have been travelling in excess of forty miles an hour. Sometimes I would see him from the top of my bus home as he gained on it down the hill and whizzed past on the outside. When I later asked him if he was scared, he replied that it was all part of it and even if he'd wanted to stop he would have been unable to. So, like a skier, if an obstacle got in his way, he simply went round it.

I was drawn to him through our shared sense of humour and his infectious, deep laugh, which when it started would set me off till tears ran down both our cheeks. Ironically it was tears of a different nature that brought us together.

It was during one of my few assertive moments at school that an argument developed between us. I am not a scrapper, but whatever it was about I wanted some satisfaction, and a scrap was proposed in the changing rooms, out of sight of the masters who patrolled the playground.

We entered the changing rooms and squared up to each other. I knew I would have to get in first, as once my anger had diffused I would want to call it off. I took a swing at Les, he ducked, and my fist crashed into the wall. I recoiled in pain and Les burst out laughing. My follow-through punch hit him straight in the eye, which shut him up completely. It was plain from the silence that followed that I had hurt him and that he couldn't see to defend himself, so I didn't hit him again. Instead I insisted that I walked him home with his bike as I nursed my bruised hand and pride.

By the time we got to his house we were getting on like the proverbial house on fire, and the next day when I asked how he was, I was delighted to find we were still friends. And friends we remained long after marriage, moves and music combined to split us up in our mid twenties. It wasn't long before I was going home to Les's house at lunchtime from school, where we listened to records and smoked roll-ups in bits of newspaper.

Eventually I gave my dinner money to his mum and she gave me the same as she gave Les. She was only a slightly better cook than the ones at school, but that didn't matter as at least we could have a laugh and a smoke in peace. She was a hard, thin woman but no disciplinarian; she knew we were smoking but said nothing. Mr. Lester was a round-featured man with thin grey hair and remarkably short arms which only just poked out of his jacket. His fingers were always extended as if to compensate, and like Les he couldn't say his 'R's properly.

In conversations about dads, our friends in turn spoke of their fathers' exploits during the war. I proudly revealed that mine had been a Desert Rat, and Les, who had said nothing at the time, afterwards revealed to me that his dad had been what he called a 'cellar rat' during the war. That is, he had gone down the cellar and not come up for the next six years except to impregnate Mrs. Lester.

The Lesters' eldest son Colin was a very bright lad, but had dropped out of grammar school and was working as a milkman. He said little, but usually could be relied upon to sell us the odd cigarette. Les's sister was a striking redhead of fifteen. To have a sister who was apparently sexually active whilst *still underage filled me with optimism, as I fell in love daily with girls on the bus going to the school up the road.*

All in all they fascinated me; they were quite unlike any family I had ever met. They seemed to cope with what life threw at them, and our lunch breaks were full of laughter and merriment before facing the uphill walk back to school.

As we ambled out of Brighton that Sunday afternoon, such thoughts were far from my mind. Here we were again on the way to 'find out', in trouble of sorts but neither of us could have cared less. I don't suppose more than half a dozen words were said without one or both of us chuckling. I can see him now, his slightly bow legs striding purposefully forward, a cigarette between his fingers, whilst his small bright blue eyes screwed up to pinpricks of merriment as we spoke in Stanley Unwin language to amuse ourselves.

As our inability to stop a car became more apparent, our laughter turned slowly to mild hysteria. Hours slipped by and we debated as to whether the best place to stop was where we were or back down the road—or maybe just around the corner. As it was, the two unluckiest hitchhikers in the world spent the next eight hours on the A23 trying to get a ride.

In desperation near the King's Head pub at Pease Pottage we jumped out in front of a Mark Two Ford Consul, whose driver gave us a lift to Redhill and lied that he had planned to stop for us anyway. We eventually arrived home after catching a Green Line bus, on which we both fell asleep, our 45 mile journey having taken thirteen hours.

From then on I hitched alone until I left for abroad with Max Faulkner in 1962.

One Saturday morning our friends had decided to travel to Brighton, and as usual I started out on the Purley Way just behind my house. After what for me represented a very short wait (about an hour), a van stopped and I clambered aboard. Lying in the back were two blokes who had hitched the van from further up the road. I had seen one of them before and knew him as Rod; the other one was unknown to me. After acknowledging my existence with a nod, they started to talk in a kind of beat shorthand which was a mixture of Kerouac, the Goon Show and the boogly boogly shoe.

Rod was disdainful in manner and was decorated in hip London garb, his hair was long and back-combed and he wore gloves with rings on the outside and a black jacket. Even before he cut his first record Mr. Stewart cut quite a dash. I got to see him in places up the West End on several occasions, but I particularly remember him at Brighton one day on the seafront. The beatnik element used to gather at a place called the old fish market and by now a few players would arrive on the weekends and play a little Trad. This always pulled a crowd, and many of the onlookers stopped just to gaze at the unwashed hordes who sat around trying to look interesting.

One of our number (Trev) suddenly got up. Without a hint of embarrassment, and using the deserted market as an echo chamber, he burst into a stagey version of *Nobody's Child*. The effect was incredible. Money was thrown from the people above, and some said that women had actually shed tears at his plaintive rendition. We all certainly looked like nobody's children.

After a half-hearted attempt to auction an alarm clock, a scuffle broke out and there on the beach in front of us a fight was in progress between Rod Stewart and a girl. We were all dumbfounded, but none of us could take our eyes off what we were watching. Like most scraps it was over in minutes, but my abiding memory is one of pity for Rod as he was in tears of frustration and rage and obviously very deeply hurt. He had no sense of shame at his crying and seemed oblivious to the reactions of the other blokes around him.

That of course is not how we described the incident to friends later. Rod was one of many names that were characters on this scene; in particular I think of Italian Tony and Horse-Head Clive, John the Road and Gnome Pat, as well as Steve and Terry from Croydon and Trev from the Cocalina coffee bar in George Street.

The Cocalina was the first real coffee bar I went to. It was owned by a Mr. Block and it had a small dance floor where I would watch entranced as boys and girls performed their strange, mannered dance routines. Fashions were changing once more, and a weird hybrid style was emerging.

The girls were wearing tight skirts and tops with their hair back-combed at the crown and fringes in the front. The boys were wearing suits of tailored quality, striped shirts with detachable collars, slim ties without Windsor knots and often handmade boots in dark green or blue leather.

Terry Atkinson was an adherent to this style, and so was his friend Brian Ash, who went out with a very striking girl. This couple were wonderful to watch, and together the whole group of kids at the Coke were known as 'Modernists'. They showed a degree of sophistication that would not be around again in youth culture for a very long time. Gradually they evolved into proper Mods, but their first incarnation was what impressed me most.

Having neither money nor scooter, Les and I adopted a style somewhere between mod and Teddy boy as we couldn't bear to do our hair styles à la mode, and so clung to our traditional Tony Curtis cuts.

We started making regular visits to the Streatham Locarno ballroom on Wednesday evenings, but remained poor pathetic dancers in spite of that. It was actually torture to look at the incredibly pretty girls and still be too shy to ask them to dance. We would get dressed up in our Blake Brothers jackets and black cavalry twill trousers, black suede shoes and elaborate post-Teddy Boy hairstyles. These creations were held together with Brilliantine, sold in Woolworth's for a shilling a tin. You could sculpt your hair into amazing shapes, and it would normally hold up until you got really hot. Then a trickle of lavender-scented sweat and grease would run down from your sideboards.

Usually we went on the bus, and Les would stay over at my place. The order of the evening would be to wander around the gallery and gaze at the girls down on the floor, and for me to watch enviously as boys who were much more stylish and bold with their fashions would expertly swing, glide and turn, in what seemed the height of sophisticated, distracted elegance, with equally posed and pretty girls with bouffant hairdos and slim fitting skirts. After another circuit at floor level, Les used to aim for the bar, and in truth he did not seem to mind that he was as partnerless as I was as the end of the evening, because he was often quite merry by then.

My yearnings were soon forgotten as we reminded each other of particularly stunning girls we had seen on the dance floor. Each time I promised myself that next week I would get up and ask a girl to dance.

Once on the floor, all the kids had a way of seeming disinterested in their partner. It was as if being with someone enabled you to express your style in a way that would have been impossible on your own. It was the combined effect that was the art. Hands connecting, heads turned at the right time, and turns executed with unspoken understanding.

For my part I had to count. This was partly to remember my moves but also to distract myself from the intoxicating nearness of some lovely creature who had the power to turn me to jelly. The feel of a waist or the suspicion of a breast as your arm passed under hers to direct a turn. Of course inevitably even the most studied disinterested partner could hardly fail to notice my lips counting one- two- three- four or whatever, and this probably seemed as if I was talking to myself. I just could not manage the studied cool of most of the boy dancers. Still it was great to wander about amongst the kids of our own age and pose and smoke and fantasise.

There were two live bands at the Loc. They had a revolving stage, and at some point in the evening it would begin to rotate, with the other band, already playing the next tune, swinging into view. Some of these bands were really good, but even then the brief period when they played actual records was the one the kids loved best. As the bass notes of The Marcels singing *Blue Moon* started there was a rush to the dance floor that neither band could engender.

The kids who flooded the floor were terribly stylish in their south London chic. Some of the fashions and hairstyles had not yet reached Croydon a mere mile or two down the A23. The boys were beginning to back-comb their hair and were wearing cashmere polo neck sweaters, and some even had what looked suspiciously like bell-bottom trousers. Les thought they looked like poofs. In fact they were mostly tough South London lads with an eye for style, and some of them were starting to arrive at the Loc on super little Vespas and Lambrettas. All the boys wore suits and/or the fashionable sweaters or celluloid collars. None of them wore lavender scented Vaseline hair grease or bought their jackets from Blake Bros. of West Croydon. Les and I must have stood out like a couple of hicks.

This particular evening I had been watching the same blonde girl in a black shift dress all night. Most of the time she had been dancing with her mate, and once I was sure that she was without a bloke (I did not fancy one of the legendary punchups that sometimes occurred) I waited for a slow tune, then walked quickly over to her and asked formally if she would like to dance. That was the only time she looked at me, and after grinning to her even prettier mate we took to the floor.

All my 'between the beds' and 'back door' rehearsals for this moment had not prepared me for actually feeling the softness of a real partner in a shiny dress, and I managed to tread on her foot at least once as I affected the mandatory disinterested pose of the young dancers. I was erotically charged and hot, with a trickle of lavender scented perspiration running down my cheek and ready to propose marriage. However, before I could say anything to her she said 'thanks' and quickly returned to her mate, where they both sat giggling. I walked away with a strange walk in an attempt to hide my manhood and a broken heart. Someone later told me that the girls 'up the Loc' always turned you down after one dance to keep you keen, but how was I to know that?

Les was impressed, though more with my nerve than my expertise. Anyway, by now he had discovered scotch and orange and usually went home pissed and content.

∾

singer

More and more lads were turning up to the Loc on scooters, and some of them were spectacular. One bloke who always wore a brown suit and winklepickers had a Vespa GS whose panels had been electroplated in copper. He'd also had it tuned so that when the boys pulled away from the front of the venue after the dance, his machine would burn off the rest in a satisfying throaty purr. These little machines were very quick and considered not in the least unmanly.

Some of the boys had started wearing parkas, as the Modernists gradually metamorphosed into Mods. Les and I saw ourselves more as rockers at this time, but couldn't have afforded a motorbike (although I had driven a BSA Bantam down Factory Lane and loved the thrill). However, one day whilst looking in a sweetshop window we saw a car for sale, so we bought it.

It was a 1939 Singer Super Twelve with overhead camshaft, and we got it for ten pounds. The bloke that sold it to us never questioned our age, so I suppose we looked old enough. I can still see Les's look of concentration as we pulled away round the block to test-drive it.

"You'll soon get used to that clutch," said the vendor.

"I had a little trouble at first," said Les, lurching round the bend.

"Yes, you have to mean it when you want to stop it, she's a heavy old girl. It's a lot of car for ten quid." We stopped millimetres from a parked car in front of us.

"I think I'll try reverse gear," said Les knowledgeably.

"You try anything you like mate," said the man, and as Les noisily found reverse he added, "One of the first overhead camshaft motors, you know."

"Yeah, it makes such a difference," said Les. Sitting in the back seat I had to look out of the window to hide my laughter as Les once again struggled to shift into the next gear.

"You'll find it best to double de-clutch going down through the gears," said the man helpfully.

"What about going up through the gears?" asked Les.

"Well yes, it helps if you do it going up as well." As I wondered what the hell a double de-clutch was, Les had lit a Woodbine to help steady his nerves, and the smoke was getting in his eyes as his lips gripped the end in concentration. With smoke now drifting up his nose and half blind, he suddenly sneezed, which caused his foot to slip off the accelerator and made the car lurch almost to a standstill.

"Ah, testing the compression," said the man, and turning to me gave a knowing wink. "There's nothing wrong with the compression, and it hardly burns any oil either," he lied.

Having sprayed the windscreen with his sneeze, Les endeavoured to clean it with a bus ticket, and then seemingly using all his strength to turn the wheel, he manoeuvred it into a suitable parking place and told the bloke we'd have it.

Les pulled out ten one pound notes (Les worked two paper rounds) and slowly—and I thought very maturely—counted them out. How he did it without laughing after the ballsup he'd made of the test drive I don't know, but by now the madness of what we were doing had taken us over, and we were in a play that would only end when the curtain came down.

And this was only scene one. As the chap handed over the log book and keys he said, "I'm probably selling it too cheap and in a few years it'll be a classic. There you go, easy come easy go." Then the classic remark from the man that's just sold you a pup: "Good luck with the car, boys."

"Thanks a lot mate," we chirped, and in a cloud of blue smoke and grinding gears we lurched off down the road.

I was very impressed with Les's ability, as he had only once before driven his brother's car, and then only down the street. And here we were, motorised! There was of course the small matter of insurance, and come to that a licence for which neither of us would have been eligible for another year anyway.

But this was the least of our worries as Les battled valiantly to keep our vehicle on a straight course down the road. There was about eight inches play on the steering wheel before the wheels were moved, so the faster we went the more stable the car became. Les had to move the wheel sixteen inches in each direction more or less all the time just to have some tactile contact with the direction in which he wanted to travel. We pulled up a couple of streets away from where he lived and parked the car. It was only then I noticed how much my friend was shaking.

We stayed put while we smoked a cigarette, and then Les said, "Right, let's go, I'll drop you home and have a chat with Colin about learning what a double de doobie is and we'll go for a drive tomorrow." With that we ground a bit more metal off the first gear cog and lurched off down the road to Croydon.

For a few days we were content to drive about locally and as a precaution against getting a tug from the police had borrowed the full driver's licence of an acquaintance. As we drove about Croydon with Les double de-clutching beautifully, we would repeat the mantra:

Here we are in the Singer Super Twelve
Nineteen thirty nine
With plush interior and overhead camshaft
With Derek J. Lester driving
On Patrick B. Bowman's licence.

After about a week we were ready to venture further afield. Not really having a better idea I suggested Banbury, where my pretty cousin Christine lived. With only a glance at the map we were off. At one point the car achieved the heart-stopping speed of between 65 and 80 mph (the speedo needle oscillated violently between the two marks). It sure was thrilling and we cheered the old girl on as we trundled towards Banbury.

Once there I telephoned Christine, who must have been surprised to hear from me, especially when I told her we were in town and would she meet us in a little pub near the Town Hall. She agreed, saying she would bring her friend Eileen. Les and I rolled up to the pub, majestically parked the old car and went inside.

We ordered two light and bitters and sat down in the corner in the shadows. We attracted only the attention any stranger attracts in a small market town, and although by London standards we were pretty plainly dressed it was clear from our garb that we were from out of town.

We were only halfway down our drinks when a bloke in a mackintosh walked in and said in a loud voice, "Does anyone here own a Singer Super Twelve?"

My heart sank and Les looked anxiously at me.

"Say nothing," I mouthed.

"What if it's the cops?" Les mouthed back.

I shook my head and prayed that it wasn't, then in my anxiety spilled the best part of a quarter of a pint down my swish London gear.

"Does anyone here own a Singer Super Twelve?" repeated the man, louder this time. Most of the bar looked around at us as we buried ourselves in our pints.

"All right, suit yourselves," said the man with just a hint of exasperation in his voice, "only it's on fire outside."

Les and I looked at each other, then jumped up at the same time and rushed to the door to find smoke pouring out from under the bonnet. On lifting it up it was clear that there had been a short circuit of some kind, as all the wiring to the headlights was burning like a slow fuse on a cartoon stick of dynamite. As we stood there helplessly, a helpful local asked for the keys and after jiggling them about in the ignition managed to stop the burning.

"Don't worry boys, she'll still drive but you'll have to wait until tomorrow as you won't have any lights."

"Oh good," said Les.

"Thanks mate," I said, and we trooped back dejectedly to the pub as Christine and Eileen arrived. Somehow we had a bit of a laugh and Les and Chris seemed to hit it off. When everyone had gone home and the little town was dark and silent, Les kissed Chris goodnight, I shook hands with Eileen and we crept back to our car. Starting it up, we limped with one lamp to a quiet street where we tried to grab a few hours' kip.

At first light we headed off back to London. Most of the way back Les was silent and even the mantra failed to produce the normal effect. The truth was that Les was smitten by my cousin Chris, and I felt a kind of glow for him.

Les and I eventually stopped going to the Loc. My wardrobe was changing from the pre-mod styles of the early sixties, along with my taste in music. I stopped using hair Vaseline and began washing it every day with egg shampoo from Mum's chemist. For spots I spent a fortune on Valderma balm that did not work, and I switched from Blake Bros. in the High Street to Millets at the top of Surrey Street market. There was a dress code even for the beat crowd.

Dances, however, were still the best places to mix with girls, and it was at one such evening at the college that I found myself talking to Susan. Of all the girls at college she was the most out of reach for me, as she was always deeply involved with one or two of the more sophisticated blokes. Currently it was Adam, a striking lad who unfortunately tucked his jeans into his black suede boots. He looked like Jack in search of a beanstalk, and he had landed the sexiest girl in the college.

Still, he had forsaken the beautiful Susan for a girl with shiny hair—which Susan pointed out was because she only washed it once a week, whilst her own was washed every day. I instinctively breathed in her hair aroma and was even more intoxicated.

She wore a perfume called Apple Blossom, and sometimes when walking past the fruit counter in a supermarket I am still reminded of her. She prattled on about this and that, and I was hardly able to believe that she was talking to me. She kept pushing her hair behind her ear like girls do when they are deep in concentration. The unposed naturalness somehow conveyed an unguarded, little girl look. Christ she was sexy in the dim light of the hall. She giggled, fidgeted and smiled, and all the time she was looking and talking with me. I leaned against the wall as much to hold on to something as to appear casually interested. She babbled on about Adam and her and I nodded where it seemed appropriate.

Suddenly she stopped talking and looked at me with a softness in her smiley eyes. It was not exactly a come-on but I found myself unable to stop, and I leaned forward and kissed her and she kissed me back and I felt like I was starting to float from the floor. I tried to appear nonchalant as I lit a Park Drive, which stuck to my lip on the first drag and pulled off a small but painful piece of skin. She didn't seem to notice, and I offered to see her home. I hardly recognised my own voice which seemed to have temporarily returned to choir boy pitch. Again Susan failed to notice. She took my hand and we headed for the door.

312

I was almost overcome with excitement as I sat next to the fragrant-haired girl whose head was lightly resting on my shoulder, and the six-mile, two-bus journey took no time at all. I dabbed at my torn lip with my bus ticket until it was quite specked with blood and wondered if she was thinking of me or Adam. Would she regret this move? Had she planned to make Adam jealous? I checked my packet of cigarettes to make sure that I had enough to last the night, and enjoyed her snuggled up form sitting next to me on the almost deserted upper deck rear seat on the 112 bus.

Soon we were at her front door and suddenly she was kissing me goodnight and it was the most wonderful moment and suddenly I was in her house and we were going to have coffee and suddenly we were almost out of control.

Then, in no time, I was having to leave and catch my bus, my untouched coffee cold in her kitchen, the beautiful Susan waving and smiling on the doorstep, her hair ruffled and her small green eyes sparkling. The last bus had long gone and I had to frequently rest as I staggered home, my head full of plans, my heart full of hope and my loins feeling like they'd been kicked by the milkman's horse.

We were fairly cool at college because she was still sort of going with Adam, or at least not arousing his suspicions that there might be someone else. I was confused as to what my role in all this was, but our evenings compensated for our lack of contact during the day; in fact they made it more delightful.

Susan's mum seemed to like me, and we were always left alone in the front room. There was a pencil drawing of Susan's father on the sideboard. He had died a few years before and I imagined him watching us both as we got as near to consummation as she dared.

I think Susan liked me for what she perceived as my feral qualities. Certainly I was more rough-hewn than her other boyfriends. I had not quite developed into a Beat and I was not a Mod; I was rather drab in appearance, but I tried to be considerate and I did seem able to make her laugh. At this time, all I wanted was sex, whereas most of the girls seemed to want a long-lasting deep relationship. Susan, however, did not. It was as if she was prepared to learn about certain intimacies so as to be prepared for her Jack and the Beanstalk man. I began to feel a little used. She seemed more consumed by curiosity than either love or passion, and once or twice I caught her looking over at Adam in the common room where I was supposed to be cool and not show real signs of our 'togetherness'.

The so called swinging sixties were not all free love and sexual abandon. Most of the kids I knew at college were still virgins at sixteen; I felt light years away from most of them and indeed as far as life experience went, I could not relate to many of them at all. Even so, as far as virginity was concerned, I was in the same boat. There were a few steady couples that may have been having a more intimate relationship, but most of us were still at the fumbling stage, and certainly most of the girls I met had a sort of code as to how far they would let a boy go with them. In many ways this only added to the excitement. Most still lived at home, and the lack of facility to explore, and the certainty that even if you were left alone together there would be an authority figure nearby only added to the intensity and urgency of pre-Pill gropings.

At Easter, Les drove the three of us in the Singer to the Mitcham Fair. I wandered around the stalls and was amazed to find so many familiar faces still working there. The boy who wanted comics from me was now in charge of the rifle range, and I was relieved that he did not recognise me, but the old lady on the 'Pick A Straw' stall was long gone. The hierarchy of the fairground remained, with the lads now my age taking change from the punters whilst balancing on the swirling whirling machines with Bruce Channel's *Hey Baby* blaring from distorted loudspeakers. The shrieks of excited girls and the posturing of young lads amongst the coloured lights was stimulating, as I searched amongst the weather-beaten faces and tattoos for people I had known from my short stay with the fair.

Les was patient and happy, occasionally slipping off to ride on some machine by himself whilst Susan and I wandered over the cinders, breathing in the smell of fried onions and candy floss on the air. Susan did not share in my nostalgia, and after one or two rides she said she was cold, and could we go back to the car. I thought this was a little bit odd but there was something in her eyes that suggested she really meant it.

I borrowed the keys of the car, and while Les had a few extra turns on the 'Whip' and the 'Waltzer', Susan and I climbed into the back seat. Soon the windows steamed up and there behind the trailers and caravans, amid the thump and smell of the diesel generators mixed with the scent of apple blossom, leather, woodwork and chrome, Susan finally dared; and through the hubbub of swirling, heightened senses over the rattling loudspeakers, Little Richard expertly articulated the moment: "Awopbopaloobopalopbamboom."

&

whitgift

Les was often quite moody at this time, partly I suppose because he couldn't see Chris as much as he would like, and partly because the car was getting less reliable. His mum had found out about it and naturally wanted him to get rid of it. One sunny evening we were driving through the old part of Croydon at the bottom of Scarbrook Road when the old girl came to a halt and refused to start again. This was really it, and after a great deal of swearing we pushed her round the corner, took our bits and pieces out of it and left her to the vultures on the estate at Salem Place. As we walked around the corner, the Whitgift Arms appeared in front of us and suggested that we went in for a cheer up drink.

The public bar was a long narrow room with a dartboard at one end and the gents toilet to the left. Just inside the door and to the right was an elderly piano and running away from it along the window was a settee. Further into the room was the bar itself and opposite it and extending all the way up to the toilets were benches. It was early evening and there were only a couple of people in the place.

As we walked up to the bar, a kindly looking bloke with a neat tie and Fair Isle pullover asked, "What'll it be, gents?"

I looked at the prices that were scrawled in chalk on the barrels that rested on the counter as I felt around in my pocket for change. As well as a few coppers, I felt the reassuring weight of a half crown. I can still remember the prices:

Bitter @ 1/10d per pint
Gaymers cider @ 1/2d per pint
Coates cider @ 1/3d per pint

"Two pints of cider please," I said, pointing to the barrel of Coates. The barman turned the squeaky spigot on the cask and dispensed the liquid into two rather greasy glasses.

Hot from our efforts to start the car, we drank the stuff far too quickly and Les ordered another. Cider is so easy to drink when you are young; it's only a short stop from apple flavoured cordials. We were only halfway down the second pint when the alcohol kicked in and for some unaccountable reason the bloke next to us started to twitch and nod his head quite violently in agreement with nobody.

Les found it very funny and as usual I found Les's laugh dangerously infectious. At first it was under control, but the more we tried to stop ourselves laughing the more hilarious it got, until Les finally broke out with a huge "HA HA HA HA HA!" and the flood gates opened. I joined in and soon we were near helpless with merriment. The bloke next to us nodded and twitched knowingly and gave the barman a wink which said the cider's got to the young fellows. The barman nodded and the bloke next to us said, "W-W-Well aren't you going to let us in on th-th-th-the j-j-joke?

As he spoke his head twitched violently to the right and left then once up and down.

His friend leaned round to look at us and blinking in an exaggerated way added, "Come on lads what's so funny?"

This was all too much for us. When Les did manage to get a word out, all he could say was, "Blimey there's two of them," and then more laughter.

I managed to come up with, "It's our motor, it's just blown up and we're just seeing the funny side of it."

The two regulars half smiled, twitched, blinked and resumed drinking and I helped my friend outside into the bright evening sunshine. We wandered off towards south Croydon with a really great cider buzz on and resolved to meet back at the pub for more of the same the next evening.

The two men we met that afternoon were Big Eddie, who was a kitchen porter, and Reg, who worked for a firm called Skinner's Removals. The landlord was called Maurice and his wife was called Rene (pronounced Reen). They were a kindly, tolerant couple, and thanks to Les and I, their little cider pub became a hang out for half the dropouts and art students in Croydon. Most of their regular clientele were in advanced states of cider addiction but there was hardly ever any trouble there.

Cider was so cheap that for 3/9d (three pints) we'd all be "silly as a box of night lights" as Georgie would say. Georgie was a dustman and a perfect Teddy boy, who'd never given up on the old style and music. His authentic appearance was only diminished when he opened his mouth to speak: poor Georgie's voice had never broken and he sounded like a five year old who had learned to swear. He was in most nights and always spotless with a clean neckscarf tied sailor-like round his throat. Then there was Danny, an Irishman from Cork city who no-one but me could understand because of his accent (my childhood neighbour Mr. Connaughton came from Cork, so for me it was fairly easy). To finance his drinking Danny did a bit of caddying up at Croham Manor golf course.

Gypsy Tony was a tiny man almost bent double with a curvature of the spine. He was about seventy when I knew him and had been a soldier in the 1914-18 war.

"I was in Kitchener's army in the Pioneer Corps 'cos I weren't too fit an' they 'ad me pickin' up bits o' bodies an' puttin' 'em in bags out in France. I said fuck this an' I took a penn'orth. They tol' me I was lucky not to get shot them bastards. For desertin' you see."

Tony was a sweet guy and I always sat with him for a while down the pub. He had lost part of a finger in the war but had never had the amputation done, so from where his first joint should have been a piece of stained bone protruded, which was a bit grisly, but which he seemed to use to his advantage in rolling cigarettes.

One night after a few drinks in a serious moment he reached over and clutched my arm and said, "You're an educated chap Ralph an' I want to ask you somefin'. Do you fink it's wrong for a man to interfere wiv hisself?"

At first I wanted to burst out laughing, but then I saw the concern in his eyes; this dear little old man was really troubled.

318

"You see I'm a caflick and the church says that a man should not interfere wiv hisself."

I knew from previous conversations with Tony that he was once married and that his wife had died. I looked into his sad deep brown eyes and with all the authority I could muster at sixteen or seventeen said, "If you believe in God and he gave you eyes to see and you didn't use them or legs and you refused to walk or a tongue and you refused to speak, what would God say? When you do whatever you do perhaps you think of your wife and in a way you celebrate her memory and the things you once had, how could any god be angry with that?"

I looked him in the eye and he looked straight at me, still clutching my arm as his large brown eyes filled up with tears that splattered unchecked down his cheeks on to the table.

"Thanks Ralph," he said, wiping his face on his cuff. He turned away and we never spoke about it again.

Bill Coomber made up the trio with Big Eddie and Reg and every night they joined in close harmony and sang. Bill struck me as officer class; he was always immaculately dressed and wore a bow tie every evening. He always sat in the same place at the end of the bar and kept an eye on the rest of us. Bill had a natural ear for close harmony and sang instinctively a third above the melody line against Eddie's clear baritone and Reg's crooning tenor. I loved these goodnight songs that eased us all into the night as we went our several ways home.

"It's long and thin
It dangles down your chin
Have a guess, Yes yes
It's spaghetti"

they sang, and then the *Whiffenpoof Song*:

"We're poor little lambs that have lost our way," they warbled, oblivious of the plaintiveness and accuracy of the description.

Big Eddie had a solo:

"When I was a wee wee tot
They took me from my wee wee cot
And put me on my wee wee pot

To see if I could wee or not
And when they saw that I could not
They took me from my wee wee pot
And put me in my wee wee cot
Where of course I weed a lot."

He sang this nearly every night and always with the same response: everyone laughed politely at the end and Eddie accepted the applause with many a nod and twitch. One night, his Northern Irish wife who had been waiting outside for him for ages came back in and demanded that he leave with her now.

"Away w-w-with you w-w-woman," he said playfully and gestured with the back of his hand his feeling that she was trifling with more important work. As she stormed out of the bar Eddie burst into the *Wee Wee Tot* song. As he reached the last line, she strode into the bar, grabbed a full pint of cider from the counter and poured the whole lot over his head. Eddie just kept singing, his last note held as never before. That was the best it ever went down.

"He shouldn't have done that," said Bill Coomber in my ear.

"Why?" I asked. "You mean he should have shown her more respect?"

"No," said Bill, "that was my pint she poured over him."

News of the Whitgift spread quickly. There was a happy mix of younger and older generations united by the need for cheap drink and good company. Guitars appeared some nights, piano players on others. We always deferred to the older crowd and they in the main tolerated us. Drunkenness was common but was seldom followed by aggression.

Paddy from Dublin had also fought in the First World War. He was a passable pub piano player, but that job was usually done by an old boy with thick lensed glasses and a flat cap. He always blamed the cold temperature in the bar for his frequent mistakes, which was a cue for someone to buy him a drink. However Paddy the dep had another weapon at his disposal: he used to carry a chanter in his top inside pocket and would wail away on some forgotten named slow air or a jig if he had the puff. A chanter is the practice pipe of the uileann or Irish pipes and the sound is made by blowing through a small reed rather like an oboe; it has a mournful note when played without the drones and regulators.

"It was the gas in the war you know. The gas got me chest," he would gasp before breaking out into such terminal-sounding coughing that someone always bought him a drink.

"Ah no," he would decline, "A beer's no good to me, I better have a little Irish. It's the same price you know."

This little parlour trick usually resulted in the old devil getting two drinks for his performance, for if the benefactor went to pick up the pint to exchange it, the old boy's claw would strike out like a snake, and with surprising strength for one so close to death he would grasp the wrist that threatened to carry the drink away and rasp, "I might manage that if you give me a minute to get the whiskey down."

Over the next two years, hundreds of kids must have visited the place, and not just from our neck of the woods. Beatniks from London's Duke of York in Charlotte Street appeared, together with couples from Brighton, and kids from Mitcham and Purley, Carshalton and Streatham, Thornton Heath and Norbury. Art students and bikers, poets and rogues all crammed into the tiny bar.

Amongst the girl regulars were Pat and Cathy, in duffel coats and dyed black hair, Margot, who was Indian and very tiny, and the Croydon Beat chapter of Steve, Val Liloff, John Kercher, Brian, and, recently returned from Spain where he'd grown his hair long, Terry Atkinson, former Modernist and now complete beatnik with a travelling past.

Terry had actually done it: he had hitched to Spain, picked grapes for his living, and travelled along the Côte d'Azure. He'd written poems and philosophised about the travelling life and I was captivated. Terry was always complimentary about my guitar playing and come to that, my attempt at painting. He gave me the kind of support you can only get from someone who is older than you are, and it was through Terry that I met Max.

❧

olive tree (foam at last)

It is hard to convey just how barren and bleak towns were for kids of my generation. There were very few places where youngsters could get off the street and hang out.

My introduction to beatnik culture had begun at the Wimpy bar near East Croydon station where the three or four principal Croydon beatniks nursed weak coffee and talked the evenings away with passionate discussions about Steinbeck, Kerouac, Corso and Ginsberg. I loved these debates and although very far behind intellectually, felt quite elevated by this search for knowledge. Without the sidetrack of religion and with a growing appreciation of the musical accompaniment of beat literature and poetry – modern jazz – I felt that a greater understanding of the meaning of life was just around the corner.

Perhaps it was a hand-bill or more probably word of mouth that alerted me to the opening of a new coffee bar in the south end of Croydon. This new place was to be launched with a publicity stunt. I wondered what this could mean. Youth culture was not yet an industry and a publicity stunt was as intriguing to me as an electric tram might have been to an Edwardian. This event was to take place fairly early on a Saturday morning and I think I might have been on my way to the Saturday gardening job I had with the Tickle family who lived fairly near.

When I arrived at the event I was a little surprised to find hardly anyone there. The coffee bar was a converted shop in the middle of a terrace of houses, the kind you see all over England. The name written over the window was 'Under the Olive Tree'.

What could that mean I wondered? I would have understood if it had been called 'The Olive Tree' but the name did not make sense beginning as it did with a preposition. Bands were still named after nouns in those days: names like 'Everything But The Girl' were not in common parlance. I had no way of knowing how advanced this name was, it just sounded odd to me.

I deduced who the owner might be by the stress and anticipation on his face. A photographer from the local paper arrived and I overheard their conversation; the event was about to happen and the participants were on their way. By now there were a few more spectators but hardly a crowd, more bemused onlookers really.

Eventually a truck and trailer arrived and, after a bit of manoeuvring, pulled up by the kerb in front the entrance. The cameraman moved into position at the back of the trailer and a tiny man in a long green overall and peaked cap went round to the back door and released the bolts. As the ramp was lowered the back end of an animal was revealed and it was clear that it was not a happy creature. The little man jumped into the trailer and grabbing a handful of reins attempted to get the beast to reverse down the ramp.

The animal in question was a dromedary and a very elderly one at that . It seemed to be in a state of moult or perhaps a terminal state of mange with great swathes of dark brown fleece hanging off its body. It looked as if it had been removed from a museum's discarded specimens and somehow resuscitated.

The poor creature was extremely stressed and highly agitated having been dragged from its cage at Chessington Zoo for this opportunity. Even though there were fewer cars on the Brighton road in those days I doubt that the animal would have experienced anything like Croydon's bustle and noise in its semi-rural surroundings at the zoo. It seemed to be very strong and the little keeper looked like a dangling mascot or lucky charm fixed to the reins. He seemed to have no control over the moth-eaten panicking animal as it reversed down the ramp. Suddenly it evacuated its bowels and I instinctively took several steps back from the clattering hooves as they slithered and hammered on to the roadside, spraying a liberal amount of waste on to the hapless keeper, the pavement and its own back legs.

The dromedary turned to look straight at us accusingly with a mad and dangerous stare showing red eyes and the whites of its eyeballs. It was foaming at the mouth like an overfilled washing machine and when it shook its head a great scud of froth flew through the air and landed on the keeper's peaked cap and into his eyes. The next violent shake produced a streamer of foaming saliva and decorated him like a South American general in ribbons of yellowish-white gunk down the front of his green overall.

The keeper manfully wiped the mess off his face with his too-long overall sleeve and smiled willingly at the camera. He tried to get into position for the picture but the camel (it was supposed to be a camel for obvious reasons) did not want anyone else near. Another violent shake of the head threw more froth over the heads of the onlookers and splattered the window. All the while the keeper kept up a willing grin for the photographer in case he was ready to shoot.

By now, I was in mild hysterics and did not know where to look for fear of offending the diminutive foam-covered handler. The poor man was not in control of the animal which constantly tried to break free. Each time it did so, it nearly lifted the tiny chap off the ground and simultaneously threw phlegm and foam in the general direction of the onlookers.

The keeper was sweating profusely from the sheer physical effort of holding on to the creature. He had now more or less abandoned trying to keep his dignity and was just trying to keep himself clean. The camel was breathing heavily and producing more foam which it periodically shook over the scene. Suddenly, the animal went off at the other end. The pair manoeuvered themselves into a different position with the splattered shop front behind them.

I honestly thought the creature would crash through the window at one point but eventually the picture must have been taken and the publicity stunt was brought to a close. The panicking animal traipsed through its own excrement and slithered and slid up the ramp looking grateful to be back in its trailer. The keeper sort of bowed to the crowd which ought to have applauded but didn't – Croydon audiences are notoriously hard to impress.

The event had been organised by a Mr Parker who had entered this enterprise with his wife Anne. I guess 'The Olive' (as it was always known) deserves its own book as so much occurred there over the next few years. Between the Whitgift Arms and 'The Olive', relationships were begun, consummated and ended. A raggle-taggle of artists, beatniks, radicals, dancers, posers, strummers, mods, rockers, bikers, hitchhikers, charmers, self-harmers and kids who simply needed somewhere to hang out populated the place. In retrospect we were all very lucky to have 'The Olive' in our lives.

My younger brother Bruce got a job there with a school friend of his called Ricky Martin. I think they were both about fourteen at the time and they only left when the imminence of exams and a threat to blow their legs off by some disgruntled biker with a shotgun caused them to reconsider life in the catering business. Somehow this small place managed to house a disco and live music and even a folk club on Sunday afternoons where the likes of Martin Carthy, Davey Graham and Wizz Jones graced the tiny performance area. It was also where I first performed with a dedicated 'old timey' banjo player called Phil Allacker – we got our first mention by a young Robin Denselow in the Croydon Advertiser newspaper.

~

max

Max Faulkner was older than me by a couple of years, and when you are seventeen, two years is a big gap. He was a great character. At nineteen he had a face that was lived in and a voice that sounded like it broke in the womb. In reality he lived with his mum. He was certainly the biggest bloke in our group of friends, weighing I should guess fourteen stone (I weighed eleven). His hair was starting to go back at the temples and was combed forward, Nero-like, in a short curly fringe. He walked incredibly erect and sort of bounced on the balls of his feet, his step sure and his whole demeanour exuding confidence. His ever present acne would have turned a more sensitive soul into a monk in a silent cloistered order, and his crowning glory was his huge scarred nose.

If you didn't know him you would have thought "Who is this arrogant ugly bastard?", but because you did know him and because his couldn't-give-a-fuck attitude was genuine, and because there was no harm in him and he had such a great smile, all the girls loved him. If we were all left wing beatniks, then Max was a redneck. He loved cowboy songs and the Carter Family music and, without noticing any irony, the songs of Woody Guthrie too. We soon hit it off really well, learning all sorts of songs together. Max was the guy I taught *San Francisco Bay Blues* to, and he showed me an E minor chord in exchange. We'd often play down at the Whitgift and at other outings that somehow got organised.

Through him I met at least another dozen kindred souls and soon we were getting invited to parties if we'd bring our 'boxes'. This of course was great because we never had to bring any drink, and until I got too drunk to play I had a wonderful time. The down side to all of this was Max's party piece.

After picking the night away and having plenty to drink, he would disappear into some room in the house only to reappear naked except for his bush hat. I have tried to indicate that Max was a big chap, and he was big in all departments. He would march into the main room with lights full on smoking a Pall Mall cigarette without a hint of shyness, and enjoy the gasps of amazement from the girls and the looks of envy from the boys as he performed forward rolls on front room carpets all over south London. I can still see the slap of his tackle as he rolled head over heels amongst the Axminster and Wilton. At one do, a very bonny and well-endowed girl called Sally joined him in his display. They became more of a double act than Max and me, and if we were planning to go to a party or crash one the question always came up: "Will Max and Sally be there?" Not surprisingly, they became lovers.

As the summer of '62 washed over me, I moved through friends and acquaintances like a bird in some migrating flock. We were all travelling in the same direction but no-one knew where we were going. Sometimes I was at the front, usually around the middle section, seldom at the rear. The two years penance spent at college had been a bit of a waste; my second year attempt at improving my exam results had only produced an A-level in Art. Earlier friendships had been temporarily outgrown, and though I didn't realised it at the time, music was the force that would drive me from now on. This was the summer when people I had met in the Soho pubs turned up again closer to home. In particular Henry Bartlett, who has been a lifelong friend since those days. Henry lived in Mitcham, and his mum and dad were constantly warm and encouraging to this young guitarist.

One weekend we all went down to the river at Richmond. We hired a couple of skiffs and rowed them and hauled them up weirs and waterfalls to Hampton Court. On the way back, our boat suffered a glancing blow from a pleasure steamer and sustained damage that nearly cost us our lives, let alone our deposit. Somehow Les replaced the shattered wood by the rowlocks and balanced the splinters like a vertical jigsaw, and the owner failed to notice as we tied up just a little way from the boathouse. That night we slept out in the shelter at the back of the towpath. We had our sleeping bags, or in my case an old World War Two army blanket and a couple of safety pins, as I had decided that sleeping bags weren't cool.

I was cool all right and as usual shivered the night away. Eventually, as the morning arrived, I gave up on any sleep and looked over to where Les was lying in exactly the same position he had adopted the previous evening. He had borrowed a couple of deck chairs and after predictable slapstick setting them up, had managed to make some sort of bed. I shall never forget the look of total repose on his face as he lay there. Partly through envy, but mainly because I was still a bit unsure about the other 'friends' that were sleeping out with us, I woke Les up.

Once we'd had a cigarette, we determined our strategy for the day. We were both hungry and had no money as usual, so Les did the milk round (meaning picking up a pint from a doorstep before the householder brought in the bottles). By the time he got back, Max and Henry had woken and were smoking and coughing and getting adjusted. Les triumphantly presented three pints of milk to the gathering and without saying much we all took huge grateful swigs from the bottles as they were passed round. This milk business did not sit well with me. I often put myself in my mum's position, where the loss of a bottle of milk would have caused some hardship. The unspoken rule was that you never took a single bottle but if there were three or more on the doorstep you could take one.

From the corner of my eye I noticed Henry getting himself together. Henry had always intrigued me. At the tender age of seventeen he'd grown his first beard (or more likely had simply never shaved), he was a huge fan of the Mickey Ashman jazz band and lived for music. This morning he was clearing his throat and smoking his first Senior Service of the day. The large intake of milk first thing had caused a cloying sensation in our mouths and several of the lads were spitting manfully.

This was an art that I had mastered when young, and I could spit with alarming speed and accuracy. So when Henry decided to bring round a waste basket that was in the shelter and pose as a waiter with a spittoon, I saw a chance to impress him. I got myself ready and when it was my turn, I let go a gobbet that should have blown a hole in the bucket. Unfortunately I missed the receptacle completely and shot the contents of my mouth straight up his arm holding the bucket. I was mortified. Les started his distinctive chuckle, whilst my mumbling apologies were sounding wet, and in spite of my cool adoption of a blanket for my image I was looking pathetic.

Henry was determined to drag out the incident for all the comedy it was worth. Without once meeting my eyes—and sensing that everyone was staring at us both—he first looked at his soiled sleeve still holding the bin, then slowly looked at those on his right, then more slowly looked at those on his left, then even *more* slowly his eyes, beginning at my belt buckle, moved slowly up my body until they met mine—and then and only then I could see that his face was slightly contorted in an attempt not to laugh himself. Henry had an operation for a lazy eye when he was a child and when he looked at you a certain way, one of his eyes involuntarily looked upward and it was doing it now. It was all too much for me and we both just cracked up.

Max was his usual ebullient self. We picked away on our guitars, and in a fit of bravado started to play to the crowds walking over Richmond Bridge. At the end of a song, a bloke shouted to us and threw down a half crown. Then a few more coins clattered on to the pavement. We played another couple of songs and got some more coins and made fourteen shillings in three numbers. It was an absolute fortune, and as we went off and bought bacon sandwiches, Max said to me, "Well Woody," (he often called me Woody after the great man and it made me feel good), "I think we may be ready to hit the road!"

Plans were drawn up to go to Greece. Henry was to make his way with June and Stan would find his own way Max and I were to travel together and meet Beau and Sally at Munich main railway station. We left England in the September; I had never been more excited about anything in my life.

The fare across the channel to Ostend was £2-2s. We had decided to go that way for ease of access to Germany. As the boat pulled into the harbour after the four hour crossing, my eyes feasted on all the sounds and sights that greeted them. Everything was different, the cars, the clothes, the voices.

"Listen Max, they're talking in French!"

"That's because it's their language," he explained. The sarcasm was wasted because I was thrilled with everything I saw and heard. I had my blanket roll and a small duffel bag with nothing much in it and my Harmony Sovereign guitar in a soft plastic shaped case over my shoulder. Max had his guitar in a hard case, and a huge rucksack that was packed by his mum. On his head was a ridiculous bush hat and down in his boot was a bowie knife. He had actually written a list of things you might need on the road and one of them was this bloody knife. It worried me.

We found our way out of the port and on to the Ostend-Brussels road. In my pocket I rubbed my lucky farthing and we raised our thumbs in high spirits in anticipation of our first lift. After six hours and a whole packet of duty free Pall Mall cigarettes we had travelled about four hundred metres. I wondered if it was Max's big hat or his enormous rucksack. Perhaps they had X-ray vision and could see through his Levis to where the bowie knife was strapped to his leg. Now I ask myself, 'Would I have stopped for two largish men, one with huge hat, both carrying full size guitars, a duffel bag and a rucksack that could have passed for a double garage?'

Our attempts at nonchalance would probably have been seen as arrogance as we stood puffing away on giant American cigarettes. After the next ferry's shipload of travellers had been accommodated and we were still standing there, I decided to hide some of our gear in the bushes at the side of the road. Sure enough we got a lift in a lorry. Lesson one had been learned and we rattled our way almost to Brussels before the driver put us down and turned off the main road. An early evening mist had begun to fall and we were dead tired. The mist became a fog, and we were stumbling on blindly through it when Max said, "Fuck this for a game of soldiers, I think we ought to try and get some kip."

My heart sank as I fondled my blanket roll; I suppose I had expected that we might sleep under cover but it was no use, we couldn't see anything and the fog had muffled the sound of traffic. I was sure we were no longer on the main road, as what little traffic there had been had dried up to a trickle and no-one could see us until they were on top of us. Max's huge nose and hat would appear out of the fog at the oncoming drivers, which could only have made them want to hurry home to their wives and families and make themselves a comforting hot drink. That was certainly what I could have done with.

With the mist now turning into drizzle and not much of anything moving on the road, we stopped. Max opened his rucksack and pulled out a tiny two-man tent that he had brought with him without telling me. We put it up somehow, and after Max had installed his rucksack, the two guitars and himself, I was invited in with my damp piece of rag posing as a cool bedroll.

The night passed in moist misery. I became aware of the noise of vehicles passing perilously close to our little home, and I poked my head out of the tent flap to be greeted by a terrifying sight. We had only got halfway across a dual carriageway and pitched the tent on the tiny grass central reservation. Traffic was thundering past in both directions at less than a metre from each side. I woke the incredulous Max, and as carefully as we could we packed our gear and found our way to the right side of the road for Brussels. This time I hid in the bushes along with both guitars and Max's rucksack, and this became the pattern for the rest of the journey to Munich.

We arrived in Brussels, had a cursory look round, ate some chips with mayonnaise, and headed out on the Aachen road. That night the weather improved and we slept in the open by a bridge somewhere. For some reason it had seemed wise not to take a map, so I cannot say what our route was but the next city was Cologne. We did eventually find a free map in a petrol station and it helped a bit. Try as I might, I do not remember eating anything else on this trip. We were stuck by the side of the road waiting for lifts, and only if the driver felt like stopping for a coffee in a roadhouse would we get a chance to eat.

As usual I had hardly any money and what I did have (maybe a fiver) was meant for Greece in case we were not able to go busking. Until Frankfurt I survived on coffee and cigarettes, and mostly felt tired rather than hungry.

All my life I had regarded Germany as the enemy, responsible for the loss of a Dad and the misery of our poverty. I expected the Germans to be hostile, and frequently cursed them when they failed to stop for us. However they seemed to bear no malice towards us, and instead wanted to talk in English and to know all about us and what we were doing and where we were going and why.

I found it hard to explain my reasons, and must have looked and sounded very young and vulnerable. It took us about a week to make it to Frankfurt. There we picked up a ride with two American servicemen, who made cracks about the quaintness of the German language; in particular the word Ausfahrt amused them, and us too at first. Then they spoke of the obliging nature of the German girls and generally treated us like manly equals with much chortling and thigh-slapping.

A stye appeared on my right upper eyelid, and my gums started to bleed. My two packs of cigarettes had been consumed and I was now reliant on Max for smokes. He was generous at first, but soon I felt obliged to wait and ask for his 'twos-ups'.4 In Frankfurt we met a gypsy musician who noticed our big guitars. He struck up a halting conversation with us and suggested we go for a beer with him and play some music.

My instinct was to decline, but that was not what we came here for. Off we trooped to some place he knew. Once inside he was greeted like a long lost brother. His guitar was brought to him, drinks were provided and he started to play. It was a German Framus cello guitar, and he was one of those incredible players with a different chord for each beat of the tune. He sang in an unintelligible dialect with a voice that cracked and split in a way that indicated a life of cigarettes and shouting. He was impressive.

He signalled that it was our turn. Max and I removed our guitars from their cases and tuned up. I still hardly ever have a drink in the daytime, and at that age and starving, this beer had gone straight to my head. I played enthusiastically but not well, and after two numbers the people were talking to each other louder than we could play. I reached in my bag, pulled out my harmonica and harness and to much derision, strapped it on and we did a version of *Hard Travelling* that I thought was pretty good. At the end of it the Gypsy guy strapped on an incredible looking machine with six mouth organs fixed like spokes on a wheel. He could play in virtually any key and proceeded to play some unbelievable Austro-Hungarian type melody that made our efforts sound lightweight. With as much dignity as we could muster, we staggered out into the bright Frankfurt sunshine, half pissed and ready for some chips at least. We both fell asleep in a park and woke feeling rotten, but we did manage to get on the road south and spent a night in some trees at the side of an autobahn.

We spent the next two days at the side of the road with nothing to eat and in my case nothing to smoke. I had stopped asking Max for twos-ups and he was flicking his dog ends into the road so that I now had to climb over the barrier to retrieve them. I was beginning to get fed up with him; I had now got another stye on my other eye, my gums were bleeding every time I tried to clean my teeth, and I was running out of toothpaste as I was snacking on it from time to time in my hunger.

To pass the time, I wrote a diary for about five days and letters of description home which my mum failed to keep, saying only that it was good to know that I was all right. From that time on, I have only sent her postcards and she is happier with that than anything else I have ever done.

We eventually arrived in Munich and walked right through the imposing city. Finding our way to the railway station was easy, but we were very tired by the time we settled down with a beer. I managed to find some rolling tobacco, and in the hustle of the main concourse we were hardly noticed, looking for all the world like travellers ourselves, which of course we were. I say 'hardly' because the man who sold the 'warm Wurst und Brot' that was to be our diet for the next week had certainly noticed me, and whenever I looked in the direction of his kiosk his eyes were following me.

That first night we slept down some stairs but were awakened by the general noise of Munich waking up. We got washed in the public toilets that were conveniently near to our resting place. I remember finding it a little disconcerting having a lady sitting there whilst we took a pee, but like everything we got used to it and so long as we left some small change, she didn't mind us making the place our own. My eyes were slowly closing up with the appearance of more styes, my gums still bled, and I couldn't have weighed more than ten stone. My money was totally gone by now and I was beginning to realise that I would soon have to go busking or starve.

I was nearly sick with fright at the thought of playing in public. Max was still OK and had enough bravado for both of us, but he was not pushing too much the idea of playing live. Time, though, was running out. After five days of waiting for the London train it began to dawn on me that Beau was not going to show up. It was typical of the unreliable bastard. Finally one evening we struck up outside the toilets and nervously played our first session, making about eight marks.

This was a great morale boost, and I was able to buy some warm wurst from the sausage seller who was always looking at me. I should have been thrilled with the new opportunities, but I wasn't and I dreaded the next occasion when we would have to play.

I was sleeping in shop doorways wrapped in my pathetic blanket, and shivering the whole night long as merry Germans poured through the station concourse, while not so merry Polizei variously prodded and poked and on several occasions woke me with a boot in the side. My right eye looked as bad as my left, and I could now insert a match into the huge pocket that had appeared behind my front teeth. In spite of being able to eat the warm wurst I felt increasingly miserable. Each night the crowds of people coming through the station ought to have provided us with ample funds to travel anywhere we wanted, but my nerves just let me down and I cried off.

Neither of us could understand where all the people where coming from or going and then the posters advertising the 'Oktoberfest' began to make sense: we were in the middle of the biggest beer festival in the world. We decided to pay a visit. It was huge, on a scale like nothing I had seen before. Max saw it as a great opportunity to busk, but when at last I had the courage (after investing in a couple of beers) the little crowd that gathered thought we were playing out of general bonhomie rather than our lives depending on it. They clapped politely at the end of our couple of numbers and dispersed.

Still, I had to laugh; a couple of the styes had burst and things were looking up! After looking at the rides and the thousands of Germans happily swigging away on huge steins of beer, I began to feel resentment creeping up on me. Part of me, I am sure, knew that if I were able to ask for help or food, these people would have been just as kind as any other, but another part of me was angry. Couldn't they see my ribs poking through my shirt or see my infected eyes? Jesus, some of them were eating legs of pork that would have fed a couple of British families for a week. I mean who won the fucking war anyway? And, more insidiously, what were those songs that they were all singing as they staggered home through the station at night? It sounded to me like I'd heard those songs before.

Beau and Sally's arrival date came and went and Max and I soldiered on as best we could. Max had plenty of dough left but could not show it as it would only underline the difference in our two states. I think he had found some compassion for my situation, and although I know now that all these little distractions would have passed, when I suggested that we return to England he did not resist. I was heartened by this, and took it to imply that despite his bravado he wasn't confident to go it alone, or else he genuinely felt sorry for my predicament. We decided to go home via Paris and immediately perked up at the prospect.

Meanwhile in Greece, Henry had arrived and for the next several weeks dutifully went to the meeting place every day at twelve o'clock to be disappointed at our non-appearance. Stan, who had been out on the camp site with him, finally upped sticks and headed east, and none of us saw him again for nearly two years.

In Paris the two of us hauled our weary way to the Gare du Nord (why does every lost soul head for the station?). I remember nothing of our journey to France, because I slept as soon as I got comfortable or warm in a car. Not much company for the kind person who had stopped for me. Certainly by the time we had arrived we'd had enough and decided that once back in England we would take a train home from Dover. Max generously offered to buy me a meal and we settled on a small workman's café near the station.

"Well Woody, have anything you want," offered my friend.

"You know what I really fancy, Max?" I said. "Egg and chips."

"So do I," he replied and we ordered the meal. I didn't want to take advantage of Max's sudden generosity. Back home the cost of such a workman's lunch would have been about 1/3d. The food arrived and I noticed we had been given two eggs, but nothing prepared us for the shock of the bill when it was presented. The bill came to twelve shillings and sixpence for the two of us! In that time 12/6d was a day's money for a labourer! I felt awful and not having enough French to argue the toss we dejectedly left the place and tried to cheer ourselves up by visiting the Eiffel Tower. This in itself was no mean feat as we had to drag all our bedraggled belongings everywhere we went.

Visiting the tower was not cool (only tourists did things like that and we were road soldiers) but who would know if we didn't tell? We surveyed the city from the top and felt very distanced from the life that bustled below us. I threw a piece of newspaper off the top and watched it vanish as small as a postage stamp below and far away. It was time to go home.

∾

Outside by the wall
Where snails have crawled
Leaving tinselled trails
Shining in the moonlight
Pale
Lovers
Promising nothing will change
The things they share
Breathing promises
Of cloudy vapour disappearing
In the frosty midnight air

pad

The idea of leaving home again and setting up in Poole, in Dorset, came from Tony Dickinson, who I knew from college. Tony was the younger brother of Beau Dickinson, who was very nearly a true Beatnik in the sense that he had not an iota of responsibility, was not the slightest bit creative (except when it came to making up excuses as to why he had broken yet another promise), did not approve of work, and loved modern jazz.

Beau was a very handsome man and the girls adored him. He had black curly hair which he kept unfashionably short on top and a little longer at the back, and a luxuriant black beard to match, which made his beautiful white teeth seem even whiter. His eyes always sparkled with mischief, his nose was large, and he smiled all the time. Tony was a few years younger, and although softly spoken like his elder brother, was much less striking: his eyelashes curled upwards, and though his eyes sparkled just the same, they were smaller than his brother's; and if anything he had an even bigger nose.

Tony was very secretive, which I found annoying because I felt that he thought I didn't understand his allusions and inferences. But to be honest I thought him immature; his professed love of modern jazz seemed unreasonable in one so young, and I assumed he must be doing it for effect. Tony knew of my love of guitar music and I can only think that it was for this reason that we got introduced to this circle of people, as at this time there was a very healthy bunch of aspiring country blues players to which we were introduced almost immediately upon our arrival at the 'pad'.

Poole High Street was a very different place in 1962. It had a Georgian feel, and it was all a little run down. There was the usual selection of seaside cafés, cheap restaurants and small shops but no supermarkets.

The pad itself was situated over a betting shop down at the end of the High Street. Access was through a passageway, past the door that led into the shop and up a wide stairway to a landing. There was a bathroom with a bath which was not connected to the water supply. Up a little further to another small landing, where you could either turn left to the main living area or right to several other rooms on various levels and half levels. There was also a lavatory which was mercifully connected to the mains. The living room was L-shaped, with a primitive kitchen arrangement on the left of the door as you entered; the living area was round to the right where there were a couple of old chairs, a distressed sofa, and an open fire on which were burning some old fish boxes. In fact the whole place smelt slightly of fish and I soon discovered why.

The whole of the upstairs was deemed unfit for human habitation and was owned by a local fish shop who leased out the downstairs to the betting shop and for a very modest rent allowed the rooms upstairs to be used as an artist studio for one of the residents called Dick. Naturally enough when Dick saw how much room was available, he quickly filled it up with fellow students so that the rent was hardly felt by anyone and always promptly paid, which in turn meant that no-one ever checked up on us. At one time there were at least eight people living, cooking, playing, loving, and occasionally even painting in the place.

When I arrived at the pad I had about £2 to my name, a sleeping bag, a spare shirt and underpants, a toothbrush and razor, a towel and a Harmony Sovereign guitar with a spare set of strings and a capo, which were unsafely housed in a white hardboard case with a red lining. The clothes I stood up in were a blue cotton shirt, an old military combat jacket, a pair of genuine 28-inch waist Levis (priced 42/6), two pairs of home-knitted socks in green wool and a pair of suede moccasins.

As Tony and I shuffled awkwardly into the main room we were greeted by Phil. He was tall and slim with a huge brown beard and moustache that completely hid his mouth. He welcomed us into the place and introduced the others who were there. Sitting on the sofa was Dai and his girlfriend Sue, him with real red hair and her with masses of eye makeup. Next we met Dick, who was standing by the record player feeling the power cable (he hardly took any notice of us at all).

"For this thing to be bloody red hot," he said strangely.

The music playing was *Porgy and Bess,* and I asked Phil, who seemed to be the friendliest, who it was playing trumpet.

"It's Miles Davis with the Gil Evans Orchestra," said Tony before Phil could answer. One or two of the bunch seemed impressed and I was embarrassed not to have known.

"That's right," said Phil, smiling, and Tony blushed bright red.

On one of the chairs by the fire sat a very pretty girl with a very wide mouth and strong jaw line. Her hair was an unnatural red/brown colour and she too wore lots of makeup around the eyes. Perched on the arm of the chair sat a curly blond haired bloke of about 25, strumming loosely on an acoustic guitar.

"This is Anna and Pep," said Phil.

Anna said hello. Pep managed a nod, then asked, "What kind of axe have you got man?" I told him and he seemed quite impressed. Then, "What kind of music do you play man?"

I said a bit of Jesse Fuller and Jack Elliott, and within a few minutes I had the guitar out and was playing my small repertoire to an admiring audience. This was totally against my natural reserve, but whenever I moved locations during these early travelling days I was aware that it was a chance to assume a different identity, and although still terribly shy I could on occasions push that to one side, especially if I was among strangers. What made this show different was that Tony was with me and he knew me a little bit. Perhaps it was in defiance after not recognising Miles Davis.

"You blokes will have to share a room at the back," said Phil after a while and he showed us back out of the room and over the second land-ing to a cubbyhole with no windows except a small skylight about a foot square up in the roof. Fish boxes were piled up on one side of the room and there was an elderly army-type iron bedstead on the side under the skylight. Tony insisted that I had the bed, and he made himself a bed out of the upturned fish crates. We stacked most of the other boxes outside except for two which we used for bedside tables. There was no light in the room except what came through the skylight, but fortunately we found a light bulb the next morning for the single socket. That first night the boys fed us with rice and a sort of tomato sauce. We drifted off to bed very late.

Tony spent much of the time writing little stories in a childish hand, and although he wouldn't show them to me, I knew they must be very profound. Tony also would not reveal his age, and in company with the other blokes kept very quiet. To be honest I found him a bit of a bore and anyway, a bond was developing between myself and Pep. All the guys in the pad were middle class. Of the four, I suppose Dai and Pep were the closest to my own roots, although they too had accents that would have stuck out in Croydon.

Phil was very kind to Tony and me—almost paternal, or at least big brotherly. Dick was genuinely upper class; typically he was the most outrageous in his eccentricity and his descent into the squalor of the pad was total. He wandered about the place in a state of dishevelled undress, bearded and unkempt, and he had affected a mode of speech which several of the fringe of students were using. If he wanted to know the time he would ask, "For me to be wondering what time it's to be?"

After he had been told the answer he might add the construction, "For me to be thurbing into Bournemouth for something," by way of explanation.

'Thurbing' was a general verb that was used in place of any other. "What a bunch of dicks," I thought, but within a short space of time I was using the word myself.

Pep never used this mode of speech. He lived with Anna away from the pad and he had very strong opinions about everything—always sounding off about something or other—but what flattered me most was that he actively sought my company and took me around with him. One morning he took me over to the art college annexe to show me a marijuana plant that he was growing in a pot. He said the principal had adopted it and always paused to water it whenever he visited Pep at work. Pep loved the idea of someone in authority being duped into caring for a banned plant: "Stupid cunt," he said. His liberal use of strong language added to his personality; I'd never heard anyone who spoke so well swear so much.

Pep was a potter, but that title does not come near to describing his involvement with the craft. He didn't just throw pots, he lived and loved them. He was one of the first of the few men I have met that could inspire you with their passion for the work they loved; he taught me how to distinguish between Chinese and English porcelain and explained in breathy detail the secrets of different glazes. As he would speak of the ancient potters' search for the elusive red glaze, his voice would become dreamy and he'd show me pieces where there might be a hint of red on a pot after firing. He talked with real reverence about old pots that he had acquired, and years later prided himself that he'd been able to fool one of Sotheby's experts with one of his own imitation Siamese dishes (after he was happy with the glaze and so on, he tied the little dish to a piece of string and dragged it up the garden path to make tiny chips on the rim to 'age' it even more). I'd never even thought about such things before, and now I was becoming an expert.

Pep's second great love was country blues by the likes of Sleepy John Estes and other more obscure artists. He was always picking away on his guitar, but he was not very good; his timing was erratic and he sped up alarmingly. But he knew a few riffs and he also knew that he wasn't very good. He seemed to get a lot of pleasure out of watching me play and always wanted me to play my bit of Blind Boy Fuller or anything in my primitive ragtime. Sometimes we would play together, though I am sure he got more out of it than I did.

Pep's third love was Anna. He was passionate about her and very jealous; she was a little younger than me, and I was convinced that she was mad. Everything about their love was so intense, and Anna was constantly seeking reassurance or railing against some insensitivity that he had shown her; often she would be in inconsolable floods of tears. An empathy grew between us that became quite strong, and although I didn't fancy her, I enjoyed her turning to me until it finally occurred to me that Pep might get the wrong idea.

One day he took me over to Bournemouth to a pub at a place called the Landsdowne. There was a bloke playing a beautiful 12-string guitar and singing in an unbelievably loud voice, in a style not unadjacent to Leadbelly. His name was Jonathan, and he wore a little pillbox hat with a tassel on it. He spoke thurbish all the time, which was annoying, but he was a very good guitar player. His mate, who was just as posh as Jonathan, spoke the same way and played a stovepipe.

In those days blues records were as rare as rocking horse shit and all us would-be country blues players played the same songs, which were copied from the same few albums that were circulating. One such album was called 'Blues Fell This Morning' and on it was a track by someone called Stovepipe Number One. I'm sure when the recording was made it was supposed to be a novelty, but I can remember the earnestness with which they were discussing the correct materials to make the best bass resonance. Just watching other blokes playing was wonderful, and hours were spent soaking up music and chatter in the living room of our pad. I never got to know Jonathan better, but he came several times to the Poole house and played to an audience that were arguing with much passion about art, music and the meaning of life.

Somewhere beyond the High Street was a small pub called The Angel which sold cider. There was the usual assortment of characters that this kind of place attracts. It was here that the blokes went to relax further as everyone was pretty laid back anyway. Drinking was never really heavy as no-one had enough money to get really pissed, but somehow we did manage to get a drink and so long as it was not interfering with the other customers we were allowed to play guitar and someone always bought me a drink. At some time amidst the general friendliness of the place and the warmth of the drink we got introduced to Mr. and Mrs. Dawes, who had a lot of children aged from about seven to sixteen.

Mr. Dawes was an old-looking fortysomething with his hair swept back and a jovial demeanour; his wife was about the same age, with a wonderful Dorset accent and the looks of a Romany: jet black hair and dark brown, darting eyes. She was slightly stooped and had a protruding belly. These two saw nothing unusual in the set-up in the pad, and one or both of them often turned up for a coffee or a chat. Their kids were allowed to wander where they pleased, and several of them used to pay regular visits to see the 'beatniks'. Somehow we all rubbed along together, cadging roll-ups and wondering how long it would be before we had to get a job and start paying our way. We survived on coffee, rice and occasional spaghetti, but I don't really remember eating anything substantial until the arrival of George.

∾

george

One morning I rolled out of bed and was drinking some coffee in the kitchen when in walked a rumpled-looking chap somewhat the worse for wear.

Phil looked up and asked, "Can I help you?"

"Well that depends, brother. Where the fuck am I?" he demanded whilst scratching his belly through a large tear in his string vest.

"You're in a private flat in Poole High Street." answered Phil.

"Well thank gawd I'm still in the same town I started out in last night. Foulser's the name, George Foulser. I got pissed up last night and someone must have brought me here. Could I possibly have a cup of coffee, mate?"

"I'm afraid we've run out of milk," said Phil.

"Don't worry about that," said George. "Black'll be fine. With four sugars."

Then Dai walked in. "Good to see you up and about," said Dai. "How are you feeling today?"

George said he was pretty good and wondered how he got to be with us. Dai explained that he had been found outside asleep in the gutter at about 1 am. Dai and a bloke called Francois had dragged him upstairs and put him in an empty room, where at least he would be dry if not warm. Armed with a cup of hot sweet coffee, George roundly thanked us all for our great kindness. Then he tapped someone for a roll up, sat down on one of the fish boxes in our 'kitchen' and informed us that what we had done was in the true spirit of socialist and student/worker relations. Between noisy sips of his drink he began to take in his new surroundings.

"Who the fuck put that gas oven in?" he asked accusingly. When it was explained that Dick had done it, he pointed out that we could all be blown sky high, and offered to make it safe for us. The offer was gratefully accepted, but to tell the truth it didn't look much different when he'd finished. It was a fairly primitive bodge-up of hose pipe and jubilee clips, but it was true that it smelt less of gas in the pad than before.

George knew loads of things and had opinions about everything. That evening we went to the pub where he bought us a drink and we talked and talked. Several of the blokes got bored, but I just loved to listen and though I'm not a cockney, I found the sound of his working class accent reassuring and his colourful language inspiring.

"Blimey, this wire is red hot," he exclaimed as his fingers brushed the electric cable that powered the record player, and as his eyes followed the wire I noticed for the first time that the cable powered everything.

"Christ that's dodgy," said George. "That wire isn't strong enough to feed all the lights and the record player as well. I'll be happy to sort that for you if you like."

"Oh er thanks," mumbled Phil, preferring not to get drawn into the conversation about the electrics, for he had a problem about the morality of hot-wiring our place illegally from the betting shop downstairs. He needn't have worried; the wires continued to almost glow and nothing was ever done about it.

George didn't move in, as he had nothing to move; he just didn't go away. He was a political agitator and a published author. His book was called *The Seaman's Voice*, and I was delighted to find a copy some years later in the library. Until then I only had his word for it (but I believed him anyway).

George was a blacklisted merchant seaman and had just been rumbled and given his papers in Poole Harbour, off a small steamer that moved down the south coast delivering coal. So in time-honoured fashion he decided to drink his money and worry about what to do next when his hangover cleared. He appeared to own nothing and desired even less; all he seemed to want was someone to listen to him, a couple of drinks and the occasional bunk-up. He had to wait a long time for the latter.

As a young man full of the songs of Woody Guthrie and already a confirmed socialist, this was like having my own guru. No matter what subject came up, George was ready with an opinion and an intuitive socialist response. Much of what was said went over my head, and you can't really discuss much when most of us were left wing and agreed with everything he said anyway. Thus George was forced to take an even more radical line so that someone would disagree with him, and then he could get back on his horse again. It wasn't long before the words 'middle class' were being used as an insult, for George had no sense of tact as far as his student landlords were concerned. "Fuck 'em," he said defiantly.

Of course this led to a cooling off between him and some of the lads. But Anna, Pep and myself still enjoyed his company, though Pep often wound George up just to watch the sparks. And as Pep and Anna's relationship rocked on, soon Anna was confiding her troubles to George as well as me.

George was really a caricature of what you would expect a seaman agitator to be. When we found him, he was clad only in a shirt and working trousers and lace-up boots. But on the dust sheet of his book he was wearing a donkey jacket and roll neck sweater; his hair was a short back and sides 30's style, brushed straight back with the very shortest hair above his ears sticking straight out. His skin was quite pale for a drinking man and he had a nose like a potato stuck on his face; he also had several teeth.

He was soon convinced that Anna fancied him.

It is well known that there is a correlation between food and love-making. There was never any attempt to organise meals together; it would have been against the whole spirit of the place. However I was not involved in any relationship, and hunger was quite often on my mind. The cooker was mainly used for boiling kettles for coffee, but one day George blurted out, "Don't any of you lot ever eat anything? How does a bit of roast lamb and potatoes sound to you?"

It sounded great to me and I said so. It was soon pointed out that we had no money but George would have none of it.

"Let's have a whip round," he suggested and between us we raised about three or four shillings.

"That'll do," said George, and off he went, returning in about half an hour laden with groceries. He slapped his shopping on the table and pulled out a huge tin of peas, some Oxo cubes, a load of potatoes and some meat. We all stared in amazement, our eyes widening further as he plonked down enough change to buy a pint of scrumpy with as well.

"How did you manage that?" I asked,

"Well I'm glad you asked, Ralph, and I'll tell you. I paid for the veg what they was asking, but the meat I blagged. You've got to get the meat first, otherwise there's no point. What you do is walk up to the butcher's shop and stare at all the stuff in the window. Once you've been noticed by the butcher himself you scurry off for a few minutes and then come back and do it a couple times more until you are quite sure he's seen you. Then you go in and without looking him directly in the eye, you ask him if he's got sixpence worth of scraps for your dog. 'Course sometimes that's exactly what you get, and you can still make some sort of stew out of a tanner's worth, but if you go in at the end of the day and they've had a good 'un, they'll usually work out that you look so down on your luck that even if you'd had a dog you'd probably already eaten it so they figure you might be just out the nick or be really down on your luck and they'll throw in three breasts of lamb or a bit of stewing steak and there you go. Then you hand over the tanner and as you pick up your bundle you make sure you squeeze his hand and you say, Thanks pal I won't forget this, knowing full well that he won't forget you and so long as you don't take the piss you can go back some other time and do it again."

That evening we dined like kings; what a man was our George.

Things of course got tighter and various members drifted off to eat with friends in the evenings or else they stocked up in the college canteens. Tony got a job as a washer-up in one of the seaside cafés called the Galleon and usually managed to smuggle a few leftovers back to the pad, and I kept my eye on George to see when his next miracle might take place.

One evening when there was only him, me and Pep in the place, George suddenly burst out with, "Ain't there no bleedin' allotments round here?"

346

I looked nonplussed and so did Pep, then we both realised what he was thinking and I was appalled. I found myself thinking of my uncle Reg and his carefully nurtured rows of lettuce and carrots.

I blushed deepest red, but felt I had to declare, "That's stealing! I'm sorry George, but I think that's wrong—after all these are the gardens of the working man, the ordinary blokes who have no land of their own. You can't nick from them."

George said nothing but reached over and opened his tobacco tin and slowly manufactured one of his 'Black Beauty' rollups. Once satisfied that it was perfect he licked the glued edge, stuck it in his mouth, lit it, inhaled a medium sized drag, blew it out, luxuriously tapped the cigarette prematurely on the ashtray and looking sort of over, past and through me said:

"To each according to his need. From each according to his ability. I know I don't have to remind you who said that, and furthermore we won't be nicking from one geezer. For a start you notice I asked for an allotment not a garden, that's so we can take a little from all of them. All blokes with allotments grow more than they can eat, it's only natural, if you've got a certain amount of plot you're going to fill it up. Otherwise you're wasting it. You content yourself with the knowledge that you can be charitable and offer your neighbour some of your surplus, only the chances are he'll have too much left over as well and it'll get thrown on the compost heap anyway.

"The other reason for taking a little from all of them is that they can commiserate with each other about being pilfered from and in a couple of days they'll have forgotten about it all. It is quite legit socialistically speaking, after all our need is greater than theirs, so we take according to our needs. 'From each according to his ability' will be about our ability to climb over that bleedin' fence around the allotment."

George felt very pleased with himself after this and took another pull on his fag, which this time caused him to start another bout of lung-wracking coughing.

"I still don't think it's right, George," I said.

"Then you don't have to come," he said, leaning over the table at me and stubbing out his cigarette at the same time. "Now, who's going to tell me where the nearest one is?"

It is one of my small regrets that I wasn't one of The Few who went over the wall that night, for to see them when they came back covered with dirt and scratches, flushed and animated by their adventure, made me feel pathetically moralistic. Especially when I saw what a small amount they had taken: there were some carrots and a swede or two, some tomatoes and a few onions; but the biggest haul was of rhubarb.

The spoils were spread out on the table like harvest festival for us all to admire, and George promised us all a stew the next day. When I came in that evening the pot was bubbling merrily on the stove. This time George had got the stewing steak, and after crudely chopping everything up had thrown it all into the pot. Including the rhubarb. We still had a few spuds left: they were boiling away on the other burner, and the smell was fantastic. Eventually the meal was served up and I was duly offered a bowl. Nothing was said but I could feel George looking at me through his spoon.

"No thanks," I said, "I've already had something," and I went up to the room I shared, took out the guitar and seriously thought about leaving the pad and going back home. After a few seconds' strumming, I went back to the kitchen to claim my bowl, only to find that it had been democratically shared out amongst the rest.

Life drifted on. More and more people called by as the reputation of the flat grew, and although I sometimes felt as if we were viewed as freaks by our guests, I still loved it. No-one ever thought about turning in until 2 or 3 o'clock any night of the week and every night was like a weekend. One weekend Henry turned up with Linda and June and we all hung out together.

Until now I had survived on fresh air, cigarettes and the charity and kindness of the chaps at the pad—and George's odd miracle—but now that Tony had got a job, the pressure was definitely on me.

Living was cheap. Clothes were washed by hand and jeans were scrubbed in the yard with a broom and rinsed in the bath on the landing. One day it was brought to our attention that some of the clientele from the betting shop had been seen pissing in it.

This presented us with a dilemma; we did not want to rock the boat by complaining to the landlords, because we were not supposed to be living in the place anyway, to say nothing of the bath's water supply being disconnected. Nevertheless George had a bit of fun one day when we'd seen two fellows go up to our landing to relieve themselves in the bath. George slipped off his shirt and walked purposely into the bathroom with his moth-eaten old towel over his arm and my toothbrush in his hand as if about to perform his daily ablutions. His feigned shock and horror at what he found on entering not only produced a grovelling apology from the two embarrassed offenders but a couple of quid to get the place cleaned.

There was never enough hot water to perform anything more than a sponge down, but we managed to wash bits of ourselves at a time on an irregular basis. When I see how my own kids feel filthy if they don't shower every day, I often wonder what they would have made of the generation that bathed once a week whether they were dirty or not.

One day Les turned up at the pad. He had become very strange, and was living in a park somewhere in the town. He'd had a very hard time in Belgium where he'd been travelling and had been drinking rain water from puddles. He had formed peculiar opinions about the Belgian people and picked up some fleas. Large spots were clearly visible through his patchy beard and I was really worried about him. He was on a mission to find out about himself and there was nothing I could do to change his direction.

He stayed with us for no more than a couple of days, then he was back to the park and off on his travels again. If anything, Les's appearance probably added credibility to the presence of Tony and myself amongst our middle class hosts. They must have been alarmed by his appearance; he certainly scared me and I worried about him for a long time afterwards.

The Dawes kids, who were allowed free rein all over town, were less regular visitors to the pad, except for the youngest, Jeannie, and her older sister Shirley. We were something of an odd collection and the two kids were intrigued by our lifestyle. They were both very familiar and would wander into any and every room to see if we were in, and because we were all very young—more like older brothers than uncles—this did not seem odd to me. Little Jeannie would climb over any of us, laugh her little gap-toothed husky chuckle as she pulled the boys' beards or got us to play our guitars. She was very fond of Pep and Anna, and would crawl up on to the sofa between them for company.

Pep looked like a leftover teddy boy; he had his blond curls pushed back and wore very tight jeans and desert boots, usually a workman's blue shirt and often a rollneck sweater. There was no attempt to impress his persona on people as he honestly couldn't have given a fuck what anyone thought of him.

Then Anna found she was pregnant, and, true to his unpredictable form, Pep married her.

❧

gill

As the pad became part of the established student tourist route, more and more kids from the colleges spent the odd night there; most however left before morning, and for most of the residents the novelty of staying up late began to wear thin. I was one of the last to give in as I was one of the last to get a job.

The wages at the Metal Box company paid about £5 a week after tax, but it made an enormous difference to me. I could buy George the odd drink and at least afford fresh tobacco. One day over the Angel, I sat down near the door with my drink and slowly took in the faces around me. Although I was firmly part of this little scene, I by no means knew everyone that gathered there. As I worked my eyes through the crowd, I suddenly noticed a girl that made my heart jump. She was without doubt the most beautiful girl I had ever seen.

Years later in *The Godfather* I was to read of the 'thunderbolt' that hit the young Michael Corleone during his enforced exile in Sicily when he first saw his bride to be, but at that time I had no words to describe the effect her appearance had on me. She simply looked stunning, her long blonde hair all the more blonde against a navy blue duffel coat, her smile somehow still unsure though huge, the slightly awkward way she held her cigarette; she was a little too clumsy in her movements to be obviously sexy, but she had a smouldering effect on me. I couldn't take my eyes off her and I couldn't understand why the boys weren't all over her. I knew she was middle class by the way she moved, and I knew that I was losing myself and I knew I must meet her and I knew it would not be tonight and what was her name and where did she come from and she didn't even notice me and she went out with some geezer and as she walked out she didn't even notice me again.

When I had judged a cool time had passed I ventured as casually as I could to ask (without my voice breaking up), "Who was that girl in the duffel coat?"

"Oh, that's Gill," someone said.

"What does she do?" I asked.

"She sort of hangs around the college."

"Is she a student?"

Phil looked up at me and said, "No, but she sometimes models for the photography class."

Something about the way he spoke indicated that he might have sort of fancied her himself. I decided that enough had been said and changed the subject. She was certainly lovely enough to have been a model and I knew her name. I would have to be content with that, but of course I wasn't. I had to get to know her—but how?

The pain of longing for someone is never so intense as when you are young; the effect that this state has on you makes your whole body and mind behave oddly. The intensity of feeling, the appropriateness of every silly love song to your situation and the deep dark knowledge that the object of your affection and the causer of your pain isn't even aware of your existence let alone your name, yet everywhere you look hers is written in huge capital letters, and even when you gaze out at the stars through the tiny skylight in your fish box smelly bedroom you see 'Gill' written in the sky.

The next morning I awoke in what I thought was a muck sweat. My sleeping bag and cover were soaked and I thought I was paralysed, as I could not move my head. With great relief I found I could move my feet and then, thankfully, all my other parts. I called to Tony to help me. He hopped out of bed and came anxiously to my side.

"I can't move my bloody head," I bleated.

"Why are your covers all wet?" he asked.

"God knows. I'm more worried about my neck."

Tony looked at my bed, and then his gaze went up to the ceiling. Suddenly he said, "No wonder you can't move, there's no bloomin' glass in the skylight."

It was the first night's rain since we had arrived at the pad. Not having any glass in the roof meant that it had just rained on me, and now my neck had locked. How could I approach the most beautiful girl in the world with my head locked securely on one side? Perhaps she would think I looked knowing or quizzical. I tried squinting, cowboy-style, whilst leaving my head at its jaunty angle. No, she would probably think I was deformed. She might go out with me because she felt sorry for me. Oh the pain of love. Oh the pain in the neck.

I kept myself indoors that day, but the next morning was horrified to find that I was no better. There was nothing for it but to go to the hospital. The doctor who examined me suggested a neck collar. I decided against that, and stumbled back to the pad. After a couple more days of misery, with just about everyone asking me what was the matter, George offered to help me out with some Chinese massage he had learned in Hong Kong. I declined, but he passed on the secrets of the Orient to Tony, who crept up behind me and, grabbing me by my forehead and the back of my neck, gave it an almighty jerk. It caused me to utter a rather unmanly shriek, but freed up the spasm.

Weeks passed and I never saw Gill. The atmosphere in the pad was changing. Phil was clearly under pressure either from work or the bombastic nature of George, who had by now become the patriarch amongst those who still hung on to every word.

We hardly ever saw Dai or Sue till early evening, and Dick was about his work and only showed up on odd days, recounting strange snippets of dreams. Once he said, "For me to have had the strangest dream the other night. I'd been plating this girl and I was sort of hiding from my mother with a huge dollop of cold cream on my nose."

Another gentle soul arrived at the pad; his name was Ian, and everyone reckoned that he was the best painter of all of them. Ian dyed his hair blond and was the first bloke I'd ever met to do so.

George had acquired an old typewriter from Anna and was busy tapping away in his room. His papers had finally arrived, and with much pride he undid a parcel tied up with string. After shuffling through piles of stuff, he produced an article he'd written for the *Observer* about the similarities between the Norwegian language and the Geordie dialect. He had noticed whilst on board ship that these two groups of sailors could converse with each other. It was just another bit of glamour that added to George's reputation.

I questioned George about what he was writing and he told me it was an article called 'The Pad At Poole'. I was terribly impressed, and when it was finished and sent off to town I waited anxiously for news of its impending publication. Once George had the bit between his teeth we hardly saw him. He locked himself in his room and tapped away at his article. When asked where all the concentration came from, he pulled a small bottle from his jacket containing some tiny pills.

"Ephedrine," he smiled smugly. "A great little helper, keeps the ideas flowing."

When we asked what ephedrine was, he told us it was supplied to asthmatics to help them breathe but it also was a form of speed and it was cheap. Though officially it was a prescription drug, with a rattling chest like George had, it was easy to find an old chemist who would sell you a few pills 'as you'd left ship without them'. Pep knew all about 'ephies' because of a real need, and though speed was always a popular recreational drug, I just did not fancy trying them in spite of George's offer. It was a long time before I even tried the 'purple hearts' that were only threepence each at the time.

George eventually received a rejection slip which stated that the article was not of the quality of his previous one, but that they would be pleased to hear from him if he had anything else to offer. George said he couldn't really give a fuck, though he seemed disappointed. He never let any of us read it, but he did tell me that we were all mentioned in it.

The novelty of George was beginning to wear a bit thin. Some of the blokes were deliberately avoiding him, and there were those who suspected that George, like the puppy, might just be for life. The whole point of being in a gang of your contemporaries is to debate and let off steam and not be constantly reminded of where you were going wrong, or that your arguments were based on false premises and so on. I can still hear Phil's voice cracking with near hysteria as he tried not to lose his temper with George. There was also the class thing—perhaps that was another reason that I continued to get on with George, as I think I still had enough Croydon accent to sound more like a fellow Londoner.

"You know what, Ralph," he said one day, "I'm beginning to think that you're bad luck. I ain't had so much as a sniff of a bit of skirt ever since I been in this place."

Is that right, I thought to myself—well some of us had been waiting considerably longer than that (unless I counted Susan, but she would have probably denied it).

I was still in touch with Henry and the gang from Mitcham and sometimes I would give him a call at his home just for a little chat when I felt low.

One day he said, "We're all going to the Richmond Jazz festival. Why don't you hitch up and meet us there?" Things were slow at the pad so I said yes, and immediately felt better. Once I got there and it was good to see all the friendly faces and to partly impress them by my authentic appearance. Linda was there, with June and a few other faces from home, plus some from our flirtations with the West End scene who were more stylishly attired.

The day was overcast but intense. There were skip jivers and Cy Laurie dancers; a sea of combat jackets, beards, berets and cider. I wandered in and out of the company through the grounds when suddenly, walking by herself smoking a cigarette, clad in Levis and a loose sweater, I spotted Gill.

Sometimes in life one is hardly responsible for one's actions; impulse or bravado can often outweigh the carefully considered remark or action. I remember in a pub once a fight had broken out, and one of the protagonists was lying on the floor with the other standing over him. The standing one picked up a chair and was about to hit the other one over his unprotected head, and in the time he had raised the chair over his head, I had realised what was about to happen, leapt to my feet, grabbed the chair from the bloke and wrestled it out of his grip, threw it violently across the bar and was sitting back in my chair holding my drink.

So here I was and there she was, and there was no time to think. I walked right up to her and said, "Hello, you're Gill. I've seen you down at the Angel in Poole, you're a friend of Phil and Dick from the pad in the High Street, I'm staying there at the moment but I'm up here with some friends from Mitch— I mean London. Would you like to meet them?"

She smiled at me or maybe even laughed, but I was feeling faint and my heart had risen to my head and was beating to the tempo of *Tiger Rag.*

"You must be Ralph. I've heard about you, you play the guitar. Pep thinks you play well."

At that moment I couldn't have cared less what Pep thought; this beautiful girl knew my name and I was sure I was about to pass out. I found her walking with me the few hundred yards to where I'd last seen my mates; I must have said something, but by now the huge rush of adrenaline that had enabled me to make the initial move had deserted me, leaving only a rush of words and a tangle of tongue and lip sounds speaking biblical babble.

With trembling fingers I attempted a roll up. The paper stuck to my perspiring fingers and half the tobacco spilled on to the ground and when it was finally ready to light my beloved Zippo had run out. I dextrously pulled out the inner tank from the cover and blew down the end to force the remaining gas up to the wick. On the first flick of the wheel, it caught and lit the cigarette all down one side and the burning tobacco fell out over my shirt and the most beautiful girl in the world said, "Would you like one of these?" and offered me one of her 'tailor-mades'.

I remember nothing of the rest of the day except that after a fairly decent interval she left to rejoin her friends and I was left with only the sound of her voice and the helpless sense of loss and doubt as to whether I had impressed her at all and if she would be coming to Poole again.

Days passed and only the sound of Miles Davis with the Gil Evans arrangements filled the languid atmosphere of the pad as summer began to assert itself on the late spring. Now Francois was spending more time with George, and George seemed to be glad of a new audience. Francois was becoming interested in getting on a ship and maybe even a union card. George and he made frequent trips down to the harbour, and eventually George got him a boat. It was only a coastal run but, just like riding a bicycle down a road you always drive along, the world from Shoreham to Portland is full of sights, smells and sounds that seem entirely new.

Francois was black-haired, swarthy and foreign-looking, but his speech was like that of the aristocracy as far as I was concerned. He too spoke thurbish, and that would have to go if he was going to make his way as a seaman. When we next saw him, he was a different bloke; the accent was the same but his manner had undergone a huge transformation. Most of those on board his vessel were foreign so they did not notice his upper-class speech, and he was able to help the ship's master with translations. The crew all thought him the bee's knees and that was the last time I ever saw him.

Once while I was at Croydon Tech I had all but enlisted in the Merchant Navy, until someone asked incredulously, "What do you want to join up with that bunch of poofs for?"

The very thought of Paul Potter or Harry Barnet (my neighbours from Croydon) having anything to do with poofs was absolutely unthinkable. But here it was again—the rumour that homosexuals were attracted to the Merchant Navy. It was enough to put me off and it did. I told George that I nearly signed up and asked him his opinion as to whether it was true.

He said nothing for a while, and proceeded to roll a cigarette.

"Yeah, it's true," he sighed after a while and blew a stream of blue smoke from his nostrils. "You mainly get them on the ocean-going boats but there are some on these inshore runs, you see no-one bothers them and they've got their own little scene going, they've got their pubs and so on and they don't bother straight people that much when they know you ain't bent."

"Have you ever come across them?" I asked.

"Oh yeah, oh yeah I have, Ralph, and I hate them bastard nancy boys. It ain't in my nature any of that old game but we'd been out at sea for weeks and I got pissed up one time and a couple of them come on to me and I never realised what was going on till it was you know like and I ain't proud of it and I try to keep away from them bastards now."

I felt a little nauseous at the thought of it and when I looked back at him there was a tear of regret—or was it a fonder memory? I would never know.

Then with a "hrumpf!" and a cough he changed the subject slightly: "Anyhow, how's your luck? I hope it's better than mine—I made a pass at that Anna and she's gone all tearful on me. I think you're a fuckin' jinx on my love life, Ralph."

Well, I've just met the most beautiful girl in the world, I nearly said. But thankfully it came out as: "I met this girl at the jazz festival and she's from round here, so I'm hopeful if you get my meaning."

"Well good luck to you, mate. I hope I get to meet her when she stays over."

When she stays over? Christ, I hadn't even got that far in my mind. I was still wondering if she had wings. Gill did not have wings, but she did have a Lambretta motor scooter, and a few days later she paid a visit to the pad and took me out on the back.

I was totally besotted with her, and she must have found me amusing as she didn't seem to mind making the journey over from Bournemouth, where she lived, to see me.

I was deeply jealous of everyone who said "Hello Gill" to her, and there were lots of them, mostly boys so much more sophisticated than me that they failed to walk out of the room backwards when in her company. Some of them were even able to speak to her without getting tongue-tied or sweaty. Many were clean and had some money; none of them paid much attention to the brooding obsessed skinny Brando/Dean figure that skulked in her shadow. They obviously failed to recognise the Brando/Dean reference, and in fact barely observed the scruffy skinny kid acutely aware of his own insecurities and lack of money, transport and confidence.

Gill was the second daughter of a clerk at the local family allowance office. Her mother was a little stuck up, not to say snooty. She had her father's small features and long limbs, while her elder sister looked like their mother. Gill was not very academic, but she loved horses and was a good rider; I suppose she was barely out of that schoolgirl crush some young girls have with horses when I met her. Men would fight for her attention, and even be prepared to kidnap her from me. Looking back, I probably rushed things, but at the time I felt I was playing it as slow as I dared. Luckily for me she responded to my attentions and we became a couple.

Back at the pad things were changing too. Sad to say, Phil was becoming odder, Dick seemed to want to move on elsewhere, and Pep was the father of a little girl with Anna, who was still crazy. Francois was at sea on a coastal steamer and looking like something out of a fifties black and white movie, and George had got lucky at last (not Anna of course, but allegedly someone we all knew—I suspect it was Mrs. Dawes[4]).

Before the pad broke up entirely, Pep's relationship with Anna was floundering and he was flirting with heroin. Tony had made up his mind

[4] Some years later my attention was drawn to a piece in a newspaper about a family called Dawes who had found a way into an old crypt. The kids kept bringing artefacts to school and it's doubtful that the teachers' suspicions would have been aroused if it hadn't been that one of the boys overstepped the mark when he brought a human skull into the class for the nature table. These days George seemed to have money on him and none of us knew where it came from. Some alleged that he and Mrs. Dawes had gone into partnership as a couple of middle-aged burglars but the whole idea seemed preposterous. They did however go exploring deserted houses for 'left-behinds' and perhaps that's where the confusion arose.

to become a vibes player, and as soon as he had the money he bought a set which were installed at his family's home. He dedicated himself to learning this instrument and indeed became very proficient, though he never gained any real recognition. He started to wear three button suits and slim ties and the distance between us grew until I eventually lost contact with him.

A couple of years ago I was walking down Northcote Road market when I bumped into Judy, a girl I'd not seen for years. As we talked of the old days we both agreed how sad it was about Les and Beau dying, and then she mentioned Tony's suicide. I nearly passed out with shock; Tony, it transpired, had been gay, and when his lover had found religion and abandoned their relationship, Tony had found the future too awful to face alone and hanged himself. Once the enormity of this story had sunk in, I found myself trawling the past for clues as to any of this. I did remember once talking to him in the pad and closely questioning him about motives for what he was doing. Really I suppose I was asking him if he thought his work was any good, and probably I was trying to help him grow up and realise that just because you want to be a writer or musician, the intent doesn't necessarily make you one.

He laughed, and then, his eyes full of compassion and the beginnings of tears, turned round to me and said, "You don't understand, do you Ralph?" His eyes now overflowed with tears and all the time he was smiling as he spoke.

There was no hint of anger in his accusation and I thought little at the time beyond being sorry if I had hurt him. Now as his words came back to me, I wondered if he was seeking to confirm something of deeper significance. I never saw Tony with a girlfriend and in those days before gay lib, his life must often have been lonely. Perhaps his dedication to the vibraphone was made easier to understand in this context.

Ever since the army, I had always been either with a girl or after a girl, and though not yet completely au fait with all the mechanics of sex and its delicate relations, I was doing a lot better than most of my friends. My technique was simple: someone would tell me so and so liked me, and if I liked her too I would ask her out. I think Gill was the first girl I had boldly gone after. With the others I'd had a start. Fortunately for me Gill was on the phone, and when I was unable to see her at least I could talk to her, which I did every day. I was desperate to make love to her but

359

she made me wait a long time. I know she had been badly hurt by some arsehole from the college who tried to worm his way back to her once word got out that she was seeing this skinny proto-Beat character 'from London', and I often dreamt of avenging her pain in a fist fight.

There was a lightness and romance to this part of my life that was not to come again until Paris. All sensations were exaggerated by my circumstance and freedom away from home, and the fact that we did not actually sleep overnight with each other until some time later. In the meantime there was still some order in our lives, as she had to be in at her parents' house in Cranleigh Gardens by a certain time most nights. Though I don't think she got on that well with her folks, she was wise enough not to make waves. We saw a great deal of each other.

She taught me to drive her scooter and, helmetless with her hair in our faces, we zipped all over Bournemouth and the roads to Poole. I would have been the happiest kid in the world if only I hadn't needed reassurance in just about everything to do with her. Bournemouth is home to countless foreign students, all of whom fancied Gill. She was known to most of the kids at the college as a part time model; all the musicians knew her because pretty girls always get to meet musicians; people on motorbikes waved to her, and it was clear to me I was going to have to make our own story if I was to lose my doubts or jealousy.

I resolved to go abroad the following summer, earn my keep through busking and take Gill with me. I only achieved two out of the three.

❧

shiver

After the pad at Poole broke up, I moved into a house on Southbourne High Street which Henry was renting with Beau.

The house was owned originally by the Lady of Brownsea Island, who had it built as her chauffeur's residence. It comprised a cellar, kitchen, lounge and bathroom and two bedrooms upstairs. The whole place was fixed to the garage, which was big enough to hold three cars at least; it was empty but locked and off limits. The house was within a few yards of the beach, but the sea held few attractions for us, especially under the moody skies and the cold wind which should have warned us of the harshness of the time to come.

By the time I arrived at the place, Beau had already split, owing Henry money for rent, and Pep, who was working with Henry as a train washer, suggested Keith, a potter from Lytchett Matravers, as a reliable and steady subtenant. 'Irish Mick' and I arrived with a handful of belongings and my by now well-travelled guitar.

Henry was genuinely pleased to see us and was more effusive than usual in his introduction of both of us to Keith. A friendly face means a lot when you are broke and a bit scared as to where the next bit of food is going to come from, and so it was with Henry at our meeting. Keith was a smashing bloke and a genuine artist; he already knew Gill from the art college, and as well as being a good potter he was immensely practical and was in charge of glueing all the bits and pieces of electrical sound systems together. He'd even fixed up a speaker in the kitchen so that we could have sounds on when it was our turn to do the washing up. This order was achieved by means of a rota and it worked surprisingly well, the only problem being that there was hardly anything to wash up—Henry was out of work, Keith ate at the college and Mick and I had neither work nor money.

I had met Irish Mick in Croydon. His surname was Doyle, and he was a Dublin man. Mick wore his curly black hair in an elaborate Tony Curtis. He had the gap between the front teeth and walked with a slight swagger which did not denote any overbearing, just a confidence in himself that was both casual and reassuring. We were an unlikely pair of mates in many ways; he laughed a great deal and he just made me feel good. How I wished I could be so light of heart; Mick worried about nothing at all, and if there was any *craic* to be had out of a situation he would find it. Nothing daunted him and he was practical if not always morally sound as far as I was concerned. We all had reason to be grateful for his amorality before very long.

Henry showed us up to our room, which overlooked part of the garage. We found two beds on opposite sides of the room but no bedclothes; there were a pair of floral curtains forlornly hanging from the window and a bit of carpet on the floor.

I dropped my bag of belongings on the floor and said, "I'll take this one then."

"Okay," said Mick, "and I'll take this one so." We looked at each other and burst out laughing.

"We're going to be feckin' comfortable tonight all right," said Mick. I was almost at the point when I would laugh at anything, and that sort of near hysteria has always made everything else seem even more ridiculous. Mick, momentarily gaining control of himself, said, "It's going to be feckin' freezin' up here tonight."

"I know," I responded and then burst out laughing again. This only made Mick start again and by the time we wandered back downstairs to the other lads it looked as if both of us had been crying.

"Now lads, have ye anytin' to eat?" asked Mick boldly.

"I was afraid you might ask that," said Henry.

"All we got is some potatoes," offered Keith and for the first time I noticed his rich Dorset accent.

"Right," said Mick, going into the kitchen, "let's have some potatoes." By making use of just about everything that was left in the cupboard—salt, pepper, tomato sauce, a bit of milk and the last of the Echo margarine—he produced a meal of mashed potato that whetted everyone's appetite for more. Unfortunately there was no more.

The place was getting colder by the hour, and then by the minute, and we were all moving about and looking at the two-bar electric fire that was the only visible form of heating in the room.

"When does the feckin' heat come on then?" asked Mick.

"Not yet," came the curt reply from Henry. "It's on a meter and we've only got a shilling so we're saving it till it gets really cold."

"Well I'm really cold now and I still have a shillin' so if one of youse fellows will show me the meter I'll be glad to share me bob wid ya," said Mick.

Henry took Mick out of the room and showed him where the slot machine was, and within a few seconds they were back downstairs and all four of us sat huddled round the one bar.

"It lasts twice as long," observed Henry cleverly.

"Yeah, but two bars would be twice as warm," reasoned Mick. We all ignored this wisdom and started smoking and chatting about this and that and the price of potatoes and where we were likely to get a job.

Most of us would convince ourselves we were warm if some part of us was heated; perhaps a warm thigh or shin would be enough to make us ignore the north wind at our backs or the draft blowing up a trouser leg. Indeed some of the women on the estate back in Croydon had burn marks on their legs from sitting so close to the fire. All was merry and the pain of hunger began to dwindle in the glow of the electric fire and the banter, when suddenly the bar went off with a click.

"Is that it?" demanded Mick. "Jesus we're only after sitting here a feckin' minute or two."

The remaining shilling was reluctantly inserted in the meter. Keith put on some Woody Guthrie, and we smoked some more cigarettes and when the last shillingsworth ran out we stayed up until our teeth were nearly chattering with tiredness, hunger and cold. I said my goodnights and went upstairs to the dreaded bed. I emptied out my bag of bits, put most of them on and spread the rest over me and lay there shivering wondering what the hell Mick was going to do. All he had were the clothes he stood up in, and there was nothing I could see in the house that could possibly have helped to keep him warm.

A few minutes elapsed before Mick entered the room with much blowing and bustle. With the enterprise we would come to expect from the man, he had purloined all the towels from the bathroom and stuffed them inside his corduroy jacket and had swathed around his shoulders the carpet runner from the landing.

"Jesus it's feckin' cold wha' boy?" He spoke loudly to himself, but it was also a check to see if I was listening and still awake. I said nothing. From the corner of my eye I could see him scouring the room for more comfort materials, and finding none, resignedly sighed. He turned off the light and fell into the bedsprings with a chorus of pings and boings that started me silently chuckling in synchronicity with my shivers. There was a great deal of tossing about with musical accompaniment before, with a huge groan, Mick got out of the bed, threw on the light and threw off his carpet. He walked over to the window and proceeded to tear at the curtains, ripping them from the rail.

At this point I could hold in my laughter no longer and burst out, "For Christ sake Mick hold on, I'll give you a hand with that." Having more carefully removed the curtains, which were only of light summer material, the only thing to do with them was to wrap them around ourselves and climb back into our respective instruments of torture.

It was obvious that we were not likely to get any sleep like this, and during a brief pause in the giggles Mick said, "Look Ralph don't get me wrong but why don't I get into your bed? We'd both be better off with the warmth of our bodies being shared."

I was so surprised that I stopped laughing, then the silence was broken by a huge guffaw from both of us at the same time as we realised the absurdity, and soon the two of us were lying, albeit uneasily, back to back on the one bed, each hardly daring to move for fear of giving out the wrong message to the other, before sleep eventually came and we were woken by the light pouring in from the curtainless window. Somehow during the day we managed to obtain some sleeping materials and we slept separately from then on.

Henry hated his job as it started so early at 5 am, and Pep, who was by now sharing the work, was also getting ready to quit. The search for work was desperate and we combed the paper nightly looking for jobs. I got a job as a tyre fitter, but on reflection decided that it was not a good idea as a budding guitarist, so I never turned up for the first day. Both Mick and I were putting off the start as we just wanted to hang out and have some fun.

The evenings were best; someone would turn up with some food or cigarettes or a new record, and we would sit around talking and joking. A girl called Barbara came to see us quite a lot. She desperately wanted to be part of the group, but was so far removed from us by class and culture that she was tolerated only out of kindness by the boys; her parents were horrified at her association with us. She used to cycle over to hang out, and looking back she probably fancied one of the boys, but which one I've no idea even now. She had been told that any foodstuffs would be appreciated, and usually obliged with sausages or some potatoes or cigarettes. One night Mick and I managed to hang her bike up a telegraph pole, but the sight of her tears of desperation took all the fun out of it, and to make it up to her I let her buy me a Rev. Gary Davis album from a shop in Bournemouth. She really tried to get into the music contained in those grooves, but I think it was all a bit beyond her. Some of it was beyond me too.

I wonder sometimes if we feel as intensely about music as we get older. In this place music was played constantly and all of it was different and all of it was good. I was heavily into the mysteries of Blind Boy Fuller, and Mick had become fascinated by an album of Woody Guthrie and Cisco Houston—especially a track not penned by Guthrie called *The Bold Philadelphia Lawyer*, which he tunelessly warbled around the house. Keith loved Jimmy Reed and John Lee Hooker, and Henry was seriously into Charles Mingus and an album containing the track *Oh Lord Don't Let Them Drop That Atomic Bomb On Me*. At the time, I found Mingus pretentious and unmusical but I/we had to tolerate it for fear of being shown up as musically inferior to Henry's advanced appreciation. Only Mick had the honesty to tell Henry what he thought of the strange sounds from this record.

The weather grew worse and the house grew even colder. Money got scarcer and the battle for the chair nearest the electric fire became intense. The shilling per night frugality finally became intolerable and one night Mick snapped.

365

"I have an idea about how to get more from the meter," he said confidently, and walked out of the room and up to the loft. There followed a couple of loud bangs and then like a miracle the fire suddenly came back on.

"How did you manage that?" we chorused in admiration as he came back into the room.

"It's just a little trick I learned in my last place," said Mick. We all were massively impressed as Mick climbed over the chair and sat warming his hands and grinning at us all whilst basking in our amazement. I was first up to my room that night and on the way I decided to take a look at Mick's engineering skills as I passed the loft door. I pulled it open and looked at the meter and there with the shattered padlock lying on the floor lay a hammer and screwdriver, the tray containing one solitary shilling was pulled open and I wandered dismayed down stairs to confront Mick.

"Ah, don't be givin' out to me," he chuckled, reading the expression on my face. "We're all feckin' freezin' to death here and when we get a job we'll soon make it up and pay back what we owe and at least we'll have some warmth."

For once his laugh did not amuse me.

"Where's all the money from the meter, Mick?" I accused.

"Oh Jesus, you don't think I'd steal the money do you? I put it in the shilling jar in the kitchen. I thought we could buy sometin' to eat with it tomorrow. After all it's our money and we're only borrowing it till we get fixed up."

I bought breasts of lamb for a shilling and Mick came back from the grocery simply laden with stuff: vegetables and spaghetti in a carrier bag but, more worrying, other items like sweets appeared unwrapped from his pockets. The others declined to notice and nothing was said. That night we let Barbara come round and had a great feast, except Barbara left most of hers so Mick ate it as he took away the dishes. I caught him gnawing on the bones as he walked to the kitchen.

"Wha?" he laughed as we walked past each other in the hall. Mick put on his Woody record and stood humming tunelessly along with the speaker on the wall as he swilled the kettle full of water round the greasy dishes in the sink. We sat in the other room smoking tailor-mades and thinking things weren't too bad after all. I pondered the morality of what we were doing but only for a little while.

Snow fell in the next few days, and a few days after that it settled and stayed the whole winter long. Henry didn't even try to get up for the train coach washing job. The house got even colder and some of the pipes froze. Then one evening I had a great idea. There were radiators all over the house, and in the cellar I had discovered behind some rubble an old boiler, so all we had to do was get some fuel and surely we would be warm as bugs in a rug. The only trouble was that we had no money to buy any with. Mick decided we should 'borrow' some coal.

There was an old portable toilet down in the cellar with a huge handle, and it seemed perfect for the job in hand. Although I knew that what we intended was wrong, I found myself enormously attracted to the idea of nicking a little heat; like stealing food for one's babies, it did not seem such a crime.

That night Mick and I ventured down the quiet suburban streets of Southbourne armed with a hand shovel and the toilet-sized bucket. We were leaving fresh tracks in the snow wherever we walked, but the cold made us reckless and when we were a good few streets away from home, we crept up our first garden path. Having made our way round the back we searched for the coal bunker. It was situated just past the back door, and suddenly as we crept nearer to it there was the most unbelievable crash. A dog the size of a polar bear had thrown its body against the back door and commenced a terrible deep barking.

"Feck!" said Mick.

"Shit!" I agreed, and we turned and ran slithering down the path dragging the toilet behind us, over the front lawn, straight down the street and round the corner. Finally we stopped, about a hundred yards from the foiled attempt, and collapsed into a privet hedge in fits of frightened laughter.

"What in the name of Jesus was that feckin' thing?" said Mick. I blew on my frozen fingers and wiped away the laughter tears that were already beginning to freeze on my face. We were luckier with our next attempt, as we seemed to have found an empty place, and once we had knocked the frozen chunks of coal apart, we shovelled away uninterrupted until the bucket was full. Warmed from our efforts but covered with snow and coal dust, we stood up and made to leave, but now the toilet was so heavy we could hardly move it. A car went past and we instinctively ducked down behind the bunker.

"We're going to have to empty some of it out," observed Mick.

I really couldn't believe what we were doing. We left about half of the coal by the back door and resolved to come back the next day and collect it.

"What are we going to say if someone stops us?" I asked Mick, but he said nothing. We staggered off down the path, leaving even deeper footprints in the snow that continued to fall. We had to rest every few yards as the thin metal handle cut into already painful fingers, and the trail we left behind became even more intriguing as the pairs of footprints were accompanied by a circle every so often as we set down our stolen burden. We were within sight of home when I saw the lights of a car approaching on our side of the road.

"Just act natural," said Mick.

"Natural? What's natural about two blokes walking out in the coldest night of the year dragging a portable toilet between them half full of stolen coal?"

As the car approached, Mick moved in front of it and adopted a pose of studied nonchalance; leaning in an unnatural bent-kneed crouch with one elbow on the rim, he took out a packet of Park Drive and offered me a smoke. The car drove past and I nearly fell on the floor. I was still chuckling as we dragged the bucket into the house to the not too admiring glances of Henry and Keith.

"That's not much, is it ?" said Henry.

"You try feckin' haulin' this stuff!" said Mick, not really angry. "Have ye prepared the fire in the boiler?"

Henry and Keith had, and after two or three attempts at rebuilding it we got a burn going. Keith checked outside and reported that smoke could be seen coming from the chimney, and we began placing lumps of coal on the fire. There was a series of different stopcocks connected to various pipes, and Keith, being the most technical, thought it best to open them all so that the water would have free passage all around. Once the fire was well and truly going, we all ran round the house feeling the pipes for any change of temperature.

From downstairs I heard Mick's voice shouting, "This one's warming up!" and after a minute, "I'm having the first bath!"

The very prospect of heat started to warm me. Suddenly there was a huge bang and then a crash which emanated from the bathroom downstairs. When I got there, the others were standing dismayed as they surveyed the scene. A pipe in the wall had exploded and blown plaster and brick work into the bath. The place was a mess and we just looked disbelievingly at each other. Fortunately we had Keith, who immediately went and turned off various stopcocks and valves, preventing the heating system from adding flood to our lists of woes.

Henry looked close to tears as he wondered what we would tell the landlord. That night as once again I lay shivering in my bed smelling comfortingly of coal dust, my thoughts turned towards home; the meagre comforts there seemed luxurious in comparison to what we had to contend with in freezing Hampshire. When we awoke next day to cold, hunger, penury, something akin to bomb damage, and partial flood, we could now add drought.

That night, the temperature dropped dramatically. When we arrived downstairs in the morning one by one, we checked the toilet and bathroom, hoping that by some miracle the wall would have righted itself and the damage repaired. But of course it had not and there was more to come. During the night someone had got up and had a crap, and though they may have flushed the toilet, the biggest turd in the world had not gone away and was lying there in a few inches of frozen water. Worse still, the toilet could no longer be flushed as the water in the earthenware cistern had frozen and the expansion had cracked it. All the water pipes inside were frozen and we didn't even have enough in the system to make a cup of tea. We all stood around wondering what to do next, half amused and half amazed that whoever had dropped that log in the drain could still walk unaided, let alone keep a straight face in denial.

I wandered out into the garden and filled the kettle and a saucepan with snow—about a foot had fallen overnight—and by this means we were able to get something hot to drink. Then we tried to flush the toilet by pouring boiling water down the loo, attempting both to disperse the turd and to defrost the bend. We were only half successful and the thing stayed with us for several days, which meant number twos had to be taken in the public toilets down on the wintry sea front until lots were drawn—which I lost—and the offending article was fished out and buried in the garden. From then on we had to flush the toilet with melted snow because when Keith did eventually get our water supply back, there was still no way we had money to repair the cistern.

Somehow we soldiered on and Mick kept us going with an assortment of items from the corner shop. The old bloke in the shop was very slow and would take forever to find things. By now Mick knew where everything was kept, so he would send the old chap across to one side of the shop and liberate an item from where he was standing. Then he would do the same in reverse and something else would vanish under his brown cord jacket. Afterwards I remonstrated with Mick that this was stealing and that he would probably put the old guy out of business. As usual Mick's defence was laughter and he pointed out that I had been enjoying the fruits of his providence on several occasions already. I protested that I had done this only because I didn't know they were nicked and swore never to eat any of Mick's supplies again.

That night as the boys tucked into a bowl of cornflakes and watered down milk, I sat smoking my dog-end mixture and thought how good it felt taking the moral high ground. Then I recalled something that had come up in conversation with George Foulser in the pad at Poole. One night the subject of the new trend towards supermarkets had come up and George had talked of how the system should have been adapted to the socialist ethic, where huge outlets could provide food at low cost for the masses.

To make conversation and to show concern for the well-being of my fellow man, I had said, "What will happen to the little corner shop keeper?"

"What will happen to the little corner shop keeper? Fuck the little corner shop keeper! Some of them are the biggest thieves going, selling stuff that's gone off and short measures! They're bigger robbers than the bastards who run the supermarkets, and most of them these days won't give any tick," George had stated calmly, making me feel like a naive twit.

As soon as I thought about it I knew he was right and I ought to make up for all the times I had been gypped over the years. I walked into the freezing kitchen and casually asked the lads if there was anything left in the packet, but of course there wasn't and so I made the tea and glanced into the cupboard in the vague hope that there would be a few scraps of something left—but of course there wasn't, except for about a dozen bits of old spaghetti in a blue packet. I made tea and poured myself a cup.

"Go easy on the milk!" the other three chorused, and I wandered off to sip the brew in the room with the two bar fire. As I sat there warming my hands round the mug I was joined by Henry and Keith, each with a tea.

"That's the last of the sugar gone," said Henry smugly.

"We're going to have to get some money somehow," we all agreed.

"Where's Mick?" I asked and Keith told me that he was doing the washing up.

"But it's not his turn," I protested (we had a strict rota and no-one ever volunteered out of hand).

Perhaps he feels guilty, I reasoned to myself, about stealing or eating all the cornflakes. Anyway, it meant that it would be another day before I would have to do it and that suited me as I have always hated getting my hands in water too long, for the feeling you get afterwards always makes my teeth go on edge. At that point Mick came into the room and put on his favourite Woody record and pressed the switch that sent the signal to the kitchen.

"Jest a bit of music while I work," he explained. I picked up the guitar and strummed along to the songs and soon we were treated to Mick's tuneless warbling from the kitchen and my accompaniment from the living room.

Henry started to chuckle. "Hark at that, that's the worst singing I've ever heard."

Suddenly Keith said, "I have an idea, maybe we can record him by using the speakers in the kitchen as microphones."

"How would that work?" I asked, relishing the prospect of hearing Mick on tape and seeing his embarrassment.

"Well you see a speaker is only a mike in reverse," said Keith, "so in theory if you shout into a speaker that is connected to a mike input you should be able to get enough signal to record."

"Oh go on do it do it," I implored.

As soon as Keith turned off the record player, Mick shouted from the kitchen, "Oi, turn it on lads."

"We will as soon as I've fixed it," said Keith. "Something's gone wrong but it won't take a minute."

"Good," said Mick, "it's just coming up to me favourite, the *Bold Philadelphia Lawyer.*"

Keith started unscrewing things and taping bits of wire and cable together, and of course without any music Mick stopped singing. After a few minutes Keith announced that the job was done and we listened anxiously to see if we could hear anything. Keith turned up the volume on the tape recorder and sure enough we could hear Mick banging about in the kitchen; we looked at each other with wonder and back at Keith with admiration.

Amongst the sound of plates and knives and forks we could just make out a low tuneless hum which suddenly broke out into, *"...two shadows he saw on that wall..."* out of tune and with gusto. There then followed a bit more tuneless humming, and then, *"...one less Philadelphia lawyer in old Philadelphia tonight..."*

"Quick quick, record him," I shouted urgently at Keith.

"I am already," said Keith, and Henry and I sat there relishing every out of tune moment as Mick went through his repertoire of song and hits of the day accompanied only by the clatter of pots and pans and the sound of kitchen work going on.

I suppose we had recorded some ten minutes of these sounds when I suddenly said, "How long does it take to wash up three bowls and a couple of cups? He's taking a long time to do such a little bit of work."

We all stopped to listen and all we could hear this time was the clatter of a spoon and bowl.

"He's eating something," said Henry.

"Don't be daft," I said, "there's nothing to eat."

"Let's take a look," suggested Keith and the three of us carefully opened the door to the living room and crept up the darkened hallway to the closed door of the kitchen. The three of us started to sniff the air. There was definitely something cooking. I grabbed the door handle and like the three musketeers we burst into the kitchen together. Mick was standing over the draining board with a bowl held almost Chinese style to his lips, and a fork cramming a few strands of spaghetti into his mouth. It is hard now to communicate the gravity with which we viewed this situation; our friend and colleague was cheating on us and had kept back some food for himself.

All laughter had ceased and we stood frozen like statues in the doorway with our mouths gaping open like fledglings in nest waiting to be fed. It is a wonder that Mick didn't walk over to us and drop a worm of spaghetti into each incredulous mouth. Instead he just stood there frozen like us, except he was in mid-mouthful. At last he could suppress the comedy of the scene no longer and sprayed us all with the contents of his mouth as he collapsed into a great wail of released guilt and laughter. "Jesus lads I was so feckin' hungry, I can't sleep at night with the hunger on me, Jesus lads I'm sorry." He set the bowl down on the draining board.

"Where did you find anything to eat?" asked Henry as we all moved closer to inspect the remains of his bowl. As hungry as I was, I have to confess that Mick's snack looked distinctly unappetising. He had taken the remaining twelve strands of spaghetti and boiled them up quickly in a solution of watered milk and a spoonful of marmalade that he'd scraped from a jar that had been 'finished' that morning. None of us wanted the ancient pasta and now Mick was unable to finish the few seriously *al dente* bits left in the bowl.

"Look lads, I'll make it up to you," he offered, and we knew he would. Nevertheless we let him stew in his guilt for about ten minutes before we remembered that the whole scene was being recorded in the front room. We hurried inside to rewind it and play it back to an incredulous Mick, who was still standing by the draining board as the awful strains of *The Bold Philadelphia Lawyer* reversed out of the speakers to an utterly amazed Irishman.

"YOU feckin'... How the feck?... is dat me you feckin'... Jesus that sounds feckin' terrible turn it off... you bastards!"

Soon we were all in hysterics as we relived the entire experience again; at that moment in that freezing house we were warmed by laughter and companionship. The next day Henry and I got jobs, and a few days later so did Mick, and naturally our fortunes changed.

∾

robbery

Henry's job was as a trainee Hoffman presser in a laundry; I became a kitchen porter in a hotel in Bournemouth. We both had early starts and, of the two jobs, mine was the easiest, because after the breakfast rush there was a great meal for the staff. Then after lunch I was left alone to wash all the pots and I usually made myself a huge ice-cream sundae. I managed to find my father figure in Len, the sous chef. He was about forty and from Lancashire. He taught me how to wash pots properly and how to make new potatoes out of old ones. He covered for me when I was late in and said I could do better for myself than being a KP.

This taking of lowly jobs on my part was quite deliberate; I had become fascinated by the life of Woody and his praise of the working man and, in order to rightfully claim my place alongside all working heroes, I felt it necessary to try as many different jobs as I could. Later on, when I read George Orwell's account of life as a plongeur in Paris, I realised I was not the only one who had slightly patronised the workers by accepting menial jobs below his ability. Truth to tell, with my qualifications I think my only options would have been office trainee, but I loved manual work and I still do; anyway I suspect Orwell of having masochistic tendencies.

My work at the hotel was boring in the extreme, but the lads at the house were grateful for any little bits I could manage to bring home. Len, realising our predicament, often gave me the nod to take an odd bit of chicken or a bit of leftover bacon. This of course was added to with a few sausages that were never missed.

My wages were £6 per week and I suppose all I could eat. Henry's wage as a trainee Hoffman presser was five pounds a week, but this rose to seven pounds after training. This was a con as it turned out, as anyone with a little sense could learn the game in a day or so. Henry taught Mick how to do it by demonstrating using the kitchen table as a press, and we thought very little of Mick's interest in the art until he turned up one day at the depot posing as a trained presser. He'd blagged his way in and explained discrepancies in style as having learned the trade in Ireland; as a skilled man his wage was seven pounds a week.

After two or three weeks I jacked in the KP job and signed on with the two other lads as a trainee, and we were all united once more. Bollom's had shops all over the county; vans collected the gear and cleaned it in a central place, and then it was given to us to press and bag up before returning. Some of the poor bastards were on piece work and worked like machines. Mick was pretty quick, but refused to go on bonus, while Henry and I just plodded along and did enough not to be sacked.

I was the only one in a relationship; with the late hours and lovemaking, I was very tired during the day and needed a lot of stimulus and conversation to keep me awake. Because of the subterfuge regarding Mick, Henry and I had to pretend to get to know him, and we had a foreman who did not allow idle chat between pressers. Anyway Mick was on the other side of the building to me, so I had to be content with Peter, who was very strange.

He was thirtyish, with curly hair and the thickest glasses I'd ever seen. It's awful how you suspect anyone with a slight affliction of being odd or unsavoury, but the truth is wherever I have worked in places that are cut off from the chance of social interaction, be it a warehouse or packing department or dispatch office, I've come across weird people.

There was a bloke at Philips who only went with whores and admitted he detested women and anyone who drove cars; if some poor unfortunate ever stopped him to ask directions it was his pleasure to misdirect them. He was an unsightly man with uneven teeth and a very upright posture with splayed feet. He reminded me of Trotsky with his tiny glasses, and although he had no beard there was always the hint of one as he was

375

never able to shave himself properly; it was as if he shaved parts of his face leaving patches completely alone. As we worked together loading TVs, I would sometimes hear him muttering horrible threats to the women he could see in his mind. There was a time that I felt he was ready to kill, and I spent long hours promising him that there was a woman out there who would love him for who he was and that they weren't all bad. When he asked me how I thought anyone would ever fall for someone who looked like him, I was stumped for a minute. Then I said, "Perhaps you could find a blind girl?"

Another time, I came across an anarchist who was so withdrawn that it broke my heart, and I really worked on him to win his confidence. When he trusted me completely, he revealed that his main ambition in life was to get a machine gun and go out into some crowded place and mow down as many people as he could before they got him. As he told me his plan, his colour changed and little foam clusters formed at the side of his mouth; his eyes widened and he positively seethed hatred.

My pressing partner Peter was not as mad as these two, but he was very withdrawn and strange, and the worst thing was that he never wanted to talk. This was torture to me, as I needed some human communication to lift me above the drudgery of the work and the constant hiss from the presses that makes you think you've lost the top end of your hearing. I was convinced I was sounding like old Mr. Cox, the husband of our landlady at the Waldrons, who was so deaf he never pronounced his 'S's and neglected most of his 'T's too.

As well as the noise there was the smell, for even after the garments have been washed/cleaned with carbon tetrachloride and dried so that there are no dirt deposits, they still smell of their owner's sweat. If you've ever walked into an charity clothes shop, you will be aware of that smell. Now if you imagine that warmed up and add humidity, you will understand what I'm talking about. We all looked forward to tea breaks and there were two a day; each lasted ten minutes, which was just time for tea and a fag. The company was so mean that they only supplied the tea on a subsidised basis, and we had to buy our own sugar.

It was Mick (of course) who noticed that our sugar was going down a lot faster than the others. He suspected that the tea lady, who was also Irish, was doling it out to her favourite lads; she made no secret that she did not like any of us. To catch her, Mick devised a simple plan. The next day after the afternoon break, he produced a small bag from his pocket and emptied the contents into our sugar bag before returning it to the counter in the canteen for safe keeping. The next day we were all deliberately late for morning tea break and none of us took our sugar; we just sat down and waited for the fun to start. One by one people began to gag on their teas; some spat it out, swearing, and others sniffed their brew or tried stirring it more vigorously, to no effect. Blokes started to go back to the counter to complain and Mick, Henry and I were there to hear them.

"There's salt in this tea!" was the universal charge, and indeed there was.

"Now then missus," says Mick, "Do you still say that you're not puttin our sugar in their teas?"

"No, no, it wasn't me," she denied, but of course it was, and everyone knew it. But still she persisted in her innocence. It was the first time I'd ever seen anyone caught in a flagrant lie and deny it, and it confused me greatly. Mick just laughed as usual, but our fate was sealed and it was not long before I'd had enough and quit the pressing game, and the others followed suit as the atmosphere in the place deteriorated. Soon we were all broke again like before, but spring was with us and optimism was in the air. Gill and I were making plans to travel abroad and we had the freedom of the scooter and each other. An easy camaraderie prevailed in the house. Then Norman arrived.

Norman's crimes were that he was one year younger than all of us, had very frizzy hair, couldn't say his 'R's properly, had too much confidence, and was from a different class than the rest of us. Henry had persuaded us to allow him to join us because the extra rent money would help out. We tolerated him, but he was always questioning everything we did and trying to find more sensible ways of doing things when he should have been more respectful. No-one got on with him and he failed to notice.

The business of rent was a sore point, as Mick and I continued to pay whenever we could, but unfortunately Henry forgot to pay the landlord. Norman soon got a job and was not really much trouble, and anyway he would share his fags with us, which at least took away the necessity of delving into the stinking dog-end jar. One night, Keith happened to mention that he'd got a job as a steward at a country point-to-point meeting. He explained about how everyone was so trusting and that money was left lying about for anyone to pick up once they were inside the compound. Mick's ears pricked up immediately.

"Is there money really lyin' about?" he asked quietly.

"Well you know it's not locked away or anything," said Keith, a little more cautiously.

"Well where is it then?"

"It's kept in the steward's hut. It's like the money from the betting tote. It's just sort of left in a cardboard box on the table," said Keith, beginning to look worried.

"Can you get into the hut?" asked Mick, his voice steady but insistent.

"Course I can," said Keith, "that's my job—I go in and put the money in the box and generally help around the site."

"Could we get into the compound?"

Keith bent his head low to the table and said in a relieved tone, "No, only people with an official sort of badge can get in." He looked round at us two for support before saying, "So whatever you were thinking you can put it out of your mind."

Mick was insistent. It would be easy to pull this one off, he said. I was grinning, allowing this fantasy to continue for as long as it lasted, knowing full well that we would never attempt a robbery in real life. Henry looked bemused, and with nostrils flared to suppress his bemusement sent glances back and forth between Mick, Keith and me. Norman's eyes were like saucers.

Keith drew a sketch of the area, the approach roads, and the outline of the low security fence where the bookies were, and in a few moments Mick seemed to have come up with a plan. The important thing was that no-one should actually be able to connect the theft to Keith, and this could be accomplished by all of us arriving at different times wearing clothes that we didn't usually wear. Each one of us would handle the money for a short time as links in a chain that would culminate in him (Mick) getting on the back of Keith's motorbike and being driven away steadily by Henry, who had a licence.

I was to act as lookout and receive the stolen cash from Keith over the fence. I was then to move quickly up the hill to where the bookies were all positioned and hand the dough to Mick, who only had a short walk to the motorbike. I was to return to hanging about down at the compound so as not to arouse suspicion, and after a discreet time leave for home, discarding my disguise before catching the bus. By this time, Henry and Mick would be home, and after Keith had spoken to the police, he would get a lift to his girlfriend's place before taking the bus back to the house. It all sounded so simple and professional. There was to be no job, however, for Norman.

"Oh go on, let me do something, please," begged Norman.

"No," we chorused.

"You're fuckin' mad," said Henry.

"Now come on lads, what could be simpler?" demanded Mick.

"Sounds a doddle," said I, still believing that reason would prevail. "How much do you think would be in the kitty, Keith?"

"About two hundred pounds."

"You wouldn't, would you Ralph?" asked Henry, his eyes wide with incredulity.

"How much, two hundred quid? Sure, why not?"

"Two hundred, you could do a lot with two hundred couldn't you eh wha'?" chuckled Mick.

"Well if Ralph's in, then I'm in," said Henry loyally.

"That only leaves you, Keith. Are you with us or against us?" demanded Mick. We all looked at Keith.

"Oh all right then," Keith agreed.

I couldn't believe what was going on—they actually intended to go through with it. There was no going back even if I'd wanted to, because waiting in the wings was bloody Norman, and anyway the others were already discussing their ideas of what we would wear.

That night I hardly slept with the anxiety of it all, and the next day it was the only topic of conversation. We rehearsed our moves around the house and garden and kept on trying to anticipate problems which we solved on the spot, and then we'd talk about what we'd spend it on or go all mysterious on poor old Norman, who had been totally frozen out of the plans. It didn't stop him, however, asking if we would give him some of the loot if and when we'd pulled it off. Perhaps it was my time in the army, but I insisted that we practise our routines properly, and came up with a really original hiding place for the money: we would secrete the notes inside the lining of the fridge door. Perfect! I was almost beginning to look forward to the caper.

On the actual day I got up early to find Henry and Keith making Marmite sandwiches without margarine, and I joined them for a cup of black tea, sweetened with jam, as we were once again without milk or sugar.

"We're still going through with this then?" was about all I could manage. Henry gave me one of his withering looks, which were always the more withering in the morning as his wayward eye looked vaguely up at the ceiling, giving him a look of exasperation and disgust.

"Just remember the plan and don't screw it up," he intoned with a dark authority. Keith busied himself with his final preparations and hardly looked at me.

I watched the two of them leave, and heard them kicking over the motorbike a couple of times before it started. The two friends climbed aboard and drove off down the road into the fine spring Saturday morning to commit a robbery. I felt sick.

Henry dropped Keith some way from the course and went and hid both bike and himself in a field. Keith walked the last distance by himself. When pressed as to where his machine was, he would later explain that he had hitchhiked to the course. Mick and I took a bus, talking all the way in our disguises. The clothes were not that different to what we might have worn anyway, but I had parted my hair in the middle and had, by listening to Keith, perfected—or so I thought—a pretty passable Dorset accent.

My whole subterfuge was set off by a brown tweed jacket borrowed from Alan, a kindly friend of Gill's. Mick had borrowed a pair of someone's prescription glasses, though I suspect just to satisfy me that he was trying. His late Tony Curtis hairstyle had been lapped down, but he still looked different to most people in the area. The glasses made him look ridiculous. A lad that wore his clothes like that would not have been seen dead in specs like those.

We tried not to let others know we were together, but the journey was a long one. We were nervous and were soon laughing at things that weren't even funny, becoming highly conspicuous.

"Well I'll be seein' yez all later," said Mick in a huge Irish accent in the middle of darkest Dorset as he climbed off the bus some way from the ground.

"So long Fred," he shouted pointedly at me, before nearly missing his footing as he half fell off the bus.

The point to point itself was a colourful affair, but I was so nervous by now I didn't take a lot of it in. Sure enough, everything was laid out pretty much as Keith had described it, although it was smaller than I had imagined. Bookmakers were setting up shop, and horses were everywhere; people walked in and out of the compound below with no checks, and cars arrived all the time. By now I was hungry, and to my deep disappointment I realised I had no money to buy anything. From the top of the bank I saw Keith in the compound, and he gave a sly signal that he wanted me to come down to meet him.

"Oh no," I thought, "he's already done it," but I realised he only wanted to give me some instructions. Before I slithered down to the fence, my heart pounding, I signalled that I understood, and by pointing to my mouth and rubbing my stomach managed to infer that I was both hungry and nonchalant. It is hard to limp when sliding down a grassy bank, and my gait must have looked more like a man suffering from St. Vitus' Dance than a crippled local. I wondered if my act might be a little over the top.

Keith said nothing, but as I drew near, he bent down to do up his shoelace and left an envelope on the grass at the foot of the fence, then turned and walked briskly away. My heart was banging away so fiercely I thought I might pass out as I picked up the package and commenced to try and run up the still dewy bank. But something told me that this was not the right envelope as it was not full enough, and as soon as I could, I opened it to find a steward's badge and a hastily scrawled note from Keith to the effect that the badge would get me into the enclosure. Therefore I wouldn't have to hang about the perimeter drawing attention to myself. When the time was right, he would signal me to move outside and take up the prearranged position.

I didn't like this. Already the plan was changing, but I put on the badge and as my heartbeat returned to somewhere near normal, I affected my limp and stumbled off with my centre parting and my Dorset accent at the ready in case anyone should talk to me, praying that no-one would, and wondering if everyone else was as scared as I was.

When your intent is criminal, it seems as though everyone is looking at you suspiciously, like when you walk through Customs and you feel as if you might as well have a pound of heroin secreted about your person. I limped around the paddock trying to look as if I knew what I was doing. It was odd passing by Keith all the time and not being able to say anything. Once or twice I nearly blurted out something as my tension rose. Surely it was time to move: our deadline was the three o'clock race. Keith walked past me once more, and as he did so he raised his eyebrows in an inquiring manner which suggested 'are you ready?' He mouthed something which I couldn't interpret and suddenly we were on.

As quickly as seemed reasonable, I limped off in the direction of the rendezvous by the fence and was halfway across when I realised I was limping on the wrong leg. I quickly changed over, looking round to see if anyone was noticing, but they paid me no attention. Over my shoulder, I saw Keith purposefully entering the shed where the money was, and I felt sick again. As I rounded the corner of the paddock, I saw Keith lay a package down on the grass between the fence and, as planned, he walked over to another official and started conversing with him. This was it.

My limp had acquired manic exaggeration as I raced round to the pickup point. I stooped down and gave the brown paper an instinctive squeeze. It was money all right. Stuffing the parcel down my shirt, I once again slid and slithered up the bank, and with a strange music and drumming in my ears, hurtled through the crowds sometimes forgetting my disability but managing not to hit anyone either. Up past the bookies I went and towards the car park. There was no sign of anyone.

Oh Christ, I prayed, where the fuck is everyone? Then I saw Mick over by one of the bookies studying the form.

"Jim," I shouted (it was his agreed alias). There was no response.

"Jim!" I bellowed. Again, nothing.

"JIM!!" I screamed like a soul demented, and the sheer desperation in my voice made almost the entire course turn round in my direction. This time he noticed me and as surreptitiously as he could ambled over to me.

"What's the matter with you Mick, you were supposed to be here," I wailed, close to tears.

"Ah come on, we're all right. Have ye got it?"

"Yes," I said as we exchanged jackets out of sight of the main throng.

Mick grabbed the package and was just about to unwrap it when I almost screamed at him, "For Christ's sake get going you idiot!" Stuffing it in his shirt, he raced across the car park to the spot where Henry had been revving the bike for nearly ten minutes, attracting comments from other racegoers about noisy yobbos.

Mick flew through the punters and leaped onto the back of the bike, which caused Henry to let out the clutch too quickly and the engine stalled. Henry then flooded the carburettor and it was some little while before the two of them actually got away. I was oblivious to this as, my limp now miraculously cured, I took myself off to join the racegoers. I saw the end of the four o'clock race before I casually left the course and aimed for the Bournemouth road.

At six o'clock I was still walking. I got my first brief lift at around seven, and walked the last six or seven miles home to the house, my stomach roaring with hunger but the pain tempered by the warmth of the spring evening, the birds singing, and the certain knowledge that the raid had been a success. Me and the boys would be on easy street. My steps quickened as I neared the front door, where I could see Keith's motorbike leaning against the wall. Unusually the door was closed and I had to ring the bell. Keith answered, saw it was me, turned, and walked into the kitchen. His lack of greeting took me aback. After a second I stepped inside, slammed the door and hurried into the room where the three of them were sitting.

"Well?" I said beaming, but just my first glance told me there was something wrong.

"Well what?" said Henry, giving me his world-weary look.

"Where's the money?"

"Oh, the money," said Henry, faking surprise. "He wants to know where the money is." Then, looking round at me, he said slowly, "There ain't no bleedin' money. Tell him, Keith."

Poor Keith, he looked so downhearted, though slightly flushed with the wind and sun.

"They didn't do what they normally do. They had a safe in one of the caravans and only the race marshals were allowed in there and even if I could have got in there I couldn't have got it out without the combination." He looked close to tears as his voice droned on in more detailed description, but I heard no more of what he said as a peculiar humming had begun between my ears and my legs had suddenly began to ache severely. I began to feel dizzy and angry and I did not believe a word of it.

"You're kidding me!" I looked imploringly from one to another as I reached for a chair and collapsed down into it. "Please tell me you're making it up," I tried again.

Suddenly Mick, who had been avoiding my gaze, burst out into one of his huge guffaws.

"So you were kidding!" I smiled with relief.

"Ah no," said Mick, "I just can't look at your face without laughin'.

We didn't get a thing."

"But what about the package?" I persisted.

At this Henry reached over to the draining board and picked up my prize and gently dropped it on the table. "Have a little look."

I picked up the brown paper parcel and gently opened it to find... two soggy Marmite sandwiches!

"You signalled to me that you were hungry," offered Keith, "so I dropped the packet by the fence for you. The next time I looked round all I could see was you disappearing above the bank and on your way. There was nothing I could do to stop you, so when I was finished I just picked up me money and came straight back here."

Slowly and with great deliberation I picked up the first sandwich and started to eat it, and in a couple of seconds I had demolished the second one too and I sat there with crumbs falling out of my mouth with my three friends in hysterics and soon I was laughing with the rest of them. Then I had an idea. Norman had not yet come in from work. I couldn't bear the thought of giving him the satisfaction of knowing we'd screwed up.

"How much have we got between us?" I asked.

Someone answered, "Not as much as we had this morning."

Of course Keith had his thirty bob for the job, and when I explained my plan they all prevailed upon the uncertain Keith to lend us his money. By the time an excited Norman arrived back from work, Mick and I had been to the shop and bought five mannequin cigars, ten Woodbines, a large bottle of cider and a few cheap candy bars. Back at the house we gently prised open the lining of the fridge and inserted a ten shilling note so that the corner just stuck out enough to reveal what it was. We put on the music, turned up the volume, filled the room with cigar smoke and dealt out the playing cards, and with the aid of matches were to be found gambling away our ill-gotten gains at three-card brag.

Norman threw open the door took in the scene and yelled, "You did it you bastards you bloody did it! How much did you get?"

"Two hundred and seventy quid," said Henry casually.

"TWO HUNDRED AND SEVENTY QUID?"

"Keep it down!" we cautioned.

"Where is it?"

"In the fridge," said Mick. "Where else would you keep hot money?"

Norman leaped to the fridge and yanked open the door.

"Where in the fridge?" he asked disbelievingly.

"In the door," I said.

"Christ there's a note sticking out," he said. "Can I have it?" But before there was time for any of us to say no, Mick had leaped to the door and plucked it from the lining and stuffed it in his own pocket.

"Have a cigar, Norman," he offered magnanimously, and he lobbed the last cheroot in Norman's direction. It was like having pulled off the perfect crime. The only trouble was that we were still broke.

By now the backlog of owed rent was insurmountable, and one night Henry's dear old dad drove down to Southbourne, threw everything in the car that he could and whisked Mick and Henry back to Mitcham.

I had already left for a short stay at home as Gill and I had definitely decided to hitch to Spain. Keith was getting a place in Bournemouth, Mick got a job in Thornton Heath as a Hoffman presser and eventually Henry did the same and even got to manage a few shops. I started working in one of them as well, before my bad timekeeping forced the other workers to get Henry to ask me to leave. That was fine with me; I had other plans anyway. The summer was on us and the road was calling me again, and this time it would be great.

olé

Terry and Mandy were the first of our friends to get married, but to be fair they were older than us. Terry Atkinson was two years older than me, and Mandy was two years older than him. No-one was surprised—and anyway, lots of working class kids got married in their early twenties. However, the first to get engaged was Les. Whatever was between him and my cousin Chris had not been possible to maintain for reasons of distance and other diversions, and slowly but surely a deep friendship and then love built up between him and Margot Rossario. She was of Indian background, but as Croydon as the rest of us, and her two friends Cathy and Pat were part of our coterie of friends from the Whitgift Arms. All three of them were very pretty and Margot had the added attraction of being the tiniest and most exotic.

For the life of me I cannot think what brought them to the place, but they were happy to spend many evenings there. Cathy soon fell in with a nice bloke called John, who was from Northern Ireland and a scaffolding ganger, and they became inseparable. Pat started to go out with Steve, and I was deeply in love with Gill but she lived in Bournemouth and I only saw her on certain weekends when she hitched up to London to be with me.

There was now nothing in the way of our plans to hitch around Spain, and with a few possessions and a determination that this time I would be able to make my way with the guitar, we left for France.

Popular knowledge warned about trying to get a lift from Calais to Paris, so we took the train and arrived in the Gare du Nord. We ate a *sandwich jambon* as I now knew not to have egg and chips, and after a coffee and my first Gauloise we walked right through Paris with our bags and my guitar.

Somewhere near the start of Route National Seven we stopped a car. It was a Citroen Big Six and I fell in love with it and knew that one day I would have to own one of them. In my halting schoolboy French I told our driver how much I admired his *voiture*. He was only a young man and he beamed at my compliments. We had travelled quite a distance before we realised that the N7 is not the best way to go to Spain and that we needed to be much further over, but I was so delighted with the short wait that I hadn't really thought about direction.

Gill was an incredible asset. Drivers nearly caused accidents whilst attempting sidelong glances at her. We slept out in the open and ate little. Gill was optimistic and confident, while I was excited and so happy to have her with me all the time that at first I didn't worry about the attention she was getting.

The weather was warm and the scents of the countryside intoxicating. Even hanging around for lifts was not a problem, as we had each other and cigarettes. And because she was so stunning, I didn't even have to hide in the hedgerows.

Each time we got on board a lorry, I glowed with the solidarity of the working class; to travel this way was truly in the socialist spirit and all truck drivers were comrades. We were stranded for some time on the Spanish border, and I discovered some old ruins and had a scout about whilst Gill sat on the roadside above the bank. After a good look round, I climbed back up the bank and sat with my arm around Gill listening to the birds and looking back up the road towards the border with France. Here we were in Franco's Spain armed only with optimism, a few quid and a handful of Woody Guthrie songs. As the shadows lengthened, I took out the guitar and sang for the pleasure of being part of the picture we were both in.

There were very few cars or trucks at this time and I began to wonder if we should stay where we were, just off the road. Then I heard the slow clop of a horse's hooves, and from round a little side turning appeared a cart pulled by a very elderly horse. The cart was built round an X frame and was not able to carry very much, which was fortunate as I don't think the old horse could have hauled much more than he had already. It was such a picturesque sight that both of us smiled at the old boy sitting up the front with a big yellow cigarette stuck in his face. He gestured at the back of his wagon. We looked at each other for a moment, then grabbing our stuff, threw it on the back and climbed up. The old horse did not even break step, and we rolled through the Pyrenees on a bed of newly cut grass, with the sounds of the day giving way to those of the evening as cicadas and crickets took over from the birds and the sun slipped behind the mountains.

We eventually arrived in Barcelona's outskirts and saw the sea. Lifts had been regular and easy, but our overall progress was slow. We had no destination in mind; just being together and travelling was all we wanted. Again I hadn't bothered with money as I was confident that I would be able to earn it by playing. I had the experience of Germany behind me, so why not? Between us I think we may have had as much as twenty pounds when we started out.

I wrote to Woody Guthrie from Fascist Spain, telling my dying hero that I was playing his songs to the working people. Which I was, in a way, sitting by the side of the road waiting for rides, but also in towns and villages whenever we stopped.

Somehow, though, I always managed to find a reason not to go busking. Gill did her best to give me confidence, but it seemed that I needed more reassurance than she was able to provide. I ate very little and Gill had no great appetite; the weather was beautiful and the heat of the noonday sun hotter than anything either of us had experienced before. We thriftily inched along the coast road towards Valencia, Gill a cheerful counter to my worries about everything from money to food to where we were heading. She was happy and beautiful and we were very much in love. We tanned by the roadsides, and her hair if anything became even blonder.

One day, high up in the hills where we had been trying for a lift for hours, we heard the slow grind of a lorry steadily climbing below us and I knew that this would be the one that was going to stop. As it hove into sight round a curve, I could see that it was painted sky blue and carried the biggest load of hay I had ever seen. The driver, who had plenty of time to take us in as he approached, leaned over to the passenger side. Without stopping, he threw open the door and motioned us to hop aboard.

Lifting Gill up first and then running alongside the cab backwards and forwards to where our little heap of stuff lay on the side of the road, I managed to get it all on. I scrambled, sweating, on to my seat next to Gill, who squeezed my arm happily. If you have never hitched a lift, it is difficult to communicate the feeling of those first few seconds, as with relief you climb into the cab. You start off by thanking your driver and then begin to work him out. Ours was a small thickset man in his forties. His name was Alphonso and he was going all the way to Valencia.

Gill sat between the driver and me. The truck had about thirty gears and in spite of this was terribly slow. I was nevertheless content to lean with one arm on the open window, taking in all the countryside and delighting in the lumbering progress of the huge *camion*. Neither of us spoke Spanish, but with my smattering of French I was able to convey our gratitude, which became greater when Alphonso stopped and bought us little snacks on the way.

Conversation was inane and minimal given my weak vocabulary and the thunderous noise from the engine, but gestures and smiles and affectionate looks from this benevolent driver were reciprocated by me as far as possible. It took us a couple of days to get to Valencia. The first night Alphonso slept in the cab while we slept outside. We lay in our two separate sleeping bags but in each other's arms under the stars, and wondered what it would be like in Valencia.

As we moved further south the sun got hotter and my right arm was as brown as a nut by the time we arrived in the city. Alphonso drove us around the city to the football stadium. I was not the least bit interested in football but I had to admit the place was impressive. He was obviously proud, strutting about gesticulating at the pitch and the goalposts and the vastness of the place. He spoke incomprehensibly fast to his friend who had allowed us to look inside, and I could see that he admired Gill by the way he kept shooting glances at her. It was the colour of the stadium's grass that I found striking. I wondered if it was it as green as that back home. Spain was all brown and greyish-green, bleached like a workman's shirt by the sun, but this was so vivid it almost hurt my eyes.

Later he took us to a restaurant and bought us a dish made from mussels in a black sauce. The nearest thing to this sort of food I had eaten was fish and chips. Perhaps it was the wine that Alphonso was pouring for me so profusely, or maybe the strange clear liquid that he insisted I try, but suddenly I felt bewildered and very sick. Time after time I threw up, and eventually Gill came and found me outside the restaurant. When she had cleaned me up a bit, she ran over to the lorry and took our little pile of stuff out.

She indicated urgently that she had to get away from our driver, and after staggering down some back streets she stopped, held on to me and burst into tears.

"What's the matter?" I wanted to know.

"It's Alphonso, Ralph, you don't know what he's been like," she said, her voice trembling. "Every time you got out of the cab, even for a pee, he was all over me trying to get me to leave you and go with him, and every time you nodded off in the cab he tried to touch me."

By now the tears were running down her face, and I was struck dumb. All the time I was talking to him about the working people and how we must all stick together, he was trying to stick it to my girl. I knew immediately what to do, but threw up again instead. My head was spinning and I was becoming delirious; my legs wouldn't work and sweat was pouring off me. Finally I passed out.

I awoke in a small room that apparently I had managed to walk to. A kind passer-by had directed us to a pension. The tiny room had a sink and a tap, so I cleaned myself up as best I could and went through all the facts of last night. My feelings of betrayal and stupidity hurt me deeply, and I begged Gill to let me know if it ever happened again and we would live with the consequences.

The room was cheap but still I was anxious to get out of it and back on the road. However, neither of us cared to venture further south. Instead I suggested that we try the South of France as we knew that there would be an opportunity to make some money there. We started to retrace our steps back up the coast. We blagged our way into a Youth Hostel and sat drinking a mixture of cognac and coke until we got quite silly. We watched the sun go down in a dusty square sitting on the edge of a fountain.

We still had little inclination to eat much and got by on tomatoes and bread, with sometimes a little cheese washed down with *Gassos*, a primitive but delicious lemonade that was about a penny a litre. Our journey was positively speedy in sleek DS Citroens, swaying 2CVs, huge lorries with chain smoking drivers and, on one occasion, the back of a tractor.

One of the large Citroen vans that were never imported to Britain pulled up and a youngish chap with a huge moustache leant over and invited us in. There was a seat for him and part of a seat for Gill, but I had to crawl into the back amongst piles of disorganised angle iron and roof supports, so that I was coiled through the parts like a snake. If he'd had to stop—indeed if he *could* have stopped suddenly—I would have been chopped in half, as the soft parts of my body were pressed up against sharp metal. The journey was slow and noisy as night descended and the difference in the countryside reminded me how far from home I was.

Every so often the guy glanced back to me as I lay amongst the twisted metal like some crash victim and yelled, *"Ça va?"* and I would yell back, *"Oui!"*

As the light faded and the roads grew smaller it seemed our journey would never end but at last we arrived at a little house in a village somewhere and I was able, just, to uncoil myself and climb out of the van. We were invited into the driver's home and introduced to his pretty wife, who could not seem to work out what we were doing or why we were doing it. As if we knew! She attempted to talk with Gill, who could not speak any French, and eventually took her to wash while the guy poured me a glass of wine. Later he showed us up to a room where they had made up a bed for us. I was quite overwhelmed by this hospitality. He then asked if we were married. I tried to say that we were engaged, but that failed to ease the situation, and with much consternation he consulted his wife, who made some suggestion. He seemed pleased with the proposed compromise and came again upstairs with a pillow, explaining that because I was not married Gill should have the bed and I was to sleep on the floor. Then he bid us *"Bonne nuit,"* and left, only to return again a few minutes later with a metal bucket and a toilet roll.

"Bonne nuit!" he said again, and Gill got the giggles at the sight of the bucket.

That night, in spite of the nearness of Gill, I did indeed sleep on the floor.

❧

riviera

Lorries, cars, hunger and tiredness, dust and thirst, insects singing loudly at the sides of roads, us getting confused and wandering down wrong turnings, complaints and blame all fuelled our long journey back towards the Mediterranean.

We arrived in Fréjus on a beautiful sunny day and bought bread and tomatoes. Someone had told us that you could get a night's stay in the local hostel for a few francs and we were ready to have a bed for the night. I was generally opposed to Youth Hostels as I thought them soft, but I became increasingly appreciative of them. Although I never joined up, I was grateful for the few nights I managed to blag my way in.

Gill and I were separated. I slept fitfully dreaming that I was in a series of car crashes; Gill was being bitten by mosquitoes. Perhaps because of my darker complexion I had been spared, and though Gill was a mite sorry for herself, her feelings soon changed to pity for a poor girl we met later on the road to Cannes. She too had spent the night in the hostel and the result was like nothing I have seen before or since. One side of the poor girl's face was as big and swollen as a football, her eye was barely visible with the swelling, and her neck was covered with infected bites.

The two of us on the French Riviera was a joke. I made the mistake of buying an orange juice that cost as much as a night's rest in a hostel, and took my shirt off, exposing my body for the first time in years. I resembled a neopolitan ice cream, my body all differing shades of red, pink and brown. I don't think I removed my shirt in public for the next six years. The contrast between us and the people that moved around the place we were in was huge. My resentment was growing, for if we had parity with the poor people of Spain, here we could just about afford a glass of water. I wondered how anyone acquired such wealth; they couldn't all be bank robbers.

All I wanted to do was get the hell out of there, and that is what we did. The next lift we got was with an Italian dentist who nearly crashed his DS several times from staring at Gill and muttering, *"Bella, bella."*

In French he asked me if all English girls were as beautiful as her?

"Yes," I lied, "there are many beautiful girls like her in England." He might have had a lovely car but I had Gill. I still had not found the courage to play in public.

Charlie was a very experienced hitchhiker, having travelled all over the States. Charlie explained that he felt the reason most hitchers take so long to get lifts is that their appearance puts other people off.

First of all, he reasoned, never carry a rucksack, as it suggests camping; wherever possible use a suitcase instead as it implies that you are only resorting to this method of transport because of an emergency. Secondly, be clean shaven (how much is a razor blade?) and keep your hair short. Next, avoid jeans and wear a pair of plain grey trousers or slacks that you hang up each night to keep the creases in. Wear a white nylon shirt that you can rinse through and have dry by the morning. If you are carrying a coat, drape it over your arm: the whole effect will make you look like this is something you don't normally do and the rides will come effortlessly.

I could find no fault with this logic, but for me the whole point of travelling was that it was a part of self-expression, and what I wore was part of that. If I had to wait twice as long as he did, I at least was a true martyr to my own style. In fact I had to wait more than twice as long as Charlie. I know this, for we met up several times along the Côte d'Azur and he was always there days before me even though I was travelling with the beautiful blonde-haired girl.

We arrived in Cannes and it was raining. Not unpleasant cold rain, but big warm dollops of it. It was getting dark, and for once we were both hungry. We found ourselves in an area where there had been an open air market of some kind. Still determined to hold on to the little money we had, I started looking for fruit and stuff that had rolled on to the floor under the stalls, while Gill sat at a small pavement café having a coffee. Looking up, I saw her being approached by two men.

As I walked over to where they were talking, Gill was just uttering her standard response to allcomers, *"Je ne parle pas francais."*

"Qu'est-ce que vous voulez m'sieurs?" I asked in as friendly tone as I could manage. The two turned around and I saw that they were both North African. The younger one was only three or four years older than me and thin, with quick nervous eyes, black tight curly hair, shabby sports jacket, slacks and sandals. The elder of the two was scary; in his late thirties, and taller than his friend, with a hideous scar that ran from somewhere near the top of his head across his right eye and down under his ear. His right eye had been removed—that is to say, most of it had been removed, because underneath the lid that would not quite close there was something floating about. I didn't look too closely.

They were alarmed to see such a pretty young thing sitting on her own, and wondered if they might assist her to her accommodation, or perhaps keep her company. In spite of my fear at the sight of them I used the sign that seems to be understood throughout Europe to indicate when two people are together: I extended my two first fingers and, holding my hands out with palms down and thumbs tucked in, brought my hands together three times. The older one nodded his understanding. The younger one of the two just stared at Gill. Good manners have led me into some dreadful predicaments and here I was not only getting myself into hot water but possibly dragging Gill with me.

Whilst the younger one stared with open admiration at my girl, the older one asked if we had eaten anything. When I said that we were about to eat he insisted, much to my horror, that he would join us and that he would pay for us all. Gill looked at me incredulously as they joined us at her table.

"Don't worry," I breathed, "we'll have plenty of time to slip away." We ate a thin steak and chips which was delicious, and as the warming effect of the wine took hold—and neither man was drinking—I began to wonder if my judgement was a bit hasty. The younger of the two continued to gaze at Gill while the older one told us of his life. He was a soldier, and I told him that I had been in the army too. He was impressed by this and after we had taken coffee he asked where we were staying that night. It was hopeless—I had not yet had time to figure that one out, so I just said that we would find somewhere. Of course he would have none of that and insisted that we stay at his home.

"Where are we going?" Gill asked.

"He is going to find us a room," I said, half truthfully.

We crossed the road and after about two minutes' stroll we turned into a little courtyard. We were bidden upstairs to an old door which was unlocked and walked into a tiny room. All that was in there was a table with a bowl and two army style beds with a mattress on one and a few blankets on the other. The elder one gestured to the beds and indicated that we should take them.

"But what about you?" I asked as Gill looked at me with widening eyes.

With a sweep of his hand he indicated the floor. I told Gill to get into her sleeping bag and pretend to fall asleep while me and the old soldier talked. He reached behind the table, pulled out a bottle of cognac, and poured out a glass for me and a monstrous one for himself. The younger one just stared at the sleeping form of Gill as I sipped at the spirit. The half blind one warmed to the drink, and when he checked that she was asleep he decided to show me his battle scars. He pulled off his shirt. Oh my God, I thought, we're both going to get it.

I was wrong. The old soldier went on to explain that most of his injuries had been caused fighting in Algeria and he had been caught in the tail blast of a grenade that had pierced his back and gone through his lung. The eye had been mostly lost in some other skirmish, and the drink (which was against his religion) was to relieve the pain in his shoulder. He was an awesome sight, a big man covered with campaign scars like a sailor would pick up tattoos.

I noticed the young one was yawning and was slowly leaning more and more towards the floor, then taking off his coat, he rolled it up, said something in Arabic to his friend and adopted a sleeping position. The old soldier gallantly did the same and lay down in front of the door. Within a few minutes he began to snore, at first softly then louder, so that I had confidence to lean across and whisper to Gill, "Are you OK?"

"Yes, are you?" she answered softly.

"Christ I'm tired," I said, and Gill told me to get to sleep. I tried but I couldn't really go under. Some time in the night, between sleep and dreams, she shook me gently and whispered, "He's trying to get into my sleeping bag."

I quickly realised it must be the younger one because the elder was still snoring.

"Just tap my shoulder next time he does it," I whispered back. I contrived a view of him by twisting my head and looking slightly over my raised left shoulder. I saw him move to climb on to her bed at exactly the same time as she tapped my shoulder and, with a gigantic stage movement and a roar like an animal in pain, I swung over on to my left side as if tormented in some terrible nightmare and caught him a fearful slap across his face.

I have never seen a reaction like what happened next outside of a cartoon. He leapt into the air like a cat, clearing the bed entirely and landing back in the corner from whence he had begun his stealthy encroachment.

The rest of the night slipped by without incident—I know because I was awake all night, even after I heard the steady snores of the younger one joining the sleepy sounds of my exhausted partner.

If I had been surprised at the opulence of Cannes, I was appalled at the excess in Nice. We could not afford to have any luxuries in cafés and I began to get angry. I suspect that my mood was as much affected by my inability to play the guitar in public as my inability to provide anything but the most meagre support for my girlfriend. Gill still did not complain. Further into the town I found a little grocery and bought one or two bits. It was cool in the narrow lane and shadowy light, and holding my purchases behind my back I walked up to Gill and said in a hammy actor's tone, "Lush and ripe fruit from the orient I bring!"

Then with a flourish I whipped the paper bag off the biggest tomato that either of us had ever seen. She laughed so much, I just loved her even more. All the time I was conscious of how inadequate I was. Around this time I wrote home to Henry, and wondered if he might be planning to come out to France on his scooter. I remember saying that if I saw his face sticking out of the crowd I would surely have the confidence to perform. Although this was for the sake of both Gill and me, it made her really sad. She told me that she wanted to be the one who could give me the confidence, and that we should not need Henry, even though she was as fond of him as I was. Her sadness made me feel even more useless. Of course she was right. Soon, I assured her, I would be ready to go to work.

Work, however, was to come from another source. Someone in the place we were staying told us about a little engineering store in some tiny back street that needed stock takers for a couple of days. The old guy that owned the place was glad of our cheap labour and we were really happy to get two days' money each from the incredibly boring work. There were several other kids there from the Youth Hostel and the atmosphere was light and friendly. Predictably it was me who got restless soonest and with our funds replenished somewhat, decided that as we were so near we would go to Italy. Because we had money now, I decided that we could be separated for the night and we'd stay at the hostel that was perched high above the town in a small house facing the line of the incoming sea.

There was an incredible view from the top, but after climbing the steep hill we found that there was a huge queue of kids waiting to get in, and by the time we got to the door, it was full. Night had fallen and we were too tired to return to the town. Instead, we walked some way up the road, and in amongst some trees we found a concrete platform with a wall round it. As we unrolled our bags, we could see the odd car headlights way off through the trees. Behind where we lay was the hill, below us the town , and above us the stars as bright as a Van Gogh painting. The concrete was still warm from the day's sunshine, and although the ground was hard on my boney body, I drifted off into fitful sleep.

I was awakened by a gentle tugging on my sleeping bag which at first I ignored, then I became aware of being almost bodily moved and my eyes blearily opened to see in the still starry night two shadowy male figures carrying a sack away from me. From out of the sack a slim arm was hanging on to my sleeping bag and that arm was attached to my Gill. I was always scared of losing her, but I never imagined that she would be physically dragged away. In the darkness all I could see were her eyes, full of fear, and her lips moving with no sound coming out. I was wide awake. I knew not to make any sudden movements. I took in my surroundings whilst my mind worked at what my alternatives were. Yes I had got it. After thinking through all the options, I had worked out that our situation was hopeless: I would be killed and she would be raped and then killed.

Slowly, very slowly, I raised my torso off the ground, and addressing the man holding her feet I cleverly came up with, "What the fuck are you doing, what's going on?" and then, *"Je m'excuse, qu'est-ce qui passe?"*

At this burst of English and schoolboy French, the one who had her arms let her go and jumped over to me pressing his knees into my neck as the only thing appearing from my sleeping bag was my head. I was still trying to get my arms out of the bag. In retrospect this was the best thing that could have happened. The one who still held her feet had to put her down and he moved away from her and spoke something in Arabic to his accomplice. Gill was by now shaking uncontrollably at my side and slowly I reached out one hand showing it to be empty and reached out to comfort her. The guy behind me was scared, I could feel that as his knees started to tremble fiercely in my back and his hand went to grab my forehead.

I shook my head and in a loud voice spoke to the other one, *"Nous sommes Anglais. Voulez vous voire nos passeports?"*

I don't know where this came from but it seemed to work. It suggested that we might have been in the wrong by being there and that they were there in some official capacity.

"Oui, vos passeports?" the one at Gill's feet ordered.

Easing my other hand slowly towards my back pocket, I allowed the sleeping bag to fall from my shoulder till I was half clear. As I handed the man my passport, I hooked the bag so that I was sitting on it and now I was halfway out of it. With both hands free, I motioned towards my scruffy white holdall and implied that I was getting Gill's passport. The one behind, whose knees were almost knocking, moved away from me and spoke agitatedly in Arabic to his friend.

Feigning some trouble with the zip on the bag, I managed to get right out of my bag and with the confidence that gave me I demanded, *"Votre pass!"*

"Nous sommes agents du police," he declared and entering the double bluff pulled out an identity card.

I leaped to my feet and yelled, *"C'est une carte d'identé! Vous n'etes pas des agents!"* Then, in a huge roar as if I had only just worked out what they were attempting, "You bastards! I'm calling the police!"

At this bellowing, the nervous one shot off in the direction of the road beyond the trees whilst the other one muttered something about radioing the police station and walked, altogether more steadily, towards the direction his friend had disappeared.

"You bastards!" I screamed after them as we heard a Deux Chevaux start up and putter off as fast as it could back down the road. For a long time Gill was unable to speak, and after she had stopped shaking we sat holding on to each other.

"Ralph," she said, "I was so scared. That guy, the one who stood behind you, had a huge knife. He was holding it just above your neck. I thought you would be killed."

"Don't worry," I said, "This is the last night we sleep outside. We'll go to Italy tomorrow. Things will be different there."

∽

returns

W̲e crossed into Italy via Menton. It was exciting to be visiting another country; the people seemed friendlier, and not so many quizzical glances came our way.

We soon learned to say, *"Due cappuccini, prego?"* and I delighted in repeating the magic number *cinque cent cinquante cinque* just for the sound of it.

Our few francs translated into massive amounts of lire, and some of the notes were the size of newspapers and had to be folded several times in order to be pushed into wallets. Unfortunately not *our* wallets. There was a note of optimism in the air as we worked our way down to Genoa, where we had been told about an inexpensive youth hostel. Once we arrived we instantly felt at home in the place: a rambling villa with floors on different levels and a large communal dining room. There was somewhere to shower and it was easy-going and kindly. We washed our clothes and at least they smelled cleaner for being washed in Wright's Coal Tar soap.

We did not leave the place for the first day and just sort of recovered from our travelling. For a hundred lire you were provided with a meal of spaghetti and tomato sauce with a little cheese on top that was absolutely delicious. It was my first real taste of Italian cooking and I was totally captivated by it. Along with a salad and a little cheap red wine we thought we had arrived in heaven. Of all the places I went in those days, I can still recall that food the best. Every so often I might be eating a spaghetti and something about it will remind me of that taste and I'm back in Genoa and it's 1963.

Sometime in the evening, showered, shaved and with clean pants, socks and shirt, I brought my guitar into the garden. There were some steps and big evergreen conifers dotted about and old stone walls and carved banisters around what must have been a beautiful family villa. Groups of kids lounged about, some writing postcards or reading, some chatting animatedly in groups. Most of them were not English and all of them seemed young and immature. In the warm evening watching the shadows grow longer, I became aware of the sweet smell of marijuana floating on the breeze. I continued to strum away—maybe just a little louder in the hope that the smoker might declare himself.

We did not have long to wait. I pretended not to be aware as from behind a wall at the end of the courtyard appeared the blondest bloke I'd seen since my brother's hair darkened to yellow when he was about ten years old. He was a couple of years older than Gill and me, and walked with a slow, bowlegged gait; he wore a white shirt and white trousers with the kind of Indian sandals you still see in Kensington market, and his skin was the shade of brown that only Scandinavian skin seems to go. He was bearded, with piercing grey blue eyes, and because he was smiling as he listened to the music, I could see that his front tooth was slightly crooked. He looked a little out of it.

"Hey man, you play nice guitar," he said.

"Thanks," I responded.

He went and fetched a little red wine from the canteen and soon we were talking. He was a bit stoned, and we started to feel the effects of the wine. It soon emerged that we had no money, and he said that if I could play like that it would be easy. Gill confirmed that she had been telling me the same thing, and after a few more swigs of wine our new friend suggested we went down to the harbour.

"Bring your guitar man," he ordered, so I did.

His name was Olaf. He was Norwegian, and an ex-merchant sailor. I knew about Norwegian sailors from old George Foulser down at Poole and whilst checking him out, it was clear to me that he had joined as a career move and not because he was in need of an enclosed environment in which to express himself. This was further reinforced by the way he kept looking at my Gill. Christ he was a handsome confident sunburnt experienced exotic Scandinavian bastard. I liked him, and off we set for the harbour.

It was early evening when we arrived and the local population were on their promenade. Europeans go out for evening walks for the sheer pleasure of looking at each other or trying out new clothes, to improve their appetite for their evening meal, or to walk their dinner off. It was all new to us and pleasant to see all the sights and the general buzz around the harbour. Every now and then I saw old ladies selling loose tobacco and cigarette papers, so in the end I bought some. It was very cheap and I was happy to have saved some money. It smoked alright too. I had my guitar in its case and Gill was holding my other arm.

Suddenly Olaf walked up to some poor geezer who was transfixed staring at Gill and demanded in English, "Do you want to hear some music?"

The bemused Italian signalled that he did not understand, so Olaf signalled back that he would get me to play if the man so wished.

"*Si Si,*" said the bloke, who probably was relieved that he was not about to be stabbed by this jealous Norwegian with the piercing eyes.

Olaf turned to me and ordered in a loud voice, "Play!"

So that is what I did. I took out the guitar, played a chord of C and launched into a passable version of *Guitar Shuffle*. The Italian looked bemused and seemed to enjoy this entertainment just for him and at the end he sweetly gave me a round of applause.

"*Cento lire!*" ordered Olaf and after just a moment's quizzical glance at me. who was just as surprised, the 'audient' handed over one hundred lire.

"*Grazie,*" said Olaf taking it, and immediately handed it to me.

"Easy isn't it," he smiled, showing his crooked front tooth again.

Gill was positively beaming, for she was sure that now I had broken my nervousness, and as the prospect of a measure of financial independence grew, we three breezed about the market area and bought some more cheap wine.

The following day Gill and I wandered about and talked about our new acquaintance. We agreed he was likeable but a bit domineering, but what I was really interested in was whether Gill fancied him. The more we travelled, the more I realised how scared I was of the responsibility of caring for us both, and on several occasions I was glad to be in the company of blokes.

In most of these youth hostels there were boys and girls our age. Unlike us, they were protected with money, monster rucksacks and good walking boots. The worst of these organised travellers were the Germans, who were always complaining if anyone was in late and then proceeded to be the first up singing what sounded to me like marching songs to the tuneless drones of their accursed electric razors. We usually bought the roll and jam that was on offer before wandering downtown to meet up with Olaf and to maybe try a little busking. Usually my nerve failed but we made a bit of money before I felt we should move on. I noticed that the cigarettes I was making were giving me a cough.

You cannot be in Italy and not see Rome, so one hot and humid morning Gill and I said our goodbyes and hit the road south. When we arrived at the hostel, in the hottest weather I have ever experienced, we were told that there was no room—but because Gill was a girl they let her in. I slept outside. The air did not move that night and I didn't even have enough money to buy an ice cream. I was getting resentful of these kids who seemed to have so much more than us, and as for the Italian boys, well my temper was always on edge because everywhere we went there were whistles and comments and I could only guess at their meanings.

I finally cracked one day on the road when a group of them were calling after Gill as if I was not even there. There were at least six of them. Tired, hungry, and now totally pissed off, I dropped my bag, put down the guitar and raced across the road towards them. God knows what I would have done if they'd turned to face me, but to a man they turned tail and ran away.

I'd had enough; the heat was formidable and the city moved at breathtaking speed. I had no money for any accommodation and would have had to sleep outside, so without so much as a glance at a Roman ruin, I declared that we were leaving. We headed back north to France. Once again my confidence had failed me and I became morose and difficult.

It didn't help when I found out how the old ladies could sell their loose tobacco so cheaply. One day I saw some poor old thing picking up dog-ends from the gutter and generously offered her one of my loose tobacco rollups. This simple gesture between two souls with a mutual need united by common poverty was met by a very odd look and then a gesture to her bag which rested by the side of the road. Sitting alongside of her dog end bag was a tray of the type that the old ladies used to display their wares. Then it dawned on me. This was what I was smoking. These old girls collected cigarette ends and nipped off the ends and then opened the stubs and recycled the remains. What some old boys referred to back home as 'roadside returns'. I was pretty choked off by this realisation but such was our condition that I refused to throw my stash away and smoked it all until it was gone and then I switched to another workman's brand called 'Nazionale'. Faced with the choice of food or fags I would take the smokes every time.

By now we were both flat broke, and with my depression creeping up on me, my attitude towards Gill became strange. All the time she tried to reassure me, but it was no good and somehow our desultory travelling led us far away from the south of France and back towards Paris. One night we were travelling across the *Massif Central*; my mood was as dark as the hills that I could not see, Gill was asleep with her head resting on my shoulder and the driver and I were filling up the cab with Gauloise smoke. Thankfully he did not want to talk and I was content to stare out at the murk.

Suddenly there was a flash of lightning and for a second the whole countryside was as clear as day. You could clearly see trees and even animals in fields, mountain peaks and roads. The only strange thing was the colour of the sky which was a sort of yellow, then pitch darkness again. I gently shook Gill from her sleep just as a mighty thunderclap began and then shortly afterwards another flash of lightning.

When we reached Lyon, there was a fair going on. The whole city seemed to be celebrating and once again the opportunity to play presented itself. There was the smell of chocolate and hot dogs in the air, and in the evening the sight of people out to enjoy themselves with money to spend. My morale, however, was so low and we were so broke and hungry that I knew what we had to do. Gill was all for heading south again back to Spain where she thought we might get a job. She may well have been right, or perhaps the thought of being back with her family was even worse than the situation that faced us. I only blamed myself, for she was optimistic to the last, but she was my responsibility and I'd had enough.

With our very last centimes we bought some grapes and a piece of bread. I made some enquiries and found the British consulate in Lyon, and it wasn't difficult to convince one of the officials there that we were in need of some help. They provided us with a travel document to get us back to England and stigmatised our passports with an official stamp in the back to the effect that the British consular office had advanced us ten pounds to repatriate us. More importantly, we were given a little money to buy some food. I don't think we ate egg and chips.

I was a cowboy
out on the prairie
Life sure is easier
back home in the alley

podger

I felt totally miserable on my return to England with Gill. With just a little more confidence—actually confidence raised to the power of ten—we could have been in Morocco, or anywhere but bloody Croydon. Not only that, I had a repatriation stamp in my passport. This was the worst aspect because I knew that Woody would never have gone cap in hand to his embassy to get home. He would have got a job on a Liberty ship washing dishes, kept his dignity, and written another 58 songs about it.

Gill had tried so hard to reassure me that we would be OK, and she was more than prepared for whatever was to come our way. The truth was that I had found myself lacking when it came to my responsibility towards Gill and her safety on the road. It should have been fun—and often it was—but we had no safety net as we had no money, except what I could earn by playing. I think that would have been tough for just one person—but two?

Gill was beautiful even before the sun had made her hair stunningly blonder and turned her skin to an irresistible golden tan. It had become a battle to keep drivers' eyes on the road and their hands to themselves. And I had no plan whatsoever—all I wanted was not to stand still. My life was all musical discovery and Gill. We had sort of agreed to be engaged before we left on the trip, but I found I was faltering on this commitment too. Gill seemed to understand, and lightened of my burden of travel bag and guitar, along with our 'understanding', life returned to some semblance of normality.

Gill returned to Bournemouth, and later that year I got a job as a storeman-cum-checker at the Philips electric factory across the Purley Way in Croydon. Gill hitchhiked up to be with me every week, to the amazement of my mates. As I recall, Gill had no trouble hitching in England. She never waited at the roadside for more than four minutes and she could time her journeys to the half hour.

Naturally these forced breaks between us meant that every reunion was consummated at the first opportunity—given that I was back home with Mum and Bruce at Miller Road. Our outings were mainly confined to the Whitgift pub and friends' homes, where we would listen to music or play guitars. I was now totally obsessed with the guitar. If it was not in my arms then Gill was, or at least by my side. Parting was misery, and queuing at the end of the road for the public phone brought only temporary relief from the torture of separation. My wages precluded moving into a flat, and besides I was still wary of deeper commitment.

The job at Philips was a nightmare of boredom. It consisted mostly of weighing the contents of boxes and stocktaking, with a little dispatch work. Old Bob, the foreman, was deeply suspicious of my career intentions, deducing correctly that I was the student type and had no real interest in the wacky world of grommets and screws. I became quite fond of him; he was a kindly and gentle man who had been there since the factory opened. He always wore the same brown overall and was completely content in his work. I started to bring the guitar into work so that I could play it in the lunch break. Above the noise of the factory floor we bellowed pleasantries to each other and he often covered for me although I was perpetually being docked wages for poor timekeeping. I hated the clock which we had to use to punch our times in and out of work. Woody Guthrie once made a drawing of a fist smashing into the face of a time clock as a reward for its passive tyranny. That's what I felt like doing.

Part of my job was to collect huge pallets of television sets or boxes of Lord knows what, and this we did with the aid of a clever piece of equipment that levered the pallet off the floor just a few inches and then locked it into position so that we could drag it to the next storage area. I discovered that if I lifted the handle to an upright position and stood on the chassis, by rocking from side to side I could create a forward motion and soon I was able to get the jacking trolley up to quite alarming speeds. The wheels were metal, and there was no need to alert fellow workers that I was on my way as you could hear me coming from all over the place. Soon other lads were travelling down the vast wide corridors in the same fashion. Perhaps because it raised morale nothing was said against it.

Every afternoon the dreaded 'Music While You Work' used to come on the Light Programme on the radio. This was a show that was originally broadcast to help keep up spirits during the war effort. Old Bob used to whistle away contentedly to every tune, and it was only after several weeks that I noticed the same songs were played every day. I couldn't believe that no-one had noticed or seemed to care. Old Bob didn't seem to mind. I thought it was grounds for a general strike.

It certainly hastened my need to depart. Through Cathy down at the Whitgift, I got a job with John, her boyfriend from Northern Ireland, as a scaffolder's labourer.

My life as a scaffolder was short. You seldom see scaffolders over the age of thirty five anyway; I was nineteen when I started and nineteen when I quit. You have to know when it's time to hang up your podger when you do this job and I found out quickly that it was not for me. Like most young men I was greedy for experience, but the only competition I wanted was with myself. I ran everywhere. Walking was too slow and after the army I ran even more. I was so fit compared to my mates back home that on several occasions I found myself running on in front and then walking back to them because I couldn't stand their slow pace. As a kid I loved to climb trees though I remember once not being able to get back down and having a hell of a job convincing my mum that I needed help.

One of my recurring nightmares is that of being stranded on a high functionless building with only the faintest hand hold and no earthly means of escape: my hands tire, my anguish increases, I am too far beyond human contact to be heard if I cry for help, and finally I fall.

I do not like heights, yet I am obsessed with tall buildings and have dragged unwilling friends up all the classic skyscrapers in the world, from the monument in Billingsgate when it was sixpence to the CN tower in

Toronto with a hungover Bert Jansch and Martin Jenkins.

In Croydon, the dominating presence at the end of the street was the old gasholder and I knew that one day I would climb it—and I did, several times. And when the new Greyhound building was almost completed, Colin (Dan) Archer and I climbed up the inside until the stairs ran out and from there up the outside scaffold till we were on the top. From twenty-three storeys up I took a pee off the top as I gazed down at the buses the size of matchboxes passing below. Dan had to relieve himself in a different way (and left his mark covered by his flat cap... I often wondered what the men returning to work must have made of that).

Even though we had both had a few ciders from the Whitgift, the fear was not really diminished as we walked across narrow walls and hauled ourselves to the top, but the sweaty palms and thumping heart were all part of the thrill. I was so high on it that I had to do it again and I was almost sorry when it was possible to climb all the way to the top via the stairs.

I was telling someone about my adventure down at the Whitgift when I was overheard by John, a scaffolding ganger, and he asked me if I wanted a job, as he was short of a labourer. What could I say? I had to accept, and so with trembling hands and thumping heart I turned up at Robstart Street in Streatham to begin work.

A scaffold gang comprises three men: a ganger, a fixer and a labourer. It was a lovely sunny, frosty morning but as I looked up at the proposed eleven storey building that was already up six floors, my heart sank. John introduced me to the other member of the gang, Marty, and suggested that I try bringing up five by five tubes, that is to say five tubes that were five feet long to where the two of them were working.

Even though the sun had been on the pipes for a couple of hours they were still frozen together and had to be prised apart and loaded on to my shoulder. The method is simple and obvious—but I had to be shown as each of the ice cold pipes wrestled and squirmed over my boney, ill-clad shoulder. John showed me how to load three on first and two to bind them. Then, raising my arm higher than looked casual, in order to raise the muscle to a height to cushion the weight, I would advance towards the almost vertical ladder rungs that ran to the sixth floor.

My progress must have been hilarious. For a start you only have one hand to grab at the ladder, so you have to develop a rhythm that allows you to throw yourself lightly at the rungs as you step. At first you take a step, then bring your other foot on to the same rung, then move your hand, then your leading foot, then bring your other foot on to the same rung, and so on. You can always spot the new boy on the job.

By the time I got to the top I was sweating and hot, though my hands were numb with the cold and my legs were shaking with exertion and fear. Suddenly there I was on a two plank platform six storeys up with no hand rail. I was carrying the hand rail. I lowered my frozen burden and Marty grabbed one and expertly fixed it to two of the uprights and then connected a larger tube to it and I felt a little more secure. I had been much higher before, yet it was more scary being up these mere six flights than climbing twenty three after the pub. It was a good view from where we were. Once I realised that neither of the guys were showing off and that they were only trying to help me, my nerve improved, and by the end of the day I was quite getting the hang of it. By the time I got back to my place, though, I was completely shattered. Dreams of wet planks and skidding off open ended platforms kept me twitching and hopping all night but I was there again the next day on time and we had tea in the hut before starting work.

By my third day, I had worked out that John was mature beyond his years, patient and kind, and that Marty was mad. Why else would he wear plimsolls in the middle of winter and refuse to use the ladders, preferring to climb up the outside tubing? He might have been older than John but he didn't act it. I asked about falling and John told me that he had fallen four times; the greatest distance was thirty feet and he survived it with just a broken leg.

"In those days we weren't obliged to build traps to stop falls like we are now," he said, motioning below us to where corrugated iron sheets leaned out at a reassuring angle a couple of floors beneath. "The biggest danger is not from falling off but from letting things fall off, like joints that are heavier than a house brick or the odd time you let go a tube. If that happens you just have to shout as loud as you can and pray there's no-one underneath. When I started, my ganger dropped a twenty-one foot tube from the top to show me what happened to it. Believe me, it looked like a hairpin by the time it hit the bottom."

I shuddered inwardly and hoped that I would never let go of a tube. The weather was good and I improved a little, though to be fair I wasn't really tested. While I was with them we never 'struck' a building, and that requires real teamwork as anyone who has had the time to observe

411

a good gang at work dismantling a scaffold would agree. The labourer stands at the bottom of the building with a short hessian sack between his hands and catches the heavy joints in its cradle soundlessly, whilst in between drops he receives the tubes and slides them on to the lorry. Up top, the fixer moves along the boards with podger in hand twirling the joints apart and passing them to the ganger who drops them below.

The biggest test of bottle comes when you are fixing the big twenty one foot verticals in place; John let me practise this on the ground. The technique was as follows: first you balance the tube on its end and then, lifting it clear of the ground, you lean it back slightly over your right shoulder at a very slight angle. Keeping your left hand under your right and about a metre apart, you pull the bottom of the pole and push the top, and this way you and the pole are stable. Once the pole is completely at the right height to drop on to the spigot, you advance to the edge of the board and place your tube on to the waiting spigot. You then change hand position so that your left hand steadies the pole and quickly tighten up the spigot with your podger. Sounds easy enough until you find yourself on a wet plank six storeys up in the pouring rain moving steadily forward to the edge of an unprotected drop with fifty pounds of freezing cold steel at least twenty five feet over your right shoulder waving about in the air. John only allowed me to attempt it with the smaller tubes, which is probably why I am still here and able to write these lines.

Our principal job was the one in Streatham but we moved about a bit; mostly small jobs because basically all the scaffolder has to do is stay in front of the brickies, especially if they're on piece work. Halfway through the third week we moved to another job on top of a block of flats where we were to build a hanging scaffold to affix a cradle for some window cleaners. That was where I decided that I would prefer to donate one of my kidneys to science without anaesthetic than to continue my career as a scaffolder's labourer. The weather had got worse and we were slipping about on a wet flat roof, dangling tubes over the edge as John designed and made instructions for the support system for the cradle that the men would use. The whole process terrified me. I wasn't getting on with Marty particularly, and when there's only three of you, any lack of enthusiasm or lack of weight pulling is felt immediately. All I needed was a reason to leave that didn't smack of cowardice.

Fortunately I picked up a minor lesion on the site. My leg swelled up and became red hot and I could not put any weight on it. There was no centre to the swelling and it just got bigger and angrier. Because of my presumed allergy to penicillin, I was only taking mild antibiotics and the leg just got worse. The only thing to do was to rest and not go out until it got better. So I went out every night as usual and walked through the pain. Finally my mum suggested that she should try to draw the infection with one of her father's old cures. I remember her telling me of things he did for carbuncles and warts with bits of raw meat, pieces of cardboard and knitting needles, and the thought that I might have to spend the next week or so with a dead rabbit tied around my knee and an onion in each sock would normally have put me off, but something had to be done.

On the Sunday afternoon Mum prepared a poultice of bread and a bowl of scalding water; there was no sign of an onion or dead rabbit so I sat down and she worked on the leg. First the poultice, then the hot water and so on until the water cooled, and then repeat. The infection was localising; she said she could feel it, but it was too painful to touch and she would have to let me do it myself. So it was that, gritting my teeth with the pain, I finally managed to exert enough pressure to express the poison.

If it had not been my own leg and my own poison that I was working on, I would definitely have passed out. As it was I felt faint with the sight of it, but almost at once the pain vanished and I began to feel better. Mum just took it in her stride; no wonder half the street came to her if anyone was injured, bleeding or otherwise.

John was kind enough to collect my money and deliver it to my house on the Sunday evening. The money was the most I had earned to date: it worked out to a little under £17 a week.

engaged

Gill got an interview and then a job at Bourne and Hollingsworth's department store in Oxford Street, in London. Along with the job came residency at the store's own hostel for its female employees in Gower Street. This of course meant that we could be together more, although there was a strict 'no men' policy in force at the hostel. So we met and walked the streets and alleys of the West End every Wednesday night, and Gill came down to Croydon on the weekends.

She seemed to enjoy the job and I was scared that I might lose her to the temptations of London life. In this mood we once again became engaged. This time it was official, and Gill found a little gold ring in a jewellers in Goodge Street. It was shaped like a tiny flower in turquoise and it cost £5.

Since Southbourne we had never been able to spend a whole night together. While we were travelling, the people who kindly sheltered us expected us to stay celibate until we were married, and the hostels were separated anyway. Somehow we kept up the torture of pretence that we were waiting to be married whilst making love at each and every opportunity. When I heard Robin Williamson's *The First Girl I Loved*, with the line "never slept with you though we must have made love a thousand times", it was reassuring that another young couple were forced into that.

We found little places for intimacy everywhere. Although there was room at home in Miller Road, the idea of staying overnight would have been an impossible suggestion. One day in November 1963 we were walking down Charlotte Street talking about what we were going to do about setting up together—or was it setting off on another trip to Europe that summer—and wandered into a small coffee bar. We were the only ones in the place and the radio was playing quietly in the background as we sat down with two instant coffees in glass cups and saucers to extend our goodnights.

Suddenly an announcer interrupted the music with the message that President Kennedy had been shot. Gill reached for my hand and we stared at each other. The woman behind the counter looked at us kids and then back to the radio.

"What did they say?" I asked. I looked back at Gill and her tears splashed down on the table.

I was aware of the politics of the blues and the early songs of Bob Dylan which were related to the civil rights movement, but my own politics were unfocused and slightly patronising—if a nineteen year old could be patronising. Kennedy was youthful and smiling. He was one of us somehow; we sensed that he understood that we were going to change the world for the better. I was aware of the Bay of Pigs debacle but had not disentangled the Cuban situation from my general idealism, which was still loosely rooted in the rights of man and a folksy Woody Guthrie philosophy of the left, without actually embracing communism (unlike many of my friends).

It was like discovering there was no Santa Claus. Idealism could be blown away by an assassin's bullet. Just as the civil rights marchers had been disposed of and union leaders in the states, now it seemed even the president could be dispatched at a whim of a madman. The prospect was numbing.

As I wandered home it was like being stoned yet angry—there was nothing to grab hold of to steady oneself. People were bewildered and silent on the tube and train home. I still did not abandon some belief in man's greater goodness, but the seeds of cynicism and doubt were planted that evening and nothing would ever be quite the same again.

Going down the Whitgift was becoming a nightly habit. I would run all the way there and stumble back. Small dramas unfolded and relationships floundered and flourished, all accompanied by a cider-induced late-teenage beatnik logic. Songs were sung, pianos played, gropings rebuffed, undying friendships confirmed. Les finally cemented his relationship with tiny Margot and they were married at Croydon Registry Office.

Les and I had become a little estranged, but so much drink was taken on the night before the wedding that I was only a little hurt when Les asked that Steve should take care of him. Steve failed to live up to the challenge and Les rebuffed all offers of help to get home. Somewhere up Scarborough Road, he fell into a hole being dug for the gas board. After several attempts to get out he decided to stay overnight.

He barely had time to get home in the early morning to don his suit and stumble back to the Whitgift where Maurice the landlord lent him a tie. After the brief ceremony they were driven off by Max in his ancient Morris 8 convertible. There was a rather drunken reception paid for and attended by Margot's family and some of Les's. Margot's dad made a speech in which, in an almost stage Indian accent, he told several jokes which he then explained. Les's huge sobbing guffaws got the whole place rocking—which Mr. Rossario found encouraging and set him off on even more banal stories.

In the photo that exists of the event, Gill and I are standing apart. I am wearing the suit that Steve would wear to Court and Tony would wear to a job interview. I would get married in it, but not to Gill.

Henry had started to organise some Sunday afternoon sessions at the Olive Tree coffee bar where my brother Bruce worked, which had a tiny stage and dance floor downstairs. They were loosely-run affairs, but people came along. Phil Allacker and I put together a few tunes and played there as residents, and I loved it, though it wasn't so good for Phil; he would throw up before going onstage. Poor Phil, he suffered a lot; I was nervous but he made me look positively devil-may-care.

Whilst we were probably awful, people continued to fill that little downstairs area to hear us and Jacqui McShee with Little Chris Aldous and the other aspiring players. This was also the second time I saw Wizz Jones playing to the small but enthusiastic crowd.

Others who performed there included Davy Graham and Alex Campbell, who gave me my biggest compliment by inviting me to join him as his accompanist. Of course we neither expected, deserved or were paid for these sessions, but it was great to get applause and I loved the guitar so much that friends said I was practically welded to it.[5]

I would never be over my nerves before playing, but I was improving; and some people even seemed to like my singing, which really surprised me as I never even thought about that side of things. I needed work if Gill and I were going to have another attempt at travel; this time we thought India would be a good idea; after all, Stan was doing it and he couldn't even play an instrument.

After jacking in the scaffolding job, I applied for work on the building site on a Tuesday and got an immediate start for the Wednesday. It was a very odd feeling going back to my old school—only this time wearing old jeans and a tattered shirt.

The job was to build a school for girls. It was the re-siting of the Coloma Grammar School for Girls, a catholic school. The firm was an outfit from Crawley. They seemed too small for the job, and definitely short of hard-bitten labourers. There were two or three sikhs, a handful of Irish lads, a pipe layer called Les, a student called Andy, an Aussie called Pete, a site foreman called Fred, another guy called Fred, a Liverpudlian ganger called Ron, an old labourer called Bob—and me.

It was a grey miserable morning in January 1964 as I stumbled out of bed much earlier than I had been accustomed to of late. It had been raining for several days. I had to run for the bus as usual and joined the coughing chorus upstairs on the 130 to New Addington. I wiped a hole in the steamed up window and looked out over the familiar suburbs printed in my mind from schooldays, as the bus was joined by some early kids on their way to my old school. I jumped off the bus at the old familiar stop and, with just a glance at the old building, turned right through the gate and made my way to the site office.

"You're late lad," said a Liverpool accent in a cloth cap pulled over one eye. "If I say eight o'clock I don't mean ten past. If you're late tomorrow

---

[5] I incidentally picked up my first media mention at this gig, playing with Phil in support of Wizz. It was in the Croydon Advertiser in a review written by a young Robin Denselow. I also remember Sandy Jones, Wizz's wife, sitting somewhere behind the stage with the dribblingest baby I had ever seen, Simeon, now a very accomplished sax player, university graduate and father of two.

you'll be docked half an hour. OK, pick up a shovel from the store and come with me." I followed him out of the shed and across the upturned ground that resembled a bomb site, as all newly-begun jobs do.

Ron the ganger pointed to a pile of earth that was about as big as the shed we had just left and said, "I want tha' lorra 'oggin over there purover there an there's a barra so get shovellin'!" Loosely translated this meant take that lot of whatever it was over there and put it over there. For a brief moment I was glad of my time in the army where I learned how to understand dialects.

Andy was a middle class boy waiting to go to university. He worked like two men, but had the piss taken out of him unmercifully by some of the blokes because of his accent. Sometimes when he was addressed by our ganger, he looked around to the rest of us for help, as his ear never really got tuned to Liverpudlian. In the end this became a source of amusement to Ron himself, watching Andy's brow furrowing in consternation as he wrestled to interpret his wishes.

Over my shoulder and to my right was the outline of a building. The area had been filled with hardcore and was now awaiting a layer of hoggin to be compressed by means of the whacker which would provide a more level surface for the first skim of concrete. Hoggin is a mixture of clay and pebbles, and it is always tricky to shovel as you are never able to get a clean sweep at it without your shovel stroke being brought up sharp by hitting a pebble or two. Manipulating the substance is further complicated by its stickiness, and to relieve the shovel of its load you are often forced to bang it on the side of the wheelbarrow. Add to this the frost factor, making the heap almost as hard as concrete.

I hadn't done much manual work recently and handling scaffold tubes had not hardened up the skin very much. I tried to remember the tips I had learned as a gardener for the Tickle family: not to hold the shovel too tightly, to spit on my hands, and to get into a proper position and have the wheelbarrow in the right place. Once lined up correctly, I took a swing at the pile, only to watch my shovel bounce right off with an ear-piercing clang and an impact that hurt my elbows and rattled my fillings. Like all new boys I was convinced all were watching me, so I redoubled my effort and with my second swing managed to collect two pebbles and three heaped tablespoons of clay, which I tapped into the waiting barrow (which suddenly seemed huge).

I then decided to attack the heap from nearer the top and succeeded in dislodging almost half a shovelful and so proceeded in this manner wandering up and down the heap until after about fifteen minutes, I had managed about half a barrow load. Then in order to make some impression on my ganger, I went to wheel my tiny load across to the hardcore. Unfortunately my efforts had made me very sweaty and out of breath and by suddenly standing up from the semi-crouched position needed for shovelling, I had become dizzy and slipped sideways causing my barrow to empty half its contents on the ground. The rest stuck obstinately to the side of the barrow.

I righted it and was scooping up the spillage with my bare hands when Ron said helpfully, "We normally find it's a bit quicker to use the shovel, lad." He walked past with his big wellington boots turned down pirate-style.

Over the next hour I had managed three respectable loads. I had acquired two fairly substantial blisters on one hand and a spectacular one on the other. My limbs were trembling uncontrollably and I was feeling faint. I realised that I was not going to last until lunchtime unless I improved my technique.

Help came in the form of a short man in a cap and an orange sweater, his trousers tucked into his boots. His name was Gupta Singh; he was a Sikh but had cut his hair. Without patronising me he showed me how I was wasting energy and how by using the inside of my knee against the top of my forearm, I could increase my leverage and double my strength so that I no longer sounded like a demented woodpecker tapping away ineffectually on my hill of stones. He then showed me that I should dig from the bottom of the pile so that any stones dislodged higher up fell loosely on to the ground to be retrieved on the next shovel load, and to get round the uneven surface on which I was digging he produced an old piece of once corrugated iron which we ran into the heap at ground level and as I cleared each section I replaced up against the pile. By lunch break I had hit rhythm, but was incredibly tired and very shaky as I sat down with a cheese roll and huge mug of tea. Peter, the Aussie, sidled over and asked me how it was going. I lied that everything was all right and then he noticed the blisters on my hands.

"Shit mate, you better piss on them."

"Yeah," I said, nodding in agreement but not knowing why.

I looked out of the window at the shed-high heap that awaited me and considered creeping out of the gate and catching the bus home.

Then a Liverpool accent bellowed through the door, "All right lads let's be havin' you," and as we piled out from the tea hut, "Well done there lad, you're getting the hang of it, now get stuck in and shift that stuff."

There was just the right amount of encouragement in his expression to lift my spirit, but the shovel felt twice as heavy as I went out to resume the attack on the hill. A soft drizzle had continued all through the day and in spite of the waterproof jacket that I had worn all afternoon, I was still damp when I arrived home. It was a tired boy indeed who met his friends down at the pub that night.

I was awoken the next morning at seven in order to get to work on time, and as I tried to lift my head off the pillow, I became aware that I had become an invalid overnight. There was an excruciating pain in my neck and shoulders and my back had locked in the position that I had fallen asleep in. My hands were too feeble to grip anything without aching and my thighs felt as if they had been run over by a lorry. My stomach muscles were inflamed and I was unable to bend my body in any direction without agony. I was not so much in panic as in a quandary as to how to go about getting out of my bed. In the end I managed to roll out on to the floor and from this position ease myself into a half crouch and from there on to my feet. I limped into the bathroom and washed carefully, then into the kitchen where I ate some cereal.

Getting dressed was painful. Going down the stairs to the front door had to be done by resting on each step as I had done on the scaffolding ladder on the first day. Even Mum laughed as I limped up the path to the gate and hobbled down to the bus stop. The step up to the bus platform nearly had to be abandoned and if it hadn't been for the general crush of people getting aboard I would not have made it to work. Getting off was just as painful and once again I was late.

"You'll be stopped half an hour for that," said Ron, "an' fer Chris' sake liven yourself up a bit lad. That's the trouble with you young lads, up all night shaggin'."

I picked up my shovel and staggered over to my heap. It had grown during the night and as my shovel chipped away at the first barrow load I wondered if an office job might be more suitable.

By tea break I thought I would have to quit, but as our ten minutes ended a brick lorry arrived and I was diverted from working on the hoggin to unloading. This made for a change, and I was put in with the other lads. We were issued with strong rubber gloves, and hopped on to

420

the stack which was already about six feet high and therefore at a good height to walk off the bricks from the lorry. By watching and trying you learned how to pick up and catch the bricks in groups of five and soon your judgement enabled you to throw them in line and tight up against other bricks. It was labour intensive work as each brick was handled several times, but before pallet loading, every brick on a building site was handled at least eight times before the mason actually laid it in a wall.

It was not unpleasant work because of the banter and craic from the other lads. There was also the element of competition, as boys used to see how many bricks they could hold together in a line. One lad managed fifteen before the middle three dropped out like a sagging piano accordion. Working through the pain eased my aching muscles, and I felt a lot better at the end of the delivery than I did at the start. Working as hard as this was a buzz and a new experience. I took delight in performing on terms with the other lads, and keeping my eyes and ears open, learned quickly the skills and knacks that you need to get you through even the simplest tasks.

As the last few bricks were put into place one of the boys said to me, "Now smell your gloves."

I slipped them off to see my blisters had burst and the skin was all soft with the sweat that had accumulated through the loading. My hands smelled just like a pair of sweaty feet and as I recoiled, a couple of the others smiled and I began to feel all right about my new job.

The banter in the tea hut was louder than the previous day, partly because I was now part of it. I sat opposite old Bob, the head labourer who entertained us with jokes and ribald comments.

As I finished my cheese roll, he grabbed one of my hands and turned it over to where my blisters were shredded and new ones forming and remarked, "You better piss on them boy before they get worse. And don't wash either."

"Yeah too right," I agreed, still not comprehending what on earth this instruction could mean. Then I was back to my heap and Pete was assigned to help me. We worked an arrangement so that sometimes he filled and I wheeled and vice versa, and the afternoon sped by more quickly. As I climbed aboard the bus home, I began to feel like I belonged and looked forward to the next day.

I woke up the next morning, convinced I was paralysed. Once more I was reduced to rolling out of bed and climbing to an upright position like an evolving species of man ape. I swallowed down some tea and a piece of toast and sort of lowered myself down the stairs leaning heavily on the banister before limping up the road and clawing my way on to the bus platform. I could not face the climb upstairs and so spent the entire journey on the lower deck. At the site I sort of fell off the platform and staggered through the gate.

"Don't try to amuse me with them funny walks lad, you only just made it in time," said the dry voice of my ganger. "Get over on that 'oggin now." I grinned at his sarcasm, and though painful, my back soon felt better than when I got up.

∽

'oggin

The days began to fall into a pattern of work where we continued with whatever we had been doing the day before, to be interrupted by the arrival of lorries carrying materials that had to be unloaded by hand. Although this was hard work, it provided a break in the monotony, and all the labourers got to have some fun together and talk about the weekend or last night. As the sweat got up with the increase in effort, the temptation was to take off the gloves and this proved to be very unwise especially with the arrival of a load of flittens. These are bricks cast from very rough moulds and when they have been fired and turned out, there are sharp edges of terracotta sticking out from every edge. By letting them slip through your hands and into place on the stack, these sharp bits slice into your skin and cover your hands with minute razor scratches. After my first load, both my hands were bleeding from cuts and one of the Irish lads said to me that I ought to piss on them. Blisters from my first day had not healed up and now there were new ones and cuts and slices across my palms as well.

At last my pile of hoggin disappeared and was laid in position for the hardcore, which was a lot easier to handle. Broken bricks and old concrete were run from a huge heap across barrow runs of boards and offloaded in heaps that, once levelled out, would be compressed into the hoggin by means of the whacker.

The whacker was operated by Sid, a powerful but simple lad of twenty two with piercing blue eyes and a shock of black curly hair that was kept under a red and black striped cap, with a tiny ornamental buckle at the back. He wore a scarf throughout the time that I knew him, and in winter and summer his nose ran constantly. He was given undemanding tasks by the ganger, who understood that there were many elements to keep together for a site to remain happy, and one of those elements was to have a lad like Sid about. When it came to unloading a brick lorry you could never find him, but he would miraculously appear with a broom once the work was done to sweep the lorry of dust before it left the site. And when it came to being in the front of the queue for tea, he was always there.

The chaps on site had fun with Sid, but there was always someone to make sure that things never got out of hand. Ron decided as a reward to let Sid operate the whacker. Sid was always fascinated by this piece of machinery and it would be impossible for any harm to come to it, or Sid, because it was only propelled by its own vibration and was only operated within the confines of the room about to be hardcored. I was working some way off when I heard the cries of panic and saw a very distressed Sid wringing his hands and looking around desperately for help. I dropped the shovel and ran over.

"Oh Ralph, the fuckin' thing's gone mad!" he wailed.

I looked over at the machine and you could just about see the piston pot above the hoggin as the whacker had vibrated itself deeper and deeper into the earth. Obviously as usual, Sid had become distracted by something he had seen and paused to watch, The machine, sensing its chance, had whacked itself into the ground and like a struggling man in quicksand, wedged its way further down into the ground with each vibration. I leaned over and switched the engine off and looked at him. The poor lad started to cry.

"Don't worry, we'll soon have it out of there," I told him, and ran over to get one or two of the other lads. As if a life depended on it we freed the machine and replaced the hoggin after telling him that he had to keep it moving from now on and no dreaming. We cleaned it up and got it going again and before anyone had noticed, he was back at work with a big grin on his snotty face. At tea break I tried to avoid sitting with him but he always found me; the thought of him drinking his tea with a good portion of what was coming out of his nose filled me with revulsion.

I was not the only one who felt this way, and one lunch time things came to a head when one of the blokes burst out with, "For fuck's sake wipe your bleedin' nose Sid," and in the general agreement from the others that he should do something about it, old Bob popped out his top set of false teeth and dropped them in Sid's teacup. I just sat there in amazement and looked around at the others, most of whom were either stunned to silence or collapsing with laughter in anticipation. For some reason Sid did not slurp his tea down in the normal fashion, instead he kept turning his head to try and focus on where the seat of the fun was coming from. Sid always ate with his mouth wide open so that food fell all over the table, and his ability with liquids was not much better. At last the moment of truth arrived and Bob's false teeth slid to the mouth of the cup and lay grinning at the drinker, who unable to believe his eyes at first, pulled the cup away from himself, the better to focus. As he did so, the teeth once more vanished from view.

Sid then plunged a pair of mud-stained digits into the brew and after a second or two's groping, fished out the top set. By now the whole tea hut was in uproar and even old Jack, the oldest tea boy in the world, was smiling. Sid held the teeth between thumb and finger and just stared at them as if unable to recognise what they were. The laughter in the hut grew even louder at his bewilderment, and then suddenly the penny dropped and the horror hit him. With a demented scream he flung them without aim as far from him as he could.

"Oi," shouted Bob, "careful, thaths my thmile you've got there thun," and rushed to retrieve his teeth from the floor. After giving them a quick rinse in his tea cup, he popped them back in his mouth. The merriment in the tea hut was enormous but Sid came close to having a fit; he was screaming and shouting and crying all at the same time and it took a little while for anyone to realise just how serious the situation had become. Even old Bob, who Sid normally worshipped, could not calm him, and it was only when Ron the ganger came in that order was restored. The way Ron handled it was to severely reprimand old Bob in front of all of us so that Sid became open-mouthed and calm as he listened to the dressing down the old labourer got. There was much winking and knowing looks exchanged and eventually Sid and Bob went out to the site together and Bob minded the boy for the rest of that day.

Old Bob was an extraordinary man. He had been a gunner in the war and lost one eye and the hearing in one ear for his pains. He was forty seven when I joined the job and had a birthday in the time I was still working there. He looked about ten years older and had not an ounce of fat on him. He was incredibly strong and uncomplaining about any job that was assigned to him; he was also an alcoholic. At the time I joined he was already subbed a week in advance and this was against any builders' policy as it meant that the firm had no security against you leaving.

By the time I left, Bob was subbed ten days in advance and every penny was spent on beer and whiskey. When he lost his digs, they let him stay in the tea hut where he ate the stale rolls from the day before. As far as I'm aware, that was all he ate, except on Saturdays, when someone would treat him to a hot pie in the pub up the road. Every now and then, he would claw back a bit of his debt by doing a bit of unpaid overtime, but by Monday he would sub it back again and so it went on. Ron assigned me to work with Bob on some trench work for the pipe layer, as the latter had complained about my meagre allowance of room for him to work and the fact that like most new boys, my trench always tapered as it got deeper and made work more difficult.

Bob was a terrific trench digger and he taught me how to do them properly, using a fork held at a forty-five degree angle and thrown down the sides to loosen the material before using the shovel to throw out the debris. Soon I could make them as straight as Bob and what is more, I enjoyed doing it. Even now, I get quite pedantic about the right and wrong way to build a trench.

When two men are working together, the subjects discussed are usually quite wide-ranging. Not so with Bob, who only wanted to talk about drink or how to get his hands on some money for drink.

One day he came out with, "You know, sometimes I get a bit of luck, it ain't always good luck though! I remember a time someone put me on to a soft touch and I got a tenner out of him straight away and fuck me when I went back for more he gave me more as well, I took him for another tenner. He was some kind of religious nut and as long as you promised to try and reform he gave you money."

"Where was this, Bob?" I asked, thinking I had heard this story somewhere before.

"Miles from here, in a place called Thornton Heath," said Bob, without breaking stroke in his digging.

I waited a moment carrying on shovelling and then asked, "It wasn't a bloke called Waters in Whilkes chemist was it?"

There was a sudden silence as Bob stopped forking down the sides of the trench and the fork fell from his grasp. He turned to face me, his face pale.

"Me and my fuckin' big mouth, do you know him then?"

"Yeah, my mum worked there for years[6]."

"You ain't going to tell him about me are you?"

"No, I just guessed that it must be him. How much did you get from him in the end?"

"Over ninety quid. I had digs there then, I was pissed for two weeks."

Just up the road from the site was a pub, and a few lads used it at lunchtimes particularly on Saturdays when we finished at around one o'clock. Whenever Bob had some change, he would go up for a pint or two. There was a very well defined hierarchy to the site. Ron, for example, would not have drunk with the boys, and the big boss would not have drunk with Ron, and yet there was a happy atmosphere on site which was due to several factors: the mixture of different types; Sid; tough but honourable conditions, and not least our ganger Ron.

Rather like a good publican, Ron wandered round the site telling a joke here or repeating one he'd heard from someone else. Occasionally he reprimanded someone for not pulling their weight or winding someone up if they had become too familiar. In this way he was everybody's mate, yet they were still eager to impress, and this made a perfect combination for work and respect. He clearly had his favourites, and amongst the young lads it would have been Pete, who looked like a young Tyrone Power and worked uncomplainingly on whatever job was assigned to him. He worked as hard as the Irish gang who kept themselves very much to themselves, and even they showed a grudging respect for his

---

[6] I later asked my mother if she remembered him, and she did.
"But his name wasn't Bob Wesson then," she recalled.
"What was it?"
"I think he said it was Bob Jamieson," she answered. From then on I always referred to Bob as Mr. Jamieson. The other lads assumed it was a reference to his preference for Irish whiskey, and in a way of course it was.

427

strength and commitment. He even played the guitar, and once on a Saturday I brought mine in and he played an extremely intricate version of *Deep Purple* from the sheet music.

Whenever we worked together, I found myself upping my rate to keep up and stay the distance. As the months went by, my strength improved, and work that would have crippled me earlier I could now take in my stride. Ron would share a joke with me and treat me like an old soldier and that made me feel good. I don't know if they were paying under scale on this job as there was a low turnover in labourers and once on the site most were content to stay for about five shillings an hour.

In that part of Croydon working up to the Shirley hills, the soil is waterlogged and of very thick clay. We were told that machines to dig would be inefficient and so there were several gangs working on the 'footings' around the many outlines of buildings that made up the school. The Irish lads worked on part of the project; their leader was a hard farm boy from Kerry, who had a difficult accent and a manner to match. I was at the concrete mixer one day when he approached the site hut with his band of five other lads and asked to see the foreman. These six great slabs of men stood lined up with their forks and turned down boots and when the bewildered face of the kindly Fred came to the doorway, Ron announced that they wanted a few words with him. Clearing his throat and banging his fork on the ground for emphasis whilst raising his voice to be heard over the roar of the clattering mixer he spoke.

"Me and the lads are not satisfied that this job is paying what it ought to. We're here sloggin' away in this clay for five and two an hour and the job has to be worth five and six and in any case they're payin' five and six an hour for diggin' in chalk over at Riddlesdown and there'd be more satisfaction there although it's hard enough on the wrists and shoulders but here it's frustratin' pulling out clay like toffee from off your fork and five and six an hour would be barely enough but we'd take it if you'd offer it, now."

This speech was offered at breakneck speed and was completely misunderstood by Fred, who looked forlornly at Ron and asked, "What did he say?"

"They want a raise," explained Ron.

"How much?" asked Fred.

"Five and six an hour," translated Ron.

"Well, I'm afraid that's impossible."

"Right then lads, we're off then," said Liam the spokesman.

And without an attempt at negotiation, they shouldered their forks, shovels and bits and bobs and like a small army of mercenaries, trooped off the site and off to Riddlesdown and were never seen again.

I stood there open-mouthed. Ron lifted his cap from his head and at the same time scratched his head, not because it itched but because he needed a second to think.

"Where are they going?" asked Fred staring after the little army.

"They've quit," explained Ron.

"But their cards and so on?" queried Fred in a tone that now sounded hurt.

"They'll send for them from Riddlesdown I expect. In the meantime we need some new lads." And turning to me he asked, "Have you got any pals need a start Ralph?"

I knew Stan my mate needed a job, but Ron was not so much requiring an answer as filling in a few seconds to gather himself for what to do next. There is always a deadline and these blokes would be hard to replace. They were on twopence an hour more than the rest of us, and they were asking for a paltry fourpence an hour more which would have cost the company about eight pounds a week. It sounds incredible today.

I got Stan the job, and around this time the labour force was augmented by several others, among them a short wiry Irish lad called Michael.

The weather was awful and we were often rained off, but unless it was hopeless, we worked through it. Digging was laborious and Ron would constantly rotate the lads so that they did not get too restless. On the major excavation, which was for the boiler house, the water was actually visible coming out of the sides of the area that had been dug. A pump was put in place, but it was like working in a quagmire, slippery and exhausting.

It was proposed to dig a sump hole and this was to be about four foot square by five foot deep. There was no problem with this, except the weather was so wet that the sides constantly fell in and work was abandoned until there was a dry spell. It never came. The rest of the job was going well and one day in the tea hut, Ron offered the proposition to all who could hear:

"Does anyone want to earn tuppence an hour more digging out the sump hole?" This was accompanied by a large stage wink delivered on Bob's blind side.

"I'll have that," said Bob immediately, and so it was agreed. On the strength of this arrangement, he conned a few bob out of one of the new boys and sloped off up the pub for lunch break and came back with at least four pints in him. Most alcoholics don't need much to get them going again and lunchtime drinking has a quicker effect than at other times. When Bob returned from the pub, he was pissed.

The rain was still steadily falling as Bob donned his waterproofs including a strange sou'wester hat, and along with his shovel, bucket and barrow, he gingerly climbed down the ladder and got ready to work. I was working alongside young Michael some way from the boiler room but I had to barrow run soil past where Bob was working and I could see Ron standing on top of the side walls looking down at him.

"Come on Bob lad, get stuck in!" he encouraged and then seeing me, he looked round and winked. Ron motioned to me to climb up the bank and join him. There below us was our man sliding about with barely a grip on the muddy surface, digging away at the sides of the sump hole and trying desperately to retrieve the mud and load it into his wheelbarrow, which tipped over, unloading its contents back into the hole.

Bob scrabbled about as if he had just strapped on ice skates for the first time. If it hadn't been for the shovel to support him, he would have gone over many more times than he did. I started to laugh at the sight of the scene below and soon I was joined by one or two others. Bob's usual pallid complexion was now quite red from the exertion, but he did not give up scooping the slurry in his bucket into the barrow, which kept tipping over with him sliding about getting more hot and bothered with each stroke.

"Come on Bob, keep it going!!" shouted Ron.

"I am keepin' it fuckin' going," called back Bob irritatedly. Ron called out again, "Come on Bob! It's started to rain a bit more and we've got to get the job done."

"What's the matter with ya, I'm going as fast as I can for fuck's sake," shouted the mud splattered veteran of a thousand trenches as he almost slithered over. Then with a comic's timing Ron delivered the killer blow.

"Look Bob, if you can't do better than that I'll 'ave to take you off and give the job to a younger bloke."

"What?" shouted Bob, looking up for the first time and seeing us all lined up at the top. He wiped a muddy hand across a sweating brow, blew snot from one nostril and hurling his shovel as far away from himself as he could, uttered the words I will remember to my dying day.

"Well fuck you and fuck the job an' all!" Then turning round on to his blind side, he took one slippery step and disappeared head first down the sump hole.

For a few seconds nobody could do anything but laugh, then we slid down the walls of the boiler room, grabbed the only visible sign of Bob (his legs) and hauled him to safety. After a cup of tea or two, Bob seemed to be relishing his new found status, and Ron got the company to pay up Bob's subs. Once again Bob had gone down the pan but come up smelling of roses.

grapefruit

The relentless drizzle of winter gave way to early spring and the journey to work was made more pleasant by the cherry blossoms that filled the streets and suburban gardens. Gill had got digs in a terraced house in Broad Green, and although she was not allowed visitors to her room, we had other ways of spending time together. She had got a job at Allders in Croydon on the make-up counter. She was a Cyclax representative and she looked quite stunning.

We met most evenings, and either stayed in at 17a Miller Road or went down to the Whitgift to see friends and play music. I had recently come across the song *Dirty Old Town* and it could have been written for me: "I met my girl by the gasworks croft." Every evening we would walk past on our way to the pub that had become our second home. The words gave a dignity to both my roots and my aspirations. The cooling towers and gasholders were as monumental as cathedrals in the dark lane that led from our road to the brighter lights of the town.

Our plan at this time was to leave England with some money. I had tried travelling without money and it didn't work. I remembered a statement made by a bloke called Steve I met somewhere on the road. He had obtained a monkey in India. "Times were hard," he said, "and just when

I'd trained it to go without food, the fuckin' thing died on me!"

This time we would eat and stay overnight indoors, so we were saving as well. I was as happy as I'd ever been at this time; I liked my job, and with the warmer weather my spirits soared and the prospect of more adventure spurred me on.

With the approaching summer the job was coming on; although there was still digging to do, there were other jobs as well, like running hardcore, and now the laying of concrete on beds that we had so carefully prepared. Often the heat would allow us to strip down to our trousers and boots, and already we were getting weathered and sun-tanned. Add to this the fact that Stan had decided to bike to work on his old fishtail Velocette and the anticipation of summer was complete.

Stan and I were a good pairing when it came to rider and pillion, so much so that on more than one occasion I fell asleep on the back. The whole secret is trust, and acquiring that trust needs bravery, in particular leaning into corners at high speed. Stan had learned the hard way when he only had his old trials bike, a Greaves which he truly loved. With Linda on the back, he lost it on a bend when she had tried to correct a lean. When he saw Linda stagger to her feet unhurt he went to get up too, but his shin had broken and was poking through his leg so naturally he fell down. He always walked with a slight limp and had a foot that turned inwards after that, but he was gentleman enough never to have blamed her, and the hideous scar was a kind of masculine result of a rite of passage. Stan was the first bloke to come to work in shorts.

I had learned to ride Gill's scooter and felt ready to get a bike of my own. I heard about a Francis Barnett that was being sold by a friend of the family. I bought it for £65, and I loved it. Because Gill was qualified as a driver, I could travel with her and it was great spinning about the countryside with her on the back. She was pretty trusting, though you couldn't throw the thing about like a more powerful machine. It was only 175cc but it was fast enough for me. Especially when I came off it. In those days helmets were not compulsory and all I wore was a cloth cap like my brother, who had earned some respect in the neighbourhood when he bought an old 500cc Matchless.

The second time I came off, I hit my head on the road and was surprised at how hard it was. I was pretty impressed by my head as well. The third time Gill was on the back, and coming into a roundabout a bit too fast, I felt the bike going and her trying to right it. Somehow she managed to step off and was completely unhurt. I, on the other hand, broke the fall with my chin and eyebrow, which I left somewhere amongst the gravel with the bike on top of me, which rubbed a hole in my knee almost to the bone. Fortunately, I knew someone close to where the accident happened, and left the bike there along with my pride. I never went to pick it up again, and sold it for about the same as I paid for it, as I reasoned there might not be a fourth time I would walk away from a crash. From now on Stan would ride and I would partner him.

As the spring moved towards summer and our trip abroad grew nearer, so the shape of the job became more apparent. On one side of the building, a real stonemason was at work cutting and laying white Portland stone and all the shapes of things to come were clearly visible. There was still some digging to be done, and along with young Michael, I was working at the far end of the site. We were maybe twelve feet down and throwing up to six feet, and from there up to the top. At this depth the walls of a trench should be supported with boards and acrojacks, and were shored up as soon as was possible. Down at the bottom of the trench it was cool out of the sun.

It was hard getting any conversation out of Michael. He was a typical shy boy from the west of Ireland. I felt very sorry for him and persuaded him eventually to come out with us all for a drink at the Whitgift, which he was reluctant to do until he had some money for some clothes. I remember coming into the bar on the appointed Friday evening to see this young man, almost unrecognisable in an obviously new blue suit that was at least a size too big for him and a Windsor knot in his tie that was almost as big as his head. We of course looked little different to the way we went to work, except that we were marginally cleaner. Every time Gill or one of the girls tried to talk to him, he blushed so deep I thought he might blow a blood vessel. In spite of all efforts to relax him, he steadfastly refused to let go of his glass until it was reasonable for us all to disperse and go home. It was seeing him in the suit that I realised how young he must be. Barely a hair on his lip and hardly a teenage pimple on his clean skin.

"How old are you, Michael?" I queried the following Monday.

"I'm fifteen, but sure I work like a man and I'm entitled to me wage am'nt I?"

"Yes Michael, you certainly are," I agreed.

434

The final big trench progressed well and soon we were sent old Bob, who Michael liked. Bob's old body was showing signs of considerable wear and tear, though it never occurred to him that he might try something a bit easier. He was as hard as nails and to watch him go to work was an inspiration. Michael's hands were sore just as mine had been when Bob told him to piss on them.

Ron kept up his amiable rounds and as I had been on the site as long as most, he would relax a bit with me but at the same time make sure that Michael did not think he could get away with anything.

One day Michael was on the platform above me shovelling out, and I was down the bottom rolling a cigarette when Ron passed by and looking down called out, "I don't mind you smoking on the job but I do object to your manufacturing them when you're supposed to be workin'. Now get on with it Ralph!"

I lit up and smiled; it was a gentle reminder that he was paying us for our time. There were few idle breaks, but once I remember saying to Michael words to the effect that it must be strange for him to be working in a big city like this when it sounded so different to where he came from, and he answered, "Yeah, it's a long way from Clare to here."

Summer progressed, and our young bodies got deep brown tans, except Michael's whose remained obstinately pink. The *craic* was good and the ride home on the back of Stan's Velo a celebration of the day. We began stopping for a pint at the pub at the bottom of Sumner Road and we'd be the only two in the bar. From the window as we sipped a pint of Ind Coopes bitter, we could see the sun beginning to fall behind the gasometer: "Dirty Old Town, dirty old town..."

Gill and I had picked a departure date in the first week in July and if the weather in England was anything to go by, we were going to have a hot summer. A few changes had taken place on the job, but Bob was still there and Aussie Pete, although he had announced that he would be leaving soon. Stan was prepared to stay on for, like me, he was happy on this site and both he and I were as brown as Gupta Singh and his smiley slow fat mate, who had forsaken his turban and worked with his top knot showing. Stan and Gupta now worked the mixer between them. It had an automated shovel that hauled vast amounts of stone aggregate into the open upturned mouth of the drum and was controlled by hand levers; as to its voracity, that was controlled by its operator. Everyone was yelling for concrete and a big dumper truck had recently arrived on site to make things quicker than the barrow running that had been the norm.

There was still the last hand digging to be done and as it neared completion, young Michael, old Bob and I were allocated the deep trench. Things were going well enough; Bob and I were throwing the earth up six feet and Michael was clearing. The trench was half shuttered and we clambered out using the acrojacks. Bob was a little slower but managed well enough, so anxious was he not to be thought of as infirm in any way apart from disabilities earned in the defence of the realm. It was coming up to our lunch break and I could feel a cheese roll coming on.

I looked up to where Michael was shovelling and called, "What time is it?"

I never heard his reply for suddenly I saw the wall of one side of the trench move slightly and responded with, "Christ what's happening to the sides?"

"Jesus God the trench's collapsing! Quick get out!" shouted Michael.

"Quick Bob move!" I shouted. "The fuckin' trench is collapsing, get out of there!"

I was screaming at him as I grabbed at the acrojack in front of me and swung up to the next one. Michael was already on the top and grabbed my hand as I leapt over the side. Old Bob had at last responded to the cries and had got up to the first stage, but the earth was still moving and a huge part of the top of the trench was poised like a giant apple bite to fall in on top of him. Michael and I both knelt down over the trench and offered him our arms.

"Quick Bob, grab hold!" we shouted together. Bob grabbed Michael's arm but did not immediately see mine as it was on his blind side. At that moment the wall caved in. I got hold of the same arm as Michael and as the tons of soil collapsed we dragged the old boy as high as we could. He cried out with the pain as he took all his own body weight on the one arm but we hauled him up regardless. Nevertheless we couldn't clear him from the hole before he was held by the waist and screaming as his legs had been forced into crossing themselves and his balls were trapped between them. Michael and I tore at the earth with our shovels as near to the poor bastard as we dare; other lads had run over to us on hearing his cries, and for a while we all lost our colour as we worked away with only his whimpering to speed us on.

By the time we had freed him we were all shaking, pale and sweaty. We laid him out and called for help, but Bob insisted that no ambulance was called. The site foreman Fred agreed under sufferance not to call them after Bob whispered something in his ear. I can only guess that it was a deal he struck right there, where he waived all claims against the company or else he was shit scared that the authorities would be able to trace him over some misdemeanour or other. Whatever the reason, the poor man could not be persuaded to get any help, so we carried him carefully on a plank to the tea hut where he rested all that day and night.

In the morning he was much improved but only just able to walk, and according to Ron, "His balls are like two black grapefruit."

I was almost sick. We only saw the old fellow at tea break and as the days passed, he was seen to be making good and soon they got him on light work painting window frames and doors which had arrived recently. When I did manage to talk to him, he gave me a huge wink and said mysteriously, "Don't you worry about me son, I'm doing better than you think."

∾

dumper

With a week to go before our intended leave date, all the hand-digging was finished and most of us were concreting in gangs of three. I found this enormously satisfying once we had mastered the basic skills of levelling, agitating and tamping. We arrived each morning to find the work from the previous day set in stone, as it were. Barrow runs were constructed across walls and we literally did run them. I watched with admiration the subcontracted bricklayers hollering for more muck (cement) from their hod carrier, and marvelled at his dexterity and strength. He kept at least five men working and ran all day with a hod the size of a small shed.

Legends grow up around certain of the building trades. After the nutting up lump that roof tilers get on their chests, or the stamina required to be a plasterer's labourer, I guess that hod carrying comes next. There is always talk of legendary men at this trade and stories abound about the size of specially adapted hods that can carry twice as much as a normal one. All hod carriers have one shoulder bigger than the other and all have calluses where the little spur catches them as they offload the cement. All hod carriers file this spur off. So why do they have it there in the first place then? In spite of some considerable strength, by now I knew that I could not carry the hod on my skinny shoulders, although I would have loved the status and the money.

We were just finishing laying a concrete floor when Ron arrived and asked, "Can any of you lads drive?" No answer came. "We need a dumper driver," he explained.

"I can drive a motorbike, Ron," I offered.

"Go on then, see how you get on. Come with me." I followed him up to the mixer.

"Now, that there is yer clutch and you only need two gears, forward and reverse, the third gear is for if you have to go on the road and you won't be needin' that. Now the clutch is just on or off, you can't slip it, just give it some diesel and let it out and away you go. Try to see things in advance, as she steers from the rear wheels as you'll have seen, and when you're takin' a load put the brake on and don't overload the skip." I climbed up and perched on the metal saddle and engaged first gear.

"Away you go then lad," said Ron, and away I went, smoothly enough.

"Just like a real one," complimented Ron as I drew up cautiously to the mixer for my first load.

"Not too much Stan," cautioned Ron, "let him get used to it first." Stan filled up the skip on the front to about halfway.

"Right," said Ron, "take that down to where you were just workin' and yer mates'll be there to spread it when you unload."

I had never driven anything with four wheels before; it felt good and carried some kudos. I merrily chugged down to the lads and dumped the half skip and returned for more, giving the throttle just a little more this time now that I had the feel of it.

"Fill her up Stan!" I shouted with bravado, and Stan almost filled it to the brim. I made a bad reverse move and slopped a load of it out, but soon turned it round and headed off in the same direction just a little faster than the first trip. Suddenly there was a clank, and the steering wheel was wrenched from my grip as the back wheel hit a huge piece of rubble in the track. This caused the dumper to change direction, and as I panicked, I must have jabbed at the accelerator and the vehicle shot forward straight towards an unmanned trench that contained the upright metal rods which signify the steel fixers' craft. I was heading straight for it. It was time to abandon ship. I swung my left leg over the saddle and in one movement leaped from the machine only to slip on the dry dusty ground and the whole of the back wheel rolled over my left leg that was lying over my right.

It was maybe just a few seconds before the truck crashed into the trench and probably only a moment or two before someone found me lying on the ground, but the pain was immediate. I grabbed a couple of pebbles that were in the dust and just squeezed and pressed them into my palm to distract myself from the agony I felt in my leg. Although I had more experience of accidents than many, I knew there was something wrong. The pain was tempered by a feeling of stupidity as I could see the dumper nose down in the trench with one wheel spinning inanely, and though I told Ron (who had drained off at the sight of me on the ground) that I was all right, he insisted that I lay there till the ambulance arrived.

In a mixture of pain and shame and under the hot June sun, I went into a delirium, one that I have had on several occasions since: I am a first world war soldier in a shell hole in no man's land, and no-one can hear my cries for help.

Although someone was with me the whole time, when you are in pain I think you lock yourself into it to the exclusion of everything in order to cope. I have seen this manifested in others, especially in a woman who is in labour. The ambulance arrived, strangely out of place, so clean and scrubbed in the dust and rubble of the building site, and one of the men gave me a cursory examination. As, like most of the lads, I was wearing shorts and wellington boots turned down, this only took a glance. It was plain to see the wheel track over my calf as the tyre tread was perfectly reproduced on my skin in blues and mauves.

"You'll be all right son, we'll take you in for an X-ray but there's nothing broken."

I nodded with relief and thought at least I'll still be able to get on the road with Gill.

Seven hours later I was still sitting on a wheelchair in my work clothes in the casualty department of dear old Croydon General Hospital. The pain was greater than when the accident had happened, and here it was seven thirty, when a nurse who had been refusing me even an aspirin for the pain came up and breezily asked, "Right now what have you been up to?"

I told her and she told me to take off my wellington but I couldn't so she cut it off with a scalpel. There on the white part of my leg was the bruise where the tyre had gone over.

"Is this where the wheel went over you?" she asked.

"Yes."

"Well nothing seems to be broken, but we'll give you an X-ray and have a look at you. Take your sock off." Unfortunately this was not possible either so she cut it off too. What was revealed underneath it was not too pretty. My ankle was cut in two places although it had stopped bleeding, but it was now bigger than my knee and almost the size of my thigh and a horrible pink purple colour.

"Oh dear," I thought as I looked down at it.

"Oh dear," said the nurse. "That doesn't look so good. Let's get you off to X-ray."

The photo confirmed that the weight of the dumper had snapped the ankle bone where it took the weight of the back end of the vehicle as it was the only part of the leg that was in contact with the ground. Because I was young they had decided not to screw it back in place but would set it under anaesthetic. In six weeks I would be up and able to walk on crutches, and after about sixteen weeks I should be able to do everything I could do before.

"Now you will feel a little prick in the back of your hand." Not half as big a prick as I felt now as I lay there in pain and confusion.

"I want you to start to count backwards from ten," said the surgeon's voice.

"What will I say to Gill?" I wondered. "Ten nine eight seven six..."

I opened my eyes to find myself looking up at four or five people in masks and uniforms. I tried to raise myself up and started to speak but my brain did not properly oblige. However I did sort of sit up, and a man's voice shouted, "What the hell is he doing awake?" Someone forced me back down and placed a mask over my face and the lights faded and I came to again on the way to the ward kissing the hand of the nurse and swearing undying love. She was nice, though old enough to be my mother, and it was she who finally allowed me to have a drink of water. Once more I drifted off to sleep.

When I awoke and looked around me I was at the far end of a ward of about fourteen beds. Next to me was a gentle chap in his sixties. His right leg was in traction, and next to him there was a bloke in similar circumstances. Next to him someone was sleeping, then another leg case and I think someone recovering from an appendectomy. Across the other side was a very old man with cancer; next to him was a Scotsman who spent most of the day moving about the ward and bringing people tea; after him was another youngish fellow with an arm and leg injury, and opposite me there was an empty bed. I was wearing a hospital pyjama jacket and had a crate over my legs to stop the sheets from pressing on me. I had no trousers on and was conscious that the blokes opposite would by now know more about me than my own mother.

My left leg was encased in plaster up to the knee and the pain was excruciating. It was only the sight of the other poor sods that stopped me from bursting into tears, not from the pain so much as the realisation that I would not be going anywhere for a while.

I still had not been washed properly when Gill came to see me that first day. Her concern was obvious as she walked into the ward and hurried towards my bed. It is hard to convince anyone that you are in pain when you look well, and I don't think I have ever looked better or fitter. All winter and spring I had worked out of doors using muscles that had seldom been employed so rigorously. The sun had shone and all of us worked stripped to the waist and in cut off jeans so that all the labourers except some of the Irish lads were now tanned a deep rich brown down to the tops of our turned down boots. I lay there trying my best to look wounded and ill but the first thing she said after asking me how I was and me telling her, was that I looked so well. I showed her my cast and she asked where my trousers were. I had been promised a modesty sheet and we both laughed a bit and I felt so sad and soon her visit was over and she kissed me good-bye and I watched her slim frame in her blue flowered dress leave the ward.

I looked up and noticed that every other pair of eyes in the place had watched her leave too and I knew how lucky I was to have such a beautiful girlfriend and that they were all jealous and I loved her more at that moment than I had done for a long time. She visited every day and so did my friends and family and the sun shone outside of the window and the pain did not diminish and I began to think that they might have done something wrong in setting it. I felt so miserable, but eventually I began to study my fellow patients. I got a drawing book and wrote maudlin little notes to myself and bits of poems, and sketched the other blokes and drew pictures of my own foot.

There are some rituals to hospital life for the bed-bound that tend to strip one's dignity, particularly the morning ablutions. For supplying and removing bedpans, nurses should get immediate access to Paradise. The morning began with being woken, if you had managed to get any sleep amongst the groans, grunts, talking, muttering, screams, shouts, snoring and other sounds of the night, by a nurse with a bowl of water and some soap and towel. This all happened at about eight, after which breakfast would arrive and little Eddie the Scotsman would shuffle round with the papers. This would be followed by the arrival of bedpans to those who called for them, and there was no escape because in the afternoons on doctor's round or Sister's you would always be asked that ominous question, "Have you opened your bowels today?"

Once the pan has been delivered, there is the problem for some as to how to get on the thing unaided, which is further exacerbated if you are in pain. For those same unfortunate souls, there is the assisted dismount, from which there is no escape.

As the screens were drawn around various beds, the true morning chorus began: audible straining grunts and farts echoing into the metallic echo chamber beneath them. Men struggled to retain dignity and balance in equal measure in the knowledge that everything could be heard by everyone else. I resolved then and there never to use one. But to no avail. I was forced to break my resolution on the second day and join the rest in the morning ritual.

There was safety in numbers, and as sure as what goes up must come down, so what goes in must come out. I still had not discovered the joys of food. Helped by what was on offer at hospital, I hardly ate at all, so I was never on the pan very long and soon had the screens pulled and continued reading the paper as the others surrendered their offerings to the wonderful nurses who had to deal with this part of all our days.

My tension was relieved every morning by a loudly-spoken bloke whose bed was second from the end; he was always addressed as Mr. Evans and I never knew his first name. He always called for the pan a good half hour after everyone else. Like Old King Cole he would call for his bowl and with the assistance of two nurses be hoist up on to it behind the screens. The rest of us would be tackling the crosswords when from the second to end bed would emanate the sounds of an elephant greeting the dawn. Sometimes there would be a series of short sharp bursts like rubbing a wet finger on the side of a balloon, on other occasions there would be just a high pitched whistle as his anus imitated the embouchure of a trumpet player trying for a note higher than Maynard Ferguson. If we hadn't known better, we would have said that Mr. Evans was making the noises on purpose to entertain us. When he was finished, the two nurses would arrive to remove him, and the screens would go back. Without a hint of embarrassment, he would wash his hands and pick up his paper and the day would continue.

After a couple of days I still had traces of concrete on my legs, although I had tried to clean myself as best I could. I mentioned this fact to my kindly neighbour and he told me that I would probably have a blanket bath eventually.

I was always asking when I might be able to get out of bed. One afternoon the windows open to let in the warm summer air, two of the young nurses came up to my bed pushing a trolley. They both spoke with West Indian accents and had a delightful way of laughing after almost every statement.

"Well Mr. May, Sister has decided that you have to have a blanket bath and spirit rub down, so please take off your jacket. You can start by washing yourself on the top." She giggled and looked at the other girl. By now I had been given the 'modesty sheet', half a bed sheet that I was supposed to drape over my more private parts to shield them from the eyes that could see me through the tunnel over my legs. I carefully positioned it and removed my pyjama top. The water was warm and it was good to wash and towel myself down.

When I was finished, I handed them the towel and said, "Thank you very much," to which they replied, "You not finished yet, you got to roll over and we do your back."

More little giggles as my neighbour lightly snored beside me. Getting myself in the new position was not as easy as it sounds as my leg still hurt, but somehow I contrived to move my body over whilst attempting to cover my backside with the pathetic modesty sheet.

One of the nurses began to gently wash my back. It was a lovely feeling and very sensual. She seemed to be taking a long time over it and then she pulled down my sheet to expose my white bottom. Both of them giggled at the same time and I could feel myself blushing fiercely. Removing the wretched sheet altogether exposed my legs which were as brown as my torso, so that the effect was that I looked as if I was wearing a pair of white swimming shorts. This amused them even more and while one of them dried me the other one went to bring one of the other girls down. I was beginning to feel a mixture of freak and curiosity as there were now three of them looking at my bottom.

I tried laboriously to turn around when one of them ordered, "Lie still Mr. May, you got to get your spirit rub."

"What for?" I pleaded pathetically.

"So that you don't get any bed sores," the other explained, and one of them gently massaged some medicinal smelling spirit into my back, shoulders, and the top of my behind. Here I was, a fit and virile young nineteen year old, used to intimate relations with his girlfriend but now deprived of such pleasures, being gently massaged by one of three giggly girlish black nurses who were enjoying the effect they knew they were having on me.

"Right, now you can turn over," said the same voice.

"No, I think I'll just lay here for a minute," I said weakly. I was feeling a bit dizzy as the blood left my head and if I had turned over it would have been obvious as to where all the blood had gone.

"Come on now we'll help you," said another voice, and a hand reached for my shoulder.

"No," I cried out, and then more softly, "I'll turn myself round in a couple of minutes." They definitely knew the effect they were having on me. I knew some lads who would have certainly turned round if asked but I was not one of them. I waited several minutes before I felt able to resume my position and several minutes more before my composure returned. The thought that it would be weeks before I could resume normal relations with my girlfriend was depressing, and I wondered if she would mind the leg being in plaster. Well, it was something to look forward to.

Days passed, and then weeks. The pain I had was still great and I had to be reminded that others were suffering too. The old gent next to me had broken his thigh in two places and his shin in one place. He told me that as a boy he had been cycling past Allders department store in Croydon when his front wheel had got stuck in a tram line and he had been knocked off his machine by a tram and his leg received the multiple fractures. Being a young fellow, they had been able to fix him up with only a plate and two screws. I had never heard of screwing bones together and felt sick at the thought of it.

All had gone well until forty years later when he was leaving late from the office after attending to some paperwork. As he called goodnight to the cleaning lady, he slipped on her newly scrubbed floor and fell, popping out both screws and plate in his leg. He had been in hospital for nearly a year and things were not going well.

Each morning he luxuriated in the things he was able to do, like wet-shaving himself and carefully combing his hair. His wife brought in his own pyjamas, and he had more than one dressing gown which he would put on in the evening. He was pale from lack of sunlight and once a month received holy communion from a C of E vicar who did the rounds. We talked of all sorts of things from religion to politics, and though I did not always agree with him, I never really took him on about anything, as I wanted to be his friend. So the apprentice beatnik and the insurance executive became buddies and he talked of stocks and schemes and I talked of travelling.

Mr. Evans had broken his leg spectacularly in four places while out walking his dog, when his foot went down a rabbit hole. Scottish Eddie had been admitted with head injuries from falling in the street after drinking a copious amount. He had lost his false teeth somewhere that night, and although looking suspiciously healthy was able to convince the doctors that he was not ready to be discharged. He was a sweet guy and only too happy to do anything for you. I think he had an alcohol problem, but had weaned himself off whilst inside. Having the few jobs of bringing the tea and papers round had given him a purpose that might have been lacking elsewhere. His conversation was lacking in substance and unintelligible to many in the ward, but I could pass the time of day with him and I sometimes translated for the others.

Next to him was the most ill-looking person I had ever seen who could still talk. He was about forty, with prematurely grey hair and skin the colour of oven paper. Most of the day he lay with his eyes and mouth half open. Shortly before I got out, he was sent home to die with his family, although a month later I saw him in George Street when he should have been dead. I was going to speak but in the end I said nothing, though I see his face still, the clearest of them all.

Men came and went and we just stayed. I remember the first time someone died and there was an empty bed in the morning by the door. I was very shaken by this and realised the nearer to the door they put you, the sooner they expected you to leave. The shortest stay was an old man, who came in quite lucid if a little fearful. As the ward was full, his bed was placed lengthways down the middle of the ward. I could chat to him easily, and helped him with hospital routine. He ordered the *Daily Telegraph* for the first three days, but by the fifth day he was incontinent and placed in huge nappies. By the seventh he was demented, crying and shouting, and by the end of ten days he was dead. I found the loss of reason and dignity more frightening than the prospect of loss of life.

Shortly before I was allowed out of bed for the first time, I awoke from a fretful sleep to see a poor fellow being brought into the ward. It was in the small hours and although he was still under anaesthetic, he was moaning as the nurses fussed around him, wiring him up to some equipment and fitting a plasma bottle to his arm. I later learned that he had been run over by a fairground truck and had his hips smashed. He was in the most complicated traction that any of us had so far seen. As they worked away on him, he was coming to, and they still had one more job to do on him, the insertion of a catheter. I could not see what they were doing but I will never forget his cries as the pain brought him round. I could hear him whimpering for some time after the staff had gone. Eventually I fell asleep.

When I woke in the morning, little Eddie was chatting away to the new bloke, whose name was Jim, and had brought him some tea. He was a gypsy lad and over the next few days he provided a nice contrast to the dear old boy next to me. I don't think he could read or write but every morning he bought a paper, and to find out what was going on he would pick up on a photo illustrating a story and say something like, "Funny about that Princess Margaret."

I would ask, "What do you mean?" and then he would try and deduce what the picture was about to get a handle on the story. I soon figured this little ruse out and so often would start the conversation going from news in my paper, and in this way we would swap stories. If I couldn't work out what he was talking about, I would just say, "I don't think that's in my paper." I would then borrow his and explain what the essence was.

There was also a white West Indian boy from St. Lucia in my ward. I had seen him around the town; he had an accident to his arm that required pins and plates, and when they took it all down and removed the plaster, his arm had mended in a bent position. He freaked and had to be sedated as they had to break it and begin again. It was strange to hear the familiar litany of black curse words coming from his mouth, and his rage was scary. He threw punches at the nurses and succeeded in really hurting one of them before he was restrained.

My first steps out of bed were painful and they did not improve with

447

time. My toes were always deep purple and after just a few steps I had to rest. When I was allowed to leave, the joy was tempered with sadness for my next door neighbour, who was still not out of bed and I think was sorry to see me go. I wrote to him once and got a letter back but I did not try to keep in touch after that. A camaraderie of 'bedfellows' builds up as you all become a team, but you quickly drift back into your old roles and underlined differences once you are free.

I know of no real friendships forged in hospital, although I assume they exist. It is just that we seek reassurance from each other when we are ill, so that together we can beat this thing and overcome our pain; often we complain about the food, or the attitude of those trying to help us, but it is only our determination to survive. We are united in our infirmity and vulnerability and our only way of showing any fight is through complaint. Later we can only marvel at our carers and the compassion, dedication and kindness we have been shown.

∾

reg

I was sixteen weeks on crutches after leaving hospital. The lads on the site had a whip-round and raised enough money for me to buy a cheap tape recorder, with which I made some recordings of my playing. The pain in my leg was still considerable and my toes a perpetual purple, sticking out of the cast. Gill had gone home to visit her family, and I decided to hitchhike down to see her. For some reason I decided to take my new tape recorder as well as my guitar. I felt confident that the sight of a crippled lad standing on the side of the road with these large and cumbersome objects would engender sympathy and kindness, and that I would be in with a chance of breaking my Croydon to Bournemouth record.

Well, I did break the record—it took me nine and three quarter hours to get there, and I was faint with tiredness and pain when I arrived. I stayed the night with Pep and his girlfriend, and I don't recall how we all got back to Croydon.

Once I could operate without sticks, I was invited back to the site and put on light duties, like sweeping. I was terribly weak and although Ron was still there, all of the lads I had worked with had moved on, the craic was missing. Already the air was alluding to autumn, and the drizzle of leaves and the slimy feel of waterproofs added to the gloom.

I was sweeping an area of concrete flooring when there was a cry and a thump. I looked over and a young brickie had fallen through a stairwell on to the floor. He survived the fall, but he was taken off the site.

"You're a fuckin jinx," joked Ron under his breath to me as he passed.

It was all the excuse I needed to leave the job. Bad luck follows you about, and once you get that kind of reputation, all misfortunes will be laid at your door. To be fair to the firm, they advised me to sue and I was awarded £100 compensation for my injury.

After a short time I got a job in the carpet department at Allders department store in Croydon.

I joined the department as a labourer and sometime van boy on deliveries, and once again was surrounded by a peculiar band of dropouts. It shocks me to think that I was one of them.

My boss was a slow old Welshman called Fred. His number two was an old asthmatic called Alf, who could sometimes be persuaded to tap dance in the arcade when we were loading carpets. Alf was a dear old bloke but his chest was awful. He wore a jacket and pullover over a shirt and vest, and in the stifling heat that helps lull shoppers into a trance as salesmen purr at them, the fluff and lint in the air conspired to induce the most awesome hacking.

After a particularly horrendous bout of handkerchief-filling expectoration, he would lean exhausted on the stacks of underfelt with sweat pouring off his forehead and mutter wheezily, "Phew, that's better, now you mind the shop while I go for a little smoke." Off he would totter a little drunkenly, and have a few pulls on a Woodbine to steady himself before coming back in to the store to breathe in more fluff.

There was another strange bloke there, a bit older than me, who used to wear Fair Isle pullovers and clonking leather shoes; he had dreadful teeth but a very posh accent. He was always complimenting me on my strength and telling me I looked like Michelangelo's David. I did not want to disappoint him so I kept my shirt on. Strong I might have been, but I was shamefully skinny. One day I heard him say the same thing to a new bloke and realised that he was queer. Without either of us acknowledging the fact we got on all right, but kept our distance.

The huge broadloom carpets were brought to the front of the store where the lorries parked on the High Street. We had special dollies that we put the rolls on and pushed them back to the store where they were fixed to the giant rollers from which lengths were cut. I must say I delighted in being able to throw these massive weights about, and with some bravado used to fly down the arcade, steering and scooting these massive lengths with some skill if not a little recklessness.

Department stores are like warehouses, in as much as they often house people who are only one step away from institutionalisation. In stockrooms and cubby holes lurk some very odd folk. I soon found some and as usual befriended them, even attempting to drag them down to the Whitgift and include them in my coterie of misfits, strummers, failed philosophers and political extremists.

It's as if in a big department store they are part of a family. There is a canteen and a simple hierarchy. The rules are simple and soon you can set your own agenda: best not to make waves, and no-one will really notice you. There were some very deep thinkers among many that I met in these places. Doing a mundane, undemanding job leaves your mind free to ramble and your thoughts roam in the delicious freedom of dreams.

People often asked me what I was doing with my life working in these places. I tried to explain that I knew what I was doing and that I was enjoying a kind of freedom of the soul. Also, I would like to have had as many jobs as Woody Guthrie. I even managed to get my guitar into work, and I would play round the back of the carpet stacks in my lunch breaks.

Occasionally I was seconded to help with the delivery of a particularly big carpet to the shop where they made up the fitted stuff. These were cut and sewn by a small group of ladies with an earthy sense of humour. I looked forward to these excursions as the old girls seemed to like me. The driver on these trips was Frank. He was from Dorset and had a great accent. When his van boy left I managed to get on the delivery rounds with him. This was terrific, as we went somewhere different every day. We would deliver mattresses and washing machines, carpets and lino, and I would have the map book. I still am tempted to turn the map round to face the direction I am going in, and Frank told me that was what girls did. I tried to read the thing like a man and that was why we ended up taking the long way around.

Frank couldn't read the map either without his glasses, and he could never find them anyway. He showed his displeasure by crashing through the gears of the various old trucks we had to use, and swearing the most incredible oaths at all and sundry. He was always in a state of sexual awareness, commenting constantly on every female on the street, making ribald comments the whole time and fantasising about the women who would open the doors in their night-dresses to welcome us in to deliver their mattresses that they would prevail upon him to try out. These little fantasies would calm him between gear crashings. On the longer journeys out to the suburbs of Croydon he would entertain me with tales of his youthful sexploits. Sometimes he would relish the telling so much that he would take his hands off the steering wheel for a moment and rub them together and utter the sound, "Ooooh..."

Sometimes he could be quite poetic. Once when talking about a particular girl from back in the mists of Dorset time he said, "'er little fanny was as soft as a mouse's earhole." He was big-hearted, bowlegged and bald with twinkling brown eyes. In spite of a slight limp from a dodgy knee he had an earthy spark and the ladies loved him.

Then there was Reg.

Reg was an absolute joy. He was lazy, fat, helpless and smiling. I had never met anyone like him and he fascinated me. He was always courteous and pleasant. His personal security systems were simple but had to be adhered to. Shaving every two days; highly polished shoes; and at tea break he went across the road to Lyons and had a pork pie, which he cut into several slices like a miniature birthday cake. He then smeared one side with English mustard and ate each portion, Oliver Hardy style, with the little finger held out. Whenever I eat a pork pie, I cut it this way and think of Reg.

Reg had suffered a nervous breakdown. This information was a long time coming and although I suspected something was wrong, it took him a while before he confided in me. My natural curiosity insisted on inquiring as to what made him tick, and what a revelation he turned out to be. He was about thirty five years old and rather tubby; his eyes were tiny and twinkling, he had a huge grin and walked in a quick energetic way, which implied more effort than he actually put in. When it was time to go home he donned a short blue raincoat and a small pork pie hat.

Reg liked music in general and was interested in my efforts, but his real love was jazz. His knowledge was extensive. He could name session and sidemen, chapter and verse, so long as the music was recorded after

1938. He favoured big band jazz, especially Duke Ellington, and had been to see Stan Kenton at the old Davis cinema in Croydon, and more recently Dave Brubeck at the Fairfield Halls. He and his brother, who he always referred to as Duke (he pronounced it Dook), went to see every visiting American musician they could, and Reg boasted how a certain bass player wanted to go off with his brother's wife and how they had all become great friends. Whenever he spoke about Americans (his interest spread to movie stars as well) his accent became more and more western until he sounded like a player from a cowboy film. I was careful not to take the piss but I did point it out to him eventually, by which time I had gained his confidence and he told me this story.

"I've always been a little overweight and as a result I had trouble with girls. Not talking to them, I never had trouble talking to them, but getting them close they always ran off like. My brother Dook was better looking than me but he wasn't so good at talking to them like I was if you understand my meaning. So we sort of became a double act, he usually got the best girls but at least I got a girl sometimes." He chuckled at the thought, his eyes flickering from side to side and only occasionally fixing on me.

"We would mostly work the weekends and bank holidays in the summers after I'd come out of the 'merchant'. What we used to do was to pretend to be Yanks. It was easy, I brought back a few suits from the States, big ties and them shiny black shoes that all the tourists have."

I knew what he meant; growing up after the war we became aware of these strangely garbed colourful people in powder blue suits and crew-cuts, their wives bedecked with huge sunglasses and accompanied by shrill voices with which they shrieked and bellowed at each other at close range. Draped with cameras and shoulder bags they trooped around London tipping cab drivers and photographing everything. Though hugely benevolent, they were still a bit resented from the war, when they were regarded as 'oversexed, overpaid and over here,' and I suspect there was the dawning realisation that in spite of Britain's enormous sacrifice, Blitz spirit and stoicism, we would not have won without them. Still we were happy to take their money, sell them Nelson's Column and Tower Bridge and were often bemused by their naïvety.

Reg and Dook turned that all around with their little subterfuge. Dressed up to the nines in powder blue and bright checked sports jackets, they cruised the sights where they knew the US visitors would be expected to be seen. Both sporting huge cameras (usually without film in them), dazzling, flat topped and gum chewing, they would engage young girls in conversation about everything and nothing in a loud mid-Atlantic drawl. By Reg's account it was flawless and foolproof.

In the early fifties before rock'n'roll, Britain was suffering all the benefits of a defeated nation: rationing, poor housing, shortages, grey buildings, grey skies, homes painted in browns and creams and kitchens in dark greens. Summers were yearned for whilst the melancholy of autumn tried to prepare us for winters that were cold, foggy and damp. The comedy shows on the radio helped to prop up spirits in the wartime manner of 'we can take it', but spring brought blessed relief as the daffodils and the Yanks arrived and colour was added to the monochrome. Reg and Dook must have looked like they had arrived from another planet.

"We'd stand outside Buckingham Palace like, and when we saw a couple of sorts who looked likely I would walk up to them and say something like, 'Say Miss, can you tell me who lives here?' and they might say, 'Why the King, of course,' and Dook might say, 'The King of England? You don't say. Hey Brad (that was my nickname) is that him looking out of the window?' and we'd all look up and Dook would pretend to take a photo or something and the girl might say, 'Don't be silly, he doesn't look out of the window,' and I might say, 'I thought I saw someone wearing a crown sweeping the steps earlier,' and one of them might laugh ("if you get them laughing you're on your way," Reg confided). Then Dook might ask something stupid like, 'Why do the guards wear those great big hats and what are they called?' And so on. It's good to ask questions that they would know the answers to, that way they think they're helping you and then the killer one is once you got them laughing, Dook would ask them to take a photo and hand them this camera and they wouldn't have a clue how to work it and then you can get close to them and help them to work it and stand behind them and lean over their shoulders and smell their perfume and their hair..."

At this point he trailed off and his eyes went glazed. Then with a shake of his head he came back to earth and chuckled, "And there you go!"

I stood staring at the little fat man in front of me, impressed by his elaborate subterfuge and preparation. To look at him now, his confidence shot, living at home with Mum and hardly venturing out. This man had been in the merchant navy, learned sophisticated manners as a steward and developed a taste for good films and jazz; now here he was, a porter in a department store, and this is where he would remain, ambition shot and insecure.

Could he have made all this up? I doubted it, and later he even produced a dog-eared photo of him and his brother fully attired as Americans in London to prove it. Taken in Leicester Square with Eros appropriately at their backs, it showed the two Croydon boys grinning from ear to ear with a couple of pretty girls on each side of them.

"They was from Yorkshire them two," said Reg distantly.

"Have you got any other pictures of girls you pulled?" I wanted to know.

"No," said Reg, "but they're all stored up here." He pointed to his head and one of his eyes produced a small tear which he brushed away immediately. I pretended not to notice.

"Do you ever get up West any more?" I asked after a while.

"My old stomping ground? No, only when I've saved up a bit, I sometimes go up for a brass," and his look signified that there were to be no more questions on this subject.

I persuaded him to come down to the Whitgift pub once or twice, and some years later when I met the Dook he told me that Reg had enjoyed these days but that he had been poorly of late and hardly went out at all any more.

Even the delivery men at Allders were characters. Quite early on, an old style three-wheeled Scammel British Rail tractor and trailer pulled up and the driver checked in to the carpet department to get us to come and unload. He was a bit odd-looking but not wild; he wore an old-fashioned train driver's hat and a waistcoat and seemed very old to me. He was probably in his mid-forties. He was either prematurely bald or else he shaved his head and eyebrows; perhaps he had been ill. We followed him out to the street and he began a running patter that he must have routined dozens of times before.

"Do you believe we have been visited from outer space?" he began. Reg said, "Oh sure."

"What about you?" he directed at me.

"I'm not sure," I responded cautiously.

"I can't see how anyone could doubt it," he went on. "Of course there is a conspiracy of silence—the Yanks have got dead aliens locked up in freezers over there. There have been loads of sightings."

"Have you seen one?" asked Reg.

"No, but there are lots of things I haven't seen but I believe they exist," he said. "Like, do you believe there's a God?"

"Yes," said Reg.

"Well have you seen him?" asked the driver.

"No," said Reg (at this point I was glad he didn't ask me because of course I had seen God, but I doubt if our descriptions of him would have tallied).

"Well that's my point," insisted the driver. "I mean Jesus was a Venusian."

"What?" said Reg.

"He was from Venus," the driver said, warming to his theme. "You see all the world's great leaders come from outer space. Julius Caesar was a Martian, so was Alexander the Great. Mahatma Ghandi, he was a Venusian as well. I mean look at your bible, it's full of stories about visitors from outer space." Reg looked blank, but then he so often did.

"Take Ezekiel and the whirling wheel," he continued, "that was obviously a flying saucer." I remembered the story of Ezekiel and Woody had sung a song about it too. I said nothing.

"Moses was a Venusian as well. The Venusians had begun to colonise the earth and they designed the pyramids and they were going to guide us to better ways but they had an emergency back home and had to leave a few representatives here. Every now and then they return and bring us another leader to stop us killing ourselves and destroying the planet."

I was intrigued. I pushed the first great broadloom back to the store. When I got back to the truck he was still in full flow. Reg had climbed up on to the tailboard of the lorry and was listening intently (and resting at the same time).

"Take the three wise men, they knew that a great leader was going to be delivered to the world and they followed the space ship for days. It wasn't a star in the east it was a bleedin' flying saucer come to deliver the baby to Mary. No wonder the shepherds were scared. Bloody great space ship coming from outer space and frightening the sheep and all that."

"How can you tell a Martian from a Venusian?" Reg wanted to know.

"Your Venusian has a slightly higher forehead," the driver explained patiently.

I glanced at Reg and his receding hairline and just for a moment I wondered... no no, not Reg, although he might well have come from *somewhere* out in space. We hoisted the last broadloom on to the trolley and our ufologist hoisted up the tailgate.

"Keep your eyes on the skies," he advised, and we nodded and manoeuvred the heavy carpet up in the direction of the arcade.

"I think he was a bleedin' Martian," said Reg.

Gill had by now been working at Allders for a while. She had to wear a lilac-coloured uniform and wear her hair up. I thought she looked prettier with it down because this made her face seem smaller.

She was on her own on the counter and she was getting more and more unhappy. I am sure I was mostly to blame, as the feelings of freedom and possible adventure began to stir in me again. The spark between us had diminished and we talked of ways of restarting our adventure. Through a friend, she had heard about an opportunity to get to America, and Gill resolved to get a job there.

Within days, it seemed to me, she had found work as a children's nanny in Los Angeles. I failed to get the significance of this job at the time, and before I could take it all in Gill was off and I was on my own.

As soon as she had arrived in America I realised how deeply I loved her, but by now it was too late to get her back, and the deep ache I felt was only slightly alleviated by the letters she wrote to me twice weekly. All those soppy songs about waiting in agony for the postman now came to have tremendous significance. I know we had both been irresponsible in our relationship, but we were young and constantly in need to express our love physically (well, I certainly was: once we sent away for a trial contraceptive pill, but I became too impatient to wait the prescribed time for it to take effect and we both got the giggles and did it anyway). I realised the main part of the blame was mine and I determined to either get to the US as soon as I could, or to at least stay faithful to her until she was ready to return. I managed neither.

Gill seemed to settle in with her new family straight away and soon became very close to the two little girls that were her charges. The young couple who employed her were kind and considerate. Gill began to renew her confidence and I wrote long letters of longing for her to return. Gill did not respond to these entreaties and I applied for my American visa to go and meet her in California. One of the questions asked if my purpose for coming to America was to assassinate the president. After what seemed an age the visa was granted, but I was told that I would not be allowed to work. So, daunted once again, I continued the correspondence of hope for her return.

Although it surprised my mum when Gill left, I think she was relieved. She had guessed the depth of our relationship, and knew me well enough to know that I was a very long way from being ready to settle down, especially as a young father as well as a husband, but she said nothing.

∾

amaranthus caudatus

It's not my arms, but my heart that aches.
Cradling this burden
Of emptiness.
Your look that said that
"This was done for us
This was meant to be."
That meeting, the concern that was
For you and me.

The neap tide that washed away
Our sand written future
With the turn of a wave
And hurled us with our makeshift plans
Into the undertow
And beached us on to separate shores.

I was always looking out to sea
Did you see it coming
At what cost, and what price?
For your decision and my backing.
And to show for it?
Nothing.
An emptiness, a crushing weight.
No towel round your shoulders
No shawl of comfort.

I wonder now
With the gap of time
If you were persuaded by our drifting?
Neither of us ready,
And even if you were, and I not,
We were not ready, us.
What we had made together, once destroyed
Would leave no claim from one
Upon the other;
Father, Mother.

No-one blames the honey bee
Lost in nectared ecstasy
For bringing pollen to the need
Of flower to gestate fruit or seed

He impregnates through innocence
Not by divine providence
Seduced by colour, movement, scent
It is design not accident

Who could deny the natural power
The wiles and ruses of the flower
To summon when and as they please
Helping intermediaries

And sometimes in their common names
We see reflected joy and pain
As if perceived humanity
Co-exists with mystery

By memory of old flames cheered
Jack by the Hedge, Old Man's Beard
Humour used against our fears
Love in a Mist and *Solomon's Tears*

Alice Sit by the Fire we're told
The warmest name for Marigold
Whilst *Crown of Thorns* and no *Heart's Ease*
Suits random dismal days like these

When petals blow across a lawn
Heaped in little drifts forlorn
No wicked truth or holy lies
Or mitigating alibis

For touch and reflex, fusion's spark
The bruised and fallen fruit is marked
Where autumn's drunken wasps are feeding
Spring's memory slowly receding
A dying sting for the unheeding
Forget-me-not, while
Love Lies Bleeding.

∾

harmony

Absence is always made harder when you wait for letters. If someone just goes away or you part under a cloud you just have to live with it, and eventually a day passes when you don't think about the one you are missing. Our situation was not like that; every day would start off with anticipation of some news, and if a letter had arrived, I would always feel there was not enough information. I would trawl each line for any indication of diminishing affection, and delve between the lines for a sign that there might be someone else. The pain of that doubt was so destructive. As a young man used to a full relationship, there was also the absence of sex; and as we had promised to stay faithful to each other, I took refuge in the Whitgift Arms.

Gill's letters were all about LA and the little girls that she was looking after and the young couple who were paying her wages. She missed me, she said, and indeed I missed her terribly. I poured out my heart in letters that I hope Gill destroyed: yards of soppy love letters full of doubt, insecurity and promises that I would be more understanding and would she please come back. This was all in the first two weeks.

As the weeks became months, my aching grew and I turned increasingly to drink for the sweet comfort of melancholy, and whilst sober felt lost, cowardly and miserable. Henry, my old friend, was a great comfort to me during this time and we often went out together in the old car that his Dad had taught him to drive in.

The pattern was established and gradually her letters spread out into the wider world of California. Her circle of friends grew and she mentioned some crazy girls who said things like "Far out" and "Out of sight". I thought to myself that it sounded a bit stupid, but before long we were using the same terms in England. It's funny how kids' slang changes. Our mob used a form of New York jazz slang mixed with more obscure cockney rhyming and other bits of patois from the street. A guitar was an axe; everyone was "man"; if someone was a good harp (mouth organ) player, his description might be, "He's terrible on the gob iron!" She still said she missed me and sent all her love.

My guitar and the admiration and encouragement of friends was a real stick to lean on during this time. I became bonded to my guitar in the way of a child with its comfort blanket; I doodled and played constantly and my fingers became calloused and strong in a way that has seldom been repeated. I often dragged the box into work or down the pub, shyly eager to share my new tunes with a few friends.

My obsession with the guitar had helped to introduce me to lots of other music lovers, and players too. Apart from Max there was Chris Ayliffe, Buck Polly and Pete Brown, and Little Chris Alldous, who accompanied Jacqui McShee (he was probably one of the best guitarists in our little circle) and could already penetrate the intricacies of the playing of Fuller and Broonzy. Jo-Ann Kelly had begun to play too, and her marvellously uninhibited voice was already showing the depth of tone and commitment that is thankfully preserved on record. Her brother Dave was also playing, and he too was blessed with a great blues voice from somewhere on the River Wandle delta.

Then there were the record buyers. I am grateful to Mick Hubbard ('M.B.') who lent me records and introduced me to other blues players and as this music filtered into our culture I was able to avail myself of dozens of LPs, which were avidly listened to on my Dansette, soon to be replaced by an Ultra.

"Listen to that bass," I would enthuse, as some thirties recording was played at maximum volume through the mighty six-inch elliptical speaker. One great record loaned to me by one of my brother Bruce's friends was called 'The Rural Blues', compiled by Sam Charters. All the songs were great, but one in particular leaped out at me: *Statesboro Blues* by Blind Willie McTell. The impact of this track on me was as great as Jack Elliott's *San Francisco Bay Blues* had been. The clear beautiful voice and intriguing lyric pulled me deeper into the tune, but above all it was the sound of that twelve-string guitar. I had to have a twelve! I found one advertised in the Melody Maker at Pan Music Studios in Wardour Street. It was another Harmony Sovereign and it was a bastard to play. All these extra strings and a high action, but it sounded wonderful to me. With my ear pressed up against the sides it sounded like an orchestra.

Once more I was in love. I played it until my fingers all but bled. The first tune I learned on it was *The Bells Of Rhymney*. I had heard Pete Seeger play this magnificent song somewhere, and I thought it the best British protest song I had ever heard for the miner. It uses a beguiling nursery rhyme format as the bells toll out their message. It was a poem written by a Welsh schoolmaster called Idris Davies, and underlined for me the importance of getting the lyric as near to a poem as possible before you add the tune, if indeed that is the order in which the components come. Seeger's tune remains I think his best, and the fact that he tuned the bass string down to D gave the whole song an unequalled majesty. I soon learned to play it and discovered that this was the same tuning that Blind Willie had used for *Statesboro Blues*. I was on my way.

Previously I had heard Buck Polly play his monster twelve string, and when he died from a heroin overdose, my friend Chris Ayliffe inherited his guitar and taught me the clawhammer lick (even the names of American guitar styles are cool). This opened up all sorts of possibilities for me. Soon I could make a passable stab at *Statesboro Blues*, and was beginning to get a minor rep as a picker. What a confidence booster this was, and some tiny compensation for the emptiness I felt in Gill's absence. So many songs seem to articulate my feelings, and I guess by standards set by a lot of the blokes that were playing, some of my preferences would have been considered soft. Because I could play fingerstyle and some blues tunes, and because at one time my right hand flat-picking was as fast as a bee's wing, I was judged OK with the chaps. Back home, though, I played Guy Carawan's adaptation of *I Love My Baby (and she's bound to love me some)* and I truly hoped that she did.

And the flimsy aerogramme letters kept arriving regularly from the

States and were eagerly opened with trembling hands. Sometimes longer letters arrived with accounts of people that she had met, but all I really needed was the signing off that she still loved me, because all the other news just made me ache. The shadow of the gasholder was over me; I relieved the pain of separation with music and cider, and tortured myself with thoughts of Gill falling for another.

The evenings in the Whitgift were now vital and I always drank too much. It was easy to get a bit of dope and I took to smoking it, only after a skinful the effects of this were fairly awful and I frequently experienced the 'swirling pit' sensation before passing out in some place or other. Some of our mates could be sick at will but ever since the times I was force fed at the nursery school and vomited when the spoon touched the back of my throat, I have had a dread of being sick. No, I always processed my alcohol and as a result built up quite a tolerance to it.

Bob Dylan's second album arrived, and already some of my mates who had disliked him from the first album were positively damning on this one. Commercial, sold out, crap, were just a few of the expressions used. I did not buy any of this, but I also did not buy the album. I loved his white boy interpretations of *Corrine Corrine* and the way he helped himself to old blues lyrics. He had adopted an Okie accent and talked and sang like some hillbilly and not a middle class boy from the mid-west. At the time I knew none of this and there was great cause for optimism through Bob's music. I could already play guitar better than him and I could certainly play the gob iron better. Now there were proper harmonica harnesses available and I guess there it ended.

I always loved Bob's voice. There was an energy and commitment to the interpretation of his own lyrics, and his vocal range is astounding as he can seamlessly soar from tenor to near falsetto with no crack in the voice as it moves from man to boy. Later on he astounded me with his baritone, and even in the hacked out rasp of recent albums there is a quality unequalled by any other singer. There are hundreds of singers now who have adopted his style based more on Jack Elliott than Woody Guthrie, but essentially Dylan invented modern rock singing and enabled a large number of people who cannot sing to make it, by adopting one or other of his styles.

Then there was the songwriting. I was already captivated by *Song to Woody* from his first album, which I would love to have written. Bob cleverly laced Woody's own words into a song of dedication. This could have been viewed as theft by some but in Bob's case it was respect and humility at source and the effect was profoundly moving to those who loved Woody's work and were growing to love Bob. Then there was *Girl From the North Country*. I was told that he had got the tune from Martin Carthy, but this is only half true. Sure it does have an English format to it, but it was the ambiguity of the chords around it and the straight declaration of the sentiment that bowled me over. It was of course about Gill. How did he know? How could he have understood every thought and doubt, each regret and uncertainty. How did he know her hair hung long? True, the rivers seldom freeze in California but I was prepared to overlook that. This was my song; I learned it straight away. Lots of other people learned it too and it seemed everyone played it slightly differently. However I was the only one I knew who did have a girl 'in a north country fair'—well, west actually, but the song was certainly the most powerful in my growing repertoire.

Other guitarists liked the contribution the sound of the twelve gave to their guitars, and I was often found playing guitar with other pickers. One of these was Eddie Parsloe, who had taken over Tubs' room at the Olive Tree (and, he alleges, some of Tubs' other diversions as well). He was singing with Jacqui McShee's sister, Pamela. She was slightly older than Jacqui and had an almost identical voice. I first heard them sing together at the Olive Tree, and they sang in unison with indistinguishable tonality. Pam was very pretty, with huge brown eyes, and quite one of the most gentle people I have ever met.

Soon the three of us were playing and singing together, and we even got a few gigs. Each Wednesday Pam would travel over from Merstham, and we would practice a repertoire that was more folky than bluesy, but nevertheless very enjoyable. Those evenings were a marker in my week, and it was also a night that I did not end up down at the Whitgift.

When Pam got married, Eddie and I motorbiked down to the church and formed a scruffy honour guard outside with our guitars, as she and her husband emerged. My Levis were a near-perfect washed-out blue, but they had also aged, and in getting on the bike they ripped from seam to seam at the knee. In the surviving photo you can clearly see a huge safety pin holding the trouser leg together.

One day Henry said to me, "Why don't you make a record?"

"Eh?" I responded.

"You can make a record at RG Jones Studio in Morden for ten quid. Little Chris has already made one."

Henry went on to explain that you simply went to the studio and they recorded up to four songs and then after about a week you got a record in the post. This sounded so exciting to me. Was I ready to record and more importantly did I deserve to record? We used to look at records as a sort of medal of musical achievement back then. Maybe I could send one to Gill and she would hear in my voice how much I missed her; maybe she would love me more. I resolved to make a recording. It was simplicity itself. They put two mikes in front of me and I recorded *I Love My Baby (and she's bound to love me some)*. I went into the control booth to listen. They played it back through their big speakers and added a little reverb.

I was so excited. I went out and recorded *Drybone Rag* as an instrumental and then *Girl From the North Country*. I finished up with *Bells of Rhymney* on the twelve and went in and had them play it all back to me. Christ it sounded all right. Of course I could not take the recordings home, but I was definitely encouraged by the sound I was making. A few days passed and then a small parcel arrived and inside were two single sized acetate EPs. I stuck one straight on the Dansette and out I came. It sounded nothing like as powerful as it did in the studio, but I was fascinated and called up Henry who came over and listened. He said little but grinned a lot at my obvious pleasure. I played it to Mum and Bruce and anyone who came by, and of course sent the other copy to Gill.

She wrote back as soon as it arrived. She made me feel so good about it. She still loved me, she said, and was so proud of me. I should have been very happy but there was a growing dilemma. Here was I promising to be true, and everywhere there were beautiful girls.

In our own little group I was aware that I would not have had to make much effort to have enjoyed female company, but to be honest I had that anyway. It was difficult to go without the sexual side of a relationship once you had become used to it. I drank enough in the evenings to lose my inhibitions, and by the reactions of some of the girls around in the company, I was able to guess who might be available. There was some sympathy with my condition from several of our girlfriends. I almost blew it on a number of occasions but I did remain faithful.

There were parties that we gatecrashed and this gave me more opportunities to get smashed and make passes that were never reciprocated. There seemed to be at least one every weekend. I don't know how we found out about them, but we ranged all over the place in a twenty mile radius and met all kinds of people who seemed to tolerate our raggedy appearance and bottles of rough cider.

I was still working at the store and it was full of pretty sales girls. One of them more striking than the rest. She was going out with a bloke from my old school who was a carpet salesman (from behind the broadlooms I would watch him and the other salesmen strutting about and a certain smugness used to creep up on me—this was their career, they were trapped, and soon I would be off on some other adventure). I did not have much to do with him. He was a little bloke and dangerous. He drove a Triumph 650 Bonneville with clip-on handlebars very fast, and was utterly fearless. He had fallen out with this girl and in the way that these things happen, the canteen rumours made it plain that she liked me. She was very attractive, and eventually I asked her out to the pictures.

She had a soft lisp and beautiful brown eyes. She was very gentle and sweet, and things could easily have gone further but there was nothing else there. She had nothing to talk about and no opinions on anything. She just faded out of the scene, and I don't even remember saying goodbye; she just seemed to disappear in front of me. All the other blokes thought I was mad to let the best girl in the place slip from my hands. I had no regrets. It was strange to be free of all the responsibility of a monogamous relationship and be unable to enjoy the freedom.

Around this time I was invited to join a great band who went under the name of the Hickory Nuts. They were three young, talented musicians from Dulwich, and I think they saved me from drowning in melancholy. We hit it off from the start and our rehearsals and get-togethers were bonded by laughter. I was never really sure about the politics of blue-grass music. I loved old-timey music, but bluegrass had the stigma of redneck right-wing connotations. My doubts were rapidly dispersed by these guys, who just loved the sound of clanking banjos and mandolins. Pete Chalkley was the leader on banjo, Ray Tassey played breathtaking mandolin, and Mick Lewis played the double bass. The boys had decided to go fully pro and had all abandoned their day jobs. They had clubbed together and with their entire savings had bought a brand new Morris

J2 van. A national tour was booked and we started to ramble. After two or three gigs which went down brilliantly, it was obvious that the agent was bent as we never got any money from the venues. We finished up in Birmingham busking in the Bullring to get enough money to buy our petrol back home.

We played a gig at the Accrington Stanley Supporters Club. It was a Wednesday and both supporters, enthusiastically playing the one-armed bandit and steadfastly ignoring the band. Within 45 minutes we had exhausted our repertoire, so I did a few tunes on my own. After an interval we played our whole set through again and no-one noticed the join.

Some time during the evening some other folks had dropped in and we were invited back to a pretty girl's house somewhere in the town. The streets were cobbled and the houses built with huge square pieces of brick made to look like stone. It was drizzling and the gas lamps threw muted reflections across the distorted surfaces of the streets. Somehow the girl and I dropped back from the others as we walked towards her house.

"You'll have to be quiet in case you wake me dad," she cautioned.

As she unlocked her front door I relayed the message to the rest of the lads. We walked into a two up two down, back to back cotton town house and immediately Pete and Mick almost blew it as they pointed at the wallpaper. It was imitation brick over real brick. I thought this a bit snobbish of them but I had to stifle laughter as well. The girl put her finger to her lips signalling us to be quiet whilst she went to the kitchen and put the kettle on. We tried to talk in low whispers and not to keep laughing.

Suddenly a voice boomed out from upstairs, "'ave you got someone down there Mary?"

"No Dad," said Mary, bringing in a tray with cups of instant coffee into the room. "I'm just 'avin' a coffee meself and then I'm goin' to bed."

"Right then. Don't be long," said dad.

More restrained laughter, then from above our heads we heard the sound of someone getting out of bed and the pling of elderly bedsprings. We all fell silent and looked at each other. Was he coming downstairs to check on Mary's honesty? We heard the footsteps across the room and the door open at the top of the stairs. All five of us were frozen in that moment when the silence was broken by the sound of a heavy tap being turned on and run into an amplified bath tub. We looked towards our hostess.

"Me dad's 'avin' a pee," she mouthed at us. The loo being outside, the old man was relieving himself into a bucket at the top of the stairs. Coffee cups jangled and spare hands were clapped over mouths as her dad enjoyed the longest pee in the history of the world.

At length there was a muttered, "You 'urry up and get to bed," and the footsteps returned to the plinky bedspring over our heads. It was no good, we couldn't stay; we were all nearly out of control. Leaving our coffees, we left as quietly as we could and ran down the road where we let out an explosion of suppressed laughter. I looked back up the road to see Mary under the gas lamp. She gave a little wave and we found our way back to the van.

∿

olaf

Hey man, what's happening? Why don't you come out to Italy, I'm high and stoned on grass at the moment. I am writing this to you from Genova. Come on out and we can make some music.

Love, Olaf

The address was 'Poste Restante Genova' and the writing scrawled by a stoned hand. I turned it over to see if there was any other information on the missive but that was all it said.

I turned over the short letter again and read the garbled message. How really uncool to tell me that he was stoned, I thought to myself. Did I really want to see this bigheaded bloke again? What had I got to lose, stuck in Croydon, with my girl in the States and a boring job? I handed in my notice and left the next day for France.

It was summer and once again the enforced solitude of the road gave me time for dark thoughts of how I could have let Gill and me drift apart. As usual my progress was pitifully slow, and in order to make some progress I took lifts in directions that were not exactly where I wanted to go. At least they were vaguely south, and I was at any rate on the move.

Over the two or three nights I slept out on the road a kind of acceptance crept over me and I fell asleep to the sound of rustling grasses and chirping insects, staring at the stars and dopily wondering what it was all about. I was terrible company for whoever picked me up. For a start my French was appalling. Expounding my 'philosophy' proved difficult for I had great problems explaining why, if I was headed to Genoa, I had arrived in the direction of Spain. Usually though, I was so tired from hanging about that within a few minutes, the rocking of the car or truck sent me off into deep and undignified sleep. I would frequently wake up with my head bouncing off the door window, mouth wide open and arms flailing, having been lost in a dream that we were hurtling into a brick wall.

As my terrified driver glanced over at me I would grin sheepishly, at the same time checking that I had no dribble down my chin, and as cheerfully as I could explain, *"Une rêve. Je rêve, je m'excuse."*

Once I actually slapped a driver on the ear and though he said it was all right, he told me that he was turning off the road and put me out only to continue in the direction I wanted to go. I couldn't blame him in all fairness.

This irregular sleeping meant that at night I was quite often awake and several times hitched through the night. One night, way off track I was in a huge *camion* and a huge moon low in the sky lit up the trees and bushes as we trundled happily through the countryside. As we slowed down to enter a small village, I saw in the truck's headlights what appeared to be a chicken sat in the middle of the road. I drew the driver's attention to it but he had already seen it and slowed down. We must have been nearly on top of it when the creature suddenly leaped up and hopped down the road in front of us. It was the biggest toad I have ever seen and once again I was reminded by this alien creature just how far away from home I was. Eventually after a few metres, the driver passed over it, between the wheels and as I looked back I could clearly see the creature still in the middle of the road until the next truck came by.

Over the next couple of days, I zigzagged my way in the approximate direction of Italy.

Somewhere still in France in the early evening by the side of a quiet country road, I had begun to look for a suitable place to sleep for the night when a 2CV pulled up. It was driven by a smart little bloke wearing white socks and beige leather shoes, pale trousers and a yellow sweater. As I gratefully jumped in he grinned at my enthusiasm. He asked me where I was going and when I explained that my eventual destination was Italy, he shrugged and mentioned a place that I had seen on a signpost which I knew was in the right direction. Off we lurched and as we drove, I realised that he was glancing at me over his shoulder. I also noticed that he had a ring with a jewel in it. This is not a bit unusual today but at that time it usually indicated a slightly effeminate man.

I remember an old guy that used to cruise the London to Brighton road looking for boys. His name was Wally, and when I told some friends of my meeting him, they all knew him and said what a nice bloke he was. One of my mates had even let him buy him a dinner and no favours asked. Once you had explained that you were not that way, he was fine. He still enjoyed the company of young men, but never tried anything on. On several occasions I'd got lifts with blokes looking for more than just company, and my usual way of dealing with unwanted attention was just to ask them to pull over and let me out, and that was all there was to it.

"*Quel age avez vous?*" he wanted to know. I told him.

"*Si jeune!*" he exclaimed, slapping himself gently on his right cheek. "*Vous n'avez pas peur sur les chemins?*"

"*Non, pourquoi j'ai peur?*" I responded with bravado that I should know the meaning of fear, and I lowered my voice to an even more manly tone to indicate my lack of gayness.

"*Pourquois, alors les voleurs, bandits ou peut-être homosexuels!*" At this last word he turned and looked directly at me so that the car started to head for the other side before he corrected it with a quick "*Ooh la la.*"

I searched in vain for the words to indicate that I would be able to take care of all eventualities because I was strong and aggressive and a great and fearless fighter but I think it came out as, "*Je lui donne un coup de pied,*" and for emphasis, I slammed my fist into my hand with a crack that surprised us both.

My driver muttered something I couldn't understand but added "*si jeune*" once more before pulling up by the side of the road and telling me that this was as far as he was going. I'd only been in the car for a few minutes and he had stopped about a mile from the town in front of us. He then proceeded to drive off into the town that I was now obliged to walk through. Any hitchhiker will tell you that you can never get a lift before a town, you just have to walk through and out the other side.

However much I cursed that bastard, it was a lesson well learned, and next time I would keep them sweet at least until we got out the other side.

I walked right through the town and paused only for a coffee and some cigarettes. As long as I had a cigarette I was OK. That evening I slept all the way to Switzerland in the cab of a giant truck driven by a German who was surprised that I was English; he said that he thought by my colouring that I must be Spanish. I was pleased to be taken as exotically foreign, and by now my skin was quite tanned from all the standing around I had done. I can remember walking through Geneva and admiring the lake and by now being almost completely broke not daring to spend my last few coins, that were French in any case. I could not believe the price of everything, and entered and left that country without spending any money. It was still not possible for me to contemplate playing guitar for money; I was still too scared.

At last I arrived in Italy and immediately became aware of a lighter mood. I was able to order coffee in fluent Italian: *"Due cappucinni prego?"*

When two coffees arrived, I was too embarrassed to send one back. Another reminder that Gill wasn't with me, so I drank them both. The weather had turned a little sour and it was cloudy with a warm drizzle. I was close to my destination and refused to let my spirit be dampened. By the time I had rambled into Genoa I had been travelling for a week. I was in serious need of a bath, or at least a clean pair of socks.

The hostel in Genoa had been a fine old house and was now full of boring kids who seemed to me to be so young: Germans who went to bed early and got up early, and one or two squeaky-clean American hitchhikers who were out of my class as they had enough money to get across the Atlantic to start with, so as far as I was concerned they must have been rolling in wealth. That evening, tired and hungry, I swallowed down the spaghetti and asked about my old acquaintance. By now it had crossed my mind that he might well have moved on; he certainly did not know that I had left home yet. To my relief I was told I would find him in the garden and sure enough there he sat with a few people around him. He was strumming a twelve string guitar and he had the chord changes made correctly. I was impressed.

"Hello man," I said as coolly as I could, "How's it going?

He looked round and stared at me I could see he had been smoking.

"Rolf!" he burst out after a while. "You made it man, hey what's happening"?

"Nothing's happening, I just decided to come out and see you."

"Shit man I'm so stoned I have to think for a minute, you came out. Far out man, far out. Hey do you want a smoke it's good grass."

It seemed churlish to refuse and we smoked a small joint out of sight of the rest of them.

"Where's your axe man?" he suddenly panicked. "Surely you brought your guitar!"

"Yeah I got my guitar," I told him.

"Get it man, let's play some music, hey this is great, you came, you really fucking came. I can't believe you came to fucking Italy man, far fucking out!"

At this point I had started to feel pretty cool myself, after all I had done precisely that. We played and he was OK, not great but the chords were right and as always the twelve-string hides your inadequacies. My old Harmony was as loud or louder than the twelve, so I could still lead. After a while I looked up to see that we had acquired a few admirers and we basked for a while in the glow until the curfew came and we had to retire. I fell asleep quickly and the next day we hit the streets of Genova big time.

After breakfast of milky coffee and cigarette, the two of us ambled out into the sunshine. I was down to my last smokes and we stopped at a Tabaco shop and I bought a soft pack of Nazionales. I lit one up and began to take in my surroundings. Olaf knew the routes into town and he had money for the tram fare. I was rested, and felt so positive about what we were about to do that it was only when I opened my guitar bag to pull the instrument out that the full realisation hit me. I think we were back in the dock area somewhere and there were people walking about. We started playing in front of an open guitar case, and after just a few seconds people started to throw small coins into it. After a few tunes (all the tunes he knew actually) Olaf stopped playing and bent down to collect the change. I finished off and the group of people who were listening gave a little applause and dispersed. In a small café Olaf counted out the change.

"Man we are rich!" he informed me, and in fact we had earned enough to buy our dinner already. I grinned with satisfaction. That night we went out again and made enough to pay for our rent and we drank a little bottle of wine and some grappa that Olaf insisted was the right thing to do. It tasted like cleaning fluid and the next day I felt as ill as I'd ever been.

~

disharmony

Always frugal, I soon had more money from my busking than I'd left home with—about £10. With affluence came confidence, and soon the attractions of Genoa began to pale and the desire to move on took over. We decided to visit Pisa. After an attempt to hitch together, we abandoned this method in favour of solo travel. My normal skill at the art continued and I arrived a day after Olaf. I can clearly recall, as I set out, that feeling of anticipation mixed with excitement at the prospect of playing music, because it is still with me. The petty anxieties of arriving in time for the gig and the wonder that people enjoy what you do sufficiently to pay you for the thing that gives you pleasure. It is a rare privilege.

Pisa was as magical to me as it must be to all who see it for the first time. I stood staring at the tower for a long time. It was raining, and the green of the grass around it provided a contrast to the whiteness of the building. It seemed to me that someone had noticed that the thing was leaning and had tried to correct this by altering the angle of the higher storeys, but I pushed this silly notion from my mind as Olaf and I climbed up the slippery marble steps. With all the bravado of an experienced scaffolder, I advanced perilously close to the edge of the landing and surveyed the town.

With sweaty palms I nonchalantly explained to my friend, "Heights don't trouble me. I was a scaffolder, you know."

I could see that Olaf was impressed, though he said nothing. Just as I got to the unprotected edge of the floor, my foot slipped and I made a grab for the pillar. Olaf grinned and shook his head in admonition of my bravado. I'd like to think that my grin in return was not sheepish.

We busked around the town and stayed in the youth hostel. Soon we moved on and in turn, I was moved by Florence and the beauty of Michelangelo's murals and appalled at their desecration by tourists who had stolen bits of the plaster or written their names on the bits they could reach. I returned on several occasions and considered stealing a bit of paint myself, but refrained. From my vantage point up in the gallery, I watched a congregation below take Mass. First there was a sort of procession followed by the movement of the congregation up to the altar to take the host and drink the wine, and not for the first time I felt a pang of envy at their corporate act of worship and belonging to something. I was still trying to come to terms with my growing atheism, but it was always threatened by such acts and great art. Here in this building, both were combined. It occurred then and still does that all great creativity comes either from religion or sex, and why wouldn't it, as they are the great forces of life and death?

Meanwhile I strummed on with *San Francisco Bay Blues*, and in the evenings played my fingerpicking pieces to the small groups of admirers. That stretched the evenings out till the hostel doors were closed and the German kids complained that we were making too much noise.

Florence was full of American tourists, and although I was a bit embarrassed singing only American songs to them from street corners, they tipped well and once a middle-aged guy asked me if I was from Texas, which made me feel authentic. When I asked him, however, he explained that it was my Levis that had made him wonder, as he had only seen cowboys wearing them "at home". I was happy with that explanation and even happier with the dollar bill he gave me, which I saved and took out to admire from time to time whilst I was travelling. I wondered what all the strange symbolism meant with the pyramid and the all-seeing eye suspended above it.

We found a spot on the famous bridge that crosses the river, and set up a pitch where we played for several days. Never overanxious to milk the scene, I left as soon as I thought we had enough to see us through the day. It was still raining and in the photo that survives from that episode I was damp but undaunted, and though sometimes deeply missing Gill, I was busy and had begun to consider moving further afield. Although Rome would have been the obvious place to work, I still had the memory of the last time to put me off going back, and so I suggested playing in Turin.

Once more I was lost on the road with my thoughts, daydreams and daymares. I would set myself problems and try to solve them in my head, think of friends at home, try to analyse my motives, blame myself for losing Gill, wonder if I really liked this Norwegian I was travelling with, and sometimes fleetingly consider leaving for home. In between all these ramblings I would wonder why I could not get a lift. Cars streamed by, trucks rumbled onward, motorbikes thundered and sometimes a bicycle would move silently past me.

As I stared down the road from my hitching point I saw, way off in the distance, two figures walking one behind the other. As they got closer I could see that the one at the rear was carrying a double bass, then as they got even closer that the one in the front had a huge accordion on his back. I sensed that they were gypsies, and experienced the thrill that I always get in their proximity. As the pair walked by me they took in my situation without pausing, and both spoke in greeting and one of them mentioned "guitarra" so I considered myself blessed by these two road soldier musicians. They asked me for nothing (just as well); they had sensed that I was sincere in my intent. They obviously could not seriously contemplate hitchhiking with such unwieldy instruments and so walked on. I watched them go and as they became dots on the long straight road, I realised that I still had this smile of bonded brotherhood on my face. At last I got a lift, and several hours later the grin of recognition returned as the two figures once more came into view. The pace of their walk had not diminished as they trudged purposefully onward.

I arrived a day after Olaf and found my way to the hostel, which was some distance from the main part of town. After I had checked in, I decided that I had to wash some of my clothes. This is not easy using cold water and toilet soap, but I managed to 'clean' my spare socks and pants and felt thoroughly pleased with myself. I am sure that today there are just as many travellers on the road, but I cannot imagine them to be as fired-up and evangelical as we were.

For my generation, unencumbered by the need to shower and wash our hair every day, to say nothing of a clean set of clothes each morning, the road represented a freedom that could only be imagined by today's kids. Nearly everyone has been abroad by now with the advent of package holidays, but at that time the only way to see the world was to join the navy. To leave the austerity of the fifties behind and break the future that seemed ordained for you by class or birth was totally exhilarating. Everything was different to the way it was at home. From the vehicles on the road to the taste of their coffee and cigarettes. Each corner you turned threw up new sights and sounds and you could be anyone you wanted to be. You could affect the walk that was done by that really cool kid down the road, or keep an Elvis sneer on permanently (though I'm not sure it helped with the hitchhiking). You could adopt that devil may care attitude and appear to shed the everyday anxieties that burdened you at home and be the coolest cat around, only to catch yourself in a mirror sometimes wide-eyed and gob-open at some visual feast or other.

Standing at the side of roads for hours on end was the most static I have ever been. As a kid I was always on the move, and I cannot think of any time apart from in hospitals when I would have been still. If I was on the move before my army days, I was even more so after. I ran everywhere, impatient to be with my friends to divert myself from melancholy or to share the company of my girlfriend. Perhaps I sought company precisely to avoid my own thoughts; I know I have always dreaded not being able to sleep, and as a little boy can clearly remember listening to the Croydon Town Hall clock chime away every hour from ten o'clock until it was time to get up at seven thirty.

Here on the kerbside there was no escape. I tried walking in the direction I was going with my thumb stretched out, but this method did not truly indicate the seriousness of intent that a true traveller must have. In the end there was nothing for it but to stand and try to look attractive or presentable and face the oncoming traffic with an air of studied indifference and fatalism. Unfortunately I was unable to do this, and constantly rearranged my stance, and in so doing, my body language. Thumb high, thumb low, square on or sideways, half-smile or no smile at all, big sweep of arm or just a flick of the thumb, guitar hidden in the bushes or bag at my feet. Each time I got a lift I examined my technique to see if a pattern emerged. I now know that there is none.

Trieste was full of colour and kids with carefree attitudes and loads of money. They all seemed terribly young and silly, not a bit deep and fascinating like myself. Where did all these people get their money from? Why did they all wear reds, yellows, pinks, oranges and fey pastel shades? How come they all had scooters and impossibly beautiful 'girl-child' type chicks riding side saddle on the backs? What was I doing with this Norwegian who couldn't play very well and always dragged the beat? Why did I not have a girl? What was I doing here?

It was inevitable that I would go into one of my moods sooner or later and it might as well be here. Olaf sensed it but did nothing to help; in fact he went off to town on his own, which meant I didn't even have anyone to moan at. There was this tight-assed English bloke with a very long face wearing a blue fisherman's sweater and sandals with socks. He was washing some clothes like me and I noticed he had been crying. I asked him what the matter was; he said that he was all right, but his eyes were so pink they made mine water. He looked a complete jerk, but I felt sorry for him and badgered away until we got round to the subject of his eyes. It turned out that he had contact lenses and hay fever. My interest waned when I realised he was not in trouble.

It is strange to think that in a perverse way I was a style victim. As I stood in the cool washroom pitying this bloke, he had actually got it right. The fisherman's sweater would have been very useful at night when it got cold. The shorts would have kept him cool in the hot sun and helped to give him a youthful appearance, whilst the sandals would have meant that he need not wear socks every day. Here on the other hand was I, wearing my prized brown leather jacket, Wrangler shirt (hard to wash) original Levis, hot airless leg coverings, socks hand-knitted from wool unpicked from older socks, and desert boots that had sweat marks creeping through the uppers during the day and white salt marks by the morning. My outfit was an understatement of road chic. It was based on the travel methods of a mysterious bloke called Don that my brother Bruce had met down at Brighton. His philosophy was simple and practical (but perhaps a bit too minimalist):

• All belongings should fit in a bag no bigger than one foot square by nine inches deep. A school duffel bag would make a good alternative. Rucksacks were definitely out and deeply uncool;

• One wash one wear, i.e. two T-shirts, two pairs of pants, two pairs of socks;

• One bar of soap, razor, toothbrush (no toothpaste, use soap);

• One penknife, needle and thread, aspirins and plaster;

• One baby's nappy instead of a towel. With practice you can learn to dry yourself adequately with one of these even after a bath. The secret is to push off as much surface water with your hands before you pick up the nappy and then use only a small part of it for each limb leaving the torso and hair till last.

All these items will fit into this small receptacle and you can travel that light.

My only concession to luxury was toothpaste.

When Olaf returned he was enthusiastic about the prospects of earning. By now my mood had changed, and although another attack of stage fright had hit me, I didn't let him know. That evening we did quite well playing at an outdoor terrace where several restaurants spilled out on to the square, and afterwards the two of us got pissed and wobbled back home just in time to get into the hostel—only to be loudly rebuked by some Germans. I told them to fuck off, Olaf managed a very loud fart and we both collapsed into the bunks in fits of giggles.

We were woken in the morning about seven by these same geezers loudly shaving with electric razors (uncool). I had lost some of my aggressive bravado from the night before, but I managed a few swear words. Olaf did better. Swinging his legs over the side of his bunk and landing soundlessly on the floor, he walked over to the shaver and pulled his plug out of the wall and threw the lead out of the window, then leaning very close to the geezer's half-shaved face he uttered in English, "Later."

The German was so shocked he said nothing, then as he began to complain Olaf leaned over the side of his bunk and putting his finger to his lips made the 'sh' sound. I turned over and pretended to sleep. I was proud of him. Maybe he was really that cool; perhaps we could be the all-conquering pair. I would reserve judgement till later. That evening we were thrown out of the hostel.

As we sat considering our fate on the wall outside the hostel, Olaf looked round at me and asked, "Why don't we go to India?" Before I could say anything, he quickly added, "We know we can earn enough to get by, we probably shouldn't be able to play in Yugoslavia, but Greece would be OK. Then it's just across the border into Turkey and by then we'll know how it's going and we can adjust our plans accordingly."

He seemed so assured that I hardly knew where to begin my protestations. I had nothing really to go home for. I'd never been to any of these places and I found the idea of visiting a communist country very exciting.

"Don't we need a visa for Yugoslavia?" was all I could manage.

"We can sort it all out later, but if we're going to do it we should maybe earn a little more money."

I clearly remember the thrill of just saying, "OK, let's do it."

As we commenced the long coastal walk into town my mind started to think of the thwarted attempts I had made before. Gill was always confident in me and our ability to make it, but I couldn't have done it with her. I suppose it was the feeling or realisation that I might as well have a go at it rather than having to look after someone I cared about. I felt strong and I had clean socks on. My thoughts once again strayed to the possibility of some female company, but I had sworn to stay true and I fully intended to keep my promise.

In fairness this promise was made easier by my appearance and road style. I was in stark contrast to the bright and gaudy Italian lads that zoomed about the streets on fizzing scooters. I was the colour of woodland in November gloomed in the streets of this north Italian city; Olaf on the other hand was the first person that I had met with that impossible combination of blond hair and beard complementing deep tanned skin. Whilst not muscular he was athletic-looking though just a little splay-footed.

He was also the first person I had ever met wearing the Indian sandals that became ubiquitous during the sixties and somehow still cling to credibility today. Olaf only ever wore white, which of course enhanced his tan, except when he wore black T-shirts which of course enhanced his tan… He spoke English with the mid-Atlantic accent of many Scandinavians, spoken in a deep monotone. He had travelled quite a bit, and wore the best white canvas trousers that I had ever seen. They even had the Levis back pocket chevron sewn into them. They were made from sail canvas and had been put together by a tailor who kept all his broken needles to show Olaf how hard the job had been.

By the time we had met, these trousers were as soft as corduroys but stronger than a new pair of Yankee jeans. The only thing that blew his cred for me was that most of the time he smoked a pipe. True, it was not always tobacco, but the idea of a bloke not yet 22 smoking a pipe did not sit with me. In fact I was glad that he had this road imperfection and that I could play better than him, otherwise he would have been perfect. I watched enviously as all the girls looked up when he entered a room. He affected not to notice them. They'll soon go off him when they see that pipe lit, I mistakenly thought.

That evening Trieste was busy and warm, and there was a good feeling in the air. We played for longer and made a few lire more than usual. Later in a café I took out what remained of the tatty map and we looked at Yugoslavia. It was simple: the main road stretched from Ljubljana to Belgrade and then south to the Greek border. It was pointless riding together, so we split up the next day and arranged to meet in Thessalonika. Olaf suggested about three days for this trip.

For once I picked up a lift quite quickly and spent the next several miles wondering how I had managed this. The truck was driven by an Italian, who wondered if I was going to look at the stalagmite caves. As if I was interested in things like that; I was about much more cool motivation than mere tourist visits. In fact I really did not know why I was travelling, which made it hard to explain why I was on the road. So I told him that I was going to look at them. The kindly man then drove me out of his way and dropped me at the entrance of the attraction before turning off down the road—and for all I knew heading for Greece.

Having neither money nor desire to see the bloody caves, I spent the next few hours trying to hitch back to the main road. Progress was painfully slow. There were few private cars, and the elderly trucks that thundered past belching diesel did not seem attracted to the frowning youth who stood by the road. That night was the first of many that I spent sleeping by the roadside in the open. One night I threw the bag down and climbed in only to find that I had lain it in a puddle, but as the water slowly seeped through it into my jeans I was just too exhausted to do anything about it.

Of all the places I had been this was the most different. Communist birds sang in communist trees and the sun shone. In the north, fields were green, yet there was somehow no colour. I confess to a feeling of horror when I realised that I actually missed seeing advertisements. Traffic was very slow, and apart from occasional German cars full of passengers, the lorries seemed to lumber past at a rate of about one every fifteen minutes, but perhaps I had got on to the wrong road again. More time for contemplation as I stood, trance-like with tiredness and hunger, wondering if I would ever get to Greece.

The off-white concrete sectioned roads stretching straight into the distance in both directions as far as I could see only enlarged my sense of isolation; then, shimmering like Omar Sharif in *Lawrence of Arabia*, a soundless apparition would emanate from the horizon and metamorphose into a truck that slowly became audible, and once again the heartbeat would pick up as it drew near. Each time I would try to remember the stance taken on my last success, only to have to revise my memory as the great smoking beast dopplered away from me to become another shimmering apparition on the opposite skyline.

The further south I went, the more alien I felt. As soon as you left the city, the people seemed to change. Even at the time I knew that amongst them there would be kind and gentle souls, but at the same time there was a hardness apparent in some of them, and a lack of sophistication that was present in even the lowliest working people that I had come across on my journeys so far.

My own social skills, such as they were, had no currency here and I sensed an 'every man for himself' attitude that upset and depressed me, for as a committed socialist I suppose I had hoped for more. I guessed some of my harder-left friends at home were right and that Yugoslavia was not really a communist country, but a bunch of different states held together by communism. I even contemplated taking a train for part of the journey, but after joining a rabble of people who made no attempt to form a queue for what seats remained on one of the trains, I walked the other way and took my place back on the roadside. I have always had trouble with queue jumpers, and in the terrible tragedy of modern day Yugoslavia, I recall that brief experience with horror at what things must have been like when it was truly a matter of life and death.

I have no memory of Belgrade except that of walking right through the city and out the other side. I slept on the side of the road most nights, and once a truck driver woke me where I lay, believing me to have been killed. Indeed I was lucky not to have been, as when he found me I had rolled off the kerb and into the road and could easily have been crushed by a truck as it roared by.

This driver offered me a lift and a small piece of bacon that he had in his pocket wrapped up in a grease-sodden piece of newspaper. I was warmed by the solidarity of the working class and the brotherhood that binds the poor together. I had nothing to drink for hours, days even, and this bit of salty bacon was the last thing I needed, but I had to accept only to find that it only smelt like bacon as it was actually a piece of fat with the tiniest hint of meat on it. The great globule stayed in my mouth a long time before I could muster the courage to swallow it. How I managed not to vomit I will never know.

Eventually the truck pulled into a petrol station wittily called 'Benzin', and not for the first time I missed the familiarity of brand names on fuel and longed for the presence of adverts and posters along the way to brighten the journey. I found the 'toilets' and for once there was a tap that had water running out of it. I drank as much as I could, which had the effect of having to make me stop the truck after a short distance in order to have a pee. The sun was coming up and as we rolled into Zagreb I spotted to my astonishment the two musicians plodding methodically onward, double bass and accordion slung across their backs. I wanted to greet them somehow, but we rolled past in the truck. After the driver dropped me, I too slung my bedroll across my back and walked through the town and out the other side.

Days passed and my progress had almost stopped completely. I was starving hungry and could feel spots and pimples proliferating on my forehead. Somewhere on the main road I waited for three days and on the third day, two rather large jolly Australian girls arrived at my bit of lay-by.

"G'day mate!" they chirped as they set down their two enormous uncool rucksacks. "How long have you been waiting?"

"Three days," I croaked hoarsely. I'd spoken to no-one for at least that time.

"Three days?" they chorused in disbelief. "Gee, we never wait more than a few minutes."

Very helpful, I remember thinking. Perhaps it was the pimples or maybe my near-starving, mad-eyed state that warned them away from me. Perhaps my crazed grin looked lascivious, and by now I was suffering from hay fever, which probably added to my attractiveness with red rimmed eyes and a snotty nose.

"Well as you were here first, we'll move a bit further down the road so you get the first shot," they chirruped merrily.

"Thank you," I croaked wearily, and then under my breath, "I suppose a..."

The next truck that came along drove straight past me and screeched

486

to a halt in front of the two girls. As they clambered aboard one of them gave me a cheery wave and shouted, "Good luck!"

I grinned my acknowledgement back at her and waved stupidly. The next afternoon I too got a lift but it did not go very far. The road on which I stood was now even longer and straighter than all the others I had ever waited beside. Things really felt desperate. The trucks seemed to have dried up completely, and with no food inside me, I decided to take out the guitar and play for a bit. Perhaps this nonchalance would make me look more interesting to the drivers as they whistled past, their heavy wheels thumping rhythmically over the sectioned concrete.

I opened my case and stared in disbelief at the sight that greeted me. The body of the instrument was concertinaed into itself, the sides had split and the front had compressed into the back. The neck was intact and the strings still in place, but no way could the instrument be played. At this point I felt as low as I have ever felt. My situation now seemed utterly hopeless. Without the guitar I had lost even that precarious support. After loosening the strings, I gently laid the broken box back in the case, and a big boy's tear plopped down my cheek.

ᕲ

crossroads

My guitar in pieces, I tried to assess the situation as my thoughts tumbled over each other. I stared at what I supposed was the direction of Greece to my right, then turning left I looked at the direction from which I'd come. Traffic moved at about the same rate in both directions, and the patch of scrub across the two-lane concrete highway looked just as appealing as the bit I was sitting on.

"I might as well cross this road and head back," was the thought that entered my head at last. Then, with a thump in my chest of real determination I thought, "What the hell, I may as well continue, things have got to get better."

I stood up, dragged a hand across my eyes, looked down the long road in front of me and took out one of my last three cigarettes. I flicked open my Zippo lighter and found that it had run out of petrol.

"Shit!" I thought, "I will not be denied!" I looked long and hard at the fuelless lighter. It still had flint in it, so how could I turn that spark into a flame? With half an idea and half in desperation, I stuck the end of the cigarette into the wind shield around the wick aiming it at the source of the spark. Furiously I spun the flint wheel whilst at the same time drawing air through the cigarette. Within a few seconds the taste of smoke reached my tongue and I removed the end of the cigarette to see that one edge had caught and by licking that edge and pulling even harder, I could get the thing to burn evenly, and soon I was puffing away merrily on one of the foul cigarettes that were all I could get in that country. They came in a blue box; inside there was not even any silver paper to glamorise them, and the brand name was something really subtle like 'Tabbac'. But that was one of the best smokes I'd ever had. My small victory in lighting it announced my new determination to overcome my difficulties.

That night I slept again by the road and woke early, shivering in the dawn. Thoughts of what had happened to my guitar kept returning. I had not played it the whole time I had been in the country, and had only spent one night under cover and that was in a student hostel that I had come across by accident. It was a crowded, hot place, and to add to my sense of loneliness, no-one spoke English. I had a reasonable night's rest but wondered if the geezer in the bunk above me had stepped on my guitar deliberately or accidentally during the night. In my mood at that time I surmised that it had been a deliberate act.

The sun rose higher in the sky. There was little shade and it was very hot. Once again I was in a dilemma whether to move to a better place or to sweat it out where I stood. In the end I was moved by thirst to find a drink of water. Everyone had advised against buying any Yugoslavian money, but I had a few notes and found somewhere to buy a coffee and a glass of water before resuming my vigil on the roadside. The day settled into an insect-buzzing, hazy, close, still afternoon. Not a soul disturbed my sojourn and the transport that passed me did so even more rarely. As my eyes sleepily stared up the road I became aware of a smaller shimmering figure that bustled along the same side of the road as me. It was a long time before I could see who it was. For a while it seemed that I would be passed by a woman in a long flowing dress before I was able to tell that it was a man in a habit.

He was in his fifties, his hair long and straggly. The sandals on his feet were almost falling apart, and the habit which at one time must have been brown was now bleached yellow on the shoulders. In his hand he carried a black tin box which he set down on the roadside.

He addressed me in a language I did not recognise and I indicated my incomprehension and uttered the single word, "English."

He nodded, his brow furrowed with compassion as he made the sign of hunger by pressing his fingers to his thumb in a cluster and pointing to his mouth. I indicated that I was OK, but he remained unconvinced. Then, leaning down he opened his metal box and pulled out half a loaf of bread wrapped in a piece of newspaper. He broke it into two approximate quarters and placed one of the pieces back into his case, handing me the other. As I took it and indicated my thanks I could feel that it was as hard as a rock. The old guy then put a hand on my shoulder and muttered something I guessed might have been a prayer of some sort. As I grinned rather inanely he turned and walked off down the road. Once more his form became androgynous before he began to shimmer. I put the bread to my lips and attempted a mouthful. It crumbled like sawdust into my dry mouth and I turned to show the monk that I was eating his gift, but by now he had disappeared into the growing shadows that indicated the beginning of evening.

I found this whole vignette incredibly moving and a very pure Christian act. I did not want to think like this; I was trying hard to be an atheist, but the old guy who obviously had nothing had shared his pittance with me. I was even more determined to carry on, and in the late evening got a lift that took me a long way in the right direction.

The road was long and straight and the surrounding countryside flat and dull. My last lift had turned off the road to some small village and I was left high and dry.

High through lack of food, and dry for lack of water. I mused on the lesson of Steve's monkey. Just when I had learned how to go without food or water I died. Way down the road was a bridge. I toyed with the idea of walking towards it, but decided as the road was so straight there was little purpose in moving from where I was. The sun was high in the sky; it must have been around two in the afternoon (you get to read shadow lengths after a while). I was gritty and sore-eyed, in need of a shower, irritable with the lack of traffic, and resigned to the unlikelihood of getting a lift.

Ever since I was a little boy I had set myself rituals that could either make things happen or stop bad things from happening, like not treading on the lines in paving stones in case the lions got me, or counting the telegraph poles that whizzed past the train carriage window to stop the train from crashing.

At first I tried not looking at an approaching vehicle until the volume of its engine had reached a certain level. Next, using the international signal of sticking out the thumb I held my Zippo in my fist. After several hours I remembered my lucky farthing (it had got me through the eleven-plus), but couldn't find it. Then I began to intone, mantra-like, the destination "Greece Greece" whilst using a rhythmic movement with my hand in synchronised movement with my lips. It must have looked to the oncoming lorry drivers as though I simply had a mad grin and St Vitus dance.

I was beginning to crack. Here I was, broke, starving, no money, a bag of grubby bits and pieces and a bundle of splintered wood and strings inside my guitar case. And my magic was not working.

I decided to move on down the road towards the bridge. As I got nearer I could see that it spanned a single track railway line which continued stretching as far as I cold see over the flat landscape. I was aware of standing in the centre of a cross, the road running north to south and the railway east to west. Leaving my small bag and my broken guitar on the other side of the road, I crossed over to lean on the railing and look out eastward. Underneath me stretched the rails, and in front of me was a largish pond, with a dead tree near the water's edge. The bark had fallen off from a large part of the trunk and my eyes slowly climbed up the tree to the skeletal bare branches at the top. There, completely at peace and a still as a statue, sat a heron.

My first sighting of this dignified bird was the day my brother Bruce stopped the train. We had been on a trip to see Grandma and Grandad in Brackley. The railway line to Brackley had recently been converted to a mere connecting service with a two-coach diesel shuttle, where previously we had been able to travel all the way there by steam train from London.

My mum and her sister had been visiting their parents, and Bruce and I had gone off to the 'echo bridge' with my pretty cousin Christine. She had been intent on picking moon daisies, and in order to impress her both Bruce and I had picked bundles. There was an abundance of flowers in the fields, but the best ones grew on the bank of the railway cutting, so we clambered down to pick them. There was never any thought of danger as we scampered about running backward and forward across the single line. Suddenly in the warm air there was a sound completely at odds with the humming of summer, as a train siren shattered the stillness. I was at the top of the embankment and Christine about halfway up. Bruce was at the bottom and the driver of the train had clearly only sought to warn us of his approach. We all looked in the direction of the train and I shouted unnecessarily at my little brother to come up away from the lines. The train looked so small and far away, but I was still concerned for Bruce; he however merely walked on to the track and assumed the position of a copper on point duty holding up his arms in the formal position of stopping traffic.

Christine and I screamed at him to move out of the way as the train grew larger and the danger more imminent. Still he stood there. The train applied its brakes and I swear it only came to a halt about six feet from where Bruce stood. Chris and I were both nearly hoarse with screaming and terror. Once the train had stopped Bruce hightailed it up the bank and the three of us scurried away over the fields.

Secretly I was impressed with his bravado, and I am sure he had hoped that Christine was as well. We soon pushed the incident to the back of our minds in the ripening fields as insects buzzed the afternoon away. After an hour or two we began our journey back to Grandma's, and after calling our names to the echo bridge and before the last stile, we saw the heron.

It was standing so still at the water's edge in the bend of the Ouse. Even though it was in its rightful place, it made me jump to see it. I thought it was beautiful and couldn't wait to tell everyone about it. As we ascended the last field before the main road a policeman apprehended us. I was terrified again, guessing correctly what he wanted.

He asked where we lived, and he escorted us home, where we were sent out in the garden whilst he warned our two mums about the seriousness of what had occurred. It finished up, so I am told, with Mum and my aunt offering to go around and scrub the police station steps so long as it was all forgotten.

In the end the railway police got involved, and I was promised a thrashing by my headmaster in front of the school, but this was finally reduced to being let off with a caution. Having experienced Mr. Wilson's savagery with a cane before, I was very relieved but still very cross with Bruce.

When I eventually told Mum about the sighting of the heron, she told me that Grandad had once found a moorhen's nest at that point and had taken some of her eggs and fried them for breakfast. It seemed wrong to steal the eggs and eat them, but somehow I was glad that Grandad, who did not seem to get much, at least had that little treat.

I stood looking at the heron on top of the tree. It was so still that I deliberately made a noise to see if it was real. A lorry thundered past, and it merely looked in the direction of the road. Eventually a train of three or four coaches passed under the bridge and into the vast middle distance and oblivion: the bird did not even acknowledge its passing. I re-crossed the road to where I could watch the bird and look towards the horizon in every direction. Then I found my lucky farthing in my Levis mini pocket.

A truck passed me and there was a shudder of brakes as he pulled up some yards away. I grabbed my bag and broken guitar and ran to the truck and surprised myself by my leap into the cab. The driver indicated that he wasn't going far, but that was OK; I was on the move again and the border was getting nearer. He let me out at a gas station and I filled my lighter with a few drops of fuel left in one of the pipes from one of the pumps. Luckily I survived the thick black smoke that came from the wick each time I lit up. The fuel soon evaporated and I rationed my cigarettes. The driver bought me a coffee before we parted and he turned off the main drag, and I trundled onward down the road and watched the shadows grow.

That evening an old Opel Rekord pulled up with four Greek guys and two English girls crammed into it. Even my broken guitar failed to put them off giving me a lift, and in great high spirits they rearranged the interior and somehow got us all back into the vehicle, its back axle periodically giving out ominous sounds as we lurched onward until, singing and shouting, they joyfully approached the border of home. The two girls and I had to get out before the border whilst our hosts did their paperwork, and we simply walked out of Yugoslavia and into Greece.

Just over the other side, the car pulled up again; we were invited back in and carried to the remains of some ancient courtyard where there was an abundance of fresh flowing water. Some of the blokes in the car stripped off and proceeded to wash themselves and so, cautiously, did I. My own skinny white body with the brown arms in contrast to their muscled olive torsos: I wondered if we were cleansing ourselves from our journey or baptising ourselves for our arrival? Suddenly the sound of jangling bells combined with ground shaking thundering made me lift up my head. Round the corner of the remains of the wall, apparently out of control, roared a horse and cart. The horse looked as shocked and surprised as we were to find anyone else there at this fine time in the morning. Soon the men were all shouting loudly and happily together, birds were singing, the sun was just clearing the horizon and there was a bright freshness at the start of this day. The contrast between the two countries was extreme. We were inside Greece and there were advertisements and posters to look at and happy people, shouting and joking together, *and* there were these two girls.

They were both from Manchester and had taken two days to hitchhike through Yugoslavia (it had taken me a week). One, called Diane, was deeply attractive; the other one was a sweet blonde girl with larger features and her name was Margaret. Neither of them took much notice of me, but they did say they were headed for Thessalonika and maybe Athens, so I said that I would see them again. They wished me good luck and climbed back into the car with the Greek lads who had been guest Arbeiters in Germany and were returning with pockets of cash to their various villages. They told me I was welcome to join them but they were far too overcrowded; I declined and they waved me goodbye.

As the old car took off down the road with them all singing again, I took out the packet of cigarettes. There was still one left, and using my fuelless method, lit up and took a big drag. Greece looked wonderful; the early mists were clearing, and the bloke with the horse gave me a lift back to the main road with my bundle of firewood and strings rattling inside the guitar case.

From my pocket I pulled a piece of paper that had the address *'Oddos Pringiposs Nickalau'* written on it. This was the place that I was to meet Olaf and possibly these two girls. I wondered how this word was pronounced, but figured once into the town I would soon find someone who would point me in the right direction. Saloniki (as the locals call it) was a wonderful place, old and crumbling in places, with people spilling out on to the pavements and spending all day over one cup of coffee.

Outside the hostel and across the road, groups of impossibly handsome young men lounged around eyeing the girls that went in and out of the old wooden door of the student hostel. It was run by an old bloke and his wife, who were very easygoing. Olaf had been there for several days. When he saw the remains of my guitar his sympathy was great and his help practical. One evening he had been strumming along by himself and a group of young lads about fifteen years old had gathered round to watch him. Eventually one of them (Nick) had approached Olaf and struck up a conversation. Olaf had told them about this friend who could play and it seemed they were most anxious to meet me.

"They'll know someone who can help, I am sure, Ralph," he said. I was further reassured when I met these kids. They were very polite and spoke just a few words of English. Olaf got me to play his twelve-string and they told me they knew this old guitar repairer in the town who they thought could fix the wreckage of my instrument. The only problem was that I had no money now and did not feel like playing on my own with Olaf's guitar. The boys, however, had a plan. The next day when they came to take me to the luthier, they explained their scheme.

On Saturday afternoon at the local cinema there was a matinee for young people. The boys had an electric guitar that I would play, and had fixed up a microphone. They had told their friends that they had met this singing star from England and that I could play a Bob Dylan song and could play the guitar really fast and that I would perform for them all. It did not seem likely that my nerves would let me do this, but when I saw the inside of the old craftsman's shop I felt confident enough to leave the guitar with him, and now I had to have money to pay for the work, I agreed to their plan.

The weather was very hot, and as the day grew nearer, I started to wonder what a rock'n'roll singer would wear for the occasion. My wardrobe was scant, but at the bottom of my bag, and by now very crumpled, was my jean jacket and I decided that this would be the item to wow them in the aisles. A good jean jacket has been a fashion item since *The Grapes of Wrath* and I would have loved a genuine Levis one, but of course they were too expensive to take as road wear. Mine came from Millets. It was at least two sizes too big for me—and at six foot two, that made it very big indeed. But I wore it with the sleeves rolled up and was quite content.

On the morning of the show I thought very carefully about which crumpled t-shirt I should wear. In the end I opted for my denim shirt. By midday the weather was unbelievably hot, and once inside the cinema it was stifling. The noise from the audience was deafening. Finally young Nick went out and tried to calm them down before announcing me, and out I walked to an enormous noise and applause. Nick handed me the horrible guitar and plugged it in and off I went.

Immediately sweat coursed down my forehead and my hands were wringing wet within the first number. Afterwards Olaf asked me how I had managed to produce so much liquid, for after half a dozen songs I came off as if I had just swam twenty lengths. The audience went wild, and I realised at that moment what pop stars experience and knew that, although it was fun, it had nothing to do with what I hoped for from music.

On the Wednesday I went to the luthier for my guitar. He expressed doubts that it should be strung with steel strings, but I explained through Nick that it was an American guitar and he said that he thought it was a very fine instrument. I beamed with delight in the reflected glory of ownership and amazed at the price he charged me for the repair. It worked out at about three pounds, and as I had earned five for my performance, I was delighted. That night Olaf went out and played the local cafés and added to our little pile of drachmas.

There were piles of young hitchhikers and travellers passing through the town, and one day the two girls who I'd met arrived in the hostel. I introduced them to Olaf, who made his usual impression, and by the end of the evening Diane was obviously besotted. For the next few days they came out and bottled for us and we did quite well. Diane and Olaf became very intense, and I was sort of lumbered with Margaret, who wasn't romantically attracted to me but was at a bit of a loose end without her mate. We had nothing in common. Although only a working class lad from south London, I was interested in the arts and music in particular. Margaret was interested in hairdressing and in the mornings emerged from the girls' side of the hostel as if she was going to the Streatham Locarno. With coiffed hair, lipstick and makeup, she made the best of herself, but for the life of me I could not fathom what she was doing on the road (in fairness, I would have been hard pressed to explain my own motives).

Margaret was very down-to-earth, and in spite of appearances very practical, whilst Diane was not so bright and rather languid. Her skin had turned a lovely golden colour whilst Margaret was sort of pinky red and she frequently looked overheated with tiny drops of perspiration on her top lip. There is no doubt that the two girls increased our turnover, but as company I didn't really want to be around them.

Olaf was happy to be getting his oats, but slowly he realised that Diane was not the woman of his dreams. One morning I noticed bruising to her face. The sullenness from Olaf was deep and dark, and I was horrified to think that he may have beaten her. About this time I began to feel a bit of resentment towards Olaf, as I felt he contributed little to our income. He was not a natural musician but had taken up the guitar rather like

496

growing your hair long: it was more a badge of belonging than a desire to make music. He seldom practised and had not improved at all since we started. And he hardly ever sang.

As I was doing the lion's share I felt I should be getting more out of it, yet I had to admit I was still not ready to go it alone. I never questioned Olaf about the intimacy of his relationship. He must have assumed that I knew; he did not attempt to hide his annoyance with Diane, and frequently ignored her and went out with me in the evenings. By now we knew our way around Saloniki and had found some cheap places to eat and drink. I had my first retsina there, and as all the meat seemed to be grilled and there were chips with everything I was very happy. I even began eating olives and relished the tomatoes that were served with everything.

Olaf frequently drank to excess. He could drink until he was almost incapable of speech, then go out and throw up, only to begin drinking again. He would stagger to the door and roar out into the street "I'm a focking Viking! We drink, we fall down, we throw up and then we focking drink again." With that he would poke his fingers down his throat and chuck into the gutter. Not always accurate, he would often soil his shirt and trousers, but in the morning express no remorse or contrition. I found this embarrassing. I even thought his pronunciation 'focking' sounded stupid. I was definitely getting the ache with him.

To get away from all of this I made an aborted attempt to go to Athens. My hitchhiking hit an all-time low on this trip, and I found myself stranded miles from anywhere when the heavens suddenly opened. There was no shelter anywhere, and within a few seconds I was drenched to the skin. As it was too late to do anything about my own condition, I transferred my thoughts to the guitar and to my relief spotted a bridge over a dried-up river bed. I scurried over to it with my belongings and watched in disbelief as the rain thundered down. As I gazed out from underneath the parapet, I became aware of a new sound. It was a gentle but insistent roaring, and as I looked up the river bed, I could see way off in the distance a wall of water moving down the dry bottom of the course. I reached into my bag, pulled out the little camera and jumped down into the middle of the dry stream. I looked through the viewfinder as the wall of water got ever closer. Wait—wait—nearly... right now! The water filled the frame, I pressed the shutter and let the camera drop to my chest.

When I looked up at the scene before me I nearly died of terror. The viewfinder had made the water seem small and a long way off, when in reality it was huge and only a few feet away from me. I barely made the safety of the bank before a six foot wall of water swept past which would have certainly carried me away. I sat under the bridge shaking for a long time before venturing back on to the roadside again.

Once back in Saloniki I resumed playing, and in spite of warnings by the police that it was not allowed, Olaf and I got quite blasé about the risk of arrest. A certain recklessness had begun to creep into our lifestyle and personally I felt too far away from home to think about going anywhere but onward, so I had shed what remained of my natural caution. We were enjoying a modest but reasonable lifestyle for two road rats, and for me, apart from the odd unbelievable hangover, life was fun.

I stayed most of the time in the hostel and Olaf stayed in different places with Diane, but their relationship was floundering and it was plain that they should part. It was just that to get regular sex with a pretty girl was hard for Olaf to turn down even though the result of it revealed a darker side to his nature. I was jealous but not envious of his situation; I was not tempted to pursue Margaret and was determined to keep my promise to stay true to Gill. And I was a martyr to that promise until one afternoon a beautiful sun-tanned girl called Carol arrived with two others at the hostel. Her hair was black and she wore a simple shift dress in sun-faded deep pink. She was beautifully tanned and she moved around in a totally uninhibited way with just a hint of gaucheness. I was stunned; she had a wonderful figure and my eyes followed her everywhere. She was oblivious of me, and although I was sure she must have noticed my open-mouthed staring over the next couple of days she gave no indication of having seen me. Her voice was raspy and quite deep but her accent was bloody awful. This helped me when I was all but convulsed with lust for her. Anyway, she was a party girl and had already caught the attention of some of the Greek boys who hung around the hostel. I realised I had no chance.

The next night, after repeated cautions, I was arrested and taken to the police cells. It was actually not too bad and I was not perturbed by the experience. For some reason Olaf was not banged up with me, so the following day when I was released, I seemed to have gained some cachet. As I sat outside at the café I noticed that Carol was looking at me—though she looked away as soon as I caught her eye. My heart thumped.

I could no longer play in the street without real risk, so it was definitely time to move on. That night, however, there was an outing arranged with some of the kids and a boat trip across to some beach café. This did not sound hip to me, but I was at a loose end, so I went. Carol was very close to me for part of the way, but I managed not one word. We tipped off the boat and trooped to the café, where I was surprised to find a number of Greek gentlemen, some in their forties, sitting at the tables we were to occupy. Food was ordered, and being close to Carol again I could only pick at mine. All the time I puzzled over our mixed company. I was suspicious, but I can only say that these suspicions were unfounded or plans thwarted, because at the end of our meal, with much jollity and wine, we were decanted back to the boat. Carol, who was all but falling out of her dress, was a little tipsy and was talking to me in her horrible accent, now slightly slurred.

I, too, had drunk quite a bit, and one thing led to another. By the time we were on our own we were both consumed with passion and had absolutely nowhere to go. I remembered the showers downstairs, and there in the darkness, fumbling and groping, we were about to consummate the evening. Suddenly the door swung open and a fat German kid entered wearing only a towel and proceeded to have a cold shower. His appearance had the effect of a cold shower on Carol, who hurried from the scene, and I limped off to my bunk in pain and frustration.

The next day she shipped out early, leaving me an address in Cambridge. I reasoned that it was probably for the best and my vow was still intact. I felt righteous and I really had to go. I had my reserve couple of English pounds and my dollar bill, but my drachmas were getting low. In order to soften Olaf's split with Diane, we took her and Margaret as hitchhiking companions part of the way to the border. Poor Margaret, she could not believe how long she had to wait for a lift with me. I, on the other hand, could not believe how easy it was with her.

Actually, travelling with her was good fun. We had decided to enter Turkey via Greece instead of Bulgaria, and she was happy to accompany me. She was ready to go home and our lack of emotional attachment meant that we could have a few laughs on the way—though she was worried about Olaf's temper, and thought her friend was being a silly cow. At a prearranged place the two girls met up and we said our goodbyes. We swapped addresses and I walked down the road first, leaving Olaf to sort out his departure without me looking on.

Once out of sight I felt again that delicious sense of freedom from any responsibility that I have only glimpsed since on one or two occasions. I guess you have to have a sense of responsibility in the first place in order to experience it, and there are those who need to feel it all the time. For me, though, the feeling comes so rarely that I remember each time with relish, and as I walked down the proverbial dusty road with my bedroll and guitar on my back, cigarette in my mouth and a few coins in my pocket, I was about as happy as I've ever been.

I never saw Diane again, though I did meet Carol once more one November. How strange her appearance seemed then: sallow not tanned, woollen-stockinged not brown-limbed, hair combed and parted not free and sun-bleached.

There was a detachment of the Greek army at the border, and relations between the two countries were intense. That night I slept in a noisy field where huge creatures of the night rustled and grunted, fussed and scampered all around me under a sky full of the brightest stars. I felt free and unencumbered again, and kept awake by the marvellous heart-racing Turkish coffee that the last lorry driver had bought me.

The border was a very uptight spot from the Greek side, but once across, the Turkish soldiers were just hanging about, leaning on walls and smoking, hardly taking any notice of me. True, there was not much activity at the border, and virtually no vehicles seemed to be crossing, but nevertheless they were pretty laid back. It was a very hot day and there was a lot of dust in the air; my eyes and nose were streaming as I squinted westward, searching the dry terrain for vehicles. I suppose I had been walking and thumbing for about an hour or two, when a battered saloon car screeched to a halt in a cloud of dust and a youngish bloke beckoned me in.

The inside of the car was full of dust, and my jeans resembled those of a plasterer's labourer as soon as I sat down. The road was rocky and bumpy and the driver was anxious to show me how fast he could negotiate the obstacles in our way. After a couple of miles, he stopped and picked up a German couple, and seemed to be more at ease with them than me. He even managed a few words of German. He then stopped for another Turkish hitchhiker, who dominated the conversation as we rattled onward.

We were a dust storm on wheels. If we closed the windows it poured through the gaps in the ancient ill-fitting doors and we nearly suffocated in the heat, so we opted for leaving the windows open and trying to breathe through the sleeves of our shirts. The good news was that he was going all the way to Istanbul. Perhaps my luck was changing.

∼

bosporus

If I had felt alien in Yugoslavia, I felt like an extraterrestrial in Istanbul. The city is awesome, not just for its magnificent appearance but because each building that glorifies God is in support of a different belief system. Here I was, trying to shake off the burden of Christianity, in the midst of a culture that I was totally unprepared for. In my boldness to reject, I had not realised the comfort still to be had from crucifixes on top of churches I had no plans to visit. Here on top of these stunning buildings rested something that to me resembled a pair of horns. Old burial grounds, their graves marked with pillars and spheres, promised a different paradise and comfort.

There was so much to feast my eyes on, and the smells of the place too, for at every street corner there was something being cooked over charcoal, and sharp smoky smells drifted in the sultriness of an overcast sky that was being jabbed by these needle-like minarets. Add to this the sounds of strange meandering music of quarter tones and cymbals, and the cantors calling the faithful to payer with the sound of sirens from ships on the magnificent Bosporus.

I was lost in a movie in which I had no useful lines to utter, and had no door by which I could leave. Of course I had no money but that was not a problem. I was approached all the time by rough looking blokes offering to change any western currency that I did have. I still had a few lire left and two English pounds that I had planned to save for an emergency and this was it. I hustled a bit and got quite a good rate of exchange, I thought, and made my way to where I was advised I could get a cheap room at the American student hostel, near the Topkapi museum.

I eventually found my way there, but it was way too expensive for me and anyway the sort of people that were staying there were on holiday! Not like me of course... Thankfully Olaf, who had arrived before me, had left me a note telling me to meet him at the Guilharne hotel which was not far away. I was unprepared for how happy I was to see him again. After a few days it was quite like old times, as there were no girls involved and we were back working the streets around the Gelata Bridge that links Europe and Asia.

The hotel was tiny with hardly any facilities apart from our tiny cell of a room in which there were three beds. We found another young English bloke there called Tim and we soon got him switched to our room and became friendly. He was younger than me and very confident in himself. I guessed correctly that he had been to boarding school. He was dressed beyond street fashion in white jeans and a checked cotton shirt and wore heavy brogues and woollen socks. He had an enormous suitcase. In spite of his confidence and our warnings, he managed to lose his passport by being bladed in the Bazaar. What happens is that the thief walks behind you and, with an incredibly sharp knife, slits your back pocket down one side from the bottom to the top. This action cannot be felt by the victim and if the thief is patient it is only a matter of time before the item slips out on to the ground.

As Tim walked into the room one night I had the satisfaction of telling him that I knew he had lost his passport because I could see the pocket flapping open. I had sewn a pocket inside my jeans where I kept my passport and pathetic valuables. Poor Tim handled his embarrassment well, and we were all supportive. After the usual bureaucratic hassle he got a new one issued in Istanbul, which was rather special.

It was noticeable how much less we were able to take from the punters on the street. At first it was such a novelty for the local population to see two western European kids busking (in reality, begging) that we did OK, but I found myself getting very uncomfortable about the numbers of dreadfully deformed beggars who were forced to make a living from our same customers, especially when I found out that they had to pay rent for their wretched pitches from street landlord gangsters.

At first, though, it was great. During the days I would wander about for hours walking in the Bazaar until the locals stopped trying to sell me things. Sometimes the merchants would invite me in to take *chai*—small glasses of tea with a sugar lump—and I would talk a little about England and tell them how wonderful it was. I bought Gill a tiny but perfectly painted segment of an ivory bracelet; I can still see the stylised face of the woman painted in miniature on its surface. The whole thing was only about three quarters of an inch square, but it was very old and I knew she would love it. I bought my mum some earrings, fashioned, I was assured, from pieces of harem jewellery (which she still has), and from my proceeds of busking I bought myself a suede jean jacket.

I am confident that this was one of the first ever suede jean jackets, and for days I worked on the tailor to get the best price from him. When we finally agreed, he asked me to let him borrow the one I was wearing for a model, and I happily left it with him. A few days later it was ready, and I can remember the excitement I felt as I went to collect it. It was made of the very softest brown suede with suede-covered buttons. The stitching was in a slightly darker brown thread and the workmanship was of the highest quality. It was a faithful copy of the original jacket that I had loaned him, and like the original it was misshapen and two full sizes too big for me! I could not believe at first that he had done this, but realised that it was all my fault because he had asked me incredulously at the time if I was sure that I really wanted it like this. I had merely been amused because I thought his implication was that I should have let him build me a beautiful coat from the high quality suede and not a lowly jean jacket. I now saw, too late, that it was the quality of the mother garment that he had alluded to. Instead of one pathetic misshapen ill-fitting coat, I now had two. Never mind, it was the price one had to pay to be a Trend Setter.

Food was cheap and mostly we ate on the street. There were street vendors all over the place, selling grilled corn on the cob to fishermen, and sardines, fresh from the Bosporus, cooked on tiny stoves in the boat and slapped between a bread roll with a sprinkle of salt. You could buy these for the equivalent of twopence in old money, and I ate one of these every day. There were kebabs, and in the evenings an occasional ice cream to complement the little hash we managed to score.

Hash was easy to find. It came wrapped in cellophane with a little crown or insignia pressed into the substance to guarantee quality. We used Olaf's pipe, and wandering around the old town in this state was a particularly pleasant experience. So was the ice cream.

One night, the most pungent smells were emanating from the next room, accompanied by the playing of the Turkish lute and flute. The smells were clearly very high grade marijuana, and the music was getting more excited and way out. Olaf insisted that we should check it out, and we knocked on their door. The occupants shouted something and we walked in. There propped up on a bed against the party wall sat three very stoned geezers, who just grinned at our look of astonishment. One of them was playing the lute, and perched on a small chair at the end of the bed sat the flute player. Without a hint of shyness, Olaf gestured rather grandly that they should continue playing, for which they needed no encouragement.

Tim, Olaf and myself crammed into this tiny room with these poor men, all of whom were manual workers and amateur musicians; they were stripped down to ragged vests and tattered work trousers whilst we were dressed in comparative finery of dirty Levis and grubby shirts. We grinned and made signs of approval at their music across a tiny overcrowded room full of smoke and sweat. It was great, and, a little bit stoned, Olaf insisted that I get my guitar and play for the men, which I did. It doesn't matter that one is no good, it is only important that music is shared.

Our mutual destination was still India, but I was beginning to be unsure. The poverty around us was impossible to ignore. I always dropped my very small change in the lap of a young lad with withered legs who sat on the pavement near the bridge where we liked to play. He certainly knew me by the end of my stay, but he never acknowledged me or thanked me for my small donation. I think I accepted this lack of appreciation as silent admonishment for doing what I was doing not out of real necessity but for adventure, whilst his very life depended on it. Certainly my life depended on this method of fund-raising, and I contented myself with the knowledge that Olaf depended on it as well.

Then there was Wendy and Tina. I cannot recall how we met, only that they appeared on our scene and, with a great deal of bravado, offered to bottle for us for the usual ten per cent. They came from Portsmouth, and were brave and fun to be around. They had great accents and seemed ready for anything, and soon they were our regular bottlers. Our income went up and we were all happy with the arrangement.

We had no particular work times, but we favoured a pitch on the Gelata Bridge where there was a slight indent, so we could stand and play while people could still pass by. Soon, with these two pretty girls bottling and the strange music emanating from our guitars, we had a huge crowd around us. I was beginning to get concerned as the crowd spilled over from the path into the road. The only thing we could have done would have been to stop playing, and we were on to too good a thing, so I just looked the other way.

Down below us in the waters of the Bosporus, boatmen ferried their craft under the floating bridge in both directions; some hauled huge numbers of barges behind them as they skilfully manoeuvred them between the stansions on the pontoons. To my horror, I looked down at an approaching boat with at least five container barges in tow, each one being about thirty feet long. He had made the mistake of slowing down slightly, the better to see what the crowd gathered on the bridge was all about. In so doing, the last barge had begun to drift round to his right and was now totally out of alignment with the arch on the bridge that he was intending to steer through.

I momentarily stopped playing to wave to him to look round at the back of his boat, but the poor man thought I was waving a greeting at him and he waved back to me. He even slowed down more and I shouted to Olaf to have a look at what was about to happen below us.

By now the last barge had pulled two more craft out of line and itself was lying at a perfect right angle to the bridge. Olaf and I stopped playing and waited for the inevitable. The boatman below us entered the arch under us at about the same time as the rear boat crashed into the upright. The whole bridge shook as the little convoy of carriers wrapped themselves round the bridge, and a great tide of swearing and shouting greeted our ears. The crowd surged forward, and we were nearly pushed over the bridge before we grabbed our instruments and threw them into their cases and made off just before the cops arrived to add to the chaos. Thereafter we selected less prone places to play.

There was a flat roof on the hotel which overlooked a small mosque, and I often sat there watching the ragged faithful going to prayers. I became fascinated, and several times visited the place with or without the congregation. It was perfectly still inside, and good to sit in contemplation from time to time. From the roof I could watch the caller psyching himself up for the job of uttering the faithful's call to prayer; he would spend several minutes walking around the platform of the minaret coughing and hawking, before a few warm-up notes emerged. Then once ready, he brought forth the most amazing noise from somewhere in his medium-sized frame. I sat partly hidden by the wall as his voice yodelled expertly between quarter tones of beauty and spirituality. Then, slowly through the door of the courtyard below, would come a trickle of men, who slipped off their shoes at the door and made their way inside for prayers.

Eventually I entered the Blue Mosque and was filled with awe at its beauty. I knew little of Islam and did not need to know much to find once again how affected I was by the corporate act of worship. Sat at the back of this magnificent building on ancient Turkish carpets, I looked towards the illuminated holy place at the front near the Imam as he took the men through their rituals. On the left stood a huge grandfather clock, to my mind oddly out of place, its slow tick there to remind us that our time is short on this Earth. I felt I had plenty of time and always felt refreshed and immortal after these short visits.

∾

spies

My daily rounds were spent in a regular fashion. For someone who had covered considerable distances overland, I moved very little from the immediate surroundings of my lodging. I would amble down to the ferry port for my bread and sardines or maybe a corn cob, and from there to the bazaar or a stroll in the Topkapi park—although I never thought of looking in the museum. I was content to soak up the atmosphere of this remarkable city and ponder not only the belief in Islam but the fact that here was the first country I had ever been in that was allied to Germany during two world wars, which felt strange. My lack of adventurous spirit provoked Olaf into suggesting a ferry trip to some places out on the Bosporus, and once convinced that I could afford it we agreed to go. The boat was reasonably modern and had a small lounge where we took chai. It was a slightly overcast day but the weather was warm. It felt odd to be travelling without the guitar, but once on our way, very pleasant.

We stopped once or twice and at the third place Olaf decided that we should have a beer. This inevitably led to another, and another, and though not drunk by any means we found ourselves relaxed enough to miss the ferry and discover that was the last one until the following day. We had nothing to get back for, and in Olaf's usual way he struck up a conversation with some local blokes who turned out to be fishermen.

As the effects of the beer wore off, the possibility of a night trip with them emerged—and as there was no way that I could get back to the city, the opportunity grew more and more attractive. Olaf had communicated that he was an ex-sailor, and they welcomed us aboard their small but efficient craft. We left the port under a beautiful sky and slid quietly over the velvety waters of the Bosporus and into the mysterious Black Sea. Slowly but certainly the night descended until the lights from shore were invisible and all we could focus on were the lights and characters on board. There were stars above us and the boat rocked gently to the hum of the diesel. It had been a long day and my eyes started to get so heavy that for once I owned up to tiredness and was shown a bunk on deck to use. In fact it was no more than a shelf that I slotted myself into. There was an incredibly smelly blanket which I gratefully wrapped around myself against the cold, and I fell into a dream-filled sleep.

I could only have been off for about an hour when my nightmares were interrupted by so much screaming and shouting that I banged my head on the low roof. I crawled out of my slot and dizzily remembered where I was. The boat was now rocking much more vigorously with the bigger swell. All around the boat, the crew of about five were screaming at each other as they pulled and hauled on nets that were bulging with an enormous catch. Olaf had his hands full and in a moment so did I. After a good fight we dragged the net over the side and a huge flipping and flopping and threshing mass of fish filled up the passageways and all around our feet, so much so that I instinctively tried to leap out of the way in case I hurt one of them. The fishermen were grinning hugely and pointing at Olaf and me as if we had been responsible for this windfall catch.

My God, I thought, how are they going to kill all these fish humanely?

My mind flashed with horror to a scene on Brighton pier during a Sunday School outing when a man, obviously in some kind of fishing competition, brought a beautiful shining mackerel from the sea and handed it to another man with some scales. My eyes wide with wonder I gazed on its shining colours as he cleverly removed the hook from its mouth and then with his index finger, he poked into the fish's gills and ripped them open. A gush of blood poured into the brass scale pan and I recoiled in horror as the creature gave a last desperate thrash and blood splattered across my arm from the twitching tail.

It soon dawned on me that this would not be the way of dispatching all of these. I remembered seeing someone once pick up a fish and beat its head on a rock to kill it and thought that this must be the way. But how long would that take? Suddenly there was a terrible scream and we all turned to face the direction of the cry. There on the other side of the boat, dramatically lit by the gas lanterns on the wheel house, was one of the fishermen, reeling and clutching his arm. All around his feet thrashed the recent catch, and lying where it had fallen from his arms was a giant ray which had bitten him.

One of the stricken man's colleagues rushed to his aid through the knee deep fish while another picked up the ray by the tail and beat it heavily against the wheel house as if to punish it for biting his friend. The ray began to die and the man it had bitten began to pass out. There was more shouting as he lost consciousness. By now another was at his side and with a knife slit open the dim mark on his arm, and like I had seen in films all my life, began to suck and spit out into the sea the poison that had paralysed his friend. The fish thrashed and the engine throbbed like some detached heartbeat.

I looked at Olaf. He looked grimly back. The injured man was now silent and I thought he had died. Blood dripped from his friend's mouth and wild eyes looked from face to face as if to see if they had missed something that might have helped the situation. Finally the man could be seen to be still breathing and was wrapped in a blanket and one of his friends sat with him as the boat turned round and headed back in the direction from which we had embarked hours before. Olaf and I had suddenly turned from good luck mascots to the bringers of misfortune; all fishermen are superstitious and we could feel their doubts. All I hoped was that we could make it back to shore before someone blamed us directly and threw us both overboard. I almost wished I was German and could remind them how we had stood together in common cause at Gallipoli. Fortunately, the man began to come round and we all gathered around him to commiserate, and as we were reassured and the atmosphere relaxed I crawled into a vacant slot and fell uneasily asleep again, to the diminishing sound of the last dying fish slapping out their long goodbyes to the evening and their unwilling participation in it.

I was awakened by a firm grip on my shoulder and being shaken by Olaf who whispered to me, "Don't say anything, just stay where you are and do not on any account move from here, I will be below you in the next bunk. An American patrol boat is pulling alongside. We've been seen trespassing in Russian waters. We must just be still or there could be a lot of trouble for all of us."

What else could go wrong? This fucking day-trip was becoming a real nightmare. I could hear the approach of the patrol boat and muffled voices speaking in English. The response in Turkish meant that there was a lot of bluff and playing dumb going on, but the clincher was the injured man who, though recovered, was putting on a good show of pain and injury. We were nearly home now and the light was coming up in stripes across the water. On inspection of the wounded man's arm, the patrol let the boat go with a stern warning. In a way our presence, which had landed them the catch and by so doing caused the injury, had paradoxically got us all out of another dangerous situation; we were once more the golden boys as we emerged from our bed-shelves blinking in the morning light.

Amongst the catch, we had brought up a beautiful orange conch shell, and as soon as he had removed the resident from its rightful place, one of the men handed it to me as a souvenir. He grinned at me, and as we said goodbye I think Olaf and I felt vindicated for all the luck we had brought them. [8]

As we stepped from the ferry that finally arrived and took us back to the city, I again experienced a lightness of step and a feeling that there was a lot of time on my side. But what I really wanted now was some sleep. Because of the size of our tiny room, I dragged my sleeping bag up to the roof of the Gulharne hotel and slept until evening when we went out to play.

I may have felt immortal, but I was not immune to the effects of an unbalanced diet and generally keeping in good health. The Turkish system of sanitation at this time was not great. True, we could flush the toilet and take cold showers, but only at certain times of the day. The reason given for this was that there was a crack in the main reservoir which supplied the city, and rather than face the cost of repair it was cheaper to turn off the water between certain hours. Of course we soon learned not to use the lavatory during this time, but some residents did. These places always stank, but during the hot weather, even after the

---

[8] I took the conch shell home for Mum, who gave it pride of place on her shelf in the living room until a horrible smell was traced to the inner ear of the shell. After a vigorous shaking some flies and maggots fell out, and we realised the fisherman had not quite removed the entire contents. We cleaned it all properly after that, and my mother has it still.

toughening-up process of life on the road, I was still nearly sick each time I had to use the place.

Hand-washing was also difficult, and washing of my nappy 'hand towel' simply never took place; it never even occurred to me to do so, and I barely had the opportunity to keep clean socks and pants together, let alone the other stuff. I did wash my jeans in the yard with a scrubbing brush, but this was more to keep them the right colour than for cleanliness.

Tim had moved on to Izmir, and Olaf and I had a Turkish bloke back in our room. I was the first one to get ill. It happened one afternoon that I began to feel hot and dizzy with stomach cramps. I barely made it back to the hotel, whereupon I threw up and had diarrhoea. I knew not to eat anything and even a drop of water went straight through me. After a day in bed in this state with just sips of water, I began to experience feelings of detachment and delirium. The bedclothes were too hot or too cold and constantly wet from sweating. I soon used up my aspirin, and knew enough to know that I must have mild dysentery. I couldn't bear staying in bed and after only a few days dragged myself up to the roof, where I rested as best I could. If you don't eat you can't throw up, so I didn't eat. After a week I was able to get about a little, and I began by eating a boiled egg, which I had to force down with a little dried bread.

Olaf had been very concerned for me, but suddenly now it was my turn. He became mega sick; his delirium was greater than mine and he was laid in a bed bath of sweat for two days. Often he was not able to hold on to the tiny amount of water that he had to drink in order not to dehydrate completely. Unfortunately this passed straight through him and soiled the already grubby bed coverings. This meant friendship above and beyond even what he had done for me, but thankfully he threw up mostly before it could arrive at the other end.

After several days in this state I eventually got him to eat an egg, and though we were both very weak we dragged ourselves out with the two girls from Portsmouth, who had begun to miss the few coins commission we had been able to provide. We must have lost about a stone between us, and we could ill afford that. Wendy and Tina were great; they both had such positive attitudes. I thought them invincible and they would have made great road companions. Wendy was the more glamorous of the pair; she wore a light denim shirt and tight blue jeans. Tina wore a dark green T-shirt and jeans, and both girls wore flip flops.

I mention this because by our standards even then, this mode of dress wouldn't have seemed provocative, but to the average Turkish male it was hard to control the passions aroused by their appearance. Olaf and I were totally unaware of any problems, then one day after a session which was cut short, Wendy suddenly burst into tears, and Tina soon joined her in floods. I was deeply shocked.

"What on earth is the matter?" I asked them.

"Oh Ralph, it's terrible out there," sobbed Wendy. "All the time they touch us and stroke us and I just can't take it any more."

I couldn't believe how naive I had been. I felt betrayed, and what compassion I may have felt for the poor repressed Turkish male vanished in a puff of righteous resentment for the way they had abused these two girls. Stupidly I had believed that the success we were enjoying was due to the strength and rightness of the music we were playing, when in reality these men (and they were all male) saw it only as an opportunity to fondle two young girls. I could only imagine the feelings of being cheap and available for these opportunistic thrill seekers. I did my best to comfort them, and indeed wished that my relationship had been a closer one to enable me to have done more, but it seemed that just being able to cry was therapy enough.

The whole Istanbul effect threw everything into a world of unreality: the minarets and wailing prayer callers, the sound of the music that wafted without beginning or end in a frenzy of what to our untutored ears sounded like acid ramblings (Turkish music is on the whole less melodic than music from further east). The strange smells and culture where ordinary men walked hand in hand down the street, the impression that dope gave that everything was vacillating between feelings of true adventure, alienation and homesickness; add to this the semi-hallucinatory and nauseous state we were in through illness, and I began to feel as if I was losing it.

Later, I realised that the reputation of English women was at an all-time low, due to various political scandals and stories of loose morals that filled the world's press. I supposed the Turkish men were rather like teenage boys who'd been told that if you blew smoke into a girl's eye without her noticing, she would not be able to resist any advance made to her, and would surrender her most intimate secrets. These ignorant boys/men must have felt Wendy and Tina were there for the taking.

Anyway true to past form, the two girls recovered themselves. Having a good cry both relieved their tension and also reassured me that they were not as tough as they would have liked us to believe (I still felt they were probably tougher than me). I determined that we would not work with them again so they should not be exposed to such treatment, and if we had to, just the pair of us would play, and so it was. I also decided that I did not want to go on any further east and I think that the girls, who had talked about accompanying us, decided that this was far enough for them too. I wanted to attack the men who had done these things, and I didn't like the way I had been made to feel. There was some satisfaction to be had when Wendy told me that she had drawn blood with the aid of my harmonica harness as she fended off a late advance from a bloke who was still trying to touch her even as we were packing up. I felt sick.

That evening I told Olaf that I'd had it and that I wanted to go back to Greece. He too had abandoned his plans to go on. There was only one problem: he felt unable to make the journey at that moment and he knew that I could not face playing on my own even though I was fed up with his contribution and felt that I did all the work.

"I've thought of that," I countered. "When I get to Saloniki I'm going to sell some blood at the hospital."

Olaf blearily looked up at me from the bed.

"You're focking mad man, you're not well enough to sell blood. You need all the focking blood you got at the moment. Stay a few days, we'll find another couple of chicks to go bottling and then we'll head back."

My mind was made up, and his inference that I was weak immediately strengthened my resolve to get back on the road to where I felt I could cope. I said goodbye to the girls, who looked a bit sad, and left for Greece the next day.

The sun beat down and I was cold and shivering one minute then sweating the next. In the cars that stopped I slept fitfully, to wake with my collar soaked. I could force no food down me, but at least I could manage to keep water inside. I arrived in Saloniki, and with almost my last money checked into the hostel and fell asleep on the bunk in the shared room. The next morning I bought a yoghurt and ate some bread. Outside, the heat was fantastic, but I felt better from my night in a real bed, even though the sounds of disjointed conversation drifted in and out of my half sleep.

With the sun blazing down on me, I wandered off to the hospital and joined a queue of hopeful donors, all about my age, who had gathered to sell their blood. My turn came to be assessed and the nurse strapped on the blood pressure measure. I was turned down out of hand. I was deeply upset and near panic; I had been relying on the thirty drachmas that I would get for the pint and felt that this would have been enough to get me through Yugoslavia. I staggered out into the bright sunlight and a young American came out after me. He was looking at the tiny plaster that covered the vein in the crook of his elbow, like a kid admires his first tattoo. We looked at each other and he grinned.

"That wasn't too bad," he said.

"They wouldn't take mine," I told him.

"Your pressure was probably too low, try running around the block, someone tells me that works."

I watched him move off, still looking at his plaster. It was worth a go, I decided, and off I set around the donor clinic in the midday heat. The queue when I returned was now much smaller, but I failed to make the test again and wandered despondent into the waiting room to rest. Suddenly, without explanation, I was summoned to a screen and a small sample of blood taken for analysis. I said nothing and after a little while a nurse came back into the room and told me they would take my pint in a few minutes. I don't know what made them change their minds, but I was very reassured that at least I would have enough money now to get back to Italy.

It was very nearly my turn to go into the donor room when a young bloke with glasses and a pretty girlfriend, who had been talking earnestly for several minutes, stood up and made the following statement:

"Listen everybody, I think that there is something you ought to know. The blood you are planning to sell is being paid for by gangsters. Yes, I know that sounds hard to believe, but these unscrupulous men pay you a pittance for your blood and then sell it to the needy patient for whatever they can make these poor distressed people pay."

He paused to let the enormity of this fact sink in. I was appalled, but desperate for the thirty drachmas.

Christ, I thought, I know what he's going to do, he's going to organise a strike for more money. I'll back him up. I stood shakily to my feet.

"Hey man, we're with you, that's a terrible thing to do to someone who needs blood, What do you want us to do?"

I had noticed this bloke around the hostel and he seemed a thoroughly decent chap, he'll see us right I thought.

"Thank you brother," he said looking straight at me.

Brother, I thought. The man's a socialist all right, he'll get us more money from these bastards.

"This shameful exploitation of the impoverished working class must stop and this is what I propose..."

Absolutely, I thought. Here we are, the working class on the roads of Europe armed only with good intent and our music, not wishing to harm anyone, and these ruthless bastards were prepared to prey on us like parasites, literally bleeding us to provide them with a living.

"Go on brother," I urged, "tell us your plan."

"Thank you for your support brother," he said again, and then turning to the other rag tag crew he continued, "This exploitation can only stop if we the suppliers get together and attempt to break their grip on the supply."

By this time one or two others were looking up and offering some solidarity, it was quite stirring actually. Our spokesman continued.

"I have been discussing it with my girlfriend and this is what I suggest we do. We give our blood..."

"Yes, yes..." I hung on to every word.

"and when they come to give us their lousy thirty drachmas..."

"Yes yes..." I was still with him.

"We tell them we don't want their lousy blood money..."

"And we demand more!" shouted an excited American across the room.

"No, no, on the contrary," continued young Lenin, "we tell them we are donating it to the hospital for free!"

At the delivery of his final comment he glanced around the room, his eyes blazing with passion, and they alighted on me. Up to this point I was sure that he was going to demand at least double for the blood, and now faced with a much more honourable choice, I was scuppered.

"What do you say brothers and sisters?" he demanded. Some of the crowd (maybe two others) agreed, and I was reluctantly about to do the same when his girlfriend chimed in, her pretty face glowing with indignation, "Well I'm selling mine! We've got no money left to speak of and he's typically trying to prick your consciences over some stupid principle that won't change anything."

Ignoring her, young Trotsky shouted once more, "All those in favour please raise your hands!" I did not raise mine and instead went out of the room for a smoke. When I got back the two young socialists were donating and I was called next and went into the bright room.

The needle was blunt when it was plunged into my arm, and the poor girl had several painful lunges before she got a satisfactory purchase. By now I was feeling sick, and they told me to pump my hand open and closed to help fill up the jar. After about five minutes and not a drop in it, they worked out that there was a blockage in the needle tube and so had to start again. Once more the bloody blunt tube was poked into another part of the vein, and this time, with the pressure I had built up, blood spurted into the jar. Of course I made the mistake of looking round at this point, and it was as if the blood in the jar was leaving my brain in equal measures. I started to pass out.

After a little while I came to, only to find that the needle tube had come loose and a rather large amount of blood had spilled on to the floor. A nurse shouted helpfully at me and lifted my now dead arm on to the bed and told me to pump my fist open and closed again. This I did until my hand was barely able to move and my whole arm was aching. Finally the same nurse came over, pulled the needle tube from my bloody lacerated arm, slipped a piece of lint over the wounds and told me to place my hand on the shoulder until the bleeding stopped. This was easier said than done, and after several checks and it was still bleeding, I tried to eat the dry biscuit they gave me but was unable. I swallowed down the tiny glass of orange juice, signed a piece of paper written in Greek and staggered out into the blinding heat of the afternoon and back to the hostel. I was nearly at my room when consciousness left me.

I came to two days later and Olaf was sitting by the bed telling me what a fool I was, as if I needed telling.

☙

517

tenner

Olaf, who had arrived just that morning, was perturbed by my condition and grateful for my support in Istanbul while he was ill, but as weak as I felt I just wanted to get away and get back to Italy where I felt that I could repair the damage I had done to myself and earn some money without the risk of arrest again; I had already spent one night in the cells here. I literally dragged myself out of the bed, and after sharing a coffee with Olaf I told him I was heading off to Yugoslavia. I left that afternoon.

I got one lift to somewhere near the border and then walked across the border once more. The road soon became little more than a track and I was dry, covered in dust and half delirious from lack of rest, blood and food. The sun poured down on my emaciated form and dust thickened my hair as sweat ran streaks down the side of my face, leaving small salty deposits under my chin.

Lorries passed infrequently and cars were even rarer. Not for the first time I cursed the weight of the guitar, and the weight of my bag with its few new acquisitions from the Istanbul bazaar. Each time a truck rolled by, I held my breath for two reasons: one, in case it stopped for me; and two, to avoid breathing in another lungful of the white chalky dust that blew up everywhere around me. I had decided to walk away the time because I found this made me less melancholic than standing still. I wished I was at home, I wished I was with Gill, and I decided that my attempt at dalliance in the showers that time in Istanbul did not count as a lack of faith. Then I wondered if Gill was still true to me, and the thought that she may have found someone else—or worse, made love to someone else—almost made me cry.

Self-pity turned to anger and resolve that I would see this journey through and get it over with. It was a sobering thought that I was no longer enjoying this trip, and especially dreading this crawl back through Yugoslavia, scene of the demolition of my guitar and people with haunted faces and suspicious looks at 'wealthy' strangers like me.

A truck in high revs roared along the road behind me. From around the bend all I could see was a cloud of dust then a sudden increase of noise as it hurtled into view and headed towards me. I stuck out my thumb and it thundered onward and then as if the driver had a second thought, it braked violently and shuddered to a halt. As tired and hot as I was, I managed to run to the cab and climb in, grinning at the driver. I put the guitar on the floor behind the seat under the fold out bunks and nearly knocked over a box of plums that were resting between the two seats. It was a refrigerated truck and his cargo was fruit. It was a large vehicle designed for long distance driving, noisy and high off the ground. I had to clamber into the cab by resting my foot on the wheel studs.

The driver was a thickset Greek with the traditional half tan that truck drivers wear with pride. I suppose he was about thirty seven years old. He spoke no English, but he did have a little French and some German, and with the aid of signs and looks we were soon able to communicate.

Andreas was smoking a Greek cigarette and soon he offered me one. I settled into my seat and smoked as I looked out of the window. The countryside was yellow and dry, but I was all right. He offered me some of the fruit which I had knocked over as I clambered into the cab, and I accepted a couple of apricots. I was touched by the look of concern in his eyes, and as I reached over to take the fruit, he noticed the plaster over the bruised area in the crook of my arm and asked me what had happened. I managed to explain that I was short of money and that I had sold blood in Thessalonika to try to make it back to Italy. He nodded his understanding but clicked his tongue to indicate that I was perhaps foolish to have done this as I looked weak and in need of sustenance.

As the hot day progressed, the thump of the diesel and the bumpy road rocked me into the best sleep I'd had for several days (I still sleep great in cars). I woke as the first shadows of evening were lengthening, and we took a left hand turn into a sort of road café area. Andreas directed me to a water tap in the yard, where he stripped down to his trousers and gave himself a refreshing sloosh. I did the same and with hair dripping and still a little damp we entered the café, where he ordered some food for both of us. It was my first hot meal for days and it tasted great. It was only a thin steak with chips with some tomato ketchup, but I can taste it still. Afterwards I offered my pathetic leftover dinars from my trip through the country, but magnanimously he refused, waving the few coins away with theatrical emphasis. I mused on the solidarity of the working class and the fact that we were all brothers and should help each other in our times of need; my faith in human nature was restored.

I felt terrific, restored even, and we were on our way all the way to Belgrade as well. I had no idea how far we had already come, but the light was fading fast and I noticed that with each passing hour the yawning from my driver was getting louder and more frequent. I judged the time to be well past midnight when I noticed his eyes begin to close whilst still driving, so I loudly cleared my throat. Fortunately this woke him immediately, and for the next hour or so I kept him awake in this fashion as we steadily lumbered into the mountains. Virtually no cars or trucks were coming the other way and no lights shone in the distance over a welcoming town. It became obvious that we would have to rest up for some time, and with a grin Andreas noticed my anxiety and pulled the lorry over in a sort of lay-by above a ravine and, heaving on the handbrake, brought the hissing truck to rest.

He got out and took a piss and as he got back in I thought I should do the same. As I clambered back inside the truck I could see that he had lowered the bunk and had climbed in having moved my guitar and bag and placed them on the engine housing inside the cab. Outside the sky was overcast because in spite of the altitude there were no stars visible. With the engine off it soon became chilly even inside the cab. I shuffled down on my seat and tried to make myself comfortable as my friend snuffled and snorted until his breathing became quite steady as he began to fall asleep. I decided to have a last cigarette and opened the window just a little to let out the smoke. As I finished and threw out the dog-end,

Andreas grunted that there was room for me to lie down on the bunk where I would be more comfortable. For a second I wondered if I would be safe, and then realising how ridiculous any doubt would have been, I crawled over the seat and lay down.

I pondered the day and all the days and thought of Gill and where we might be at this moment. I thought how good it would be to be back in Italy, where I was sure I would be able to go out busking. I tried not to move too much in case I disturbed my host, and I was very nearly asleep when I felt a bristly chin on the back of my neck. At first I thought that I must have moved into his space and moved my head forward, but within a second or two the regular breathing had been replaced by silence as this huge macho lorry driver started placing tiny kisses on the back of my neck. I froze in terror, then I cracked and my sense of betrayal turned to unbelievable rage.

I leaped up from the bunk and started shouting at him in English, "You fucking bastard what the fuck do you think you're doing? What gave you the fucking idea that you could try this on with me? You fucking bastard what am I supposed to do where the fuck can I go? If you try to touch me again I'll fucking kill you, you fucking horrible piece of shit you stinking queer how dare you lay your fucking hands on me you fucking piece of shit."

I was frantically trying to pull my bag and guitar over towards me in order that I should get out of the truck and then I realised that there was no shelter for me and if this bastard had wanted to, he could have probably overpowered me—or worse, clubbed my head in with a rock and tipped me over the ravine. I stopped my hysterical ranting, noting that my outrage had no effect on him. After a while his breathing returned to the steady snore and whistle, and I slept holding my bag on my lap with my head lain on the door window dozing on and off awake all night until the threads of the dawn slowly crept over the hills and a different reality came to rest on my jangling red-eyed consciousness. Slowly the form of my driver stirred and in one movement, swung his legs over the bunk and into his work trousers. I noted with horror that he was down to his underpants in readiness. I was still fully clothed, and with trepidation wondered what he would say now with me still sat there like an idiot.

He said nothing, but opened the door on his side got out and took a piss, I did the same on my side and got back in. It was actually cold outside and without a word he started the engine and we pulled out and on to the highway again. After only half an hour he pulled into another café area and insisted that I had a coffee and some bread with him. It was then that he apologised for his advances the night before, explaining it away by stating that he had not had a woman for over a week. I was nonplussed by his excuse, and although grateful for the food and appreciative of the fact that he had sort of said sorry, I could not comprehend that he did not understand my feelings of outrage. I was totally shaken. All my judgements about people were under threat: my fellow feeling for the working class; doubts about myself; what of self-control? Had I somehow given him a signal that I might be open to this type of advance? I felt as if all my values were under threat and this bastard had managed it all with just one misjudged move. I did not say anything to him about his excuse and when he turned me out before he turned off the main road, he pointed out the way I should go. He waved me off, and it was as much as I could do to wave back. It was with a heavy step that I wandered into the centre of Belgrade. I don't recall how I made it to the border with Italy, but somehow I did.

I met Olaf in Trieste as we'd arranged—again he had beaten me to it. He looked even thinner and a little road-weary, but he still looked better than I felt. How come he always got there first? I even started to wonder if he took the train. Did he cheat? Cheat at what? Was this a game with rules? No, of course not. The rules of the road are get there any way you can. If you have the money, take the train; if you have the money, eat steak. I still couldn't get out of the habit of saving just a little bit, so consequently I was always poor or felt poor. In spite of these doubts it was good to see him, and it sure was good to be back in Italy ordering *due cappuccini* and smoking the old Nazionale again. We got some accommodation for a night, earned some money playing and then sat up for a long time telling each other about how we got back to where we had just met. Olaf listened patiently to my tale of near rape at the hands of the lorry driver and helpfully opined that if it had happened to him, he would have waited till the man was asleep and then stoved his head in with a rock.

"Oh yeah," I countered, "and just how far do you think you would have got on a mountain road covered with blood in the middle of fucking Yugoslavia?" He said nothing, and I added, "I wouldn't have minded but he never even blew smoke in my eyes."

It was good to have company again. We drank more wine and smoked more cigarettes (by now I had a spectacular hacking cough), finally turning in after discussing where we might go next. Olaf wanted to go to Venice where he was sure we could really earn a fortune, but I was tired. I had not embarked on it to see things and tick them off like a tourist; Venice held no more attraction to me than Frankfurt. I had begun to travel to be in it, to be part of the scenario, playing my small part in the events mundane or special, like a time traveller who momentarily interrupts the ordained course of events—and I could do that anywhere, I didn't need Venice. Then suddenly I decided to give it another go, although my resentment at Olaf's lack of musical progress was getting me down.

It's only now that I see my attitude may have been that way because I was still not ready to go it alone, and somehow I blamed him for it. I also failed to see that my slightly better musical skills were what provided equality in our relationship; if he had not been an admirer of what I could do, our relationship would have been impossible, as he was superior to me in many ways and much tougher and more confident.

Olaf had taken to wearing shorts, and was constantly going on about his elegant legs, which were if anything on the skinny side. He was luxuriating on his new meerschaum pipe, and kept on repeating how you should only smoke it wearing white gloves, so that your fingers didn't mark the bowl and make it colour unevenly. I was really starting to get irritated, but our combination still worked well, and after a brief rest I wearily plodded my way to Venice.

The place we stayed was somewhere around a heavy industrial complex—I recall power stations or electricity substations—but the hostel was old and adequate, and I met a French bloke who wanted to swap me his rather smart Fred Perry shirt for a set of guitar strings. I had brought a few spares and had been very fortunate in breaking hardly any on the trip, so I was able to cobble together a set. And I loved that red shirt. It was my lucky shirt, and I still had it in 1970 at the Isle of Wight festival.

We had to take a ferry across to Venice itself. Sadly its crumbling grandeur was lost on me. Busking was a bit difficult, but we did OK in a very short space of time as the tourists were as plentiful as the pigeons in St Mark's Square. I added the tower to my collection of tall buildings when I climbed it one day. The truth is that my abiding memories are: a comparison of the way the tourists looked and my by now tramp-like appearance; meeting a young harmonica player from Norfolk who could play Sonny Terry style; and a photograph on a café wall somewhere of the pigeons that had been persuaded to feed on carefully laid out letters of the Coca-Cola label.

The weather was warm but overcast and I was incredibly tired, the canal stank and I wanted to move on. Milan sounded promising, and Olaf, the harmonica player and I made plans. A photo of Olaf and I exists showing us outside the hostel and we both look surprisingly fit. I am proudly wearing the red shirt and leather flip flops, looking more like starting out than ending a trip.

I headed off for Milan on my own as usual, but once there met up with the other two who—surprise—were there before me. We must have sounded quite good, as the harp player was always asking when we were next going out to make some money. It amazed me to see that he actually saw this as an earner, when all I was worried about was just making enough to get by on, and once that had been achieved I wanted to have the day off. I guess I'm still the same. It was all right for these two, as neither felt competent to go it alone and I was resenting taking a third share when I felt I was holding it together. I had conveniently forgotten that I was still too scared to go it alone, and needed them just as much as they needed me.

I had found a room which I shared with Olaf, the harp player and another bloke called Nick. This guy was about three or four years older than me and very cool. He wore glasses and had his hair cropped unfashionably short. He stayed silent while he listened to our various tales, but when he did talk I found myself quite mesmerised by his understanding. This still happens occasionally. Generally speaking, experience is available to all, though we learn at different rates. My favourite comparison is that of someone who drives around a big city for years and then makes a 'wrong' turning that leads to a street he already knows. The relief at the discovery of familiarity is the same as when someone is able to link the things that you already know so that you don't feel stupid; on the contrary, you have been guided to a conclusion that you would probably have come to after a 'wrong turning' just a little quicker. So it was with Nick; over many long night chats and discussions, he shepherded my rambling thoughts and steered them safely into pens where I could call on them as proper themes rather than rambles. Such are the building blocks of reason.

I remember nothing specific of our conversations, except that he was incredibly knowledgeable about the coded messages wrapped up in the radio series *Beyond Our Ken*, which he revealed was a show written for the enjoyment of camp and gay audiences. My recent close encounter had not exactly endeared this minority to me, but as he explained the strange jokes and mummers lingo, I was entertained and couldn't wait to tell Les (who thought this was the greatest show on the air) what it all meant when I got back.

Nick had worked for the BBC and had been in the theatre, and although I was not sure at the time, I am now positive that he was gay in a very non-camp way. One by one as I delivered my prejudices and fears about 'queers', he demolished them with reason and humanity that made me a little ashamed.

When I protested at my recent experience he told me, "The ultimate fantasy for a gay man is to be loved by a straight one; this is not possible, and therefore a gay man's ultimate fantasy is never possible."

Even after my outraged feelings, I could see the poignancy and sadness in that situation.

Olaf moved to other accommodation nearby, and an American named Gerald Bergstrom moved in. He was a friendly geezer, and knew something about the music I loved. He offered to collect for us, and for a little while things slid along in an easy manner. A couple of times Olaf cried off from busking; he was getting stoned a lot and I went out with the harp player, until one afternoon he left my bag of harmonicas at the railway station where we'd been working. I'd had enough by now, and with Olaf throwing more moodies, I decided I was strong enough to head home.

It was Nick who casually said one evening, "Why don't you take the train, it's only ten pounds to Victoria."

It sounds little enough now, but it was a fortune to me and I said so. Nick immediately offered to lend me the money as he could tell that I would post it back to him. I gratefully accepted, and within a day I had said my goodbye to Olaf and the lads and was on my way. So exhausted was I that I slept nearly all the way. In any case I had no money for food and this is a good way of suppressing appetite. I had my cigarettes, a couple of snide lighters, a conch shell, the remains of some socks and underwear, my mended guitar, a glass animal from Venice and some jewellery from the bazaar. I also had two ill-fitting jean jackets, one in flimsy denim and the other in top quality suede. My passport was full of stamps, and I had what I feared at the time might be terminal athlete's foot.

A few days after I got home, my small gifts shared and my suede jean jacket sort of admired (it was strange explaining that the man who had made it was a master craftsman as it looked like it was tailor made for Quasimodo, but all admired the quality of the material), I was frantically trying to sort out the ten quid that I had borrowed to pay back Nick in Milan when a note arrived from Olaf from an address in Milan:

Dear Ralph,

I am sorry to have to ask you but I know that things are not good between us. I hate to ask you for money but I cannot turn to anyone else. Please send me some dollars to the address on this letter.

Olaf

I was overwhelmed with compassion and guilt, for without me Olaf was unable to support himself. By the end of the week I had raised the dough. I changed it into dollars (ten pounds worth) and sent it off.

Six months later the letter was returned to me with the money still inside, with a message that simply informed me that my letter had remained uncollected. I was completely puzzled and finally found Olaf's original letter and checked the return address. To my horror I saw that I had sent it to American Express (which for some reason was where all travellers normally got money sent to) when Olaf had asked for it to be sent to Thomas Cook's.

I wrote several times to his address in Norway to apologise and explain what had happened, but my letters were never acknowledged and I never heard from him again. He talked of going to work in the city of Brasilia—I hope he made it.

As for the ten pounds, Nick knew I would return it to him. I regret to say that I still owe him it!

And once I walked a million miles
All of the way to Yugoslavia
And I carried you all of the way
For where I was, then there you are

Now I cannot speak for everyone
For they got their reasons
All on this road
But heron, would that I had your wings
For then I'd know where I would go

tubs

Almost certainly I first met Tubs at the Olive Tree coffee bar in Croydon. The Olive Tree was just a little converted shop, so above the ground floor were a few tiny rooms that were occupied by a vague assortment of beatniks or apprentice beatniks, and in one of these dingy little rooms lurked Tubs.

The first thing to say about Tubs was that he was not fat. He had a shock of blond hair that was so thick and curly that the only thing he could think to do was to part it down one side and try to make it lie down. He showed a great deal more imagination about every other aspect of his life, however. He'd lost a couple of teeth along the line, though you would never know unless he deliberately showed you. He had a penchant for white jeans and leather shoes that clicked as he walked. His eyes were small and never stopped moving about. He had less of a Croydon accent than me in; in fact at first I thought he might be posh. He'd attended secondary modern school when he'd felt like it, and though he was capable of better things, he just wasn't interested.

Tubs's family were what I would describe as upper working or lower middle class; he once told me that his father worked at the Savoy—'bowing and scraping' Tubs called it—then imitating the characters in the

Styx cartoons he would flex his fingers as if tapping in exasperation and say "Scra-a-a-a-a-pe". This was one of his trademarks that we were all to copy. To me he had a strange sense of humour, in as much as he admired comedians like Jack Benny and Bob Hope alongside such British stalwarts as Peter Sellers (my all time comic hero) and Frankie Howerd. Tubs's speaking voice was sort of smoky and cracked in tone, and was a fairly unreliable accompaniment to his playing; his laughter was a wheezy, almost silent chuckle that frequently brought tears to his tiny mischievous eyes. He was one of the few people I've met that laugh out loud at cartoons or jokes in newspapers. One such joke from a Playboy magazine (no-one else I knew would even admit to reading such an item, but Tubs had no problem with this) showed two city gent type characters walking down a street passing a skeleton with a begging cup in front of him, with a card reading 'thank you' around his neck; one gent turns to the other and observes, "Some people can't make a go of anything!"

Tubs thought this was so funny, I must have heard him repeat that punchline dozens of times. He was also a master of the double take, reacting to movements that in no way threatened him as if he was about to be slapped.

Tubs was ideally suited to the apprentice beatnik lifestyle, but had adapted it so as to dispense with the search for enlightenment through poetry and jazz, preferring to reach the answer by sleeping, shagging and getting pissed as often and as cheaply as possible. He did however have a flirtatious interest in acoustic blues guitar, especially a number by Big Bill Broonzy called *Hey Hey* which he played all the time. Tubs seldom arose before mid-afternoon and had somehow convinced the owner of the coffee bar to employ him behind the jump on a 'live-in' basis.

Val Liloff lived downstairs below Tubs's room. Val was of Polish origin and was full of all the angst and passion of the true beatnik. His bible was the Alexandria Quartet and he was engaged in an impossible affair with a middle-class girl from the suburb of Shirley, who was probably a lot brighter than he was, but who seemed to enjoy the intensity of the relationship as much as Val loved the constant arguing and passionate raging this love provoked. He was never more fulfilled than when he carried the weight of yet another breakdown in their on/off affair. Val knew that the best way to understand the meaning of life was through art, literature and music, though frequently he would resort to the *Sporting Life* for relief from his pain. Sometimes he would drag me with him to the betting shop, and we would sit next door in the little Greek café whilst he daydreamed over the heavily pregnant wife of the owner.

"Isn't she beautiful?" he would ask me, and eventually I began to see why he found her so sexy. I ventured that most men have a mild attraction to waitresses and a pregnant one is even more dominated by man, as she wears the proof of carrying his child as evidence of her willingness to serve his every wish blah blah blah, but Val said it was just the way she moved and the tiredness in her languid movements and he'd just seen *The Fugitive Kind* and was in love (sort of) with Anna Magnani. We both wanted Marlon's snakeskin jacket, but it was Val who had noticed Leadbelly's signature on the guitar Brando carried.

One night Val introduced me to Tubs as "the noisy bastard who's got a thing for Ma Parker". It transpired that Tubs knew I played and liked what I did, and thus was born our musical friendship, which spilled over to the Whitgift Arms. Maurice and Rene were happy to tolerate this younger breed of drinkers to enliven the place from the usual type of cider head with their twitching hands, stammering and eye tics. We strummed guitars, got drunk, groped girls, swore undying friendships, fought and fell in love just like any normal post-war broken-homed teenage kids.

There was always a bit of grass about, and also some purple hearts which we could get hold of. But I was already going off that and I'd never been into speed really, so I suppose you could say that I was fairly relaxed on the subject of dope. Tubs, however, was fascinated and would constantly ask me about it—what was it like, what did it do? No-one openly sold any gear down at the Whitgift, so Tubs, like the rest of us, had to be content with the stuff you could get across the pub counter. I enjoyed the feeling of being more experienced than him, at the same time knowing or sensing that Tubs had an almost dangerous obsession with finding out as soon as possible what it would be like to turn on.

Henry had started to get heavily into the Cyril Davies Band that used to play at Eel Pie Island on the Thames at Twickenham. He still loved his jazz, but for sheer excitement and what we took for pure authenticity, Cyril's band was hard to beat. The journey to the island was part of the adventure; a platform ticket from East Croydon station, change at Clapham Junction for the Twickenham train and either get off at St. Margaret's and walk, or pay from St. Margaret's at Twickenham the 6d fare. However once at the island it cost 2d to go over the bridge, where two little old ladies used to stand in all weathers to take our tolls as they huddled round a paraffin stove. Wearing plastic raincoats in a little sentry box, they addressed everyone as 'dear'. They never looked up as they took the money, so I couldn't say what they looked like.

The venue itself was a great big abandoned hotel with a sprung dance floor and a stage at one end. It was between two and three shillings to get in most Saturday nights. Once when one of our friends complained about paying half a crown and asked who it was that should command such a high price he was told, "The Paul Butterworth *(sic)* Blues Band."

There was a huge long bar in another room which also sold strong cider and I remember a handwritten note on the wall high above the bar under the outline of two footprints with the legend 'Mr. Bunce jumped 10 feet'.

The plot was to freight up with a few pints and then bop and dance away to the great sounds of Cyril Davies and later Long John Baldry. During the break we would repair outside for some air or occasionally a draw and a few pulls on a joint. Weed had not taken any real hold on me. My preference was for rough cider, cheap, and in the quantities that I drank it, cheerful. I seldom bought dope as I could never achieve the precise balance to gain the desired effect. You knew where you were with cider, and you also knew where that extra pint would take you. Also I seldom if ever had a drag on any dope without having had some drink first. This is a dangerous way to handle things. A couple of hits was all I usually wanted anyway, and only then where music was involved. Up until this time all smoking materials had been marijuana or Golden Virginia and odd 'tailor mades'.

Stan had just returned from India after more than a year on the road. His hair was an admirable below-shoulder length and he was a rich golden brown colour. His Levis were the colour we all wanted ours to be, and above all he looked the real thing; a gentleman of the road, a beatnik. But although he had managed to smuggle a couple of pounds of hash across a dozen borders and convince the Egyptian authorities that he was probably a holy man and should not have his hair cut when he was arrested for begging, he was still Stan Tether from Mitcham who couldn't wait to get back on his 350 Velocette and go ripping round the lanes and roads of south London again. I was totally impressed by Stan, who had achieved what I had always hoped to have done, but I had been beaten back by hunger, insecurity and cowardice, and had on one of my early trips suffered the indignity of repatriation from the British consul in Lyon. Perhaps it was the fact that Stan was not really arty, although he loved music like the rest of us.

In the end it was music that was the glue that held us all together, but it was not his driving force. Stan was practical, good with his hands, that sort of thing. I questioned him constantly as to how he made out, and to this day I wonder if his travels changed him in any major way. In the end it didn't matter. We had returned home after brief adventures whilst Stan trekked onward through to India with not a penny to his name and did not return until the call of the Velo was louder than the pull of the road.

When I asked him how he'd managed to keep the dope hidden across all those borders, he just said that no-one seemed very keen to question him and that he only carried the most distressed of his few undergarments on the top of his travel bag, so that whenever it was opened no-one delved very deep. Stan sold his stash slowly in small amounts for about ten shillings a deal, which was a cube of hash about the size of a dice for a game of snakes and ladders. Hash was fairly new to us at this time; we soon learned to love the ritual that went with the preparation of the joints, but Stan simply broke a bit off with his thumbnail and smoked it in a conventional briar pipe with a bit of Old Holborn.

One Saturday in September I went to Eel Pie Island with Tubs and a bunch of friends. Having recently returned from the Istanbul adventure, there were still some physical effects, and as usual there was the anticlimax of home, where you find little has changed and people don't seem to be impressed with your exploits, especially post-Stan. And there was of course Gill's continued absence. Whatever the reasons, I was desperately unhappy and went for the drink even harder than usual.

I lost Tubs somewhere during the evening, and staggered outside during the break to where I knew someone would be smoking a bit of stuff. I found Stan with a couple of other mates and Stan's pipe, and their joints were soon being passed round and I greedily had my share. On my return to the dancefloor I surpassed myself with my technique until the pillars were moving with the walls and ceiling. Soon I entered the swirling pit and threw up all over myself before collapsing on the sympathetically heaving sprung floor. My friends realised I was in some trouble and dragged me outside and were persuaded by me to leave me on the steps where I promptly vomited again. People were now giving me a pretty wide berth and although I can remember events clearly, I was in no state to do anything about it.

It was here that Tubs found me, and in all honesty would probably have left me if I hadn't mentioned the word dope to explain my predicament. His first question was as to whether or not I had still got any on me. I think he'd had a few on board anyway and without much resistance from me decided to help me across the bridge and take me home.

"Good night dears," cooed the paraffin stove ladies as Tubs manfully hauled me over the bridge where I threw up again—this time partly over him. "Ne-e-e-e-xt," said Tubs (his favourite catchphrase). He dumped me on a bench and disappeared from my blurred double vision.

I began to enter the swirling pit again when I became aware of a scuffle. It seems my friend, in a misguided attempt to help me, had decided to steal a motorbike and had been observed by three off-duty policemen trying to kick over at least five different bikes. His excuse that he was drunk and couldn't remember what his machine looked like had not impressed them, and they were about to cart him off to the nick when he kindly remembered me. When the cops realised that I was unable to walk unaided, they deduced that I was intoxicated and arrested me for being drunk in a public place. We were both taken to the Twickenham nick and banged up for the night in different cells, as even my friend could not stand the smell of my regurgitated cider and was given his own room. I doubt they would show the same consideration to an offender today.

In the small hours of the morning, some other mates turned up and bailed us out, took us home and returned us to court the following day where I was fined £5 and Tubs £15. Rumours started that we were both under the influence of drugs and it now became a matter of urgency that Tubs get hold of the real thing. Up until this point I had attempted to keep him away from the gear because I knew there would be no half measures with Tubs. Now having disgraced myself in a marvellous exhibition of not being able to handle it, I could no longer ignore his incessant nagging to score a deal for him. In the end Stan relented and sold Tubs his first ten bob deal. He soon became an expert in rolling and scoring, quickly building up his own network of contacts for his needs.

Before long he was travelling up to the Front Line in Brixton and talking in West Indian patois, until one day when slightly high he got one of their swear words confused with a term of endearment: he greeted a black guy in a doorway with the salutation, "To Ras clart mon," and was immediately nutted, knocked to the ground and given a kicking. Although bewildered by the experience, he continued to make regular journeys up there. Soon Larry, a small time dealer, was part of our group, and Larry explained to me why it was OK to smoke hash.

"You see man, when they go into the tomb of Christ an' found him gone, they look around and them find only traces of his dried blood from his wounds. Them take it a sign and the roll up the dried blood of Jesus man an' them smoke it ya hear sah. Then they have visions and all things are clear to them man. Thas why it OK to smoke the blood of Christ!"

What could anyone say against that? Larry had almost turned it into communion. The religious significance was of no matter to Tubs, and I am absolutely sure that, although up until the island escapade he had not partaken of anything stronger than his mum's slimming pills, he was determined to make up for lost time.

waterloo

When I had asked Gill to marry me, I had actually asked that question. Some people asked to get engaged, which is different, like asking for a trial period. We had been through that. However marriage was never on my mind, although I supposed one day we would get married. I just wanted her to know that I only wanted her and, equally if not more importantly, that I wanted to be assured she would not look elsewhere. Engagement was really a way of making a claim on someone. I offered her nothing except my company and some slightly rudimentary guitar playing. She did however say yes. We never lived together, although we did once go and look at a flat. It was dismal and my wages would have confined us to the two rooms. I never wanted to get a career job, and I could stay at home until the summer came and we could be off again.

Gill never pressured me. I know it was not just my apparent lack of commitment that may have helped her make up her mind to go to the States. We had been through a great deal together. Some price had to be paid for the reckoning of the equation of reckless love over fun, divided by responsibility for each other and our actions, multiplied by intensity of needing to possess without proper sharing.

Gill's American employers thought I might be able to get a job playing out there, but I was still too worried about my ability to consider working as an illegal alien. Besides, I had no money to buy a ticket and so continued to beg her to return.

Her social circle widened a little more, and of course it was not long before her beauty effected introductions to more people. At one time she was an escort to a gay Hollywood minor celebrity who needed to have a pretty girl to be seen with. She found him amusing and I was mad with jealousy.

In the summer of 1965, rioting broke out in downtown LA, in the black area called Watts, and Gill tried to interpret for me the causes of the unrest. My politics were naive, and her views and interpretations were perceptive and more mature than my vague grasp. The civil rights campaign held no real resonance with me as there was no really disenfranchised minority I was aware of, at least until six years later in Northern Ireland. Of course I supported the aims of the movement, and as a very left-wing young man deeply suspected the true motives of some of the shirt-tail grabbers attached to the protest movement.

All the time I was aware of Gill's growing maturity and broadening horizons. My only concern was when I would see her again. It's not that I didn't want Gill to be happy; I just did not want to be unhappy. Her absence seemed to be the cause of my unhappiness and therefore if she returned I would be happy. And she...?

Finally my begging and pleading worked. Perhaps she was tired of it all out there (who was I kidding? I mean what could sunny California and open-topped cars possibly have to offer compared to Croydon in October?). Gill talked to her employer, and the understanding couple released her from her contract and wished us both well hoping that we would be happy.

I had no plans in place as to how we were to carry on, but once she got back something would work out. I had kept my promise to stay faithful almost to the end. I had been faithful to her in my mind. I would deal with this lapse eventually, I promised myself. But what if Gill had slipped? The realisation that she might have was almost too hard to bear. In the end the thought of seeing her again vastly outweighed that doubt. Her ticket home was booked and I did my best to prepare myself.

On the day of her return I found myself at Heathrow Airport in a state of inner turmoil. Most of my feelings began with "what if...?"

I stood at the arrivals gate of Terminal 2 awaiting her appearance with my heart pounding as the minutes ticked by. I knew she had landed because it said so on the board. Might she have changed her mind at the last minute? I watched other passengers coming through the terminal gate. I paced up and down and moved further away from the exit and then after a short gap in the passengers coming through, there she was.

Grinning and waving, she came hurrying over to me. I was overwhelmed and tongue tied. She was brimming with affection and confidence and I was the same way I was when we first met, stumbling, mumbling and feeling slightly weak and wobbly-lipped.

Taking her back to the dismal flat in Miller Road was in such sharp contrast to California, it is hard to imagine how she felt. Mum made up a bed in our tiny front room and Gill was soon asleep. I lay in the room I used to share with Bruce wondering if all was as it should be. Something was different; I was scared. Naturally I wanted to consummate our relationship as soon as possible and to start where things had ended. We had a little time together the following morning, but things were not right; conversation was stilted and I had so little to tell her except to confess my one slip-up, and this was not the right time.

Gill had so much to tell, but I could not differentiate her enthusiasm from the thought that she might have met someone else, and I didn't want to hear about all I had not been able to participate in.

She had to pay a visit to her parents' home. I decided to go with her, frightened to let her out of my sight. We left the next day for Bournemouth.

Waterloo.

Within a day of her being back, Gill and I were on the train to the south coast. Her parents were anxious to see her and I could not provide anywhere for her to make her stay longer in Croydon.

We had been alone together but there was an uncertainty and a coolness that had settled on Gill and I did not know how to deal with it. The feeling was like having a hunger that no food could satisfy and experiencing the same weakness resulting from lack of sustenance. Your arms and legs sort of lose their strength and all attempts at light conversation sound mundane and ordinary. The little jokes and asides that lubricate conversation dry up and you sound like a stumbling fool. I could only evince one or two words from Gill, despite my best efforts. Most of the journey was spent with me trying to make conversation and Gill seemingly wishing that I would stop talking. Finally I could stand it no longer. My voice was faltering and I was trembling slightly. I asked her to step into the corridor of the train so that we could talk without being overheard by the other passengers.

"You're just not sure are you, Gill?" I said.

The empty pit of my stomach seemed to appear as a hole in the floor of the train, and as she answered quietly "No," I began to slide into it.

Through the blackness of the outside a few lights were appearing as we neared our destination. Rain distorted the view and I was aware of the train slowing down as my heartbeats increased. The train stopped. My heart pounded and I felt myself moving along the corridor. The door had become so heavy I had to push hard to open it on to a small platform. I half stepped and half fell out and without a backward look slammed the train door behind me. I walked steadily to the ticket barrier, there was no-one to take my ticket. I had no idea where I was except that it was near Bournemouth. I felt faint and the rain fell on me.

I was in a film. I could not stop the camera; the train was pulling away. I had no money as usual. Out on the street the cars went by, people scurried to wherever they were going. No-one knew me or what had just happened. No-one knew what I had just done. To these strangers it was just a rainy night and they were going home. To me it was like the world was ending. Nothing eased my feelings of desperation and numbed senses. I did not write songs then but if I did this would be my first one.

My girl left me—no that wasn't right.

I left my girl at the station—where was I? I looked around and saw that I had alighted at somewhere called Pokesdown.

Fucking Pokesdown for Christ's sake! There was a name that was never going into a romantic song of love and loss.

What could I do? Should I try to get to Bournemouth and see if her family would put me up? I thought if Gill tells them it's over they would already have the bunting hanging out by the time I got there. The evening drizzle had soaked through my coat shoulders and I was crying but no-one would have noticed. I would have to hitch home. Where was the London road? Shop signs and traffic lights reflecting on the otherwise unyielding pavement. My desert boots are sodden, I can feel the water inside my socks. I am drowning from the feet up. My balance is affected,

I am disorientated by the immediate and waterlogged confusion spreads like ink on blotting paper in my head.

"...the road is so hard..."

That time I took the bend on the motorbike
and Gill sensed I wouldn't make it;
she jumped off and came to no harm,
I landed on the road and my jaw hit the gravel
which also scraped the skin off my knee down to the bone.
My leg was so shocked that it forgot to bleed for a while
and then it poured.
My chin swelled up on one side
and I couldn't shave for days until the cut had healed.
My eyebrow was torn like a boxer's.
I did not mind the torn eyebrow.
I left the racing green Francis Barnett in New Addington
and sold it a few days later.
My motorbike time was at an end.

Gill had got off the bike, now I had got off the train.
"Do you know where the London road is?" I asked someone.
"No mate."
Where the fuck is the London road?
Curtains are being drawn in houses along the way. Slowly I am being shut out. There are fewer and fewer people on the street as I wander working my way out towards the road to London via the urban road signs. Now and then I make huge shuddering sighs. Past more shops closing and shutters going down.

"The riots are all about prices in the Watts district being too high for the poor black people who live there. All the shops are owned by white people. From where we are we can see the smoke and everyone is worried," wrote Gill.

Civil rights and the back of the bus. I have no money for any part of the bus. I just keep on walking.

"...I'm going where the weather suits my clothes," sings Woody.

Dear Woody,
I am writing to you to tell you that I have sung your songs in Franco's Spain.
I have your picture inside my guitar case.
Yours sincerely with huge admiration, Ralph May.

Dear Ralph,
Thank you for writing. Keep singing, signed Marjorie Guthrie.

My first lift is taking me the wrong way towards Bournemouth. I ask to stop, at least I am on the right road, should I continue or cross the road—how different will my life be? My next lift takes me near the New Forest.

Hide and seek
the smell of summer
insects buzzing
soft bracken
two days to go before she flies.

"…baby please don't go…"

"…I love my baby
and she's bound to love me some.
she used to throw her arms around me
like a circle round the sun…"

My head is bouncing gently off the window of the car Gill is nudging me.
I am on the wrong side of the vehicle. Where are we? Italy.
"He keeps touching me."
"I'll kill him," I murmur.
"Don't hit him, he'll crash the car. Let's get further down the road," whispers Gill.
"I won't fall asleep," I say, but I do.

I am woken by my head banging against the window. I am on the left side. My clothes are warm but damp.
"Are you all right mate?"
"Yeah."

"You had a bad dream?"
"Yeah."
"How long you been waiting?"
"What time is it?"

"Does anybody know what time it is?"
Brighton beach. March.
Christ it's cold
lying on the pebbles
with Judy in the bag.

"About two hours I suppose."
"You look like a drowned rat!"

Rats swimming around in drains
dragging the debris pulling it under.
In the red sea an arm waves.
It's OK it's already dead.
They go for the throat.

I sit up.
"Do you mind if I smoke?" My eyes are so sore.

"...I love my baby
and she's bound to love me some..."

"Here have one of these."
"No, I roll my own." My hands are shaking still the tobacco falls on
my lap. I make the smoke; it is badly rolled; I inhale deeply.

The windscreen is misty and everywhere is black except the dashboard
and my red glow from the roll up reflection. I drift into a red miasma...
rat's teeth nip at my skin jerking me back to startled wakefulness. I am
shivering in short rhythmic bursts just like Teddy Wolf.

My donkey jacket smells like a blanket. The car steams like a wintry
stable.

She is riding over the hills and New Forest,
her hair blowing in the wind.

541

Her hair flicks at my face
as we drive the coast road on the scooter.

"...she used to throw her arms around me
Like a circle round the sun..."

I doze; the car is heading for a wall, I instinctively lean away; my head hits the driver's shoulder as we drive straight on. "Sorry," I say.

"You OK mate?" he asks again.

"Yeah." I roll another fag. It stops raining and he drops me outside of Epsom. I walk and walk, eke out my tobacco. My Zippo held tight in my fist. Maybe she will write in a few days.

I knew she wouldn't.
She needed more time.
She was jet-lagged, except the term had not been invented
and it would have meant nothing to me.
This is not a nursery game, ending prematurely.
I am not a baby, I am a man.
This is not some lovesick teenage boy here.
These are a man's feelings—does she not know?

"...you should have gone to the States man..." chorus the nipping, squeak-ing, red-eyed rats.
She cannot know.

"...baby please don't go..." sings Big Joe.

I am sinking like a stone,
I am drowning,
I am being pulled under a red river.
The headlights are rats' eyes in the dark.
I am not waving.

I never wavered, except once or twice.

I am back on the train.
Some soldiers share some cake with me
and my mum says it's OK to eat it.

The men laugh a lot and offer her a cigarette.
She politely refuses. I think they like her.
The cake is nice. It came out of a mess tin.
I am on the train; her eyes have a deeper knowledge than me.
They look at me but I am barred from access to move her heart.
Shutters have been pulled down.
The victim cannot forgive.
The judgement extenuated.
The jury is excused.
We will never forget.

"Now you understand.
This is not to hurt you,
the teeth marks will fade.
You will swim away one day," sings the wind through the pylons on Fac-
tory Lane.

I am under the shadow of the gasholder and it has been raining for the last hour. I tap the letterbox. Eventually my mother answers the door.

"What on earth is the matter?" she asks with a worried look.

"It's over," I say, and the tears fall again.

"...the sun gonna shine on my back door some day
And the wind's gonna get up and blow my blues away..."

∽

543

timber

Once again the cast of thousands that populated these years came to my rescue. I spent my 21st birthday alone and drunk, but friends were supportive and in their pre-hippy way tried to offer advice and comfort. Between bouts of severe melancholy I did begin to eat again, although I lost an awful lot of weight in a few weeks.

Jobs were quite plentiful and I found work in a timber kiln drying unit in Beddington Lane, Mitcham, where I worked with Tubs' bosom pal Bunny Doyle. The job was actually quite a gas, and soon we had Tubs working with us as well. We had a great little cockney foreman called Fred, from Rotherhithe. He looked at us with a mixture of pity and curiosity. We had decided to eat in the modest staff canteen, and the normal boys' talk was interspersed with political chat and conversations about obscure jazz musicians. We discussed news items and general issues whilst wading through the typical English stodge that passed for food for the working man. Our little foreman listened to us and threw in the odd comment now and again. Once when Tubs was recounting a time when he managed it four times with a very pretty girl called 'dirty Di', Fred stood up, shaking his head in disbelief.

"Four times in one night?" he said. "You must be like bleedin' bunny rabbits, that's all I can say. When me and my missus is finished we're both completely knackered and sweating hot." It was not a pretty thought but a good point.

Once when we were talking about child psychology, little Fred told us, "During the war my old man bred rabbits. We was all allowed to call one of them our own but we didn't realise he was breeding them to eat did we? So one day my little sister is watching out the window when she sees my old man going to her hutch. He takes out her rabbit, Snowy was his name as he was nearly all white. And the next thing, bosh! he kills it ready for the table. Well you know my sister went really peculiar after that and got St Vitus' Dance and had fits. Funny that..."

Fred had been listening to a conversation about capital punishment. We were all fervently against it and were deeply engrossed in argument with one of our number. He was a real racist called John. Lunch break was nearly over and none of us had made any advance on John's view.

The bell sounded to resume work, and as we stood up from the table Fred solemnly announced his philosophy thus: "If you debolish the hangin' you ain't got no detergent!"

Tubs' last mouthful of mashed potato hit the wall opposite, and this phrase entered our vernacular for years.

Jacqui McShee and I were friends from the Olive Tree, and our common love of music was one of the bonds that saw us on a weekend away with Henry, who had newly passed his test. Henry had acquired an elderly hand-painted Bedford Dormobile with a sliding side door that was very good at sliding open, especially on bends.

Somehow we made the long and pleasant journey back to Poole for old times' sake and spent the day ambling about the old place washed in nostalgia for events that had only occurred a couple of years before. I had my Harmony Sovereign and soon we were sitting outside the Angel pub; I was playing songs and Jacqui was singing along, with a small group of admirers watching us.

I guess we must have impressed, as after a short while a tall young fair-haired fellow came up to us and engaged us in conversation, saying that he had really enjoyed our playing. Henry acted as intermediary as we discussed music in general and guitars in particular.

"Actually I have a guitar I want to sell," said the young fellow.

"Oh, I'm suited," I said. "I love this guitar, I've taken it all over Europe and I hope to get a Gibson."

"I think you'd like this guitar I've got," interrupted the young bloke. "It's called a Martin."

"A Martin—" blurted Henry as I kicked out at him and hit him smartly on the shin.

All of this was duly noted by the young bloke who said, "I know what a Martin is. I know they are valuable but all I do is keep it under my bed and polish it. I can't play it like you would, so I'd like you to have it."

Henry and I looked suitably chastened. Henry asked, "How much do you want for it?"

"Well it's very old, it's a 1936 00028. It's smaller than your guitar but it sounds great and I think you ought to have it."

Martin is the acknowledged Rolls Royce of acoustic instruments, and as such was completely out of my class. The only people I knew who played them were pro musicians who needed them for their work or their ego. In the days before PA systems in folk clubs the Martin reigned supreme as it was both beautiful in tone and huge in volume. The guitars also started off at about £200. My Harmony had cost me £29 and that had taken me a year to save for.

I repeated Henry's question: "How much do you want for it?"

The young man seemed to think for a moment as if trying to access what we could reasonably pay and then he said, "I must get £25 for it."

He might as well have said two hundred. As usual I had a few coins and my emergency ten bob note folded into my Levis 'pick pocket'. Jacqui had a couple of quid, and Henry said, "Twenty five quid? I've got some money but not that much."

"Well why don't you come and look at it?" offered the bloke.

We agreed and drove him to his address where, as he told us, the instrument was stored under the bed. He pulled out the old shaped case and opened the lid and there, nestling in its faded blue lining, was a near-perfect vintage 00028 Martin guitar. I carefully took out the in-strument and smelled the strong aroma of lavender polish and must that accompanies old instruments kept in cases.

The strings looked like they had never been changed, but the sound! The sound was of bell-like clarity and I gawped in wonder at its simple beauty. The back and sides were of rosewood and the top a splendid piece of pine; the bridge and finger board were of ebony and the body was bound in herring bone purfling. It had a slotted head and the Grover machines were adequate, if not perfect. There was a small mark on the front and the usual little scratches earned through proper playing and ownership.

"It used to belong to the guitar player in the Billy Cotton band," the bloke informed us. I looked at Henry and Henry looked at me. Jacqui looked at both of us and we all looked back at the bloke. We simply did not have £25 between us.

"It is beautiful," I said, "but it's not really my guitar." In truth the action had risen over the years and I could not easily get the response from it that the instrument merited but it was almost a religious experience to hold the thing.

"Look," said the bloke, "I know it's worth about £250 but I really would love you to have it." Henry told me he had his holiday money on him and that if we pooled all our dough we would have sixteen pounds ten shillings. We told the bloke more to provide him with the information than in hope that he would be interested.

"Are you going back to London today?" he asked. We nodded that we were. "Can I get a lift with you then?" he said.

"Yeah," said Henry, "I suppose so."

"Well maybe I'm mad, but you can have the guitar for that money and a lift to town," he said, so we shook hands all round and gave him literally all our money and the guitar was mine.

It was a Sunday evening and Henry wanted to get back to the Red Lion in Sutton, where we met some old friends. I shared the news with them and Cliff Aungier who was the guest that night at the folk club there.

"You jammy sod!" he laughed. Everyone was slightly incredulous at my good fortune. We had dropped off the bloke somewhere along the line and all the time I was wondering if the guitar could have been stolen. The bloke had got the guitar from an old Irishman he had met in a pub. It all seemed a bit shady.

As soon as I could, I wrote to Martin Guitars with the serial number; they wrote back to confirm that it was shipped to England in 1934 and that it had never been reported as stolen, and I sighed a huge sigh of relief. It was a long time before I tried to get it worked on and made easier to play.

Over the years, I have used it on record and Bert Jansch once borrowed it for a recording. It is a real treasure of a guitar and it is still in great condition. I have never played it on stage, but I once used it in public a few years ago when I performed with John Williams on a Melvyn Bragg programme to publicise a concert we gave for Chile.

I do hope the bloke who sold it to me happened to be watching, because the last words my generous guitar donor uttered to me before leaving Henry's old Bedford were, "You never know, one day I might see you on the telly playing my guitar and that will be great."

A week or so later, Henry, Jacqui, a girl called Alison and I went for a mooch about in Cornwall. I was never one for camping, but during our short stay in the West Country that was what I was forced to do. My clearest memory, sharpened by some photos, is staying in a caravan near Penzance and playing and singing together. We heard about a folk club down at Bottalack, near Land's End, called 'The Counthouse'. We managed to play two or three numbers there. We were received well, and who could fail to be impressed by Jacqui's marvellous voice and Henry's jug blowing?

I am pretty sure that I wrote *Sleepy Time Blues* in the rainswept caravan park just behind the heliport in Penzance. It was somewhere in St Ives that Henry bought his first fisherman's smock and I remember his dad asking me what I thought he looked like. I responded that he looked all right, I supposed.

"All right?" he queried, "I think he looks like a bleedin' terrapin."

Back at the timber yard, Bunny managed to keep me from the deep darks by his enthusiasm and ever-optimistic plans. Bunny's dad was Irish, and for some reason had settled in Alderney. From his accounts it was a very quiet place, which was amazing because Bunny had a sense of survival and an eye for a situation that was so far in front of us town boys; he shamed us all and he would have a go at anything. He was the sort of bloke who wouldn't impress Mums but, providing he was not trying to get off with your sister, might impress your Dad.

I think it was Bunny who first realised that one of the black guys used to come back from lunch with a big grin on his face, and it wasn't long before we were all sitting in his old Jag having a draw after the canteen. It was as a result of this partnership that the three of us started harmonising whilst we were loading the timber on to pallets on rails for the kilns. We used to get off on it and no-one ever took the piss so I guess we sounded all right. I remember one time as we stood in the machine shop on wet time, we even started harmonising with the lathes, creating dissonances and eastern tones as well. Most of the other workers were sure we were quite mad, except the black guys who just shook their heads and smiled.

One day in late November or early December, we were loading stacks of timber in the pouring rain when Bunny suddenly said, "Sod this, why don't we fuck off to Paris?"

I knew that Gill would not call me again, so after thinking about the proposition deeply for about ten seconds I said, "I haven't got any money."

Bunny said, "Where would you rather be broke?" We both climbed off the stack and turned the job in. Within two days Bunny and I were in Paris.

◡

matuzzi

The Hotel du Commerce was already a well-known cheap lodging on the Rue de la Montagne Ste Geneviève. To say it was run-down implies that at one time it must have been fairly decent. Its present state belied that it was ever anything other than dark, dingy and smelly, with minute rooms barely big enough to take the bed, a cupboard and an evil smelling hand basin, set off with oddments of lino and rough painted walls. My army days were only five years behind me, and to give myself some sense of order I tried to make my bed most days—or at least to straighten it out. Once I even stripped the sheet away from the mattress, but the sight of what lay underneath lives with me still. The mattress looked as if it had been used as a dissecting table for about thirty years, which was probably half its real age. To this day I try never to read other people's love letters written on mattresses.

The whole place was presided over by Madame Matuzzi *"et mon fils, Jean."*

She was five foot two with eyes of blue and about the same size waist measurement, grizzled grey hair, rolled down stockings which revealed varicose veins and a jovial face with a ready smile. I can't recall her smoking but she sounded as if she did. After living there about a month I was awoken one morning by a lot of activity outside; Madame et Jean were hanging out bed sheets, and that night when Bunny and I got back to our room we had different linen—I can't bring myself to say clean, but it was not the same as we'd had up to that point. It cost eleven francs per night and we paid every night after working the cinema queues.

Madame appreciated our promptness, and not only got us a room on the ground floor out the back in the courtyard near a WC (there was another one on the first floor landing) but one night she insisted that we had a little drink from a bottle that she kept hidden.

"Attention flics!" she used to say, rubbing the side of her nose with a grubby finger. She dropped a sugar cube into each tiny glass and bade us throw it down. It was so strong that after two glasses we had to go and lie down. I seem to remember saying something about alcohol made from wood, but anyway we didn't notice the dampness of the beds that night.

Another little act of kindness towards us was the provision of a small paraffin stove which she put in the room one freezing cold night in January. The problem was that all the wallpaper left its moorings as the heat pulled moisture from the walls and steamed it off on to our beds. The next day the stove was gone and dry wallpaper had been pinned up on the crumbling plaster with drawing pins.

There was no doubt that Madame quite liked us, mainly I suppose because we paid nightly for our accommodation. But rough as we were, we were positively upmarket compared to the usual clientele. Across the courtyard from us lived two ladies of the evening who entertained their noisy punters through the small hours, but in the end we took hardly any notice of the crashes and bangings, and I never even saw them in daylight—though Bunny did, and commented that you could understand why they only went out after dark.

The two WCs that served all the patrons were of the 'bomb aimer' type and were really awful even by Paris standards. The one on the first landing had a wooden shed-type door and the walls were covered in graffiti in most European languages (plus Arabic). One notice in French had been translated into English as 'Please do not flush the dismembered bodies of your unborn children down the toilet as it blocks the drains.'

Because of the late hours many of the guests kept, and the occupations of some of the others, the front door was always open, enabling anyone to get in. There was little reason to lock the door as no-one living in this place would have anything worth stealing. There was the little window in the hall behind which Madame used to sit, fat knees apart, scratching her veins which ought to have been a deterrent to anyone planning on gaining entry for any criminal intent, and in front of her window were the stairs to the first floor.

One morning as we were leaving the hotel, I happened to notice that someone had taken a shit on the uncarpeted third stair, just out of sight of Madame's window. It remained there for several days. Neither Bunny nor I liked to say anything about it in case it was construed as a complaint. I don't think Madame Matuzzi knew anything about what went on upstairs, as she found moving about a bit of a nuisance as well as tiring. Although she would probably not have approved of the wording of the notice, she would have gone along with its practicality. I doubt if Jean could read, and if he could have, would have cared. As for the turd, no-one would have noticed the smell.

Madame Matuzzi favoured the toilet on the courtyard level as it was near her lair. Unfortunately it was also adjacent to our room. The smell from it was unbelievable, so the door was always left open to help disperse the build-up of dangerous gases. If you required privacy when forced by nature to enter this foul cabinet, it was necessary to turn the little lock on the door which was cleverly arranged so that a light went on at the same time. Unfortunately, once the electrical circuit was complete, you also received a rather nasty shock. I personally could not bear to go inside unless I had first thrown in a lighted newspaper in order to obliterate some of the excess smell (it brings a whole new meaning to taking a newspaper to the loo). Then by skilfully adapting a rubber band and hooking it over the lock, privacy and light could sometimes be obtained.

Usually though, by the time you had got properly into position with any degree of confidence that you might be on target, you began to get overcome by the fumes once more, and were forced into running the gauntlet of a short sharp shock and bursting into the morning air of the courtyard having aborted your mission. Besides, the local café was just around the corner and marginally less pungent.

Madame Matuzzi however was made of stronger stuff and was far more practical; she simply didn't bother closing the door.

"Bonjour mes enfants!" she would shout as we attempted the near impossible task of walking past her without looking directly at her,

responding only with as nonchalant a *"Bonjour madame!"* as we could manage whilst she grunted and puffed, poised in a most precarious position that was not quite squatting and not quite standing. As far as anyone could tell though her aim was perfect and she never missed the hole.

"For fuck's sake don't start her talking mate, we'll never get away," Bunny would warn me. I would find something deeply fascinating to study on my left sleeve as we scurried by.

"Il fait beau ce matin eh?" she would offer. *"Attention flics mes enfants eh!"*

"Oui Madame, a toute a l'heure," we limply chorused down the hall past the turd on the third step.

There was a bar on the corner of our street and the Rue des Ecoles, and we would start the day with a cup of coffee and, in my case, a hard boiled egg and a piece of baguette and butter. Then I would either go back to the hotel and play guitar for a while or mooch about the area of St Michel. My only source of income at this time was busking, which I dreaded.

The day we arrived in Paris I had just five pounds in my pocket. It must have been Bunny's idea to go to this particular area, as it was all new to me.

We stood on the Rue des Ecoles—bag in one hand, guitar in the other—and Bunny said, "Well how about it then, are you hungry?"

"Yes," I replied.

"Well let's go to work then."

"What right here, now?" I enquired, the nervousness creeping up on me.

"No mate," said Bunny, "there's these two cinemas down the road. We'll play there." So we made our way along the road to where two small cinemas were situated, one on the corner and the other just inside a tiny turning. To my relief there was no-one there, so I reasoned with my mate that there was no point in playing. So he explained to me the way Paris cinemas work: people do not enter the picture house once the film has begun, preferring to form a line outside where of course they are a captive audience. My heart was now beating as fast as it does before going on stage, and as we sipped a coffee across the road and watched, a queue began slowly to form at first one and then the other movie house.

Bunny and I had played together before on many occasions, and he was a very competent strummer with a slightly nasal voice with a good bit more penetration than me, but our repertoire was very esoteric, made up of 1950s blues, bluegrass and folk songs.

I wondered if we perhaps should have had something better known, but it was far too late to worry about things like that now. Both queues were now considerable and I knew it was time to move. My hands were trembling and I needed to go to the lavatory. The awful thing was, every one of my friends knew that I had carried myself around Europe playing guitar for a couple of years already, but due to my shy personality I had always played where the people had an option to avoid paying me anything, i.e. street corners. Here we were on a street where the audience had only the option of refusing the hat when proffered.

"I need to tune up," I announced as I returned from the loo. We managed a rudimentary A-string agreement and in a rare act of French café proprietor kindness, he allowed us to leave the guitar cases in the café and we crossed the road ready to take up position to play. As we drew near I excused myself again and went for a little stroll around the block to try and calm my almost uncontrollable shaking.

By the time I had regained my composure enough to play, Bunny was really agitated. "Come on mate for fuck's sake, they're about to let them in."

There was nothing left but to go for it, and as soon as the sound from my old Harmony Sovereign boomed out I was OK. Halfway through the second number the queue started to move. Suddenly Bunny stopped playing, put his guitar down and ran to the front of the queue. He pulled his cap out of his pocket and started bottling the line. I manfully continued on my own until the last of them had gone in. There was no time to count the money as the second queue had started to move.

"Oh shit man," said Bunny, "we'd better hop it, lively, lively."

With pockets jingling we ran across the road and over St Michel to the Rue Racine where there was another small picture house. Here we did our first proper busking, playing four numbers which became our staple show over the next few weeks.

We began with *San Francisco Bay Blues*, then *Hard Travelling*, followed by *Roll in My Sweet Baby's Arms* and finishing with *The Saints*. The first number was played halfway down the line; the next was played on the hoof as we slowly moved up towards the front. For the third we moved

554

back down the line, bottling as we went; and the fourth we played as an unrequested encore. This generous performance was soon cut to three numbers, with the bottling being done by a third party for 10% of the take.

After our little show we returned to where we had left our cases and excitedly counted our small change. I don't remember how much we got, but it was more than we expected and we were able to pay for our drinks, a snack, and most importantly a room for the night.

Some people would have gone on to do much more playing, as there was certainly a good living to be made on the street if you were bold enough. I was content just to get by; in those early Paris days we got merry and occasionally pissed but we didn't drink a lot.

∾

musketeers

All northern European cities are cold in winter, but Paris, so far inland, was bitter. Part of the reason we played such a short set on the street was that we could not feel our fingers after the first number, and whilst sensitivity is not normally a quality that is in high demand as a busker, it does help to know what string you are pressing down. String breakages were common, but because there were always two of us we could cover for each other and we'd get away with it. I remember one freezing night I broke a B string and carried on playing, and at the end of the number I noticed that it had entered the back of my hand. To my amazement as I pulled it out I realised that it must have penetrated nearly half an inch and I hadn't felt a thing. Luckily it did not become infected—I don't suppose any germs could survive in that temperature.

I have always been a creature of habit, and I never ventured very far out of this small group of streets around St Michel. I hardly remember eating anything hot but occasionally one of those thin steaks and chips that you can get in nearly all French cafés. I drank coffee, developing a strong taste for espresso, and smoked Gauloises *sans filtre*, hardly slept, played guitar, laughed a lot, talked about what it would be like when Tubs came over, and in the main loved this existence.

I still experienced this terrible void whenever I thought about Gill, but in my heart I knew it was all over. I knew that somewhere she was living, working, maybe even loving someone else. When these thoughts of her came to me, the emptiness I felt almost made me sick. Since we were seventeen we had done everything together and now she was gone. I had tried to be faithful to her while she was in the States, but had slipped a couple of times, only to be consumed with guilt afterwards.

I knew in my heart that she would have erred as well, because no girl as beautiful as her would have been able to avoid the attention of men for very long. I knew that some of the time she had been the escort of some gay bloke who worked out of Hollywood but needed not to be perceived as homosexual. I also knew that there was a guy that she occasionally mentioned in letters, and if the thought that she may have loved him hurt me then, the pain I now felt was hardly bearable. I constantly went over our last few days together, wondering if it had all been my fault or was it just the payoff line for all my immaturity and insecurity. I constantly asked how she was feeling and constantly told her how I felt. Most of the time when I looked at her I could not believe she was mine, and the fact that she was so completely mine and had gone through so much with me made the pain of her going even harder. Sometimes I just felt like crying out like a wounded animal, such was my desolation.

My companions knew of as much of my hurt as I chose to tell them, and as the pain produced by the awful realisation that our affair was over began to subside, I found as any young man does that pretty girls still affected the vital parts, if only the heart would mend.

In truth the city provided so many distractions, and instead of a constant ache, the pain used to suddenly flood over me like a wave that hits you when your back is to the sea. Gradually the gaps between the waves grew further and further apart until, like giving up smoking, a whole day might pass without thinking of her at all. I had to wait a very long time for that to happen.

I also knew I had to do something about the female situation. I would have loved to have met a French girl, but it was as if they were on another planet as far as we were concerned. Also you have to put out the signs that you are interested in becoming involved with someone new. I guess I was still walking around wearing my mourning in a very visible way. Of course there were girls all around us from all over the world and even at street level there was a foreign community of sorts that we were becoming aware of. This area centred round the Boulevard St Germain and Odéon but I guess through shyness or British reserve we made very slow progress. Except for Tubs, who was convinced that everywhere we went girls were undressing him with their eyes.

Just before I left England I'd had a brief encounter with a girl called Anita. She was really beautiful, tall and slim with a lovely complexion, blue eyes and a pretty mouth and a cascade of blonde hair which she pulled up at the sides in a ponytail and left some to fall over her shoulders. She had a lovely south London accent, but after the admiration of her beauty there was not much to be said to each other really, and after a couple of dates I went cool. I was so lonely in Paris for girl company that somehow I prevailed on her to pay a short visit to Paris.

It was not a great success, and after the brief joy of a companion in my room/bed I lost interest and was unable to disguise my lack of depth of feeling for her. I'm sure her feelings were hurt; I just felt like a heel. I needed some sexual satisfaction and I really convinced myself that we could make it. Maybe that is the difference between my generation and the one my children have grown up in. It's funny how my generation never seemed to have friends of both sexes. We were all ensconced or involved sexually; working class kids got engaged then, and I had been engaged to Gill for about two years on and off by this time. Now it was most definitely off.[9]

At some point I decided I had to go home at Christmas. This again was probably an obligation that I felt towards my mum, and anyway I

---

[9] Years later I chanced to meet 'Slim Tony' and MB (two old mates from the sixties) in a pub in west London. It was one of those chance things when someone you haven't seen for years turns up out of the blue and you stand reminiscing over a few pints. Both blokes had been part of our late adolescent scene and we had lots to reminisce about.

At one point MB went to the gents toilet and Slim Tony said to me, "You nicked the best looking bird I ever had."

I was stunned and certainly couldn't remember at that point who he could mean.

"Her name was Anita and you pulled her off me at a Bonzo Dog Doo Dah Band gig at the Old Tiger's Head in Lee Green."

"Did I?"

I could not deny knowing Anita but I had no recollection of pulling her from anyone. I certainly went to plenty of Bonzo gigs with Henry, and Anita came from somewhere. Actually I had only to look at him as he spoke these words. The look in his eyes clearly showed pain even after all the intervening years. I felt terrible and thirty years later found myself apologising for something I did not remember doing. He laughed and said it didn't matter now but for a moment there in his eyes I saw all the pain of remembrance and knew that he had experienced that aching void that I had gone through with Gill.

have never spent a Christmas away from home to this day. I was back in Paris before New Year. If anything it was colder, but we still had our cinema queues and Bunny had met some more people. Tubs had arrived and we all shared the fortunes of the streets.

Tubs had brought a friend from Croydon who couldn't play guitar but who wanted to earn his living with us. His name was Robin Best and he had earned something of a reputation back home for being somewhat difficult and dangerous.

Robin was older by a few years than all of us and walked in subtly different worlds to our little trio. It was years later that I found out that he had been rejected by his mother and raised by his grandmother, which gave him a very strange attitude to all his women. Nevertheless he was from the now almost obligatory broken home, and was attracted like all of us to the music that gave us commonality. I had to believe it was the music because he was so successful at all other aspects of his social life. If it had not been the music I doubt very much if our paths would have crossed at all. Robin was a real predator and enormously experienced as far as girls were concerned. He was possessed of very good looks and more front than Blackpool. Even if a girl showed immediate distaste for him it would seldom put him off and whatever his formula was he never had any trouble pulling a new 'chick'. I had not taken to him and I was prepared for the worst.

Although the Olive Tree was the place where most of us met in Croydon, there was another coffee bar called 'The Chalet Suisse' which was frequented by a different class of kid altogether. Most of them had cars or access to them, and all of them had money that they did not earn. I suppose they were all middle class young people from the more prosperous parts of South Croydon and the suburbs of Selsdon and beyond. I only ever went in the place once, but Robin, who spoke with a posh accent (to my ears) used it on a regular basis, only latterly becoming a visitor to the Olive. Tubs was a sometime visitor to the Chalet Suisse and I suppose that's how their friendship developed. Robin had a reputation as a good man in a fight; the only trouble was that it was often he who started them.

I remember one night on the door of the Olive there was a little fracas and Robin who was smoking a small cigar stepped in to help out. Quickly weighing up the situation and realising that actions would be more effective than words, he moved into the group and hit the first one with a straight right hand which caused the chap's nose to sort of explode. The blow sent the chap reeling back down the narrow passage of the club entrance taking his three mates with him. There was no room for a full scale bundle and they were soon thrown out the door humiliated and damaged, with the promise they'd be back. They never did.

Robin sauntered back up the passage and leant forward to the girl taking the money and jutting out his chin wordlessly bade her take the cigar from his mouth, he then stepped into the gents to wash his hands (of blood) returning a few seconds later to jut out his chin to receive his cigar back from the girl. This all happened so quickly hardly a word was said. I thought it was pretty cool.

Some time later I learned that for a very brief period Robin had been an apprentice policeman but had decided to hold up a petrol station for some cash and had been nabbed as he drove off straight into the path of some of his colleagues. He had spent his twenty first birthday in the nick. Robin was very volatile and had little tolerance of gentler souls except for women. Up until this point I'd hardly ever been in a fight, and hearing of Robin's impending arrival I feared the worst. I needn't have worried however, as the bloke who arrived in Paris was very different to the one we knew in Croydon, both in looks and personality.

Bunny and I were out on the street as Tubs and Robin arrived, we were coming back from Place Contrescarpe where we occasionally went for an evening beer and had just arrived at Rue des Ecoles as they walked up Rue de la Montagne.

"Jesus, look at Bestie," sniggered Bunny. "What does he fucking look like?" Then after a moment, "Fuck me, he looks like Barnacle Bill the Sailor!"

We both burst out laughing. I have to admit it was embarrassing. There was Tubs in a white polo neck sweater matching jeans and jean jacket, leather Chelsea boots with guitar slung over his shoulder and a carrier bag holding his worldly goods.

'Bestie', on the other hand, looked like he'd done a smash and grab raid on Millets and a fancy dress shop. He was wearing flared sailor's trousers, a reefer jacket and white leather boots, and to top it all off he had a peaked naval cap on his head. His bag of belongings was vast by our frugal standards, and over his shoulder sticking out of a military duffel bag was what looked suspiciously like a guitar. Definitely uncool, I thought!

Gone was the over-confident swaggering self-assured bloke from the smart set of Croydon and in his place stood this risible caricature of what he thought a busker should look like—and he couldn't even play an instrument. Bunny was unable to hide his amusement but I started to feel sorry for the poor sod. Robin was plainly excited by the prospect of Paris street life and it showed in his eyes that were taking in everything we said. I remember thinking that we'd better enjoy his brief moment of insecurity because it wouldn't be long before he had it sussed.

The implement he carried in the duffel bag turned out to be a collapsible bass guitar which he intended to learn to play so that he could earn his share of the take. This was all very well, but no-one knew how to play one and no-one even cared about Robin's position—after all he'd let others suffer plenty of indignities in the past. I realised this wouldn't do however, and later spent some time showing him what not to hit if he could help it. After a week the bass was abandoned and Robin took up the job of bottling, at which he was superb. Though some of his methods for extracting money may have been illegal; I think particularly of the very firm thrust of the hat under the rib cage if someone refused to donate, and the long cold stare that implied he might be waiting for them after they came out of the cinema. For whatever reason, our take went up when Bestie bottled the queue.

Until this time we'd had a girl called Marie, who appeared from somewhere and offered to do the job, which she did very thoroughly and for 10% of the take. She was an Irish girl who had spent a bit of time in London and was here in Paris for reasons she never explained. Bunny was sure she was a 'brass' and Tubs hoped she was and certainly tried it on, but she wasn't having any from us boys.

It was extremely hard to determine her age because she wore so much make-up and was from a very different world to us, but I liked her. She had lovely unusually deep brown eyes and she always turned herself out well for us when she worked the queues. The boys were sure she was dipping us, but I think that would have been beneath her dignity. When Robin took over she accepted it without complaint. Once to see who was the best we let them both do the queue and though we let her go first, Robin still managed to get nearly as much again.

It soon became obvious that Robin's pride would not allow this situation to last, and one afternoon after he had got rid of the offending bass implement and acquired a Spanish guitar, I gave him a start with a few rudimentary chords. By the time I returned to Paris after Christmas, Robin was just about holding his own with the others and well on the trail of female company.

One Saturday morning just after New Year I met Marie with four of the roughest looking blokes I'd seen in a while. It was not yet midday but they were drinking champagne and were on the way to getting pissed. They could not have been more conspicuous as they had arrived in Paris in an old London taxi cab. Marie introduced me to them, herself a little squiffy, and they all offered me drink. I definitely didn't fancy getting to know them better and after about two weeks they all mysteriously disappeared.

Marie later confided what we already sussed—that they had done a bank job somewhere around London and were having a bit of fun in Gay Paree. I deliberately did not get close to them but it was a matter of some pride to me that Marie chose to confide in me, and I was proud that I managed to keep her confidences. I found it amusing watching the villains getting slowly more bored with their high life; the cultural differences began to wear them down and their frustration with the language and inability to communicate with anyone but themselves started to lead to tensions.

One of them in particular, called Pete, was a nasty paranoid piece of work, who thought everyone was taking the piss out of him. His hair was very dark and he had a pointed undamaged nose. One of the things that was pointed out to me early on in my travels is that it is sensible to respect a man who has a broken nose because he probably sustained it in a fight. The fact that he wears it like a badge warns other men that he might be dangerous (what it also signifies is that he has been hit and if he's been hit once he can be hit again). Anyway Pete, after flaunting his new money and getting pissed, his chat-ups misconstrued and misunderstood, just got angry.

"Who's he fuckin' lookin' at?" was his most commonly spoken or shouted remark, and several times before they all got bored and went back to England, the others had to hold him back from dangerous close calls with the locals. In a way I felt sorry for Pete as he would probably have enjoyed his trip to Paris if the others had let him have a punchup.

I am convinced that robbers don't steal just for the money, because when they have had a result they usually can't wait to get rid of it and usually in the most ostentatious manner. This unloading of spoils seems to

562

give them a little satisfaction but cannot be the reason for robbing in the first place. Over the intervening years I have met a few villains including 'Jacka' Goody, the Great Train Robber, along with several other lesser ones, and most of them say they do it for the rush.[10]

1966 had come in on Boulevard St Michel with a chorus of car horns and a slight uneasiness that the general movement against America's involvement in Vietnam and the call to rational debate about politics, drugs, the meaning of life and the awareness fostered by the music of Bob Dylan had permeated the consciousness of French student life. The city was buzzing and we three musketeers had learned a Donovan song!

As someone who had written to Woody Guthrie, sung his songs all over Europe, defended Dylan's actions and songs from the outrage of some of my contemporaries (one of whom had accused Bob of 'crawling over the dying body of Woody Guthrie to success'), and as someone who loved the work of Bert Jansch, I was deeply resentful of Don. He has since become a good friend, but at the time I perceived him to be an exploiter of the vacant position of British Bob Dylan, and to my mind he did not deserve it. But then some have greatness thrust upon them, and Don handled it as well or better than most would have done. He's given the world a bunch of memorable tunes, loads of hits and has always been generous with his patience and time with others. Of course at the time I didn't know any of this, and having taken the piss out of his song about contagious flatulence, I ended up singing it on the Paris streets in fairly close Everly Brothers harmony with Tubs and Bunny. The French cinemagoers loved it. Thanks, Don.

∽

---

[10] One long-time friend of ours and almost reformed minor villain used to say when describing armed robbery, "Ralph, it's better than a bunkup."

joints

Snow had fallen some time in early January and settled around our neighbourhood. Christ, it was cold. As the boys and I wandered home to the Commerce at night we frequently saw 'clochards' sleeping over the hot air gratings above the metro, often with their boots under their heads to prevent them being stolen. Occasionally we would leave the smallest of our change in a shoe if it was visible, and we became on friendly terms with one or two old winos up at the Place Contrescarpe.

We were stunned to learn after a few nights elsewhere that one of them had frozen to death on the street the previous night. It was perhaps a couple of days later, turning left out of the hotel, that I noticed a pile of snow about a metre high begin to move. A couple of people shook the blanket that had covered them free of snow and brushed themselves down. I began to form the idea of a song about the poor people of Paris, but that had been done before. Maybe Paris boulevards or Paris streets? Streets of Paris even? I put the idea on hold for a while but it never left me.

Thinking only of ourselves and being away from English media, I was largely unaware of the things that were going on at home. Sometimes we glimpsed a copy of the Herald Tribune which was sold each evening by a very self-contained Finnish girl who was very fanciable in her blue jeans and jacket and fair hair. The odd perusal of tabloid French papers indicated that there was growing unrest with the influx of foreign flotsam that was finding its way to Paris. As spring approached, more and more penniless kids arrived: Americans, Dutch, some Germans, more English and soon every busking site was a jealously guarded property. On more than one occasion encroachers had to be reminded that these were our pitches, sometimes with threats levelled at their instruments and more rarely at their person. Pitches you could protect, but street corners were up for grabs and on every street corner there was someone doing something: conjurers, fire eaters, sword swallowers and strummers of every type of ability and nationality.

One street entertainer caught my imagination, and some years later I wrote a short instrumental and named it after him (*The Wino and The Mouse*). This little old man used to sit outside the self-service restaurant on St Germain des Prés on a piece of cardboard. He played little meandering notes on a penny whistle whilst a little mouse ran up and down the length of the instrument in an appearance of dancing. It was not a great show and not much else happened, but it was enough to catch the eye and earn the old boy a little change.

One day I observed his preparations for the performance which entailed dipping the tiny creature into a glass of water which along with the mouse's showbiz nerves and the extreme weather conditions made the poor thing shiver which added to the dancing effect. I liked to think that he was able to warm his little mouse hands over the warm air coming out of the finger holes on the instrument. Usually though the corner musicians would be strummers, and Bunny's most often repeated judgement was "crap" as he walked past, usually loud enough to be heard.

Nat Schaeffer was a piano accordion player from London who every year came over to Paris to play for the tourists.

"What do people come to Paris for?" Nat would ask rhetorically. "I'll tell you, they want to see the Eiffel Tower, the Mona Lisa, the Seine. They want a bit of romance and they want piano accordions. And if the French don't want to dress like Frenchmen and play their accordions, I will."

Nat was about forty five years old, of medium height and slim with a small French-style moustache. For professional purposes he wore a beret, striped matelot tee-shirt and black trousers. Although some of the buskers were really getting on our nerves, for Nat the situation was almost intolerable. One night Tubs was sitting in a café in the Rue Seine when he overheard Nat talking soothingly to some young girl at a table just behind where he was sitting. By his tone of voice he was obviously trying to pull her and as it became more and more obvious that he wasn't going to succeed, his tactics turned from trying to impress her to sympathy for his situation. His pleas grew more plaintive and desperate as he realised the situation was moving further away from his grasp, whilst nearby Tubs (who had probably had a joint) was finding the situation more and more hysterical. Tubs reported it this way.

"I know what it is, you think I'm too old for you don't you, you want another drink, I suppose you think I'm trying to get you drunk, listen babe I could have any woman I want in this town, you think you're special, you're not so special, is it because I'm old, listen there's many a good tune in an old fiddle, it's because I play accordion isn't it? I suppose you like them bleedin' guitar players don't you? why? they can't play, do you know most of them learn to play on the boat coming over here..."

At this point Tubs could hold his laughter in no longer and sprayed whoever he was with with beer, and having made such an outburst attracted Nat's attention, which alerted him to the fact that he may have been overheard, so Tubs had to pretend to have been hit by a really good punchline to some joke to divert Nat's attention. When the situation was back under control Tubs swore he heard Nat lean over to the girl and ask in a softer even more hurt tone, "Is it because I'm Jewish?" After spraying everyone for the second time Tubs was forced to make his excuses and leave.

One night on the Rue de Medicis we were playing the queues as usual when a young American made himself known to us. He had been standing in line for the movie, but decided that we looked more fun. He was with his wife Melinda, and after our performance they joined us for a coffee across the road in the bar, then invited us back to their hotel, the Juliana.

Gary Petersen had recently turned twenty one and had inherited a trust fund from his dad. Mr. Petersen Sr. was a very wealthy man who had many wives and offspring. To satisfy his obligations to his children he had created these funds that became available on maturity. Gary had managed to convince the draft board of his unsuitability for service by affecting to be homosexual and then mentally unstable. He was frighteningly thin, with barely enough on his hips to hold up a pair of Levis.

He made a passable lisping gay boy, although he was totally straight. However I'm sure he got out of service on the grounds of being mentally unstable.

He was a very strange but enormously talented young man. He ran from California for New York where, while studying guitar with the legendary Rev. Gary Davis and jazz with Les Span, he met, fell in love with, and married Melinda Patton. Gary was kind and generous and Melinda was warm and eccentric. They were a wonderful crazy irresponsible couple who slept a lot and smoked an enormous amount of dope in a little pipe with no tobacco. With his trust money Gary had purchased a Gibson Les Paul, a 1941 vintage Martin D-28 and two one-way tickets to Paris with his new bride. What I was to hear later that night would change my life again.

The two of them were so nice that we could not resist the invitation to visit. After offering us a smoke, which we accepted to be sociable, Gary took out his beloved Martin and played for us. That night in their hotel room I heard the best live guitar playing I'd ever heard in my life. The moments flew past as if he was a weaver of magic. Notes of unheard syncopation floated around their tiny room as Bunny and I sat totally entranced whilst Melinda shyly relished our enjoyment of her young husband's ability.

Amongst my friends I was regarded as a pretty good guitarist, but in Gary's company I was a rank beginner. His classical ragtime playing was sensational; my jaw literally dropped at the things he could do and it stayed dropped. The boys got me to play my bits of Blind Boy Fuller, Anji and so on, and although Gary was complimentary I knew he was out of my class. When I got back to my place I tried to emulate what he had done. I managed to get some way with his version of *Buddy Bolden* which I subsequently recorded on my first album under the wrong name of *Blind Blake's Rag*.

When I had learned to play the guitar there were no songbooks to teach you, like there are now. My method comprised lifting the needle on and off a record, listening carefully to try and work out what was going on. Even with the best ears in the world this was a highly unreliable plan, and I often convinced myself that something was correct only to go back to a piece years later to find I was miles off.

Gary not only had a remarkable set of ears, he also understood music in an intellectual way, he could actually tell you what chord something was just by listening to it, e.g. E minor 6th flattened 13th sus 4th. What to me was even more amazing was his deep affection for country blues, never 'correcting' musical naivety with what would be the correct musical thing; if someone played a twelve-and-a-half bar blues, then that's how Gary played it. Obviously if you can sit at the feet of someone like the Rev. Davis you are in touch with a living thread with the past, and you learn an even deeper respect for these masters of their instrument. Gary also composed tunes of wonderful melody coupled with beautiful bass harmonies as he employed his almost double-jointed finger style to tremendous effect.

For example, Gary often played the A chord in the first position with the first joint of his second finger only! It was awesome for us skifflers and because I'd grown up playing with guys who jealously guarded all their knowledge to the point of turning away when they were about to play a particular part they knew you wanted to know, I could never look directly at Gary's fingers for fear he would hide his skill from me. On the contrary, he was generous to a fault and I was mesmerised by his ability and so grateful for his willingness to share his talent.

I think if you truly love music there are few things in the world that compare to making it: the first time you can cleanly play the (aptly named) F chord, the first time you play a tune you have composed all the way through, the time you share a newly completed song with a trusted friend, the thrill of anticipation you get when you open your guitar case to take out your instrument to play. That's how I felt again with Gary; each day I was learning something new. I was discovering new harmonies and my right hand was beginning to master the mind-over-matter techniques required to play ragtime properly. On top of this, Gary and I were beginning to play together, though he never contemplated busking with me; his playing was too subtle for the street.

Gary and Melinda had a friend called Isobel from New York; she was very interested in pornography and delighted in telling us all about her goofy cousin who could only achieve a climax if a woman abused him by calling him names and making him lie on the floor. It was all a bit strong for me, especially as I felt sorry for the poor bastard, but she said I shouldn't be, because he was very happy with this arrangement. Through Isobel we met some other Americans; I particularly remember George who was a genuine draft dodger. George had a slight lisp and was nearly broke, but he always produced some candy after everyone had been smoking for what he called the 'munchies'. We would meet up at Gary's room and play guitars, smoke dope and wander round the streets of the quarter.

These sessions were never enough for Tubs, who always wanted to get that bit further out than everyone else. The joints he rolled were twice the size of anyone else's, and he developed a technique of using loads of 'skins' when manufacturing. His preparations for take-off became more and more elaborate and pedantic. Soon he realised that the paper that tampons were wrapped in was as thin as the cigarette papers he used. He started to collect them, and to ask girls of our acquaintance if they were having a period. If they replied in the affirmative he would ask them for their wrappers and ask them to open them as near to the end as they could manage. After mixing the tobacco and other materials together, he would painstakingly stuff the empty wrapper, making the roach out of cardboard and putting this in the open end resulting in him having what resembled a white cigar. He would then smoke until he could hardly move.

I was becoming concerned for him. All he seemed to want to do was get wasted. The strange thing was that he was not unhappy, but he was increasingly drawn to the low life and the junkies that you can find anywhere if you try. He became fascinated with an American banjo player called Curran, and whilst I was away in England began to call round to see him, allegedly to play music together. Curran was a junkie and Tubs was fascinated by the ritual of preparing his fix.

Tubs wasn't using at this time, but under supervision he helped Curran with his strap and spoon and learned how to load the syringe. It was, from what Tubs told me, an almost doctor/patient relationship. Tubs watched enthralled as Curran became stoned and spoke softly to his new friend. Their bonding was confirmed when one day Tubs called round unexpectedly to find his friend collapsed across the sink in his tiny room, blood all up the wall from a fix that had gone wrong. Tubs relished his role as saviour and was very soon using the needle himself. It was classic, him trying to convince us that he had it all under control and that he was cool, and to be fair he was still smoking and drinking.

We all gave him our fears and advice but he ignored all of us and did his own thing. He was always looking for quick money and hatching crazy schemes. Sometimes he would seem mildly deluded, saying things like "that girl over there keeps on undressing me with her eyes," or "she fancies me gutless."

We found this way of talking quite amusing, but sometimes I wondered what was going on in his brain. Our morning rituals gradually began to change, and more and more we found ourselves across St Germain where we might eat a croque monsieur or spin a coffee out for an hour or two. Around Rue de Seine there were a lot of small bars and all sorts of fascinating characters. Most of them had money of some kind and I think we had a little kudos by virtue of the fact that we took care of ourselves via the streets.

One little group caught my eye who always sat at the next bar to us but in the way that bars touch each other on the crowded streets we could all hear each other's conversation and anyway these three guys were American, and Americans always seemed to talk to each other in public as if they were deaf. These blokes couldn't care less who heard them. They always seemed to be having a good time, and it slowly dawned on me that they were always stoned.

Tubs was fascinated by them, especially when it became common knowledge that they could get LSD. It also became clear that they were gay. I was intrigued by their behaviour and astonished to hear that they spoke to each other just like the gays back home, only with American accents. The ringleader was the most outrageous in his mannerisms and I doubt he would have been able to flaunt his sexuality with as much abandon back in the USA. He was going for it, and we all found it quite amusing and just another rich seam of the eccentricity that so enhanced our Left Bank days. Soon rumours started to go around as to how they used some of these new drugs to seduce young boys, and we all watched in helpless fascination as one young fellow was gradually absorbed into their clique. He seemed happy enough, so then there were four of them.

Tubs had made friends with another strange bloke, a South African called Dennis. He was a classics scholar and a very intelligent and funny guy. He was both fascinated and appalled by Tubs. Dennis seemed so straight, with his spotless shirts and immaculate pressed trousers, and always clean-shaven. Tubs kept up appearances in the main, but he was starting to let go a little. It appeared that Dennis liked to let Tubs draw him into these scrapes he would not ever allow himself to have entered on his own. I particularly remember his shame when I enquired what was in the bottle he was carrying wrapped up in a paper bag. He leant towards me to confide that it was a lotion for the treatment of 'crabs' (crab lice).

He blamed Tubs for this problem because he got them from some chick that he and Tubs pulled somewhere. But if he hadn't been somewhat proud of this street-cred affliction, why hadn't he lied about it? None of us would have ever known. We later heard that he'd had a terrible bad trip on some acid in the States and never came back from it.

One day I bumped into Tubs by the Café Seine and he was quite animated.

"I've got a great ruse afoot," he said, "a ru-u-u-u-se." He stretched the word to enjoy it the more. "I've got wind through one of the blokes in the Café Bussey that there's this African diplomat that's coming through and he wants a white girl for the night and he'll pay 10,000 new francs for the privilege."

"Tubs," I said, "that would make you a pimp or a ponce. You're not going to be able to get any girl to do it."

"We'll see about that. I've already got someone in mind," he replied mysteriously.

Nothing more was said, but a flurry of excitement went round our small community as speculation began as to whom the girl might be. Tubs enjoyed the task immensely; chatting up girls was always something he enjoyed, but this quest added a whole new piquancy to the challenge. As the day grew closer and no candidate had emerged it began to seem more unlikely that the arrangement would take place, but Tubs had not given up and with about one day left to find a girl he was successful. Far from being a brassy type, she was a slightly round mousy little thing, American and broke. She was trepidacious but had no problem with the morality of the thing. Talking to her before the event, I was amazed at her matter-of-fact attitude. Croydon seemed very far away.

The assignation duly took place in some small hotel nearby on the appointed day. Tubs confirmed that it had taken place, but we didn't see the girl for some days and when we did I was shocked. She was wearing shades but she was still bruised under the glasses. She was shaking a little, wearing no make-up or stockings, smoking heavily and not saying much. I felt a mixture of compassion and curiosity. I never heard the details, but it was clear she had been very badly abused, and to make matters worse she was never paid. Tubs was vaguely sympathetic but uncontrite. We began to drift apart, and anyway I had met Nanna.

nanna

I first saw Nanna standing outside the big bar at the end of Rue des Ecoles: a very pretty girl wearing a very green coat and black suede boots that were too wide for her slim legs. Her haircut reminded me of Leslie Caron. Her friend Karen was American; she had long dark hair and huge brown eyes. She too was pretty but not as slim as Nanna (the suede boots belonged to her). The two girls shared a room in the Hotel Welcome in Rue de Seine with a Swiss girl called Eve that Tubs fancied.

Eve had a job but the other two girls were broke and found it quite a gas to work with us. Nanna was Norwegian and engaged to an American army guy; they had been together some time and Bill had visited Nanna's folks back home. Karen was unattached. Tubs introduced us all and as far as I could tell I made very little impression on either girl, but it was so nice to have female company again. I found that I was prepared to shave in the freezing cold water that came out of the smelly sink in my room before going out and meeting the girls. Some nights after playing we would meet some of their acquaintances and everyone would sit and talk quite frankly about their lives and morality. My recent past was still too painful to discuss so I told them of my days as a boy soldier. They seemed to be impressed.

As far as getting money from the cinema queues went, neither of them was very good. Nanna was far too gentle to bully the small change out of the reluctant Parisians and we were all beginning to feel the growing unrest amongst the locals about the foreigners who found their way to Paris expecting to find a living there. Stories had started to reach us about arrests and even instrument confiscation, as well as the proceeds from buskers who were nabbed by *les flics* (the police) whilst bottling the crowd. We were all a little wary and tense with the situation. Once or twice we ventured out of our quarter as far as the Champs Elysées, where the money was very good but the chances of getting nicked were even higher. Sometimes we played sidewalk cafés and this too could be good. But, creature of habit that I was, I still preferred my own patch that we'd managed to cling on to. Our circle of friends was changing too, and my friendship with Nanna was changing at the same time. She still saw Bill, but we two were keeping company even when we weren't working the cinemas.

Somewhere around this time I'd met a German called Bernard Grey. He was a lot older than me and as Tubs was more and more working his own scene and still being a very nervy street performer I threw my lot in with him and we started to play together. Bernard found it necessary to call himself Grey after his 'Scottish' grandmother. I never believed his granny was Scottish, but it clearly suited him not to have a German name.[11]

We all got along together, but I think Bill was beginning to get the ache with me. Although Nanna and I were still just friends, I was certainly harbouring stronger feelings for her and I hoped she felt the same. Nanna spoke very good English with a charming Norwegian uplift at the end of sentences. In spite of her knowledge she still made small mistakes with her vocabulary. One evening we were playing some sidewalk cafés near Pigalle and it was pouring with rain. I thought I might get a few more sympathetic francs from the punters by continuing to ply my trade as the rain came down. I sort of stood outside the awnings over the cafés with the guitar just under the protection of the material. The effect was that I became quickly drenched and my old Harmony guitar stayed dry. Unfortunately the audience found more humour than sympathy in my

---

[11] A couple of years ago I was looking through some snapshots in Pete and Gill Brown's collection from their days in Paris and among the names like Alex Campbell and the Thompson Brothers from Croydon and an earlier time, I spotted a snap of this Bernard who was working the streets or just hanging out at least three or four years before I arrived.

plight. I seemed to be making out all right, though, and I suppose I was trying to impress Nanna with my boyish, devil-may-care bravado.

We finished playing one café, and as we hurried across the boulevard she looked at me and said with real concern, "Oh Ralph, you must get your wet clothes off or you might catch nymphomania!"

I hoped that it might have been a Freudian slip. It gave everybody a few laughs in repetition. Nanna had by now met Gary and Melinda and we increasingly went around together. One day they took us to see a concert by an experimental group who were playing instruments of extraordinary construction. Mainly glass rods of various lengths and thickness, some had long wires attached to them and reflectors for the sound; they were variously tapped or struck but mostly caressed with fingers or gloves to give an ethereal sound of immensely soothing effect. The piece was continuous and apparently improvised, occasionally dissonant but never discordant and harsh. We were transported and delighted, perhaps enhanced by a little dope beforehand but certainly abetted by our now mutually growing feelings for each other. The effect was both intoxicating and erotic, and later that afternoon in my grotty little room Nanna and I became lovers. From that moment everything changed.

Paris, they say is made for lovers. I don't know if this is any more true of the Latin Quarter than, say, Sutton Coldfield—lovers are probably so self-centred that they just think the world smiles on them wherever they are.[12]

The thing was, we were in Paris, spring was on its way, we had some-where to stay together, our lives revolved around music, and we had mad and eccentric friends. So all things considered, we were in with a chance. We also had Bill.

To say that Bill was not best pleased with the situation was an un-derstatement. News filtered back to us that he was determined to seek revenge. I was very uneasy and wished that Robin was still around, instead of having departed with his three chords to Geneva in an MG. I saw Bill everywhere and once even thought he was skulking around the inside of the hotel. The locks on the doors were not strong enough to repel a cat so we slept with a large piece of wood under the pillow. It was an uneasy time.

On Rue Xavier Privas there was a little bar called the 'Bombarde', and this became a hangout for us as we could sit for hours with a beer and

---

[12] As my old manager Joe Lustig used to say, "When you're in love the whole world is Jewish!"

play guitars quietly—which made a big change from having to thrash it out on the streets every night. We actually became friendly with some French people, in particular a youngish guitar player who thought I was the bee's knees because I could play finger-style.

It's hard now to realise the effect guitarists who played with their fingers had on other musicians, because nowadays so many use this method, from Mark Knopfler in the world of rock, to Jerry Donahue in country rock, and all the folkies from Bert Jansch on down, but at that time it was almost the exclusive preserve of British and American players who had acquired the techniques from their black American cousins. I am sure that most guitarists will admit that the first time you hear some picker playing Scott Joplin's *Maple Leaf Rag* is a moment you never forget, that an instrument with just six strings and with only one hand to be able to project the melody, rhythm and bass all at the same time is really awesome (the other hand meanwhile is as it were manufacturing the notes on the fretboard).

I really enjoyed my moments of fame at the Bombarde, and when I got to persuade Gary to come and play there too our reputation was secured. Gary would seldom sing and when he did it was a strange sound, somewhere between the voice of an old lady and a guy that had had a couple to get him going. He sang *Diving Duck* and *Buddy Bolden* and would patiently accompany most of my repertoire. He loved some of the Beatles tunes and did a stunning version of *My Babe*. I did not however share his passion for endless and repetitive twelve bars, which seemed pointless to me. Tubs would get loaded and quite cheerfully spend a half hour vamping away on his three chords. This part of the session usually had the effect of me leaving the smoky room and going for a wander outside.

One day Melinda noticed an advert in the paper saying that Memphis Slim was playing in a bar called 'Le Chat Qui Peche'.

"Why don't we go and play there?" asked Gary with a huge stoned grin.

"You must be joking!" I said. "Because we're not good enough."

"Oh yes we are," said Gary, and try as I might I could not get him to relinquish the idea. We began to practise more earnestly together, but when we heard how much it was going to cost to get in I felt relieved because now I certainly would not be going. Then Melinda bought the tickets for the four of us and I reluctantly dragged my guitar with me to the club where Gary and Melinda were already seated.

Gary had been smoking extensively for the whole day and was fairly relaxed by the time I arrived. Memphis Slim was genial and clearly enjoying being in Paris. His style is not my favourite but if I hadn't been so nervous at the prospect of our impending debut I would have enjoyed him. When the great man took a break Gary went up with me and asked him if we could play.

"Oh you can play the blues can you?" said Memphis Slim.

"Yes sir," answered Gary politely and smiled his stoned friendly grin.

"Sure!" said the great man. "Let's hear what you can do."

Perhaps I was wrong, but I thought I detected a patronising note in his response, and that was enough to undermine me completely. I told Gary I couldn't join him, but Gary didn't seem to mind. He went up on stage and played his old Gibson L5 and sang in his creaky stoned nasally voice. He should have played the old Martin, because there was poor amplification on stage and even a great guitar like an L5 can sound tinny. The public largely ignored Gary's efforts and Melinda sat breaking the contents of an entire box of matches into tiny fragments before her new husband left the stage to indifferent applause. I certainly respected Gary for his courage and could never have done what he did myself. I felt I had let him down, but Gary was pretty pleased with himself. I am afraid that I was embarrassed and after a discreet interval we left, went back to their hotel, smoked a little dope and played guitars together.

Around this time we met Cindy, an American girl who was striking without being pretty. She was several years older than us and had money. She lived in a nice hotel near the island in the Seine. She had captured a huge young, shy, probably virgin male football college student who was attending the University of Hawaii, and they were hugely happy.

One day Cindy announced that a hamburger bar had opened on the Champs Elysées and it was her intention to introduce all of us lowlifes to the culture of the good ol' US of A by treating us all to a burger. For a lad who had only had the Croydon Wimpy Bar experience to go on (where the likes of Kercher, Liloff and Atkinson discussed Ginsberg, Corso and Ferlinghetti whilst being waited on by Shirl the fat waitress), a real hamburger was quite a treat—if a little decadent and frivolous. Our days were like that, often punctured by spontaneous indulgences. Nanna liked ice cream and sweets which I thought immature and unhip, but I found myself joining in with these moments. Maybe I'd been old too long. Gary and Melinda were much the same and after my initial reluctance to let go, I joined in with them too.

Rumours greeted my return that an even more disgruntled Bill was on the prowl again. In spite of Nanna's assertion that their relationship was already over because of his assumption that it was OK to pick up other girls, Bill was not able to come to terms with this fact. One night I had arranged to meet Nanna at the Bombarde, and when I arrived there was quite a crowd of us. As I sat down I was immediately approached by Cindy telling me that Bill was in the place up at the bar and was seriously pissed off. I decided that I'd had enough of all this cloak and dagger stuff and I went over to talk with him in a reasonable way.

"Look Bill," I said, "it's crazy going on like this. Nanna wants this to be over between you and her, and she's going out with me now so can't we just try to get on together?"

"I'm not talking to you, you fucking bastard," he hinted. "I want to talk with Nanna."

I went back to Nanna and explained the situation. "Why don't you see him just for a minute," I asked, having not read the madness in his eyes to be anything other than hurt pride.

Against her better judgement, Nanna went outside to talk with him on the street and the heavy wooden door of the club swung shut. For some reason we sensed that all was not well and Cindy opened the door to look outside. Bill in his rage had knocked Nanna to the ground and started kicking her. Cindy screamed, at which point I jumped up from the table and raced round to the door, but Cindy's cry of shock had alerted Bill who pulled a huge Bowie knife from his boot. The next few seconds flew past.

"Christ he's got a knife!" yelled Cindy, as everyone rushed for the door. I could see what was happening, but as I struggled to get out of the door it was pushed wide open as the huge bulk of Cindy's boyfriend from Hawaii hurtled past. In the time-honoured manner of all heroes I was still trapped behind the door as Bill took off down the tiny street. Everyone was running and girls were screaming when Cindy's boyfriend produced what can only be described as a near perfect American football tackle, the kind you dream of making. He dived full-length with no thought of his own safety or the solid nature of the road and grabbed Nanna's assailant around the knees at the same time that his shoulder crashed into Bill's waist.

The effect was spectacular as both of them careered through a restaurant plate glass window and landed on a table where a couple were dining, showering glass and food everywhere. Nanna was on her feet being comforted by Cindy, so I ran past her into the restaurant and hauled Bill to his feet, pulling one of his arms behind him and forcing it up his back. I was shaking with anger and fear and so was he. I wanted to kill him for what he had done and I wanted to die for what I'd been unable to do.

I had to be content to hold the creep until the police and ambulance arrived. All hell was going on around us with people screaming and men shouting. Bill said nothing and waited without resistance until the authorities arrived. I felt so frustrated just holding him there. I really wanted to hurt him, trapped as he was and unable to escape, but apart from giving his arm the odd tweak to let him know I was still there I took my lead from the quiet American from Hawaii who calmed the proceedings down with his height and unassuming authority.

Later Nanna told me that Bill had watched his mother kill his father with a shotgun.

Nanna was allowed out of hospital later that night with severe bruising, but sadly the woman diner on whose table the two Americans landed had her leg broken, something we all deeply regretted. The hardest thing to come to terms with was that, as Bill was an American GI, he was back out on the street within hours of his arrest. I had a few sleepless nights thinking I could still hear him creeping about the Paris streets, but he never troubled us again. For as long as I live I will wish it was me who had rugby-tackled the rat.

⌒

fin

Life on the street was improving as the weather got warmer, and consequently playing got easier, though my rituals before performance remained fairly elaborate, just as now, nearly thirty years on—just one more cigarette, one more tune up, mislaid the pick etc. etc.

In early spring, Bernard told me he was going to Brussels to visit his girlfriend and did I fancy a change of scene? I told him I did. On arrival Bernard got me a room and deposited me in the Café Welkom—and that was the last I saw of him for two days while he made up for lost time. I only have so much time for 'café society'—the endless hanging about doesn't sit easily with me and I usually find that I get impatient with circular discussions about art and the meaning of life.

The same goes for sitting around someone's pad smoking joints and giggling or hammering out endless twelve bars, or worse, tuning guitars. It was interesting to be somewhere else but I wondered how long I would be able to stand not doing anything. I was sitting halfway down the bar when a group of young people about my age came in, and after lighting up and ordering coffee they began to talk in very loud voices, arguing and bantering like students everywhere. I had decided that they were very un-hip but I had nowhere else to go so I stayed put and tried to understand a little of their conversation. It appeared that they were mostly talking about the night before when a generally good time seemed to have been had by all. Then suddenly in the chatter I heard the name Derroll Adams, and shortly the name came up again.

There could only be one Derroll Adams, surely; my heart picked up a bit and I concentrated even harder to understand what they were saying.

Derroll Adams, in partnership with the wonderful Jack Elliott, had made one of the most influential albums of the sixties as far as those of us who wished to follow in the footsteps of the great Woody Guthrie were concerned. The album was called 'The Ramblin' Boys' and had changed the lives of several people that I knew who had willingly bought into the lifestyle and philosophy contained in the grooves of this record. Could Derroll be in Brussels? Did he live near here? Finally I plucked up courage to ask in French, *"Excusez moi, mais je pense que j'ai entendu le nom Derroll Adams, est-ce qu'il habite ici?"*

"Yes, he lives here," said a tall young man in English. "You can meet him if you like." Some of the other kids tittered in the background, and I was embarrassed. I asked if this was the same Derroll Adams who played the banjo and was assured that it was. The tall young man explained that usually by prior arrangement somebody accompanied Derroll to the bar as he was often unsteady in the mornings due to drink. I felt I understood and asked if I could bring him to the bar the next day. Would he mind being met by a stranger? The young man assured me that it would be OK and I felt quite excited by the prospect. The young man turned out to be more simpatico than he first appeared as we chatted—then he revealed that he was the grandson of the artist Marc Chagall. My trip to Belgium was really becoming an adventure.

I woke early the next day and followed the directions to where Derroll was living, located the number of the apartment and nervously knocked at the door. After a few seconds the door half opened and a harassed looking youngish woman looked out,

"Je m'excuse, je viens à accompanier Derroll au bar," I offered.

"Oui, je le sais," she replied in a heavy resigned tone and pushing the door to a quarter closed, called in a soft voice to Derroll to come to meet the stranger out on the street.

I wasn't prepared for the sight of the man who arrived on the doorstep and carefully stepped down to the pavement. He looked like a real old man. He was taller than I'd imagined he would be and very pale. He was unable or unwilling to speak, and his walk was unsteady. Supporting him slightly on my arm I began a non-stop babble of how pleased I was to meet him and what his music had meant to me and how Max Faulkner and I had hoped to emulate him and Jack by hitching across Europe playing guitars and trying to become the Ramblin' Boys of Croydon...

Derroll's response to this was zero and we shuffled along to the bar where some of yesterday's crowd were already sitting. Most of them acknowledged him in some way, but none of them afforded him the respect I felt he deserved. I asked him what I could get him; he motioned towards the bar with a wave of his hand and one of the students whispered that Derroll would like a whisky and coke. I happily ordered Derroll's usual and was only slightly shocked when I was given a quarter bottle of the stuff and a single small bottle of coke. I had to help Derroll get the top off the whisky as the poor man had little strength in his hands. He took a moderate swig and then topped up the amount he had swallowed with a little dribble of coke. By the time he was halfway down the bottle he had begun to talk. At three quarters down the bottle he began to take an interest in me, though clearly he didn't remember my meeting him at his home. I told him of my desire to sort of follow in his footsteps, quickly adding "not all of them" and I asked him if he had any plans to play.

"I don't play much any more. It's the drink," he explained in his gentle bass baritone voice, but for once I wasn't going to stand for 'no'. I worked on him for a long time and eventually he agreed to get his banjo. It duly arrived from somewhere, and after more drink and tuning the thing to his satisfaction, he began to finger the instrument. For me it was a moment of pure joy and as I just happened to have my guitar with me I asked if I might pick along. He played so softly that my guitar kept drowning him out and he kept telling me to play quieter. I found this so hard to do because of my excitement and pleasure but I had several flat picks and eventually found the softest one so that he didn't object to my duetting.

I was so happy and was able to offer accompaniment to most of what he could play—which wasn't much because drink had made him forget lyrics and a lot of tunes—but his demeanour improved so much so that I managed to get him to agree to do a little busking with me in one or two places nearby. Reluctantly he agreed, and I am proud to say that I worked a couple of bars with the great man. He kept telling me to play

581

softer and I ended up using a shirt collar stiffener to strum lightly behind him. The only words he could remember went with a song called *Little Birdie*, and of those the only ones which came to him were "little birdie little birdie." It was not a session of great variety but I shall never forget it. Derroll cannot recall any of it!

We have become good friends and still meet occasionally, most recently at a concert that Billy Connolly gave in Glasgow when he invited me and Derroll to be his special guests.

As my memorable night with Derroll came to a close and he became more and more lucid, he confided in me, "You know Ralph, the thing with an alcoholic is that when most people say, 'Boy did I get drunk yesterday,' I say, 'Boy did I get sober!'"

I left Bernard in Brussels and returned to Paris; I was missing Nanna and wanted to tell someone about my adventure. It was good to be back even after such a short time away. We got to know different people and our circle of acquaintances continued to grow. After getting the minimum from the street to sustain me and pay my rent, Nanna and I would wander slowly through our patch and make our way to Rue Xavier Privas and into the dark womb-like safety of the Bombarde, where we were regarded almost as regulars.

Gradually over the evenings spent there we became aware of a quiet and intense young guy who always wore black gloves. He was an American and gradually he was pulled into our company. Our conversations were rambling, funny and disjointed and I suppose we all assumed that because we were in Paris, we were bound together by some obvious arty interest. At best our politics would have been described as vaguely left wing. Sexual matters were discussed with more candour than I was used to especially in mixed company. I know now that it is one of the most commonly used tricks to show how liberated one is. Those of us with girls were usually the first to leave the company, but Nanna and I often stayed up until the very early hours. I always preferred the softening to the conversation that female company brings. The young American was called Steve, and apart from the eccentricity of his refusal to ever take off his gloves he was a funny, average sort of bloke.

Late one night he told us that he had seen active service in Vietnam. This was a war that had hardly registered with most of the people we were with. We listened eagerly to his stories. All I knew at this time was that it had been Kennedy who had sent the US soldiers into southeast Asia, but we were all largely ignorant of the horrors of that conflict.

The stories and coverage that we knew about were somehow related in my mind to the riots in Watts in Los Angeles that Gill had brought to life in her eagerly awaited letters to me whilst she worked there. My knowledge of the civil rights movement was still concerned with the very basic and sentimental views that were all mixed up with the songs of Bob Dylan and my early attempts at songwriting.

It took a little time before Steve really trusted us enough to stop trying to be funny all the time. He definitely wanted to unload on us, but just as he seemed to be nearly ready he would change tack and make a silly joke. Slowly as his confidence grew his stories gained a greater intensity and it began to emerge how deeply affected by his war he had been. At one point, when our naive understanding of the rights of the people of North Vietnam to self-determination was being aired, and by implication our support for the Viet Cong, he leaned forward, his eyes blazing and said in an eerily calm voice, "They use little kids you know."

My politics at this time were pretty far left, so obviously I sided with the people of Vietnam to decide their own destiny; this was all right so long as I was in England and perceived the US army as a bunch of John Wayne types slaughtering poor peasants in a land far away. Here in Paris, though, these soldiers were as young or younger than me, often confused by their role and needing to unwind. These were young men made old by their experiences and wanting to be young again. To find people that were my age and who looked like me, yet had quite different views, was a shock.

"I went into this village one time," he continued, "and we were just mopping up. We'd practically wiped the place out, when suddenly out of a doorway steps this young girl about nine years old with a grenade in her hand."

At this point he paused while we confronted the scene in our imaginations.

"So what did you do?" I asked.

"Do?" he responded, "I blew her fucking head off!"

I can't possibly describe the effect of these words on those of us listening to him, and seeing them written down doesn't convey it either.

"It was her or me," he explained.

I understood, and in that one short sentence the real horror of that terrible time came home to me. There was simply nothing more to be said.

We were looking at a man who had knowingly responded to his training and shot dead a nine year old girl in the name of what, I wondered? Unlike Pilate he could never wash off that stain; gloves would have to do.

My main busking associate now was Tubs, though I felt his performances lacked conviction. He often arrived late and would never rehearse new numbers, and yet we made a living. The tightening up on the street people was making me very nervous, as police were regularly to be found in cinema lines. If they got you, you would be cautioned and your money confiscated. Adding to this was Tubs' cavalier attitude, my run-in with Bill and the growing intensity of my relationship with Nanna.

The lines outside the cinemas contained the money that only needed to be extracted from the punters. They had also contained the police that had on one occasion stepped from the queue and arrested me, only to release us after confiscating our takings. It was from one of these lines that Gary and Melinda had emerged and become good friends. I had begun to come up with little riffs and finger style driven melodies; I think it was Melinda who first suggested I write some words to one of these songs, and that's how *Nanna's Song* was born. Now the queue on Rue de Medicis was about to throw up another adventure.

One evening Bernard and I were working, and a small Frenchman in a red shirt and glasses stepped out and asked me in an excited voice if I could play the guitar finger style. I could not quite make out what he was driving at, so Bernard translated for me and answered that I could. The Frenchman asked us if I would like a job off the streets, and when I said that I would, gave me a card with his name on and asked me to report to the address on the back the following morning. I said that I might, and we finished our show and crossed the road to the bar to divide our tips. Bernard was staring at this card and finally he said, "You know, I think this could be very important. I think I'll come with you."

I must have looked up with an 'oh yeah?' look, because the next thing he said was, "They want you to play an audition at l'Olympia, my friend!"

L'Olympia is one of Paris's most famous music theatres; Piaf played there and countless others. It was like being summoned to the London Palladium. The next day the three of us duly arrived, to scenes of utter chaos. I was soon glad that Bernard was there because at least he could speak French well enough to find out what was going on and to make sure we were in the right place when the time came. Backstage musicians were riffing and tuning up, scene shifters were shifting scenes, people were shouting, a bearded giant of a man was mooching about and the little Frenchman with the red shirt and glasses was conducting it all with much gesticulation and screaming. A beautiful Swedish girl kept walking on stage and I became aware of a very gangly French lad about my age who was keeping a nervous eye on everything.

At last in the chaos I was summoned to the centre stage. Bernard came with me and translated. The little Frenchman said something like *"Commencez s'il vous plait,"* and Bernard said, "Play something really fast like *Freight Train* or *Railroad Bill.*"

At the end they all clapped and said *"Formidable!"* and Bernard announced that we'd got the job. What job, I wondered?

The music of Bob Dylan had finally reached France, and just as France had its own Elvis in Johnny Halliday, they now needed their own Bob Dylan. His name was Antoine, the skinny lad I had seen earlier at the auditions. His backing group were called 'Les Problemes' and the bill also comprised a skiffle group from Belgium featuring the bearded giant I had seen earlier and the pretty Swedish girl with her backing.

I was employed to play the accompaniment to two quiet songs in the middle of the show called *Pourquoi les Cannons* and *Je Vie Comme Je Veux* (which couldn't have been further from the truth). This was the moment of the show when he was supposed to truly communicate with his audience in a very intimate manner. He had to sit on the edge of the stage languidly picking his guitar but not actually touching the strings whilst the music was provided by me. There was even a subterfuge here as well, in case the audience might have been too impressed with one guitarist making all the music, they made three of us stand on stage (that's where Bernard came in, and another slightly plump French guy who lived at Robinet) and in case any of the audience might find any of us attractive we all had to wear 'le Smoking' (tuxedos) to add to our anonymity.

When asked what they should play, the other two were told, *"Faire un blanc."* In other words, pretend.

I was horrified by the level of deceit and showbiz; surely this was not what the new music was about! I had severe problems with all of it, but because the whole thing seldom rose above the level of farce I managed to see the funny side.

The contrasts between the acts was quite extreme to begin with. The

Belgian skiffle group had a singer with a voice that could stop a train, which was in direct contrast to Antoine, whose voice would have had trouble stopping a bicycle. The Swedish girl was mostly decorative and everyone wanted to screw her; stories were fed to the press which upset her because they were all lies. The promoters needn't have worried, as the shows were all sold out, even the matinees.

The papers were also full of stories about the clean-up of foreign bums from the streets of Paris. It seemed our timing was good for once and we were in the warm with guaranteed money. Les Problemes had an excellent lead singer and though I can't say much about the content of their songs, they were professional and competent. As they only had a couple of songs on their own they gave them their best shot. When they came on with Antoine it was a different story. The stage director had decided that the band should be arranged on a system of ladders and planks, but had not allowed for the bass player's vertigo. I will forever remember his expression of total fear as he perched in the middle of a plank between two trestle ladders moving involuntarily with his own slight weight. Every time there was a sudden movement by one of the band he took his hand off the bass to steady himself, which didn't do a lot for his rhythm.

Les Problemes also had another problem: the keyboard player. He was a perfectly ordinary chap and one of the better musicians, but he was a little overweight, and they made him stand behind a curtain so that he wasn't seen. I found this both unnecessary and cruel. I still see the hurt in his eyes, and as far as I remember none of his so-called friends in the band protested on his behalf. Whatever I could have said would have been ignored, as we were so low down the pecking order we didn't even have a dressing room.

Bernard always wore his sunglasses on stage, which I thought a bit over the top, but I soon realised that it was so that he might be remembered—or at least noticed—as we walked out the stage door and pushed our way past the adoring fans that nightly clogged the passage up the side of the theatre.

Antoine had long hair, and although certainly this had been the fashion for some years at home, most of us hip chaps had rejected that style. Indeed, Tubs and I were both totally through that phase, and Croydon chic dictated we cut our own hair and slightly back-combed the crown for effect. In Paris, though, there was no time for all that old moody so we just kept it fairly short but always looking grown out.

France it seemed took no notice of long-haired foreigners any more, but Antoine was French and his hair was a sensation. Suddenly, French kids were all turning up with shoulder length hair. This fashion spilled over to the student population and consequently they got lumped together with the rest of the street bums. I've often pondered whether the crackdown on the streets was observed by French youth and in some way contributed to the student unrest that finally degenerated into the violence known as the Paris riots. It's odd to think that a hairstyle might have had something to do with it.

The Antoine shows were a huge success and sold out for every single concert. I must say I enjoyed my fifteen minutes of fame as his backing guitarist, although any kudos I might have gained was diluted by the presence of the other two guys who had to pretend we were all making the music. Each night we would change in the wings and step out into the rainy early spring streets. Bernard usually hesitated for a moment and looking around through his sunglasses in the darkness flared his nostrils in a thespian way. Actually his nostrils were already flared now I think about it.

One afternoon after the matinee performance I became very disorientated. I found my way to an empty room near the side of the stage and passed out on the floor. I was still in my tuxedo when they found me. A sort of paralysis had kept me locked on the floor. I was pretty scared and totally aware of not being able to move or get up by myself. A doctor was summoned and he gave me a shot of something, which enabled me to get up and eventually be able to perform in the evening show.

It was a very frightening experience, and from what I gathered later had been brought on by exhaustion and lack of proper food. This situation improved slightly for soon Nanna found a friendly restaurant back in our area of the Quartier Latin. We were looked after by a youngish waiter who had an incredibly deep voice. We always ordered the same meal of spaghetti and we always got huge portions. Paris did seem to have a special understanding and regard for lovers, and people smiled at us and were sympatique and gentil. Our waiter was working like a slave and probably raising a couple of kids on his meagre salary and tips, yet he was kind to us and we appreciated it.

The last Saturday's performance had a special appearance from Dave Dee, Dozy, Beaky, Mick and Titch. They looked like creatures from another planet, which I suppose was their intention. These events only served to point up more emphatically that the music I wanted to play, learn and eventually write would have nothing to do with show biz if I could help it.

At the end of the run, the musical director who had found me in the cinema queue came and asked me to go on tour with the company. The show's phenomenal success meant that the provincial theatres were crying out for the production and I was offered good money by busking standards. I was flattered, but to be truthful I'd had enough of *Pourquoi* and *Je Vie*.

I also suspect that young Antoine was a bit disillusioned with the 'biz'. We spoke only a few times, but to me he seemed sincere and had had the mantle of 'the French Bob Dylan', or perhaps more accurately that of Donovan, thrust upon him. The culture of France at that time could not have coped with his gentle rebel image, and without the media, who had a field day inventing stories about the artists, especially the pretty Swedish girl, he could not have enjoyed such success. I declined the invitation to join the tour and wondered what to do next. The comparative security of the Olympia had softened me a little and the prospect of running the gauntlet of le flic busting the busking fraternity helped me to make up my mind. There is no doubt a lot of confidence had returned to me; my guitar playing was rated enough to be taken on tour with a top act.

I was in love with a beautiful girl who also loved me. There was so much I wanted to do but I did not know what it was. There were still places I wanted to see but I did not know where they were. My original street friends were otherwise disposed. Tubs was by now addicted to heroin although he maintained that he was 'cool'. I was hurt that I had absolutely no influence on the guy when once I seemed to have so much. I soon learned that you can't argue with a junkie. Tubs was resolute and had formed a business plan. He would return to England where he would become a registered addict and then sell his surplus prescription to produce income. I could not persuade him against his logic but having observed his intake going up all the time I feared the worst. Bunny, arguably Tubs' best pal, had all but given up on him too and had plans to quit the 'overplayed' streets of Paris for Geneva. He wanted me to go with him, but I was drained by recent events and missed my friends in England, like Henry, who were perhaps less radical than my Paris mates.

Robin was about his business and progressing well on his quest to be self-sufficient with his guitar playing. I did not see him again for eight years as he set off around Europe on his own adventure. Gary and Melinda were talking about coming to England. My excitement for the guitar that was glowing pleasantly was now blazing merrily with the new breath of life breathed into it by the insights revealed by Gary's wonderful playing techniques. I had begun to write songs. The depth of feelings I had for Nanna worried me too. We were in love and never out of each other's company, but I was not ready for any new real commitment. It was 1966 and the last year had been a roller coaster of a ride. Nanna, who had also been through a difficult time, understood that it was probably best to put some space between us and we agreed to part for a while.

It was April when we said goodbye. She on the train to Oslo and I on the boat to England. Spring was occasionally promising Summer, lightening my footstep and expectations. In a lower key, the turn of the ship's screw hummed the deep rumbling song of freedom again. I stood on deck and watched the white cliffs come into view. As the ship rhythmically dipped and rose through the water, it seemed to harmonise with my mood. Down with one wave, and up with the next. A sad developing acceptance for things past, only to have the sickly comfort of melancholy lifted by the next. A glow from knowing that although we were apart, I was a mere stretch away to things not entirely out of reach.

I was once more back on the lorry that took me away from Parkhall Camp and my brief military service. The wind and spray on my face was exhilarating. The offshore breeze sent a shiver through my two-shilling jacket and thin clothes, but part of the shiver was anticipation.

Something else was in the air.

❧

In my dreams you're dancing
In the embers of an evening
And I'll hold your hand a little tight
As if by this I'd stop the night
From running into morning light too soon